MW00390779

THE BOOK OF ESTHER BETWEEN JUDAISM AND CHRISTIANITY

The book of Esther is one of the most challenging books in the Hebrew Bible/Old Testament, not only because of the difficulty of understanding the book itself in its time, place, and literary contexts, but also for the long and tortuous history of interpretation it has generated in both Jewish and Christian traditions. In this volume, Isaac Kalimi addresses both issues. He situates "traditional" literary and textual, theological, and historical-critical discussions of Esther alongside comparative Jewish and Christian interpretive histories, showing how the former serves the latter. Kalimi also demonstrates how the various interpretations of the book of Esther have had an impact on its reception history, as well as on Jewish–Christian relations. Based on meticulous and comprehensive analysis of all available sources, Kalimi's volume fills a gap in biblical, Jewish, and Christian studies and also shows how and why the book of Esther became one of the central books of Judaism and one of the most neglected books in Christianity.

ISAAC KALIMI is Research Professor of Hebrew Bible/Old Testament studies and Ancient Israelite history (emereitus) at Johannes Gutenberg University Mainz, Germany. He is one of the most important and influential scholars in our time. His scholarly output has been prodigious and has encompassed a wide variety of fields. He is an ordinary member of the Academia Europaea and author of numerous books and articles, including *The Reshaping of Ancient Israelite History in Chronicles* (2005, reprinted 2012; R. B. Y. Scott Book Award of the Canadian Society of Biblical Studies 2006); *An Ancient Israelite Historian* (2005); *The Retelling of Chronicles in Jewish Tradition and Literature* (2009); *Fighting over the Bible* (2017); *Metathesis in the Hebrew Bible* (2018); *Untersuchungen zur Jüdischen Schriftauslegung und Theologie* (2018; Franz Delitzsch Prize 2019); and *Writing and Rewriting the Story of Solomon in Ancient Israel* (2018).

THE BOOK OF ESTHER BETWEEN JUDAISM AND CHRISTIANITY

The Biblical Story, Self-Identification, and Antisemitic Interpretation

ISAAC KALIMI

Johannes Gutenberg University Mainz, Germany

CAMBRIDGE
UNIVERSITY PRESS

Shaftesbury Road, Cambridge CB2 8EA, United Kingdom

One Liberty Plaza, 20th Floor, New York, NY 10006, USA

477 Williamstown Road, Port Melbourne, VIC 3207, Australia

314–321, 3rd Floor, Plot 3, Splendor Forum, Jasola District Centre, New Delhi – 110025, India

103 Penang Road, #05–06/07, Visioncrest Commercial, Singapore 238467

Cambridge University Press is part of Cambridge University Press & Assessment, a department of the University of Cambridge.

We share the University's mission to contribute to society through the pursuit of education, learning and research at the highest international levels of excellence.

www.cambridge.org
Information on this title: www.cambridge.org/9781009266123

DOI: 10.1017/9781009266147

First published 2023

A catalogue record for this publication is available from the British Library.

A Cataloging-in-Publication data record for this book is available from the Library of Congress

ISBN 978-1-009-26612-3 Hardback

אָנָה הָלַךְ דּוֹדֵךְ הַיָּפָה בַּנָּשִׁים? אָנָה פָּנָה דוֹדֵךְ וּנְבַקְשֶׁנּוּ עִמָּךְ?
דּוֹדִי יָרַד לְגַנּוֹ לַעֲרוּגוֹת הַבֹּשֶׂם, לִרְעוֹת בַּגַּנִּים וְלִלְקֹט שׁוֹשַׁנִּים (שיר השירים ו,א-ב).

"וללקט שושנים" – לסלק את הצדיקים שבישראל. מה בין מיתת זקנים למיתת
נערים? רבי יהודה ורבי אבהו, ר' יהודה אומר: הנר הזה בזמן שהוא כבה מאליו יפה
לו ויפה לפתילה, ובזמן שאינו כבה מאליו רע לו ורע לפתילה. רבי אבהו אומר:
התאנה הזו בזמן שנלקטת בעונתה יפה לה ויפה לתאנה, ובזמן שאינה נלקטת
בעונתה רע לה ורע לתאנה" (שיר השירים רבה ו,ח).

נר זכרון
לנשמת אמי חוה (נאנאג'ן) ואחותי תעוז, עליהן השלום,
שנקטפו באיבן בארץ נוכריה,
ולא זכו לגדל בנים ובני בנים, ולא זכינו לגדול בצל אהבתן ותמיכתן.
תהי נשמתן צרורה בצרור החיים לעולמי עד.

Contents

Figures

Abbreviations

Biblical Books

Gen	Genesis
Exod	Exodus
Lev	Leviticus
Num	Numbers
Deut	Deuteronomy
Josh	Joshua
Judg	Judges
1-2 Sam	1-2 Samuel
1-2 Kgs	1-2 Kings
Isa	Isaiah
Jer	Jeremiah
Ezek	Ezekiel
Hos	Hosea
Joel	Joel
Amos	Amos
Obad	Obadiah
Jon	Jonah
Mic	Micah
Nah	Nahum
Hab	Habakkuk
Zeph	Zephaniah
Hag	Haggai
Zech	Zechariah
Mal	Malachi
Ps	Psalms
Prov	Proverbs
Job	Job
Song	The Song of Songs (Song of Solomon or Canticles)

Ruth	Ruth
Lam	Lamentations
Qoh	Qohelet (Ecclesiastes)
Esth	Esther
Dan	Daniel
Ezra	Ezra
Neh	Nehemiah
1-2 Chr	1-2 Chronicles
1-2-3-4 Macc	1-2-3-4 Maccabees
Jub	Jubilees
Matt	Matthew
Mark	Mark
Luke	Luke
John	John
Acts	Acts
Rom	Romans
1-2 Cor	1-2 Corinthians
Gal	Galatians
Eph	Ephesians
Phil	Philippians
Col	Colossians
1-2 Thess	1-2 Thessalonians
1-2 Tim	1-2 Timothy
Tit	Titus
Phlm	Philemon
Heb	Hebrews
Jas	James
1-2 Pet	1-2 Peter
1-2-3 John	1-2-3 John
Jude	Jude
Rev	Revelation

Frequently Cited Reference Works and Periodicals

AHR	*American Historical Review*
AJP	*American Journal of Philology*
ANET	J. B. Pritchard (ed.), *Ancient Near Eastern Texts Related to the Old Testament* (3rd ed. with Supplement; Princeton, NJ: Princeton University Press, 1969).
BASOR	*Bulletin of the American Schools of Oriental Research*

BBR	*Bulletin for Biblical Research*
BDB	F. Brown, S. R. Driver, and C. A. Briggs, *A Hebrew and English Lexicon of the Old Testament* (Oxford: Clarendon, 1907).
BibInt	*Biblical Interpretation*
BibSac	*Bibliotheca Sacra*
BSOAS	*Bulletin of the School of Oriental and African Studies*
CAD	*Chicago Assyrian Dictionary* = I. J. Gelb *et al.* (eds.), *The Assyrian Dictionary of the Oriental Institute of the University of Chicago* (21 vols.; Chicago: The Oriental Institute / Glückstadt: J. J. Augustin / Winona Lake, IN: Eisenbrauns, 1956–2010)
DSD	*Dead Sea Discoveries*
ET	English translation (where verse numbering differs from the Hebrew)
HAR	*Hebrew Annual Review*
HTR	*Harvard Theological Review*
HUCA	*Hebrew Union College Annual*
IEJ	*Israel Exploration Journal*
JAJ	*Journal of Ancient Judaism*
JBL	*Journal of Biblical Literature*
JBTh	*Jahrbuch für Biblische Theologie*
JNES	*Journal of Near Eastern Studies*
JQR	*Jewish Quarterly Review*
JR	*Journal of Religion*
JTS	*Journal of Theological Studies*
LB	*Linguistica Biblica*
LXX	Septuagint (the Greek version of the Hebrew Bible/Old Testament)
MT	The Masoretic Text (the traditional Jewish text of the Hebrew Bible)
NETS	A. Pietersma and B. G. Wright (eds.), *A New English Translation of the Septuagint and the Other Greek Translation Traditionally Included under that Name* (New York and Oxford: Oxford University Press, 2007)
NRTh	*La nouvelle revue théologique*
PAAJR	*Proceedings of the American Academy of Jewish Research*
RevQ	*Revue de Qumran*
RRJ	*Review of Rabbinic Judaism*
SAK	*Studien zur altägyptischen Kultur*

VT	*Vetus Testament*
WA	M. Luther, *Werke: Kritische Gesam(m)tausgabe* (121 volumes; Weimar: Hermann Böhlaus Nachfolger, 1883–2009)
WZKM	*Wiener Zeitschrift für die Kunde des Morgenlandes*
ZABR	*Zeitschrift für altorientalische und biblische Rechtsgeschichte*
ZAW	*Zeitschrift für die alttestamentliche Wissenschaft*

CHAPTER I

An Introduction

I The Story of Esther

The biblical book of Esther tells a short but horrifying story about the threatened annihilation of all the Jews in the Persian Empire, a near Holocaust/Shoah, which is averted only thanks to the rapid, courageous, and decisive actions of courtier Mordecai and Queen Esther, who took a tremendous amount of risk on herself in order to save the Jewish people. The catastrophe is turned upside down as the threat of annihilation is not merely cancelled but instead inflicted on the enemies of the Jews, resulting in them suffering the violence and death that they had intended against others. Set in the Elamite city of Shushan (/Susa), the book mixes reality, drama, humor, irony, and sarcasm to create a series of tragic–comic moments – all expressed in a fluid and appealing style, sophisticated literary performs, and rich language – in order to attract its audience to the frightening and dramatic story that hides an important theological and social message.

II Esther, Jews, and Christians

Among Jews, *Megillat* (i.e., the Scroll of) Esther is included with the Five *Megillot* in the Hebrew Bible, namely: The Song of Songs, Ruth, Qohelet, Lamentations, and Esther. Among Christians, the book of Esther comes under the umbrella of the historical books of the Old Testament, alongside books such as Joshua, Judges, Samuel, and Kings, and located after Chronicles, Ezra, and Nehemiah.[1] In both Jewish and Christian Bibles, however, Esther and the Song of Songs stand out: Despite their differing

---

[1] For the form and location of the book in Christian canons, and the differences compared with the Jewish canon, see Chapters 8, §II and 10, §III.

I

literary genres, they are the only biblical books that explicitly do not mention any form of God's name or religious practice, cult, or institution.[2] No
wonder, therefore, that both books were discussed in early Jewish and especially Christian societies, whether they should be included in the canon of
the Holy Scriptures or not,[3] though in the end, they were accepted in both
canons.

Yet, concerning the Song of Songs, the two sister religions, Judaism and
Christianity, both maintained allegorical approaches to the book,[4] reading
it as a poem on divine love, while disputing its precise allegorical meaning.
Each religion allegorized the "bride – groom" of the biblical text, according to its own unique theological orientation: either as "God – Israel" or
"Jesus – Church."[5] In contrast, when it comes to the book of Esther, there
is a gaping chasm between these two religious denominations. Generally
speaking, Jews adore the book of Esther and grant it a central place
within their interpretation, theology, liturgy, festivals, literature, and art,
while Esther does not play any role in Christian theology or liturgy, and
Christians have usually neglected the book, often even condemning it and
the Jews and Judaism with it.

---

[2] The ending יָהּ of the *hapax legomenon* שַׁלְהֶבֶתְיָה in the Song of Songs 8:6 is not an abbreviated form
of God's name (*contra* W. Rudolph, *Das Buch Ruth. Das Hohe Lied. Die Klagelieder* [Kommentar
zum Alten Testament 17,1–3; Gütersloh: Gütersloher Verlaghshaus Gerd Mohn, 1962], pp. 179–
180: "Jahweflammen"; *New Jerusalem Bible* [Garden City, NY: Doubleday, 1985], p. 1040: "a
flame of Yahweh himself"). Rather, it is a third feminine singular pronominal suffix (referring to
אהבה), or a sort of superlative (see D. Winton Thomas, "A Consideration of Some Unusual Ways
of Expressing the Superlative in Hebrew," *VT* 3 [1953], pp. 209–224 esp. 221), and should be
translated as "a blazing flame" (*Jewish Publication Society Hebrew-English Tanakh* [3rd ed.;
Philadelphia: The Jewish Publication Society of America, 1999], p. 1739), or "a raging flame" (*New
Revised Standard Version* [Oxford: Oxford University Press, 1989], p. 697). G. Gerleman (*Ruth.
Das Hohelied* [Biblischer Kommentar Altes Testament 18; Neukirchen-Vluyn: Neukirchner
Verag, 1965], p. 216), translated: "eine gewaltige Flamme." On p. 217, Gerleman expounds: "sehr
wahrscheinlich [יה] ein Intensivsuffix ist. מַאְפֵלְיָה 'tiefes Dunkel' [ist die Intensivform von מַאְפִּיל]...
In ähnlicher Weise scheint שַׁלְהֶבֶתְיָה eine Intensivform von שַׁלְהֶבֶת zu sein, also 'eine mächtige
Flamme'"). Thus, Meinhold's statement that Esther is the only biblical book that does not mention God's name יהוה is inaccurate. See A. Meinhold, "Esther/Estherbuch," in H. D. Betz *et al.*
(eds.), *Religion in Geschichte und Gegenwart* (4th ed.; Tübingen: Mohr Siebeck, 1999), vol. 2, pp.
1594–1597 esp. 1596.
[3] Although it should be stressed that the book of Esther is much less disputed in Judaism than in
Christianity, and also much less disputed than the Song of Songs; see Chapters 7, 8, and 10, §I and
§III.
[4] Regarding the Song of Songs among the Jews and Christians, see G. L. Scheper, "The Spiritual
Marriage: The Exegetic History and Literary Impact of the Song of Songs in the Middle Ages"
(Ph.D. dissertation; Princeton University, 1971); J. P. Tanner, "The History of Interpretation
of the Song of Songs," *BibSac* 154 (1997), pp. 23–46, with references to the primary sources and
bibliography.
[5] For a recent discussion on this and other issues regarding the Song of Songs, see I. Pardes, *The Song
of Songs: A Biography* (Princeton, NJ: Princeton University Press, 2019).

III Challenges and Purposes

Generations of exegetes, theologians, philologists, historians, and folklorists, particularly Jewish but also some non-Jewish, have sought to comprehend and interpret the book of Esther from various viewpoints. Indeed, Esther is one of the most challenging books in the Hebrew Bible/Old Testament, not only due to the difficulty of understanding the book itself in its time, place, and literary context, but also for the long and torturous history of interpretation it has provoked in Jewish and Christian traditions.

This volume addresses both challenges: a focus on the book itself as well as its reception history among Jews and Christians. In other words, it treats the book's canonical validity and different traditions and usage in Judaism and Christianity, without neglecting the fundamental questions regarding the book in scholarship.

The volume strives to accomplish these goals through a meticulously structured approach to the subject matter, in which attention is paid to providing the building blocks for the reader to follow the line of argumentation. Accordingly, it divides the argument into three overarching subject areas, which lay out my approach: Part I provides a comprehensive introduction to the study of the book of Esther, as an essential background for the following parts and for better understanding of them. I contextualize this within the comparative reception history in the Jewish and Christian traditions in Parts II and III. The latter examines the contrasting place of both the book and the characters (i.e., Esther, Mordecai, and their important literary companions) within the Jewish and Christian communities, and the impact that it has had on the relation between the two communities and community identity. Thus, the latter is a description of the different historical receptions, impacts, and continuities of the former. Let us turn our attention to these in some detail.

The first part of the volume concentrates primarily on the book itself. It opens with a presentation of the book's story, investigation of its date and place, and questions its literary unity and possible textual development, literary genera and stylistic features, noble characters, historical setting, historicity, and the apparent core theological message of the composition. All these issues have played too important a role in modern scholarship to ignore. Furthermore, these explorations contribute not only to a better, deeper, and more appropriate comprehension of the book of Esther itself – issues which are significant for their own merit – but they also serve as an essential background for a closer reading, understanding, and evaluation of the reception of Esther in biblically oriented societies, namely Jews and Christians. In different words, by means of the issues that are discussed in the first part of the volume it will be possible to comprehend, support, or challenge the positive or negative approaches to the book of Esther and its reception that will be addressed in the remaining two parts of the volume.

The second and third parts, which comprise almost two-thirds of the volume, focus on the "after life" (*Nachleben*) of the book and its key characters, their reception history (*Rezeptionsgeschichte*), and their impact, treatment, and roles (*Wirkungsgeschichte*) in Jewish and Christian societies, religions and cultures, from earliest times to the modern era.[6] The volume does not intend to be merely a survey of Esther's reception, as is commonly done in the field regarding some other biblical books. Instead, it endeavors to evaluate the uses, reuses, abuses, as well as various interpretations and misrepresentations of the book of Esther across centuries, among Jews and Christians. It presents and compares the two sides of the reception history of Esther and shows that still there is some positive approach toward the book among certain Christians, and there is also hostility to Esther among some Jews.[7] Nevertheless, the latter cases are relatively in the minority in both religious groups. Thus, the volume contrasts the embrace of Esther by most of the Jewish people, tradition, and literature, with the condemnation of Esther by many Christians and in Christian tradition, especially since Martin Luther.

IV   Sources and Approach

The core basis for discussion of the Esther story here is its Hebrew version – the Masoretic (i.e., traditional) Text, and most likely the oldest version – while the differing Greek and Aramaic versions are discussed distinctly and included in the discussion of the book's reception histories.[8] The volume utilizes the valuable contributions of classical Jewish exegesis and literature, without overlooking the results of up-to-date modern exegesis and historical-critical research.[9] It integrates the discussions in

---

[6] For the reception of Esther in Islamic contexts, see A. Silverstein, *Veiling Esther, Unveiling Her Story: The Reception of a Biblical Book in Islamic Lands* (Oxford Studies in the Abrahamic Religions; Oxford: Oxford University Press, 2018).

[7] As we will see, the hostility to the book of Esther is not only among the strict religious Qumranic community in the far distant past, but also among certain modern Reform Jewish scholars, each group for its own unique reasons.

[8] See the detailed discussion in Chapter 2, §IV and Chapter 10, §I (Greek versions), and Chapter 8, §IV (Aramaic translations).

[9] Unfortunately, a classical Christian exegesis of Esther is not available; see Chapter 10, §IV.

the most recent studies of the historical, philological, literary, interpretive, and theological aspects of the book, with differing written sources in several languages throughout many eras and locations, as well as the archaeological finds from ancient Near Eastern and Mediterranean cultures. The approach adopted here is interdisciplinary, addressing multilingual, multicultural, and multireligious communities across Esther's origins and reception, and crosses ethnic, linguistic, and geographical borders.[10] Thus, the volume combines the analysis of Esther's various aspects with an exploration of its receptions. Finally, texts and terms from foreign languages are translated to English in order to make the volume accessible for a large readership.

V State of Research

The Jewish reception of Esther has been addressed to some extent in a few studies. This includes Barry D. Walfish, *Esther in Medieval Garb*,[11] who devotes a chapter to medieval Jewish debates concerning some issues in the book. In one chapter Walfish refers to medieval commentaries referring to the faithfulness or unfaithfulness of Esther and Mordecai in allowing her to marry a gentile king, and the justice of the Jews slaughtering their enemies at the end of the book.[12] In another chapter, Walfish reviews the diverse ways in which Haman's accusation is elaborated upon by medieval commentators,[13] an issue that will be taken up much more broadly and from a different angle in Chapters 8 and 9 of this volume.

In his monograph, *Reckless Rites: Purim and the Legacy of Jewish Violence*, Elliott Horowitz explores the history of violent accusations and acts associated with the book of Esther, particularly in relation to the Purim festival that is based on it.[14] The first half of the monograph focuses on the question of whether the book of Esther celebrates vengeance or hidden divine rescue, on the contrast between Vashti and Esther, the significance of Mordecai's refusal to bow to Haman, the supposed parallels to Haman's hostility toward the Jews, and finally the reception of Amalek.[15] The second half of the monograph then focuses on the accusations of violence since late

---

[10] All translations from non-English languages are mine, unless noted otherwise.
[11] B. D. Walfish, *Esther in Medieval Garb: Jewish Interpretation of the Book of Esther in the Middle Ages* (New York: SUNY Press, 1993).
[12] Walfish, *Esther in Medieval Garb*, pp. 121–141 (ch. 6).
[13] Walfish, *Esther in Medieval Garb*, pp. 142–155 (ch. 7).
[14] E. Horowitz, *Reckless Rites: Purim and the Legacy of Jewish Violence* (Jews, Christians and Muslims from the Ancient to the Modern World; Princeton: Princeton University Press, 2006).
[15] Horowitz, *Reckless Rites*, pp. 21–146 (chs. 1–5).

antiquity, by and against Jews, in association with Purim.[16] Though only very rarely, Horowitz argues that Purim celebrations have sometimes led to real or imagined violence against outsiders or their symbols.[17] At the same time, however, non-Jews have also frequently pointed to Purim and its celebration to support accusations of Jewish violence, usually with no real basis. They have blamed the Jews for ritual murder and bloodthirsty vengefulness and used this to justify their own violence *against* Jewish communities.[18] There has been a tendency among many Jews to identify later oppressors with Haman in their celebrations of Purim, for example, dressing up "Haman" to look like contemporary oppressors, in Purim plays, theatrical shows, and public processions.[19] Also, local "Second Purims" have often been established, in which particular communities celebrate later moments of deliverance from violence according to the models provided by Esther.[20]

Horowitz's monograph explores the reception of Esther and its characters, especially in relation to the seeming legitimacy of violence. In contrast to my volume, Horowitz does not explain and situate the book of Esther itself in its original form. He does not discuss the original content or context of the book, its unity and textual growth, and offers no detailed discussion of the purpose of Esther itself – its main theological and social-national message, its historical setting, or its time of composition, literary features, and historicity.[21] Horowitz also does not discuss in detail the approach to the book as a whole in the Christian tradition from earliest times onward, as this volume does.[22] For instance, he briefly mentions Luther's attitude to the book,[23] but he does not dedicate any deep analysis to why, when, where, and in which contexts Luther said what he said, nor to explain how this might be correlated with Luther's attitude toward the Old Testament in general, the Jewish people, and Judaism.[24] Although he refers to some followers of Luther, he does not discuss the full spectrum of later Christian reception and interpretations of Esther, and does not make any effort to analyze and question the common Christian allegation that Esther portrays a "Jewish pogrom" against Gentiles.[25]

---

[16] Horowitz, *Reckless Rites*, pp. 147–316 (chs. 6–10).
[17] Horowitz, *Reckless Rites*, pp. 149–185 (ch. 6).
[18] Horowitz, *Reckless Rites*, pp. 187–247 (chs. 7–8).
[19] Horowitz, *Reckless Rites*, pp. 248–278 (ch. 9).
[20] Horowitz, *Reckless Rites*, pp. 279–316 (ch. 10); see Chapter 9.
[21] See Chapters 2–5.
[22] See Chapters 10–13.
[23] See Horowitz, *Reckless Rites*, p. 12.
[24] See Chapter 11.
[25] See Chapter 12.

Horowitz's focus is purely on the conflicting ways in which later readers have interpreted and used the book, and he makes no attempt to evaluate the degree to which these later readings adapt, distort, or reject the key themes of the biblical book itself.[26] Even more extreme, his chapter on the different ways that Haman has been used as a model for later oppressors of Israel does not devote *any* discussion to the characterization of Haman within the biblical book itself or to ancient parallels to Haman's accusations.[27] All in all, Horowitz's monograph and my volume have different focal points and different approaches in general, and mainly cover different sources from different perspectives. Moreover, his specific conclusions do not always line up with mine. For instance, he emphasizes much more strongly than I can accept that violence against outsiders – again, real or only imagined – has commonly played a part in the celebration of Purim.

The most comprehensive study of Esther's reception history available to date is Jo Carruthers' commentary in the Blackwell Bible Commentaries series, *Esther through the Centuries*.[28] She offers an overview of the book's reception, with chapters devoted to each major section of the book. Carruthers also offers a short review of previous scholarship on Esther's reception, and a bibliography organized into categories. However, while she refers to Horowitz's monograph in her bibliography, she does not engage with it directly. Due to her general approach, Carruthers also does not focus on the specific issue of Esther's use by both Jews and Christians to demonize their opponents and glorify themselves.[29]

The most recent monograph on the context and early reception of Esther among the Jews is Aaron Koller's *Esther in Ancient Jewish Thought*.[30] His focus is on the "politics" of the book of Esther: how it reflects early Jewish views of the Persian Empire, and how subsequent Jews struggled to explain and accommodate its message. He argues that the book deliberately challenges several core beliefs common in Persian-period Judaism, particularly regarding the centrality of Jerusalem, the Persian emperor as God's agent, the necessity to strictly separate themselves from all foreigners and their practices, and a commitment to the Davidic dynasty.[31] For this

---

[26] For instance, regarding Mordecai, Horowitz spends only half a page on his characterization within the biblical book, noting the similarities between his refusal to bow to Haman and Vashti's refusal to appear before the king, before turning to the diverse later explanations and evaluations of Mordecai's refusal. See Horowitz, *Reckless Rites*, pp. 63–80 (ch. 3).

[27] Cf. Horowitz, *Reckless Rites*, pp. 81–106 (ch. 4).

[28] J. Carruthers, *Esther through the Centuries* (Blackwell Bible Commentaries; Victoria: Blackwell, 2008).

[29] Cf. the brief discussions of these issues in her chapter on Esther 9–10; Carruthers, *Esther through the Centuries*, pp. 254–279.

[30] A. Koller, *Esther in Ancient Jewish Thought* (Cambridge: Cambridge University Press, 2014).

[31] Koller, *Esther in Ancient Jewish Thought*, pp. 45–53.

reason, Koller claims that many early Jewish allusions to and interpretations of Esther, particularly in the Land of Israel, were negative rather than positive, and that this only changed after the destruction of the Second Temple.[32] At that point, according to Koller, Esther's popularity expanded significantly, and its more subversive and problematic aspects were widely ignored or given novel explanations in order to correspond better to mainstream Jewish belief, though some still continued to question the book, its characters, and its overarching story. Thus, Koller's book parallels some portions of the present volume, namely regarding the meaning of the book and its early Jewish reception. However, I take different approaches, and deal with different questions and themes. Here the main goal of the book of Esther is explained very differently than Koller does.[33] Moreover, he does not address the Christian reception of the book in ancient, medieval, and modern times, and pays little attention to certain key aspects of its Jewish reception that will be explored in this volume.[34] These include, especially, the tendency among both Jews and Christians to use the book to demonize their contemporary opponents while glorifying their own legacy.

In fact, Koller downplays the role that the respective contemporary interpretations of the book have played in its reception history, focusing on Jewish attempts to read the book for its own sake, even when their readings were extremely creative and non-literal.[35] Furthermore, Koller's book is marked by a number of oddities, perhaps the most significant of which is a broad willingness to speculate beyond the evidence. Nowhere is this more apparent than in his extended reflections concerning the thoughts and desires of the author/editor. For example, Koller describes in detail what he imagines the author of Esther thought about the parallels between Joseph and Daniel, and states: "This was quite a brilliant use of allusions, Marduka [a term he uses to refer generically to the anonymous author/editor of MT Esther] thought. What he found maddening was that the storyteller made

---

[32] Though Koller finds positive use of Esther in 2 Maccabees (which he takes to be a work of the Diaspora; see Koller, *Esther in Ancient Jewish Thought*, pp. 109–112), and of course, in the expanded Greek translation of the book of Esther (ibid., pp. 113–123), he points to Qumran as evidence of its rejection by other Second Temple period Jews (ibid., pp. 129–135). However, Koller overlooks that the Qumran community was a marginal minority among the Second Temple Jews; see Chapter 7.

[33] See Chapter 4.

[34] See Chapters 7–13.

[35] For example, Koller asserts that "much of the rabbinic interpretation is not focused on the relevance of the biblical text for the Rabbis' own time. Although there are of course such contemporizing readings within rabbinic literature, much of their exegesis is academic in nature: they are interested in interpreting the Bible, as a whole and in all its details, for the sake of plumbing the meaning of the sacred texts" (Koller, *Esther in Ancient Jewish Thought*, p. 171). While this may be true of some interpretations of Esther, there are many exceptions, as we will see.

his hero [= Daniel] *superior* to Joseph."[36] How Koller can know what the author of Esther found "maddening," is an unexplained enigma. Additional points in Koller's presentation will be challenged in later chapters.

To sum up, among the previous studies of Esther and its reception, this volume is exceptional. It suggests innovative avenues and fills in a gap in biblical, Jewish, and Christian studies. It demonstrates how the different interpretations of the biblical text have essentially impacted on those receptions as well as on Jewish–Christian relations. This particular form of engagement of "traditional" literary, textual, theological, and historical-critical discussion of Esther situated alongside comparative Jewish and Christian interpretive histories, while exemplifying how the former serves the latter, is indeed unique in scholarship of any biblical book. Additionally, this volume sheds a new light on and contributes numerous fresh insights throughout its three parts that moves us beyond the current state of scholarship in the field.

VI Outline

Following this introductory chapter, the volume addresses the content and context of the book itself in Part I, "Esther: Story and History, Literary Features and Theology." This part presents the book of Esther and examines a number of the central discussions stimulating research on the book and analyzes certain themes regarding it – themes that play an important role in the later progression of my arguments. It includes five chapters.

Chapter 2 introduces the Esther story, and then discusses the presumed place and time of the composition, dating it to the fifth century BCE. It discusses the literary unity, textual development (Hebrew and Greek versions) of the book and prioritizes the witness of the Masoretic Text over the Greek versions. It presents the portrait of the noble characters in the book – Vashti, Esther, and Mordecai – as they are reflected in the Hebrew Bible.

Chapter 3 examines the virtuosity, literary style, and features of Esther story: The book as a world masterpiece literature, its secular presentation, its variety of literary techniques (e.g., *inclusio*, chiasmus, and chiastic in parallel, antithesis, structures of reversed fate, *talionis*), the author's overstatements and exaggerations, satirical and humoristic descriptions.

Chapter 4 questions whether the book of Esther is just a humorous and purely secular tale designed to entertain the reader as some scholars consider it; or whether it is – even with its humoristic style and the absence of God's name – a thoughtful story about the dangerous destiny of the

---

[36] Koller, *Esther in Ancient Jewish Thought*, p. 40, cf. pp. 30–34, 37–44.

Jews in the Persian Empire, a religious text with an important theological message – particularly addressed to the Jews in Diaspora – that should be read cautiously and earnestly? And, if so, what precisely is that theological message, and why does the name of God not appear explicitly in any form, even once, among the entire 3,044 words of the 167 verses of the ten chapters of the Hebrew version of the book? The chapter discusses this issue within the book of Esther and its biblical contexts (further supported by extra-biblical sources), that is: the fear of total annihilation and hope for salvation by God, who is loyal to his covenant with Israel.

Chapter 5 investigates the historical setting and historicity of the book of Esther. It challenges both the view that Esther is a completely reliable historical account, and the assumption that Esther is a completely unreliable, fictional, or even mythological story. It calls for a balanced approach, arguing that Esther is best understood as a "novelistic history," combining both plausible and implausible elements. Through a comparison with biblical and extra-biblical sources from Persian, Greek, and Jewish authors, as well as archaeological finds, it reveals that many elements in the Esther story are most likely grounded in historical reality, including the core theme of the threat to exterminate the Jews. Other topics addressed in this chapter include the empire and the imperial hierarchy; the identification of the king and his portrayal; the queen and harem; the capital city and the royal court; royal annals and imperial archives; the postal delivery system; the legal system; tolerance toward minorities; and conspiracy and murder in the royal court. The extended discussion of the historical setting of the book serves the dual purpose of bolstering his dating and of providing a historical matrix for the book's composition. Although the central events of the book as related in Esther may not reflect what actually happened, the themes reflected in the book's main narrative are, however, indicative of issues faced by the Jews living within the Persian Empire. Expanding on this theme, the volume adduces ancient parallels for the threats faced by the Jews in the book of Esther at the hands of Haman, which are discussed in Chapter 6. The parallels from several different ancient sources for Haman's accusations against Jews in the writings of many Jew-haters support the claim that the accusations of Haman as stated in Esther are not fictional.

Part II, "'Oh, How Much They Love the Book of Esther!'[37] – Esther among the Jews," is concerned specifically with the reading and reception of Esther in Jewish thought through the ages. It shows how Jews have

---

[37] M. Luther, *Werke: Kritische Gesam(m)tausgabe* (121 vols.; Weimar: Hermann Böhlaus Nachfolger, 1883–2009), vol. 53, p. 433, lines 17–19; see Chapter 11, §III, note 20.

interpreted, addressed, grasped, modified, and adopted key aspects of this late biblical book. It demonstrates that the book of Esther has long been one of the most beloved biblical books within the Jewish community in spite of its lack of any explicit mention of God. This centrality of the book within Jewish reception history may be attributed to its understanding as a scheme providing hope to an exiled community living during precarious times that, no matter how bad the situation, there is always hope for redemption and salvation. Hence, it is a deeply theological book despite the apparent absence of the divine from the narrative. Indeed, as shown in Chapter 9, the book of Esther has been paradigmatic for Jewish confrontations with peril throughout the ages, including both during and after the Holocaust.

This part comprises one relatively short and two very large chapters. It opens with Chapter 7 that treats the intriguing absence of even a tiny fragment from the book of Esther amongst the hundreds of surviving manuscripts – mostly fragmental – of the Dead Sea Scrolls. Is this just incidental or accidental, or rather a reflection of the attitude of the Qumran community toward the figure of Esther and the book which bears her name? The chapter surveys some previous suggestions and proposes a few fresh ones.

Chapter 8 discusses Esther's place in Jewish tradition, culture, and thought more broadly, emphasizing the portrayals of its central Jewish characters, Esther and Mordecai, Haman, Agag, and Amalek in Jewish thought, the significance of the Megillah and the festival of Purim in Judaism over the centuries, and its place in Jewish art, play, music, and film. The chapter closes with a review of the attitude of some Reform Jewish scholars toward the book of Esther and the feast based on it.

Chapter 9 examines explicit Jewish identifications of particular persecutors and Jew-haters with the biblical Haman. Through creative applications of the book of Esther, they invented new "Hamans" and "Purims," and formed new "Megillot" in different Jewish communities, in various places and periods. A particular discussion devoted to the Esther story and Purim in the "Third Reich" Nazi Germany. An appendix to this chapter questions whether the "relief and deliverance" that was predicted by the author of Esther indeed characterize the Jews' long and bitter Exile. After this long history of Jewish persecution, and its horrific culmination in the Holocaust, is Esther's central theological message that God is always loyal to his covenant with Israel, as argued in Chapter 4, still credible? How do the major socio-religious streams of the Jewish people currently struggle with this problematic matter?

Part III, "Divine or Demon? – Esther among the Christians," examines the book of Esther in Christianity and Christian communities. This part comprises four chapters, and in fact stands in sharp contrast to the previous part.

It demonstrates that the book of Esther has at best a marginal place in Christianity, usually neglected or treated negatively, and even loaded with anti-Jewish and antisemitic assertions and allegations.

Chapter 10 points out the major differences between the Jewish "Megillat Esther" and the Christian "book of Esther." It addresses the anti-Jewish trends already present in Esther's Greek translations, which the Christian forms of the book of Esther follow. The chapter presents the authority, place, and name of the book of Esther in the Christian canon. It shows the general lack of interest in and neglect of Esther in Christian societies and literature. It discusses Esther in Christian theology in general, with a focus on the first Christian commentary on the book by Rabanus Maurus, and the negative attitude of Martin Luther to Esther. Luther's harsh critique on the book of Esther and his long-term influence on generations of Christians scholars are carried forward in Chapters 11 and 12. Chapter 11 focuses on Luther's complicated and conflicting attitudes toward the book of Esther and its Jewish characters: a friendly attitude toward the characters, and an extremely negative one toward the book itself. This chapter suggest a new understanding of Luther's viewpoint, against the background of his attitudes toward the Old Testament, the Jewish people, and Judaism in general.

Chapter 12 demonstrates how Luther's negative attitude toward and assertions against the book of Esther, Jews, and Judaism crucially affected Christian society, including the scholarly world, crossing the boundaries of territories and nations, throughout numerous generations. There is ample unjust hostility toward the book among Christian commentators, theologians, and thinkers, especially – but not exclusively – in Germany, the homeland of Luther and Protestantism. This chapter shows how the anti-Judaic agenda of some scholars has had a decisive impact on their misreading, mistranslating, and misinterpreting the book of Esther as a whole, and its various parts and particularities. It then suggests that a close reading of Esther from historical, literary, linguistic, and hermeneutical perspectives within its broad biblical and extrabiblical contexts, leaves no space for any anti-Judaic interpretation of the book. It shows that Esther is not a story of an "antisemitic pogrom of the Jews against their gentile persecutors," but instead describes a just self-defense of the Jews in a hostile society, against a ruler who attempted to annihilate them.

Yet not all Christian interpreters followed Luther's hostility. Chapter 13 lists and analyzes a handful of positive voices among Christian scholars regarding the book of Esther and the Jews, before and after the Shoah. Finally, Chapter 14 offers a comprehensive summary, synthesis, and conclusions to the entire volume.

PART I

Esther: Story and History, Literary Features, and Theology

CHAPTER 2

Esther's Story
Composition, Literary Unity, Textual
Development, and Noble Characters

I The Story of Esther

In the preexilic period the relationship between the Israelites and the Persians was very restricted, if any existed at all. This situation changed when the Judahites were exiled to Mesopotamia, and particularly when they came under control of Cyrus II, the Great.[1] A range of royal decrees regarding the Jews is attributed to the Persian kings in late biblical literature. Of these, two are particularly well known and even revolutionary: a positive one – the "Cyrus Decree," recounted in Ezra 1:1–3 (// 2 Chr 36:22–23)[2] – and a totally negative one – the "Haman Decree," recounted in the book of Esther (3:13–14).[3]

The book of Esther is the story of a beautiful orphaned Jewish girl who became queen of the Persian Empire (Esth 2:16–18). Together with her cousin Mordecai she successfully saved her people from total ethnic annihilation (or, if you wish, from an inclusive antisemitic pogrom/holocaust), which Haman, the vizier of the king, had planned and attempted to execute.

The geopolitical setting of the Esther story is far from the Jewish homeland, Eretz-Israel (the Land of Israel), which in fact is not mentioned even once in the entire book. It takes place in the Diaspora, at the court of a foreign king, King Ahasuerus of Persia and Media, in the Elamite city of

---

[1] See Chapter 5, §IV.

[2] The final execution of the Cyrus Decree took place in the reign of Darius the Great (522–486 BCE), who canceled the prohibitions that had in the meantime been imposed on the Judeans due to the strong opposition and malicious words of their surrounding neighbors (Ezra 4:17–24), and allowed the rebuilding of the Jerusalem Temple – as Cyrus had promised. Darius even provided funding and supplies for the Temple services (Ezra 6:1–11 esp. 1–5). Some scholars dispute the historical authenticity of the Cyrus Decree, in my opinion without any solid justification. For a survey of such opinions, see J. Liver, "Cyrus," *Encyclopedia Biblica* (Jerusalem: Bialik Institute, 1962), vol. 4, pp. 55–64 esp. 62–63 (Hebrew); P. Briant, *From Cyrus to Alexander: A History of the Persian Empire* (Winona Lake, IN: Eisenbrauns, 2002), pp. 46–48.

[3] And, of course, the counter-decree of Mordecai (which was written in the name of King Ahasuerus), that canceled Haman's decree (Esth 8:7–14).

Shushan/Susa, one of five capitals of the Persian Achaemenid Empire.[4] Therefore, it is no wonder that there are similarities between the Esther story and the stories of Joseph, Daniel, Fourth Ezra, and Aḥiqar, which also took place in the courts of foreign rulers in the diaspora.

Esther's story is concerned, first and foremost, with protecting the Jewish people from those who wish to destroy them. It is an example of the classical story of the Jews' struggle to survive under foreign dominion (in this case, the Persian Empire), controlled by an unpredictable, absolute autocrat (the Persian king) and his capricious official(s). As such, the book narrates the struggle between life and death, between light and dark, between liberty, tolerance and plurality of religious beliefs and opinions on the one hand, and the tyranny of racial and religious fanaticism, hatred, prejudice, and intolerance on the other. Indeed, threats against Jewish existence like that recounted in the story of Esther have frequently repeated themselves in various ways and at different times and places throughout the long and bitter history of the Jewish people. In that struggle the Jews have often turned to Esther to ground their trust that God will keep his covenant with them, and – in one way or another – redeem his people from annihilation (cf. Esth 4:13–14).[5]

II   Place and Time of Composition

Prior to studying any text, it is important to clarify where and when exactly it was composed, or, if that is not possible, at least the geographic area and the historical era. It is essential to read the composition within its sociocultural environment and its religious and historical settings.[6] In the case of Esther, it is hard to say exactly where the story was composed. Adele Berlin suggests that, in principle, it could have been written anywhere in the eastern Jewish diaspora.[7] However, since the author is so familiar with Susa,[8] it is reasonable to assume that Esther was composed there.

There is no doubt that the book of Esther originated at some point in the Second Temple period. However, scholars have suggested a wide range of potential dates for the composition of the book within that framework.

---

[4] On Shushan/Susa see Chapter 5, §II, 5.
[5] For more details see Chapters 4 and 9.
[6] See I. Kalimi, "Placing the Chronicler in His Own Historical Context: A Closer Examination," *JNES* 68 (2009), pp. 179–192 esp. 179–180.
[7] Cf. A. Berlin, *Esther: A Commentary* (Mikra Leyisra'el; Jerusalem: Magnes Press / Tel Aviv: Am Oved, 2001), p. 28 (Hebrew).
[8] See further Chapter 5, §II, 5.

These run from the early Persian period to the early Hasmonaean period. There is a gap of about 340 years between the earliest and the latest suggested dates, with many or additional options proposed between these two extremes. For example, Shemaryahu Talmon and Edwin M. Yamauchi date the book "in the beginning of the Persian era. The traditional setting of the book in the days of Xerxes I cannot be wide off the mark."[9] Robert Gordis dates the book to "approximately 400 B.C.E."[10] Carey A. Moore is of the opinion that "it is most likely that Esther reached its final form in either the late Persian or early Hellenistic period," though the first edition was probably even earlier.[11]

In contrast to these datings of the book in the Persian or early Hellenistic periods, Wesley J. Fuerst thinks that "the present written form of the book may be traceable to the *early part of the second century B.C.* in Palestine" (italics added).[12] On the basis of some similarities between the book of Esther and the book of Judith, Ruth Stiehl classifies the book as a typical Hellenistic novel that includes erotic elements, and dates the composition of Esther to the Maccabean era, sometime around 140 BCE.[13] Elias J. Bickerman asserts that "It was in the Hasmonean period, in which Esther was written, that mass conversion to the true faith began …."[14] Most recently, Beate Ego puts it only slightly earlier, arguing for a "pre-Hasmonean origin for the book."[15] However, such late dating of Esther by Stiehl, Bickerman, and Ego are particularly problematic, as will be discussed below.

At the least, the book of Esther could not have been written *before* the time of the historical figure, King Ahasuerus/Xerxes I, who reigned in the

---

9 See S. Talmon, "'Wisdom' in the Book of Esther," *VT* 13 (1963), pp. 419–455 esp. 453; followed by E. M. Yamauchi, *Persia and the Bible* (Grand Rapids, MI: Baker Book House, 1990), p. 228 (he miscites it as p. 449). See also S. B. Berg, *The Book of Esther: Motifs, Themes and Structure* (Society of Biblical Literature Dissertation Series 44; Missoula, MN: Scholars Press, 1979), p. 2: "not far removed from the events it describes," that is, ca. 485–465 BCE.

10 See R. Gordis, *Megillat Esther: The Masoretic Hebrew Text* (New York: Ktav, 1974), p. 8.

11 See C. A. Moore, *Esther: Translated with an Introduction and Notes* (Anchor Bible 7b; Garden City, NY: Doubleday, 1971), pp. lvii–lx. See also J. D. Levenson, *Esther: A Commentary* (The Old Testament Library; Louisville, KT: Westminster John Knox Press, 1997), p. 26.

12 W. J. Fuerst, *The Books of Ruth, Esther, Ecclesiastes, the Song of Songs, Lamentations: The Five Scrolls* (Cambridge Bible Commentaries on the Old Testament; Cambridge: Cambridge University Press, 1975), p. 40.

13 See R. Stiehl, "Das Buch Esther," *WZKM* 53 (1957), pp. 4–22 esp. 6–9, 22.

14 See E. J. Bickerman, *The Jews in the Greek Age* (Cambridge, MA: Harvard University Press, 1988), p. 247.

15 See B. Ego, "The Book of Esther: A Hellenistic Book," *JAJ* 1 (2010), pp. 279–302, and most recently in her commentary: *Esther* (Biblischer Kommentar Altes Testament 21; Göttingen: Vandenhoeck & Ruprecht, 2017), pp. 59–69. See also H. M. Wahl, *Das Buch Esther: Übersetzung und Kommentar* (Berlin and New York: Walter de Gruyter, 2009), p. 25; For a further survey and bibliographical references, see Yamauchi, *Persia and the Bible*, pp. 226–228, and Ego, "The Book of Esther."

years 485–465 BCE (*terminus a quo*),[16] but it also could not be written *after* the composition of 2 Maccabees (ca. 143 BCE; *terminus ad quem*), which affirms that the "Day of Nicanor" (the 13th of Adar) is "the day before the Day of Mordecai" (πρὸ μιᾶς ἡμέρας τῆς Μαρδοχϊκῆς ἡμέρας; 2 Macc 15:36), which is called "Purim" (in plural!) in Esth 9:26, 28, 32. This implies that at the beginning of the Hasmonaean period, the Purim Festival was already well known also among the Jews in Judea.[17] Since 2 Maccabees referred to one of the key figures of the book – Mordecai – and the festival of Purim in some form that related to him, the author was most likely aware of at least the main story of Esther.[18]

As is usual in the biblical literature from the Persian period, such as Ezra-Nehemiah and Chronicles, the language and style of the *Megillah* are Late Biblical Hebrew.[19] It contains several Aramaic words, for example, אנס ("force," Esth 1:8), יקר ("honor," 1:20), איגרת ("letter," 9:26, 29), פתגם ("decree," 1:20), and, even more significantly, many Persian loanwords, such as פרתמים ("nobles," Esth 1:3; 6:9), דת ("law," 1:8; 3:14; 9:13),[20] פתשגן ("copy," 3:14; 4:8; 8:13), אחשתרפן ("satrap," 3:12; 8:9; 9:3), אחשתרן ("courier/ courser," 8:10, 14), and Persian names such as Zeresh (5:14) and Vaizatha (9:9).[21] On the other hand, the book of Esther lacks any Greek word,

---

[16] On Ahasuerus/Xerxes I, see the discussion in Chapter 5, §II, 2.

[17] See the detailed discussion by B. Bar-Kochva, "On the Festival of Purim and Some of Succot Practices in the Period of the Second Temple and Afterwards," *Zion* 62 (1997), pp. 387–407 esp. 387–402. For the inaccurate opinion that the Festival of Purim was unknown in the Second Temple period, see A. Oppenheimer, "The Historical Approach: A Clarification," *Zion* 61 (1996), pp. 225–230 esp. 227–228; idem, "Love of Mordechai or Hatred of Haman? Purim in the Days of the Second Temple and Afterwards," *Zion* 62 (1997), pp. 408–418. All three articles are in Hebrew.

[18] Interestingly, Mordecai and Esther are not mentioned in the "Praise of the Fathers" in the Wisdom of Ben Sira 44–49, which was composed ca. 180 BCE, but this need not imply that the book was only written after that date. On "the Day of Mordecai," see also Chapter 8, §I and §VIII.

[19] For the language and style of the Megillah, see for example, H. Striedl, "Untersuchung zur Syntax und Stilistik des hebräischen Buches Esther," *ZAW* 55 (1937), pp. 73–108; M. Z. Segal, *An Introduction to the Hebrew Bible* (Jerusalem: Kiryat Sepher, 1967), vol. 3, pp. 718–728 esp. 725–727 (Hebrew); R. Weiss, "The Language and Style of Megillath Esther," *Mashot beMikra* (Jerusalem: Reuben Mass, [1976]), pp. 114–128 (Hebrew); R. Bergey, "Late Linguistic Features in Esther," *JQR* 75 (1984), pp. 66–78.

[20] On this word see Chapter 5, §II, 8.

[21] There has been much written on the Persian words and names in Esther. See for example, H. Gehman, "Notes on the Persian Words in the Book of Esther," *JBL* 43 (1924), pp. 321–328; A. R. Millard, "The Persian Names in Esther and the Reliability of the Hebrew Text," *JBL* 96 (1977), pp. 481–488 (indeed, the conclusion of Millard regarding the foreign names in Esther is valid: "the Old Testament text has often been disparaged, yet when the evidence of its own contemporary world is evaluated beside it, it is seen to be as reliable a source as any newly excavated inscription"; p. 488); R. Zadok, "Notes on Esther," *ZAW* 98 (1986), pp. 105–110 (Zadok's notes are concerned with proper names); Berlin, *Esther: A Commentary*, p. 19; M. Hutter, *Iranische Namen in Semitischen Nebenüberlieferungen – Faszikel 2: Iranische Personalnamen in der Hebräische Bibel* (Vienna: Verlag der Österreichischen Akademie der Wissenschaft, 2015). See also Chapter 5, §I, 2, A.

name, idiom, or anachronism from the Hellenistic era. Moreover, in the Megillah the Elamite capital city is called שׁוּשָׁן (Shushan), that is, Akkadian Šušanu, and not by its Greek name Σοῦσα (Susa). Thus, on this basis it is reasonable to assume that Esther was composed sometime in the Persian Achaemenid period, that is, between the time of Xerxes I (485–465 BCE) and the final collapse of the Persian Empire with the conquest of Persepolis by Alexander the Great (330 BCE).[22]

Yet, if the main story of Esther could have been composed around 340–330 BCE as Moore suggests, then why did its author choose to ascribe his story to the time of Ahasuerus/Xerxes I who reigned about 145 to 165 years earlier? Why didn't he ascribe the story to the time of one of the last kings of the Persian Empire, such as Darius III (336–330 BCE)? Indeed, the Esther story ridicules the Persian king and his court in many ways, as will be detailed below (Chapter 3, §XI). But these kinds of descriptions of a Persian king and court do not necessarily require us to date the composition of Esther to a time when the central government was very weak and dying or even after its collapse. Probably, it would still have been possible to compose such a story in Hebrew even when a powerful Persian emperor was in control, as later parallels attest. For instance, if Maimonides could call Mohammad "crazy" and "insolent" while serving in a Muslim royal court in twelfth-century Egypt, Persian-period Jews could have produced a satirical account of a Persian Emperor in Hebrew as well.[23]

It appears that the core story of the book of Esther was probably composed either sometime during the reign of the historic figure, Ahasuerus/Xerxes, when at least some of the events of the book took place, or within a generation or two after that, let's say sometime between ca. 475 to 425 BCE. As we will see below in Chapter 5, the author of the book is intimately familiar with a variety of aspects of the Persian court and the empire, and the core of his story is broadly plausible within that context.

III Structure and Literary Unity

The book of Esther has been preserved in quite different versions: a short one in Hebrew (the Masoretic Text, the *textus receptus* of the Jewish Bible), and two versions in Greek that each contain considerable additions and

---

[22] In fact, officially it was destroyed with the conquest and destruction of Persepolis, in 330, by Alexander the Great.

[23] Regarding Maimonides' comments, see I. Kalimi, *Fighting over the Bible: Jewish Interpretation and Polemic from Temple to Talmud and Beyond* (The Brill Reference Library of Judaism 54; Leiden and Boston: Brill, 2017), pp. 116, 119–120, 254, and the references there to primary literature.

variations. Whereas the Greek versions of the book are not coherent texts, overall, the Hebrew version seems relatively unified.[24] It comprises two major parts:

1. The first and the largest one is the core story/narrative of the book in chapters 1:1–9:19 and 10:1–3. Here the author presents the full story with fixed structure: Prologue (or exposition; 1–2), the story (3:1–9:19), and closing section of the epilogue (10:1–3, see later).
2. The second part regards the origin of the institution of the Purim festival – two "Purim letters" (9:20–32). Here the establishment of the feast of Purim on the 14th and 15th of the month of Adar is recounted, the explanation of why the feast is called "Purim" is provided, and why it takes place on two different days in different places is explained. Mordecai and Esther call the Jews to observe the feast forever. The call is stated by two Purim letters: one from Mordecai (9:20–28), and another from Esther together with Mordecai (9:29–32).

Some scholars are of the opinion that Esth 9:20–32 and 10:1–3 is secondary, a late addition.[25] In what follows, I will discuss this issue in three parts: (1) 9:20–28 – the first Purim's letter; (2) 9:29–32 – the second Purim's letter; (3) 10:1–3 – the closing chapter of the book.

1   Esther 9:20–28 – The First Purim Letter

In my opinion the paragraph in 9:20–28 is part and parcel of the original book. This paragraph together with 10:1–3, builds an epilogue to the core story of the book. In fact, there is no decisive evidence – linguistic, stylistic

---

[24] Some scholars speculated that the book was built from a different bulk of sources, see H. Cazelles, "Note sur la composition du rouleau d'Esther," in H. Gross and F. Mussner (eds.), *Lex tua veritas* (Festschrift Hubert Jonker; Trier: Paulinus, 1961), pp. 17–29; LaCocque follows him and asserts: "The book of Esther may very well be dependent upon pre-existing sources. There seems to remain an imperfectly smoothed out seam between the story of Esther and the one of Mordecai"; see A. LaCocque, "The Different Versions of Esther," *BibInt* 7 (1999), pp. 301–322 esp. 321. Niditch concludes correctly: "The book of Esther divides into sources only by the most wooden exegesis"; see S. Niditch, "Esther: Folklore, Wisdom, Feminism and Authority," in A. Brenner (ed.), *Feminist Companion to Esther, Judith and Susanna* (Sheffield: Sheffield Academic Press, 1995), pp. 26–46 esp. 32–33.

[25] See, for example, L. B. Paton, *A Critical and Exegetical Commentary on the Book of Esther* (The International Critical Commentary; Edinburgh: T. & T. Clark, 1908), pp. 57–60; D. J. A. Clines, *Ezra, Nehemiah, Esther* (New Century Bible Commentary; Grand Rapids, MI: Wm. B. Eerdmans / London: Marshall, Morgan & Scott, 1984), pp. 253, 331; idem, *The Esther Scroll: The Story of the Story* (Journal for the Study of the Old Testament Supplement Series 30; Sheffield: JSOT Press, 1984), pp. 50–63; M. V. Fox, *The Redaction of the Books of Esther: On Reading Composite Texts* (Society of Biblical Literature Monograph Series 40; Atlanta: Scholars Press, 1991); F. W. Bush, "The Book of Esther: *Opus non gratum* in the Christian Canon," *BBR* 8 (1998), pp. 39–54 esp. 41–42.

or any other – that distinguishes 9:20–28 (or 9:6–28) and 10:1–3 from the core narrative. The latter serves as a historical setting and rationale for the former. The contents of the two parts are closely related to each other: The chief figures – Mordecai, Esther, Ahasuerus, and Haman – play a role in both. The phrase הפיל פור הוא הגורל ("cast *pur*, that is, the lot"), appears in both parts (3:7 and 9:24) and connects them. The text in 9:24–27 that offers a summary of the key events in the central narrative, also connects the two parts. The purpose of the book – to show how God keeps his promises and redeems Israel by an unseen divine hand ends with thanksgiving and the celebration of Purim.[26] In this sense, Esther is the "Torah of Purim," the story behind the festival. In other words, the feast and the celebration of Purim are the outcome of the story, rather than vice versa: the latter was not composed to justify etiologically an existing old pagan festival (*ätiologische Festlegende*) whose origin is unknown. It is not a rejection of an old pagan festival and the replacement of it by the new one – Purim. In fact, all the speculative theories regarding the hypothetical "old pagan festival," which scholars consider to be self-evident, fail to match with or to explain the origin of the feast of Purim.[27] As Gerleman rightfully concludes: "That with that kind of circumstantial evidence using a very questionable divining rod becomes clear as soon as we look more closely at the literary character of the story of Esther."[28] That is, you are theorizing on the basis of what you want to hear, without proper proof, and that becomes clear as soon as you take a good look at the book of Esther from a literary standpoint. Thus, the confident assertion – without presenting any verification – such as that of Johannes Meinhold: "Only one thing is certain in this horror, this completely a-historical, bloodthirsty story, that the Purim festival of the Jews existed, and should be explained," cannot be accepted.[29] Instead, it is likely that Purim was introduced as a natural outcome of the essential events that

---

[26] For further details see Chapter 4. For the opinion that "the genre of Esther is that of *a festival etiology*" (italics original), see F. W. Bush, *Ruth, Esther* (Word Biblical Commentary 9; Dallas, TX: Word Books, 1996), p. 306 and the references there to several other scholars that hold a similar opinion.

[27] For such hypothetical theories as that suggested by Paul de Legarde, Heinrich Zimmern, and Peter Jensen, see Chapter 5, §I, 2, A. For a survey of some others, see G. Gerleman, *Esther* (Biblischer Kommentar Altes Testament 21; Neukirchen: Neukirchener Verlag, 1973), pp. 23–25.

[28] Gerleman, *Esther*, p. 25: "Daß man bei Indizien dieser Art sich einer sehr fraglichen Wünschelrute bedient, ergibt sich, sobald wir uns den literarischen Charakter der Esthererzählung vergegenwärtigen."

[29] See J. Meinhold, *Einführung in das Alte Testament* (3rd ed.; Giessen: Alfred Töpelmann, 1932), p. 360 (in the 1st ed., 1919, this quotation appears on p. 305): "Gewiss ist bei dieser grausen, gänzlich unhistorischen blutdürstigen Geschichte nur eins: das Purimfest der Juden bestand und soll erklärt werden." Similarly, Theodor H. Gaster, *The Festivals of the Jewish Year* (New York: William Sloane Associate Publishers, 1953), pp. 215–232. Edward L. Greenstein concludes that "the scroll was custom-made for

the Esther core story recounts – the redemption of the Jews. The many later "Megillot" that have been composed to tell the stories of the redemption of the Jewish community and the "Second Purims" that were consequently established and celebrated,[30] support this approach. This is not an anachronistic view, but a realistic observation concerning similar occasions that recur and follow the same pattern. So, why should one consider the similar case in Esther itself differently and search for something that we have no indication that it existed at all? Thus, all in all, we can say that Esth 9:20–28 is an integral part of the book rather than a late addition.

2   Esther 9:29–32 – The Second Purim Letter

After the writing and sending of the (first) Purim letter by Mordecai (Esth 9:20–28), why should Mordecai join with Esther to write and send the second letter (Esth 9:29–32)? Presumably Esth 9:29–32 is a late addition to the book.[31] The secondary nature of Esth 9:29–32 is clear also from the resumptive repetition (*Wiederaufnahme*) in the text:

וְיִּכְתֹּב מָרְדֳכַי אֶת הַדְּבָרִים ... וַיִּשְׁלַח סְפָרִים אֶל כָּל הַיְּהוּדִים אֲשֶׁר בְּכָל מְדִינוֹת הַמֶּלֶךְ אֲחַשְׁוֵרוֹשׁ ...

(Esth 9:20), and the words in bold type are repeated at the beginning of the "second letter" (Esth 9:29):

וַתִּכְתֹּב אֶסְתֵּר הַמַּלְכָּה ... וּמָרְדֳכַי הַיְּהוּדִי אֶת כָּל תֹּקֶף לְקַיֵּם אֵת אִגֶּרֶת הַפֻּרִים הַזֹּאת הַשֵּׁנִית
וַיִּשְׁלַח סְפָרִים אֶל כָּל הַיְּהוּדִים אֶל שֶׁבַע וְעֶשְׂרִים וּמֵאָה מְדִינָה [ב]מַלְכוּת אֲחַשְׁוֵרוֹשׁ.

Moreover, the phrase: אִגֶּרֶת הַפֻּרִים הַזֹּאת הַשֵּׁנִית ("this *second* letter about Purim"; 9:29) furnishes an additional indication for its lateness and *secondary* nature.[32]

---

the feast [of Purim]," see E. L. Greenstein, "A Jewish Reading of Esther," in J. Neusner, B. A. Levine, and E. S. Frerichs (eds.), *Judaic Perspectives on Ancient Israel* (Philadelphia: Fortress Press, 1987), pp. 225–243 esp. 226–228, 233. André LaCocque considers Esther story as *hieros logos* for the feast, and declares without hesitation that "the book was written to clean up a pre-existing, more or less pagan festival celebrated by provincial Jews of the Eastern diaspora"; LaCocque, "The Different Versions of Esther," pp. 302, 305. Adele Berlin (*Esther: A Commentary*, pp. 3–5) is also of the opinion that the main story is an etiological-historical background to justify the festival.

[30]   See Chapter 9 for further details.

[31]   Here I am joining several scholars who have already identified this passage as a late addition to the book; see, for example, S. E. Loewenstamm, "Esther 9:29–32: The Genesis of a Late Addition," *HUCA* 42 (1971), pp. 117–124; Clines, *Ezra, Nehemiah, Esther*, p. 331; *Biblia Hebraica Sttutgartinsia*, p. 1380; L. M. Wills, *The Jew in the Court of the Foreign King: Ancient Jewish Court Legends* (Harvard Dissertations in Religion 26; Minneapolis: Fortress Press, 1990), pp. 169–170; Berlin, *Esther: A Commentary*, p. 149.

[32]   For a similar late addition that was inserted into an earlier text and defined as the "second time," see Gen 22:15: "The angel of the Lord called to Abraham from heaven the *second time* ...." On the secondary nature of Gen 22:15–18, see I. Kalimi, *Early Jewish Exegesis and Theological Controversy: Studies in Scriptures in the Shadow of Internal and External Controversies* (Jewish and Christian Heritage 2; Assen: Royal Van Gorcum [now under: Brill, Leiden and Boston], 2002), p. 9 and note 1 with additional bibliography.

In his comment on Esth 9:30, Abraham ibn Ezra explained the necessity of this "second letter of Purim," which was because the feast was not well established until Esther wrote her letter, together with Mordecai. However, perhaps Mordecai's name was inserted there just to honor him.

3 *Esther 10:1–3 – The Closing Chapter of the Book*

The short final chapter of the book – Esth 10:1–3 – is not just "another appendix" to the book, in addition to "the first appendix (9:20–32)," as asserts Samuel Sandmel.[33] Why should it be considered as an "appendix," and for what purpose was such an appendix needed here? Sandmel does not clarify. David Clines, who considers Esth 9:20–10:3 as "the appendices of the Esther scroll,"[34] explains that "Est. 10:1–3 also bears all the marks of an addition, since its vague generalities contribute nothing to the concrete narrative of the book."[35] It is not clear, however, what "all the marks of an addition" that Clines refers to are. Elsewhere Clines provides a few more details: "This paragraph [i.e., Esth 10:1–3], like 9:20–28 and 9:29–32, is strictly unnecessary for the purposes of the narrative, and may well be yet another secondary addition. The style is very stilted with a conventional formula referring to the record of the 'act of Mordecai'."[36] But the author of the paragraph does not refer "to the record of the 'act of Mordecai'," rather to the "Annals (lit., the book of chronicles) of the Kings of Media and Persia" (ספר דברי הימים למלכי מדי ופרס; Esth 10:2). Also, Clines' statements that 10:1–3 "contribute nothing to the concrete narrative of the book" and "is strictly unnecessary for the purposes of the narrative" are inaccurate. This paragraph is part of the core narrative. It is sophisticatedly connected to the opening of the book that describes Ahasuerus and his empire as well. The names מדי ופרס ("*Media* and **Persia**") in Esth 10:2 repeat and stand in chiastic order to those in Esth 1:3, פרס ומדי ("**Persia** and *Media*"), and both together construct a literary form of *inclusio* to the book.[37] Moreover, Esth 10:1–3 closes the epilogue of the book, as the antithesis to the prologue of it: While the latter opens with the lewd and silly drunker King Ahasuerus who acts irresponsibly, the former closes with King Ahasuerus who rules the lands and "islands of the sea" and demands a

---

[33] See S. Sandmel, *The Hebrew Scriptures: An Introduction to Their Literature and Religious Ideas* (New York: Oxford University Press, 1978), p. 503.
[34] Clines, *The Esther Scroll*, pp. 50–63.
[35] Clines, *Ezra, Nehemiah, Esther*, pp. 253–254.
[36] Clines, *Ezra, Nehemiah, Esther*, p. 331.
[37] See also Chapter 3, §VII, 1.

tribute/taxes (lit., forced payment) from them. He accredits himself with achievements – "acts of his power and of his might." Moreover, the book opens with Mordecai the courtier, a Jew who was subjected to the whims of the evil Haman, and ends with Mordecai the vizier, who ranked "next to king Ahasuerus and was influential (lit., great) among the Jews," but still does not forget his people and continues to seek good for them.

Clines' attempt to explain the necessity of the "appendix" saying: "we may presume that some editor was unhappy with the prominence given to Esther by a book ending with 9:32 and decided to bring Mordecai back into the limelight for the closing verses."[38] However, Esth 10:1–2 speaks mainly about Ahasuerus and his reign. Besides, why should we assume the ending of the book with 9:32? Is there any textual or other evidence for such an ending? What guarantee have we that it was ever so? In this way, the research moves in a circle: one assumption leads to another, the latter is built on the unproven former.

Regarding the tax that the king imposed (Esth 10:1), Carey A. Moore acknowledges that "Unfortunately, the author does not say why this was imposed, and many scholars have had difficulty seeing its relevance to the theme of Esther."[39] Indeed, the author does not state explicitly why the tax was imposed.[40] However, he expresses the relevance of this paragraph to the theme of his book not explicitly, but rather by sophisticated literary forms and connections. As Johan Wolfgang von Goethe already affirmed: "Content determines form; form never exists without content" (*Gehalt bringt die Form mit; Form ist nie ohne Gehalt*).[41]

IV   Textual Development: The Hebrew and Greek Versions

1   B-Text, A-Text, and MT

There are two Greek versions of the book of Esther, which were produced mainly by Jews,[42] but preserved by Christians: The first one is included in the Septuagint/LXX and called simply "Septuagint" or "B-Text," the other is known as the A-Text (Alpha-Text, or the Lucianic- [= L-] Text). Of the

---

[38] Clines, *Ezra, Nehemiah, Esther*, p. 331.

[39] Moore, *Esther*, p. 98.

[40] Moore, *Esther*, pp. 98–99, cites some suggestions that attempt to explain this issue.

[41] See J. W. von Goethe, "Paralipomena," *Gedenkausgabe der Werke, Briefe und Gespräche* (edited by E. Beutler; Zurich: Artemis Verlag, 1949), vol. 5, pp. 539–619 esp. 541; see also Kalimi, *The Reshaping of Ancient Israelite History in Chronicles*, pp. 404–405.

[42] See the discussion in Chapter 10, §I.

36 preserved manuscripts of the Greek Esther, only four medieval copies preserve the A-Text.[43]

These Greek versions of Esther differ from each other: the A-Text is shorter than the B-Text, and some events are presented in a different order.[44] They both differ substantially from the MT/Hebrew version not only in many minor (and sometimes important) variants, but they also contain six major (pre-Christian) additions, comprising 107 verses altogether, which are scattered throughout the book.

2   The Six Major Greek Additions and the Colophon

The six major Greek additions include:

A. An opening prologue describing a dream of Mordecai (before 1:1);
B. The verdict against the Jews of the Persian Empire (after 3:13);
C. Prayers for God's intervention offered by Esther and Mordecai (after 4:17);
D. An extension of the scene in which Esther is presented to Ahasuerus (also after 4:17);
E. A copy of the verdict in favor of the Jews (after 8:12);
F. An interpretation of Mordecai's dream from the prologue (after 10:3).[45]

Also, at the end of B-Text a colophon appears:

> In the fourth year of the reign of Ptolemy and Cleopatra, Dositheus, who said he was a priest and Levite, and Ptolemy his son, brought this Letter of Purim, stating that it was authentic and that had been translated by Lysimachus [son of] Ptolemy, [a member] of the Jerusalem community.

The purpose of the colophon was to show the originality and the authenticity of the text: It is based on a copy of the "Letter of Purim" – Megillat

---

[43] Mss. 19, 93, 108 and 319; see K. H. Jobes, *The Alpha-Text of Esther: Its Character and Relationship to the Masoretic Text* (Society of Biblical Literature Dissertation Series 153; Atlanta: Scholars Press, 1996), p. 2 and Appendix 2 (unnumbered).

[44] See K. H. Jobes, "Esther," in A. Pietersma and B. G. Wright, *A New English Translation of the Septuagint and the Other Greek Translation Traditionally Included under that Name* (New York and Oxford: Oxford University Press, 2007), pp. 424–440. Jobes presents the English translation of both Greek versions in two parallel columns, thus one can easily see all the differences between them.

[45] For the additions and their analysis, secondary features, original language, date, and authorship, see C. A. Moore, *Daniel, Esther and Jeremiah: The Additions: A New Translation with Introduction and Commentary* (Anchor Bible 44; Garden City, NY: Doubleday, 1977), pp. 153–252 esp. 153–172; Jobes, *The Alpha-Text of Esther*, pp. 162–194; I. Kottsieper, *Zusätze zu Ester* (Altes Testament Deutsch Apokryphen 5; Göttingen: Vandenhoeck & Ruprecht, 1998), pp. 109–207; J. Trebolle Barrera, *The Jewish Bible and the Christian Bible* (Leiden and Boston: Brill / Grand Rapids, MI: Eerdmans, 1998)," p. 182; S. A. White Crawford, *The Additions to Esther: Introduction, Commentary and Reflections* (The New Interpreter's Bible 3; Nashville, TN: Abingdon Press, 1999), pp. 945–972.

Esther – that was sent from the Holy City, Jerusalem, by a priest and Levite. It also indicates that the Greek B-Text of Esther was translated by a scribe in Jerusalem, and then brought to Alexandria.[46] The colophon refers simply to Ptolemy and Cleopatra, which could refer to any of three different Cleopatras and Ptolemys: 114, or 78/77 or 48 BCE, a matter that is debated among scholars. Usually, the commentators date the colophon to 114 BCE; thus, for instance, Jolio Trebolle Barrera asserts that "the translation was made around 114 B.C.E."[47] Elias Bickerman, however, is of the opinion that it was written between "September 12, 78 and September 11, 77 B.C."[48] At any rate, we can conclude that the Greek B-Text/Septuagint was translated from Hebrew in Jerusalem in the last quarter of the second century or the first quarter of the first century BCE and was sent to Alexandria.[49]

When Jerome (Eusebius Sophronius Hieronymus; ca. 347–420) translated the Christian Bible into Latin (which became known as the "Vulgate"), he also included the Greek additions, but not in their proper places as in LXX; instead, he collected them at the end of the book of Esther. Thus, when Stephen Langton divided the Bible into chapters in 1225, he numbered the six additions consecutively as Esth 10:4–16:24, as if they formed a direct continuation of the main story found in the Hebrew text. Accordingly, Addition A became Esth 11:2–12:6; Addition B – 13:1–7; Addition C – 13:8–14:19; Addition D – 15:1–16; Addition E – 16:1–24; Addition F – 10:4–11:1.

Since the Reformation and Luther's translation of the *Biblia* into German, in the first half of the sixteenth century (see Chapter 11), this group of additions has typically been collected separately, as one of the fifteen Deuterocanonical (or Apocryphal) books that were excluded from the Jewish canon, but included in the Roman Catholic and Eastern Orthodox Bibles. Yet, some modern Catholic English Bibles, for instance, *The New American Bible*, reestablished the Septuagint order of the book of Esther including the additions.[50]

It is basically a question of whether these additions were added by the Greek translator(s), or they were already an integral part of the Hebrew *Vorlage* used by the translator(s). Trebolle Barrera, for instance,

---

[46] On the uniqueness, meaning and significance of this colophon, see E. J. Bickerman, "The Colophon of the Greek Book of Esther," *JBL* 63 (1944), pp. 339–362.

[47] See Trebolle Barrera, *The Jewish Bible and the Christian Bible*, p. 399.

[48] Bickerman, "The Colophon of the Greek Book of Esther," p. 347; see also Bar-Kochva, "On the Festival of Purim," pp. 189–190.

[49] Contra Cordoni who dates this Greek translation of Esther to the third century BCE; see C. Cordoni, "'Wenn du in diesen Tagen schweigst' (Est 4,14): Zur mittelalterlichen biblischen Heldin Ester," in C. Bakhos and G. Langer (eds.), *Das jüdische Mittelalter* (Die Bibel und die Frauen 4,2; Stuttgart: W. Kohlhammer, 2020), pp. 37–56 esp. 38.

[50] The project of *The New American Bible* was completed in 1970.

thinks that apart from Additions B and E, "these additions already form an integral part of the Hebrew text in the period when it was translated into Greek."[51] However, this still does not mean that the additions were also an integral part of the original Hebrew Esther story. Besides, in the Greek version the language of these additions to Esther is considerably better than that of the translated texts of the book. This means either that the additions are not from the same hand that translated the core text of the book, or, as Martin Hengel suggests, that "The author seems to have taken particular care over the Greek of these additions."[52] But if Hengel is correct, it would raise the question: why have these additions received such special attention, more so than any other part of the book?

3 Which Text Is Closest to the Urtext?

In 1944, Charles C. Torrey asserted that "Our standard Greek version [i.e., B-Text] deserves to be regarded as a most important witness to the original form of the Esther narrative."[53] According to him, the Hebrew and Greek versions of the book of Esther are the translation of an original Aramaic version. Moreover, he concluded: "Our Hebrew book is an abbreviated translation from an Aramaic original," and dates the "Hebrew edition ... later than the time of Josephus."[54] However, Torrey's opinion remains a single and isolated one in the scholarship. Hanna Kahana, who compared the Hebrew MT with the Greek B-Text, concludes that the differences between the two are *not* due to different *Vorlagen*, but rather due to the translator's work and techniques. According to her, the *Vorlage* of the B-Text was different from that of the MT only in some unimportant variations.[55] Moreover, while the B-Text without the six additions is a text close to the MT, the Alpha-Text even with the six additions is about 20 percent shorter than the MT, and without them it includes only about half of the text in comparison to the MT.[56]

Some scholars, such as David Clines and Michael V. Fox who followed him, have argued that the A-Text (apart from the additions) represents an

---

51 See Trebolle Barrera, *The Jewish Bible and the Christian Bible*, p. 182.

52 M. Hengel, *The "Hellenization" of Judaea in the First Century after Christ* (London: SCM Press / Philadelphia: Trinity Press International, 1989), p. 25.

53 C. C. Torrey, "The Older Book of Esther," *HTR* 37 (1944), pp. 1–40 esp. 27.

54 Torrey, "The Older Book of Esther," pp. 34–38 esp. 38–39.

55 See H. Kahana, *Esther: Juxtaposition of the Septuagint Translation with the Hebrew Text* (Contributions to Biblical Exegesis and Theology 40; Leuven: Peeters, 2005).

56 See Jobes, *The Alpha-Text of Esther*, p. 62; idem, "Esther," in Pietersma and Wright (eds.), *A New English Translation of the Septuagint*, pp. 424–425. On the Greek versions of Esther, see also C. D. Harvey, *Finding Morality in the Diaspora? Moral Ambiguity and Transformed Morality in the Books of Esther* [Beihefte zur Zeitschrift für die alttestamentliche Wissenschaft 328; Berlin: Walter de Gruyter, 2003], pp. 8–12.

old pre-MT Hebrew version of Esther.[57] Clines' assertion is sharply criticized by André LaCocque, who concludes that "the A-Text cannot be used for retrieving an *Urtext* of Esther."[58] Many other scholars, however, consider the A-Text as a reworking of the B-Text. Thus, for example, Julio Trebolle Barrera thinks that the A-Text depends on and is shortened from the B-Text, and is actually a Lucianic revision of it (L-Text).[59] Emanuel Tov has also defended the secondary character of the A-Text, but denies that it is Lucianic.[60]

4   Provisional Summary

All in all, it seems that the MT and the B-Text had very similar *Vorlagen*. The Greek translators made several minor and major changes to their Hebrew *Vorlage* – above all, they inserted into it the six substantial additions. The A-Text is secondary, a late revision and shortened version of the B-Text, from which it also kept the six additions. In other words, the Hebrew version (Masoretic Text) of Esther is probably the oldest and closest to the original form of the book, except for the late insertion of the second letter (Esth 9:29–32). The Greek translators of the B-Text added to, omitted from, and altered their core Hebrew *Vorlage* in order to interpret and to adapt it to their own religious norms, social and political needs, and time. This is true for both the minor differences and the six major additions mentioned above. Indeed, the contents of these additions change the overall themes of the book of Esther as a whole, particularly regarding the absence/silence of God, much as the additions found later also in the Aramaic translations (Targums) of the book do.[61]

V   Noble Characters

Obviously, the most notable characters of the book are Ahasuerus, Haman, Vashti, Esther, and Mordecai. Because the first two characters are discussed – in this or other ways – throughout this volume, there is no necessity to provide specific paragraphs on them here as well. I would like just to state that the author of the scroll portrayed King Ahasuerus as an unpredictable ruler, often drunk, and playing into the hands of his vizier and

---

[57] See Clines, *The Esther Scroll*, pp. 139–174; Fox, *The Redaction of the Books of Esther*, pp. 9, 127–133 *et passim*.
[58] LaCocque, "The Different Versions of Esther," pp. 301–302, 308–322; the quotation is from p. 321.
[59] See Trebolle Barrera, *The Jewish Bible and the Christian Bible*, pp. 399–400.
[60] See E. Tov, "The 'Lucianic' Text of the Canonical and Apocryphal Sections of Esther: A Rewritten Biblical Book," *Textus* 10 (1982), pp. 1–25; see also R. Hanhart (ed.), *Esther* (*Septuaginta: Vetus Testamentum Graecum Auctoritate Academiae Litterarum Gottingensis editum* 8,3; Göttingen: Vandenhoeck & Ruprecht, 1966; 2nd ed., 1983).
[61] See the examples in Chapter 4, §III.

his wife, but also as an emperor with achievements, who imposed taxes on his land. Haman is presented as an Agagaite/Amalekite – a symbol of the Israelite's bitter enemy,[62] as an egocentric and megalomaniacal person, and as a wicked mass murderer who, despite all that he has – a very high-level position, a lot of honor, a wife, sons, houses – remains unhappy unless he can see Mordecai and his people dead (Esth 5:11–13).[63] His plan was to annihilate the human beings – the Jews – but to keep and take their property; in terms of murder and also inheritance of the possession (cf. 1 Kgs 21:19).

In contrast, the figures of Ahasuerus and Haman, Queen Vashti, Esther, and Mordecai are presented solely as noble characters. Certainly, it is important for its own sake to introduce these important figures of the story. But I particularly present here the portraits of these characters as reflected in the biblical story, because of their relevance for Parts II and III of the volume. Simply, it furnishes us with the necessary background to understand and evaluate the conflicting views of them held by different later groups of Jews and Christians, as will be discussed in the subsequent parts of this volume.

1   Vashti: A Queen with Dignity and Self-Respect

The Esther story opens with King Ahasuerus' protests of his great prosperity, supremacy, and glory. It details how the king reveals to his assembled nobles and officials his enormous wealth (Esth 1:4–7),[64] and then – "when the heart of the king was merry with wine" (Esth 1:10) – he wishes also to impress them by showing his wife's, Queen Vashti's, extraordinary beauty. Vashti, however, refuses to obey the king's capricious *order*. She does not explain her refusal, and also the narrator neither discloses nor gives any indication of her motive, but only alludes to Vashti's act: She courageously maintains her self-respect and royal dignity and does not display her beauty before the lustful and drunken males (Esth 1:12). Seemingly, Vashti was aware that her refusal would make the king angry and perhaps also cause her to lose if not her life then at least her royal crown (Esth 1:10–15). The king with his council of seven "wise" men overstate the incident and conclude that Vashti's refusal to obey her husband's order challenges all the imperial social norms regarding women and could become a destructive model for others. Thus, Vashti was removed from her position as the queen of the Persian Empire (Esth 1:10–22). From here the entire story takes its starting point, and all the rest of the

---

[62] See Exod 17:8–16; Deut 25:17–19; Judg 6:1–6; 1 Samuel 15; 30:1–21; see also Chapter 4, §II, note 24.
[63] On Ahasuerus, see Chapter 5, §II, 2; on Haman, see Chapter 6, §I.
[64] For further details see Chapter 5, §II, 5.

tale is based on what is told here in this chapter about Vashti and the king. In fact, "Queen Vashti's demotion is Esther's promotion to the throne."[65]

The story implies a disparity between Vashti's brave and noble behavior and her excessive and unbalanced punishment. The biblical story gives no indication that Vashti's fate was deserved. Once again, the author leaves readers to fill in the gap and come to their own conclusions. In later generations, some rabbis attempt to find a balance between Vashti's noble act and her retribution.[66]

2   Esther: Beauty, Courage, and Wisdom

The author identifies the common Babylonian name of the heroine "Esther" (אסתר >Ištar) with her Hebrew personal name "Hadassah" (הדסה היא אסתר; Esth 2:7). Perhaps he presents that the foreign name "Esther" was given to her as she became the queen of the Persian Empire, similar to the case of Joseph, whom Pharaoh called "Zaphnath-Paaneah" when he appointed him as a vizier (Gen 41:45).[67]

The orphan Jewess, Esther, was adopted by her exiled cousin (Esth 2:7, 15), Mordecai; she behaved reasonably (Esth 2:15), followed Mordecai's instructions (Esth 2:10, 20), and finally ended up replacing Vashti as the Queen of the Persian Empire. Esther does not reveal her ethnic origin and her descent (2:10, 20), as Mordecai ordered. The narrator does not disclose why Mordecai ordered such a thing and leaves this open for speculation by his potential readers. Probably, he meant to secure her status in the palace and to avoid some obstacles on her route to the position. In any case, Esther's obedience to Mordecai at this point is crucial for the development of the story later in Esther 7, and as such it serves as an exposition of it.

Certainly, the greatest blessing of Esther was her extraordinary beauty, as stressed already in introducing her in the prologue of the tale (Esth 2:7). However, it is inaccurate to describe her as one who "wins her victories not by skill or by character, but by her beauty."[68] Indeed, in her first steps as queen, Esther plays a passive role and follows Mordecai's instructions. She had to be motivated and persuaded by Mordecai to act on behalf of her people, being told that if she does not approach the king and request him

---

[65] LaCocque, "Haman in the Book of Esther," p. 207.
[66] For the treatment of Vashti by the talmudic sages, see Chapter 8, §IV, 4, B. For further discussion on Vashti, see Chapter 5, §II, 3, A.
[67] On the names "Hadassah" and "Esther," see the discussion in Chapter 5, §I, 2, A.
[68] Paton, *A Critical and Exegetical Commentary on the Book of Esther*, p. 96.

to cancel Haman's evil decree, she will perish together with all the Jews of the empire. From that moment and own, Esther acts alone and independently until the complete illumination of Haman (Esther 7).

Although she was the wife of the king and the queen of the empire, she, like everyone else, was prohibited from uninvited visiting of the king – her husband – at the royal court, and whoever goes there without invitation risks death penalty (Esth 4:11). Still, she courageously took the risk and put her life in danger (and that is not nothing!) by going to King Ahasuerus in order to attempt to save the lives of many others to whom she owed loyalty (Esth 4:10–11, 16; 5:1–8; 7:1–10).[69] She is best characterized as an altruist, a selflessness person who is concerned for the wellbeing of her people.

The narrator emphasizes the incomparably lower status of Esther in comparison to the king through a sophisticated literary description. In Esth 5:1 he states that "Esther put on her *royal dress*," and in the same verse he stresses five times the king and his royal status, saying, she "stood in the inner court of the *king's* palace, opposite the *king's* palace; and the *king* sat upon his *royal throne* in the *royal palace*, opposite the gate of the house (i.e., the palace)" (ותלבש אסתר מלכות ותעמד בחצר בית המלך הפנימית נכח בית המלך והמלך יושב על כסא מלכותו בבית המלכות נכח פתח הבית). In other words, although Esther put on "her *royal dress*," still Ahasuerus is the king, sitting on his royal throne in his royal court, and controls all the royal authorities, and can make sudden decisions regarding her very existence!

To get a sense of how dangerous and heroic Esther's act was, it is worthwhile to cite the Greek Addition D 1–16 (// A-Text 6:1–12; Vulgate 15:4–19). Here the late author took advantage of the scene in the Hebrew text of Esth 5:1–2 and deliberately expanded it with a dramatic description of that moment, while expressing his own theological view:

> When she had passed through all the doors, she stood before the king. He was seated on his royal throne .... Upon seeing Esther, his face glowered in fiercest anger. The queen stumbled, turned pale and fainted, keeling over on the maid who went before her. But God changed the king's spirit to gentleness. The king leaped down from his throne in alarm and took her up in his arms until she revived. He comforted her with reassuring words, telling her, "what is the matter, Esther? I am your brother. Relax. You are not going to die! ... Come to here!" Then he raised his scepter, and tapped her neck; he hugged her and said, "talk to me!" ....[70]

---

[69] It is not clear on which basis Ellens argues that Esther went to the king, "*sexually seduced him*, and persuaded him thereby to hang the perpetrators and protect the Jews"; J. H. Ellens, *Sex in the Bible: A New Consideration* (Westport, CT and London: Praeger, 2006), p. 42 (italics added).

[70] For the text, cf. Moore, *Daniel, Esther and Jeremiah: The Additions*, pp. 216–217.

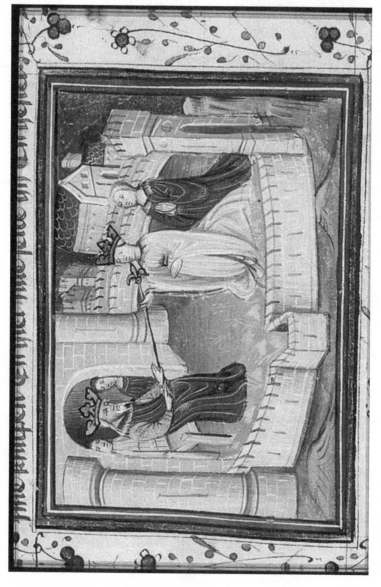

Figure 1 Anonymous Dutch master, Esther before Ahasuerus (Esth 5:1–2), Utrecht, ca. 1430; The Hague, Royal National Library

Mordecai requested Esther to go to the king, "make supplication to him, and entreat him for her people" (Esth 4:8). However, she acted differently and strategically planned everything; she invited the king and Haman to dine with her twice, and employed all her physical beauty, mental strength, intelligence, and rhetoric, as well as her personal relations with the king, in order to demolish Haman and his genocidal plan (Esther 5 and 7). Also, Esther "spoke once more before the king, and fell down at his feet, and pleaded with tears to prevent the evil design of Haman the Agagite, and the plan that he had devised against the Jews" (Esth 8:3; cf. 4:8). Thus, Esther accomplishes her goals not only with her unique natural beauty, but also with her rhetoric, social skills, and personal character (Esth 2:15, 17; 8:3).[71]

By acting so and saving the entire Jewish people from annihilation, Esther joins earlier saviors in the history of Israel, such as Deborah, Yael, and the wise woman from Abel of Beth-Maachah (Judges 4–5; 2 Sam 20:14–22), and as such she serves a model for generations to come. The figure of Esther and her actions as the savior of the Jews, shines particularly in comparison to and contrast with those of her bitter opponent, Haman, who is presented in the book as a wicked man of boundless ego and self-importance, and as a bloody mass murderer of innocent Jewish people (Esth 3:3–15; 5:11–14; 6:4–9; 7:6; 8:5).

The courageous acts of Esther were praised even by the Protestant reformer, Martin Luther, who is otherwise harshly critical of the book of Esther. In 1523, in a sermon on Luke 16, Luther names Esther as "the beloved daughter of God," for she did not care about her life but rather about the lives of her people (WA, vol. 12, p. 593 lines 1–5).[72] In contrast, the German poet, Johann Wolfgang von Goethe, describes Queen Esther in a short play (1778) as not having the courage to speak to the king in order to save her people.[73] By doing so, Goethe inaccurately reverses the sense of the biblical story.[74]

In the last decades, there is lively discussion of Esther's character in modern feminist biblical interpretation. However, this interesting and important matter is beyond the focus of the current volume. There are

---

[71] See also Talmon, "'Wisdom' in the Book of Esther," pp. 419–455; J. Magonet, "The Liberal and the Lady: Esther Revisited," *Judaism* 29 (1980), pp. 167–176 esp. 173; Niditch, "Esther: Folklore, Wisdom, Feminism and Authority," p. 39. Contra Paton, *A Critical and Exegetical Commentary on the Book of Esther*, p. 96.

[72] For further details see Chapter 11, §II.

[73] See J. W. von Goethe, *Sämtliche Werke nach Epochen seines Schaffens* (Munich: Carl Hanser Verlag, 1987), vol. 2.1, pp. 211–234 esp. 229–232.

[74] On the historicity of Queen Esther, see Chapter 5, §II, 3, A. For additional discussions of Esther's reception history in Judaism and Christianity, see Chapters 8 (esp. §V, 1) through 13.

Figure 2   Aert de Gelder, Esther and Mordechai, ca. 1685, the Netherlands

many studies on this issue in the scholarly literature, all easily accessible to the interested readers.[75]

3   Mordecai: "Seeking the Welfare of His People"

A   The Major Persona of the Book

Without a doubt, Mordecai is the major persona and the most leading figure of the book of Esther. He is the first Jewish character that the book presents in the prologue (Esth 2:5–6), and the last one who closes the epilogue (10:1–3). Mordecai initiated the composition of the Megillah, established the Purim feast, and distributed them among the Jewish communities all over the kingdom (9:20–28, cf. 29). The core story deals with him, his conflict with Haman (3:2–6), and his efforts to cancel Haman's edict against the Jews.

---

[75] See, for example, Brenner (ed.), *A Feminist Companion to Esther, Judith and Susanna*; M. McClain-Walters, *The Esther Anointing: Becoming a Woman of Prayer, Courage, and Influence* (Lake Mary, FL: Charisma House, 2014); L. Brownback, *Esther: The Hidden Hand of God* (Flourish Bible Study; Wheaton, IL: Crossway Books, 2020); C. B. R. Howard, "When Esther and Jezebel Write: A Feminist Biblical Theology of Authority," in P. K. Tull and J. E. Lapsley (eds.), *After Exegesis: Feminist Biblical Theology: Essays in Honor of Carol A. Newsom* (Waco, TX: Baylor University Press, 2015), pp. 109–122; S. A. White Crawford, "Esther," in C. A. Newsom, S. H. Ringe, and J. E. Lapsley (eds.), *Woman's Bible Commentary* (3rd ed.; Louisville, KY: Westminster John Knox, 2012), pp. 201–207; O. Avnery, "Gender, Ethnicity, Identity: Duality in the Book of Esther," in P. Machinist, R. A. Harris, J. A. Berman, N. Samet, and N. Ayali-Darshan (eds.), *Ve-'Ed Ya'aleh (Gen 2:6): Essays in Biblical and Ancient Near Eastern Studies Presented to Edward L. Greenstein* (Atlanta: SBL Press, 2021), vol. 2, pp. 1099–1121, and the additional bibliography therein. See also the discussion of A. C. Silver, *The Book of Esther and the Typology of Female Transfiguration in American Literature* (Lanham, MD: Lexington Books, 2018) in Chapter 13.

Mordecai was a descendant of a noble lineage that goes back to the first king of Israel – Saul from the tribe of Benjamin (Esth 2:5–6; 1 Sam 9:1–2). He is a dynamic, self-confident, and nonconformist who acts and advises others contrary to regulations. Thus, officials who keep the king's order and bow down to Haman (3:2) still conspire to assassinate the king. In contrast, Mordecai who does not keep that order of the king and does not bow to Haman, yet stays loyal to the king, indirectly warns him – via Esther – on time, and saves his life (2:21–23). In other words, when it is necessary, Mordecai follows the regulation and perfectly fulfills his duty. Although "no one might enter into the king's gate clothed with sackcloth," nevertheless Mordecai does so (4:2); Esther stresses the risk to life involved in coming to the inner court of the king (4:11), but Mordecai still pushes her to go there, against all regulations (4:13–14).

After the death of Esther's father and mother (the author does not say when, where, or why this happened), Mordecai adopted the orphan girl as his own daughter (Esth 2:7).[76] He is the authority behind Esther, who guides her in her first steps at the palace concerning how to behave, what to do, and what not to disclose (2:7, 10–11, 20, 22; 4:8–16).

While the villain Haman uses his influence on King Ahasuerus to destroy the Jews of the Empire, Mordecai uses his influence on Queen Esther to rescue them. He definitely did not "sacrifice his cousin to advance his interests," as Paton asserts.[77] A careful reading of the biblical text shows clearly that Mordecai did not send Esther to the king's palace, and it was not Esther's free will to go there. Rather, "when the king's command and his edict were proclaimed, and many girls were gathered into Shushan the capital, into the custody of Hegai, *Esther was taken* [also] to the king's house" (ויהי בהשמע דבר־המלך ודתו ובהקבץ נערות רבות אל־שושן הבירה אל־יד הגי ותלקח אסתר אל־בית המלך; Esth 2:8).

B   A Courtier at the King's Gate

According to the prologue of the book, Mordecai "the Jew" began his career as a courtier in the king's gate (Esth 2:21; cf. 6:10, 12), and according to the epilogue he ended as a vizier of Ahasuerus (Esth 10:2–3).[78] At first glance, one gets the impression that Mordecai was just an ordinary

---

[76] Regarding the Septuagint version here and the statement in the Babylonian Talmud, *Megillah* 13a that Esther was the wife of Mordecai, see Chapter 8, §V, 1.

[77] Paton, *A Critical and Exegetical Commentary on the Book of Esther*, p. 96.

[78] On the possibility of the identification of Mordecai with "the *Mar-duk-â* the Sipîr," and that Mordecai (or one of his ancestors) was exiled by Nebuchadnezzar from Judah to Babylonia, see Chapter 5, end of §I and §II, 4.

resident of Susa, who had a low-level court position ("sat in the king's gate"; Esth 2:21), but still he had indirect access to the king via his agent – Esther. However, the implication of the reference to "sitting in the gate" is, probably, that he served as a kind of security police at the royal court, a position that was called the "eyes of the king" or "ears of the king" or "listening-watch,"[79] and somehow, he found out about the conspiracy against the king. The "eyes of the king" was a high post. Thus, Mordecai already had an important position in Xerxes' court even before the main story begins. He was blamed for not keeping "the king's laws" (Esth 3:18), however, he was loyal to the gentile king, Ahasuerus, whom he saved from the conniving plans of the officials (/ eunuchs), Bigthan and Teresh, who probably kept "the king's laws," but sought to assassinate him (Esth 2:21–23).[80] This is just the opposite portrait of a Jew compared to the false description of the Jews by Haman that "it is not for the king's profit to tolerate them" (Esth 3:8).[81] Moreover, in contrast to some Christian anti-Esther and antisemitic interpreters, this scene shows clearly that the Jews do not hate Gentiles as such.[82]

C   The Clash between Mordecai and Haman

In contrast to some Israelites in Egypt who accused Moses and Aaron that "you have made us loathsome in the eyes of Pharaoh, and in the eyes of his officials, to put a sword in their hand to slay us" (Exod 5:21), the story of Esther does not imply that Mordecai provoked Haman and caused all the trouble for the Jews.[83] Because of the immediate proximity of the brief story regarding the conspiracy of Bigthan and Teresh (Esth 2:21–23) to the story of the appointment of Haman as Ahasuerus' vizier and his clash with

---

[79] See, for example, Aristotle, *On the Cosmos* 6 (398a-b); D. J. Furley, "On the Cosmos," in E. S. Forster and D. J. Furley, *Aristotle*, Volume 3: *On Sophisticated Refutations, On Coming-To-Be and Passing-Away, On the Cosmos* (Loeb Classic Library 400; Cambridge, MA: Harvard University Press, 1955; reprinted 2000), pp. 333–409 esp. 386–391: "The pomp of Cambyses and Xerxes and Darius was ordered on a grand scale and touched the heights of majesty and magnificence: the king himself, they say, lived in Susa or Ecbatana, invisible to all, in a marvelous palace ... fortified with brazen doors and high walls; outside these the leaders and most eminent men were drawn up in order, some ... *called Guards and the Listening-Watch, so that the king himself ... might see everything and hear everything*" (ibid., pp. 387, 389; Greek on pp. 386, 388; emphasis added). On this office in the Achaemenid Empire and later in Athens, see J. Balcer, "The Athenian *episkopos* and the Achaemenid King's Eye," *AJP* 98 (1977), pp. 252–263.

[80] On this issue, see the discussion in Chapter 5, §II, 10.

[81] This text serves also as an early preparation and background – an exposition – for the turning-point of the story in Esther 6.

[82] On this issue, see the full discussion in Chapters 11, §VII and 12, §III.

[83] Cf. D. Daube, *Civil Disobedience in Antiquity* (Edinburgh: Edinburgh University Press, 1972), p. 90.

Mordecai (Esth 3:1–15); and because the two stories are related by the phrase אחר הדברים האלה ("after these things"; Esth 3:1a), the author of the Greek Addition to Esther (A 12:6) connects these stories. It says that Haman "determined to injure Mordecai and his people *because of the two eunuchs of the king*" (italics mine). However, the fossilized biblical phrase "after these things" only indicates the sequence of the stories in the book, rather than implying an organic and causal connection between them.[84] Therefore, the proximity and the phrase cannot support the conclusion of the author of the Greek Addition.

According to the biblical story, the conflict between Haman and Mordecai stemmed from the instructions of the king that everyone must stop and bow down before Haman wherever and whenever he is present. Mordecai refused to bow down to Haman. The story does not clarify Mordecai's rationale for his refusal to do so, when all the other servants of the king fulfilled the king's instruction (Esth 3:2–5). David Daube explains this as follows: "It looks – especially when we bear in mind the opening chapter about Queen Vashti – as if it were primarily a matter of dignity and pride. While Haman is a descendant of the Amalekite king, Mordecai belongs to a noble Jewish house: Saul's father is his ancestor (Esth 3:2; 2:5).[85] He would not recognize Haman as his superior."[86] Elias J. Bickerman also stresses that "Mordechai fights for his honor."[87]

Some cases in the Hebrew Bible show that bowing down – even to a foreigner – was unproblematic. For example, "Abraham bowed to the people of the land, to the Hittites," (Gen 23:7, 12). In the beginning, Joseph's brothers considered him as an Egyptian ruler and still "bowed down before him with their faces to the earth" (Gen 42:6, cf. 43:26). Thus, bow down to a foreigner should not be considered as a transgression. However, it is plausible that Haman demanded *divine* honor (as Nebuchadnezzar demanded; Judith 3:8), and Mordecai considered this to be idolatry, which is forbidden according to Jewish law. A clear hint of this view appears in Esth 3:3–4: when the king's servants asked Mordecai, "Why do you disobey the *king's command* (מצות המלך)?" The latter told them that "he is a Jew" (הגיד להם אשר הוא יהודי). In other words, the reason that he does not obey the king's command/ law

---

[84] On this expression in the Hebrew Bible, see Kalimi, *The Reshaping of Ancient Israelite History in Chronicles*, pp. 23–24; idem, "Go, I Beg You, Take Your Beloved Son and Slay Him!: Binding of Isaac in Rabbinic Literature and Thought," *RRJ* 13 (2010), pp. 1–29 esp. 6–7.

[85] On this issue, see Chapter 6, §II, 9.

[86] Daube, *Civil Disobedience in Antiquity*, p. 89.

[87] See E. J. Bickerman, *Four Strange Books of the Bible* (New York: Schocken, 1967), pp. 179–180, and cf. Berlin, *Esther: A Commentary*, p. 95, who stresses the well-known conflict between Israelites and Amalekites as the background for Mordecai's refusal.

is because he is a Jew – in the cultural and religious sense – who is obliged to follow the ancestral law that forbids him to bow down to any human who demands a divine honor. Against this background, Haman's claim is also clearer: He tells the king, "There is a certain people … *their laws are different* from those of every other people, and they do not keep *the king's laws*" (ישנו עם אחד … ודתיהם שונות מכל עם ואת דתי המלך אינם עשים; Esth 3:8). The words דתי המלך in Haman's claim is parallel to מצות המלך. That is, Mordecai does not keep the *king's command/law*, because it contradicts his own *religious law*. If so, then this is not only a personal clash between the pride of Haman and that of Mordecai, but also a cultural-religious conflict.[88] Thus, the story is – at least to some extent – a martyr's tale (*Kiddush Hashem*, i.e., the sanctification of God's name, martyrdom) in which the hero (i.e., Mordecai) is prepared to take a great risk, even to die, rather than to deny his ancestral faith or a single one of its norms. Mordecai protested against the rule of imperial power which arbitrarily imposes new law on him (and others) – a law that contradicts his own Jewish law and religious heritage.

Indeed, it seems that already the author of Addition C (Mordecai's Prayer) in Greek Esther 13:12–14 has interpreted the refusal of Mordecai to bow down to Haman in this direction: "You know, O Lord," says Mordecai, "that it was not in insolence or pride or for any love of glory that I did this, and refused to bow down to this proud Haman; for I would have been willing to kiss the soles of his feet to save Israel! But I did this so that *I might not set human glory above the glory of God*, and *I will not bow down to anyone but you*, who are my Lord; and I will not do these things in pride."[89]

A similar explanation is proposed also by the Jewish historian, Josephus Flavius, at the end of the first century CE: "Mordecai because of his wisdom and his native law would not prostrate himself before any man" (*Jewish Antiquities* 11.210).[90] Likewise Targum Sheni to Esther ascribes to Mordecai the claim that he does not bow down to a human being, but "I only bow down to the ever-existing God who is One in heaven … who lifts up the earth …."[91] Also, some midrashic sources interpret the clash

---

[88] Cf. Daube, *Civil Disobedience in Antiquity*, p. 89.

[89] Bickerman (*Four Strange Books of the Bible*, pp. 220–221) clarifies that Mordecai's refusal to bow down to Haman, which appears in his prayer in the Greek Addition of Esther, should be understood against the background of the Hellenistic custom not to bow down to any human being, even a king.

[90] See R. Marcus, *Josephus with an English Translation* (Loeb Classical Library; London: William Heinemann / Cambridge, MA: Harvard University Press, 1958), vol. 6, p. 417.

[91] B. Grossfeld, *The Targum Sheni to the Book of Esther: A Critical Edition Based on MS. Sassoon 282 with Critical Apparatus* (New York: Sefer-Hermon Press, 1994), pp. 45–46; idem, *The Two Targums of Esther: Translated, with Apparatus and Notes* (The Aramaic Bible 18; Collegeville, MN: Liturgical Press, 1991), pp. 142–143.

between Mordecai and Haman as a cultural–religious conflict. For instance, *Pirke deRabbi Eliezer*, ch. 50 (Eretz Israel, ca. eighth century), writes that Mordecai did not bow down to Haman because the latter "had an image (צילם) embroidered on his garment, and anyone who bowed down to Haman bowed also to the abomination (תועבה) which he had made. Mordecai saw this and did not consent to bow down to his disgusting thing (שיקוצו)."[92] The same line has been taken also by Abraham ibn Ezra: "What our rabbis, God bless their soul, expounded is correct, namely that he had the image of an idol on his clothing or on his hat" (ונכון מה שדרשו רז"ל כי צורת צלם ועכו"ז היו בבגדיו או על מצנפתו).[93]

Some scholars note that the author of Esther interprets the conflict between Mordecai and Haman as the exemplary war between Israel/Jews and Amalek (Exod 17:8–16; Deut 25:17–19). "This war is represented more personally in 1 Samuel 15 as that between Israel's king, Saul son of Kish the Benjaminite, and the Amalekite king, Agag. In Esther, Mordecai son of Yair son of Shimei son of Kish a Benjaminite, plays the role of Saul (Esth 2:5), while Haman 'the Agagite' (Esth 3:1) stands in for his eponymous ancestor,"[94] and he is "the Jews' enemy" (Esth 8:1; cf. 3:6, 10; 7:6).

From the moment that Mordecai found out about Haman's evil decree against his people, he did not rest, but promptly and decisively did everything he could to cancel it and protect them (Esth 4:1–17). Later, when Mordecai was promoted to serve as the king's vizier – "next to king Ahasuerus" – and became the most powerful Jew in the court of the king, he did not forget where he came from and to whom he belonged: He constantly continued "seeking the welfare of his people, and speaking peace to all his descendants" (Esth 10:3) – "seeking the welfare of his people" and not vengeance and hatred for others; "speaking peace" and not confrontation and war. Thus, Mordecai is presented as a valiant character, in contrast to the wicked Haman, who was seeking evil and destruction for the Jewish people.

[92] The English translation follows Horowitz, *Reckless Rites,* p. 157. Horowitz presumes that "The author of this late midrash transforms Haman into a Christian bishop who proudly wears upon his chest the sign of the cross …" (ibid., pp. 157–158). Horowitz himself admits this midrashic writer lived in the Land of Israel under the Islamic rule of Umayyad. This fact does not weaken his presumption, because at that time Christians had been in the Land of Israel for more than half a millennium already.

[93] See A. Mishaly and M. A. Zipor, *Abraham Ibn Ezra's Two Commentaries on Megilat Esther: An Annotated Critical Edition* (Ramat Gan: Bar-Ilan University Press, 2019), p. 77 (Hebrew); in his second commentary on Esther, ibn Ezra put this in different words: שהיה בבגדי המן צורת צלמי אליל, על כן לא השתחוה לו מרדכי (ibid., p. 140).

[94] Greenstein, "A Jewish Reading of Esther," p. 230; see also Berlin, *Esther: A Commentary,* p. 95.

All in all, the book of Esther presents Mordecai as one who is loyal to his ancestral tradition, to his family, to his people, and to his king.[95] No wonder, therefore, that generations of Jews have identified with "Mordecai the Jew" (Esth 6:10; cf. 2:5). They considered his triumph on Haman as the triumph of the Jewish people over their foes (or, if you wish, the "Amalekites" – as a personification of the evil), the triumph of the light and good over the dark and evil. Once again, even Luther who severely criticized the book of Esther, spoke warmly about Mordecai.[96]

VI   Conclusion

The biblical story of Esther focuses on Mordecai and his orphaned cousin Esther, whom he adopted as his daughter (Esth 2:7). She became the queen of the Persian Empire, then she took advantage of her position to destroy Haman's genocidal plan and save her people.

The origin of the book of Esther is disputed, but its date of composition cannot have been earlier than the second quarter of the fifth century BCE, nor later than the mid-second century BCE. The book's use of numerous Aramaic and Persian loan words and names but the lack of Greek ones or any allusion to event in the Hellenistic era support this. The author's apparent familiarity with many aspects of Persian culture and imperial administration, also support seeing it as a product of the Persian period rather than the Hellenistic or later period. There is no convincing reason to doubt that it could have been written within a generation or two of the essential events it describes, probably in Susa.

The book of Esther has been preserved in quite different versions: a short one in Hebrew, and two versions in Greek. The Hebrew, and most likely the oldest, version of Esther contains two parts, namely 1:1–9:19 and 10:1–3 (prologue, core story, and part of the epilogue), and 9:20–32 (the institution of Purim). In contrast to the Greek versions of Esther, the Hebrew version of the book seems overall a coherent text, with the exception of one late insertion – "the second letter of Purim" (Esth 9:29–32). Esther 9:20–28 and 10:1–3 is the epilogue of the book, and, as such, an integral part of it.

The Greek versions (the B-Text, and the Alpha-Text/ A-Text/ the Lucianic [L] Text) contain not only many different minor variants, but

---

[95] On historicity of Mordecai, see the discussion in Chapter 5, §II, 4. On Mordecai in the rabbinic literature, see Chapter 8, §V, 2.
[96] See Chapter 11, §II.

also six major additions (altogether 107 verses), which were preserved in the Christian Bible. Probably the MT and the B-Text had very similar *Vorlagen*. The Greek translators made many small and large changes of their Hebrew *Vorlage*. The A-Text is a shortened version of the B-Text. The Hebrew version of Esther is probably the oldest and closest one to the earliest form of the book.

Esther's story reflects a noble portrait of Vashti, Esther, and Mordecai. They are portrayed as respectable figures who refused to give up their integrity, even before the "king of kings" – the Persian emperor who controlled their fate. Vashti refused to flaunt her beauty before the king's drunken male guests, even though it cost her her position. Mordecai refused to bow down to Haman, even though it put his life in danger. Queen Esther risked her life and acted courageously and cleverly to free her people from that danger of destruction. The admirable characteristics of Esther and Mordecai and their audacious behaviors and acts for the sake of their people were and are a guidance to generations of Jews and non-Jews all over.

Mordecai, who was "sitting in the gate" of the king, perhaps served as a kind of security force at the court. It was a high position called the "eyes of the king" or "ears of the king" or "listening-watch," and in one way or another he found out about the plot against the king and saved him. Most likely, the clash between Haman and Mordecai was a religious–cultural one.

CHAPTER 3

Virtuosity, Literary Style, and Features

I Virtuosity

The narrative quality of the book of Esther is very impressive. It demonstrates, from beginning to end, an extraordinary and artful method of storytelling. It is rich in colorful images and creative literary features, emotional insights, and lively descriptions of figures, places, and events. The acts of its characters are described in a dramatic and dynamic manner, and their interactions are marked by suspense and sharp irony. All of this is presented in a clear structure, and in a simple and fluent style that takes the reader's heart from one scene to the next. No wonder, therefore, that the skillful storytelling of Esther has been accorded broadly a noble place among the world's greatest literature. For example: "According to numerous literary critics, Esther deserves to be reckoned among the masterpieces of world literature" (Bernard W. Anderson);[1] "One of the most successful novels of world literature that even today has not lost its effect on the reader" (Ruth Stiehl);[2] "There is widespread agreement that the literary skill of the narrative is of high quality" (Brevard S. Childs);[3] "The book of Esther is a masterfully constructed and narrated work of art" (Arndt Meinhold);[4] "The supreme narrative art of the book of Esther is universally praised" (Rolf Rendtorff).[5] The high literary quality of Esther is also not ignored by some of those scholars who denounce its religious

---

[1] See B. W. Anderson, "The Place of the Book of Esther in the Christian Bible," *JR* 30 (1950), pp. 32–43 esp. 32.

[2] "einer der erfolgreichsten Romane der Welt-literatur – verfehlt auch heute noch seine Wirkung auf den Leser nicht"; see Stiehl, "Das Buch Esther," p. 5.

[3] See B. S. Childs, *Introduction to the Old Testament as Scripture* (Philadelphia: Fortress Press, 1979), p. 600.

[4] "Das Estherbuch stellt ein meisterhaft aufgebautes und erzähltes Kunstwerk dar"; A. Meinhold, *Das Buch Esther* (Zürcher Bibelkommentare; Zurich: Theologischer Verlag, 1983), p. 12.

[5] See R. Rendtorff, *The Old Testament: An Introduction* (Philadelphia: Fortress Press, 1991), p. 270.

and moral values.[6] So, for instance, alongside emphasizing the "defects" of the book, Samuel Sandmel states that "Esther discloses a tremendous narrative skill, for it is as comic a story as has ever been told ... the author never allows the recurrent earnestness of his protagonists' plight to deter him from those little touches of character and incident that mark the difference between a mere narrator and a storyteller of genius."[7]

II The Secular Feature of the Book

On the surface, the scheme and features of the book indicate that the story is anthropocentric and takes place on the level of the natural and human spheres. Like the Joseph story, there is no direct divine involvement super-natural, imaginative, or meta-physical power(s) or miracles in the story of Esther. Furthermore, in contrast to the Greek versions of the book,[8] the Hebrew version of Esther does not contain any form of God's name or any religious law, institution, prayer, custom, or ritual (except for the fasting requested by Esther, as it is described in 4:16–17; 9:31).

Moreover, the author frequently uses passive language and forms in his writing, for example: Esth 1:19 (יִכָּתֵב); 2:8 (וַתִּלָּקַח אֶסְתֵּר), 20 (מַגֶּדֶת אֶסְתֵּר אֵין); 2:23 (וַיְבֻקַּשׁ הַדָּבָר וַיִּמָּצֵא); 5:3 and 9:12 (וְיִנָּתֵן לָךְ); 7:4 (נִמְכַּרְנוּ); 8:13 (לְהִנָּתֵן); וְהַיָּמִים הָאֵלֶּה נִזְכָּרִים (9:28) וְרָאֵתָו לְהֵעָשׂוֹת ... דָּת (9:1) וְהָפוֹךְ הוּא ... דָּת; ... לְהִנָּקֵם מֵאֹיְבֵיהֶם וְנַעֲשׂוֹ).[9] This linguistic feature creates a literary effect that gives the impression that the events are happening by themselves, without any interference.[10] As such, the feature contributes also to the telling of the story in the normal human realm.

III Repetitive Style and Other Literary Elements

The book narrates a clear and accessible short story in an appealing and beautiful style. It has a pleasant repetitive style, where the author uses

---

[6] See, for example, A. Weiser, *Einleitung in das Alte Testament* (5th ed.; Göttingen: Vandenhoeck & Ruprecht, 1963), p. 273; S. Ben-Chorin, *Kritik des Estherbuches: Eine theologische Streitschrift* (Jerusalem: Salinger, 1938), p. 5; S. Sandmel, *The Enjoyment of Scripture: The Law, the Prophets, and the Writings* (New York: Oxford University Press, 1972), pp. 36, 44; idem, *The Hebrew Scriptures: An Introduction*, p. 498; L. Day, *Three Faces of a Queen* (Journal for the Study of the Old Testament Supplement Series 186; Sheffield: Sheffield Academic Press, 1995), p. 9. For a negative opinion, see R. H. Pfeiffer, *Introduction to the Old Testament* (New York: Harper & Brothers, 1941), p. 747. It seems that Pfeiffer's deep hatred for the book prevents him seeing its high literary quality. For this and other negative evaluation of the book of Esther, see Chapter 8, §XI, Chapter 11, §III, and Chapter 12.

[7] Sandmel, *The Hebrew Scriptures*, pp. 497–498.

[8] On this issue see Chapter 10, §I.

[9] Cf. Berlin, *Esther: A Commentary*, p. 13.

[10] See Berlin, *Esther: A Commentary*, p. 13.

double terms, such as: אִישׁ וָאִישׁ ("each one"; 1:8), מְדִינָה וּמְדִינָה ... עַם וָעָם ("every province ... every people"; 1:22); תֹּר נַעֲרָה וְנַעֲרָה ("the turn came for each girl"; 2:12); וּבְכָל מְדִינָה וּמְדִינָה וּבְכָל עִיר וָעִיר ("in every province and in every city"; 8:13; 8:17). It includes also double phrases, for example: אֶת עֹשֶׁר כְּבוֹד מַלְכוּתוֹ, וְאֶת יְקָר תִּפְאֶרֶת גְּדוּלָתוֹ ("the great wealth of his kingdom and the splendor and pomp of his majesty"; 1:4); יְפַת תֹּאַר וְטוֹבַת מַרְאֶה ("beautiful and of good presence"; 2:7); מִי הוּא זֶה וְאֵי זֶה הוּא ("Who is he, and where is he"; 7:5); דֹּרֵשׁ טוֹב לְעַמּוֹ, וְדֹבֵר שָׁלוֹם לְכָל זַרְעוֹ ("seeking the welfare of his people, and speaking peace to all his seed"; 10:3). There are also double or triple, or even four synonym words one after the other, such as: צָהֲלָה וְשָׂמְחָה (8:15); לְהַשְׁמִיד וְלַהֲרֹג וּלְאַבֵּד ("to destroy, to kill, and to annihilate"; Esth 3:13; 8:11); אוֹרָה וְשִׂמְחָה וְשָׂשֹׂן וִיקָר ("light, and gladness, and joy, and honor"; 8:16).

    There are also recurrent traditional repetitions in the book: Twice appear the words, וְכָל עַבְדֵי הַמֶּלֶךְ אֲשֶׁר בְּשַׁעַר הַמֶּלֶךְ ("And all the king's ser-vants who were at the king's gate"; Esth 3:2) and in 3:3, וַיֹּאמְרוּ עַבְדֵי הַמֶּלֶךְ אֲשֶׁר בְּשַׁעַר הַמֶּלֶךְ ("the king's servants who were at the king's gate said"). Similarly, Esth 8:11, לְהִקָּהֵל וְלַעֲמֹד עַל נַפְשָׁם לְהַשְׁמִיד וְלַהֲרֹג וּלְאַבֵּד אֶת כָּל חֵיל עַם וּמְדִינָה הַצָּרִים אֹתָם טַף וְנָשִׁים וּשְׁלָלָם לָבוֹז ("to gather themselves together, and to stand for their life, to destroy, to slay, and to annihi-late, any armed force of any people or province that might attack them, infants and women, and to plunder their goods"), repeats on 3:13, לְהַשְׁמִיד לַהֲרֹג וּלְאַבֵּד אֶת כָּל הַיְּהוּדִים מִנַּעַר וְעַד זָקֵן טַף וְנָשִׁים בְּיוֹם אֶחָד... וּשְׁלָלָם לָבוֹז. Three times appears, וַיִּיטַב הַדָּבָר בְּעֵינֵי הַמֶּלֶךְ ("and the saying pleased the king"; Esth 1:21) and in 2:4, וְהַנַּעֲרָה אֲשֶׁר תִּיטַב בְּעֵינֵי הַמֶּלֶךְ ... וַיִּיטַב הַדָּבָר בְּעֵינֵי הַמֶּלֶךְ. Also, three times, יוֹשִׁיט לוֹ הַמֶּלֶךְ אֶת שַׁרְבִיט הַזָּהָב ("the king shall hold out the golden scepter"; Esth 4:11); וַיּוֹשֶׁט הַמֶּלֶךְ לְאֶסְתֵּר אֶת שַׁרְבִיט הַזָּהָב (5:2); and in 8:4, וַיּוֹשֶׁט הַמֶּלֶךְ לְאֶסְתֵּר אֵת שַׁרְבִט הַזָּהָב.[11] Four times repeats the phrase: מַה לָּךְ אֶסְתֵּר הַמַּלְכָּה וּמַה בַּקָּשָׁתֵךְ עַד חֲצִי הַמַּלְכוּת וְיִנָּתֵן לָךְ ("What is it, Queen Esther? What is your request? It shall be given you, even to the half of my kingdom"; 5:3); וּמַה שְּׁאֵלָתֵךְ וְיִנָּתֵן לָךְ וּמַה בַּקָּשָׁתֵךְ עוֹד וְתֵעָשׂ (5:6; 9:13); אֶסְתֵּר הַמַּלְכָּה וְתִנָּתֵן לָךְ וּמַה בַּקָּשָׁתֵךְ עַד חֲצִי הַמַּלְכוּת וְתֵעָשׂ (7:2).

    Repetitions appear also in the form of an instruction and its fulfill-ment; for instance, Esth 6:10–11 reports that Haman does exactly as he was ordered by the king: קַח אֶת הַלְּבוּשׁ וְאֶת הַסּוּס ... וַיִּקַּח הָמָן אֶת הַלְּבוּשׁ וְאֶת הַסּוּס ("take the clothing and the horse ... then took Haman the clothing and the horse"). Likewise, in Esth 7:9–10, ... הִנֵּה הָעֵץ אֲשֶׁר עָשָׂה הָמָן לְמָרְדֳּכַי ("Behold also, the gallows that Haman had made for Mordecai ... then the king said, hang וַיֹּאמֶר הַמֶּלֶךְ תְּלֻהוּ עָלָיו, וַיִּתְלוּ אֶת הָמָן עַל הָעֵץ אֲשֶׁר הֵכִין לְמָרְדֳּכַי

---

11 Cf. Niditch, "Esther: Folklore, Wisdom, Feminism and Authority," pp. 30–32.

him on it, so they hanged Haman on the gallows that he had prepared for Mordecai"); although here the author uses two different synonym verbs (עשה and הכין) and does not repeat exactly on the same word. In these cases, the author wished to say that the order performed precisely as the king ordered.[12]

The book contains several additional literary and stylistic devices, such as: detailed description (Esth 1:2–5); conditional clauses, for example: אם מזרע היהודים מרדכי אשר החלות לנפל לפניו לא תוכל לו כי נפול תפול לפניו ("If Mordecai, before whom you have begun to fall, is of the seed of the Jews, you shall not prevail against him, but shall surely fall before him"; 6:13); אם מצאתי חן בעיניך ("If it seem good to the king"; 5:4); אם על המלך טוב ("If I have found favor in your sight, O king, and המלך ואם על המלך טוב if it please the king"; 7:3); ואלו לעבדים ולשפחות נמכרנו החרשתי ("if we had been sold as male and female slaves, I would have kept my silence"; 7:4); indirect language,[13] a metathesis (6:14, ויבהלו להביא את־המן),[14] a pun (9:24, והמן ... לְהֻמָּם),[15] metonymy (3:15, והעיר שושן נבוכה ["but the city Shushan was thrown into confusion"]; 8:15, והעיר שושן צהלה ושמחה ["and the city of Shushan rejoiced and was glad"]), metaphor (ליהודים היתה אורה, "The Jews had light," i.e., "gladness"; 8:16), and merismus (1:5, 20, למגדול ועד קטן ["both great and small"]; 3:13, מנער ועד זקן ["both young and old"]).[16]

IV   Mosaic Style

In the category of literary style there includes a unique one, the so-called "mosaic style": The author of Esther intertwined into his story in an artistic way many phrases, idioms, and expressions that appear in earlier "biblical" writings, as if they were old mosaic stones embedded within his new creative composition. This feature of inserting a "quotation" in the composition – or creating an intertextuality with other "biblical" texts – is not exclusive for the Megillah. It is known also from other late biblical books of the Second Temple period, such as Chronicles, Qohelet, and

---

[12] This phenomenon is well known from the biblical and Ugaritic literature. See, for example, Gen 1:3; the instructions to build the Tabernacle and its vessels in Exod 25:1–31:11 and the fulfillment of them in 35:4–40:33.

[13] Cf. Berlin, *Esther: A Commentary*, pp. 10–14. On the structure and style of Esther, see also Levenson, *Esther: A Commentary*, pp. 5–12 and additional references there.

[14] I. Kalimi, *Metathesis in the Hebrew Bible: Wordplay as a Literary and Exegetical Device* (Peabody, MA: Hendrickson Publishers, 2018), p. 119.

[15] Cf. W. Dommershausen, *Die Estherrolle: Stil und Ziel einer alttestamentlichen Schrift* (Stuttgarter Biblische Monographien; Stuttgart: Verlage Katholisches Bibelwerk, 1968), p. 145; Levenson, *Esther: A Commentary*, p. 127.

[16] Cf. Dommershausen, *Die Estherrolle*, p. 146.

Daniel.[17] The following list includes some examples where the book of Esther depends on earlier literature or shows some similarity with it:

1. Esther 1:3, בשנת שלוש למלכו עשה משתה לכל שריו ועבדיו ("*In the third* year of his reign, *he made a feast for all his* officials and *servants*"; see also 2:18); Gen 40:20, ויהי ביום *השלישי* יום הלדת את־פרעה ויעש משתה לכל עבדיו ("It was *on the third* day, which was Pharaoh's birthday, and *he made a feast for all his servants*").

2. Esther 2:3, ...ויקבצו ("*Let* the king *appoint officers* in all the provinces of his kingdom, *and let them gather* ..."); Gen 41:34–35, ... ויקבצו ... פקידים על הארץ ("*Let him appoint officers* over the land ... *and let them gather* ...").

3. Esther 2:6, עם יכניה מלך יהודה אשר הגלה נבוכדנאצר ... אשר הגלה מירושלים מלך בבל ("Who had been exiled from Jerusalem ... with Jeconiah king of Judah, whom Nebuchadnezzar the king of Babylon had exiled") is parallel to Jer 29:1, אשר הגלה נבוכדנאצר מירושלם בבלה אחרי צאת יכניה המלך ("whom Nebuchadnezzar had exiled from Jerusalem to Babylon; after Jeconiah the king ... had departed from Jerusalem").

4. Esther 2:7, יפת תאר וטובת מראה ("*beautiful of form and* good *looking*") is parallel to Gen 39:6, יפה תאר ויפה מראה ("*beautiful of form and* beautiful *looking*").

5. Esther 2:8, ותלקח אסתר אל המלך אחשורוש אל בית מלכותו ("*Esther was brought* to King Ahasuerus, *to his palace*"); and Gen 12:15 regarding Sarah, ותקח האשה בית פרעה ("and the woman was taken to Pharaoh's palace").

6. Esther 2:12, כי כן ימלאו ימי מרוקיהן ("*for thus were the days filled with* treatment"); Gen 50:3, כי כן ימלאו ימי החנטים ("*for thus were the days filled with* embalming").[18]

7. Esther 3:4, ויהי באמרם אליו יום יום ולא שמע אליהם ("They were speaking *to him daily, but he did not listen to them*"); and Gen 39:10 about Potiphar's wife, ויהי כדברה אל יוסף יום יום ולא שמע אליה ("She was speaking to *Joseph daily, but he did not listen to her*").

8. Esther 3:10, ויסר המלך את טבעתו מעל ידו ויתנה להמן בן המדתא האגגי ("The king *took the signet from his hand and gave it* to Haman, son of Hammedatha, the Agagite"); Gen 41:42, ויסר פרעה את טבעתו מעל

[17] See the examples collected and discussed by Kalimi, *The Reshaping of Ancient Israelite History in Chronicles*, pp. 252–255 (these in addition to the many texts that the Chronicler took from the Torah, Samuel, Kings, Ezra, and Nehemiah); idem, *The Retelling of Chronicles in Jewish Tradition and Literature: A Historical Journey* (Winona Lake, IN: Eisenbrauns, 2009), pp. 17–20.

[18] Note, while Genesis speaks about the dead body of a man (Jacob), Esther speaks about the live body of a woman.

ידו ויתן אתה על יד יוסף ("Pharaoh *took the signet ring from his hand and put it* on the hand of Joseph"). Compare also Esth 8:2, ויסר המלך את טבעתו ... ויתנה למרדכי ("The king *took the signet ring ... and gave it* to Mordecai").

9. Esther 4:16, וכאשר אבדתי אבדתי ("*If* I perish, I perish"); Gen 43:14, ואני כאשר שכלתי שכלתי ("*If* I am bereaved, I am bereaved").

10. Esther 5:9, ויצא המן ביום ההוא שמח וטוב לב ("Then went Haman out that day *joyful and with a glad heart*"), cf. וילכו לאהליהם שמחים וטובי לב ("they blessed the king, and went to their tents *joyful and glad of heart*"; 1 Kgs 8:66 // 2 Chr 7:10)

11. Esther 6:11 and 8:2, 7 use the following verbs and descriptions to describe Mordecai: ויסר ("and he took off"), ויתנה ("and he gave it"), וילבש ("and he put on"), וירכיבהו ("and he caused him to ride"), ויקרא לפניו ("and he called out before him"); the same expressions also appear regarding Joseph in Gen 41:42–43: ויסר ("and he took off"), ויתן אותה ("and he gave it"), וילבש ("and he put"), וירכב ("and he caused to ride"), ויקרא לפניו ("and they called out before him").

12. Esther 8:6, כי איככה אוכל וראיתי ברעה אשר ימצא את עמי ואיככה אוכל וראיתי באבדן מולדתי ("*For how* can I bear to see the evil that is coming upon my people? Or how can I bear to see the destruction of my kindred?"); compare to the similar expression that ascribed to Judah in Gen 44:34, כי איך אעלה אל אבי והנער איננו אתי פן אראה ברע אשר ימצא את אבי ("*For how* can I go back to my father if the boy is not with us, lest I see evil that will come upon my father?").

13. Esther 4:1, ויזעק זעקה גדלה ומרה ("*He cried out a great and bitter cry*"); compare to the similar expression regarding Esau in Gen 27:34, ויצעק צעקה גדולה ומרה עד מאד ("*and he cried out a* very *great and bitter cry*"). The words זעק זעקה and צעק צעקה are synonyms.

14. Esther 5:7–8, ותען אסתר ותאמר ... אם מצאתי חן בעיני המלך ("Then Esther said ... If I have found favor in the king's sight"), and likewise in 7:3 and 8:5 is similar to the opining Num 32:5, ויאמרו אם מצאנו חן בעיניך ("If we have found favor in your sight").[19]

15. The phrases in Esth 8:17, כי נפל פחד היהודים עליהם and in 9:2, כי נפל פחדם על כל העמים (see also 9:3), are like the one in Ps 105:38, שמח מצרים בצאתם כי נפל פחדם עליהם.[20]

---

[19] The expression that is used in similar cases in earlier biblical writings is: בי אדוני (Gen 44:18; 1 Sam 1:26), or 2) עלי אדוני המלך העון 2 Sam 14:9).

[20] Cf. also ויפל פחד יהוה על העם in 1 Sam 11:7; as well as 1 Chr 14:17, ויהוה נתן את־פחדו על־כל־הגוים (an "addition to 2 Sam 5:25); 1 Chr 18:14 (// 2 Sam 8:15); 2 Chr 20:29, פחד אלהים על כל ממלכות הארצות ויהי.

16. Esther 9:4, וְגָדוֹל הוֹלך מרדכי האיש כי ("for this man Mordecai grew greater and greater"), reminds Exod 11:3, מאד גדול משה האיש גם ("also the man Moses was very great").

17. Esther 3:1*b* talks about Haman: השרים כל מעל כסאו את וישם וינשאהו אתו אשר ("and they *raised* [= advanced] him up and *set his seat above all the officials* who were with him"). In 2 Kgs 25:27–28 the same idiom is used in the story on Joiachin, king of Judah, in the Babylonian court, מלך יהויכין ראש את מלכו בשנת בבל מלך מרדך אויל נשא אתו אשר המלכים כסא מעל כסאו את ויתן טבות אתו וידבר כלא, מבית יהודה בבבל ("In the year that he began to reign, Evil-Merodach king of Babylon *raised up* the head of Jehoiachin king of Judah from prison; and he spoke kindly to him, *and set his throne above the throne of the kings* who were with him in Babylon").

18. Esther 6:10, דברת אשר מכל דבר תפל אל ... היהודי למרדכי כן ותעשה דברת כאשר ... ("... as you have said, and do so to the Jew Mordecai ... Leave out nothing that you have mentioned"), is similar to what appears in Solomon's prayer in 1 Kgs 8:56, מכל אחד דבר נפל לא דבר אשר ככל ... דבר אשר הטוב דברו ("not one word has failed of all his good promise, which he spoke through").

19. Esther 9:22, לרעהו איש מנות ומשלוח ושמחה משתה ימי ("**joy**, and of sending portions one to another"); Neh 8:12, שמחה ולעשות מנות לשלח גדולה ("to send portions, and to make great **rejoicing**").

20. There are also pairs of words in Esther that appear already in early Hebrew literature, especially in the prophetical books:

    a. The phrase ועבדיו שריו in Esth 1:3 is parallel to ושריו עבדיו in 1 Kgs 9:22.

    b. Esther 1:22, כלשונו ועם עם ואל ("it should be proclaimed according to the language of **every people**") is parallel to Neh 13:24, ועם עם כלשון ("according to the language of **every people**").

    c. The phrase וימצא הדבר ויבקש ("And when investigated and found to be so") in Esth 2:23 mirrors the same words in Isa 65:1, בקשני ללא נמצאתי ("I was ready to be found by those who did not **seek** me").

    d. The words ומשתחוים כרעים in Esth 3:2 appear in chiastic order in Ps 95:6, ונכרעה נשתחוה ("let us worship and bow down; let us kneel"; cf. 22:29); and in 2 Chr 7:3, הרצפה על ארצה אפים ויכרעו וישתחוו ("they bowed with their faces to the ground upon the pavement and worshipped") – all regarding bowing down to God.

e. The words הקרובים והרחוקים ("both **near** and <u>far</u>") in Esth 9:20 is the plural form of the same words in the singular that appear in Isa 57:19, לרחוק ולקרוב ("who is <u>far</u> off and for him who is **near**").

f. The phrase שלום ואמת ("**peace** and <u>truth</u>") in Esth 9:30 is the same one in Zach 8:19, והאמת והשלום ("<u>truth</u> and **peace**").

g. The idiom איי הים ("islands of the sea") in Esth 10:1 appears twice in Isaiah (11:11; 24:15).

The use of the pairs of the words in chiastic order in comparison to their appearance in the earlier literature supports the proposition that the later author – author of Esther – made use of the earlier writings.[21]

21. Although the phrase מנער ועד זקן ("from young to old") in Esth 3:13 appears already in Gen 19:4,[22] it could be a part of common linguistic style or a usage of it from there.

A brief glance at these examples shows that many are shared by the Esther story and the Torah (no. 1–2, 4–9, 11–14, 16), especially the book of Genesis (no. 1–2, 4–9, 11, 16), and here particularly the Joseph story (nos. 1–2, 4, 6–9, 11–12). These links with the Joseph story and the fact that many of them reflect close verbal parallels, point to a strong linguistic similarities and patterns of content connections between the stories. Indeed, the Talmudic Rabbis had already pointed out the relationship between the stories (Midrash *Esther Rabbah* 7:8), and later on Martin Luther noticed some similarities between the Joseph, Daniel, and Esther stories.[23] Some of these literary parallels and allusions, as well as other thematic links between these stories, have been discussed in detail in modern biblical scholarship.[24] Striking are also the parallels between Esther and those in other places

---

[21] On this feature in biblical literature, see Kalimi, *The Reshaping of Ancient Israelite History in Chronicles*, pp. 232–274 ("Chiasmus between Parallel Texts").

[22] Compare this phrase with Exod 10:8.

[23] See Chapter 11, §II.

[24] See M. Gan, "The Book of Esther in the Light of the Story of Joseph in Egypt," *Tarbiz* 31 (1961–1962), pp. 144–149 (Hebrew); A. Meinhold, "Die Gattung der Josephsgeschichte und des Estherbuches: Diasporanovelle," *ZAW* 87 (1975), pp. 306–324; 88 (1976), pp. 72–93 (some of the examples listed here are taken from these studies); Berg, *The Book of Esther: Motifs, Themes and Structure*, pp. 121–142; see also the discussion of these studies by Niditch, "Esther: Folklore, Wisdom, Feminism and Authority," pp. 26–28. For similarities between Esther and Daniel, see, for example, L. A. Rosenthal, "Die Josephsgeschichte, mit den Büchern Ester und Daniel verglichen," *ZAW* 15 (1895), pp. 278–284. See also Wills, *The Jew in the Court of the Foreign King*, pp. 39–74, with a discussion of court legends in Egyptian, ancient Near Eastern, and Greek literature.

Niditch ("Esther: Folklore, Wisdom, Feminism and Authority," p. 28) believes that "the language and content that Esther shares with the Joseph narrative confirms its place in the traditional-style literature of Israel." But what about all those parallels that Esther shares with other biblical writings? Should they also be considered as "the traditional-style literature of Israel"?

in the Torah (Genesis, Exodus, and Numbers), Kings, prophetical writings, Psalms, and Nehemiah. In other words, the author of Esther knew well the earlier different "biblical" texts, particularly Torah and Prophets, used them in his composition, and created analogies between his story and those writings that probably were known to his audience. By doing so, he enriched his writing and made it attractive to the readers because it was in line with earlier Hebrew tradition. The cases from Nehemiah (no. 19, 20b) are in chiastic parallel to Esther, and likely were taken from it.

V   Synonyms and Series of Synonymous Words

In addition to the double terms that the author of Esther uses in his narration (see §III), he also often employs two, three, and even four words, one by the other, usually synonyms, in other to emphasize some point. This includes: מבהלים דחופים (8:14b); רוח והצלה (4:14); שמח וטוב לב(5:9); צר ואויב (7:6); משתה ויום טוב (8:17); שמחה וששון (8:17); צהלה ושמחה (8:15); הרגו היהודים ואבד (9:6). There is also usage of three synonymous words, such as להשמיד להרג ולאבד (3:13; 7:4; 8:11); מכת חרב והרג ואבדן (9:5), or even four, אורה ושמחה וששן ויקר (8:16). In these cases, by using a series of synonymous words the author probably wished to highlight the incredible disastrous destruction and tragedy that could be happened (3:13; 7:4; 8:11; 9:5) on the one hand, and the greatness of the happiness and joy (8:16) that its cancelation caused, on the other.

The story opens with the scenes of the great banquet that King Ahasuerus made for his שריו ועבדיו (Esth 1:3). The word עבדיו means either "his officials/ ministers"[25] – in which case it is simply a synonym to the common term שריו, and the latter interprets it – or it means "his servants"[26] – in which case the phrase is not a tautology, but the author wishes to say that the banquet was not just for a limited number of officials, but for the numerous workers of the palace – for "his officials and servants."[27] The appearance of the phrase in Esth 3:1–2, וישם את כסאו מעל כל השרים אשר אתו, as well as וכל עבדי המלך אשר בשער המלך ... ויאמרו עבדי המלך אשר בשער המלך, in 5:12, אשר נשאו על השרים ועבדי המלך, approves the latter understanding of the phrase in 1:3 rather than the former.

---

[25] Cf. 1 Kgs 9:22, "But Solomon made no *slaves* (עבד) of the Israelites. They were his soldiers, *officers* (עבדיו ושריו), commanders, and chief officers of his chariots and horsemen." Similarly, the title עבד on the bronze stamp seal from Tel Megiddo: לשמע עבד ירבעם, that is, "Shema *official* of Jeroboam" (the II); see C. Watzinger, *Tell el-Mutesellim* (Leipzig: J. C. Hinrichs'sche Buchhandlung, 1929), vol. 2, pp. 64–65. Strikingly, in the parallel text in 2 Chr 8:9, the Chronicler omits the word עבדיו and writes ושריו only.

[26] See previous note, and 1 Kgs 1:2, "And his servants (עבדיו) said to him ..."

[27] It is also possible that the author simply used here – in chiastic order – the same phrase that appears in 1 Kgs 9:22; see above §IV, no. 17.

VI   Inner Interpretations and Identifications

Occasionally, the author correlates in the narrative some foreign or uncommon words/ phrases, which he interprets by using another word/phrase. In other words, there are several inner/internal interpretations in the book of Esther, for example:[28]

1. Esther 3:7 and 9:24 (cf. 9:26) recount that Haman הפיל פור הוא הגורל ("cast Pur, that is, the lot"). The term פור derives from Akkadian – more precisely neo-Assyrian – *pūru*(m), which means "lot" or "a little cube" by which one casts lots.[29] This foreign term appears in biblical literature only in Esther. Because it was rare and unfamiliar for his audience, the author interprets it by a renowned word, saying: הוא הגורל. Indeed, the word גורל is common in the Hebrew Bible (e.g., Lev 16:8, 9; Num 26:54; Josh 14:2; Obad 1:11; Neh 8:2).

2. The phrase הכתב להנתן דת בכל מדינה ומדינה פתשגן in Esth 3:14 regarding Haman's decree, repeats with a minor variation also in the report of Mordecai to Queen Esther in 4:8, פתשגן כתב הדת אשר נתן בשושן, and in the counter decree of the king in 8:13, פתשגן הכתב להנתן דת בכל מדינה ומדינה. The word פתשגן is a Persian word that H. Gehman assumed that was borrowed by Hebrew through Aramaic,[30] and means a "written" (or a "copy" of) document.[31] Thus, most likely, the word כתב actually interprets the foreign and unusual word פתשגן.[32]

3. Esther 3:13 reports that the Haman's decree was carried out by הרצים ("the couriers," lit. "the runners"). A similar phrase appears twice also in the king's contra-decree: once in 8:10, הרצים בסוסים רכבי הרכש and once again in Esth 8:14, הרצים רכבי הרכש. The term הרצים in 3:13 and in 8:14 is an elliptical form (מקרא קצר) of [בסוסים] הרצים ("runners [on horses]").[33]

---

[28] The examples here are organized not in canonical order of the biblical text but according to their contribution to illustrating the issue in the book.

[29] See *CAD*, vol. P, p. 528a; W. Hallo, "The First Purim," *The Biblical Archaeologist* 46/1 (1983), pp. 19–29; S. Dalley, *Esther's Revenge at Susa: From Sennacherib to Ahasuerus* (Oxford and New York: Oxford University Press, 2007), pp. 167–168.

[30] See H. Gehman, "Notes on the Persian Words in the Book of Esther," *JBL* 43 (1924), pp. 321–328 esp. 326; Moore, *Esther*, p. 42; Ego, *Esther*, p. 192.

[31] BDB, pp. 837b, 1109a; Gerleman, *Esther*, p. 99: "einem vorlegenden Schriftstück angefertigte Kopie."

[32] In Ezra 4:11, 23; 5:6; 7:11 this word appears as פרשגן. It is "not clear whether פרשגן is text error from פתשגן, of from different origin, or from the same root in different stage"; BDB, p. 1109a.

[33] This phenomenon is well known in the biblical literature; see, for example, 2 Sam 6:6; Ps 18:17 and the discussion by Kalimi, *The Reshaping of Ancient Israelite History in Chronicles*, p. 73.

The word רֶכֶשׁ means סוּס ("horse"), as it reveals from Mic 1:13, רְתֹם
הַמֶּרְכָּבָה לָרֶכֶשׁ יוֹשֶׁבֶת לָכִישׁ ("You inhabitant of Lachish, harness the
chariot to the רֶכֶשׁ [= horse]");[34] and from 1 Kgs 5:8, וְהַשְּׂעֹרִים וְהַתֶּבֶן
לַסּוּסִים וְלָרֶכֶשׁ יָבִאוּ אֶל הַמָּקוֹם אֲשֶׁר יִהְיֶה שָׁם אִישׁ כְּמִשְׁפָּטוֹ ("Barley and straw
for the horses and for the רכשׁ brought they to the place where every
man according to his charge"). That the word רֶכֶשׁ means "horse,"
appears also in the Aramaic ostracon (no. 6, line 1) from Arad, and in
the Aramaic documents from Egypt.[35] Also, רכשא in late Syriac means
"horse." The word סוּס(ים) is much more common in the Hebrew
Bible than רכשׁ: the former appears 137 times, while the latter only
four times, and of which twice in Esther (1 Kgs 5:8; Mic 1:13; Esth
8:10, 14).

Accordingly, in the phrase הָרַצִּים בַּסּוּסִים רִכְבֵי הָרֶכֶשׁ (8:10), the words
הָרַצִּים בַּסּוּסִים are parallel to and interpret רִכְבֵי הָרֶכֶשׁ. Probably, the
potential readers of Esther (and of Kings) no longer comprehended the
word רֶכֶשׁ. To make it clear, the author of Esther (and that of Kings) –
or a glossator – clarified it by adding the familiar word סוּסִים.[36] It should
not be surprising that the common word סוּס /סוּסִים appears before the
uncommon word רכשׁ that clarifies it, because such clarification can
come before or after the uncommon word (see also below).

4. In Esther 2:2 the author narrates that נַעֲרֵי הַמֶּלֶךְ מְשָׁרְתָיו suggested to
    the king "Let young virgins of good presence be sought for the king."

---

[34] Prophet Micah uses the word רכשׁ rather than סוּס, because it creates word-play with the name
"Lachish" which follows immediately, just as he uses the word אכזב ("disappoint") in the next verse
because it sounds good with the name אכזב : בָּתֵּי אַכְזִיב לְאַכְזָב לְמַלְכֵי יִשְׂרָאֵל ("Achziv houses to disappoint the kings of Israel").

[35] See Y. Aharoni, *Arad Inscriptions* (Jerusalem: Bialik Institute and Israel Exploration Society, 1975),
p. 171 (Hebrew).

[36] Some scholars are not aware of the inner biblical interpretation; thus, they struggle to expound/
translate these verses in Esther and Kings. For example, Meinhold translates here as follows: "… und
schickte Schreiben durch die Eilboten zu Pferde, die herrschaftlichen Rossen, den Rennpferden, rit-
ten" ("and sent letters through the couriers on horseback, the stately steeds, the racehorses, rode");
see Meinhold, *Das Buch Esther*, p. 73. New King James Version: "and sent letters by couriers on
horseback, riding on royal horses." Berlin (*Esther: A Commentary*, p. 135) writes here: הָרַצִּים בַּסּוּסִים,
שֶׁהֵם הָרוֹכְבִים (הַמְּקֻצְעִים) עַל סוּסֵי הַדּוֹאַר הַמַּלְכוּתִיִּים, שֶׁנּוֹלְדוּ מְסוּסִים מְהִירִים ("The horse runners, who are the
(professional) riders on the royal mail horses, born from fast horses"). Similarly, regarding the word
רכשׁ in Kings: Hentschel translates as follows: "Die Gerste und das Stroh für die Pferde und *Zugtiere*
brachten sie jeweils an den Ort, für den jeder zuständig war." The German word *Zugtiere* means any
"draft animal," that is, it could be also donkey, ox, etc., not necessarily "horse"; see G. Hentschel, *1.
Könige* (Echter Bibel 10; Würzburg: Echter Verlag, 1984), p. 39. Noth is of the opinion that רכשׁ does
not necessarily mean "horse": "Bei רכשׁ ist nicht notwendig an Pferde zu denken, es könnte auch Esel
in Frage kommen." He thinks that the Hebrew רכשׁ derives from the Akkadian *rakāsu/rakāšu* that
means "bind, tie" or "clamp"; see M. Noth, *Könige* (Biblicher Kommentar Altes Testament 9,1;
Neukirchen-Vluyn: Neukirchner Verlag, 1968), p. 58; *CAD*, vol. R, p. 91a.

Now, the word נער appears in the Hebrew Bible in three meanings:
(a) a child or a young man, such as מנער ועד זקן (Esth 3:13); נער הייתי גם
זקנתי (Ps 37:25); והנער נער (1 Sam 1:24); נער יהוה את פני משרת שמואל
אפוד בד (1 Sam 2:18); והנער שמואל הלך וגדל (1 Sam 2:26); (b) a soldier,
such as in 2 Sam 2:14, יקומו נא הנערים וישחקו לפנינו ("Let the נערים come
forward and have a contest before us," see also 2:21; and 1 Sam 21:3, 5,
6; Neh 4:10, 17); and (c) a servant, such as וישכם אברהם בבקר ויחבש את
ובא נער הכהן ואמר לאיש הזבח (Gen 22:3, cf. 19); חמרו ויקח את שני נעריו אתו
ויאמר קיש אל שאול קח נא אתך את אחד מהנערים וקום לך (1 Sam 2:18);
בקש את האתנת ... ושאול אמר לנערו אשר עמו (1 Sam 9:5). In order to
provide the reader the exact meaning of the phrase נערי המלך, he adds
the word משרתיו, which interprets the idiom נערי המלך. That is to say,
the king's servants, and not his soldiers, children, or those who grow
up with him (e.g., 1 Kgs 12:10). Later in the story, the author uses
once again נערי המלך משרתיו (6:3), but thereafter simply נערי המלך (6:5).

5. Esther 2:23 recounts that the conspiracy against the king and its
prevention is written in the book of Chronicles (ויכתב בספר דברי הימים
לפני המלך). Esther 6:1 recounts את בלילה ההוא נדדה שנת המלך ויאמר להביא
ספר הזכרנות דברי הימים ויהיו נקראים לפני המלך ("On that night the king
could not sleep, and he commanded to bring the Book of Records,
the Chronicles, and they were read before the king"). Here the
author explains that ספר הזכרנות is דברי הימים, which describes the
events that took place in the royal court and in other places in his
kingdom. Those who are expert in such writings are called החכמים ידעי
העתים (Esth 1:13), in modern terms – the "historians."

It is possible that the author of Esther himself used the foreign or rare
words while compounding their meaning next to them. Accordingly,
the interpretation of the word is an integral part of the original text.
However, it is also not impossible that the word(s) penetrated Hebrew
and was used on certain occasions, but later an interpretation of it was
needed. Such an annotation is made either by a later editor or by a reader
through a gloss. Thus, the meaning of the word is not an integral part of
the ancient text but is added to it later on. In several cases it is difficult,
if not impossible, to determine the exact relationship between a word
and its meaning.

This phenomenon is not exclusive to the book of Esther. Translations/
interpretations of foreign, difficult, or rare words, phrases, and sentences
appear in several other biblical writings, for example:

1. The words מים על־הארץ ("waters over the earth") in Gen 6:17 is an interpretation of המבול (the "flood"), which probably derives from the Akkadian word *bubbulu* ("flood").[37] The same event is called in Isa 54:9, מי־נח ("the water of Noah").

2. In Gen 31:45–47, יגר שהדותא ("pile of witness") is an Aramaic phrase translated in context by the Hebrew word גלעד (also meaning "pile of witness").

3. In Lev 19:19c the legislator commands ובגד כלאים שעטנז לא יעלה עליך ("You shall not put on yourself clothes of two kinds, mixed fabric"). Although the phrase בגד כלאים ("clothes of two kinds") comes before it, it is a translation of the word שעטנז ("mixed fabric"). Though the origin of the word שעטנז is uncertain, it likely derives from Egyptian.

4. Similarly, in Deut 22:11, לא תלבש שעטנז צמר ופשתים יחדו ("You shall not wear mixed fabric, wool and linen together"), the phrase צמר ופשתים יחדו is an interpretation/ translation of the word שעטנז.[38]

There is also some identification of Babylonian names in the book: The author identifies the common Babylonian name of the heroine "Esther" (אסתר >Ištar) with her Hebrew personal name "Hadassah" (הדסה היא אסתר; Esth 2:7).[39] The late biblical books Ezra, Nehemiah, and Chronicles are still using the ordinary numbers as names of months (e.g., Ezra 3:1, 6, 8; Neh 8:2; 2 Chr 30:2, 15; 31:7; 35:1; see also Ezek 1:1; 8:1). At some point, the Judeans received the neo-Babylonian names of months: Nissan, Iyar, Sivan, Tammuz, and so on. From this point of view, the book of Esther seems to be a transitional one. Here there is an identification of the names of months in the ordinary numbers, as used in the old system, with the current neo-Babylonian names: בחדש העשירי הוא חדש טבת (Esth 2:16); בחדש הראשון הוא חדש ניסן בשנת שתים עשרה למלך אחשורוש הפיל פור הוא הגורל לפני המן ביום אחד בשלושה עשר   (3:7); מיום ליום ומחדש לחדש שנים עשר הוא חדש אדר ויקראו ספרי המלך בעת ההיא בחדש השלישי (3:13); לחדש שנים עשר הוא חדש אדר ובשנים (8:12);   בשלושה עשר לחדש שנים עשר הוא חדש אדר (8:9); הוא חדש סיון

---

[37] See *CAD*, vol. B, pp. 298–300.

[38] Note the chiastic in parallel order of the phrase in Deuteronomy:

Lev 19:19c, בגד כלאים שעטנז לא יעלה עליך

Deut 22:11, לא תלבש שעטנז צמר ופשתים יחדו

Thus, these texts are related thematically as well as literarily, and in Deuteronomy also the phrase בגד כלאים of Leviticus is interpreted as צמר ופשתים יחדו. Cf. I. Kalimi, "Jewish Bible Translations," in K. J. Dell (ed.), *The Biblical World* (2nd ed.; London: Routledge, 2021), pp. 889–905 esp. 890–891.

[39] On the names "Hadassah" and "Esther," see the discussion in Chapter 2, §V, 2 and Chapter 5, §I, 2, A.

עשר חדש הוא אדר חדש חדש עשר (9:1). Surprisingly, identification of חדש שנים עשר with חדש אדר appears constantly four times (3:7, 13; 8:12; 9:1).

VII *Inclusio*, Chiasmus, and Chiastic in Parallel

The author of Esther uses a series of literary devices in his composition. We mentioned already the usage of resumptive repetition. Like many other biblical authors, he also uses forms of *inclusio*, chiasmus, and chiastic in parallel structures.

1 Inclusio *and Chiasmus*

1. The Esther story opens with information about the greatness of King Ahasuerus (1:1) and ends with his (and Mordecai's) greatness (10:1–2), that is, the whole story is presented within an *inclusio*. Moreover, the names מדי ופרס ("Media and **Persia**") in Esth 10:2 stand in chiastic order to those in Esth 1:3, פרס ומדי ("**Persia** and Media").

2. Esther 2:13–14 recounts that a young girl could visit the king only after having been prepared for twelve months. The author formed this information within an *inclusio*:

   "And when every **girl's** time (or turn) **had come to go in to king** (ובהגיע תר נערה ונערה לבוא אל המלך) Ahasuerus,
   after she had been twelve months, according to the manner of the women, for so were the days of their purifications accomplished, namely six months with oil of myrrh, and six months with sweet perfumes, and with other ointments for women,
   then thus **came** [every] **girl to the king** (ובזה הנערה באה אל המלך)."

3. The author systematically refers to the ruler of the Persian Empire as המלך אחשורוש (1:2, 9, 10, 16, 17, 19; 2:1; 3:1, 8; 7:5; 8:1, 7, 12; 10:1, 3), and to his wife in chiastic order, as אסתר המלכה (2:22;5:2, 3, 12; 7:1, 2, 5; 8:1, 7; 9:12, 29, 31)

4. Twice it has been stressed in the book that Esther did not disclose her ethnic and cultural origin. Once in Esth 2:10:

   לא הגידה אסתר את עמה ואת מולדתה, כי מרדכי צוה עליה

   and once again, in chiastic order, in 2:20:

   אין אסתר מגדת מולדתה ואת עמה כאשר צוה עליה מרדכי

Note, there are three sets of chiasmus between the two parallel verses.

5. Esther 2:10 is formed within *inclusio*: לא הגידה אסתר את עמה ואת מולדתה
כי מרדכי צוה עליה אשר לא תגיד.

6. Esther 2:20 is formed in chiastic order: אין אסתר ... כאשר צוה עליה מרדכי

ואת מאמר מרדכי אסתר עשה כאשר ...

7. Esther 3:12:

בשם המלך אחשורש נכתב
ונחתם בטבעת המלך

8. The information that appears in Esth 5:10b-11a is within the literary form of *inclusio*, in which the opening and closing words are repeated in chiastic order in 5:14 (a, b, c … c', b', a'):

"He sent and called for
(a) **his friends** and
  (b) *Zeresh, his wife,*
    (c) and told them" (5:10b-11a)
      [account of Haman, 5:11b-13]
    (c') "Then told him
  (b') *Zeresh, his wife,*
(a') and all **his friends**" (5:14)

9. Esther 6:13, ויספר המן לזרש אשתו ולכל אהביו את כל אשר קרהו ויאמרו לו
חכמיו וזרש אשתו ("And Haman told **Zeresh his wife** and all his friends everything that had befallen him. Then said his wise men and **Zeresh his wife** to him").

10. Esther 7:5:

ויאמר המלך אחשורש ויאמר לאסתר המלכה
מי הוא זה
ואי זה הוא
אשר מלאו לבו לעשות כן

11. Esther 9:4 is formed within *inclusio* and there is also a structure of chiasmus between 4a and 4b:

כי גדול מרדכי בבית המלך ושמעו הולך בכל המדינות
כי האיש מרדכי הולך וגדול

12. The second "Purim Letter" (9:29–32) is built in chiastic structure with its center being the letter that Mordecai sent to all Jews:

(a) ותכתב

(b) אֶסְתֵּר הַמַּלְכָּה בַּת אֲבִיחַיִל

(c) וּמָרְדֳּכַי הַיְּהוּדִי

(d) אֵת כָּל תֹּקֶף לְקַיֵּם אֵת אִגֶּרֶת הַפּוּרִים הַזֹּאת הַשֵּׁנִית

(e) *וַיִּשְׁלַח סְפָרִים אֶל כָּל הַיְּהוּדִים אֶל שֶׁבַע וְעֶשְׂרִים וּמֵאָה מְדִינָה*
מַלְכוּת אֲחַשְׁוֵרוֹשׁ דִּבְרֵי שָׁלוֹם וֶאֱמֶת

(d') לְקַיֵּם אֵת יְמֵי הַפֻּרִים הָאֵלֶּה בִּזְמַנֵּיהֶם

(c') כַּאֲשֶׁר קִיַּם עֲלֵיהֶם מָרְדֳּכַי הַיְּהוּדִי

(b') וְאֶסְתֵּר הַמַּלְכָּה ... וּמַאֲמַר אֶסְתֵּר קִיַּם דִּבְרֵי הַפֻּרִים הָאֵלֶּה

(a') וְנִכְתָּב בַּסֵּפֶר.

Moreover, there is an inner-chiastic structure in the following phrases:

כַּאֲשֶׁר קִיַּם עֲלֵיהֶם מָרְדֳּכַי הַיְּהוּדִי

וְאֶסְתֵּר הַמַּלְכָּה ... וּמַאֲמַר אֶסְתֵּר קִיַּם דִּבְרֵי הַפֻּרִים הָאֵלֶּה

13. Chiastic structure appears also in the last and the shortest chapter of the book, Esth 10:1–3:[40]

(a) וַיָּשֶׂם הַמֶּלֶךְ אֲחַשְׁוֵרוֹשׁ מַס עַל הָאָרֶץ וְאִיֵּי הַיָּם וְכֹל מַעֲשֵׂה תָּקְפּוֹ וּגְבוּרָתוֹ

(b) וּפָרָשַׁת גְּדֻלַּת מָרְדֳּכַי אֲשֶׁר גִּדְּלוֹ הַמֶּלֶךְ ...

(b') כִּי מָרְדֳּכַי הַיְּהוּדִי

(a') מִשְׁנֶה לַמֶּלֶךְ אֲחַשְׁוֵרוֹשׁ וְגָדוֹל לַיְּהוּדִים ...

14. Some scholars suggest that the whole book of Esther is built in chiastic structure. Thus, for instance, Yehuda T. Radday noted the following chiastic structure:

   (a) Chs. 1–5 – annihilation threat
      (b) Ch. 6:1 – turning point
   (a') Ch. 6:2–10:3 – salvation

The third part repeats the first one.[41] Or, in some detail, as Radday presents it:

   (a) Opening and background (ch. 1)
      (b) The king's first decree (chs. 2–3)
         (c) The clash between Haman and Mordecai (chs. 4–5)
            (d) "On that night, the king could not sleep (ch. 6:1)
         (c') Mordecai's triumph over Haman (chs. 6:2–7:10)
      (b') The king's second decree (chs. 8–9)
   (a') Epilogue (ch. 10)

---

[40] Esther 10, with its three verses, is the second shortest chapter in the Hebrew Bible. The only shorter one is Psalms 117 with two verses.

[41] See Y. T. Radday, "Chiasm in Joshua, Judges and Others," *LB* 27/28 (1973), pp. 6–13 esp. 9–10.

2   Chiasmus in Parallel

1. The number "one hundred and twenty-seven" in Esth 1:1 stands in order of chiasmus in parallel to the same number that appears in Gen 23:1:[42]

   Esth 1:1 – שבע וַעֶשְׂרִים וּמֵאָה מדינה
   Gen 23:1 – מֵאָה שנה וַעֶשְׂרִים שנה ושבע שנים

2. Esther 6:12 describes that Haman went to his home אבל וחפוי ראש, which resembles when David ran away from his son Absalom בוכה וראש לו חפוי (2 Sam 15:30).[43]

3. Several phrases in the book of Esther appear in chiastic order to the similar ones in the prophetical books, as listed above in §IV.

4. There are two idioms that express the same idea, which appear in chiasmus in parallel:

   Esth 1:5, למגדול ועד קטן ("from **great** to small");
   Esth 3:13, מנער ועד זקן ("from young to **old**").[44]

VIII   Antithesis

"Antithesis is a literary device used to draw lines of contrast between the deeds or fate or other details of two characters."[45] This literary feature that is common in the other books of the Hebrew Bible, appears also in Esther, for example: Esth 3:15, "The king and Haman settled into drinking, while the city of Shushan sat dumbfounded" (והמלך והמן ישבו לשתות והעיר שושן נבוכה). As Susan Niditch properly puts this, "this brief phrase style encapsules a wonderful image of 'fiddling while Rome burns',"[46] which is attributed to the Roman emperor Nero, who played music while his people in Rome were suffering the big fire of 64 CE.

Moreover, the scene that "the king and Haman settled into drinking" (3:15), stands totally in contrast to the scene that is reported immediately in the following verse (4:1): "When Mordecai learned all that had been

---

[42] For the phenomenon of "chiastic parallelism" between texts in the biblical literature, see Kalimi, *The Reshaping of Ancient Israelite History in Chronicles*, pp. 232–274. Note, the chiasmus between the parallel texts, Esth 1:1 and Gen 23:1, is invisible in English translations as well as in other European languages.

[43] However, compare Jer 14:3, וחפו ראשם.

[44] On this phrase, see also §IV no. 14 above.

[45] Kalimi, *The Reshaping of Ancient Israelite History in Chronicles*, pp. 325–349 esp. 325.

[46] Niditch, "Esther: Folklore, Wisdom, Feminism and Authority," p. 29.

done, Mordecai tore his clothes and put on sackcloth and ashes, and went through the city, wailing with a loud and bitter cry."

There is an ironic antithesis between how King Ahasuerus represented throughout the tale – drunk, lustful, and manipulated by his wife and officials – and his final description in Esth 10:1–2 as an active, powerful and mighty emperor: "King Ahasuerus *laid tribute* on the land and on the islands of the sea. *All the acts of his power and might ....*"

IX   Structures of Reversal Destiny and *Talionis*

The reversal destiny is a central literary tool in the composition of Esther, and usually built in a chiastic form.[47] That is, a single person (e.g., Haman) or a group of people (e.g., the Jews' enemies) plans to do something but it turns upside down in reality. The author explicitly highlighted this principle in Esth 9:1 by the term *"it was turned to the contrary"*: "in the day that the enemies of the Jews hoped to have power over them, though *it was turned to the contrary*, that the Jews had rule over those who hated them" (ביום אשר שברו איבי היהודים לשלוט בהם ונהפוך הוא אשר ישלטו היהודים המה בשנאיהם). The intention is clear: to show the unpredictability of human fortune and his ability to rule the events, or in theological terms – "the man thinks, and God laughs!"[48]

This feature of the Megillah is especially emphasized in comparison with the irreversibility and unalterable nature of the Persian king's decree or law: "for the decree which is decreed in the king's name, and sealed with the king's ring, is not reversal" – even by the king himself (Esth 8:8b), while in other cases, an unseen hand turns human plans upside down. Some examples follow:

- Haman came to the king's court to ask permission to hang Mordecai on the gallows that he had prepared; but instead he should extend to Mordecai a royal honor that he had hoped to receive himself (Esth 5:14 and 6:4–12).
- At the end, Haman found his death on the same gallows that he prepared for his opponent. Haman searches for support, encouragement, and sympathy for his awful situation from his wife Zeresh and other beloved and wise members of his family and

---

[47] This issue in Esther is much discussed in the scholarship (though not using the same term); see, for example, Gerleman, *Esther*, pp. 30–32; Moore, *Esther*, p. lvi; Clines, *The Esther Scroll*, p. 155.

[48] Cf. Prov 19:21, "There are many plans in a man's heart; nevertheless, the counsel of the Lord shall stand" (רבות מחשבות בלב איש ועצת יהוה היא תקום).

friends. However, they discourage him and increase his agony (Esth 6:13).

- Haman falls on Esther's bed *to beg for his life*, but the king interprets the act as Haman's attempt to sexually abuse the queen, *leading to his death* (Esth 7:7–8).
- Even more significantly, Haman wished "to destroy, to kill, and to annihilate *all Jews, young and old, women and children* ... and to plunder their properties" (3:13).
- The Jews, however, defended themselves from those enemies and still did not plunder their properties, that is, the counter-decree of Mordecai is opposite of Haman's decree but just to some extent. Generally speaking, what the latter planned for Mordecai and his people (Esth 3:8–9), was turned backwards, "on the very day when the enemies of the Jews hoped to gain power over them, but which had been changed to a day when the Jews would gain power over their foes" (Esth 9:1).
- Thus, the month "had been turned for them from sorrow into gladness and from mourning into a holiday" (Esth 9:22; cf. 7:9–10; 3:7).

The reversal destiny has also an aspect of the divine principle of absolute justice, "measure for measure" (*quid pro quo*, or *qualis culpa talis poena*, that is, "the punishment resembles the sin in quality"), or even the principle of *talionis*.[49] We already mentioned that Haman, who prepared a gallows to hang Mordecai on, was hanged on that same gallows (Esth 5:14; 6:4; 7:9–10).[50] Haman desired to annihilate Mordecai and all his people, the Jews of the Persian Empire, and possess their properties. However, he himself, his sons, and supporters were destroyed;[51] his estate was given to Esther (who appointed Mordecai to be in charge of it, Esth 7:9–8:7; 9:7–10); and his political power was bestowed on Mordecai.[52]

---

[49] See Midrash Psalms *Shocher Tov* 22:2; S. Buber, *Midrash Tehillim* (Vilna: Reem, 1891; reprinted, Jerusalem: Ch. Wagschal, 1977), p. 181 (Hebrew); W. G. Braude, *The Midrash on Psalms* (Yale Judaica Series 13; New Haven: Yale University Press, 1959; 3rd ed., 1976), vol. 1, p. 298. That the people are rewarded or punished according to a principle and pattern of equivalent retribution, is reflected in several biblical, postbiblical and extrabiblical sources. For a discussion and additional examples, see Kalimi, *The Reshaping of Ancient Israelite History in Chronicles*, pp. 186–193.

[50] Compare these acts with the decree detailed in Ezra 6:11, ומני שים טעם די כל-אנש די יהשנא פתגמא דנה יתנסח אע מן-ביתה וזקיף יתמחא עלהי וביתה נולו יתעבד על-דנה ("whoever shall change this word, let timber be pulled down from his house, and let him be lifted up and impaled on it; and let his house be made a dunghill for this").

[51] For more on this issue, see Chapter 6, §I, Chapter 8, §VII.

[52] The only exception to this pattern of appropriate reward and punishment is the case of Vashti, who was punished unevenly; see Chapter 2, §V, 1 and Chapter 8, §IV, 4, B.

In this regard, there is also a case of contra-*talionis* in the book: Despite Mordecai saving the king from the conspiracy of Bigthan and Teresh who sought "*to lay hand on* the king Ahasuerus" (ויבקשו לשלח יד במלך אחשורש; Esth 2:21), Haman committed an offense – he "disdained *to lay hands on* Mordecai" (לשלח יד במרדכי; Esth 3:6).[53]

X   Overstatement, Hyperbole, and Typological Numbers

The book of Esther includes several ahistorical overstatements, hyperbolical and typological numbers, as well as fantastic or novelistic descriptions.[54] For example, in the *third* year of his kingship, the king held in Susa a banquet, in which "all his officials and ministers, the army of Persia and Media and the nobles and governors of the provinces were present ... for many days, *one hundred eighty days* in all" (Esth 1:4). When these days were over, Ahasuerus gave for "*all the people present in Susa*, both great and small, a banquet lasting for *seven* days" (Esth 1:2–5). Later, he made another banquet in honor of the new queen, Esther (Esth 2:18). Also, he took part in two banquets prepared by Esther (Esth 5:4–8; 7:1–8). Simply, the quantity of the banquets and their long durations – particularly "one hundred eighty days" – are beyond the reality.

The numbers "three," "seven" (days, officials, maids, years; Esth 1:3, 10; 2:9, 12, 16), "ten" (sons of Haman; Esth 9:7–10, 13, 14), "twelve" (months, Esth 2:12), as well as "180" (3×60, or 3×6 [= 2×3]×10; Esth 1:4), and 300 foes (3×100 or 3×10×10; Esth 9:15) could be real ones; after all, how could the author express himself when he needed to report something in these amounts? But probably they are typological numbers, and as such they are a legendary part of the story.

The claim that the king appointed officials in *all* the provinces of his kingdom to *gather all the beautiful young virgins* to the harem in Susa is also exaggerated (Esth 2:3). Moreover, according to Esth 2:12–14, the young girls in the harem were said to have been prepared for *twelve* months: "*six months* with oil of myrrh, and *six months* with sweet perfumes ...." Certainly, to sleep with the king demanded some necessary preparation. However, it is not clear why a naturally beautiful young virgin needed a *twelve-month* preparation with spices and lotions. This preparation for a woman is nine times longer than the preparation for a mummy, which according to Gen 50:3 took only *forty days*. Yet, if this long process resulted

---

53   Greenstein, "A Jewish Reading of Esther," p. 228, pointed out the parallel idioms in Esther, but did not see the contra-*talionis* between them.
54   Some of these features of the book are noted already in scholarship, though not fully; see, for example, Berlin, *Esther: A Commentary*, p. 13.

in an even more beautiful woman or a kind of "living mummy," is hard to say. Nonetheless, the preparation process of twelve months seems far beyond reality, and these numbers seem hyperbolic.[55] No wonder therefore, that the translator of Peshiṭta altered the word "month" in these verses to the word "days," and read: "for twelve *days* ... six *days* with oil of myrrh, and *six days* with sweet perfumes."

Moreover, Haman bribed the king with "ten thousand talents of silver" (Esth 3:9). To judge according to the Greek historian, Herodotus of Halicarnassus (*Historia* 3.95–96; written around 440 BCE), this amount of bribe is equivalent to almost two-thirds of the annual income of the entire Persian Empire.[56]

Haman made gallows "fifty cubits high" (Esth 5:14), that is, as tall as an eight- or nine-storey building. Also, according to the Masoretic Text of Esth 9:16, the Jews killed "seventy-five thousand" of their enemies – a huge number in any case.[57] The same can also be said about Esth 9:15, which reports the killing of 300 foes by Jews of Susa. Such descriptions and numbers are all hyperbolic, and enormously exaggerated, ranging between improbable and impossible.[58] Their intention is to magnify as much as possible the immense wealth of the king, Haman's deep hatred of Mordecai and his people, the incredible animosity between Jews and Gentiles, and the ridiculous treatment of virgins who will spend one night with the king.

XI Satirical and Humoristic Descriptions

On their way to conquer the Holy Land from the hands of Muslims in 1096, the Crusaders gave the Jews of Rhineland the choice: "Cross or

---

[55] Contra Briant, *From Cyrus to Alexander*, p. 282, who considers Esther's description as a realistic one. The comparison with Judith 10:3–4 does not make Esther's description more reliable. Albright suggested that this long process led to impregnation of the girls; see W. F. Albright, "The Lachish Cosmetics Burner and Esther 2:12," in H. N. Bream, R. D. Heim, and C. A. Moore (eds.), *A Light unto My Path: Old Testament Studies in Honor of Jacob M. Myers* (Philadelphia: Temple University Press, 1974), pp. 25–32. This suggestion is accepted also by some commentators, for example, Moore, *Esther*, p. 23; see also Bush, *Ruth, Esther*, p. 365. However, Clines (*Ezra, Nehemiah, Esther*, p. 289) correctly notes that "the practice of impregnating the skin and hair with the fumes of burnt cosmetics is paralleled by customs of semi-nomadic Ethiopian tribeswomen of the nineteenth century AD, a culture rather distant from the court of ancient Persia."
[56] On this issue, see below, §X.
[57] On this issue as well as for other textual versions of this number, see the detailed discussion in Chapter 12, §III, 1.
[58] See also Th. Nöldeke, "Esther," *Die Alttestamentliche Literatur in einer Reihe von Aufsätzen dargestellt* (Leipzig: Verlag von Quant & Händel, 1868), pp. 83–84; Dommershausen, *Die Estherrolle*, p. 145; Niditch, "Esther: Folklore, Wisdom, Feminism and Authority," pp. 29–32, where she refers to Hermann Gunkel's study (ibid., p. 29 note 1).

Death!" In contrast, the book of Esther recounts a horrifying story about a temptation to exterminate the entire Jewish people in one day, without even leaving an option of conversion and integration in the surrounding society. In order to soften the shock and irritation of his potential audience, the author of Esther story skillfully used humor. Indeed, the book is full of humoristic imagery, and rich in ironic description (several of the reversals mentioned above paragraph §IX are also examples of irony in the story). This literary feature is known from other ancient writings, biblical (e.g., Judges 3) as well as nonbiblical (e.g., Herodotus, *Historia* 1.8–13).[59] There are also many examples of satire. The Esther story mocks Ahasuerus and his royal court: He becomes a prisoner of the laws and decrees that he himself created or signed, without being able to change them.[60] He reigns over a great empire, "from India to Nubia/Ethiopia," but is powerless to force his wife, Vashti, to come and show her beauty to his officials (Esth 1:10–12). His sexual desires seem endless. After Vashti snubs him, he gathers "*all* the beautiful young virgins in *all* the provinces of his kingdom" to his harem, and each of them visits him for one night (Esth 2:3, 12–14). He is also presented as a glutton, who celebrates one banquet after another, drinks boundless wine, and seems to be regularly drunk (Esth 1:10; 3:15; 5:6; 7:2). Therefore, he came to be, in fact, a marionette in the hands of his vizier Haman as well as of his wife Esther.[61]

XII Conclusion

The narrative quality of the book of Esther is remarkable. It presents a notable and artful method of storytelling. It shows colorful characters, emotional insights, and lively descriptions – all in a clear and accessible and attractive style. No wonder, therefore, that the book counts among the world's masterpieces of literature.

The book combines well-crafted literary style with a concise but highly engaging story of averted catastrophe. It uses drama and humor to depict a plot by a high royal official named Haman to bring about the complete destruction of the Jewish people in the Persian Empire, in revenge for

---

[59] On humor and irony in the book of Esther, see also Greenstein, "A Jewish Reading of Esther," p. 228; Y. T. Radday, "Esther with Humour," in A. Brenner and Y. T. Radday (eds.), *On Humour and the Comic in the Hebrew Bible* (Journal for the Study of the Old Testament Supplement Series 92; Sheffield: Almond Press, 1990), pp. 295–313; J. W. Whedbee, *The Bible and the Comic Vision* (Cambridge: Cambridge University Press, 1998), pp. 129–190 esp. 171–190.

[60] On this issue, see the detailed discussion in Chapter 5, §II, 8.

[61] On the king's decision-making, see Chapter 5, §II, 2 and 8, no. 3.

a supposed insult by the Jew Mordecai. The story contains many over-statements, hyperbolic and typological numbers, satirical and humoristic descriptions, and ironic reversals of fate, which all give some legendary character to the tale. There is no explicit divine interfere in the sequence of events, and the story has a secular characteristic that the author compe-tently achieved. He presents his story in a variety of forms and fixed struc-tures, while using several literary and stylistic features, such as mosaic style, *inclusio*, chiasmus, and chiasmus in parallel. The author uses also double terms, indirect language, pleasant repetitive style, as well as several liter-ary tools, for example metathesis and pun (though just one time of each), metonymy, antithesis, formations of *talionis*, as well as inner interpreta-tion and identification. Some of these literary tools are well known from other biblical writings, others are more unique to Esther – for instance, reversals of fate.

CHAPTER 4

The Central Message of Esther within Biblical and Ancient Near East Contexts

To understand any literary composition and fully appreciate its value, the reader must know its exact nature and the author's intention. Thus, usually, the Classical and Hellenistic writers provide an explanatory preface to their works and reveal the nature and purpose of their compositions. For example, Herodotus starts his *Historia* (1.1), which is written around 440 BCE, close to the composition of Esther, as follows:

> What Herodotus of Halicarnassus [modern Bodrum, west coast of Asia Minor] has learnt by inquiry is here set forth in order that the memory of the past may not be blotted out from among men by time, and that the great and marvelous deeds done by Greeks and the Barbarians [i.e., foreigners] and especially the reason why they warred against each other may not lack renown.[1]

A similar justification for his writing is reflected in the words of the author of the first letter of Purim in that he justifies the composition of the Megillah (and ascribes it to Mordecai): "therefore for all the words of this letter, and of that which they had seen concerning this matter, and which had come to them" (על כן על כל דברי האגרת הזאת ומה ראו על ככה ומה הגיע אליהם, Esth 9:23–26 – esp. verse 26). One can deduce from these verses that he considered the story of Esther as something that actually happened, and Mordecai composed it to commemorate it for the coming generation. Nonetheless, the specific nature of the work and its genre is still disputed in the scholarship: Is Esther really just a humorous or carnivalesque book, "a happy story about a happy holiday," and "one should not read the story

---

[1] A. D. Godley, *Herodotus with an English Translation* (Loeb Classical Library 1; London: William Heinemann / Cambridge, MA: Harvard University Press, 4 vols.; 1920), vol. 1, p. 3 (with some minor changes). Similarly, Thucydides, *The Peloponnesian War* 1.1–2; Dionysius of Halicarnassus, *Roman Antiquities*, I 1.1–8.4; Josephus Flavius, *Jewish Antiquities* 1.1–26. For additional citations and discussion, see I. Kalimi, *An Ancient Israelite Historian: Studies in the Chronicler, His Time, Place, and Writing* (Studia Semitica Neerlandica 46; Assen: Royal Van Gorcum [now under: Brill, Leiden], 2005), pp. 19–20.

as a serious story, but rather as a story designed to entertain and make the reader and listener laugh"?[2] Does the book truly belong to the Ancient Near Eastern wisdom literature category?[3] Is it right that it "contains no religious element"[4] whatsoever, "a secular book [that] hardly deserves a place in the canon of Sacred Scriptures,"[5] or "the most secular book of the Bible"?[6] Is it indeed true that "the lack of reference to God probably shows that he [i.e., the author] did not intend his book to be regarded as sacred scripture"?[7] Or, is the book – despite its humoristic style and the absence of God's name – a serious story about the tragic destiny of the Jewish people in the Diaspora, a religious text with an essential theological and social message that should be read very carefully and seriously (and then its place in the canon would be self-evident)?

Furthermore, the book of Esther has long enjoyed great popularity and high esteem among the Jews.[8] What accounts for this? Does the book have any important message that warranted such a unique and central place? To address these questions, it is necessary to examine the main story of Esther concerning the threatened annihilation of the Jews and their redemption, within its contexts, as reflected in several biblical and extrabiblical sources.

I The Fear of Complete Annihilation

Several texts in the Hebrew Bible reflect the fact that the Israelites main-tained a traumatic fear of their complete annihilation. Generations were terrified for their very existence. This inner fear is rooted in, or at least illustrated by, the horrific story of the Aqedah (the binding of Isaac) in Gen 22:1–19. After several promises (Gen 12:7; 15:4–5, 7–21) and long-awaited hope, the hundred-year-old Abraham and ninety-year old Sarah had an only son (Gen 18:10–15; 21:5). Yet, God commanded Abraham to take his

---

[2] See Berlin, *Esther: A Commentary*, p. [1]: אין לקרוא את הסיפור כסיפור רציני, אלא כסיפור ... סיפור משמח על חג משמח שתכליתו לשעשע ולגרום לקורא ולשומע לצחוק.
[3] See Talmon, "'Wisdom' in the Book of Esther," pp. 419–455.
[4] See W. M. L. de Wette, *Lehrbuch der historisch-kritischen Einleitung in die Bible, Alten und Neuen Testamentes* (5th ed.; Berlin: G. Reimer, 1840), vol. 1, p. 275 (§198 b); English translation from: idem, *A Critical and Historical Introduction to the Canonical Scriptures of the Old Testament* (translated by T. Parker; Boston: H. B. Fuller, 1850), vol. 2, p. 340 (§198 b). Recently, Carruthers (*Esther through the Centuries*, p. 7) repeated this claim (without referring to de Wette) by speaking about "the book's lack of religious content."
[5] See Pfeiffer, *Introduction to the Old Testament*, p. 747; cf. O. Eissfeldt, *The Old Testament: An Introduction* (New York: Harper and Row, 1965), p. 511: "it is purely secular."
[6] See Berlin, *Esther: A Commentary*, p. 3.
[7] M. V. Fox, *Character and Ideology in the Book of Esther* (2nd ed.; Grand Rapids, MI: Eerdmans / Eugene, OR: Wipf & Stock, 2001), p. 238.
[8] For further details see Chapter 8.

beloved one and "offer him … as a burnt offering[9] upon one of the mountains that I will tell you" (Gen 22:2). Only at the last moment, before Abraham's knife touched Isaac's throat, the angel of the Lord ordered: "Do not lay your hand on the lad" (Gen 22:12).[10] Thus, the very founders of the Israelite nation are portrayed as near victims of extermination.

Later on, the fear of annihilation is reflected in Jacob's prayer: "O save me from the power of my brother, from Esau! *I am afraid of him coming and slaying me, the mother with the children*" (Gen 32:12 [ET, 32:11]). It emerges also in Jacob's reaction to Simeon and Levi's devastation of Shechem: "You have undone me, you have made me odious among the natives, the Canaanites and Perizzites; my numbers are few, and *they will muster to attack me, until I am destroyed, I and my family!*" (Gen 34:30). Indeed, the author of the story stresses that only God's interference saved Jacob's family from annihilation: "As they rode off, a panic fell upon the surrounding towns, and no one pursued the sons of Jacob" (Gen 35:5).

When the Israelites resided in Egypt, Pharaoh could not tolerate them, because they were "too many and too mighty" (Exod 1:9). He put them "under captains of the labor gangs, to crush them with heavy loads" (Exod 1:11) and ordered the execution of every newborn male Israelite child already on the birth-stool (Exod 1:16). He ordered all his people "to throw every son born to the Hebrews into the Nile" (Exod 1:22).[11] Once again, only direct interference by God saved the Israelite children from death (Exod 1:17) and redeemed them from Egyptian slavery and oppression "by a series of tests, by signal acts, by war, by sheer strength and main force, with awful terrors" (Deut 4:34; cf. Exod 20:2).

Such deep hatred toward the Israelites and the strong will to see their complete extermination is reflected not only in the biblical descriptions of "Pharaoh the enslaver" (probably Ramses II), but also in some extrabiblical

---

9 Some earlier English versions translated here "holocaust" in place of "a burnt offering," see J. A. H. Murray, *The Oxford English Dictionary* (Oxford: Clarendon Press, 1933), vol. 5, p. 344. "Holocaust" was just an English word for "burnt offering," related to the Greek ὁλοκαύτωμα, which translates עֹלָה ("burnt offering") in many biblical passages (e.g., Gen 22:2, 7–8, 13; Leviticus 1 uses a similar term: ὁλοκάρπωσιν), which came to be used in the late nineteenth century to describe cases of mass slaughter (not only of Jews), before eventually becoming the preferred term to describe the atrocities carried out against the Jews by the Germans and their collaborators during the Second World War. Due to this association, it fell out of use as a general term for burnt offerings, but this reflects how the events of the Second World War were interpreted. Cf. J. Fleet, "History and Meaning of the Word 'Holocaust': Are We Still Comfortable with this Term?" *Huffington Post* (March 28, 2012): www.huffingtonpost.com/2012/01/27/the-word-holocaust-history-and-meaning_n_1229043.html

10 See the discussion by Kalimi, *Fighting over the Bible*, pp. 149–183.

11 No wonder that in Quran Pharaoh is related with Haman (as his adviser, 28:6, 8, 38, cf. 29:39–40; 40:23–24, 36–37), who wished to annihilate the Jews; see G. S. Reynolds, *The Qur'ān and the Bible: Text and Commentary* (New Haven: Yale University Press, 2018), pp. 595–596, 603–604, 617–618, 711, 713.

sources. In the Hymn of Victory, the so-called "Israel Stele," from the fifth year of Pharaoh Merneptah II (ca. 1213–1203 BCE),[12] the first mention of "Israel" outside of the Bible is marked by deep abhorrence: *Israel is laid waste, his seed is not.*[13]

Several hundred years later, Mesha, king of Moab (ca. mid-ninth century BCE), recounts his rebellious actions against the Kingdom of Israel, and states: "As for Omri king of Israel, he humbled Moab many years, for Chemosh was angry at his land ... but I have triumphed over him and over his house, while *Israel has perished forever*" (the Moabite Stone, lines 4–7).[14]

The horrible, deep fear of complete destruction lingered among the Israelites for a long time, and one of its clearest expressions is reflected in Psalm 83:

> Do not keep silent, O God; do not hold your peace and be still, O God. For, behold, your enemies make a tumult; and those who hate you have lifted up the head. They have taken crafty counsel against your people, and consulted against your hidden ones. *They have said, Come, and let us cut them off from being a nation; that the name of Israel may no longer be remembered.* For they conspire together with one accord, they make an alliance against you ... They said, let us take possession for ourselves of the pastures of God. (Ps 83:1–6, 13 [ET, 83:1–5, 12])

Some scholars have attempted to connect this psalm to a particular event in the history of Israel in the biblical period. Briggs and Briggs, for example,

---

[12] The dating of Merneptah's reign in the late thirteenth century BCE differs widely according to various scholars; the figures here follow J. von Beckerath, *Chronologie des Pharaonischen Ägypten* (Münchner Ägyptologische Studien 46; Mainz: P. von Zabern, 1997), pp. 126–129.

[13] See J. B. Pritchard (ed.), *Ancient Near Eastern Texts Related to the Old Testament* (= *ANET*; 3rd ed. with Supplement; Princeton, NJ: Princeton University Press, 1969), p. 378a. Most probably, "Israel" in this inscription refers to a group of people or some tribe(s), because the word is written with the determinative of people rather than land. See J. A. Wilson, "Hymn of Victory of Mer-ne-Ptah (The 'Israel Stela')," in Pritchard, *ANET*, pp. 376–378 esp. 378 note 18. See also A. F. Rainey, "Israel in Merneptah's Inscription and Reliefs," *IEJ* 51 (2001), pp. 57–75. Rainey concludes: "this expression is clearly meant to indicate that Israel has been annihilated like a plant whose seed/fruit has been destroyed ... Israel was evidently one group among many *Shasu* who were moving out of the steppe land to find their livelihood ..." (pp. 74–75). It is worthwhile to note that similar idioms are used also of the Sea Peoples in Ramses III's inscription from the temple of Medinet Habu at Thebes: "Those who reached my frontier, *their seed is not*, their heart and their soul are finished forever and ever." See Wilson, "Hymn of Victory of Mer-ne-Ptah," in Pritchard, *ANET*, p. 262. Accordingly, some scholars consider this to be typical conquest language; see, for instance, K. L. Younger Jr., *Ancient Conquest Accounts: A Study in Ancient Near Eastern and Biblical History Writing* (Journal for the Study of the Old Testament Supplement Series 98; Sheffield: JSOT Press, 1990), pp. 165–194 esp. 189–194 (though not focused on the Merneptah Stele specifically).

[14] See H. Donner and W. Röllig, *Kanaanäische und Aramäische Inschriften*, Volume I: *Texte* (3rd ed; Wiesbaden: Otto Harrassowitz, 1971), p. 33, no. 181. For the English translation, cf. W. F. Albright, "The Moabite Stone," in Pritchard, *ANET*, pp. 320–321 esp. 320a; cf. also J. C. L. Gibson, *Textbook of Syrian Semitic Inscriptions, Volume I: Hebrew and Moabite Inscriptions* (Oxford: Clarendon Press, 1973), pp. 75–76.

dated it to the time of Nehemiah, "for deliverance from the conspiracy made against Israel by the neighboring nations with the purpose of exterminating him."[15] Others suggested that the psalm refers to the story about the attack against Jehoshaphat by the Moabites, Ammonites, and Meunites (2 Chronicles 20), or of Uzziah by the Philistines and Arabs (2 Chr 26:6–8), or even against Judas Maccabeus by neighboring peoples (1 Maccabees 5).[16] However, because we do not know of any warlike circumstances in which all the nations mentioned here were allied against Israel, and "since it is more doubtful whether the specified nations [in Ps 83:7–12 (ET, 6–11)] existed at all at one and the same time, and since, moreover, neither an actual campaign is discussed nor any concrete measures of defense are envisaged, but mention is made only of the enemies' plots against God and his people, we shall have to refrain from any purely historical explanation of the psalm."[17] It seems to be the case, as already affirmed by Friedrich Nötscher, that this account of the nations and their alliances is "poetically and freely composed."[18] This psalm expresses, therefore, the Israelites' fear of national annihilation by the surrounding pagan nations, an anxiety that emerges from other biblical texts as well. Here the psalmist leaves it up to God to destroy all Israel's foes.[19]

Indeed, the Israelites' fear of complete annihilation on the one hand, and the deep trust in God's redemption on the other, are reflected once more in Psalm 124 (which is dated relatively late):[20]

---

[15] See C. A. Briggs and E. G. Briggs, *A Critical and Exegetical Commentary on the Book of Psalms* (International Critical Commentary; Edinburgh: T. & T. Clark, 1907), vol. 2, p. 217. See Neh 2:19; 4:1–2; 6:1–9.

[16] See, for instance, R. Kittel, *Die Psalmen übersetzt und erklärt* (Kommentar zum Alten Testament 13; 6th ed.; Leipzig: A. Deichertsche Verlagsbuchhandlung D. Werner Scholl, 1929), pp. 277–278: "Das findet zumeist seine so gut wie sichere Erklärung durch die Beziehung auf 1 Mak 5."

[17] See A. Weiser, *The Psalms: A Commentary* (translated by H. Hartwell; The Old Testament Library; Philadelphia: Westminster, 1962), p. 562.

[18] See F. Nötscher, *Die Psalmen, Die Heilige Schrift in deutscher Übersetzung* (Echter-Bibel; Würzburg: Echter Verlag, 1947), p. 168: "Der Dichter ist kein Historiker. So ist es wohl möglich, dass hier im Ps keine bestimmte Lage mit geschichtlicher Treue geschildert, sondern eine Anzahl von Völkern dichterisch frei zusammengestellt wird, deren Feindseligkeit in Geschichte und Gegenwart sich geäußert hatte oder typisch war. Zudem redet der Dichter nur von bösen Plänen der Gegner (4–6), ohne zu sagen, ob sie wirklich zur Ausführung gekommen sind." ("The poet is not a historian. So, it is quite possible that here in this Ps no specific situation is described with historical credibility, but rather a number of peoples are poetically, freely, put together whose hostility was expressed in the past and present or was typical. In addition, the poet only speaks of the enemy's evil plans (vv. 4–6), without saying whether they were actually carried out.") This conclusion is adopted also by H.-J. Kraus, *Psalms 60–150: A Continental Commentary* (translated by H. C. Oswald; Minneapolis: Augsburg Fortress, 1989), p. 161.

[19] Weiser, *Psalms*, pp. 562–563, prefers to interpret the psalm "in the light of a cultic situation."

[20] See Briggs and Briggs, *A Critical and Exegetical Commentary on the Book of Psalms*, vol. 2, p. 452; Kraus, *Psalms 60–150: A Continental Commentary*, p. 441, with references to earlier secondary literature.

If it had not been the Lord who was on our side, let Israel now say; If it had not been the Lord who was on our side, when men rose up against us; Then they would have swallowed us up alive,[21] when their wrath was kindled against us; Then the waters would have overwhelmed us, the stream would have gone over us [lit., "our soul," נפשנו על]; Then the proud waters would have gone over us.[22] Blessed be the Lord, who has not given us as prey to their teeth. Our very selves have escaped as a bird from the snare of the fowlers; the snare is broken, and we have escaped. Our help is in the name of the Lord, who made heaven and earth.

It is impossible to suggest any specific event in the history of ancient Israel as the background for this text. The conditional words "*if*" (לולי) and "*when*" (ב), and the word "*then*" (אז) actually testify to the generalized character of this psalm, rather than to any particular historical event. Accordingly, it seems, once again, that the psalmist reflects the general Israelite fear of annihilation.

This issue is also well summarized later by the Rabbis of the Passover Haggadah, who interpreted Deut 26:5, "A wandering Aramaean was my father," as follows: "Go forth and inquire what Laban the Aramaean intended to do to our father Jacob. While Pharaoh decreed the destruction of the males only, Laban sought to uproot the whole, as it is said: 'An Aramean nearly caused my father to perish ....'"[23] The legend in the Babylonian Talmud *Berachot* 54b, regarding Og, king of Bashan, who wished to bury all the Israelites under a mountain, but God miraculously saved them – is going in the same direction: An Israelite enemy attempted to annihilate the nation but God saved them, while bringing death on him.[24]

II   Esther's Response to the Fear of Complete Annihilation

The book of Esther is probably one of the links in the long chain of biblical texts alluding to the aforementioned phenomenon. In fact, it relates that

---

[21] Compare this metaphor to Jer 51:34.

[22] This verse should not be considered a gloss (contra Briggs and Briggs, *A Critical and Exegetical Commentary on the Book of Psalms*, vol. 2, pp. 452–453). It is used as a turning point between the first part of the psalm (verses 1–4) and the second part of it (verses 6–7), as its chiastic structure with the earlier verse testifies:

verse 4: אזי המים שטפונו / נחלה עבר על נפשנו

verse 5: אזי עבר על נפשנו / המים הזידונים

[23] See also Targum Onkelos on Deut 26:5, and another quotation from the Haggadah, below in this chapter, §V.

[24] For further details, see I. Kalimi, *How the Mighty Have Fallen: The Disastrous Destiny of Arrogant Leaders in Ancient Mediterranean Cultures*, ch. 11, §VI (in press).

because of a personal conflict that Haman had with Mordecai,[25] he wanted to "destroy *all* the Jews ... throughout the whole kingdom of Ahasuerus" (Esth 3:6, 8–9). Thus, he wrote letters "to all the king's provinces, giving orders to destroy, to kill, and to annihilate all Jews, young and old, women and children, in one day!" (Esth 3:13; see also 7:5; 9:24). This would have meant the immediate and complete genocide of the Jewish people wherever they were found. The annihilation of the Jews should be undertaken by the peoples with whom they live. In order to push those peoples to fulfill his decree, Haman offers them the right to loot Jewish property.[26] Once again, the old fear of the Israelites/Jews became clear and real.

Unlike in many other biblical texts, Esther never explicitly refers to God's acting on behalf of his people. However, many see a hint of God's *indirect* action in Mordecai's words to Esther to act immediately in favor of the Jews, where he states with full confidence, without any hesitation: "For if you remain silent at this time, *relief and deliverance will rise for the Jews from another place*; but you and your father's house shall be destroyed. And who knows whether you have not come to the kingdom for such a time as this" (כי אם החרש תחרישי בעת הזאת, רוח והצלה יעמוד ליהודים ממקום אחר, ואת ובית אביך תאבדו ומי יודע אם לעת כזאת הגעת למלכות; Esth 4:14). But the narrator does not explicitly explain the grounds for Mordecai's assurance that deliverance for the Jewish people would rise somehow from another place or in another way. In fact, he leaves his audience to speculate on this issue.

In order to clarify the theological notion of Esther, I would like to compare the main lines of this court-story with another one accounted roughly in Genesis 37–50 (Joseph story) and its direct following story in Exodus 1–15. Here a young and handsome Hebrew boy – Joseph – became the most powerful official in a foreign land – in the court of the Egyptian Pharaoh. Though he assisted his family during the famine, later

---

[25] On the conflict between Haman and Mordecai, see the discussion in Chapter 2, §V, 3, C.

[26] The general picture of complete annihilation of all the Jews in all provinces of the king (Esth 3:13), is partially parallel to the concept of *ḥerem* in the Hebrew Bible. See the description of *ḥerem* in Deut 13:16–18; and 20:16–17: "But of the cities of these people, which the Lord your God does give you for an inheritance, *you shall not keep alive anything that breathes*. Rather you shall completely destroy them ..."; for dis-implementation of this law, see Judges 1; 1 Kgs 9:21 // 2 Chr 8:8–9. An example of full implementation of *ḥerem* appears in Josh 7:24–25 regarding Achan: Joshua and all Israel took "Achan ... and the silver, and the garment, and the wedge of gold, and his sons, and his daughters, and his oxen, and his asses, and his sheep, and his tent, and all that he had; and they brought them to the valley of Achor ... and all Israel stoned him with stones, and burned them with fire." Nonetheless, Haman's plan was to annihilate the human being but to keep their property. In other words, his plan sustains just part of the *ḥerem* law. Similarly, Samuel asks from Saul: "go and strike Amalek, and completely destroy all that they have, and spare them not; but slay both man and woman, infant and suckling, ox, and sheep, camel and ass" (1 Sam 15:3). However, Saul struck Amalek but took spoils and captured Agag, king of Amalek (15:7–9).

on a new king in Egypt was crowned who threw the male Israelite babies into the Nile and enslaved all the people of Israel. Then the God of Israel directly interfered, redeemed his people, and led them to the land that he promised to their forefathers – Land of Canaan that became the Land of Israel. In the Esther story, the Jews were living in exile/the Diaspora – all over the Persian Empire. A pretty Jewish orphan girl – Esther – became the Queen of Persia and her uncle – Mordecai – held an important position in the court. However, the danger of annihilation for the Jewish people was still present and was almost fulfilled, and only the intensive activities of Esther and Mordecai saved the Jews, who continued to live in the Diaspora.[27]

In earlier crises such as the one in Egypt, God acted directly on behalf of his beloved, chosen people. In the book of Esther, however, no such direct divine intervention is reported, and God himself is not explicitly mentioned. Nevertheless, Esther's point may not be that God no longer intervenes, but instead that even in those times when the direct interference of God is unseen, and clear and unusual miracles are extremely rare, in the ages of *hester panim* (that is, the "hidden face" of God, which implies his temporary silence); God will still help his people and redeem them (covertly), and the Jews can continue to live outside of their homeland, in the Diaspora. Most likely, this is the central theological theme (*die Mitte*) of the book of Esther: God will save his people at any time and place, directly and indirectly, by extraordinary miracles or by acting "behind the story" (or, if you wish, "behind the scenes"), where the particulars of his acts are hidden and invisible.[28] The purpose is clear: to strengthen the self-confidence of the Jewish communities all over the world, particularly in the Diaspora.

III   Theology without Mentioning *Theos*

Generations of commentators and theologians have attempted to explain the complete absence of God's name in Esther. For instance,

---

[27] Generally speaking, while Ezra-Nehemiah as a whole concentrates exclusively on Yehud Madinta and Jerusalem, Esther concentrates on the Jewish Diaspora of the Persian Empire. Thus, for instance, in contrast to Neh 1:1–2, 6; 2–3, where Jerusalem takes central place, apart from Esth 2:5–6, which provides the genealogy of Mordecai as one who was exiled from Jerusalem (or his ancestors were), the author does not refer to that city or to the Land of Israel. The Targum Sheni to Esther fills in this "lacuna" in the biblical text as it ascribes a prayer to Esther, who says: "inhabitants of Jerusalem move in their graves because you gave their sons to be slaughtered." Also, Midrash *Esther Rabbah* 8:3 speaks about a promise that Ahasuerus made to Esther to build the Jerusalem Temple if she has a son.

[28] In Ruth 2:3 the author refers to the unseen hand of God behind the human activity by saying "as it happened" (ויקר מקרה). In the book of Esther, the writer refrained even from giving such a note.

in medieval times this was the first issue that Rabbi Abraham ibn Ezra discussed in the brief introduction to his first commentary on the book of Esther:

והנה אין במגילה הזאת זכר השם, והיא מספרי הקדש! ורבים השיבו כי הוא "ממקום אחר"
[אסתר ד:יד], וזה איננו נכון, כי לא נקרא השם "מקום" בכל ספרי הקודש ... והנכון בעיני
שזאת המגילה חיברה מרדכי, וזה טעם "וישלח ספרים" [אסתר ט:כ] ... ונכתבה בדברי הימים
של מלכיהם, והם עובדי עבודה זרה, והיו כותבין תחת השם הנכבד והנורא שם תועבתם,
כאשר עשו הכותים שכתבו תחת "בראשית ברא אלהים" [בראשית א:א] "ברא אשימא".
והנה כבוד השם שלא יזכרנו מרדכי במגילה.[29]

There is no mention of God's name [lit. the name] in this Megillah, and still it is included among the Holy Scriptures! Many [scholars] say that he is [referred to] in "from another *place* [*makom*; Esth 4:14]," but this is incorrect, because "*Makom*" [as a name of God] is not mentioned in all of the Holy Scriptures .... In my opinion, this Megillah was written by Mordecai, and this is the reason for "and he sent letters" [Esth 9:20] ... And it was included in the Chronicles of [the Persian] kings, and they were worshippers of idols, and would write instead of "God created" (Gen 1:1), "Ashima created," as did the Samaritans. Thus, for the glory of God [lit. the name], Mordecai did not mention [God's name] in the Megillah.

Even if one does not accept ibn Ezra's opinion regarding the absence of God's name in the Megillah,[30] he is right: The word מקום in Esth 4:14 means "place" or "direction" it is not God's name as it is later found in the rabbinic sources. Nevertheless, arguably the words "from another place" (Esth 4:14) still allude to God's interference.[31]

In modern biblical study, several suggestions have been offered for the absence of divine name in the book. For example, Samuel R. Driver considers this as a reflection of the book's secular feature.[32] Similarly states Carl Steuernagel:

---

[29] The text version is according to Mishaly and Zipor, *Abraham Ibn Ezra's Two Commentaries on Megilat Esther*, pp. 57–58. Several years later, ibn Ezra composed a second commentary on the book of Esther, where he repeats on this claim, in his commentary on Esth 4:14: ויש שאלה: למה לא נכתב השם במגילה הזאת? והגאון רב סעדיה ז"ל השיב, כי המלך צוה למרדכי שיכתוב המגילה ויעתיקוה בלשון פרס בספר דברי הימים, ואלו היה כותב שם השם, היו הפרסיים מחליפים אותו בשם עבודה זרה. (Mishaly and Zipor, ibid., 148).

[30] However, still there are scholars that suggested similar explanation for absence of God's name in the Megillah; see, for instance, Segal, *An Introduction to the Hebrew Bible*, vol. 3, p. 721.

[31] Cf. C. F. Keil, *Biblischer Commentar über die Nachexilischen Geschichtsbücher: Chronik, Esra, Nehemia und Esther* (Leipzig: Dürffling und Franke, 1870), p. 640; idem, *The Books of Ezra, Nehemiah, and Esther* (Edinburgh: T. & T. Clark, 1873), p. 353; C. Steuernagel, *Lehrbuch der Einleitung in das Alte Testament* (Sammlung Theologischer Lehrbücher; Tübingen: J. C. B. Mohr [P. Siebeck], 1912), p. 434.

[32] See S. R. Driver, *An Introduction to the Literature of the Old Testament* (9th ed.; Edinburgh: T. & T. Clark, 1913), pp. 485–486; cf. Eissfeldt, *The Old Testament: An Introduction*, p. 511.

There is hardly any religious coloring in the book. The mention of God is consistently avoided, though in this case not based on the feeling that one should not associate his name with such secular intrigues and such lust for revenge (that would be quite un-Jewish), but only because in some circles of Judaism one generally avoids mentioning the Holy One directly.[33]

But is there really any purely secular writing in ancient Israel and the ancient Near East?

Steinthal states that the "author's avoidance of the name of God is due to the fact that he is a skeptic." Scholtz believes the avoidance is due to the author's residence in Persia. Paton argues that the book of Esther was meant to be read at the annual merrymaking of Purim, an occasion when people drink a lot of wine. "On such occasions the name of God might be profaned, if it occurred in the reading; and, therefore, it was deemed best to omit it altogether."[34] Close to Paton's suggestion, asserts Greenstein: "Purim was, and has always been a frivolous festival, in time for jesting and revelry. As the Esther scroll would be read only at such a celebration, it was no time to pronounce the sacred divine name."[35] Adele Berlin arrives at the same interpretation independently.[36]

However, this repeated explanation in various variants is built on a series of unproved assumptions: It presumes that the Purim fest was originally a pagan carnival/fest, which was adopted by the Jews in the east Persian Empire, and the book of Esther was written later to justify its existence.[37] But these very unproved assumptions cannot be used as a base for an additional assumption regarding the absence of God's name in the book.

Most recently, Brittany N. Melton expressed that Esther was "intended to convey a perspective on divine action held in the Diaspora. Perhaps what is chiefly being communicated is the uncertainty held by some in the Diaspora about where and how God was acting.[38] The argument for

---

[33] See Steuernagel, *Lehrbuch der Einleitung in das Alte Testament*, p. 434: "Eine religiose Färbung tritt in dem Buche kaum hervor. Die Erwähnung Gottes ist geflissentlich vermieden, jedenfalls aber nicht aus dem Gefühl heraus, dass man seinen Namen mit so weltlichen Intrigen und solcher Rachlust nicht in Verbindung bringen dürfe (das wäre ganz unjüdisch), sondern lediglich, weil man in Judentum überhaupt in manchen Kreisen eine Scheu hatte, den Heiligen direkt zu nennen."

[34] See Paton, *A Critical and Exegetical Commentary on the Book of Esther*, pp. 94–96, with references to the works of H. Steinthal and J. M. A. Scholtz.

[35] Greenstein, "A Jewish Reading of Esther," pp. 232–233.

[36] See Berlin, *Esther: A Commentary*, p. 4.

[37] On this, see the discussion in Chapter 5, §I, 2 A.

[38] Here she refers to A. D. Cohen, "'Hu Ha-Gural': The Religious Significance of Esther," *Judaism* 23 (1974), pp. 87–129 esp. 129.

religious uncertainty is undergirded by the general sense of 'uncertainty' for Jews in the Diaspora."[39]

Nonetheless, it seems that by the literary absence of God's name and religious laws, rituals, and institutions, the author of Esther meant to convey the religious presence: In order to present the above-mentioned theological notion effectively, he creates a "theology" without explicitly mentioning *theos* – any form of God's name, or any theological theme. He never implicitly refers to a religious law or cult, nor to any religious institution or custom (except the mention of fasting in Esth 4:16). Instead, he let the events and the characters talk for themselves and express explicitly his theological notion. Thus, on the other hand, he refers frequently to a variety of banquets and feasts (משתה, 20 times out of 46 in the entire Hebrew Bible).[40] Again, the absolute absence of God's name in the entire Megillah is highlighted particularly by the contrast with the frequent mentions of the "King (of Persia)" (190 times), "Ahasuerus" (29 times), and some 30 other figures' names. Thus, the attention that the book's audience has given to God's silence shows, as stated by Michael V. Fox, "that the silence speaks louder than the whole string of pious prayers and protestations."[41]

It seems, therefore, that the literary avoidance of naming God or religious elements by Esther's author has a bold theological intent, that is, God does not always *reveal* and act openly (as he did in the case of the redemption and deliverance from Egyptian slavery; Exod 2:23–14:31), but sometimes he is acting as a *hidden* God, unseen, however still working on behalf of his people behind the scenes/curtain. Furthermore, the writer of the story attempts to show the actual King Ahasuerus, the absolute ruler of the great Persian Empire, in some ridiculous behavior, as a marionette, perhaps in order to stress the existence of the "real king" – God – though he is unseen, but yet controlling all events.

---

[39] See B. N. Melton, *Where Is God in the Megilloth? A Dialogue on the Ambiguity of Divine Presence and Absence* (Oudtestamentische Studiën 73; Leiden and Boston: Brill, 2018), p. 68; here she cites S. A. White Crawford, "Esther: A Feminine Model for Jewish Diaspora," in P. L. Day (ed.), *Gender and Difference* (Minneapolis: Fortress Press, 1989), pp. 161–177 esp. 171, 173, who attests to the "uncertain world of the Diaspora" in relation to the ambiguous purpose of the book. For a survey of other opinions regarding the literary absence of God in the book of Esther – such as of Meir Sternberg, Orit Avnery, and Timothy Beal, see Melton, *Where Is God in the Megilloth?*, pp. 72–74.

[40] See Esth 1:2–9; 2:18; 3:15; 5:4–8; 7:1–9; 8:17; 9:17–19. On this issue in the book of Esther, see Fox, *Character and Ideology in the Book of Esther*, pp. 156–158; and the recent detailed discussion by P. Machinist, "Achaemenid Persia as Spectacle, Reactions from Two Peripherical Voices: Aeschylus, *The Persians* and the Book of Esther," *Eretz-Israel* 33 (L. E. Stager Volume; Jerusalem: Israel Exploration Society, 2018), pp. 109*–123* esp. 112*–114*, and there, on p. 119* note 11, additional bibliography on banquets/feasts in the ancient Near East and elsewhere.

[41] Fox, *Character and Ideology in the Book of Esther*, p. 244.

Accordingly, all the efforts of the ancient translators and exegetes to integrate the name of God – or any other religious aspects – into the book are missing this cardinal theological character of Esther, for example:

1. The so-called Greek Alpha Text (the A-Text),[42] and the First and Second Targums[43] on Esth 4:14, as well as Josephus, *Jewish Antiquities* 11.227,[44] and *Midrash Esther Rabbah* 8:6[45] – all have the name of God in this verse (although it is possible that Josephus and the Midrash just paraphrased the biblical text).[46]

2. The Septuagint (the B-Text), *Vetus Latina* (the "Old Latin"), and the First and the Second Targums on Esth 6:1 write: "That night *God* prevented (lit., took away) the King from sleeping," in place of the Masoretic Text: "That night the King's sleep fled."[47]

3. According to MT Esth 6:13, after Haman had told his friends and his wife Zeresh everything that had just happened to him, they then advised him: "If this Mordecai before whom you have started to fall is Jewish, you would not succeed against him, but undoubtedly fail." Except the Vulgate, all ancient translations add: "for God is with him."[48]

4. God's name is mentioned also in five of the six "Additions" in the Greek versions of the book of Esther (it is absent only in Addition B), which are mainly intended "to strengthen the book's religious character."[49]

---

[42] On the Greek versions of Esther, including the Alpha Text, see Chapter 2, §IV; Chapter 10, §I.

[43] On the relationship between the First and the Second Targums, see Grossfeld, *The Two Targums of Esther*, pp. 23–24.

[44] See Marcus, *Josephus with an English Translation*, vol. 6, p. 425.

[45] Cf. Midrash Psalms *Shocher-Tov* 22:5; see Buber, *Midrash Tehillim*, p. 182; for the English translation see Braude, *The Midrash on Psalms*, vol. 1, p. 301.

[46] However, the Septuagint, *Vetus Latina*, the Vulgate and the Syraic versions of the verse do not go in this direction; see also Abraham ibn Ezra's commentary on Esth 4:14. See I. Kalimi, "The Task of Hebrew Bible/Old Testament Theology: Between Judaism and Christianity," *Early Jewish Exegesis and Theological Controversy: Studies in Scriptures in the Shadow of Internal and External Controversies* (Jewish and Christian Heritage Series 2; Assen: Van Gorcum, 2002), pp. 135–158 esp. 142 note 20.

[47] See also Babylonian Talmud, *Megillah* 15b. It is worthwhile to note that the B-Text reads in Esth 6:1: "the Lord" (ὁ κύριος), whereas the A-Text uses the expression "the Powerful" (ὁ δυνατός). Moore (*Esther*, p. 66) correctly stresses that MT which does not attribute the king's sleeplessness to God "does not mean, however, that the author of the Hebrew Esther did not believe in the active hand of Providence here." Demsky properly notes that Esth 6:1–3 and Dan 5:5–28 present instances of God's messages to foreign kings via writing or reading of a text: writing on the wall in Daniel, and reading of the Persian records to the king regarding Mordecai. See A. Demsky, *Literacy in Ancient Israel* (Biblical Encyclopedia Library 28; Jerusalem: Bialik Institute, 2012), pp. 365–366 (Hebrew).

[48] See Moore, *Esther*, p. 63.

[49] The quotation is from Moore, *Daniel, Esther and Jeremiah: The Additions*, p. 153. For this purpose of the "Additions," see also his commentary, *Esther*, pp. xxxii–xxxiii. The same could be said about Josephus, *Jewish Antiquities* 11.231–232, 234, which describes Esther's and Mordecai's prayers to God (Marcus, *Josephus with an English Translation*, vol. 6, pp. 427, 429), and Targum Sheni on Esther,

5. In Esth 2:20, "as Mordecai had charged her; for Esther did the command of Mordecai," in the B-Text is added: "to fear God and to keep his commandments."[50]

There is no textual evidence, and it is hard to imagine that the name of God appeared in Esther's original text and somebody simply removed it.[51] Thus, the appearances of God's name in these ancient translations and texts should be considered late theological reinterpretations of the Scriptures. The scribes, translators and writers who added these simply failed to see or accept the ultimate theological goal of the book of Esther: to depict the salvation of Israel even when God *appears* absent.[52]

In modern biblical scholarship, Arndt Meinhold finds an acrostic on the name יהוה in Esth 5:4bα: יבוא המלך והמן היום אל המשתה.[53] One can also add something similar in Esth 7:7: כי כלתה אליו הרעה. The question is, however, if acrostic features were known at the time of the composition of Esther, and if these examples were used intentionally. If the answer is yes, the name does appear but still in hidden form! However, if these plays on the divine name were intentional, one might expect them to appear in more prominent positions within the book (e.g., in the first and last verses, or in 4:14), not buried in the middle of two seemingly random verses in the body of the book.

IV The Theological Message of Esther

The absence of God's name from the book of Esther does not mean that it is purely secular, nor that the author had no interest in theological issues. On the contrary, his message is intended for Jews in general, and for those in the Diaspora in particular, namely, that God is devoted to Israel.[54]

---

which presents Mordecai and Esther as faithful to the Torah; see Grossfeld, *The Targum Sheni to the Book of Esther*, pp. 42–43, 53–56. Similarly, one must consider also all the midrashic interpretations that insert various religious aspects into the biblical story of Esther.

50 The text of MT Esth 2:15–20 does not appear in A-Text.

51 Contra Clines, *The Esther Scroll*, p. 112, who is of the opinion that "the pluses of the AT [e.g., Alpha-Text of Esther] can more readily be explained by supposing that MT represents a systematic attempt to remove religious language than by supposing AT to present a systematic attempt to introduce religious language."

52 For a list of the "Additions" in the Greek versions of Esther, see Chapter 2, §IV, 2; Clines, *The Esther Scroll*, pp. 107–112; Melton, *Where Is God in the Megilloth?*, pp. 69–72.

53 See Meinhold, "Esther/Estherbuch," p. 1596. Recently, Konrad Schmid mentioned this acrostic (without referring to Meinhold) as a sign of hidden God in the book of Esther; see K. Schmid, *Theologie des Alten Testaments* (Tübingen: Mohr Siebeck, 2019), p. 172.

54 This conclusion completely contradicts that of Sweeney: "Esther is written to make a point, namely, human being must act to defeat evil in the world when G-d fails to do so"; M. A. Sweeney, *Reading the Hebrew Bible after the Shoah* (Minneapolis, MN: Fortress Press, 2008), p. 220 cf. p. 222.

As the earlier biblical and extrabiblical cases show, Israel has enemies (or if you wish, "Hamans") who have threatened its very existence many times throughout its history, in different places.[55] However, God is always there to keep his promise and help his people. His help is unconditional and not subject to any time or place. It could be given directly, such as in the redemption from Egypt, by taking them *out* of the land; or indirectly while acting silently "behind the scenes/curtain," such as the redemption *in* the framework of the Persian Empire, without any "new exodus." When we read the book of Esther in light of other biblical texts which affirm that God's covenant with Israel is everlasting, it can be seen as an implicit affirmation that "the Lord ... is God, the faithful God who maintains *covenant loyalty* [שומר הברית והחסד] with those who love him and keep his commandments, to a thousand generations" (Deut 7:9; see also 4:30–31; 30:2–3).[56] This is in line with the prophetic promises, such as: "For this is as the waters of Noah to me: as I have sworn that the waters of Noah should no more go over the earth, I swore that I would not be angry with you nor rebuke you. For the mountains shall depart, and the hills be removed; but my *loyalty* [וחסדי] shall not depart from you, neither shall the *covenant* of my peace [וברית שלומי] be removed, says the Lord who has mercy on you" (Isa 54:9–10); and "For just as the new heavens and the new earth that I will make will endure before Me – the words of the Lord – so will your [i.e., Israel's] offspring and your name endure" (Isa 66:22). Thus, the story of Esther about the redemption of the Jews, particularly in Diaspora, from the annihilation plan of Haman is an example of the fulfilment of the divine promise, as stated in Leviticus: "And yet for all that, *when they are in the land of their enemies, I will not cast them away, nor will I despise them, to destroy them totally*, and to break my covenant with them" (Lev 26:44).

Because the existence of the Jewish people is everlasting, the Esther story also implies that the extermination of the Jews in any form and at any time and place is unbearable to God. This reflects confidence that "Israel *is* holy to the Lord [קדש ישראל ליהוה],[57] the first fruits of his harvest, all that

---

Moreover, the concept of God's devotion to Israel is entirely different from that suggested by some scholars, that is, that the purpose of the Scroll is to provide Purim with an etiological background in order to justify the festival (see Chapter 2, §III, 1).

[55] See also the postbiblical examples detailed in Chapters 6 and 9.

[56] Compare 1 Kgs 8:23 and, especially, Neh 1:5; 9:36.

[57] Many Christian translators and commentators read Jer 2:3 as "Israel *was* holy to the Lord ...." See, for example, the King James Version, Revised Standard Version, Luther Bibel, and Zürcher Bibel, ad loc.; W. Rudolph, *Jeremia* (Handbuch zum Alten Testament 12; Tübingen: J. C. B. Mohr [P. Siebeck], 1947), p. 10; J. A. Thompson, *The Book of Jeremiah* (New International Commentary on the Old Testament; Grand Rapids, MI: W. B. Eerdmans, 1980), p. 159; J. Schreiner, *Jeremia 1–25,14* (Die Neue Echter Bibel; Würzburg: Echter Verlag, 1981), p. 18 ("Heiliger Besitz *war* Israel

devour him shall offend: evil shall come upon them" (Jer 2:3). Therefore, Jews' confidence in God's salvation should be complete, since the enemies "Take counsel together, and it shall come to nothing; speak the word, and it shall not stand; for God is with us" (עֻצוּ עֵצָה וְתֻפָר דַּבְּרוּ דָבָר וְלֹא יָקוּם כִּי עִמָּנוּ אֵל, Isa 8:10).

This is the central theme emerging from the book of Esther for everyone, Jews and non-Jews. These and similar texts are the grounds that the narrator (and Mordecai) have to be so certain that Jewish people would be helped and redeemed (Esth 4:13–14). Seemingly, the narrator expects that his audience would read Esther's story within the context of other parts of the Israelite literary heritage, particularly the Torah and prophetic literature – in some form. In other words, the story of Esther probably sends the message that is well summarized later by the Sages in the Passover Haggadah:

> והיא שעמדה לאבותינו ולנו שלא אחד בלבד עומדים עלינו לכלותנו
> אלא שבכל דור ודור עומדים עלינו לכלותינו והקב"ה מצילנו מידם.

And it is this [same promise] which has been the support of our ancestors and of ourselves, for not one alone ["Haman"] has risen up against us, but in every generation, some have arisen against us to annihilate us, but the Most Holy, blessed be He, has delivered us out of their hands.

This notion appears not only in the Passover Haggadah, which Jews read once a year on that Exodus holiday's night, but also in the liturgy of every daily Evening Service, following the reading of the *Shema Yisrael* and related texts (Deut 6:4–8; 11:13–21; Num 15:37–41):

dem Herrn"); R. P. Carroll, *Jeremiah: A Commentary* (Old Testament Library; Philadelphia: Westminster Press, 1986), p. 118; W. McKane, *A Critical and Exegetical Commentary on Jeremiah* (International Critical Commentary; Edinburgh: T. & T. Clark, 1986), vol. 1, 26; P. C. Craigie, P. H. Kelley and J. Drinkard, *Jeremiah 1–25* (Word Biblical Commentary 26; Dallas, TX: Word Books Publisher, 1991), p. 22. Thus, these Christian scholars imply through their translations that the election of Israel is a past event and see themselves as a direct continuation of "Biblical Israel" in replacement for the election of the Jews.

In contrast, Jewish scholars read Jer 2:3 in the present tense and understand it as a testimony to the eternal election of Israel. Indeed, the following words are better understood to refer to the present and future: כל אוכליו יאשמו. Consequently, קדש ישראל ליהוה has been interpreted by ancient, medieval and modern Jewish commentators and translators in the present tense. For example, Targum Jonathan: קודשיא אינון בית ישראל קדם יהוה, Rashi (who cites Targum Jonathan), and David Kimchi; S. D. Luzzatto, *Erläutungen über einen Theil der Propheten und Hagiographen* (Lemberg: Verlag A. Isaak Menkes, 1876), p. 4 (Hebrew), כקדש הם לה' כתרומה (Israel *is* to the Lord as a sanctuary donation and tithe"); L. Zunz, *Die vier und zwanzig Bücher der heiligen Schrift* (Berlin: Verlag von Beit, 1838), p. 427, "Ein Heiligtum *ist* Israel dem Ewigen"; the *Jewish Publication Society* ("Israel *is* the Lord's hallowed portion"); A. J. Rosenberg, *Book of Jeremiah: A New English Translation* (Judaica Books of the Prophets; New York: Judaica Press, 1985), ad loc., "Israel *Is* holy to the Lord"; Y. Hoffman, "Holy Is Israel to God," in M. Haran (ed.), *Companion to the Biblical World: The Book of Jeremiah* (Ramat Gan: Revivim, 1983), vol. 11, p. 29 (Hebrew), ... בהיות ישראל עמו של האל, קודש לה' ("Israel is God's people, holy to the Lord ...").

... כִּי הוּא יהוה אלהינו ואין זולתו, ואנחנו ישראל עמו.
הפדנו מיד מלכים, מלכנו הגואלנו מכף כל העריצים,
האל הנפרע לנו מצרינו, והמשלם גמול לכל אויבי נפשנו ....
השם נפשנו בחיים, ולא נתן למוט רגלנו [תהלים סו:ט]:
המדריכנו על במות אויבינו, וירם קרננו על כל שונאינו.

... because he is our Lord God, and there is none but him, and we are Israel, his people.
He redeems us from the power of kings, our king who delivers us from the hand of all cruel tyrants.
He is the God who exacts vengeance for us from our foes, and who brings just retribution upon all enemies of our soul ...;
Who set our soul in life, and did not allow our foot to falter [Ps 66:9].
Who led us upon the heights of our enemies and raised our pride above all who hate us.

This is the uniqueness of the book of Esther in the Hebrew Bible: It shows not the implicit and open acts and miracles of God, but rather strives to display explicitly his hidden existence and acts in history as well. God acts also behind the screen on behalf of Israel. This is Esther's answer to the fear of annihilation: God stands with Israel in this or other ways – whenever, wherever, and forever.[58]

V   Is the Presumed Theological Concept of Esther Innovative?

The basic theological concept of Esther is not entirely innovative. It would seem to be the outcome of similar theological lines that are already expressed in the Torah. Thus, for example, the idea of the "hidden face" (*hester panim*) of God, that implies his short-term silence, followed by his redemption of Israel, is affirmed at various times in Israelite history, including in Deuteronomy 31:

> And the Lord said to Moses, "Behold, you shall sleep with your fathers; and this people will ... break my covenant which I have made with them. Then my anger shall be kindled against them in that day, and I will forsake them, and *I will hide my face from them, and they shall be devoured, and many evils and troubles shall befall them*; so that they will say in that day, 'Are not these evils come upon us, because our God is not among us?' And *I will surely hide my face* on that day because of all the evils which they shall have done." (Deut 31:16–18)

It is not a coincidence that throughout the book the author used precisely the name "Esther" (אֶסְתֵּר) – and not "Hadasah" (הדסה; Esth 2:7) – which is spelled similarly (apart from the Masoretic pointing and additional י) to

---

[58] Still, the fear of annihilation expressed by Rab in early third century CE, see below, Chapter 6, §I.

the Hebrew verb meaning "I will hide" (אַסְתִּיר). On the one hand, this could be because Esther herself hides her ethnicity, homeland, and religion for a while (2:10). On the other hand, it could also allude to the use of the expression to describe God's own hiding in Deut 31:18, הַסְתֵּר אַסְתִּיר פָּנַי ("I will hide my face").[59] The latter is used in this passage to describe God's judgment against Israel, but thereafter – at some later point – he also rescues his people, even when they cannot see him working. Indeed, in the same book, the ultimate divine redemption of Israel is also stated in the following chapter, in the Song of Moses (*Shirat Haazinu*, Deut 32:1–43), which he was directed to compose (Deut 31:19):

> He [= God] shall relent regarding His servants [= Israel], when he sees that their power is gone, neither bond nor free remaining .... For I [= God] lift up my hand to heaven, and say, I live forever. If I whet my glittering sword, and my hand takes hold of judgment; I will render vengeance to my enemies, and will requite those who hate me ... Rejoice, O you nations, with his people; for He will avenge the blood of his servants and will render vengeance on his adversaries .... (Deut 32:36b, 40–41, 43, see also 32:20)[60]

In line with such passages, in the book of Esther God does not appear explicitly, but he is still there and acts "behind the curtain" on behalf of his people, to redeem them from annihilation. The narrator of Esther preferred not to state this straightforwardly, but rather indirectly alluded to it in various ways:

1. He expresses through the saying ascribed to Mordecai that somehow an act [most likely of God] will appear on behalf of Israel: "For if you remain silent at this time, then *shall relief and deliverance arise for the Jews from another place* ..." (Esth 4:14).
2. The three days fast of the Jews in Shushan as well as that of Esther and her maids (Esth 4:16–17), were surely accompanied by prayers to God. Therefore, Esther's successful visit of the king (Esth 5:1–5) alludes to the hidden hand of God, for whom they fasted and to whom they prayed for help.

---

[59] Cf. also Gen 4:14, וּמִפָּנֶיךָ אֶסָּתֵר; Deut 32:20, אַסְתִּירָה פָנַי; Ezek 39:23, וָאַסְתִּר פָּנַי; Micah 3:4b, וְיַסְתֵּר פָּנָיו מֵהֶם. Note that already the Talmudic sages related the book of Esther to this passage in the book of Deuteronomy, though in their own unique midrashic approach; see Babylonian Talmud, *Chullin* 139b, and the discussion in Chapter 7, §III, 1. The idea that the book of Esther addresses the hidden face of God is stated also by some modern scholars, for example, T. Beal, *The Book of Hiding: Gender, Ethnicity, Annihilation and Esther* (Biblical Limits; London and New York: Routledge, 1997), p. 117; M.-D. Weill, "Le livre d'Esther et la face cachée de Dieu, *Hester Panim*. Une lumière sur la Shoah," *NRTh* 138 (2016), pp. 367–384.

[60] See also Deut 4:25–31; 30:1–10; 1 Kgs 8:44–53.

3. As already mentioned, the narrator avoids mentioning any form of God's name as well as any religious institution or custom (except for the fast). He stresses this point also by frequent references to the king and his name (together with other figures) and banquets. Thus, the reader is not confronted with any direct interference of heavenly power, although it is still there to help Israel, even in the most secular gentile environment of banquets and wine.

Thus, Esther recounts a story in which God is never mentioned, but the story is centered on a heroine whose name recalls that divine hiddenness, who finally redeems his people, similar to what is already detailed in Deuteronomy.[61]

VI   Conclusion

Some scholars claim that Esther's story lacks theological content altogether and is simply an attempt to authorize the festival of Purim or entertain the people. In my opinion, however, the book of Esther is not just a literary masterpiece, but also a religious and theological *magnum opus*. It expresses one of the worst fears of the Jewish people: fear of complete annihilation, which is also well documented in the Hebrew Bible and has left traces in some extrabiblical sources. Esther acknowledges that fear, exemplifies it in this breathtaking story, and gives voice to the theological message that God will not abandon Israel, even when he is not explicitly named, or his acts are not clearly seen. It is not a secular book, intended only to entertain people. Though literary features and humorous elements are included in it, this is not for their own sake, but to attract the attention of the audience to the book's main theological themes.

Thus, the absence of God's name from the book of Esther does not mean that the author has no interest in theological issues. The central theme which emerges from the book of Esther is that God is devoted to Israel and he is always there to keep his promise and support his people directly or indirectly, while acting "behind the scenes/curtain." This runs parallel to other biblical texts (such as those in Isa 54:9–10; 66:22), which state that God's covenant with Israel is eternal, and that he keeps the

---

[61] That God acts "behind the scenes/curtain" on behalf of Israel, is also revealed from the prophecies of the Second Isaiah regarding the redemption of Israel by Cyrus king of Persia (Isa 44:28; 45:1–3); see A. Rofé, "Isaiah 59:19: Read: 'A messenger (ציר) will come as light' – The Vision of Redemption by Trito-Isaiah," *The Religion of Israel and the Text of the Hebrew Bible* (ed. by Y. Segev; Jerusalem: Carmel, 2018), pp. 382–389 esp. 382–383 (Hebrew).

prophetic promises. In other words, Esther expresses the message that "the Strength of Israel will not lie nor repent; for he is not a mortal, that he should repent" (נצח ישראל לא ישקר ולא ינחם כי לא אדם הוא להנחם; 1 Sam 15:29). Because the survival of the Jewish people is everlasting, the book implies that the destruction of the Jews in any form, at any place, and in any era is intolerable to God. That is, "Israel *is* holy to the Lord, the first fruits of his harvest, all that devour him shall offend: evil shall come upon them ..." (Jer 2:3). Thus, Esther has an important religious message for Jews and non-Jews as well: In national crises God stands with Israel and redeems it. As such, the book fits well into the Jewish Scriptures, and – in contrast to the claims of some Christian scholars – also into the Christian Scriptures.

CHAPTER 5

Historical Setting and Historicity

I The Historicity of the Esther Story

Alongside the question regarding the theological value of the book of Esther,[1] the historicity of its story occupies more scholarly interest than any other aspect of it. In fact, "the question of historicity seems to have loomed larger for Esther than for most other books of the Hebrew Bible."[2] Because of a lack of substantial relevant contemporaneous extrabiblical historical sources – Persian, Greek, Jewish or other – that could confirm or challenge the reliability of the story as it is presented in the Hebrew Bible, scholars are sharply divided in their opinions on this question. They run from complete acceptance of the book as a historical account, to complete negation of its historical trustworthiness, defining it as fiction. In order to address this important issue, this chapter presents a brief review of the main contrasting opinions on the historicity of the book of Esther, and then argues for a balanced approach. This is illustrated by a detailed discussion of several significant aspects of the book, which demonstrate that Esther combines both historical and nonhistorical elements in its depiction of the story and its Persian setting.

1 Esther as a Completely Reliable Story

As we will see below in Chapter 10 (§III), the Christian canon considers the book of Esther as a historical story and locates it among the late biblical historical books, after Chronicles, Ezra, and Nehemiah. Although the Jewish tradition does not count the book with the historical books, it is considered to be an accurate description of what really happened. In the last centuries, however, only some modern scholars have accepted this common Jewish and Christian traditional view. For example, in 1888

---

[1] On this issue see Chapters 4, 8, 10, 12, and 13.
[2] See A. Berlin, "The Book of Esther and Ancient Storytelling," *JBL* 120 (2001), pp. 3–14 esp. 3.

Paulus Cassel stated: "One recognizes the stamp of genuineness *in every trait of the narrative* .... The doubts which modern writers have raised against this book are owing to their deficiency in the historic sense, and to their want of a thorough acquaintance with Oriental affairs" (italics added).[3] Three and a half decades later, in 1923, Joseph Hoschander wrote a dissertation to show the historicity of the book of Esther.[4]

In recent decades, some scholars have continued to defend Esther's absolute reliability. For example, William H. Shea is of the opinion that the most common arguments against Esther's historicity are unconvincing. In particular, he attempts to coordinate between the dates in Esther and those in the Greek accounts regarding Xerxes I.[5] However, his conclusions are often speculative. For instance, he identifies the 180-day banquet in "the third year" of Ahasuerus, in 483 BCE (Esth 1:1–3), with a six-month planning session for Xerxes' Greek campaign before the Battle of Thermopylae in August of 480 BCE, although the latter occurred two to three years later. Shea explains the discrepancy by appealing to a revolt in Babylonia that could have delayed the campaign.[6] He also identifies Vashti with Amestris, and suggests that the story about Vashti's rejection as queen in Esth 1:9–22 provides the reason for Amestris' absence from Herodotus' account of Xerxes' time in Sardis in 480/479 BCE.[7] This is despite the fact that Herodotus describes Amestris as the queen of Persia during and long after Xerxes' time in Sardis (*Historia* 9.108–113 esp. 9.110; see also 7.114).[8]

Recently, Gerard Gertoux has also attempted to re-establish the historicity of the book.[9] He tries to reconcile the chronology of Esther with those of the Greek sources by re-dating Xerxes reign ten years earlier, which he thinks allows us to identify Esther with Amestris.[10] In contrast to Shea, Gertoux dates the 180-day banquet in Esth 1:1–3 to 493 BCE, and sees it as a celebration of Xerxes'/Ahasuerus' victory over the Ionian revolt recounted by

---

[3] See P. Cassel, *An Explanatory Commentary on Esther* (Clark's Foreign Theological Library 34; Edinburgh: T. & T. Clark, 1888), pp. ix–x esp. x.

[4] See J. Hoschander, *The Book of Esther in the Light of History* (Ph.D. Dissertation, Dropsie College; Philadelphia, 1923); see the critical review of this work by T. J. Meek in *AHR* 29 (1924), pp. 744–745.

[5] See W. H. Shea, "Esther and History," *Concordia Journal* 13 (1987), pp. 234–248.

[6] See Shea, "Esther and History," p. 236.

[7] See Shea, "Esther and History," pp. 238–239.

[8] See Godley, *Herodotus with an English Translation*, vol. 3, pp. 416–417, and vol. 4, pp. 284–293. Regarding Shea's explanation of the four-year gap between the removal of Vashti in the third year of Ahasuerus/Xerxes I (Esth 1:3), and the crowning of Esther in his seventh year (Esth 2:16), see the discussion below in §II, 3, A.

[9] G. Gertoux, "The Book of Esther: Is It a Fairy Tale or History?" www.academia.edu/8233800/ (accessed February 1, 2016).

[10] See Gertoux, "The Book of Esther: Is It a Fairy Tale or History?" pp. 1, 18–26.

Herodotus (*Historia* 6.31–33). Herodotus attributes this campaign to Darius I, Xerxes' father, but Gertoux claims that Xerxes had ten years of coregency with Darius.[11] He concludes that "for most historians the Book of Esther is an Oriental story, for most archaeologists it is a fairy tale, for me it is history."[12]

There are indeed many aspects of the story and its background that fit well with what is known or can be reconstructed concerning the situation in the Persian Achaemenid Empire. Nevertheless, neither those elements in the text, nor the recent defenses of the book's chronological plausibility by Shae and Gertoux, can justify Cassel's accusation that all doubts concerning the book's historicity reflect a "deficiency in the historic sense." On the contrary, Cassel, Shea and Gertoux themselves ignore substantial nonhistorical elements in the text. As we saw already in Chapter 3, there are many structures of reversed fate, overstatements, hyperbolic and typological numbers (i.e., there is no guarantee that these reflect accurate numbers), satirical and humoristic descriptions, as well as other literary features in the story of Esther that are far beyond historical plausibility. For these and other reasons, it is irrational to take some particular details from Esther (such as the celebration of 180 days of banqueting) and bend them to fit some information in the Greek sources, as Shea and Gertoux attempt. There are undeniable legendary elements in the story that by no means can be considered as historical data.

2 Esther as a Completely Unreliable Story

In modern scholarship, there are two groups of scholars that both regard the Esther story as completely unreliable historically, but for differing sets of rationales. Some consider Esther to be no more than an echo of ancient Mesopotamian myth and therefore also a nonhistorical story. Others do not consider the story to echo an ancient myth regarding gods, but still negate its historical credibility, for a variety of reasons.

A The Esther Story and Purim Are Echoes of Ancient Myth
In 1891 Heinrich Zimmern assumed that the origin of the Purim feast stems from the Babylonian new year feast, which the Jews in eastern diaspora adopted. Zimmern derived the name Purim from Akkadian *puhru*

---

[11] See Gertoux, "The Book of Esther: Is It a Fairy Tale or History?" p. 3; see also his article "Dating the Reigns of Xerxes and Artaxerxes," www.academia.edu/2421036/ (accessed February 1, 2016).

[12] See Gertoux, "The Book of Esther: Is It a Fairy Tale or History?" p. 34.

(assembly), and Mordecai from *Marduk* – the Babylonian god who took central place in the new year celebration. According to him, the book of Esther is a legend about its central figure – Mordecai – who is related to Purim, as the Babylonian new year festival was related to Marduk who sat in *puḥru* – assembly.[13] According to Zimmern, the struggle between Mordecai and Haman is similar to the struggle between Marduk and Tihâmat (/Tiâmat). He stresses that the relation between the Babylonian new year and Purim should be considered as quite sure. In the same breath he states that the assumption of Paul de Legarde (published three years earlier) that the origin of Purim stems from the Persian new year feast (or "all souls feast") *farwardîgân* is not impossible, although it is more problematic.[14]

A year later, Peter Jensen argued that the names "Esther" and "Mordecai" are derived from the Babylonian deities' names Ištar and Marduk, while the name Haman is derived from the Elamite god named Humman (/ Umman or Humban), Vashti (/ Wašty) from the Elamite goddess Mašti, and Zeresh (Haman's wife) perhaps from the Elamite name Kiriša.[15] On this basis, several scholars conclude that the origin of the Esther story was Mesopotamian mythological legend about the struggle between the Babylonian and Elamite gods, and the triumph of the former over the latter. The biblical author, they argue, demythologized and historicized the pagan tale and made it a cover for the Purim feast, whose origin was also pagan – the Babylonian new year festival (*Akîtu*).[16] However, as already stressed by Gaster, *Akîtu* fell in the month of Nisan, while Purim is in Adar; the former lasted ten or eleven days, while the latter only one day (14th or 15th of Adar); the chief god of the Elamites was not named Humman, who was just a minor god; and finally, "while it is true that the

---

[13] H. Zimmern, "Zur Frage nach dem Ursprunge des Purimfestes," *ZAW* 11 (1891), pp. 157–169 esp. 166–169.

[14] "ein Zusammenhang zwischen dem Purimfeste und dem babylonische Neujahrsfeste als ziemlich gesichert angenommen werden darf"; Zimmern, "Zur Frage nach dem Ursprunge des Purimfestes," p. 169.

[15] See P. Jensen, "Elamitische Eigennamen: Ein Beitrag zur Erklärung der elamitischen Inschriften," *WZKM* 6 (1892), pp. 47–70, 209–226 esp. 70. Jensen also denied the historicity of the Hebrew Bible and New Testament more broadly, claiming that Moses, Jesus, and Paul were all legendary characters based on Gilgamesh; P. Jensen, *Moses, Jesus, Paulus: Drei Varianten des babylonisches Gottmenschen Gilgamesh* (2nd ed.; Frankfurt am Main: Neuer Frankfurter Verlag, 1909).

[16] See, for example, K. Budde, *Geschichte der althebräischen Literatur* (Leipzig: C. F. Amelangs, 1909), p. 238; Daube, *Civil Disobedience in Antiquity*, p. 87 (the Esther story is a "myth, celebrating a war between different deities"); Bickerman, *Four Strange Books of the Bible*, p. 181 ("the name [Mordecai], which means 'man of Marduk' or 'worshiper of Marduk,' ... is not Jewish at all. We may wonder whether the hero of the original tale was a Jew"); LaCocque, "The Different Versions of Esther," pp. 304, 321. See also Chapter 2, §III, 1, and the reference in note 27.

fates of men were believed to be decided at the Babylonian New Year, it does not appear that the Festival was known popularly as 'the Feast of Lots (purê).'"[17]

Stephanie Dalley presented the mythological approach a bit differently. She traced the original Esther story to the neo-Assyrian era, soon after the Assyrians (together with the Babylonians) sacked the Elamite city of Susa in 646 BCE. She points out that the word פור (Esth 3:7; 9:24, 26) is from the neo-Assyrian *pūru* (that is, "lot"), while later the neo-Babylonian equivalent word *isqu* was typically used for "lot."[18] According to Dalley, the Esther story is a demythologized adaptation of a myth regarding Marduk and Ištar, who defeat the Elamite god Humban, in which the three gods were replaced by three humans – Mordecai, Esther, and Haman.[19] Dalley suggests that the demythologizing features of the book are due to late editorial rephrasing, even though these features pervade the whole book, almost in every verse.

However, as Dalley herself admits, "The transformation of the deities Marduk and Ishtar into the mortals Mordecai and Esther, has no parallels in other court narratives."[20] She – and others – do not explain how and why the Jews adopted a mythological legend to a historical novel. Her claim that "the wall-painting from the synagogue at Dura-Europus … shows Mordecai seated on a throne like a god,"[21] is simply wrong: the one who is seated on the throne is King Ahasuerus, and on his right side is Queen Esther seated by him, while on the left side is Mordecai, who is standing.[22] Further, the fresco is about 900 years after Dalley's own dating of the composition of Esther. Moreover, unless there is clear-cut proof that a name and a word was known only in the neo-Assyrian and neo-Babylonian periods and they went out of use in the following times, the fact that the author of Esther uses names and words that originally appears in those periods does not prove that the work was composed in either of those periods. A late author can choose from the vocabulary that he has in his pouch whatever word that he finds appropriate. In other words, the date of a composition must be determined first and foremost by its latest elements rather than its earlier ones.

---

[17] See Gaster, *The Festivals of the Jewish Year*, p. 217. For some other speculative theories regarding the origin of Purim, see ibid., pp. 217–221.
[18] See Dalley, *Esther's Revenge at Susa*, pp. 167–168. On this word, see also *CAD*, vol. P, p. 528a; W. Hallo, "The First Purim," *BA* 46/1 (1983), pp. 19–29. The equivalent word in Aramaic is: פורא.
[19] See Dalley, *Esther's Revenge at Susa*, pp. 165–226.
[20] Dalley, *Esther's Revenge at Susa*, p. 224.
[21] Dalley, *Esther's Revenge at Susa*, pp. 224–225.
[22] See Chapter 8, Figure 8, p. 187.

It seems that such hypotheses go far beyond what the biblical and extrabiblical sources affirm or imply. There is no substantial evidence that the Esther story itself derives from or refers to a mythological source, and the efforts to discover one because of the similarity of the names, are extremely speculative. Esther, Mordecai, and Haman are personal names that may be derived from foreign – Babylonian and Elamite – gods' names. But deriving human personal names from gods' names is neither unique to the book of Esther, nor confined to mythological texts. Thus, for example, the personal name Anat (Judg 5:6) is derived from the name of the famous Canaanite goddess. The companion of Moses[23] and Aaron (and probably also the grandfather of Bezaleel) named Ḥur (חור; Exod 17:10; Num 13:5),[24] which is derived from the Egyptian god's name Horus or goddess Hathor. Daniel's three friends, Hananiah, Mishael, and Azariah, also hold foreign names: Shadrach, Meshach, and Abednego (Dan 3:12). "Shadrach appears to be a deliberate perversion in spelling of Marduk … likewise Abednego is a clever deformation of Abednebo, which corresponds to Akk[adian] *arad-nabu* 'servant of (the god) Nabu. Meshach is no longer recognizable."[25] Thus, seemingly there are at least two Jewish heroes with Babylonian theophoric elements in their names in the story of Daniel 3. Is there any mythological story behind Daniel 3? Also, several scholars assume that the name שלמה (*Shlomoh*, Solomon) is derived from the Jebusite god's name שָׁלֵם (*Shalem*), which was also the name of the city (Gen 14:22–23).[26] Similarly, some scholars consider the name נח (Noah) to be the name of an Amorite deity.[27] However, in biblical literature (that is, in Genesis and Isaiah) נח appears as the name of a human being. Furthermore, "Esther" was not the given name of the queen: Her original Jewish name was "Hadassah" (Esth 2:7).[28] Dalley's speculation that the original name of Esther –הדסה – be linked with the Akkadian *hadaššatu*, meaning "bride," which is used for a goddess,[29] is unacceptable. The noun הדס in Hebrew

---

[23] Despite the Hebrew folk-etymology that has been given in Exod 2:10 to the name of the Israelite savior and lawgiver, "Moses" (משה), it derives from an Egyptian word meaning "child," and it stands in contrast to the name of Pharaoh "Ramses" (רעמסס; i.e., "child of the sun-god Re").

[24] See also 1 Chr 2:50. Ḥur appears also as a name of Midianite prince (Num 31:8; Josh 13:21); see also Neh 3:9.

[25] See P. W. Coxon, "Shadrach," in D. N. Freedman *et al.* (eds.), *The Anchor Bible Dictionary* (New York: Doubleday, 1992), vol. 5, p. 1150; see also W. Gesenius, *Hebräisches und Aramäisches Handwörterbuch über das Alte Testament* (Berlin and Heidelberg: Springer, 2013), p. 911.

[26] See I. Kalimi, "Salem," in *Das wissenschaftliche Bibellexikon im Internet* (Stuttgart: Deutsche Bibelgesellschaft Stuttgart, 2015): www.bibelwissenschaft.de/stichwort/25882/

[27] See J. Lewy, "Nāḫ et Rušpān," *Mélanges syriens offerts à monsieur René Dussaud* (Paris: Geuthner, 1939), vol. 1, pp. 273–275.

[28] On this issue see also the discussion in Chapter 2, §V, 2.

[29] Dalley, *Esther's Revenge at Susa*, pp. 168–170.

means (as she admits) "myrtle" (e.g., Isa 41:19; 53:13; Zech 1:8, 10, 11; Neh 8:15), and הדסה is just a feminine form of it. This name is like the name שושנה (Shoshana) meaning "rose" or "lily."[30] Indeed, Jews who served in foreign courts or lived in non-Jewish societies usually had two names: a Jewish one (used at home and in the Jewish community by family members and friends, as well as in synagogue when the person was called to Torah reading at Sabbath or holidays) and a foreign one (used outside in foreign society). Thus, for example, Joseph also had a foreign name given to him by Pharaoh: "Zaphnath-Paaneah" (Gen 41:45); Daniel and his friends – Hananiah, Mishael, and Azariah – also held foreign names that the chief of the eunuchs gave them: "for he gave to Daniel the name of Belteshazzar; and to Hananiah, Shadrach; and to Mishael, Meshach; and to Azariah, Abed-Nego" (Dan 1:7).[31] The custom of holding two names in this way is very common in many Jewish diaspora up to the present day.[32] Further, "Mordecai" was not an unknown name among the Jews of Babylonia (see Ezra 2:2 // Neh 7:7).[33] Meanwhile, though the name "Vashti" perhaps represents a form "which is somehow related to Vašta ... as in Imperial Aramaic Wštan ... P. Jensen's identification of Wšty with the Elamite goddess' name Mašti is unlikely, as there is no proof that its <m-> renders <w->."[34] The name of Haman's wife, Zeresh, does not derive from the Elamite name Kiriša, as Jensen assumed, but rather from the Persian female name Zairičī.[35] Moreover, Vashti, Esther, and Mordecai are represented in the story as noble human figures, rather than as warrior deities.

Following Adam Silverstein, Koller also speculates that "At some level, the story of Mordecai and Esther seems to have been based on the Babylonian creation myth, known as Enūma ēlish."[36] Though Koller notes some general parallels, he never clarifies in what sense Esther could be "based on" a myth that takes an entirely different form, in an entirely

---

[30] Did Mordecai, who served in the foreign royal court, also have a Jewish name (and for whatever reason the author does not mention it)? It is hard to say, because we do not have any record for this.

[31] The historicity of these figures is beyond the scope of this volume. What is important here is the phenomenon.

[32] Cf. Berlin, *Esther: A Commentary*, p. 83.

[33] The identification in the Babylonian Talmud, *Menachot* 65a, of Mordecai of the book of Esther with that one listed in Ezra 2:2 // Neh 7:7 is unacceptable, first and foremost because of the gap of the generations between the two figures.

[34] See Zadok, "Notes on Esther," pp. 109–110; Hutter, *Iranische Personalnamen in der Hebräische Bibel*, p. 48. Although I must note that an exchange of the letters מ/ו in the Semitic languages is known. Compare, for instance, Hebrew סיון with the equivalent Akkadian *Simannu*.

[35] See Hutter, *Iranische Personalnamen in der Hebräische Bibel*, p. 49, and earlier references there.

[36] Koller, *Esther in Ancient Jewish Thought*, pp. 36–37; A. Silverstein, "The Book of Esther and the *Enūma Elish*," *BSOAS* 69 (2006), pp. 209–223.

different context, in a different language and culture, with which it shares no significant phrasing, theme, scenes, or time.

B   Esther as a Nonhistorical Story

Also, those scholars who do not consider the Esther story to echo an ancient Mesopotamian myth regarding gods, still negate its historical credibility. Since the assertion of Johann Salomo Semler in 1772: "I leave together the *complete book of Esther*, as a whole, and explain it as a Jewish myth,"[37] several scholars have claimed that the biblical story of Esther is completely fictional and therefore ahistorical. For example, in the second half of the nineteenth century, Theodor Nöldeke stated that the story of the book of Esther as it is, has hardly any historicity.[38] In the twentieth century, Karl Budde concluded that the story is between implausible and impossible, and "there may be no historical fact at all underlying this book."[39] Lewis B. Paton categorically declares that "the book of Esther is not historical, and it is doubtful whether even a historical kernel underlies its narrative."[40]

This tendency was continued also by other scholars, such as Johannes Meinhold,[41] and Robert H. Pfeiffer, who concludes that "we must regard the Book of Esther as a work of fiction and all characters in the book, with the exception of Xerxes, as purely imaginary." Thus, he considers Haman as "a caricature of Antiochus," and claims that "The Book of Esther reflects the third, and spiritually lowest of these stages and particularly the reign of John Hyrcanus (135–104 [BCE]), who drastically forced the conquered Idomeans to adopt Judaism by compulsory circumcision. Such forcible conversions to Judaism, [are] alluded to in [Esth] 8:17 ...."[42] This supposition of Pfeiffer sounds to me "purely imaginary" and indefensible, first and foremost because Esther could not be written *after* the composition of 2 Maccabees (ca. 143 BCE), which affirms that the "Day of Nicanor" (the 13th of Adar) is "the day before the Day of Mordecai" (2 Macc 15:36);[43] and John Hyrcanus reigned – as Pfeiffer himself notes – in 135–104 BCE.

---

[37] See J. S. Semler, *Abhandlung von freier Untersuchung des Canon* (Halle: Hemmerde, 1772), vol. 2, p. 151: "Ich lasse *das ganze Buch der Esther*, als ein *totum*, beisammen, und erkläre es für einen jüdischen μῦθος" (italics mine).

[38] See Nöldeke, "Esther," p. 85.

[39] Budde, *Geschichte der althebräischen Literatur*, p. 238: "Es dürfte ihm überhaupt keine geschichtliche Tatsache zugrunde liegen."

[40] Paton, *A Critical and Exegetical Commentary on the Book of Esther*, p. 75.

[41] See Meinhold, *Einführung in das Alte Testament* (1st ed., 1919), p. 305; (3rd ed., 1932), p. 360. For the quotation of Meinhold's assertion on this issue (original German accompanied with English translation), see Chapter 2, note 29.

[42] See Pfeiffer, *Introduction to the Old Testament*, pp. 737–742 esp. 739, 741, 742.

[43] See above, Chapter 2, §II.

Theodor H. Gaster considers the book "simply a piece of romantic fiction and cannot possibly represent historical fact."[44] Similarly concluded Arndt Meinhold: "Since Esther is a literary art work, it is hardly to be expected that it is historically reliable historiography."[45] Comparable views are expressed also by Michael V. Fox, Edward L. Greenstein, and Jon D. Levenson.[46] Most recently, Adele Berlin described the story of Esther as an "imaginary tale."[47] Generally speaking, this group of scholars based their claim – more or less – on the following arguments:

1. The king reigned 20 satrapies but not 127 provinces;
2. The Persian kings married only women from the seven Persian noble families, and would not have married a foreign orphan;
3. The name of Xerxes' wife was Amestris, rather than Esther;
4. None of the Persian kings had a vizier called Haman;
5. It is implausible that Mordecai, who was exiled in 597 BCE, was still active, over a century later, in the court of King Xerxes (485–465 BCE);
6. There are several hyperbolic and legendary elements in the story (e.g., banquet 180 days; gallows of 50 cubits; the huge amount of compensation that Haman prepared to pay);
7. It is impossible that a Persian king would have allowed to annihilate his own civilians, on the one hand; or would have let the Jews slaughter his own people, on the other hand.

However, this skeptical view and the arguments claimed to support it, which are expressed in various times in different words, will be carefully evaluated and challenged in the course of the discussion in the following sections. Attention will be given also to the historical setting of the account and the plausible historicity of its core story, despite its current narrative form that contains certain literary structures, overstatements, and legendary elements.

II   Historical Setting and Historicity

In contrast to both of the extreme positions presented in the previous section, a proper evaluation of the historicity of the book of Esther must be built on a detailed comparison of its account with all various available sources on the

---

[44] Gaster, *The Festivals of the Jewish Year*, pp. 215–216.
[45] Meinhold, *Das Buch Esther*, p. 17: "Da es sich bei Esther um ein literarisches Kunstwerk handelt, ist kaum historisch zuverlässige Geschichtsschreibung zu erwarten."
[46] See Fox, *Character and Ideology in the Book of Esther*, pp. 131–139; Greenstein, "A Jewish Reading of Esther," p. 228; Levenson, *Esther: A Commentary*, pp. 23–27.
[47] Berlin, *Esther: A Commentary*, p. 5; see also her article, "The Book of Esther and Ancient Storytelling," pp. 3–14, where she specifically contrasts (Greek) historiography with mere "storytelling."

period and historical context in which the book is set. Indeed, as shown in Chapter 3, the book of Esther makes widespread use of exaggeration, hyperbolic and typological numbers, overstatement, ironic reversal, satirical or humoristic descriptions, and fixed literary structures. Obviously, these sorts of descriptions are nonhistorical. Nevertheless, these features of the present story cannot be taken as proof that as a whole it is completely fiction. Though the book's secular setting and its lack of any miracle or explicit divine intervention do not by themselves make the story of Esther historical, they do undermine the theory that Esther is nothing more than a historicized myth (in addition to the arguments presented above). At the same time, the book reflects a broad knowledge of the Persian Achaemenid Empire in the fifth century BCE, which could definitely not detract but rather support its historical credibility at least to some extent. Even though some aspects of the book's portrayal are unverified, legendary, or exaggerate the situation, a close examination of the narrative shows that it presents a mix of genuine historical knowledge with creative literary elements, and supports the conclusion that, all in all, the core of its story and its historical setting are broadly plausible.

It has already been seen in Chapter 2 that the author of Esther shows good knowledge of the languages of the Persian Empire, particularly "Imperial Aramaic," and uses some Persian vocabulary, idioms, and names. The following paragraphs will demonstrate that he is also familiar with various Persian customs, manners, and institutions, including the Empire's size, borders, and organization, the king, queen and harem, the imperial hierarchy, the city of Susa, the king's palace, Persia's archival and postal delivery systems, legal policies, and tolerance of outsiders, the danger of conspiracy and murder in the royal court, and the existence of anti-Jewish hostilities within the empire. Through a detailed comparison of these aspects of the book's portrayal of Persia with the surviving biblical and extrabiblical written sources, as well as the archaeological finds, it will be argued that the book of Esther combines historical and nonhistorical elements in a way that can best be described as a novelistic history.

1   The Empire

A   Borders and Provinces
The Cyrus Cylinder[48] states that Marduk appointed Cyrus "to be(come) the ruler of *all the world*" (*a-na ma-li-ku-tì kul-la-ta nap-ḫar iz-zak-ra*

---

[48] Cyrus Cylinder was composed between 539–530 BCE, and uncovered in Babylon in 1879 CE. Currently it is displayed at the British Museum in London.

šu- ⌐um-šú⌐ ; line 12).[49] Similarly, the introductory words of the Hebrew Cyrus Decree say that the Lord, the God of heaven, has given to Cyrus "*all the kingdoms of the world* [/ *earth*]" (כל ממלכות הארץ, Ezra 1:2 // 2 Chr 36:23). In contrast to these politically and theologically oriented texts, in his historical romance *Cyropaedia* 8.8.1, Xenophon (ca. 430–354 BCE) details the exact borders of Cyrus' empire:[50]

> Cyrus's empire was the greatest and most glorious of all the kingdoms in Asia .... For it was bounded on the east by the *Indian Ocean*, on the north by the Black Sea, on the west by Cyprus and Egypt, and on the south by *Ethiopia*.

Like the Cylinder, the Decree, and *Cyropaedia*, the Esther story also opens with a general description of Ahasuerus' empire: "this is Ahasuerus, who reigned from India to Ethiopia [or Nubia; lit. Cush],[51] over one hundred and twenty-seven provinces" (Esth 1:1). The definition of the borders is partially identical to that in *Cyropaedia*: Both mention the border-corners in the far east and southwest, *India* and *Ethiopia*. Because the narrator indicates incompletely the borders, he wished to be a bit more inclusive. Therefore, he also counts the number of the empire's מדינות (provinces): "one hundred twenty-seven." Indeed, at the end of the reign of Darius I, the Great, and the beginning of Ahasuerus' reign, the Persian Empire stretched out to its peak, and became the largest empire that had ever existed in the ancient world, not exceeded until the time of Alexander the Great (330–323 BCE). No wonder, therefore, that in the Akkadian foundation tablet from Persepolis (of which Persian and Elamite copies were found also in Pasargadae), Xerxes I (/ Ahasuerus, see below) declares: "I am Xerxes, the great king, king of kings [*šar šarrāni*], the king of the lands [*šar mātāti*; with] all kind of languages [or tribes], *the king of this [entire] great and far[-reaching] earth* ...."[52]

---

[49] See H. Schaudig, *Die Inschriften Nabonids von Babylon und Kyros' des Großen samt den in ihrem Umfeld entstandenen Tendenzschriften: Textausgabe und Grammatik* (Alter Orient und Altes Testament 256; Münster: Ugarit-Verlag, 2001), p. 552; cf. also A. L. Oppenheim, "Babylonian and Assyrian Historical Texts," in Pritchard, *ANET*, p. 315b. Probably, the motif of ruling over "all the world" is influenced by what commonly appears in the Assyrian royal inscriptions. For example, Shalmaneser III king of Assyria (859–824 BCE) states: "(I am) Shalmaneser, the legitimate king, king of the world, the king without rival"; see Oppenheim, ibid., p. 276b.

[50] See W. Miller, *Xenophon: Cyropaedia with an English Translation* (Loeb Classical Library; London: Heinemann / Cambridge, MA: Harvard University Press, 1961), vol. 2, p. 439.

[51] The form "from x to y" – for instance, "from India to Nubia" (Esth 1:1; 8:9) – is well known from biblical sources (for example, 1 Sam 3:20; 2 Sam 24:2; 1 Kgs 5:4 [ET, 4:24]), as well as from the Akkadian, Assyrian, and Babylonian royal inscriptions, for example: "(from) the Upper Sea (to) the Lower Sea" (Sargon of Agade); see Oppenheim, "Babylonian and Assyrian Historical Texts," p. 267b.

[52] For the text, cf. Oppenheim, "Babylonian and Assyrian Historical Texts," p. 316b. See also R. Schmitt, *Die altpersischen Inschriften der Achaimeniden* (Wiesbaden: Reichert Verlag, 2009), p. 152 (§2, D), who translates "Stämmen" (tribes) instead of "languages" (see also ibid., pp. 153, 155).

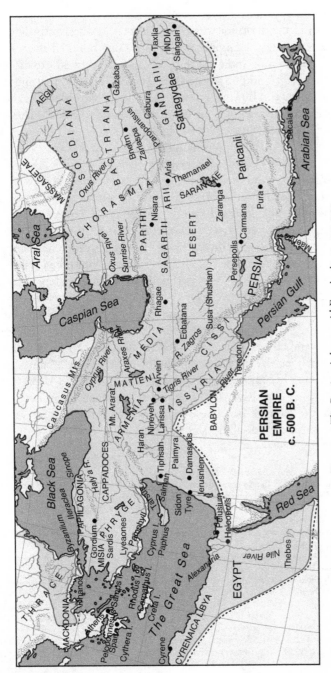

Figure 3   The Persian Achaemenid Empire in ca. 500 BCE

B   מדינה, *"satrapy,"* and *dahyu*

The number of the מדינות mentioned in Esther is identical with the one in 1 Esdras 3:2 regarding the empire of Darius I: "one hundred twenty-seven," which also spread "from India to Ethiopia." Also, it is very close to the number that is mentioned (regarding Darius I) in Dan 6:2, "one hundred and twenty" אחשדרפניא ("satraps"). But these numbers are much larger than the one mentioned by Herodotus regarding the empire of Darius I: "he divided his dominions into 20 governments, called by the Persians satrapies" (*Historia* 3.89).[53] Moreover, in his Behistun Inscription Darius I details the lands that he rules, altogether 23 *dahyu* (plural: *dahyaua*; Old Persian; "land," "province," or "people-country"),[54] and in an Akkadian foundation tablet, Xerxes counts 29 *dahyu* that he rules over, in addition to Persia, altogether 30.[55] Is it possible to explain the huge gap between these numbers, and if so, how?

Although this is often cited by scholars as a direct contradiction between biblical and extrabiblical sources,[56] it seems that the differences stem from the terms that each text uses: the Greek term *satrapy* and the Persian *dahyu* appear to refer to much larger territorial units than the Hebrew/Aramaic term מדינה (e.g., Esth 1:1; 3:12; 8:9; 9:30). The latter appears mostly in the late biblical writings,[57] and derives from the root ד"נ, in the sense of "area of judgment," "county," "district" or "province." Thus, each satrapy included several מדינות ("counties"). For instance, the territorial unit which was named *Yehud Medinta* was a small מדינה ("Province")[58] among many other provinces of Satrapy V, which was called עבר הנהר (Akkadian: *Ebir Nāri*, "Beyond the River [= Euphrates]"), which comprised: Syria, Phoenicia, the Land of Israel, and Cyprus.[59] Thus, the number 127 could refer to all small territorial units of the empire.

---

[53] See Godley, *Herodotus with an English Translation*, vol. 2, p. 117.
[54] See G. G. Cameron, "The Persian Satrapies and Related Matters," *JNES* 32 (1973), pp. 47–56; Schmitt, *Die altpersischen Inschriften der Achaimeniden*, pp. 38–39, §6.
[55] See Cameron, "The Persian Satrapies and Related Matters"; Oppenheim, "Babylonian and Assyrian Historical Texts," pp. 316b–317a esp. 316b.
[56] See, for example, Moore, *Esther*, p. xlv; Levenson, *Esther: A Commentary*, pp. 24–25; Wahl, *Das Buch Esther*, p. 28.
[57] Esther, Ezra-Nehemiah and the Aramaic parts of Ezra and Daniel, Qoh 5:7, and four times in 1 Kgs 20:14–19 (and see also verses 16 and 24).
[58] Most likely the province included Bethel and Mizpah in the north, Jericho in the east, Jerusalem, Beit Zur in the southwest, and En Gedi in the southeast.
[59] On the Satrapy "Beyond the River," see A. F. Rainey, "Satrapy of 'Eber-Hanahar'," in H. Tadmor (ed.), *The History of the Jewish People: The Restoration – The Persian Period* (Jerusalem: Am Ovid, 1983), pp. 105–116, 277–280 (Hebrew). Note that in Esther "satrap" (the person) is referred to with אחשדרפן (Esth 3:12; 8:9), which is distinguished from פחה and שרי המדינות. It seems that the author has listed the types of rulers from those who rule the largest type of territories to those who rule the smallest.

As for the inscriptions, George G. Cameron suggests interpreting *dahyu* as "a group of people."[60] If so indeed, then 29 or 30 *dahyu* may not refer to territorial units at all, but to the groups of people that comprised the empire. In that case, we have no necessary reason to doubt Esther's references to 127 of מדינת ("counties," "districts" or "provinces"; Esth 1:1; 8:9; 9:30), since both a satrapy and a *dahyu* very likely included more than one מדינת each. Alternatively, the number 127, which is not attested by any nonbiblical source, could also represent a symbolic figure.

C "One Hundred Twenty-Seven"

The distinction between the terms designating different territorial units in the Esther story and the extrabiblical sources, could explain the huge gap between the number 127 on the one hand, and the numbers 20 and 30 on the other. But why did the narrator of Esther choose precisely the number 127? Does it really reflect the historical number of מדינות in the Persian Empire, or is it a symbolic number that has a literary function?

The number "one hundred twenty-seven" in Esth 1:1 ומאה מדינה ועשרים שבע (and 1 Esdras), recalls the same number of years of Sarah's lifetime in Gen 23:1, מאה שנה ועשרים שנה ושבע שנים, but it is reported in chiastic order.[61] Similarly, according to 1 Kgs 20:29–30 the death toll of the Arameans in the war with Ahab of Israel was 127,000, that is, 1,000 × 127. Herodotus (*Historia* 8.1) recounts that in the naval battle of Salamis between Xerxes and the Greeks (480 BCE), "the Athenians furnished a *hundred and twenty-seven* ships."[62] It seems, therefore, that these identical numbers are not coincidental. Apparently, the number 127 expresses completeness and quality.[63] It unites two numbers which are considered to be complete and qualitative in the Hebrew Bible and the ancient Near East: "120" and "7." This is well known regarding the number "seven," while the number "120" is 10 times 12 – both typological numbers and regarded as complete in and of themselves, and when combined.[64] Thus, Gen 6:3 states that the Lord said, "My spirit shall not always strive with man, for he also is flesh; yet his days shall be a *hundred and twenty years.*" Moses died at the age of 120 (Deut 31:2; 34:7). The reference to 120 satraps (אחשדרפניא) in Dan 6:2 also likely reflects such a symbolic figure. Unlike Esther, the text in Daniel was not composed in

---

[60] Cameron, "The Persian Satrapies and Related Matters," pp. 47–50, 54.
[61] On the chiasmus between the parallel texts, Esth 1:1 and Gen 23:1, see Chapter 3, §VII, 2.
[62] See Godley, *Herodotus with an English Translation*, vol. 4, pp. 2–3.
[63] See M. Bar-Ilan, *Biblical Numerology* (Rehovot: Association for Jewish Astrology and Numerology, 2005), pp. 135–136 (Hebrew).
[64] Cf. Meinhold, *Das Buch Esther*, p. 23.

the Persian period; accordingly, its author perhaps was already unaware of the relations between provinces and satrapies.

From among many other numbers that appear in the early Hebrew texts, the narrator of Esther chose precisely the number 127, which occurs in the biblical literature only in Gen 23:1. The chiastic order in which this number in Esth 1:1 stands in parallel to Gen 23:1 could be a sign that the former made use of the latter.[65] Maybe Esth 1:1 (as well as its parallels in 8:9 and 9:30) uses Gen 23:1 specifically to connect the Esther story with the matriarch Sarah in some way, though it is not clear what the purpose of such a connection would be.

Alternatively, we might turn to another explanation, which is perhaps more plausible: possibly the author of the text in Esther wished in this way to inform his audience, implicitly, that Ahasuerus reigned over the whole world, including a complete number of provinces, as explicitly stated about Cyrus in the Cylinder and the Decree that carry his name, and as Xerxes expressed in his inscription. The stage is therefore set, so that when Haman later sends his decree to "the governors [הַפַּחוֹת] that were over every province [אשר על־מדינה ומדינה], and to the rulers of every people of every province ... and the letters were sent by couriers to all the king's provinces ..." (Esth 3:12–13), it is clear that he wished to annihilate the Jews of all the world! Furthermore, the phrase "one hundred twenty-seven" מדינה/ מדינות appears two additional times in Esther (8:9; 9:30), and the phrase "from India to Ethiopia" one more time (Esth 8:9), all in the context of the attempt to reverse Haman's decree. Thus, the narrator was interested in stressing, once again, that both the request of Haman from Ahasuerus to annihilate the Jews "in *all the provinces* of your kingdom" (בכל מדינות מלכותך, Esth 3:8, cf. 3:13), and the later reversal of that decree, were referring to the entire civilized world.

2   The Emperor: Ahasuerus/Xerxes

According to the Hebrew version of Esther, the head of this empire was named Ahasuerus. Is this a historical figure? Does he correspond to any Persian emperor known from other sources? The Greek translation of Esther known as the Septuagint (or the B-Text),[66] identifies Ahasuerus with the biblical Artachshasta, king of Persia, who is called

---

[65] For "chiastic parallelism" between texts in the biblical literature, see Kalimi, *The Reshaping of Ancient Israelite History in Chronicles*, pp. 232–274.

[66] On this translation, see Chapter 2, §IV, 1.

in other Greek sources "Artaxerxes" ('Αρταξέρξης). This identification is also made by Josephus Flavius (who follows the Septuagint in his retelling of the biblical story: *Jewish Antiquities* 11.184–296), and by some medieval Jewish commentators.[67] Some scholars accept this identification and set the events of the Esther story in the time of Artaxerxes I (465–424 BCE),[68] or Artaxerxes II (404–358 BCE), or even Artaxerxes III (358–338 BCE).[69]

However, as many other scholars have argued, the name אֲחַשְׁוֵרוֹשׁ (*Ahashverosh/ 'Ăḥašwērôš*)[70] is better understood as a Hebrew variant of the Old Persian *Xšayārša* that appears in Old Persian cuneiform texts,[71] who is known in the Greek sources as Xerxes (Ξέρξης) I ("the Great"), son of King Darius I and Queen Atossa. Strikingly, there are three Aramaic papyri from Elephantine that clearly verify this assumption. The first and second papyri are two copies of a single document (B4.3 – Cowley 3; and B4.4 – Cowley 2), which expresses an obligation to deliver grain, dated to the third year of חשירש מלכא (King Ahasuerus), that is, 483 BCE.[72] The third one (B2.1 – Cowley 5) is a sale document that is dated to the 15th year of חשיארש מלכא, that is, 471 BCE.[73] Thus, there should be no doubt about the historicity of the king himself; he is *'Ăḥašwērôš* = *Xšayārša* = Xerxes I.

This historical figure is mentioned also in Ezra 4:6, which lists Persian kings in chronological order and sets him after Cyrus II and Darius I (Ezra 4:5), but before Artaxerxes I (Ezra 4:7), who followed Xerxes.[74] Indeed, Ahasuerus/Xerxes I succeeded his father, Darius I, and reigned over the Persian Achaemenid Empire in the years 486/5–465 BCE. The Greek historians, Herodotus (who was born in ca. 484, that is, around the time when Xerxes ascended the throne; *Historia* 7.138–239; 8.40–96; 9.1–89),[75] Ctesias (/Ktesias) of Cnidus (southwest Asia Minor;[76] in fragments of his *Persica*,

---

[67] Such as Abraham ibn Ezra, in his commentary on Esth 1:1.
[68] See, for example, Hoschander, *The Book of Esther in the Light of History*, pp. 30–41, 77–79, 118–138; Greenstein, "A Jewish Reading of Esther," pp. 229–230 ("*ahashverosh* is certainly the Artaxerxes whose name is spelled identically in Dan. 9:1 and Ezra 4:6," without identifying which one of them he means); Dalley, *Esther's Revenge at Susa*, p. 1.
[69] See, for instance, Stiehl, "Das Buch Esther," p. 10.
[70] Interestingly, the *ketib* of the name in Esth 10:1 is: אֲחַשְׁרֵשׁ without the *vav*.
[71] See Yamauchi, *Persia and the Bible*, pp. 134–135.
[72] For these documents, see A. Yardeni and B. Porten, *Textbook of Aramaic Documents from Ancient Egypt*, Volume 2: *Contracts* (Jerusalem: Academon, 1989), pp. 106, 110, see also pp. 107–108, 111.
[73] See Yardeni and Porten, *Textbook of Aramaic Documents from Ancient Egypt*, vol. 2, p. 16, see also pp. 17–18.
[74] See also Dan 9:1.
[75] See Godley, *Herodotus with an English Translation*, vol. 3, pp. 441–557; vol. 4, pp. 39–95, 159–265.
[76] Ctesias was also the physician of King Artaxerxes II (404–359/8 BCE); see Diodorus Siculus 2.32.4; C. H. Oldfather, *Diodorus of Sicily with an English Translation* (Loeb Classical Library;

or *History of Persia*, books 12–13);[77] and Diodorus Siculus (*Bibliotheca Historica* 11.1–92),[78] recount that Xerxes marched on Athens, captured and burned it, and defeated the coalition of the Greek poleis (city-states) at the battle of Thermopylae, but he was defeated at the naval battle of Salamis, all in 480 BCE. A year later, in 479 BCE, he fought his final land-battle with the Greeks, near the city of Plataeae (Πλαταιάι), where the Persian army was badly defeated.[79]

Nonetheless, there is no hint of such military exploits in the book of Esther. Instead, this king is mocked for his personal behavior. He is presented as one who concludes important personal and political decisions under the influence of alcohol and when he is angry, without being aware of the consequences of his decisions and the decrees he signs, which he later regrets. For example:

1. On the seventh day of the grandiose banquet, when the heart of King Ahasuerus was merry with wine, he ordered his wife, Vashti, to wear her royal crown and appear in front of him and his officials, to show them her great beauty (Esth 1:10–15). The biblical description, "wearing the royal crown" (Esth 1:11), does not indicate how exactly the king desired to show his wife: dressed magnificently while also wearing her crown on her head, or – as the Rabbis later suggest – wearing the royal crown only (that is, completely naked).[80] However, Vashti's refusal to appear in front of the men made the drunk king extremely angry (Esth 1:12, "his anger burned in him"), and it cost Vashti her position as queen of the empire. Sometime later, "when the anger of King Ahasuerus was appeased, he remembered Vashti [זכר את ושתי], and what she had done, and what was decreed against her" (Esth 2:1). The word זכר here is much more than simply "remembered." In this context

London: Heinemann / Cambridge, MA: Harvard University Press, 1960), vol. 1, pp. 458–459. See also the discussion by L. Llewellyn-Jones and J. Robson, *Ctesias' History of Persia: Tales of the Orient* (Routledge Classical Translations; London and New York: Routledge, 2010), pp. 1–3, 7–18.

77 See Llewellyn-Jones and Robson, *Ctesias' History of Persia*, pp. 183–185.

78 See C. H. Oldfather, *Diodorus of Sicily with an English Translation* (Loeb Classical Library; London: William Heinemann / Cambridge, MA: Harvard University Press, 1961), vol. 4, pp. 121–363.

79 Ctesias also tells that Xerxes ordered his men to plunder the sanctuary of Delphi; see Llewellyn-Jones and Robson, *Ctesias' History of Persia*, p. 184.

80 The talmudic Sages concluded that Vashti should appear with nothing else on her but the crown. See Babylonian Talmud, *Megillah* 12b; Midrash *Esther Rabbah* 3:13; Midrash *Leqach Tov* on Esther (1:11); the First Targum (Tragum Reshon) of Esther on 1:11.

it means also that the king missed Vashti and was sorry for her removal.[81]

2. When Haman requested Ahasuerus to sign an extermination decree against the Jews of the empire, the king's behavior was quite unconventional and even irrational, presumably because he was drunk and not completely aware of what exactly the decree meant. He sold to Haman his loyal subjects' lives, the Jews of his empire, for nothing (Esth 3:8–11). Thus, Ahasuerus did not even ask for the name of the nation that Haman desired to annihilate. He turned down the huge amount of payment – "ten thousand talents of silver" – that Haman offered him, presumably for the loss of the future income tax that would result from the annihilation of the Jews, saying: "the silver is given to you" (Esth 3:11). This was no trivial sum: This amount was nearly equal to two-thirds of the entire annual income tax of the Persian Empire during the time of his father, Darius the Great, as related by Herodotus (*Historia* 3.95–96): "Therefore it is seen by adding all together [that is, 9,880 silver talents plus the value of the collected gold-dust that was equivalent to 4,680 silver talents], that Darius collected a yearly tribute of fourteen thousand five hundred and sixty talents … This was Darius' revenue from Asia and a few parts of Libya."[82] Whether this information is accurate or not, it gives some estimation. So how could the king simply turn down such a generous offer, if he consciously understood and agreed with Haman? Indeed, only later, when Esther drew the king's attention to the act of Haman, did the king grasp what had really happened, and then he permitted the Jews to protect themselves (Esth 8:10–12; 9:13–15).

3. When the king decided to send his head of ministers, Haman, to his death on the gallows (or, on picks), once again he made such an important decision when he was extremely angry and under the influence of alcohol (Esth 7:1–10).

---

[81] Cf. Gerleman, *Esther*, p. 75; Levenson, *Esther: A Commentary*, pp. 53–54. The assertion of Greenstein ("A Jewish Reading of Esther," p. 231): "he cannot even remember from 1:21 to 2:1 that he has banished Queen Vashti," is simply inaccurate.
Usually scholars compare Vashti's incident with the tale of Herodotus regarding Candaules, king of Lydia, who insisted that his bodyguard, Gyges, gaze on the beauty of his naked wife (*Historia* 1.7–12; Godley, *Herodotus with an English Translation*, vol. 1, pp. 9–17). However, it seems to Levenson (ibid., p. 48) that "the similarity is scant, and influence is unlikely." For other similar Greek stories, see Berlin, *Esther: A Commentary*, pp. 67–69.
[82] See Godley, *Herodotus with an English Translation*, vol. 2, p. 123.

4. The king was also forgetful. He forgot that he himself had permitted Haman to annihilate the Jews of the empire (Esth 3:8–11; 7:4–6). He also forgot that Mordecai had saved the king from the conspiracy of the officials Bigthan(a) and Teresh, even though it had been noted in the book of the Chronicles (Esth 2:21–23). The conspirators were hanged on the gallows, but the king overlooked rewarding Mordecai for his loyal service. To be sure, one of the Greek Additions to Esther (A 12:5) states: "And the king ordered Mordecai to serve in the court and rewarded him for these things." Josephus (*Jewish Antiquity* 11.209) follows this and adds that Mordecai remained in the palace "as a very close friend of the king."[83] However, these are late additions that attempt to improve the impression given by the original Hebrew text. According to Esth 6:1–3, Mordecai was rewarded only later, when the king accidentally noticed that nothing has been done yet for him. Only then did he correct what he had forgotten or neglected.

Similar characterizations of Xerxes as one who makes vital decisions at banquets, or when he is angry, without foreseeing their severe consequences, are also attested by Herodotus (*Historae* 9.108–113), regarding his affair with his niece and the reaction of his wife Amestris. Herodotus also attests that at the feasts of the Persians: "it is their custom to deliberate about the gravest matters when they are drunk; and what they approve in their counsels is proposed to them the next day by the master of the house where they deliberate, when they are sober, and if being sober they still approve it, they act thereon, but if not, they cast it aside" (*Historia* 1.133).[84] However, the latter ability to change such drunken decisions after the fact is excluded in the case of the king, according to Esther (Esth 2:1).

To sum up, Ahasuerus/Xerxes refers to a real historical figure, but his representation in Esther is marked by mockery and exaggeration, and he himself is characterized by irresponsible and irrational behavior and decisions. Herodotus and other Greek writers also portray Xerxes and other Persians in similar terms, but not in so extreme a manner. However, none of the above-mentioned *specific incidents* described in Esther are attested by outside sources. Nor are Xerxes' specific activities that are attested in these Greek sources described in Esther.

---

[83] Marcus, *Josephus with an English Translation*, vol. 6, pp. 414–415.
[84] Godley, *Herodotus with an English Translation*, vol. 1, pp. 172–175.

Figure 4   Ahasuerus/Xerxes, King of the Persian Empire, National Museum
of Iran, Tehran

3   The Queen and Harem

Like many kings in the ancient Near East (and elsewhere), Ahasuerus/ Xerxes had both: an official queen and a "House of Women" (בית הנשים; Esth 2:3, 9, 10, 13), that is, a harem. Let us turn our attention to these issues in detail:

A   The Queen: Vashti, Esther, and Amestris

A Persian king could have only one royal wife/queen, but as many concubines as he wished. Scholars have long noted that the claim that Esther replaced Vashti as queen of the Persian Empire stands in contrast to the accounts in the classical Greek sources.[85] Unlike a concubine, who could come from anywhere in the empire (Esth 2:3), Herodotus (*Historia* 3.84) claims that the Persian kings could only marry a woman from the seven leading Persian families. Only such a woman could be appointed a queen of Persia. Furthermore, according to Herodotus, the name of Xerxes' queen was Amestris, said to be the daughter of a Persian general, Otanes (*Historia* 7.61; 7.114; 9.112), rather than Vashti or Esther.[86]

However, Robert L. Hubbard re-examined the three references by Herodotus to Amestris, and concluded that *Historia* 7.61 refers to a male person; 7.114 suggests nothing assured regarding the activities of Amestris in 480 BCE. Thus, Hubbard says, "given their ambiguity, the two texts from Herodotus offer less reliable evidence for events and customs in Achaemenid Persia than scholarly citations generally assume." According to him, this evidence "*does leave open* the possibility that Esther and Amestris may have been the same person" (italics mine).[87] Hubbard does not refer to Herodotus' other claim that a Persian king should take a wife only from among one of the seven noble Persian families (*Historia* 3.84), which opposes the information that Ahasuerus took a foreigner, an orphan Jewish girl, to be his wife and queen (Esth 2:7, 16–18). Nonetheless, Herodotus' information also cannot be relied upon uncritically.[88]

---

[85] See, for example, Fox, *Character and Ideology in the Book of Esther*, pp. 132, 135; Levenson, *Esther: A Commentary*, p. 24.

[86] See R. Schmitt, "Amestris," *Encyclopaedia Iranica* (New York: Bibliotheca Persica Press, 1973), vol. I, pp. 936–937; online: www.iranicaonline.org/articles/amestris-gr.

[87] See R. L. Hubbard, "Vashti, Amestris and Esther 1,9," *ZAW* 119 (2007), pp. 259–271 esp. 271. Interestingly, there are common consonants between the names Amestris and Esther. Is perhaps Esther derived from Amestris, or is it simply coincidence? I tend to favor the latter option.

[88] See R. Schmitt, "Otanes" *Encyclopaedia Iranica*: www.iranicaonline.org/articles/otanes (paragraph 4; 2012).

As Edwin M. Yamauchi claims (following J. Stafford Wright), Amestris herself contradicts Herodotus' assertion, as her father Otanes is not from one of the seven families.[89]

Shea explains the four-year gap between the removal of Vashti in the third year of Ahasuerus/Xerxes I (Esth 1:3), and the crowning of Esther in his seventh year (Esth 2:16), by suggesting that this corresponds to the period when Xerxes was on a campaign against the Greeks, and stayed in Sardis, the fifth capital of the Persian Empire.[90] Shea defends the plausibility of this point as follows: "if the writer of Esther had created this story out of thin air, there would have been no reason to allow for such a time lag."[91] However, Shea's suggestion is not convincing because, as Herodotus affirms (*Historia* 9.108–113), when Xerxes returned in 479 BCE from Greece (i.e., in his seventh year), his wife Amestris was still in power. That is, she was not dismissed in the third year, as told about Vashti in ch. 1 of Esther. Further, Shea's claim that the time lag between the third and seventh years supports the historicity of the account ignores the likely typological significance of the numbers three and seven.[92]

Shea attempts to explain this by speculating that Vashti/Amestris was rejected in year three (and was therefore not with Xerxes when he had an affair in Sardis in year seven, according to Herodotus), but that it was only after Amestris reacted violently to that affair that Xerxes finally named a new queen in his seventh year. This does not resolve the contradiction, however, as Esther 1 grants no further role to Vashti after her dismissal in the third year. Moreover, Herodotus refers to Amestris as "the wife of Xerxes" (*Historia* 7.114) and still attributes great power to her even at the end of her life, when she died many years later of old age.

Moreover, some have suggested that the name ושתי (ו and שתה) is a wordplay on משתה,[93] meaning that this queen's name in the Megillah could be seen as artificial, and built by the narrator for literary-stylistic

---

[89] See Yamauchi, *Persia and the Bible*, p. 233. Yamauchi himself claims that Vashti was Amestris (ibid., pp. 230–232).

[90] See Shea, "Esther and History," pp. 234–241; see also Clines, *Ezra, Nehemiah, Esther*, pp. 260–261; Yamauchi, *Persia and the Bible*, p. 231.

[91] Cf. Shea, "Esther and History," p. 243.

[92] On this, see above, §I, 1.

[93] See B. W. Jones, "Two Misconceptions about the Book of Esther," *CBQ* 39 (1977), pp. 171–181 esp. 174.

effect rather than representing her authentic historical name. If this is correct, then it is not impossible that her original name was "Amestris." But this is nothing more than speculation.

On the one hand, Herodotus' own accounts on these matters may not be entirely reliable. On the other hand, we do not in fact have at our disposal any argument to support the possibility that either Vashti or Esther actually could be Amestris. Therefore, it seems that this issue is still open, and far from satisfactorily resolved, due to the quality and quantity of the available sources, whether Amestris could be identified with either Vashti or Esther – and the problems created by coordinating them are substantial.

B   The Harem

According to Esth 2:3, 9, 10, 13, there was a "House of Women" in Shushan/Susa, which refers to a "harem."[94] The official in charge of the House of Women was Hegai, the סְרִיס. The name "Hegai" is possibly *Hu-gaya* of the Old Persian, which means "having a good life."[95] The title סָרִיס is well known also from other writings in the Hebrew Bible, and corresponds to the Akkadian *ša-reši*, that is, "of the head" (of the king), an official. Usually, these male officials were taken to the royal courts at a very young age and were castrated.[96] Lacking any sexual desire or responsibility for family, wife, and children, they were entirely dedicated to the royal service. Isaiah 56:3b-5 refers to such eunuchs: "Do not let the eunuch [הַסָּרִיס] say, 'I am just a dry tree' [i.e., castrated]. For thus says the Lord: to the eunuchs who keep my Sabbaths,

---

[94] The term *harem* is strictly applicable only to Muslim culture. However, the institution was common to most ancient Near Eastern societies, particularly where polygamy was customary. See 1 Kgs 11:3 regarding King Solomon, who is said to have had: "seven hundred wives, princesses, and three hundred concubines" (surely an exaggeration). Note that the building in Persepolis commonly referred to as "the Harem" (or "The Queen's Quarters"; it was completed by Xerxes) had 22 rooms, which could presumably have accommodated a significant number of women; cf. "The Harem of Xerxes," *The Oriental Institute: Persepolis and Ancient Iran* (2018); online: https://oi.uchicago.edu/collections/photographic-archives/persepolis/harem-xerxes and A. Shapur Shahbazi, "Harem: i. In Ancient Iran," *Encyclopaedia Iranica* (New York: Bibliotheca Persica Press, 2003), vol. 11, pp. 671–672 and vol. 12, pp. 1–3; online: www.iranicaonline.org/articles/harem-i

[95] See Zadok, "Notes on Esther," p. 107; Gesenius, *Hebräisches und Aramäisches Handwörterbuch*, p. 266; Hutter, *Iranische Personalnamen in der Hebräische Bibel*, p. 43.

[96] See H. Tadmor, "Was the Biblical *sārîs* a Eunuch?" in Z. Zevit, S. Gitin and M. Sokoloff (eds.), *Solving Riddles and Untying Knots: Biblical, Epigraphic, and Semitic Studies in Honor of Jonas C. Greenfield* (Winona Lake, IN: Eisenbrauns, 1995), pp. 317–325.

who choose the things that please me and hold fast my covenant, I will give, in my house and within my walls, a monument and a name better than sons and daughters." Except for a few places (Gen 37:36; 40:2 // 41:10 [עבדים]; Jer 34:19), in all other biblical texts, including the one under review in Esther, the term סריס could be interpreted in both as an "official" and "eunuch"/ "castrate."[97] The Persian king, therefore, did not take any risk: He appointed the right man – Hegai the סריס, in charge of the right place – the House of Women! Whether the name "Hegai" – "having good life" – presents the original given name of a historical officer, or the narrator uses it sarcastically for the poor castrated man who was surrounded by the most beautiful women in the kingdom, yet was excluded from having any sexual life, wife, children, and family of his own – is difficult to say. Nonetheless, since the story of Esther is immersed with humor and sarcasm, the latter option cannot be excluded.

In any case, the preparations of a beautiful young virgin were required twelve months, "six months with oil of myrrh, and six months with sweet perfumes ..." (Esth 2:12),[98] and all this only to meet the king for one single night: "she was called by the king, she left [the harem] in the evening and returned in the morning." Then she stayed in another harem under the care of Shaashgaz, another eunuch of the king, until the king called her again (Esth 2:12–14). Thus, Esther was an exceptional case, because the king simply loved her the most and invited her frequently (Esth 2:15–17).

Similar descriptions of royal harems are available in the classical literature regarding various kings in the fourth century BCE, for example:

1. Plutarch reports that Artaxerxes II (Mnemon; 404–358 BCE) kept, in addition to his wife, "three hundred and sixty concubines also, who were of *surpassing beauty*" (*Lives: Artaxerxes* 27.1–2).[99] That is to say, the king had an exceptionally beautiful woman for each day of the

---

[97] Tadmor suggests that Gen 37:36 might also play on the meaning of סריס as "eunuch," by using this title for Potiphar, whose wife attempts to sleep with another man (Joseph); see Tadmor, "Was the Biblical *sārîs* a Eunuch?" p. 321.

[98] On this issue in Esther, see Chapter 3, §X.

[99] See B. Perrin, *Plutarch's Lives with an English Translation* (11 vols.; Loeb Classical Library; London: William Heinemann / Cambridge, MA: Harvard University Press, 1950–1968), vol. 11, p. 193.

year (according to the 360-day calendar followed by the Persians).[100]

2. Diodorus Siculus recounts that when Alexander the Great had accomplished his goals and held his empire without any challenge, "he began to imitate the Persian luxury and the extravagant display of the kings of Asia ... he added concubines to his retinue in the manner of Darius [III], in number not less [than] the days of the year, and *outstanding in beauty as selected from all the women of Asia*. Each night these [concubines] paraded about the couch of the king so that he might select the one with whom he would lie that night" (*Bibliotheca Historica* 17.77.5–6; italics mine).[101]

Did Ahasuerus have the same or a similar number of concubines as well? Briant is of the opinion that "this is a symbolic number that was also found in Greek tradition ... it was a number pertaining to the sacred character of Achaemenid kingship."[102] In any case, the book of Esther tells us that Ahasuerus had many concubines (Esth 2:3), though it does not offer an exact number of them. For the discussion here, the decisive fact is that Esther as well as the Greek sources suggest that a different woman was brought every night to a Persian king. In other words, the biblical text reflects a similar situation to that depicted in the extrabiblical sources.

4   The Imperial Hierarchy

The Esther story reflects the Persian imperial hierarchy as follows: On the top of the pyramid stands King Ahasuerus of the Achaemenid dynasty (550–330 BCE). Below the king comes Haman, the vizier who was above all the officials/ministers, and before whom everybody should bow down, by the king's order (Esth 3:1–2). Later, Haman is replaced in this position by Mordecai (Esth 8:2), who becomes second to the king (Esth 10:1–3). Additionally, the king had an advisory council of seven

---

[100] On the Old Persian 360-day calendar and its later replacement (possibly during the Achaemenid period) by a 365-day solar calendar, see, e.g., A. Panaino, R. Abdollahy and D. Balland, "Calendars," *Encyclopaedia Iranica* (New York: Bibliotheca Persica Press, 1990), vol. 4, pp. 658–677; online: www.iranicaonline.org/articles/calendars.

[101] C. B. Welles, *Diodorus of Sicily with an English Translation* (Loeb Classical Library; London: William Heinemann / Cambridge, MA: Harvard University Press, 1963), vol. 8, pp. 340–343.

[102] Briant, *From Cyrus to Alexander*, p. 281.

officials of Persia and Media, "those next to the king, who had access to the king, and hold the leading positions [lit.: sat first] in the kingdom" (Esth 1:14). Only occasionally is the king said to have consulted with them (Esth 1:13–22).

Esther implies that generally the decisions were made by the king alone: He appointed Haman as vizier (Esth 3:1–2); he permitted the latter to annihilate the Jews, and decided not to take the payment that was offered by Haman (Esth 3:11); he decided to send Haman to his death and hanged him and his sons (Esth 7:9–10; 8:7–8); and he let the Jews defend themselves from their enemies (9:12–14). It was also Ahasuerus who laid tribute "on the land and on the islands of the sea," and promoted Mordecai to high honor (Esth 7:9–10; 8:7–8; 9:12–14; 10:1–2). Thus, Ahasuerus emerges from the book of Esther as the absolute dictatorial king of the Persian Empire.[103] This picture corresponds well with the nonbiblical sources. Regarding the king's unmatched authority, for instance, the Akkadian foundation tablet from Persepolis describes Xerxes (/Ahasuerus) as "the great king, the king of kings … the son of king Darius, the Achaemenian, a Persian son of a Persian, an Aryan of Aryan descent [lit.: seeds]."[104]

Regarding the advisory council of seven ministers that Esther mentions, these were most likely representatives of the seven Persian aristocratic families who are mentioned by Herodotus (*Historia* 3.83–84; see also 7.8).[105] Thus, although usually the number "seven" is typological in the Hebrew Bible (including in Esther, where it appears several times, Esth 1:5, 10; 2:9; see above), it does not exclude the possibility that it is always an accurate number, as appears to be the case here. As Pierre Briant stresses, the membership of the council was not imposed on the king, and he could overrule them and make decisions alone.[106]

Esther also affirms that the many satrapies of the empire were ruled by satraps (אחשדרפני המלך; Esth 3:12, which were of Persian origin), who reported directly to the king. Under every satrap served several פחות, that is, lower rank "governors" who were over "all the provinces" (אשר על-מדינה ומדינה), who usually came from Persia's leading families (but not always, as the cases of Zerubbabel and Nehemiah prove; Hag 1:1; Neh 5:18). Under each פחה served "officials of all the peoples, to every province" (שרי עם ועם מדינה ומדינה), who regularly came from the noble strata of the different nations (Esth 3:12; cf. 8:9).

---

[103] See also below, §II, 8, no. 3.

[104] See Oppenheim, "Babylonian and Assyrian Historical Texts," in Pritchard, *ANET*, p. 316b.

[105] See Godley, *Herodotus with an English Translation*, vol. 2, pp. 111,113; vol. 3, pp. 308–309.

[106] See Briant, *From Cyrus to Alexander*, pp. 128–129, and the references therein to the primary sources.

Figure 5   Relief of King Darius the Great and behind him his son, Crown Prince Xerxes, receiving tribute; *Apadana* ("Audience Hall"), Persepolis; National Museum of Iran, Tehran.

In the context of this general agreement between Esther's portrayal of the Persian hierarchy and what is known from other sources, what about the specific figures of Haman and Mordechai? Regarding the former, no contemporaneous surviving sources outside of Esther explicitly mention a royal vizier named Haman, nor describe any of the specific actions attributed to him in the book. Some have connected his name to the Old Persian word *hamanā*, meaning "illustrious," and his ten sons do have genuine Persian names (Esth 9:6–10), but unless Haman is to be identified with the "Omanes" mentioned in some Persian sources, no references to him survive.[107]

In 1941 Artur Ungnad identify the Persian royal official in Susa from the first year of Xerxes, named "the *Mar-duk-ā* the Sipîr" (i.e., Mordecai the Scribe) of Barsipa/Borsippa (ca. 25 km, south of Babylon), who is mentioned in a tablet from Amherst Collection (no. 250, line 9), with Mordecai the Jew in Megillat Esther.[108] Some scholars, such as Yamauchi, accepted this identification,[109] while others, such as Arndt Meinhold and Jon D. Levenson, reject it. The former does not provide any explanation for his rejection,[110] while the latter objects that:

> Given its association with the Babylonian god-name "Marduk," one should not be surprised to find the name of Mordecai paralleled in literature of this period, but the notion that Mardukā in the Persian inscription and the Mordecai of the book of Esther are the same individual strains credulity and cannot be used to support the historicity of the biblical book (though it often has been). One might as well argue that the appearance of the name "George" as a colonist in North America in the eighteenth century proves accurate the old story of Washington and the cherry tree.[111]

This argument of Levenson is not compelling. The *Mardukā* in this inscription is not just any Persian, but the name of one of Xerxes' officials, precisely what Mordecai appears to be in Esther, and even if the name were common – which has not been demonstrated – that is no disproof of the possibility that this could in fact refer to the same Mordecai as in

---

[107] See J. M. Wiebe, "Haman," in D. N. Freedman *et al.* (eds.), *The Anchor Bible Dictionary* (New York: Doubleday, 1992), vol. 3, p. 33, with bibliography.

[108] See A. Ungnad, "Keilinschriftliche Beiträge zum Buch Esra und Esther," *ZAW* 58 (1940–41), pp. 240–244 esp. 243–244. As a German who lived in Falkensee near Berlin in 1941, the peak of the Nazi regime, Ungnad notes – though it has nothing to do with the topic under his discussion – that "Xerxes himself was free of that Aryan race-consciousness" ("Xerxes selbt fehlte jedes arische Rassenbewußtsein"; ibid., p. 243). Presumably, he attempts to explain how the Aryan Xerxes hired the Jew Mordecai to work in his court.

[109] See Yamauchi, *Persia and the Bible*, pp. 234–236 esp. 235 with bibliography.

[110] See Meinhold, *Das Buch Esther*, p. 32.

[111] Levenson, *Esther: A Commentary*, p. 24.

Esther, who is also described as an official of Xerxes/Ahasuerus in his third year (Esth 1:3).[112] Of course, this remains only a possibility: there is still no conclusive proof that these *were* in fact the same individual, rather than two people who carried a common name.

That a foreigner could serve in a Persian king's court is reflected also in the book of Nehemiah. Similar to Mordecai, Nehemiah was a Jewish official in the Persian court in Shushan (Susa), during the reign of King Artaxerxes I (464–424 BCE; Neh 1:1; 2:1–9), the successor of Xerxes.[113] Moreover, this phenomenon is possibly known already from the time of Sennacherib king of Assyria (705–681 BCE), if we accept the possibility that the Rabshakeh (or Rab-šaqeh) who spoke in Hebrew to the Judahites on the wall of Jerusalem (2 Kgs 18:17, 19–35 // Isa 36:2–20), could have been an Israelite exile.[114] A more certain set of examples of foreigners at the neo-Assyrian court is the role of Aramaeans there. Thus, for example, the consort of King Sennacherib, *Zakūtu*, or according to her Aramaean name, *Naqi'a*, was the mother of Sennacherib's successor, Esarhaddon. In the latter's reign the wise Aramean counselor, Aḥiqar served in the royal court.[115]

According to Esth 2:5–6, either Mordecai or one of his ancestors was exiled by Nebuchadnezzar, king of Babylon, in 597 BCE, from Jerusalem to Babylonia, together with Jechoniah (Coniah/Jehoiachin), king of Judah, and many noble and capable Judeans (2 Kgs 24:8–17 // 2 Chr 36:9–10). If this refers to Mordecai himself, and if the story of Esther took place in the third year of Ahasuerus (Xerxes; 485–465 BCE; Esth 1:3), that is, in 482 BCE, Mordecai would have to have been at least 116 years old, and still active in the kings' service (Esth 2:21; 5:13; 6:10; 10:3)!

[112] Ungnad, "Keilinschriftliche Beiträge zum Buch Esra und Esther," p. 243 note 1, refers to Septuagint Esth 11:3, which says that Mordecai served the kind already in the second year of Ahauerus.

[113] For identification of the biblical Artachshasta with Artaxerxes I, see Kalimi, *The Reshaping of Ancient Israelite History in Chronicles*, p. 8; idem, *Zur Geschichtsschreibung des Chronisten* (Beihefte zur Zeitschrift für die alttestamentliche Wissenschaft 226; Berlin and New York: Walter de Gruyter, 1995), pp. 7–8, with references to earlier secondary literature. On Jewish ministers in the Persian Empire, and later on in European royal courts, acting on behalf of their people, see K. A. D. Smelik, "Nehemiah as a 'Court Jew,'" in I. Kalimi (ed.), *New Perspectives on Ezra-Nehemiah: History and Historiography, Text and Literature* (Winona Lake, IN: Eisenbrauns, 2012), pp. 61–72.

[114] That the Rabshakeh was an Israelite is already speculated on in Babylonian Talmud, *Sanhedrin* 60a, and in modern times has been put forward as a suggestion by H. Tadmor, "Rabshakeh," *Encyclopedia Biblica* (Jerusalem: Bialik Institute, 1976), vol. 7, pp. 323–325 esp. 324 (Hebrew).

[115] See Tadmor, "Rabshakeh," p. 324; E. Frahm, "Family Matters: Psychohistorical Reflections on Sennacherib and His Times," in I. Kalimi and S. Richardson (eds.), *Sennacherib at the Gates of Jerusalem: Story, History and Historiography* (Culture and History of the Ancient Near East 71; Leiden and Boston: Brill, 2014), pp. 163–222 esp. 179–180; T. L. Holm, "Memories of Sennacherib in Aramaic Tradition," in Kalimi and Richardson, *Sennacherib at the Gates of Jerusalem*, pp. 295–323 esp. 309.

Possibly, we have before us a shortened genealogy, that is, a list that omits a few names/generations, in order to connect Mordecai to his famous ancestor, Kish, who is either himself the father of Saul, or a later descendant named after him. Such shortened genealogies, highlighting significant ancestors, are common, including the common refrain "your fathers Abraham, Isaac and Jacob" (ignoring all later generations; e.g., Exod 3:6, 15–16; Deut 1:8; Jer 33:26), but also in more specific cases, such as 1 Chr 7:1–5, which traces the descendants of Issachar (one of Jacob's sons) only four generations, before jumping ahead to the time of David (800 years later, according to the biblical chronology).[116] If it is so indeed, then the narrator of Esther meant that Mordecai, who historically existed, was a *descendant* of one of those who were exiled with King Jechoniah. Thus, Esth 2:5–6 does not present a complete or accurate list. It refers to Mordecai's ancestors rather than to himself. However, if indeed these verses refer to Mordecai himself, whom the narrator wished to associate with the nobles who exiled in 597 BCE, then the narrator must not have been aware of the chronological difficulty, despite all his high literary qualifications.

5 The Geographical Setting: Susa, Persepolis, and Their Palaces

A Susa and Its Palace

The Esther story takes place, almost entirely, in the city of שׁוּשַׁן (Shushan), that is, Akkadian Šušanu, and Greek Σοῦσα. Susa is in the lower Zagros Mountains (about 250 km, ca. 160 miles, east of the Tigris River), in southwest Iran. Up to its capture by Cyrus II, the Great, Susa was the capital of Elam. Darius the Great renovated the city, reconstructed its wall and temples, built a new royal palace, *apadana* (Old Persian; "Audience Hall") and acropolis, as attested by Strabo (ca. 64 BCE – 24 CE; see below) and confirmed by the archaeological discoveries.[117] Darius also established Susa

---

[116] Similarly, in the New Testament, the Gospel of Matthew names Jesus as "the son of David, the son of Abraham" (Matt 1:1) skipping all those in between. The rest of the chapter then presents a fuller genealogy of Jesus, but it also is selective, naming precisely fourteen generations from Abraham to David, and the same number of generations also from David to the Exile, and from the Exile to Jesus (see Matt 1:2–17, esp. 1:17). Meanwhile, the Gospel of Luke presents a much fuller genealogy of Jesus, reaching all the way back to "Adam, son of God," while including many more (and different) names than Matthew does (Luke 3:23–38). Usage of "father" to refer to a more distant ancestor appears also in the rabbinic literature, see for instance, Midrash *Aba Gurion*, parasha A: ... וכשראה חזקיהו את הכסא אמר מה ראה שלמה אבי לעשות שש מעלות לכסא ("As Hezekiah saw the throne, he said, 'Why did Solomon, my father, make six degrees to the throne ...'").

[117] See in detail Briant, *From Cyrus to Alexander*, pp. 165–168.

as one of the five capitals of the empire, alongside Persepolis (which replaced Pasargadae, the capital of Cyrus the Great); Ecbatana ("Aḥmatha" of Ezra 6:2, that is, modern Hamadan, which previously was the capital of Media); Babylon (the capital of the former Babylonian Empire); and Sardis (Asia Minor; originally the capital of the Anatolian kingdom of Lydia). Xerxes/Ahasuerus continued to build and develop Susa.

In that context, Esth 1:6–7a describes the glorious wealth of Ahasuerus's palace in Susa as follows:

> There were white cotton curtains and blue hangings tied with cords of fine linen and purple to silver rings [rods] and marble pillars. There were couches of gold and silver on a mosaic pavement of porphyry, marble, mother-of-pearl, and colored stones. Drinks were served in golden goblets, goblets of different kinds.

Indeed, as Strabo declares, Susa was "a most notable city ... they adorned the palace at Susa more than any other ... the treasure and the riches and the tombs of the Persians were there, since they were on sites that were at the same time hereditary and more strongly fortified by nature" (*Geography*, 15.3.2–3).[118] Also Plutarch (ca. 45–127 CE) relates concerning the extreme wealth of Susa: "On making himself master of Susa, Alexander came into possession of forty thousand talents[119] of coined money in the palace, and of untold furniture and wealth besides. Among this they say was found five thousand talents' weight of purple from Hermione ..." (*Alexander* 36.1–2).[120] Despite the exaggerated numbers of this source, the impression it conveys is that Susa was an extremely wealthy city. Once again, the description of Susa in the book of Esther stands generally in the same line with those in various extrabiblical sources, although from later periods than Esther.

But Susa of the Esther story was not only a royal city with a magnificent palace packed with unimaginable wealth. It was also, as we saw above, full of banquets and wine, or if you wish, "bread and circuses" for everybody. In those banquets, "the royal wine was poured according to the bounty [literally, hand] of the king. Drinking was by flagons, without limit ..." (Esth 1:7b-8). The banquets for women were separate from those of men, perhaps because of serving great amounts of wine. Thus, the narrator tells also about Vashti's banquet as well as the banquet of Esther. Moreover,

---

[118] See H. L. Jones, *The Geography of Strabo with an English Translation* (Loeb Classical Library; London: Heinemann / Cambridge, MA: Harvard University Press, 1961), vol. 7, pp. 156–159.

[119] "A talents' weight was something over fifty pounds." See Perrin, *Plutarch's Lives with an English Translation*, vol. 7, p. 332 note 2.

[120] See Perrin, *Plutarch's Lives with an English Translation*, vol. 7, pp. 332–335.

the capital city also hosted numerous attractive young women from all over the empire: The king appointed commissioners "in all the provinces of his kingdom to gather all the beautiful young virgins to the harem in Susa" (Esth 2:3).

Xenophon (*Cyropaedia* 8.6.22)[121] recounts that Cyrus the Great spent in winter "seven months in Babylon, for there the climate is warm; *in the spring he spent three months in Susa*, and in the height of summer two months in Ecbatana. By doing so … he enjoyed the warmth and coolness of perpetual spring-time." Did Xerxes I keep this custom as well? Esth 3:7–8 reflects that in the month of Nisan (in early spring), the king was in Susa, and according to Esth 8:9 in the 23rd of the month of Sivan (in late spring) he was still there. In other words, Xerxes I spent spring-time in Susa. Nevertheless, according to Esth 2:16–17 he was also in Susa when Esther was crowned there as queen, in the winter month of *Tebet*. Perhaps the latter was an exception from the normal custom of the Persian kings. Thus, there is no serious challenge to accuracy of Esther's depiction, and it is similar to what is told by the Greek historian, Xenophon.

B   Susa versus *Persepolis*

The Esther story takes place in the rebuilt Elamite city of Susa, rather than in the most magnificent Persian city, which the Greeks called "Persepolis" (modern *Takht-i Jamshid*, that is, *the Throne of Jamshid*, who is an Iranian mythological figure). The latter is located in southwest Persia, in the province of Fars, near the river Pulwar, about 52 km (ca. 33 miles), northeast of the modern city of Shiraz.[122] As the monumental ruins and artifacts of Persepolis testify, it was an extremely wealthy and glorious imperial center of the Achaemenids. To cite Diodorus Siculus, "It was the richest city under the sun and the private houses had been furnished with every sort of wealth over the years" (*Bibliotheca Historica* 17.70.2).[123] It was founded by Darius I, apparently in 518 BCE, and gradually built up and developed by his successors, particularly Xerxes, who completed his father's projects such as "the Gate of All Nations" and "the Harem" (or "Queen's Quarters"). In addition to the palaces, Persepolis had reception halls, an imperial treasury, military quarters, royal stables and chariot places. The city's architecture

---

[121]   Miller, *Xenophon Cyropaedia*, vol. 2, pp. 420–421.
[122]   On Persepolis and its monumental constructions, see H. Koch, *Persepolis: Glänzende Hauptstadt des Perserreichs* (Mainz: von Zabern, 2001); I. Kalimi, "Persepolis," in K. D. Sakenfeld (ed.), *The New Interpreter's Dictionary of the Bible* (Nashville, TN: Abingdon Press, 2009), vol. 4, pp. 450–451; A. Shapur Shahbazi, *Persepolis: Die altpersische Residenzstadt* (Darmstadt and Mainz: Wissenschaftliches Buchgesellschaft, 2013).
[123]   See Welles, *Diodorus of Sicily with an English Translation*, vol. 8, pp. 318–319.

is distinguished by its numerous dark-grey stone columns (their tops were made from sculptures of lions, eagles, and double-headed bulls), decorated walls (with plants, bulls, and lions), bas-reliefs and sculptures.

Why, then, is Esther set in Susa rather than Persepolis? It seems that the setting could be explained in the following ways:

1. As hinted in Isa 11:11–12, Jews lived in Elam and most likely in its capital Susa for hundreds of years.[124] Such a hint regarding Persepolis is not available. Thus, presumably, Esther's narrator located his story in Susa rather than Persepolis, simply because according to his tradition the core of the story took place in Susa, where Jews lived. The narrator knew the city very well, and probably he was a man of Susa himself.

2. Together with Babylon and Ecbatana, Susa was the genuine political, economic and administrative capital of the Empire, while Persepolis was mainly used as a recreational site, a place for international receptions and ceremonies.

3. According to Diodorus Siculus (*Bibliotheca Historica* 17.70.1), Alexander the Great described Persepolis to the Macedonians as "the most hateful of the cities of Asia."[125] Indeed, Persepolis was one of a few cities in Asia that Alexander partially ruined (330 BCE), and "gave it over to his soldiers to plunder, all but the palaces" (Diodorus Siculus, ibid.; the palace of Xerxes was also plundered, perhaps as revenge for Xerxes' destruction of Athens in 480 BCE). It is possible, therefore, that for whatever reason Persepolis was also disliked by Esther's narrator.

6   Achaemenid Royal Annals and Imperial Archives

In addition to the king's decrees and accounts of warfare, the Esther story also claims that actions of the king's servants that relate to the king were documented within a file or book named דברי הימים ("the Annals" or

---

[124] Several biblical texts mention Elam, which was eventually annexed into the Persian Empire (Gen 10:22; 14:1, 9; Isa 11:11–12; 21:2; Jer 25:25; Jer 49:34–39; Ezek 32:24–25), and its capital Susa (שׁושׁן; Neh 1:1; Dan 8:2). In particular, the prophecy in Isa 11:11–12 regarding the messianic era recounts that the Lord shall assemble the outcasts of Israel and Judah "from Assyria, and from Egypt, and from Pathros [= Upper Egypt], and from Kush [= Nubia], *and from Elam*, and from Shinar [= Babylonia], and from Hamath [representing all of Syria], and from the islands of the sea [that is, the remote Greek islands]. And he shall set up a banner for the nations, and shall assemble the outcasts of Israel, and gather together the dispersed of Judah from the four corners of the earth."

[125] Welles, *Diodorus of Sicily with an English Translation*, vol. 8, pp. 318–319. See also Kalimi, "Persepolis," pp. 450–451.

"Chronicles"; literally: "words/matters/things of the days"; Esth 2:23) and deposited in the royal archive. This included Mordecai's disclosure of a conspiracy by Bigthan and Teresh to assassinate Ahasuerus (Esth 2:21–23; 6:2). Esth 6:1 mentions two terms, side by side: ספר הזכרונות דברי הימים ("the book of records, of the Annals/Chronicles"), in order to say that they both define one and the same royal book. Most likely, ספר הזכרונות דברי הימים is the same book mentioned in Esth 10:2 as ספר דברי הימים למלכי מדי ופרס ("the Annals/Chronicles of the kings of Media and Persia"), in which had been written "all the acts of his [= Ahasuerus'] power and might, and the full account of the high honor of Mordecai, to which the king advanced him." This seems to describe, therefore, the official Achaemenid royal annals, which were deposited in the royal archives of the Empire. Seemingly, these annals were similar to those of earlier kingdoms, such as the royal annals in Assyria, Babylonia, Israel and Judah (ספר דברי הימים למלכי ישראל/ ויהודה),[126] or even to the Greek *ephēmerides* (plural of *ephemeris/* ἐφημερίς, "diary" or "daybooks").[127]

Esther 6:1–3 recounts a notable occasion when one night the king could not fall asleep. On this occasion, he did not order his servants to bring him a concubine from his huge harem, but rather the ספר הזכרונות דברי הימים, which were read before him. It is reasonable to assume that such a book was written on papyrus or skin that was easy to carry to the king's bedroom, rather than on a big clay or stone tablet. Probably, such a book included also some interesting stories about the life and safety of the Persian kings, written in an attractive literary style that was worthy to read for a king before his sleeping (although, entertainment probably was not the primarily goal of the book). Indeed, "it was found written that Mordecai had told of Bigthan and Teresh, two of the king's chamberlains, the keepers of the gate, who sought to lay hand on the King Ahasuerus." As it is described in Esther, the reading did not lead to the king gradually falling asleep, but rather drove the sleep from his eyes. He inquired whether or not an appropriate honor and dignity had been done to Mordecai for his noble act. In other words, the king attempted to correct what he had abandoned or forgotten.

---

[126] See 1 Kgs 14:19, 29; 15:7, 23, 31; 16:5, 14, 20, 27; 22:39, 46; 2 Kgs 1:18; 8:23; 10:34; 12:20; 13:8, 12; 14:15, 18, 28. Berlin ("The Book of Esther and Ancient Storytelling," p. 7) claims that the references to official records in Esther are a *deliberate* echo of that very convention found in earlier biblical historiography, and therefore do not necessarily refer to actual annals. This overly skeptical suggestion is implausible, given the allusions to such Persian records in other ancient Israelite and ancient Near Eastern sources, discussed below.

[127] On Greek *ephēmerides*, see E. Posner, *Archives in the Ancient World* (Cambridge, MA: Harvard University Press, 1972), p. 126.

Indeed, like kings of other times and lands in the ancient Near East (i.e., the Egyptians, Assyrians, and Babylonians), the Persian kings documented their military, royal building and civil activities and decrees. In his *History of Persia*, Ctesias relates that the Persians "kept an account of their ancient affairs" in archive (Diodorus Siculus, *Bibliotheca Historica* 2.32).[128] According to Plutarch, at the naval battle of Salamis (480 BCE), many scribes sat near Xerxes, "whose task it was to make due record of all that was done in the battle" (*Themistocles* 13.1).[129] Such documents were deposited in the royal archive that was called in Aramaic, בית גנזיא (Ezra 5:17) or בית ספריא (lit., "House of Books"; Ezra 6:1). The archives were located in each of the five capitals of the empire. Thus, for example, a copy of the Aramaic version of the Cyrus Decree to the Jews was written on a scroll, as a דכרונה ("record") that was included within a book named ספר דכרוניא ("The Book of Records/Memories"): "they searched the archives where the documents were stored in Babylon. But it was in Ahmatha [= Ecbatana], the capital in the province of Media ..." (Ezra 6:1–2, see also Ezra 4:15).[130] A parallel Hebrew name of the book under review is mentioned in Esth 6:1, ספר הזכרונות. Both terms – the Aramaic as well as the Hebrew – are connected with royal archival documents. Thus, in comparison to what is known from the biblical as well as Greek and other documents, all in all the main description of Esth 6:1–3 does not sound too far from reality.

7   The Royal Postal Delivery System

The Esther story refers three times to the mail delivery system in the Persian Empire. First, Esth 1:22 recounts that Ahasuerus' letter regarding the behavior of household women was sent to "all the royal provinces," without specifying how it had been done. Second, as the narrator describes the Haman Decree it is said that "Letters were sent by couriers to all the king's provinces ... The couriers *went quickly* by order of the king ..." (Esth 3:13–15). In the third instance, the narrator describes the contra-decree which was sent by Esther and Mordecai to the Jews as follows:

---

[128] See Oldfather, *Diodorus of Sicily*, vol. 1, pp. 458–459.
[129] See Perrin, *Plutarch's Lives with an English Translation*, vol. 2, p. 39.
[130] Two versions of the Decree are preserved in the Hebrew Bible: One is in Ezra 1:1–4 (// 2 Chr 36:22–23), which is probably a Hebrew oral version that the king's messengers passed among the Babylonian Jews. The other is in Ezra 6:3–5 – an official version written in Aramaic (דכרונה), which was used by the king's officials. See I. Kalimi, "'So Let Him Go Up [to Jerusalem]!': A Historical and Theological Observation on Cyrus' Decree in Chronicles," *An Ancient Israelite Historian: Studies in the Chronicler, His Time, Place, and Writing* (Studia Semitica Neerlandica 46; Assen: Van Gorcum, 2005), pp. 143–157.

"He wrote letters ... by mounted couriers riding on *fast horses* bred from the royal herd ... So the couriers, mounted on their *swift royal horses*, hurried out, urged by the king's command" (Esth 8:10, 14). In the last two cases, and particularly in the third one, the narrator repeatedly stresses the rapidness of the royal postal delivery to all the king's provinces, because they should arrive on time – before a specific date.

The most detailed description of the postal delivery system in the Persian Empire of Xerxes has been provided by Herodotus, who also stresses the swiftness of the messengers:

> Now there is nothing mortal that accomplishes a course more swiftly than do these messengers, by the Persians' skillful contrivance. It is said that as many days as there are in the whole journey, so many are the men and horses that stand along the road, each horse and man at the interval of a day's journey; and these are stayed neither by snow nor rain nor heat nor darkness from accomplishing their appointed course with all speed. The first rider delivers his charge to the second, the second to the third, and thence it passes on from hand to hand, even as in the Greek torch-bearer's race in honour of Hephaestus ... (Historia 8.98).[131]

This Greek source confirms, without a doubt, that the Esther narrator had solid and reliable information about the postal delivery system in the Persian Empire. Moreover, it seems that the Persian delivery system could quickly reach almost every place in the empire. Places that a delivery did not reach, the Persians did not rule there.

8 The Persian Legal System

The story of Esther reflects some issues regarding the legal system in the Persian Empire:

1. The Persian word which is used to describe a decree or law is דת (e.g., Esth 1:8; 3:14; 9:13). This word is identical with the Old Persian *dt* that also appears in Aramaic and in Akkadian (*dātu*).[132] It is not related to and bears no connotation of "religion," unlike how דת is used in Modern Hebrew.

2. According to the book of Esther, the Persian authorities made special efforts to distribute also some nonsensical royal decree(s), such as

---

[131] See Godley, *Herodotus with an English Translation*, vol. 4, p. 97. "Hephaestus" was the Greek god of craftsmen, metallurgy, and fire.

[132] See I. J. Gelb *et al.* (eds.), *The Assyrian Dictionary of the Oriental Institute of the University of Chicago* (= *CAD*; 20 vols.; Chicago: The Oriental Institute; Glückstadt: J. and J. Augustin, 1956–2010), vol. 3 (D), pp. 122b–123a.

"that *every man should be master in his own house, and speak according to the language of his people*" (Esth 1:22).[133] Historically, this seems implausible, and as far as we know, there is no parallel to this in any nonbiblical accounts.

3. According to Esth 8:8, there was a unique regulation in the Persian legal system, that is: "the decrees which are decreed in the king's name, and sealed with the king's [signet] ring, no one can invalidate," not even the king himself. But, was a royal decree indeed irrevocable, even when it expressed an extremely evil, unjust and immoral demand, such as Haman's decree to annihilate the entire Jewish people – innocent men, women, and children, young and old – in one day? Was the king imprisoned within his own legal system, without any ability to change it, even in the worst scenario? In fact, no outside evidence exists to confirm this law, and it is difficult to imagine that any kingdom or empire could function properly under such a requirement. It seems, therefore, that this is only a literary-polemical feature in the book of Esther (and Daniel; see below).[134] Most likely, the author of Esther polemicizes here against the despotic (tyrannical) ideology of the Persian ruler. This idea presupposes a king who holds enormous power and authority over every aspect of society, as if he were a god. As such, the totalitarian ruler makes no mistakes at all, and therefore his decrees are irreversible! This authority, which in monotheistic religions such as Judaism has been attributed to God alone, was given to an emperor like Xerxes, and Esther's author tries to show the absurdity and irrationality of this.

4. This Persian legal norm is also reflected in Dan 6:8–9, 12, 15–16. Here, heavenly interference was required to solve the problem caused by the irrevocable order of the king; namely Daniel was saved miraculously from the lions after he was thrown into their den (Dan 6:19–24, 27). By contrast, in Esther the problem was solved by issuing a counter-decree by the king, which technically does not nullify the previous royal decree made by Haman, but in practice leads to its reversal.[135]

---

[133] The LXX does not have "and speak according to the language of his people" (Esth 1:22b), perhaps because it does not fit the context and the translator deleted it. Some scholars consider the phrase to be corrupted and attempt to correct it. For some suggestions, see the discussion by H. Junker, "Konsonantenumstellung als Fehlerquelle und textkritischer Hilfsmittel im massoretischen Text," in P. Volz, F. Stummer and J. Hempel (eds.), *Werden und Wesen des Alten Testaments* (Beihefte zur Zeitschrift für die alttestamentliche Wissenschaft 66; Berlin: A. Töpelmann, 1936), pp. 162–174 esp. 173. However, none of those suggestions is convincing.

[134] Note the same motif is also reflected in Judg 11:30–31, 34–36, regarding Jephthah's vow.

[135] It is debatable whether Daniel 6 depends on Esther at this point.

5. According to the Esther story, the Persian authorities sent their edicts and orders "to every province in its own script and to every people *in its own language*" (Esth 1:22; see also 3:12; 8:9). But the royal administrative communication in the Achaemenid Persian Empire was in a *lingua franca*, so called Imperial Aramaic.[136] Thus, for instance, a copy of Cyrus' decree to the Jews (דכרונה, "record"; Ezra 6:1–2, see also Ezra 4:15) was written in Aramaic.[137] The wide usage of Aramaic is also reflected in the Elamite tablets that have been found in Persepolis, from the end of the reign of Darius I until the seventh year of Artaxerxes I.[138] Did the author of Esther not have a genuine knowledge of the inner workings of the Persian government, and as such he did not know about the usage of Imperial Aramaic as a royal administrative language? Since there are many signs of Persian setting for the book of Esther, and it reflects (at least partially) a real historical core, it is reasonable to assume, as Jonas C. Greenfield does, that these verses in Esther refer to the explanation and translation of the Aramaic documents into the local languages.[139]

9 Tolerance toward Others

Ancient and modern historians have praised Cyrus the Great for his tolerance and friendly attitude toward the minorities and occupied nations of the empire. Thus, for instance, roughly a hundred years after the death of Cyrus (530 BCE), Xenophon wrote that "he honoured his subjects and cared for them as if they were his own children; and they, on their part, reverenced Cyrus as a father" (*Cyropaedia* 8.8.1).[140] As already mentioned (§II, 1, A), Cyrus claims in his Cylinder that Marduk appointed him the ruler of all the universe and ordered him to reconstruct the shrines of the gods. In fact, he rebuilt some Babylonian temples and released them from taxation.[141] Cyrus' decree to the exiled Jews in Babylonia, which was issued in his "first year" as the king of Babylonia (538 BCE), should be considered in this context.[142]

[136] On the use of Aramaic in the Persian Empire, see F. Altheim and R. Stiehl, *Die aramäische Sprache unter den Achaimeniden* (Frankfurt am Main: Vittorio Klostermann, 1960); J. C. Greenfield, "Aramaic Language in the Persian Period," in H. Tadmor (ed.), *The History of the Jewish People: The Restoration – The Persian Period* (Jerusalem: Am Oved, 1983), pp. 224–228, 310–311 (Hebrew).

[137] See above, §II, 6.

[138] See G. G. Cameron, *The Persepolis Treasury Tablets* (Chicago: University of Chicago Press, 1948); R. T. Hallock, *Persepolis Fortification Tablets* (Chicago: University of Chicago Press, 1969).

[139] See Greenfield, "Aramaic Language in the Persian Period," p. 225; see also below, §II, 9.

[140] For the English translation, see Miller, *Xenophon Cyropaedia*, vol. 2, pp. 439–441.

[141] See Oppenheim, "Babylonian and Assyrian Historical Texts," pp. 315a–316b.

[142] On the two versions of the Cyrus Decree, see above, §II, 6.

Of course, this political strategy of Cyrus did not stem only from his humanistic character; it also well served his imperial agenda. Henry Kissinger writes that "the Persian ideal of monarchy elevated its sovereign to quasi-divine status as a magnanimous overlord of peoples – the 'King of Kings' dispensing justice and decreeing tolerance in exchange for peaceful political submission."[143] The wise policy of the founder of the Achaemenid dynasty toward other peoples was followed by his successors. In one of his inscriptions, Darius the Great states: "Much of this evil that had been committed, I turned into good. The countries that fought each other, whose peoples killed each other, I fixed ... so that their peoples did not kill each other, and I restored each to its place. And, faced with my decrees, they respected them, in such a way that the strong did not strike nor despoil the poor."[144]

By contrast, Xerxes reports in his Akkadian foundation tablet that there were "(some) which performed (religious) service (lit.: festival) to the 'evil (god)s.' (But) under the 'shadow' of Ahuramazda I destroyed (lit.: eradicated) these temples of the 'evil (god)s' and proclaimed (as follows): 'You must not perform (religious) service to the 'evil (god)s' (anymore)!' Wherever formerly (religious) service was performed to the 'evil (god)s,' I, myself, performed a (religious) service to Ahuramazda and the *arta* (cosmic order) reverently."[145] Who were those that worshiped the "evil (god)s"? It is hard to say exactly, and several possibilities have been suggested in the scholarship. Probably that country was "none other than Babylonia," which rebelled against Xerxes I,[146] and the latter displayed intolerance toward the cult of those who "disturbed the imperial order." Otherwise, however, Xerxes seems to have continued the tolerant policy of Cyrus and Darius toward the cultic practices of others.[147]

The Persian tolerance toward other nations is reflected in the Esther story regarding their languages: They explained and translated the official documents that were written in Aramaic into the local languages (Esth 1:22; 3:12; 8:9). The Persians thus showed tolerance and respect toward foreign languages and cultures. Xerxes proudly announced that he is "the king of (all) countries (which speak) all kind of languages."[148] By contrast,

---

[143] H. Kissinger, *World Order: Reflections on the Character of Nations and the Course of History* (London: Penguin, 2014), p. 149.
[144] See Briant, *From Cyrus to Alexander*, p. 166, and reference to the inscription therein.
[145] See Oppenheim, "Babylonian and Assyrian Historical Texts," p. 317a.
[146] See Briant, *From Cyrus to Alexander*, p. 543.
[147] Cf. Briant, *From Cyrus to Alexander*, p. 549.
[148] See Oppenheim, "Babylonian and Assyrian Historical Texts," p. 316b.

the Greeks generally considered someone who speaks a different language (βάρβαρος) also as uncivilized. They demanded that all non-Greek peoples should know their language (ἑλληνικά). Hence the Greek idiom: "whoever is not Greek is a barbarian" (πᾶς μὴ "Ελλην βάρβαρος).[149]

The Esther story tells that there were some foreigners in the Persian royal service: the king's vizier was Haman the Agagite; his wife, Queen Esther, was an orphan Jewish girl (Esth 2:7, 16–18), and one of the servants at the palace's gate was Mordecai the Jew (Esth 2:5, 21–23). Later on, Mordecai was promoted to be "next in rank to King Ahasuerus" (Esth 10:2–3; see also 8:2a, 15a). Thus, the book of Esther presents the Persian government as a tolerant one, which accepts minorities and gives them opportunity to integrate in the royal service. In the biblical literature there are also other stories about foreigners who serve in the Persian government: Nehemiah was the butler of King Artaxerxes I (Neh 1:1; 2:1–9), and according to the book of Daniel, the wise Jew Daniel served in a high position in the court of Darius (Dan 6:1, 2, 7, 10, 26, 29 [ET, 5:31; 6:1, 6, 9, 25, 28]; 9:1; 11:1).

The evil plan against the Jews was issued by a high official who was non-Persian in his origin, an eternal enemy of the Jews since ever, without the complete understanding of the king, perhaps because the latter was drunk.[150] Thus, the narrator of Esther depicts the Persian king as an idiot, but not as a nasty or mean person. Later, when the king recognized his mistake, he acknowledged the rights of the Jews to defend themselves from their enemies: "By these letters the king allowed the Jews who were in every city to assemble and defend their lives" (Esth 8:11, see also verse 8). Thus, the struggle between Haman and Esther/Mordecai was a struggle between two groups of foreigners, rather than between Persians and Jews.

All in all, Esther's story implies that Persian rule basically showed tolerance toward others. Again, there are several parallel examples for this point in the Persian royal inscriptions. Other biblical texts set in the Persian period reflect a similar perspective: Both in Ezra-Nehemiah and in Daniel, the opposition does not come directly from the Persian king – who is depicted as benevolent (e.g., Ezra 1:1–4; 5:13–6:12; 7:11–28; Neh 2:1–9; Dan 6:1–5, 15, 19–29 [ET, 5:31–6:4, 14, 20–28]; an exception

---

[149] This concept is found in one of Plato's dialogues, though not the exact quotation: "they separate the Hellenic race from all the rest as one, and to all the other races, which are countless in number and have no relation in blood or language to one another, they give the single name 'barbarian'; then, because of this single name, they think it is a single species." See Plato, *The Statesman* 262d; H. N. Fowler and W. R. M. Lamb, *Plato*, vol. VIII, *The Statesman, Philebus, Ion* (Loeb Classic Library 164; Cambridge, MA: Harvard University Press, 1925; reprinted 2006), p. 25 (Greek on p. 24).

[150] See above, §II, 2.

is in Ezra 4:17–24) – but from other subjects or factions of the kingdom, who are depicted as jealous or antagonistic (e.g., Ezra 4:1–24; 5:3–5; Neh 2:10; 3:33–4:17; 6:1–14; Dan 6:6–15, 26 [ET, 6:5–14, 25]).

10   Conspiracy and Murder in the Royal Court

One example of such opposition within the Persian court is found in the second chapter of Esther, which presents Mordecai as one who saved King Ahasuerus from the conspiratorial plan of the royal court officials, Bigthan and Teresh, to assassinate the king (Esth 2:21–23). The biblical story does not explain how and why these officials wished to kill the king, nor in what way Mordecai found it out. These gaps in the biblical text were filled in by various later Jewish writers. For example, according to Josephus (*Jewish Antiquities* 11.206–208),[151] "Barnabazos, the servant of one of these eunuchs, who was a Jew by race, discovered their plot and revealed it to Mordecai ..." (11:207). Josephus does not tell how the eunuchs planned to kill the king. Each of the Aramaic translations of Esther as well as in the Babylonian Talmud, *Megillah* 13b, 15b, filled in the gaps differently. For example, Targum Rishon to Esth 2:21–23 expounds the biblical text, saying that the two eunuchs were angry with the king who promoted Mordecai rather than them, and they were worried that one day they would be replaced by Mordecai, uncle of Queen Esther. The two consulted with each other and decided to poison the king, while speaking in their native language – Tarsusian (= Tarsean, based on the sounds of the name Teresh). They assumed that Mordecai could not understand this language, but in fact he did.[152] Nonetheless, if we ignore the legendary character of these accounts, the assumption of rivals, intrigues, poisoning and killing conspiracies in the Persian royal court seems to be not far from reality. As already mentioned above (Chapter 2, §V, 3, B), probably Mordecai served as a kind of security police at the royal court, a position known as "eyes of the king" or "ears of the king" or "listening-watch," and somehow he found out the conspiracy against Ahasuerus. As a matter of fact, such a conspiracy eventually succeeded: Ctesias reports in his *Persica* that in 465 BCE, Xerxes I, as well as his elder son, crown prince Darius, were murdered by Artabanus (or Artapanus = Hystaspes), Xerxes' second

---

[151] Marcus, *Josephus with an English Translation*, vol. 6, pp. 412–415.
[152] See Grossfeld, *The Two Targums of Esther*, pp. 48–50, and cf. Targum Sheni (ibid., pp. 139–140), which is surprisingly much shorter than Targum Rishon. Targum Sheni states that the matter was revealed to Mordecai through the Holy Spirit. See also the Greek Addition to Esther (A 12:1–2).

son and chief of the king's bodyguard, and the eunuch Spamitres, who held great influence at the royal court.[153]

Indeed, conspiracies and killing – particularly poisoning – of rulers in the Persian court was not rare. So, King Artaxerxes III (Ochus; 358–338 BCE), who murdered his own entire royal family in order to secure his throne, was poisoned by his vizier Bagoas. As Diodorus Siculus describes it, "a eunuch in physical fact but a militant rogue in disposition, [Bagoas] killed him [= Artaxerxes III] by poison administered by a certain physician" (*Bibliotheca Historica* 17.5.3–6.3).[154] However, here it is worth mentioning that according to a Babylonian solar eclipse tablet (British Museum 71537), Artaxerxes III died because of natural causes: "Month VI (= Month Ululu), Umakuš (= Ochus = Artaxerxes III) died. Aršu (= Arses = Artaxerxes IV), his son, sat on the throne."[155] Nevertheless, Diodorus recounts further that two years later, the same destiny found the son and successor of Artaxerxes III, Arses, who is known as Artaxerxes IV. The latter, who was placed on his father's throne by Bagoas, was also poisoned by him in the summer of 336 BCE. In the same year, Bagoas himself was forced to drink the cup of poison that he prepared for the new king of Persia, Darius III (Condomannus; 336–330 BCE), the opponent of Alexander the Great.[156] So, when Philip of Macedonia and later his son and successor, Alexander, challenged the very existence of the Persian Empire, the royal court in Persia was already sinking in bloodbath and serial murders. It is worth mentioning that according to Diodorus Siculus, Plutarch, Arrian, and Justin, Alexander the Great was also a victim of a poisoning conspiracy.[157]

These extrabiblical sources demonstrate that conspiracies were not rare in the Persian (and other) courts in different times, and a range of kings were victims of assassination by poison. They undeniably support

---

[153] See Llewellyn-Jones and Robson, *Ctesias' History of Persia*, p. 185, §33. However, see also the legend regarding "Xerxes at the tomb of Belus and the assassination of Xerxes" by his son (ibid., pp. 185–186), and the discussion of the whole matter by Briant, *From Cyrus to Alexander*, pp. 565–567. In the end, Artaxerxes I succeeded his father Xerxes I, as reported by Ctesias (ibid.).

[154] Welles, *Diodorus of Sicily with an English Translation*, vol. 8, pp. 130–133.

[155] See H. Hunger (ed.), *Astronomical Diaries and Related Texts from Babylonia: Volume V, Lunar and Planetary Texts* (Vienna: Verlag der Österreichischen Akademie der Wissenschaften, 2001), p. 45 (Text no. 11, III, rev., lines 9–10); see also A. Kuhrt, *The Persian Empire: A Corpus of Sources from the Achaemenid Period* (London: Routledge, 2007), p. 423.

[156] On Darius III, see P. Briant, *Darius in the Shadow of Alexander* (translated by J. M. Todd; Cambridge, MA: Harvard University Press, 2015).

[157] Recently, this theory was confirmed as a reasonable possibility by scholars from the National Poisons Centre at the University of Otago (Dunedin, New Zealand); see L. J. Schep, R. J. Slaughter, J. A. Vale, and P. Wheatley, "Was the Death of Alexander the Great Due to Poisoning? Was it *Veratrum album*?" *Clinical Toxicology* 52 (2014), pp. 72–77.

the plausibility of the basic description of the failed assassination story of Ahasuerus in the book of Esther.

11   Annihilation of the Imperial Jews

The central theme of the book – the plan to annihilate the Jews of the Persian Empire – has often been denied as historically implausible, particularly the claim that the event was planned a year in advance.[158] Thus, for instance, recently Harald Martin Wahl asserted:

> The presentation of the planned pogrom and also the retribution of the Jews, lack any historical reality: Persecution and destruction of all Jewish life in an empire that reached from the furthest corner of the Indus [river] to as far away as Ethiopia and Asia Minor is consistent with poetic imagination, but not administrative and certainly not executive reality (3:9–15).[159]

However, even if *the extent* and *details* of the event described in the book of Esther are questionable, such an intended persecution of the Jews would not be unparalleled. The same might have been said later on about the clear-cut declarations of Adolf Hitler, just a few generations ago, to annihilate all the Jews in the world, in particular those on the European continent. They also might sound unbelievably imaginary: How could such a thing happen in a country such as Germany, "the land of poets and thinkers" (*Das Land der Dichter und Denker*)? However, unfortunately, Nazi Germany, with the cooperation of some other European nations, systematically eliminated one-third of the Jews on the globe. Admittedly, the plan to kill the Jews everywhere in the Persian Empire in a single day sounds imaginative, and it should be counted as a part of Haman's sick and megalomaniacal overstatement. However, the very desire – if not the plan – to annihilate as many Jews as possible across the Empire, should not be considered unrealistic, as the tragic history of the Jewish people teaches. The comparison of a case from ancient Persia with the one in modern Germany – in its big and bold lines – should not be considered anachronistic, but rather as a realistic perspective in light of the broader trends of Jewish history. In that sense, the "Haman Decree," which was the first

[158] So, for example, Levenson, *Esther: A Commentary*, pp. 24–25; Meinhold, *Das Buch Esther*, pp. 18–19.

[159] Wahl, *Das Buch Esther*, p. 24: "Das geplante Pogrom und auch die Vergeltung der Juden entbehren in ihrer Darstellung jeder historischen Wirklichkeit: Eine bis in den letzten Winkel des vom Indus bis nach Äthiopien und Kleinasien ausgedehnten Reiches durchgeführte Verfolgung und Vernichtung alles jüdischen Lebens entspricht dichterischer Phantasie, aber nicht administrativer und schon gar nicht exekutiver Realität (3,9–15)."

inclusive call for genocide, can legitimately be considered as the first "Final Solution" (*Endlösung*) of the Jews in world history.

Moreover, although Haman's decree would be the worst and the most severe persecution of the Jews in the Persian period, *hostilities* – though for different reasons than what we find in the Esther story – toward the Jewish minority in different corners of the Persian Empire are attested in biblical and extrabiblical sources. There were at least three additional such cases. Two cases are recorded in the biblical-historical writings of Ezra-Nehemiah regarding the Jewish community of *Yehud Medinta* (Province of Judah under Persian rule) in the postexilic era. They reflect a religious, social, and political tension particularly between Judah and Samaria. The first one tells that Judah's troublesome neighbors, or as the biblical writer put it: "the adversaries of Judah and Benjamin" (צרי יהודה ובנימין; Ezra 4:1–6:18), did not welcome the Jewish restoration from the Babylonian Exile. They attempted – by all means – to stop the rebuilding of the community and its spiritual center in Jerusalem, the Temple (ca. 538–515 BCE). It is worth noting that "the adversaries" stress to the Persian king that if Jerusalem is rebuilt, the Jews will not keep the imperial law: they will rebel and not pay taxes to the king's treasury: "Now may it be known to the king that, if this city is rebuilt and the walls finished, *they will not pay tribute, custom, or toll,* and the royal revenue will be reduced" (Ezra 4:13). This is similar – at least partially – to Haman's accusation that the Jews "do not keep the king's laws" due to their different religious laws (Esth 3:8).[160]

Later on, in the time of Nehemiah's government in Yehud, the surrounding enemies of Judah again did all that they could – including planning a military attack – in order to prevent the erection of the wall of Jerusalem (Neh 2:10, 19; 3:33–35 [ET, 4:1–3]; 4:1–17 [ET, 4:7–23]; 6:1–16). Indeed, these conflicts seem more like religious and political disputes than pogroms, but still they demonstrate that at least the Jews in Judah had bitter enemies who attempted by force to prevent their activities in their own land.

A third incident is documented in the Aramaic papyri from Elephantine (*Yeb*) – a small island in the Nile in southern Egypt, at the border of Nubia (or Ethiopia). The papyri are from the 14th year of Darius II, that is, 407

---

[160] The assumption of Ran Zadok ("The Historical Background of Megillat Esther," *Beit Mikra* 30 [issue no. 100; 1985], pp. 186–189 [Hebrew]) that the conflict between Haman and Mordecai reflects the conflict that is described in Ezra between Judahites and Samaritans, is far beyond what these sources can bear: the two stories are referring to different Persian kings who reigned in different periods, describing different groups of people in different places (Elam, Susa *versus* Judah/Samaria), and address different issues. The stories are also written in different languages and different literary genres.

BCE. They recount that native Egyptians, under the command of a man named Widranag (or Vidranga), the regional leader, attacked the Judean/ Jewish mercenary community in Elephantine, killed several of them, and destroyed their "temple of Yahu" (410 BCE).[161] Was this attack carried out against the community because of their unique Yahwistic religion and Judean nationality, or because they were mercenaries of the hated, foreign, Persian Empire? It seems that the tensions between the Judeans and Egyptians in Elephantine may have included a religious component, since it led to the destruction of their temple, but it also had a political component, in that the Judeans supported the Persians and fought on their side against the Egyptian rebellion in 425 BCE. The Egyptians waited until the Persian Satrap was out of the country to attack.[162] This has been described as "an anti-Jewish pogrom, perhaps the very first," which has been documented in the history of the Jewish Diaspora.[163] To be sure, this was a local incident in a distant border of the empire, certainly not sponsored by the Persian Emperor or one of his high officials,[164] and it is not at all the same as an empire-wide call for extermination of all Jews everywhere, which, according to Esther, the Persian Emperor would have accepted. Despite these restrictions, the story of Yeb testifies that a violent attack against the Judeans/Jews was not implausible in the Persian Empire, and at least in

---

[161] See A. Cowley, *Aramaic Papyri of the Fifth Century B.C.* (Oxford: Clarendon Press, 1923), nos. 27:30–33; 30:18–19, 30 // 31:17–18, 29; pp. 112, 120 (English translation, pp. 114, 121); H. L. Ginsberg, "Elephantine Papyri," in Pritchard, *ANET*, p. 492. See also P. Schäfer, *Judeophobia: Attitudes toward the Jews in the Ancient World* (Cambridge, MA: Harvard University Press, 1997), pp. 121–135; I. Kottsieper, "Die Religionspolitik der Achämeniden und die Juden von Elephantine," in R. G. Kratz (ed.), *Religion und Religionskontakte in Zeitalter der Achämeniden* (Veröffentlichungen der Wissenschaftlichen Gesellschaft für Theologie 22; Gütersloh: Gütersloher Verlagshaus Gerd Mohn, 2002), pp. 150–178; T. Bolin, "The Temple of יהו at Elephantine and Persian Religious Policy," in D. V. Edelman (ed.), *The Triumph of Elohim: From Yahwisms to Judaisms* (Contributions to Biblical Exegesis and Theology 13; Kampen: Kok Pharos, 1995), pp. 127–144 esp. 130, who summarizes the primary literature regarding Widranag's identity.

[162] Cf. Schäfer, *Judeophobia*, pp. 133–135.

[163] See A. Rofé, *Introduction to the Literature of the Hebrew Bible* (translated by H. N. Bock and J. H. Seeligmann; Jerusalem Biblical Studies 9; Jerusalem: Simor, 2009), p. 148.

[164] Whether Widranag and his supporters were punished by the Persian government is unknown. For contrasting views on this issue, cf. Schäfer, *Judeophobia*, p. 123; J. M. Lindenberger, "What Ever Happened to Vidranga? A Jewish Liturgy of Cursing from Elephantine," in P. M. Michèle Daviau (ed.), *The World of the Aramaeans III: Studies in Language and Literature in Honour of Paul-Eugène Dion* (Journal for the Study of the Old Testament Supplement Series 326; Sheffield: Sheffield Academic, 2001), pp. 134–157, with bibliography. In any case, the Jews were permitted to rebuild their temple three years later, as reflected in the letter they sent to the governor of Yehud asking for assistance to rebuild it (cf. Cowley, *Aramaic Papyri of the Fifth Century B.C.*, pp. 108–122, esp. 112–113, 120–121 = no. 30 [A4.7] lines 16–17 // no. 31 [A4.8] lines 15–16; for a recent edition, cf. B. Porten, *The Elephantine Papyri in English: Three Millennia of Cross-Cultural Continuity and Change* [2nd ed.; Studies in Near Eastern Archaeology and Civilization; Atlanta: Society of Biblical Literature, 2011], pp. 139–147 [B19–B20]).

some local districts Jews had admitted hostilities and bitter conflicts (Esth 9:2–3). In any case, these parallels support the possibility that the central theme of the Esther story has a historical kernel.[165]

Indeed, as of now there is no parallel from the Persian period for such an empire-wide persecution of the Jews as the book of Esther presents. However, far later, similar events happened to Jews by different peoples, in different times and places. The closest ancient parallel to the story to have survived (which is still more local than Haman's decree) is Antiochus IV's persecution in Judea in 166 BCE, although it started as religious and cultural persecution, rather than physical. Moreover, there are many examples from medieval times in European Jewish history. For instance: following brutal persecutions of the Jews in England, in 1290, Edward I expelled all of them from the country. In 1394, Charles IV expelled the entire Jewish population of France. About a century later, in 1492, Ferdinand II and Isabella ordered all Jews in Spain to convert to Christianity or face expulsion from the kingdom. Five years later, in 1497, the same destiny befell the Jews in Portugal. All these countries forbade Jewish existence there for hundreds of years. To cite Bernhard W. Anderson: "Quite apart from the problem of the historicity of the book of Esther or any part of it, the real issue of the book, viz., the tension between Jew and gentile, is clearly 'historical' and is as old as the phenomenon of Judaism itself."[166] Thus, numerous similar and other horrible experiences have been faced by many Jewish communities, from which they were somehow saved, and which they sometimes even celebrated as their own "Purims."[167]

III Conclusion: Esther as Novelistic History

Esther is the only biblical book that is set completely against the geographical, political, and cultural background of the Achaemenid Persian Empire and its royal palace in Susa. In that context, comparison with the biblical and surviving extrabiblical sources – mainly Greek and Persian – as well

---

[165] In Yecheskel Kaufmann's opinion, the minimum that can be said is that at some point the Jews in the Persian Empire were in great danger of annihilation, which was canceled due to the efforts of the Jewish officials in the king's court. See Y. Kaufmann, *History of the Religion of Israel: From Its Beginnings to the Babylonian Exile* (Jerusalem and Tel Aviv: Bialik Institute and Dvir, 1972), vol. 8, p. 440 (Hebrew).

[166] See Anderson, "The Place of the Book of Esther in the Christian Bible," p. 35; and compare G. I. Emmerson, "Esther," in R. J. Coggins and J. L. Houlden (eds.), *A Dictionary of Biblical Interpretation* (London: SCM Press, 1990), pp. 204–205 esp. 205: "the story has a historical basis ...."

[167] See the examples listed in Chapter 9, §II.

as archaeological finds, suggests that the book of Esther reflects substantial reliable historical data about the Achaemenid Empire, including the size and administration of the empire, the identification of the king, his harem, the wealth of the city and palace in Susa; the likelihood that the Persian king spent the spring season there; information regarding the imperial-royal annals and archives; the imperial postal system; the Persian policy of tolerance toward minorities; the danger of conspiracy and murder in the royal court, and the threat of anti-Jewish hostility among other minority groups within the empire.

Admittedly, the story also contains many implausible elements such as overstatements, hyperbolic numbers, satirical and humoristic descriptions, as well as fixed literary structures, which all in all give it a legendary character. However, the author's detailed knowledge of the historical context supports that there are some *plausible kernels of historical reality* hiding behind the story: King Ahasuerus existed in reality, and so may well have Mordecai and also some other figures. The core story concerning the attempted annihilation of the Jews of the Persian Empire should not be dismissed. After all, there are examples of Jewish communities that were attacked by their enemies in the Persian Empire. Also, accusations similar to those of Haman were and are expressed by many other Jew-haters in different times and places (see the next chapter), and the "final solution," that stated by Haman, is also not something imaginary, as the unfortunate Jewish history teaches. Thus, the book of Esther demands to be read in a way that allows a rational balance between the overly naive and overly skeptical judgments of its historicity. Against such extreme approaches taken by some scholars, the book should be considered neither a completely historical description of events as they really happened, nor an imaginative story that was completely invented by author's fantasy. To cite Moore: "neither pure fact nor pure fiction."[168] Indeed, some scholars have recognized this combination of historical and nonhistorical elements and defined the book as a "historical novel(la)." This term suggests that the book tells basically a fictional story set against a more or less authentic historical background. In my judgment, the story of Esther might be better described as a novelistic history, that is, a fictionalized story established in a real historical setting, and also based on some plausible kernel of historical event.[169] In other words, not every detail in Esther should be accepted

---

[168] See Moore, *Esther*, pp. xxxiv–liii esp. lii.
[169] For the distinction between "historical novel" and "novelistic history," see Clines, *Ezra, Nehemiah, Esther*, pp. 256–257.

as a record of historical events, since the book mixes reality with imagination. In the same breath, the story is also imbued with real historical environment, and the core of the plot is not inherently impossible. The author wishes to deliver an important message to his potential audience about the potential annihilation of the Jews, while recounting his story against the background of the Persian Achaemenid political, cultural, linguistic, social, and administrative situation. At the same time, he desired to attract as much as possible his audience through a humoristic, satirical, sarcastic, hyperbolic, fluent and attractive style, even if it meant paying less attention to the exactness and historical accuracy of every detail of his story. Obviously, the author of Esther did not write as Leopold von Ranke who wished only to present history "as it actually happened" (*wie es eigentlich gewesen [ist]*). The story is so devastating, that the author tries to present it in a humorous way to strikes a balance between the horrific content and the amusing style and literary features.

IV   Appendix: Persia and Persians in the Hebrew Bible

Persia is directly described in only a relatively small number of biblical writings, and not at all in any pre-exilic texts of the Hebrew Bible. Most likely this is due to the enormous geographical distance that separates Eretz-Israel and Persia. In addition, there are colossal differences in language (Semitic *versus* Indo-Iranic), as well as cultural and religious norms (Yahwism *versus* Zoroastrianism) between Israelites and Persians. No wonder, therefore, that in the pre-exilic era the connection between the two peoples and lands was very limited – if any existed at all.

In the collections of Oracles against Nations in the Prophets, there are two oracles against Elam (Jer 49:34–39 and Ezek 32:24–25). However, there is no prophecy against Persia. Though מָדַי ("Madai," "Media" or "the Medes" in various translations) is occasionally mentioned more broadly,[170] references to "Persia" seem confined to exilic or postexilic writings. The first time Persia is mentioned is in the book of Ezekiel (27:10; 38:5), after the Jews were forced in 597 and 587/6 BCE into exile in Mesopotamia, the western neighbor of Persia.[171] The situation was completely changed in 539

---

[170] See Gen 10:2; Isa 13:17; 21:2; Jer 25:25; 51:11, 28; 2 Kgs 17:6; 18:1, as well as in postexilic sources such as 1 Chr 1:5; Dan 8:20; 9:1; 11:1, and of course in Esther, though only at the beginning and the end of the book, namely Esth 1:3, 14, 18, 19; 10:2.

[171] Note, the "Table of Nations" mentions "Madai" (Gen 10:2), but not "Persia." Possibly, either the writer simply did not yet know Persia, or he knew it but considered it as a part of "Madai," which ruled Persia in the pre-Cyrus II era. Likewise, several biblical texts mention Elam, which was later annexed into the Persian Empire, but not Persia itself (Gen 10:22; 14:1, 9; Isa 11:11–12; 21:2; Jer

BCE, when King Cyrus II (the Great) of Persia entered Babylon without battle, and the entire Babylonian-Chaldean Empire came under his control. Suddenly the Jews found themselves under the rule of Persia. For the next two centuries, their destiny was in the hands of the Persian Achaemenid monarchs (539–330 BCE). Accordingly, Persia and the Persians are very visible in the postexilic biblical prophetic literature (for example, Deutero-Isaiah, Haggai, Zachariah and Malachi, although the word "Persia" itself does not appear). They are most prominent in late biblical historical books – Ezra, Nehemiah, and Chronicles – and in the court stories of Esther, and Daniel and his friends, where they appear explicitly 32 times.[172]

There are also anachronisms that point to the Persian period origins or editing of other texts (for instance in 1 Chr 29:7, where the use of the Persian coin *daric* is attributed to King David's times), and Persian words and names are used, including those of Achaemenid kings, such as Cyrus II (550–530 BCE), Darius I (the Great, 522–486 BCE), Ahasuerus/Xerxes (486/5–465 BCE), and Artaxerxes I (Longimanus; biblical Artachshasta; 465–425/4 BCE). Certainly, the most well-known Persian kings among the Jews, and the ones who played an essential role in Jewish history, are Cyrus II (the Great) and Ahasuerus. The latter discussed above (§II, 2). The former is mentioned no less than 23 times in the Hebrew Bible.[173] Most likely, Cyrus is the only foreign king who is called by the Israelite God "my

---

25:25; Jer 49:34–39; Ezek 32:24–25 [some sources mention Elam together with Madai]). Moreover, the prophecy in Isa 11:11–12 regarding the messianic era recounts that the Lord will assemble the outcasts of Israel and Judah "from *Assyria*, and from *Egypt*, and from *Pathros* [= Upper Egypt], and from *Kush* [= Nubia], and from *Elam*, and from *Shinar* [= Babylonia], and from *Hamath* [representing all of Syria], and from *the islands of the sea* [that is, the remote Greek islands]. And he shall set up a banner for the nations, and shall assemble the outcasts of Israel, and gather together the dispersed of Judah *from the four corners of the earth*." Though "Elam" is mentioned here among the lands "from the four corners of the earth," neither Madai nor Persia are.

[172] References to Persia or Persians appear thirteen times in Ezra (1:1 [twice], 2, 8; 3:7; 4:3, 5 [twice], 7, 24; 6:14; 7:1; 9:9), four times in Chronicles (2 Chr 36:20, 22 [twice], 23); five times in Esther (1:3, 14, 18, 19; 10:2); ten times in Daniel (5:28; 6:9, 13, 16; 8:20; 10:1, 13 [twice], 20; 11:2), plus the two in Ezek 27:10; 38:5 (though Nehemiah also takes place in the Persian Empire, and partially in Susa itself, the terms "Persia" and "Persians" never appear). Strikingly, the 34 references to Persia in the Hebrew Bible are far less than for any other major foreign lands and nations in the Bible. Compare, for example, Egypt and Egyptians (680 times); Babylonia (287 times); Assyria (150 times); Aram (133 times); or even the minor lands and nations such as Moab/Moabites (200 times); Ammon/ Ammonites (122 times); and Edom/ domites (112 times). For the biblical references for the nations, see A. Even-Shoshan, *A New Concordance of the Bible* (3rd ed.; Jerusalem: Kiryat Sefer, 1988), pp. (respectively) 962, 700–703, 147–148, 125, 110–111, 628–629, 896–897, 12–13.

[173] Fifteen times in Ezra (1:1 [twice], 2, 7, 8; 3:7; 4:3, 5; 5:13 [twice], 14, 17; 6:3 [twice], 14); three times in 2 Chronicles (36:22–23); two times in Isaiah (44:28; 45:1); three times in Daniel (1:21; 6:29 [ET, 6:28]; 10:1).

shepherd" (כורש רעי; Isa 44:28) and "his Messiah [i.e., God's anointed]" (למשיחו לכורש; "to his Messiah, to Cyrus"; Isa 45:1–7, 13 esp. 45:1).[174] Indeed, in contrast to the brutal Assyrian and Babylonian kings, who destroyed the kingdoms of Israel and Judah and exiled their inhabitants, Cyrus turned a new page in Jewish history with his declaration of 538 BCE, the so-called "Cyrus Decree" (Ezra 1:1–3 // 2 Chr 36:22–23), and let the Jews to return to their homeland.[175]

The only other foreign king who is called "my servant" is Nebuchadnezzar, in MT Jer 27:6. However, it is hard to imagine that the one who destroyed Jerusalem and its Temple, and exiled Judah, was so honored in the original form of the text. Indeed, LXX-A and B (where the verse appears as Jer 34:6), as well as the Ethiopian translation, preserve here: לְעָבְדוֹ, and in one Hebrew manuscript the word does not appear at all. Precisely due to that theological difficulty, Rudolph thinks the LXX has deliberately modified the phrase, which he considers original.[176] However, I accept Janzen and McKane's suggestion that the MT could be secondary, and consider עבדו as a corruption of לְעָבְדוֹ due to haplography with the preceding ל and the following ו (thus, originally the text would have read ... מלך־בבל לעבדו וגם ...).[177]

---

[174] There are other texts in Second Isaiah that explicitly mention Cyrus' name; and some others probably implicitly refer to him; see Isa 41:1–5, 25–26; 42:1–9; 45:9–13; 46:8–11; 48:12–16a.

[175] See also above, §II, 9.

[176] See Rudolph, *Jeremia*, p. 146.

[177] See J. G. Janzen, *Studies in the Text of Jeremiah* (Harvard Semitic Monographs 6; Cambridge, MA: Harvard University Press, 1973), pp. 54–55 (he also allows the possibility that the LXX resulted from dittography); McKane, *Jeremiah*, vol. 2, pp. 687–689.

CHAPTER 6

Ancient Parallels to Haman's Accusations

I Haman and His Accusations

In the Babylonian Talmud, *Makkot* 24a, Rab (early third century CE) expresses his fear that the prediction, "And you shall perish among the nations, and the land of your enemies shall eat you up" (Lev 26:38) might yet be fulfilled.[1] Indeed, as we have seen in earlier chapters, the story of Esther affirms that it almost happened in the Persian Empire. Haman, "the enemy of (all) the Jews" (Esth 3:10; 8:1; 9:24), was prepared to eliminate an entire Jewish people because of his conflict with one Jew – Mordecai. According to Esth 5:11–13, Haman considered his great wealth, honor, many sons, and his top political position in the royal court as worthless: "all this avails me *nothing* (איננו שוה לי)" he says, "so long as I see Mordecai, the Jew, sitting at the king's gate" (5:13).[2] Killing *all* the Jews of the Persian Empire was the only way for Haman to boost his huge ego. He simply disliked the unlike: he disliked all the Jews whose laws are unlike all others, including himself. He could not accept or live with difference and diversity of the Jewish religion and culture. Thus, to obtain the permission of the king to execute his plan, Haman was ready to pay him an enormous amount of money, "ten thousand talents of silver" (Esth 3:9) – an amount equivalent to nearly two thirds of the annual income of the Persian Empire (*Historia* 3.95–96).[3] In his argument Haman gives voice to what will become a classical defamation against the Jews: "There is a certain people," says Haman, who "scattered and dispersed among the people in all the provinces of your kingdom; *and their laws are different from those of all other people; neither do they keep the king's laws.*

---

[1] On the fear under review, see Chapter 4, §I.
[2] It is worth noting that this information appears within the literary form of *inclusio*, in which the opening and closing words are repeated in chiastic order; see, in detail, Chapter 3, §VII, 2.
[3] On this amount, see Chapter 5, §II, 2, no. 2. It is probably the payment offered to the king as substitute for loss of taxes of the dead Jews, or simply as a bribe in order to encourage the king to accept his wicked proposal and issue a decree to destruct the Jews.

Therefore, it is not appropriate for the king to tolerate them. If it pleases the king, let a decree be issued for their destruction ..." (Esth 3:8–9).

The first part of Haman's charge is true and reflects historical reality, since the Jews were scattered all over the known world. However, the last part of his claim, that by keeping their own particular religious laws, tradition and cultural identity, the Jews become disloyal, separatists who ignore the collective and social laws, is false (except that a single Jew – Mordecai – who refused to keep king's order to bow down to Haman; Esth 3:2–4).[4] Nonetheless, the conclusion of Haman, that the Jews' existence should therefore not be tolerated but rather exterminated, is extremely evil, unjustified and should be totally rejected. In fact, how and why the Jewish keeping of religious laws and rituals (such as eating kosher, blowing shofar in Rosh Hashanah, feasting in Atonement, keeping Sabbath, practicing circumcision, and so on) contradict civil laws of the king? Should keeping of the Jewish laws be considered a "dual loyalty,"[5] and as a source of causing civil and social problems?

Yet are such accusations against the Jews unrealistic, and merely in the imagination of the author of Esther? Comparison with a broader range of ancient literature shows that similar charges were regularly laid against the Jews in other biblical and nonbiblical literature, from various times. Jews repeatedly have been accused by their contemporary "Hamans" that they found 'a nation within a nation' and conspire against the non-Jews.

There were many Greco-Roman writers who expressed positive views of the Jews. They stated, for example, that "Moses is depicted by these authors as a wise lawgiver and his followers as a people of philosophers, who have one of the most exalted forms of spiritual worship. Some authors say the Jews set an example that should be followed by other nations."[6] However, a wide range of authors from that period and onward reflect an opposite perspective, repeating accusations very much like those attributed to Haman in the book of Esther – that the Jews are different from and hostile to all other people. Some even called for a comparable "solution" to this difference: the

---

[4] On Mordecai's refusal to bow down to Haman, see Chapter 2, §V, 3, C. Esther appeared in front of the king "not according to the law" (אשר לא כדת; Esth 4:16) because of the emergency situation. However, in general, the Jews keep the laws of their state. In fact, prophet Jeremiah calls the exiled Judeans in Babylon to "seek the peace of the city where I have caused you to be carried away captives, and pray to the Lord for it; for in its peace shall you have peace" (Jer 29:7). Compare Anderson, "The Place of the Book of Esther in the Christian Bible," p. 35.

[5] So, Greenstein, "A Jewish Reading of Esther," p. 237. In modern times scholars considered the Jews who are keeping their laws as "state in state," or they "serve two masters" (though without explicitly referring to the book of Esther); see Chapter 12, §II.

[6] See P. W. van der Horst, *Philo's Flaccus: The First Pogrom* (Philo of Alexandria Commentary Series 2; Leiden and Boston: Brill, 2003), p. 32, with bibliography.

elimination or expulsion of all the Jews from society.[7] To cite David Clines, "The simple fact is that Haman's death has solved nothing, relived nothing. He himself may be dead, but his evil is very much alive. And it lives on under the banner of unalterable Persia law."[8] Indeed, Clines stated this regarding the particular scene in the Megillah, namely Esth 7:9–8:6, but certainly it could be said as well on the tragic history of the Jewish people in general.

II   The Opponents of Daniel

1   Daniel in the Lions' Den

Similar to the setting of the Esther story, the Joseph story (roughly Genesis 37–50), the tale of the three boys in the Septuagint's 1 Esdras 3–4 (= 3 Esdras in the Vulgate and other Latin translations), Aḥiqar, and the story of Daniel and his friends (Daniel 1–6) also take place in the court of a foreign king (so-called *Diasporanovelle*).[9]

Daniel 6:2–25 recounts that King Darius of Persia decided to appoint Daniel over all his realm. However, the ministers and satraps became jealous, and attempted to harm Daniel. Because "they could find no cause nor blame, and no sin or fault in him" (6:4), they decided to find something against him "concerning the law of his God" (6:5). Thus, they went to the king and stated that they had all consulted each other and agreed to establish a fixed royal decree, that whoever would address a petition to any god or man during thirty days, except to the king himself, would be cast into a lions' den. Darius agreed and signed the ordinance. However, even when Daniel learned that this decree had been signed, he continued his habit of praying and giving thanks to the God of Israel three times a day, as he had

---

[7] For an overview of Greco-Roman writers' hostility toward Jews, see M. Stern, *Greek and Latin Authors on Jews and Judaism* (Jerusalem: Israel Academy of Sciences and Humanities, 1974–1984), vols. 1–3; Schäfer, *Judeophobia*; Z. Yavetz, *Judenfeindschaft in der Antike* (Munich: Verlag C. H. Beck, 1997); P. W. van der Horst, "The Myth of Jewish Cannibalism: A Chapter in the History of Antisemitism," *Israel Academy of Sciences and Humanities Proceedings* (Jerusalem: Israel Academy of Sciences and Humanities, 2008), vol. VIII (no. 3), pp. 43–56; Bar-Kochva, *The Image of the Jews in Greek Literature: The Hellenistic Period* (Hellenistic Culture and Society 51; Berkeley: University of California Press, 2010). However, these scholars do not compare any Greco-Roman writer with Haman.

[8] Clines, *The Esther Scroll*, p. 18.

[9] For the similarity between the Esther and Joseph stories, see the examples and the bibliographical references in Chapter 3, §IV. For the similarity between Esther and Daniel, see, for example, Rosenthal, "Die Josephsgeschichte, mit den Büchern Ester und Daniel verglichen," pp. 278–284; W. L. Humphreys, "A Life-Style for Diaspora: A Study of the Tales of Esther and Daniel," *JBL* 92 (1973), pp. 211–223; Berg, *The Book of Esther: Motifs, Themes and Structure*, pp. 143–145; Wills, *The Jew in the Court of the Foreign King*.

done previously. When this disobedience was discovered and witnessed by Daniel's opponents, he was thrown into the lions' den. Nevertheless, Daniel was miraculously rescued from the lions, which clearly demonstrated his innocence, as well as the truth and power of his faith.

Daniel kept his religious tradition despite the king's decree and the severe punishment for any violator. As such, the story is parallel to that of the miraculous rescue of Daniel's three friends, Hananiah, Mishael, and Azariah (also called Shadrach, Meshach, and Abednego; Daniel 3), who were thrown into a furnace for refusing to bow down to Nebuchadnezzar's golden statue, but were protected from the flames by God.[10] Both stories describe acts of *Kiddush Hashem* (sanctifying God's name, martyrdom); that is, the heroes were ready to die rather than deny their ancestors' faith and laws.[11]

2   *Is Daniel's Story Shaped According to Esther's Story?*

The resemblances between the Daniel and Esther stories are particularly notable: Both stories took place in the courts of Persian kings; in both stories the central heroes – Mordecai and Daniel – served as courtiers in the gate of foreign kings (Esth 2:21; 6:10, 12; Dan 1:1–21; 6:3); in both stories the central hero refused to fulfill a royal decree because it stands in contrast to the Jewish law. Moreover, presumably, Mordecai's refusal to bow down to Haman was motivated by his faith, and as such is also a martyr story,[12] as that of Daniel in the lions' den (and of his three friends in the furnace). For our purposes, it is particularly important to recognize the similarity between the accusation of Haman, that by keeping their religious laws and customs the Jews violate the king's laws, and the accusation of Darius' officials that Daniel's praying to his God violates the king's decree, which was made specifically to put him in a difficult situation of conflict between divine law and royal law. Further, in both stories – Esther and Daniel – the opponents request that the Jews should be killed for their (supposed) violations of the collective royal laws. The difference between the two cases is that in the case of Daniel the accusation that the law was not being upheld was explicitly directed against him personally (and so also in the case of his three friends), not at any other Jews who continued to worship their God,

[10] On the similarities and differences between these and other stories, see, for example, L. F. Hartman and A. A. Di Lella, *The Book of Daniel: A New Translation with Notes and Commentary* (Anchor Bible 23; Garden City, NY: Doubleday, 1978), pp. 154–164, 196–197. See also the references listed above in note 9.

[11] For more on this issue in the Second Temple and rabbinic literature, see Kalimi, "'Go, I Beg You, Take Your Beloved Son and Slay Him!'," pp. 14–15.

[12] See Chapter 2, §V, 3, B.

whereas in Esther the accusation was not just directed at Mordecai, who did not keep the order of the king to bow down to Haman, but against the entire Jewish people in the Persian Empire.

The story of Daniel was written after the composition of the core story of Esther: The latter was composed sometime in the Persian Achaemenid period, probably sometime between ca. 475 to 425 BCE.[13] Yet, although there is a unity of topics in the book of Daniel, it is built of several literary layers, and biblical scholars disagree on the date of the current form of it. However, Daniel 4–6 was composed probably in the second century BCE, perhaps around the Maccabean era.[14] If so, is the story of Esther used as a literary model for this story of Daniel? Let us keep in mind that the story of Esther was known in Eretz-Israel of the Maccabean time (2 Macc 15:36).[15]

III   The Counselors of Antiochus VII Sidetes/Euergetes

Yet it is not just in Jewish sources – Esther and Daniel – that such accusations are voiced against the Jews. A similar viewpoint is attributed to certain Syrian officials of the late second century BCE by the Greek historian, Diodorus Siculus (ca. 90–ca. 30 BCE). According to Diodorus, the Syrians were enemies not only of the Hasmoneans who defied the king of Syria, Antiochus IV (Epiphanes), but also of the Jews in general.[16] Thus, when Antiochus VII Sidetes (or Euergetes; see below fig. 6), was willing to terminate the war he was waging against the Hasmonean King Hyrcanus I, and abandon the siege of Jerusalem (ca. 133 BCE), he was advised by his counselors to exterminate the Jews because their way of life is different from that of all other people, the same argument which Haman raised:

> Now the majority of his [i.e., Antiochus'] friends advised the king to take the city [= Jerusalem] by storm and *to wipe out completely the race of Jews*; since they alone of all nations avoided dealings with any other people and looked upon all men as their enemies. They pointed out, too, that the ancestors of the Jews had been driven out of all Egypt as men who are impious and detested by the gods …. [After they were thus expelled], the refugees had occupied the

[13] On the time of the composition of Esther, see the discussion in Chapter 2, §II.
[14] See J. A. Montgomery, *The Book of Daniel* (International Critical Commentary; Edinburgh: T. & T. Clark, 1927), pp. 114, 116; K. Koch, *Daniel* (Biblischer Kommentar Altes Testament 22.1; Neukirchen-Vluyn: Neukirchener Verlag, 1986), p. 27; J. J. Collins, *A Commentary on the Book of Daniel* (Hermeneia; Minneapolis, MN: Fortress, 1993), pp. 38, 129; E. H. Haag, *Daniel* (Die Neue Echter Bibel; Würzburg: Echter Verlag, 1993), pp. 7–9.
[15] See Chapter 2, §II.
[16] Syrian hostility toward Jews was a constant factor whenever they were in contact; on the relationship between Jews and Syrians, see further Kalimi, *Fighting over the Bible*, pp. 227–229.

territory about Jerusalem, and having organized the nation of the Jews had made their hatred of mankind into a tradition, and on this account made utterly outlandish laws: not to break bread with any of other race, nor to show them any good will at all …. [They claimed that it was] Moses, the founder of Jerusalem and organizer of the nation, the man, moreover, who had ordained for the Jews *their misanthropic and lawless customs.* And since [Antiochus IV] Epiphanes was shocked by such hatred directed against all mankind, he had set himself to break down their traditional practices. Accordingly, he sacrificed before the image of the founder and the open-air altar of the god a great sow, and poured its blood over them. Then, having prepared its flesh, he ordered that their holy books, containing the *xenophobic laws,* should be sprinkled with the broth of the meat …. Rehearsing all these events, his friends strongly urged Antiochus [VII, Sidetes] *to make an end of the race completely,* or, failing that, to abolish their laws and force them to change their ways. (Diodorus Siculus, *Bibliotheca Historica* 34.1; italics added)[17]

What is remarkable about this passage is that its close resemblance to the accusations Haman lebeled against the Jews in Esther was not written by a Jewish author to stereotype their enemies' slanders, but was written by a Greek historian. Later on, the Jewish historian, Josephus Flavius (ca. 37–100 CE), also refers to this incident, summarizing Antiochus VII Sidetes' counselors' words in this way: "They [that is, the Jews] alone of all nations do not take part in social intercourse with other nations, and regard them all as enemies" (*Jewish Antiquities* 13.245).[18]

According to Diodorus, Antiochus VII, Sidetes, ignored this advice, and "being a magnanimous and mild-mannered person, took hostages but dismissed the charges against the Jews, once he had exacted the tribute that was due and had dismantled the walls of Jerusalem" (*Bibliotheca Historica* 34.1).[19] Josephus also states that Antiochus concluded a peace treaty on terms which amounted to a partial surrender by John Hyrcanus (*Jewish Antiquities* 13.245–247). However, this incident is noteworthy because it demonstrates the bitter hatred that burned in some Syrians toward their Jewish neighbors. The latter is also supported by Josephus' claim that another Hasmonean king of Judea, Alexander Jannaeus (103–76 BCE), refused to recruit Syrians to his mercenary army "on account of their innate hatred of his nation."[20]

[17] The English translation is from F. R. Walton, *Diodorus of Sicily: The Library of History* (Loeb Classical Library; Cambridge, MA: Harvard University Press, 2001), vol. 12, pp. 53, 55 (Greek version on pp. 52, 54).

[18] For the English translation, see R. Marcus, *Josephus with an English Translation* (Loeb Classical Library; London: William Heinemann / Cambridge, MA: Harvard University Press, 1943; reprinted 2006), vol. 9, pp. 350–351 esp. note c.

[19] The English translation is from Walton, *Diodorus of Sicily: The Library of History,* vol. 12, p. 55 (Greek on p. 54).

[20] Marcus, *Josephus with an English Translation,* vol. 9, pp. 245–247.

Figure 6   The front (a) and back (b) of the coin of Seleucid King Antiochus VII (138–129 BCE).

In the above passage, Diodorus quotes an extremely harsh characterization of the Jews, that "their holy books containing the xenophobic laws," which served as the basis for a (rejected) proposal to wipe them out entirely as enemies of all mankind. In another part of his *Bibliotheca Historica*, however, Diodorus quotes at length a similar (but less antagonistic) account of Jewish origins and tradition written by Hecataeus of Abdera in his *Aegyptiaca* (ca. 360–290 BCE).[21] For the most part, Hecataeus' account is more even-handed, though it is also full of errors about Jews and Jewish history (for example, it claims that Moses founded Jerusalem, the Jews never had a king, and they hate foreigners), but it affirms that: "the sacrifices that he [= Moses] established differ from those of other nations, as does their way of living, for as a result of their own expulsion from Egypt *he introduced an unsocial and intolerant mode of life*" (*Bibliotheca Historica* 40.3.4, cf. 40.3.1–8).[22]

IV Apollonius Molon

The Greek rhetorician and writer of the first half of the first century BCE, Apollonius Molon (Ἀπολλώνιος ὁ Μόλων; or Molo/Molonis), was a native of Alexandria, but settled at Molon of Rhodes. According to Plutarch, Apollonius established a school of rhetoric in Molon, where he studied, among others, Cicero and Julius Caesar.[23] "He is to be distinguished carefully from his older contemporary Apollonius who came from Alabanda in Caria [Anatolia] and also taught rhetoric at Rhodes."[24]

Unlike Manetho, who in his *History of Egypt* occasionally attacks the Jews (88–87 BCE), Apollonius published a pamphlet called "Against the Jews," which exclusively dealt with the Jews and attacks them.[25] Still, Josephus states that "Apollonius, unlike Apion, has not grouped his accusations together, but scattered them here and there all over his work …" (*Against Apion* 2.147). Though Josephus does not mention explicitly "Against the Jews," he frequently refers to Apollonius anti-Jewish writing in his *Contra Apionem*

---

[21] On this Greek writer, see B. Bar-Kochva, "The Jewish Ethnographic Excursus by Hecataeus of Abdera," *The Image of the Jews in Greek Literature*, pp. 90–135.

[22] For the English translation, see Walton, *Diodorus of Sicily: The Library of History*, vol. 12, pp. 281–287 esp. 283 (Greek on pp. 280–286 esp. 282). See also Schäfer, *Judeophobia*, pp. 22–23, 58–59, 68; R. S. Bloch, *Antike Vorstellungen vom Judentum: Der Judenexkurs des Tacitus im Rahmen der griechisch-römischen Ethnographie* (Historia: Einyelschriften 160; Stuttgart: Steiner, 2002), pp. 29–41 esp. 31.

[23] See Plutarch, *Caesar* 3; *Cicero* 4.

[24] See E. Schürer, *The History of the Jewish People in the Age of Jesus Christ (175 B.C.–A.D. 135)*. There is a new English version revised and edited by G. Vermès, F. Millar and M. Goodman (Edinburgh: T. & T. Clark, 1986), vol. 3,1, pp. 598–600 esp. 599.

[25] Cf. Schürer, *The History of the Jewish People in the Age of Jesus Christ*, p. 599.

(= *Against Apion*, e.g., 2.79, 145, 236, 255, 258, 262, 295). Also, a passage from the writing of Apollonius is quoted by Alexander Polyhistor in Eusebius of Caesarea (ca. 260/265–339) *Praeparatio Evangelica* (= *Preparation for the Gospel*; early fourth century) 9:19.

Apollonius harshly attacked the Jews and the essence of their religion, their laws and ancient lawgiver, personal, and national characters, and their attitude toward other people. Josephus recounts that Apollonius is "reviling us in one place as atheists and misanthropes, in another reproaching us as cowards, whereas elsewhere, on the contrary, he accuses us of temerity and reckless madness. He adds that we are the most witless of all barbarians, and are consequently the only people who have contributed no useful invention to civilization" (*Against Apion* 2.147–149).[26] Moreover, Apollonius accused the Jews "not worshiping the same gods as other people" (2.79). He condemned the Jews "for refusing admission to persons with other preconceived ideas about God, and for declining to associate with those who have chosen to adopt a different mode of life" (2.258). Apollonius also made reflections upon the lawgiver Moses and his laws, which are "partly from ignorance, mainly from ill will, have made reflections, which are neither just nor true," underlying his immorality as "a charlatan and imposter," whose demands teach just evil, no virtue (2.145).

Yet if the colophon at the end of Esther's Greek version (B-Text) was written in 114 BCE, as most of the scholars suggest,[27] then Esther and Haman's accusations presumably were known to Greek speaker scholars in the Greco-Roman world, including Apollonius. Most likely the latter was familiar with these materials due to the many Jews who lived in Rhodes and Caria already at the beginning of the second century BCE.[28] But even if one accepts the late dating for the colophon that suggests Bickerman, then, as he stresses, "Dositheus delivered the book [of Greek Esther] in 78–77 B.C., about the same time Apollonios [*sic*!] Molon published pamphlet 'Against the Jews'."[29] That is, the hatred of Apollonius toward the Jews and their laws was not something completely innovated. The similarity of Apollonius' accusations with those of Haman's is obvious, at least partially: Both stress the variances of the Jews and Jewish laws from all other people, and their worthlessness

---

[26] H. St. J. Thackeray, *Josephus with an English Translation*, Volume 1: *The Life, Against Apion*, p. 351 (Greek on p. 350). This charge repeated by Apion, see *Against Apion* 2.135: "But" (urges Apion) we "have not produced any geniuses, for example, inventors in arts and crafts or eminent sages"; Thackeray, *Josephus: The Life, Against Apion*, p. 347 (Greek: p. 346). Most likely Apion followed Apollonius.

[27] See Chapter 2, §IV, 2.

[28] See 1 Macc 15:16–24, and cf. Schürer, *The History of the Jewish People in the Age of Jesus Christ*, p. 599 and note 115.

[29] Bickerman, "The Colophon of the Greek Book of Esther," p. 347.

to exist: "And Haman said to King Ahasuerus, There is a certain people scattered abroad and dispersed among the people in all the provinces of your kingdom; and their laws are different from those of every other people ... therefore it is worthless [or, not appropriate] for the king to keep [or, to tolerate] them. If it please the king, let it be decreed that they may be destroyed" (מדינת) ויאמר המן למלך אחשורוש ישנו עם אחד מפזר ומפרד בין העמים בכל מדינות מלכותך ודתיהם שנות מכל עם... ולמלך אין שוה להניחם. אם על המלך טוב יכתב לאבדם; Esth 3:8–9). Thus, it is not impossible that Apollonius was familiar with Haman's accusations (in the Greek version of Esther), and perhaps even influenced from.

The impact of Apollonius' anti-Jewish writing on the Greco-Roman world, particularly on the Hellenized Egyptians, such as Apion of Alexandria (*Against Apion* 2.79), Hellenistic and Roman intellectuals, historians, and statements was enormous, and caused great damage to the Jewish people and Judaism. No wonder, therefore, that almost 180 years later, Josephus polemicized with him and dedicated half of the second book of his *Against Apion* (2.145–286) to refute Apollonius' poisoned assertions.[30] Josephus specially stresses: "we possess a code excellently designed to promote piety, friendly relations with each other, and humanity towards the world at large, beside justice, hardihood, and contempt of death" (*Against Apion* 2.145–146) –in contrast to Apollonius' false accusations, as well as to those (of Haman before him, and) of Apion after him.

V   Apion of Alexandria

Because of his persuasiveness and bitter hatred for the Jews, the Hellenized Egyptian, Apion of Alexandria (ca. 30–20 BCE to ca. 45–48 CE), was appointed as the leader of the delegation sent (around 38 CE) to the Roman emperor Gaius Caligula, to complain against the Jews in Alexandria, whom they wanted to restrict. In his representation, Apion alleged that the Jews refused to erect statues in Caligula's honor and to swear by his sacred name. In addition, Apion included attacks on the Jews in one of his books (all lost), the *Aegyptiaca*, referred to by Josephus, in the first part of the second book of *Against Apion*. Eusebius presumably has the same book in mind in his *Praeparatio Evangelica* 10.10-12, where he affirms that Apion "was so spitefully disposed towards the Hebrews as to have composed a

---

[30] Bar-Kochva speaks of "more than 150 years earlier"; see B. Bar-Kochva, "The Anti-Jewish Ethnographic Treatise by Apollonius Molon," *The Image of the Jews in Greek Literature*, pp. 469–516 esp. 469.

book *Against the Jews*."[31] Most likely, Eusebius is mistaken in attributing to Apion a specific work *Against the Jews*. As mentioned above, this work was written by Apollonius Molon, and Apion used it, as testified by Josephus: "I am no less amazed at the proceedings of the authors who supplied him [i.e., Apion] with his materials, I mean Posidonius [of Apameia, ca. 135–51 BCE] and Apollonius Molon" (*Against Apion* 2.79).[32] Apion has grouped his accusations together, and Josephus points to them as they appear in the third book of Apion's *Aegyptiaca* (*Against Apion* 2.147).[33]

Josephus responds to the accusations of Apion, who repeated Manetho's slanders such as that the ancient Israelites were expelled from Egypt because they were lepers, and that the Jews are not proper Alexandrians,[34] as well as some of Apollonius' charges (*Against Apion* 2.1–64). Then he quotes Apion's question: "why, then, if they are citizens, do they not worship the same gods as the Alexandrians?" (*Against Apion* 2.66).[35] Obviously, this accusation is on the same line with that of Haman, who accused the Jews that their religion/laws "*are different from those of every other people*" (Esth 3:8).

Indeed, Josephus himself states that "Greeks, as is well-known, are not the only people with whom our laws come into conflict; those principally so affected are Egyptians and many others" (*Against Apion* 2.99).[36] But the main point is that these Jew-haters use this difference against the Jews, although it does not hurt anyone. Like Haman, who attempts to convince the king that the Jews cause damage to him by keeping their own laws, because then "they do not keep the king's laws" (Esth 3:8); Apion also attempts to show that keeping Jewish laws does hurt the Romans: "Apion has consequently attempted to denounce us on the ground that we do not erect statues of the emperors.[37] As if they were ignorant of the fact or

[31] Aulus Gellius' *Noctes Atticae* (*Attic Nights*) 5.14; and Pliny the Elder's *Naturalis Historia* (*Natural History*) 37.19, also refer to Apion, but say nothing about his attitude toward the Jews.

[32] The translation is from Thackeray, *Josephus: The Life, Against Apion* (The Loeb Classic library; London: W. Heinemann and New York: G. P. Putnam's Sons, 1926), p. 325 (Latin on p. 324). Note that the entire section from 2.52–114 is missing from the Greek manuscripts – all of which appear to be dependent on a single exemplar – and are preserved only in an Old Latin translation; cf. Thackeray, ibid., vol. 1, pp. xviii–xix.

[33] Thackeray, *Josephus: The Life, Against Apion*, p. 351 (Greek on p. 350).

[34] On this issue, see G. Hata, "The Story of Moses Interpreted within the Context of Anti-Semitism," in L. H. Feldman and G. Hata (eds.), *Josephus, Judaism and Christianity* (Detroit, MI: Wayne State University Press, 1987), pp. 180–197.

[35] English translation according to Thackeray, *Josephus: The Life, Against Apion*, p. 319 (Latin on p. 318).

[36] Thackeray, *Josephus: The Life, Against Apion*, p. 333 (Latin on p. 332).

[37] Because this contradicts the biblical law, for instance: "You shall not make for you any engraved image, or any likeness of anything that is in heaven above, or that is in the earth beneath, or that is in the water under the earth" (Exod 20:4 // Deut 5:8). Instead, a sacrifice was made daily at the Jerusalem Temple in honor of Roman Caesars; see Josephus, *Jewish War* 2.409–417.

needed Apion to defend them! He should rather have admired the mag-
nanimity and moderation of the Romans in not requiring their subjects
to violate their national laws, and being content to accept such honours
as the religious and legal obligations of the donors permit them to pay"
(*Against Apion* 2.73).[38]

Because the Romans tolerated the unique Jewish law and did not consider that its keeping caused damage to them, Apion turns to accuse the
Jews with a false and horrible charge: "They [i.e., the Jews]" says Apion,
"would kidnap a Greek foreigner, fatten him up for a year, and then convey him to a wood, where they slew him, sacrificed his body with their
customary ritual, partook of his flesh, and while immolating the Greek,
swore an oath of hostility to the Greeks" (*Against Apion* 2.95).[39]

Although there is no direct literary connection between most of the
accusations of Apion and that of Haman in the book of Esther, there
are undeniable similarities between their arguments: Both Jew-haters
attempt to mark a sharp contrast between the Jewish religion and the
laws of the emperor's dominion, and try falsely to show that the former
causes damage to the latter. Both refuse to recognize the uniqueness of
the Jewish laws, which in fact do not harm anyone, and both attempt
to falsify the essence of Jewish religion and encourage the ruler to hurt
the Jews.

Since the Greek version of Esther appeared in Alexandria before the
time of Apion and was popular among the Hellenistic Jews, it is possible
that Apion knew the book and Haman's charges against the Jews, and perhaps even used it as a model for his own. However, Apion never explicitly
mentions the book of Esther or anything in it. Also, there is no evidence
that he, who was so clearly antagonistic toward the Jews, had any interest
to read widely in their literature. Even his depictions of Moses show no
evidence of having read the Torah himself, even in part.

VI   The Roman Governor Flaccus

In his work *In Flaccus* 1.116–124 (§14; esp. 116), the Jewish-Hellenistic
philosopher, Philo of Alexandria (ca. 25 BCE–50 CE), refers to the

---

[38] Cf. *Against Apion* 2.121: "he [i.e., Apion] attributes to us an imaginary oath, and would have it
appear that we swear by the God who made heaven and earth and sea to show no good-will to a
single alien, above all to Greeks." English translations from Thackeray, *Josephus: The Life, Against
Apion*, pp. 321, 323 (Greek on pp. 320, 322); 341 (Greek on p. 340).

[39] Visibly, here is a sign of blood-libel in the Hellenistic society, that later pursued the Jews, particularly in the Christian society. English translation from Thackeray *Josephus: The Life, Against Apion*,
p. 331 (Greek on p. 320).

Roman Governor of Egypt, Aulus Avilius Flaccus (ca. 15 BCE–39 CE), in a manner reminiscent of Haman. According to Philo, in 38 CE Flaccus instigated a series of actions against the Jewish community of Alexandria, culminating in the burning of several synagogues, expulsion of the Jews from all but one quarter of the city, and the torture and murder of many who attempted to escape. But in the autumn of 38 CE, Flaccus was suddenly arrested by imperial troops and brought to Rome, where he was first exiled to the island of Andros, and then, in the spring of 39 CE, he was executed.[40] Describing these events, Philo concludes that:

> The fact that Flaccus had to undergo this unprecedented misfortune, taken captive as he was like an enemy in the country of which he was governor, was I think due to his treatment of the Jews, whom he had decided to exterminate completely in his craving for fame. The moment of his arrest is also a clear proof of this, for it was the national Jewish festival of the autumn equinox, in which it is the custom of the Jews to live in tents [i.e., the festival of Sukkot].[41]

Obviously, we do not have here a direct reflection of Haman's charges, but Flaccus acted in a similar manner in seeking to destroy the Jews for his own glory, whereas Haman sought to destroy them because of his ego. Thus, in the introduction to a 1967 French translation of *In Flaccus*, André Pelletier suggests that Philo's account "recalls the end of the book of Esther."[42] Van der Horst summarized this as a claim that Philo might have modeled his depiction of Flaccus on the books of Esther and 2 Maccabees, with Flaccus as "the new Haman, Antiochus Epiphanes, and Nicanor."[43] Even though Flaccus was punished in the same measure for what he did to Jews, still Philo's writings make no explicit connection between him and Haman.[44]

---

[40] For a summary of these events, see van der Horst, *Philo's Flaccus*, pp. 34–38; for detailed discussion, cf. S. Gambetti, *The Alexandrian Riots of 38 C.E. and the Persecution of the Jews: A Historical Reconstruction* (Supplements to the Journal for the Study of Judaism 135; Leiden and Boston: Brill, 2009), esp. 167–193.

[41] Translation from van der Horst, *Philo's Flaccus*, p. 75; for the Greek and a different English translation, see F. H. Colson, *Philo in Ten Volumes, with an English Translation* (Loeb Classical Library; London: W. Heinemann / Cambridge, MA: Harvard University Press, 1967), vol. 9, pp. 366–367.

[42] "La complaisance de Philon à s'appesantir sur les tourments de l'adversaire vaincu rappelle la fin du livre d'Esther où l'on voit les Juifs obtenir de prolonger un jour encore le massacre d'ennemis dont ils n'avaient déjà plus rien à craindre (Esther 9, 13)," A. Pelletier, *In Flaccum* (Les Oeuvres de Philon d'Alexandrie 31; Paris: Cerf, 1967), p. 18.

[43] See van der Horst, *Philo's Flaccus*, p. 42.

[44] It seems that Philo never refers to Esther and its characters anywhere else either. On the whole incident regarding Flaccus, and the anti-Jewish persecution he carried out, cf. Schäfer, *Judeophobia*, pp. 136–160.

VII The Roman Historian Tacitus

The Roman historian Publius (or Gaius) Cornelius Tacitus (ca. 55–ca. 117 CE) parallels as well the key charges of Haman toward the Jews – that they are separatists whose laws are much different from all other peoples' laws.[45] Like Apollonius, he presents the lawgiver, Moses, in a negative light, saying: "Moses introduced new religious practices, quite opposed to those of all other religions." He goes further and lists several Jewish laws that are completely opposite to the laws of other nations, and which seem to him very strange if not ridiculous. Thus, he mentions that the Jews circumcise themselves, do not eat pig meat, do not work at Sabbath and every seventh year, do not make masks and sculptures, and they bury their dead bodies instead of burning them (*Histories* 5.4–5). According to Tacitus, "The Jews regard as profane all that we hold sacred; on the other hand, they permit all what we abhor" (*Histories* 5.4). He continues:

> The Jews are extremely loyal toward one another ... but *toward every other people they feel only hate and enmity* (*sed adversus omnes alios hostile odium*) .... Those who are converted to their ways follow the same practice, and the earliest lesson they receive is to despise the gods, to disown their country, and to regard their parents, children and brothers as of little account .... [T]he ways of the Jews are preposterous and mean. (*Histories* 5.5; italics mine)

Tacitus describes the Jews as "a nation which is the slave of superstition and the enemy of true beliefs" (ibid., 5.13; cf. 2.4).[46]

Indeed, not all of Tacitus' nasty notions about the Jews are entirely new. Some similar accusations had already been uttered by earlier Hellenistic writers, such as Hecataeus of Abdera (citied by Diodorus Siculus, see above §III), Apollonius Molon, as well as Apion of Alexandria.[47] Thus, we already pointed out the similarity of the negative judgment of Moses by Apollonius and Tacitus. Like Apion, who claims that the Jews "show no good-will to a single alien, above all to Greeks" (*Against Apion* 2.121), Tacitus also accuses the Jews that they hate all non-Jews (*Histories* 5.5).[48] Still, Tacitus was not just another bitter pagan Jew-hater. He not only

---

[45] See J. Borst (ed.), *P. Cornelius Tacitus Historien: Latain-Deutsch* (Zurich: Artemis Verlag, 1984), p. 552. However, some scholars date his death as late as 125 or even some years further.

[46] The translation is mostly according to C. H. Moore, *Tacitus in Five Volumes*, Volume 3: *The Histories, Books IV–V* (Loeb Classical Library; London: William Heinemann / Cambridge, MA: Harvard University Press, 1969), pp. 178–187. See also Borst, *P. Cornelius Tacitus Historien*, pp. 514–519.

[47] Cf. Bloch, *Antike Vorstellungen vom Judentum*; Schäfer, *Judeophobia*, pp. 31–33. For additional discussion of Tacitus' words regarding the Jews and their character, see J. H. Levy, *Studies in Jewish Hellenism* (Jerusalem: Bialik Institute, 1960), pp. 115–196 (Hebrew).

[48] Thackeray, *Josephus: The Life, Against Apion*, p. 341.

expressed extreme venomous accusations against the Jews, but also was an influential Roman historian and politician in Rome, whose writings caused enormous damage to Jews and Judaism.

In *Annals* 1.1, Tacitus declares: "my purpose is to recount ... without either bitterness or bias from which I am far removed" (*inde consilium mihi ... tradere ... sine ira et studio, quorum causas procul habeo*). But one can very much doubt this declaration of Tacitus, at least regarding to his writing about the Jews and their laws. The harsh statements and accusations of Tacitus should be considered in the context of his time and his political position in Rome: He had a seat in the Senate as a consul, and the international political background is the First Jewish–Roman War (66–73 CE). The *Histories* of Tacitus covers the Roman history of the period from the rise of Vespasian to the death of his younger son, Domitian (brother of Titus; ca. 69–96 CE).[49] Probably, Tacitus' attempts to present the Jews as a nasty people with strange laws in his historical writing – particularly in the fifth book of the *Histories*, which serves as a prologue to the account of Titus' suppression of the First Jewish–Roman War – was his own contribution to the struggle of Rome with the Jews. Metaphorically speaking, he fought against the Jews with his reed pen.

As mentioned above, Josephus Flavius disputed with Apollonius who lived almost 180 years earlier, and with Apion who died when he was 8–11 years old (Josephus was born in 37 and Apion passed away ca. 45–48 CE). However, he did not refute the fake accusations of his contemporary historian – Tacitus – who lived in the same city, Rome, simply because the latter wrote his *Histories* in ca. 100–110 CE, that is, around or after the death of Josephus (ca. 100 CE).

Strikingly, there is similarity between the accusations of Tacitus against the Jews and those in the First Letter to the Thessalonians in the New Testament:

> You have fared like the congregations in Judaea, God's people in Christ Jesus. You have been treated by your countrymen as they are treated by the Jews, who killed the Lord Jesus and the prophets and drove us out, *the Jews who are neglectful of God's will and enemies of their fellowmen* ... All this time they have been making up the full measure of their guilt, for the wrath is come upon them at last. (1 Thess 2:14–16; italics added)[50]

---

[49] It is worthy to note that the *Annals* and the *Histories* were published separately. Although the *Annals* covers the time from the reign of Tiberius to death of Nero (14–68 CE), it was written after the *Histories*, which covers the years ca. 69–96 CE.

[50] See Kalimi, *The Retelling of Chronicles in Jewish Tradition and Literature: A Historical Journey*, pp. 55–56.

If the First Letter to the Thessalonians was written by Paul himself (ca. 50 CE), then these sentences were expressed before the birth of Tacitus (ca. 55 CE). Nevertheless, it is possible that the Epistle was "updated" sometime after 70 CE by an interpolator, or even it entirely was written by a later Christian and ascribed to Paul.[51] If so, then it would be hard to deny the possibility of Tacitus' influence on the early Christian writer, a matter that would have fueled the hatred inherent in antisemitism/anti-Judaism.

VIII   The Greek Scholar Lucius Flavius Philostratus

The Greek sophist and rhetor Lucius Flavius Philostratus (ca. 165/172–244/250 CE), mentions Jews in his work *Life of Apollonius of Tyana*, which is probably written after 217 CE.[52] Here he attributes the following statement to a certain Euphrates, an advisor to Vespasian. Like Haman, Euphrates claims that by keeping their religious laws, the Jews have separated themselves from all humanity. His conclusion is that it would have been better to have left the Jews alone:

> The Jews cut themselves off long ago, not only from the Romans, but from all mankind, since people who have devised an unsociable way of life, with no meals, libations, prayers, or sacrifices in common with other men, have moved further away from us than Susa, Bactria, and the Indians beyond that. There was no point in punishing them as rebels, when they would have been better left unconquered. (Philostratus, *Life of Apollonius of Tyana* 5, 33.4)[53]

Philostratus might just be reflecting a popular view that resonates well with the old stereotype represented by Haman, the opponents of Daniel, the counselors of Antiochus VII, Apollonius, Apion, and Tacitus without investing much into it himself, since instead of proposing harsh measures as Haman did, he suggests that the Jews simply be left alone, but the accusation remains more or less the same.

IX   Conclusion

The accusations expressed by the biblical Haman against the Jews of the Persian Empire (Esth 3:8), particularly his claim that by keeping their own

---

[51] Nero's (reigned 54–68 CE) persecution of the Christians is well known. Tacitus mentions the death of Jesus in context with Nero's persecutions (*Annals* 15.44).

[52] Tyana is in Southwest Anatolia.

[53] English translation is from C. P. Jones, *Philostratus: The Life of Apollonius of Tyana Books V–VIII* (Loeb Classic Library; Cambridge, MA: Harvard University Press, 2005), pp. 63, 65 (Greek on pp. 62, 64).

specific laws, the Jews become separatists who disregard the communal social and civil laws, are not solely in the ancient world, though they are the earliest known ones. Similar allegations were stated across the Greco-Roman world in the Hellenistic period and then after, and have continued to medieval and the modern times, as subsequent chapters in this study show.[54] This chapter presented some examples in which ancient writers parallel Haman's accusations, and some call for actions against the Jews, similar to those of Haman. The opponents of Daniel, the counselors of Antiochus VII Sidetes/Euergetes, Apollonius Molon, Apion of Alexandria, the Roman governor Flaccus, and the Roman historian Tacitus are just some known examples of this phenomenon. All the cases condemn Jewish laws and point out the "weird" laws of the Jews and their unusual behaviors as a result, as if the Jews are misanthropes and worthless, and therefore some call explicitly for their expulsion or destruction, as did Haman. Apollonius' false assertions included, for instance, that the Jews are the worst among the non-Hellenic people, lacked any creative ability, contributed nothing to the prosperity of mankind, believed in no divinity (atheists), and were ordered by their religion to hate all other people. On the background of this broad historical perspective, it is reasonable to consider Haman's accusations and attempts to annihilate the Jews not as a fantasy of the author of the Esther story, but rather as on a realistic basis, at least to some extent.

Seemingly, Haman's defamations and genocidal plans not only became a prototype for generations of antisemites, but some intellectuals, rulers, and political leaders have even developed – directly or indirectly – his views and intentions further. Unfortunately, such horrible views did not remain an abstract dream, but became reality in many ways during the Jews' long and bitter history, while challenging the core theological message of the book of Esther, as discussed above.

The attempts of the Jews to keep their ancestorial laws, religious regulations, and cultural identity are falsely interpreted as a bold sign of hatred toward others and targeted the Jews as enemies of humanity – all non-Jews. According to this wrong set of logic, the Jew-haters demand an active action against – even annihilation of – them, wherever they exist on the globe. Indeed, a person is the enemy of what he does not know, and most likely these and other Jew-haters were (and are) ignorant of Jewish culture, values, and literary heritage.

At the end of his magnum opus, *Jewish Antiquities* (20.267–268; completed in 93–94 CE), Josephus informs of his two forthcoming projects:

---

[54] See the discussion in, especially, Chapters 9, 11, and 12.

(1) a summary of the war and the after-history of the Jews; (2) "a work in four books concerning God and His being, and concerning the Laws, why some things are permitted to us by them and others are forbidden."[55] Knowing the great damage and potential danger of the anti-Jewish statements and false accusations of the Greco-Roman writers, most likely Josephus intended in his second project to reply in detail and refute all those accusations, but unfortunately he did not achieve this goal.[56]

Apparently, here lie the roots of anti-Judaism/antisemitism, which later developed and took shape in the monotheistic religions – Christianity and Islam, which consider themselves as "Israel in spirit" and a continuation of biblical Israel – as a means of replacing Jews and suppressing Jewish religious laws. In fact, there is similarity between the accusations of Tacitus against the Jews and those in 1 Thess 2:14–16. Possibly the former influenced the latter.

---

[55] See Thackeray, *Josephus: The Life, Against Apion*, pp. xi–xii.

[56] Thackeray adds that "Neither work apparently was ever published; but the second, 'On Customs and Causes,' as he elsewhere calls it, had, as may be inferred from the mention of four books and scattered allusions in the *Antiquities* to its contents, taken shape in his mind and been partly drafted" (*Josephus: The Life, Against Apion*, p. xii).

PART II

"Oh, How Much They Love the Book of Esther!"
Esther among the Jews

CHAPTER 7

Esther, Torah's Law, and the Dead Sea Scrolls' Community

I Introduction

Among the more than 900 manuscripts from the eleven caves of Qumran, about 210 of which are biblical manuscripts,[1] the book of Esther is completely missing. There is not even one small fragment from the 167 verses of Esther to be found![2] In contrast, the book of Ruth is only half the length of Esther (85 verses), yet four manuscripts, preserving parts of all four chapters of the book, remain (2QRuth[a], 2QRuth[b], 4QRuth[a], 4QRuth[b]).[3] From the book of Lamentations, comprised of five chapters (altogether 154 verses), fragments from four manuscripts were discovered at Qumran (3QLam, 4QLam, 5QLam[a], 5QLam[b]).[4]

The only other book of the Hebrew Bible unattested at Qumran is Nehemiah. However, most likely it was combined with the book of Ezra, as is reflected in several later sources, such as Josephus Flavius, *Against Apion* 1.8; Babylonian Talmud, *Baba Batra* 15a; Eusebius; and the Codex Alexandrinus of the Septuagint.[5] Yet from Ezra three fragments have been found.[6]

[1] The majority of the biblical manuscripts are partial copies. The other manuscripts – mostly written in Hebrew, some in Aramaic and a few in Greek – are literary-religious texts of the community.

[2] See S. A. White Crawford, "Has *Esther* Been Found at Qumran? *4Qproto-Esther* and the *Esther* Corpus," *RevQ* 17 (1996), pp. 307–325 esp. 307, 325; idem, "Esther, Book of," in L. H. Schiffman and J. C. VanderKam (eds.), *Encyclopedia of the Dead Sea Scrolls* (Oxford: Oxford University Press, 2000), vol. 1, pp. 269–270.

[3] The fragments that survived are: Ruth 1:1–12; 1:1–6,12–15; 2:13–23; 3:1–8,13–18; 4:3–4; altogether 48 verses, including some duplicates; cf. E. [C.] Ulrich, *The Biblical Qumran Scrolls: Transcriptions and Textual Variants* (Supplements to Vetus Testamentum 134; Leiden: Brill, 2013), pp. 735–738.

[4] Ulrich, *The Biblical Qumran Scrolls*, pp. 749–754.

[5] See Kalimi, *The Reshaping of Ancient Israelite History in Chronicles*, p. 8 note 28; idem, *Zur Geschichtsschreibung des Chronisten*, pp. 7–8 note 26.

[6] See below, §III. In contrast to the absence of the book of Esther among the Dead Sea Scrolls, many fragments of it have been found in the Cairo Genizah; for further details see Chapter 8, §III.

II   Why Is the Book of Esther Absent from
the Dead Sea Scrolls?

There is no guarantee that the publication of the texts from the Judean Desert is complete.[7] Accordingly, it remains theoretically possible that a fragment of Esther may yet be found, but the chances are slim. The long-standing hope that Esther will be found there is merely a wish, rather than a realistic observation of the current situation.

It is also difficult to suppose that the absence of Esther from among hundreds of Dead Sea Scrolls is simply circumstantial or accidental,[8] rather than a reflection of the attitude of the Qumran community (which many scholars have identified with the Essenes).[9] Nevertheless, we do not have any written document expressing the position that any member of the Qumran community took toward the book of Esther. Thus, as far as we know, the book was neither studied nor used in the community's liturgy, although authors of some works from Qumran were presumably familiar with Esther's tale.[10] There is also no evidence that the book of Esther was the subject of *pesher* (that is, commentary) by the Qumran community/Essenes, unlike several other biblical books.[11]

---

[7] For a complete edition of all those scrolls so far known, see E. Tov (with the collaboration of S. J. Pfann), *The Dead Sea Scrolls on Microfiche, Companion Volume: A Comprehensive Facsimile Edition of the Texts from the Judean Desert* (Leiden: Brill, 1993).

[8] This possibility is expressed, once again, by J. Magness, *The Archaeology of Qumran and the Dead Sea Scrolls* (Grand Rapids, MI: W. B. Eerdmans, 2002), p. 34.

[9] The Essenes are described by Josephus, *Jewish Wars* 2:119–261, and there is a great deal of debate in the scholarship regarding whether the Qumran community represents part of the same sect or not; see, for example, F. García Martínez and J. C. Trebolle Barrera, *The People of the Dead Sea Scrolls: Their Writings, Beliefs and Practices* (translated by W. G. E. Watson; Leiden: Brill, 1995), esp. pp. 50–96; N. Golb, *Who Wrote the Dead Sea Scrolls: The Search for the Secret of Qumran* (New York: Simon & Schuster, 1995), pp. 95–115; G. Boccaccini, *Beyond the Essene Hypothesis: The Parting of the Ways between Qumran and Enochic Judaism* (Grand Rapids, MI: W. B. Eerdmans, 1998); J. J. Collins, *Beyond the Qumran Community: The Sectarian Movement of the Dead Sea Scrolls* (Grand Rapids, MI: W. B. Eerdmans, 2010).

[10] For this assumption, see J. Finkel, "The Author of Genesis Apocryphon Knew the Book of Esther," in Y. Yadin and C. Rabin (eds.), *Essays on the Dead Sea Scrolls in Memory of E. L. Sukenik* (Jerusalem: The Shrine of the Book, 1962), pp. 163–182 (Hebrew); S. Talmon, "Was the Book of Esther Known at Qumran?" *Eretz-Israel* 25 (Joseph Aviram Volume; 1996), pp. 377–382 (Hebrew), and its references to earlier bibliography. See also White Crawford, "Has *Esther* Been Found at Qumran?" pp. 307–325; idem, "Esther, the Book of," pp. 269–270; J. Ben-Dov, "A Presumed Citation of Esther 3:7 in 4QD^{b*}," *DSD* 6 (1999), pp. 282–284. Though he denies that it can be taken as direct evidence of the beliefs of the Qumran community (since he follows Talmon in denying that it was composed by them), Koller (*Esther in Ancient Jewish Thought*, pp. 141–145) argues that the Genesis Apocryphon not only knows Esther and alludes to it in its account of Abram and Sarai in Egypt, but that these allusions serve to "correct" aspects of Esther that were considered problematic.

[11] *Pesherim* have been found on Psalms (1Q16; 4Q171; and 4Q173), Isaiah (3Q4; 4Q161–165), and some books of the Minor Prophets such as Hosea (4Q166–167), Micah (1Q14), Nahum (4Q169), Habakkuk (1QpHab), and Zephaniah (1Q15; 4Q170).

A similar situation to that of the book of Esther can be seen for the book of Chronicles – which is much longer (65 chapters that comprise 1765 verses), but from which only one tiny fragment has been found in the eleven caves of Qumran, which contains no more than some words of four verses (2 Chr 28:27; 29:1–3)![12] In contrast, from the book of Psalms, for instance, 39 manuscripts with thousands of verses were found at Qumran,[13] and it was a theme for *pesher* – both clear-cut evidence of the book's broad acceptance and popularity in the Qumran community. In that light, it is likely that the lack of any Esther manuscripts at Qumran reflects a comparatively minimal interest in (or knowledge of) the book, if there was any interest at all.

It seems that in the Qumran community the book of Esther was not considered to be holy and authoritative Scripture, whether because it was not considered canonical at all by the time when the Qumran scrolls were written,[14] or because the particular community simply did not accept its scriptural status. Either way, there would have been no necessity to copy the book, explaining why there are no archaeological remnants of it. But why would the Qumranites reject the book?

In the light of a lack of *any* explicit or concrete evidence for the Qumranites'/Essenes' attitudes toward the book of Esther, scholars have pointed to various aspects of the book that would have conflicted with Qumranites' religious beliefs in order to explain the book's absence at Qumran.[15] For example, some propose that because the book was written in the Diaspora it may not have been known in the Land of Israel prior to the destruction of the Second Temple (70 CE).[16] Yet this is undermined by the evidence supporting the idea that Esther was known at Qumran or among those whose works ended up in the Qumran library.[17] Others suggest that the community may have rejected the book because of its lack of overtly religious features, particularly since the Hebrew Text does not mention God's name. However, this assumption is seriously challenged by the fact that the

---

[12] See in detail, Kalimi, *The Retelling of Chronicles in Jewish Tradition and Literature*, pp. 111–115; idem, *Das Chronikbuch und seine Chronik: Zur Entstehung und Rezeption eines biblischen Buches* (Fuldaer Studien 17; Freiburg im Breisgau: Herder Verlag, 2013), pp. 137–148 esp. 137–140.

[13] See P. W. Flint, *The Dead Sea Psalms Scrolls and the Book of Psalms* (Studies on the Texts of the Desert of Judah 17; Leiden: Brill, 1997). For an index of the passages from the book of Psalms, see E. C. Ulrich, "An Index of the Passages in the Biblical Manuscripts from the Judean Desert (Part 2: Isaiah–Chronicles)," *DSD* 2 (1995), pp. 86–107 esp. 98–104.

[14] So Stiehl, "Das Buch Esther," p. 9.

[15] For a brief survey of the various opinions, see Moore, *Esther*, pp. xxi–xxii; White Crawford, "Esther, the Book of," p. 269.

[16] See White Crawford, "Esther, Book of," pp. 269–270.

[17] See above, note 10.

Song of Songs also does not mention God's name anywhere; yet there were four fragments of it uncovered at Qumran (6QCant, 6QCant^a, 6QCant^b, 6QCant^c).[18] A related issue could be that Esther breached Jewish dietary laws as she ate with the gentile king, Ahasuerus. Other scholars, such as Roger Beckwith, presumed that the Qumran sect refrained from using the book of Esther in their liturgy since they had already established a calendar of 364 days, divided accordingly by weeks. Thus, the same date always fell on the same day of the week, so that the feast of Purim always fell on the Sabbath.[19] Because the feast of Purim was excluded from the Qumranites calendar and was not celebrated, therefore there was no need to copy and keep the book of Esther, which in its essence is the "Torah" of Purim. However, none of these is likely to be the primary reason for Esther's absence in Qumran.

III Esther's Marriage to Ahasuerus

One might posit that Esther's absence from Qumran may have been because they objected to a beautiful young Jewish girl – Esther – becoming the wife of a non-Jewish king – Ahasuerus. Even though this marriage with the Persian king led to the salvation of the Jews of the empire, it was considered a violation of the law of the Torah concerning intermarriage with the Canaanites (as well as with the Ammonites and Moabites),[20] which was extended during the Second Commonwealth era to include all non-Jews in general. The Qumran community strictly followed the commandment of the Torah as it is expounded and conceptualized in the books of Ezra and Jubilees (Ezra 9–10; Jub 30:7–10). These books strongly opposed any sort of intermarriage with Gentiles. For example, in Ezra 9–10 we read as follows:

> The people of Israel … have not separated themselves from the peoples of the lands with their abominations, from the Canaanites, the Hittites, the Perizzites, the Jebusites, the Ammonites, the Moabites, the Egyptians, and the Amorites. For they have taken some of their daughters as wives for themselves and for their sons. Thus the holy seed has mixed itself with the peoples of the lands, and in this unfaithfulness the officials and leaders have led the way. When I heard this, I tore my garment and my mantle, and pulled hair from my head and beard, and sat shocked …. Shecaniah … spoke to Ezra, saying, "We have broken faith with our God and have married foreign women from the peoples of the land …." (Ezra 9:1–3; 10:2–3)

---

[18] On this issue, see Chapter 1, note 2.

[19] See R. Beckwith, *The Old Testament Canon of the New Testament Church and Its Background in Early Judaism* (London: SPCK, 1985), p. 292.

[20] See Exod 34:16; Deut 7:3; 23:4–5, and cf. also Josh 23:7–13; 1 Kgs 11:1–2.

And Jub 30:7–10 states:

> And if there is any man in Israel who wishes to give his daughter or his sister to any man who is from the seed of the gentiles, let him surely die, and let him be stoned because he has caused shame in Israel. And also the woman will be burned with fire because she has defiled the name of her father's house and so she will be uprooted from Israel. And do not let an adulteress or defilement be found in Israel all of the days of the generations of the earth because Israel is holy to the Lord. And let any man who causes defilement surely die, let him be stoned because thus it is decreed and written in the heavenly tablets concerning all of the seed of Israel: "Let anyone who causes defilement surely die. And let him be stoned." And there is no limit of days for this law. And there is no remission or forgiveness except that the man who caused defilement of his daughter will be rooted out from the midst of all Israel because he has given some of his seed to Molech and sinned so as to defile it.[21]

It is noteworthy to mention that alongside the Torah, Psalms, and the prophetic scriptures, the book of Ezra and especially the book of Jubilees were very popular in Qumran. Three fragments from Ezra have been found there (4QEzra), and from Jubilees, no less than fourteen or fifteen manuscripts.[22] Despite the fact that Jubilees was not ultimately accepted as canonical by the Rabbis, it clearly had a great influence on the Qumran community, and perhaps was accepted among them as containing "divine, authoritative revelations."[23]

By contrast, since the book of Esther does not appear in the Qumran library, was not cited as scripture, and was not a theme for *pesher*, it was probably excluded from the sacred authoritative scriptures of the community's

---

[21] See O. S. Wintermute, "Jubilees: A New Translation and Introduction," in J. H. Charlesworth (ed.), *The Old Testament Pseudepigrapha* (The Anchor Bible Reference Library; New York: Doubleday, 1985), vol. 2, pp. 35–142 esp. 112–113. Compare Rofé, *Introduction to the Literature of the Hebrew Bible*, p. 154.

[22] For an index of the passages from the book of Ezra, see Ulrich, "An Index of the Passages in the Biblical Manuscripts," p. 107. For the book of Jubilees, see J. C. VanderKam, "Jubilees, Book of," *Encyclopedia of the Dead Sea Scrolls* (Oxford: Oxford University Press, 2000), vol. 1, p. 435. In an earlier entry VanderKam speaks about twelve manuscripts only, see "Jubilees, Book of," in D. N. Freedman *et al.* (eds.), *The Anchor Bible Dictionary* (New York: Doubleday, 1992), vol. 3, pp. 1030–1032 esp. 1030.

[23] See, for instance, J. C. VanderKam, "The Jubilees Fragments from Qumran Cave 4," in J. Trebolle Barrera and L. Vegas Montaner (eds.), *The Madrid Qumran Congress: Proceedings of the International Congress on the Dead Sea Scrolls, Madrid 18–21 March, 1991* (Leiden: Brill, 1992), vol. 2, pp. 635–648 esp. 648. For the citation, see J. C. VanderKam, "Authoritative Literature in the Dead Sea Scrolls," *DSD* 5 (1998), pp. 400–402. In the Dead Sea Scrolls there is no evidence either of a list of authoritative holy books (which anachronistically could be called "canonical books"), nor of a list of excluded books. However, since the book of Jubilees is represented in Qumran with an impressive number of copies, and since it was quoted as scripture (for instance, in the *Damascus Document*), we can presume that it was included among the authoritative scriptures of the community.

library. Accordingly, the question arises: did the Qumran community simply have a different sort of what we call "canon" than the later Hebrew canon, a "canon" which was guided by different norms and theological criteria? This is not an appropriate place to discuss this interesting issue in detail. However, the most important question is whether these texts were considered authoritative, scriptural or divine. In that sense Jubilees clearly claims to be (and seems to have been accepted as such), while Esther never even mentions God, much less claiming to be revealed by God, so it would not be surprising if its acceptance as scripture was not universal, and perhaps not even very widespread, in the Second Temple period.

Besides Jubilees, other Qumran scrolls also portray Gentiles negatively, for instance, *Miqṣat Ma'ase haTorah* (4QMMT). To cite Cecilia Wassén:

> Interaction with Gentiles in general and intermarriage with them in particular are major concerns [in 4QMMT]. According to the reconstructed, composite text, B 39–49 refers to the different categories of people who are prohibited from entering "the assembly" in the tradition of Deut 23:1–8, i.e., the Ammonite, the Moabite .... The biblical categories "the Ammonite and the Moabite" in this case serves as a label for foreigners in general ....
> B 75–82 introduces the practice of prohibited marital unions by labelling such forbidden unions as ועל הזונות הנעסה בתוך העם:זונות "And concerning the practice of illegal marriage that exists among the people." In B 77–78 such illegal union is compared to that of *kila'yim*, the improper mixing of two different kinds (Deut 22:9–11; Lev 19:19).[24]

In view of this negative position of the Qumranites regarding intermarriage, it is very likely that the marriage of the Jewess Esther with the gentile Ahasuerus also would have made the book unacceptable to the community.

IV   Boaz's Marriage to Ruth the Moabitess

Yet if Esther's marriage to a gentile was the major reason for the book's relative absence at Qumran, why was the book of Ruth popular there? The marriage of Boaz and Ruth the Moabitess is not in accordance with the law in Deut 23:4–5, which forbade marriages with the Ammonites and Moabites. Ruth and Boaz's marriage also contradicts the policies

---

[24] See C. Wassén, "The Importance of Marriage in the Construction of a Sectarian Identity in the Dead Sea Scrolls," in S. Byrskog, R. Hakola, and J. Jokiranta (eds.), *Social Memory and Social Identity in the Study of Early Judaism and Early Christianity* (Novum Testamentum et Orbis Antiquus / Studien zur Umwelt des Neuen Testaments 116; Göttingen: Vandenhoeck & Ruprecht, 2016), pp. 127–150 esp. 132–136 (the quotation is from pp. 133–134).

emphasized in Ezra 9–10; Neh 13:23–27 and Jub 30:7–10.[25] Nevertheless, the book of Ruth was accepted by the Qumranic sectarians while the book of Esther seems not to have been. The acceptance of Ruth by the sect was, presumably, due to her "conversion to Judaism" (Ruth 1:16–18), while Ahasuerus was and remained a gentile. Moreover, it may be that the Qumranites interpreted the Deuteronomistic verses concerning the Moabites and Ammonites in reference to males only, rather than to males and females, similarly to the rabbinic interpretation later on.[26] But that view also stands in contrast with Ezra, Nehemiah and Jubilees (and several other Persian period texts) that specifically condemn marriage to foreign *wives* (not just foreign husbands). Perhaps acceptance of the book of Ruth was needed since Ruth was considered the ancestress of King David (Ruth 4:18–22 // 1 Chr 2:11–15). Indeed, David's portrait in the Dead Sea Scrolls was developed even more than in the Hebrew Bible itself, "as Psalmist, and as a messianic figure whose throne and kingdom will last forever."[27] Nonetheless, the very prominence of David could have been a reason *not* to preserve Ruth, since it calls his Jewish ancestry into question, given the (later?) rabbinic emphasis on matrilineal descent.

V "Fast for Me"

Esther's marriage to the gentile Ahasuerus was not the only transgression by this Jewish woman. When Mordecai urged her to act on behalf of her people, she requested that he: "Go, gather all the Jews who are present in Shushan, and fast for me, and neither eat nor drink *three* days, night and day" (Esth 4:16). Now, since Haman's decree to persecute the Jews has been written on the thirteenth day of the first month (Esth 3:12), and assuming that Mordecai knew about the decree on the same day or even a day later, it means that Esther ordered the Jews of Shushan to fast on Passover. In other words, she ordered Jews to abstain from eating *mazot* (= unleavened bread) on the fifteenth day of the first month, the month of Nisan, and not to celebrate the Passover holiday in accordance with the Torah commandment (Exod 12:14–20; 34:18;

[25] For the purpose and time of the composition of the book of Ruth, see for example, Gerleman, *Ruth. Das Hohelied*, pp. 7–8; Rendtorff, *The Old Testament: An Introduction*, pp. 259–260; T. Linafelt, *Ruth* (Brit Olam; Collegeville, MN: Liturgical Press, 1999), pp. xvii–xx.

[26] See Babylonian Talmud, *Yebamot* 76b: עמוני ולא עמונית, מואבי ולא מואבית "An Ammonite, but not an Ammonitess; a Moabite, but not a Moabitess." See also Midrash *Ruth Rabbah* 2:9.

[27] See P. W. Flint, "David," in L. H. Schiffman and J. C. VanderKam (eds.), *Encyclopedia of the Dead Sea Scrolls* (Oxford: Oxford University Press, 2000), vol. 1, pp. 178–180 esp. 180.

Lev 23:5–8; Num 28:16–18; Deut 16:1–8). If the Qumran community was aware of this particular problem with Esther's narrative, these violations of Torah laws presumably could not be tolerated by them, even though it was an urgent situation, just as they could not tolerate her marriage with a gentile, although she was taken to the king's house against her will (Esth 2:8a). This community may have believed that Esther should have called Jews to fast sometime before or after Passover, as she should have resisted marriage to the king, even if she would have paid with her life for it. This opinion, however, would be completely opposite to that of the Rabbis.[28]

VI   Conclusion

This chapter introduces one of the vexing problems in Qumran scholarship, namely the absence of the book of Esther among the biblical manuscripts. It reviews and summarizes a variety of proposals by scholars and suggests that Esther (but not Ruth) was unacceptable to the Qumran community particularly because: (a) it centered on the marriage of a Jewish girl, Esther, and a gentile man, Ahasuerus; and (b) by asking the Jews to fast on the thirteenth day of the month of Nisan for three days, Esther was asking Jews to fast on Passover and to abstain from eating the unleavened bread and celebrating the holy day. These transgressions of Esther mean either that she, as a matter of fact, did not know the Torah at all, or she knew the Torah's laws but preferred to ignore its divine commandments. Both cases contradict fundamental theological principles of the members of the Qumran community, who built their entire lives around the Torah and were very much committed to its commandments, which oppose intermixing with foreigners and required the eating of *mazut* at Passover, rather than fasting. These reasons could be the most important ones among some other possibilities that may have caused the community at Qumran to dismiss Esther.

Nevertheless, the absence of the book of Esther altogether from among the Dead Sea Scrolls cannot be a model representing the general attitude of the Jews toward the book. One must keep in mind that the whole community of Qumran was comprised, most probably, of no more than several

---

[28] See Babylonian Talmud, *Megillah* 15a (Mordecai "made the first day of Passover pass as a fast day"); *Pirqe de Rabbi Eliezer*, 49 (M. Higger, "Pirke Rabbi Eliezer," *Horeb* 10 [1948], p. 243 [Hebrew]; English translation: G. Friedlander, *Pirke de Rabbi Eliezer* [2nd ed.; New York: Hermon Press, 1965], p. 401, here it appears under ch. 50).

hundred members.[29] As a matter of fact, this small isolated Jewish community was a marginal and unrepresentative minority among the Jewish people in the late Commonwealth era. Most Jewish people, however, had a very different approach toward this fascinating book, as we will see in the following chapter.

---

[29] This assumption is based generally on the archaeological remains at Qumran. As of today, the exact number of the members of the Qumranic community is unknown. Yet, what is known is that the cemeteries of the community hold about 1100 tombs. These cemeteries, however, served the community for over 200 years. Unfortunately, Roland de Vaux, who excavated the site, never published the final report of the data. See J. C. VanderKam, *The Dead Sea Scrolls Today* (Grand Rapids, MI: W. B. Eerdmans, 1994), pp. 14–15.

CHAPTER 8

Esther in Jewish Canon, Tradition, Culture, and Thought

I The Book's Name

As mentioned above, Mordecai is the main character of the story of Esther.[1] According to Esth 9:20–23 he also composed the Megillah, as well as established the festival of Purim: "And Mordecai wrote these things and sent letters to all the Jews … to establish this among them, that they should keep the fourteenth day of the month Adar, and the fifteenth day of the same, yearly" (9:20–21). Moreover, according to the second letter of Purim (Esth 9:29–32), the festival was inaugurated by both Mordecai and Esther: "*Esther the queen* … and *Mordecai the Jew* wrote with all authority … to confirm these days of Purim in their times appointed *as Mordecai the Jew* and *Esther the queen* had enjoined them …."[2] Despite all this, the book neither bears Mordecai's name alone, nor combines it with that of his cousin – "Mordecai and Esther." Instead, like the books of Ruth, Judith and Susanna, this book was named after its core heroine – "Esther," the beautiful queen who was ready to sacrifice her life and her position in order to save her people from Haman's evil decree.[3]

Nevertheless, 2 Macc 15:36 names the day of the celebration which commemorates the Jews' redemption from Haman decree: "the Day of Mordecai," even though the biblical story calls it "Purim" (Esth 9:26, 28, 32). Interestingly, Josephus attributes the establishment of the new feast only to Mordecai: "For Mordecai wrote to all the Jews living in the kingdom of Artaxerxes, telling them to observe these days and keep them as a festival …" (*Jewish Antiquities* 11.292–293).[4] Did Josephus not know the second letter of Purim (Esth 9:29–32)? Or did he choose that part of the biblical text that is confirmed in 2 Maccabees?

---

[1] See Chapter 2, §V, 3, A.
[2] On the first and second letters of Purim, see the discussion in Chapter 2, §III, 1–2.
[3] On the noble characters of Queen Esther and Mordecai, see Chapter 2, §V, 2.
[4] See Marcus, *Josephus with an English Translation*, vol. 6, pp. 454–455.

II The Place in the Canon

The names of Esther and Mordecai were not mentioned by Shimeon Ben Sira in his "Praise of the Fathers" (Ben Sira 44–49). This can possibly indicate that the book of Esther still was not recognized as a Holy Scripture at that time (ca. 180 BCE), at least by some Jewish Sages in the Land of Israel. But since Ben Sira does not mention *all* past Jewish figures, it is also possible that Esther and Mordecai were not considered as important as the others depicted. So, for instance, as important as Ezra the scribe was, he also receives no mention in Ben Sira, though Zerubbabel and Nehemiah do. Hence, although it is unclear the exact reason for the absence of Esther and Mordecai in the book of Ben Sira, it does not mean that the book of Esther was unknown to Ben Sira or in the Land of Israel in general.

As mentioned above, Josephus discusses the story of Esther in his *Jewish Antiquities*, and most likely, the book of Esther was included in his "canon" in the first century CE (*Against Apion* 1.38–41).[5] The existence of tractate *Megillah* in the Mishnah leaves no doubt that Esther was an authoritative book for the Tanaim (i.e., mishnaic Sages/Rabbis). However, this did not prevent continued discussion of the book's legitimacy. There were some Amoraim (i.e., talmudic Rabbis, ca. 200–500 CE) who hesitated to include the book of Esther in the Hebrew canon. Thus, the Babylonian Talmud, *Megillah* 7a recounts:

אמר רב שמואל בר יהודה: שלחה להם אסתר לחכמים: קבעוני [נוסח אחר בהמשך הטקסט: כתבוני] לדורות. שלחו לה: קנאה את מעוררת עלינו לבין האומות. שלחה להם: כבר כתובה אני על דברי הימים למלכי מדי ופרס.

Rabbi Samuel son of Judah said: Esther sent to the Sages saying, "*Commemorate me*[6] [another version continues: *write* (an account of) *me*] for future generations." They replied, "you will incite the ill will of the nations against us." She replied: "I am already recorded in the chronicles of the kings of Media and Persia."

Apparently, the statement of this Babylonian Amora, Rabbi Samuel son of Judah (ca. 290–320 CE), represents just a "scholastic exercise" ("scholastische Übung"), not a real debate about the already firm status of the book in the Jewish Bible, Mishnah and Tosefta.[7] That is, despite the reservations

---

[5] For the Jewish "canon" reflected in Josephus's *Against Apion*, see in detail Kalimi, *The Retelling of Chronicles in Jewish Tradition and Literature*, pp. 98–100; and cf. P. Brandt, *Endgestalten des Kanons. Das Arrangement der Schriften Israels in der jüdischen und christlichen Bibel* (Bonner Biblische Beiträge 131; Berlin: Philo, 2001), pp. 57–171; Ego, *Esther*, pp. 72–78 esp. 71–72.

[6] Lit., fix me, that is, the book named after me and the Purim festival.

[7] Cf. S. Talmon, "Heiliges Schriftftum und kanonische Bücher aus jüdischer Sicht: Überlegungen zur Ausbildung der Grösse 'Die Schrift' im Judentum," in M. Klopfenstein, U. Luz, S. Talmon and

of some Sages toward the book of Esther, it was already recognized and canonized as Holy Scripture among the Jews and achieved a respected place among the books of the Hebrew Bible as well as in the Oral Torah. It is located in the third part of the Tanakh – in the *Ketuvim* (the Writings/ Hagiographa), as the fifth and the last of the Five Megillot, which are usually arranged according to the chronological order of the festivals in the Jewish calendar, on which they were a part of the Jewish liturgy in the synagogue: The Song of Songs (Passover), Ruth (Shavuot), Lamentations (9th of Ab), Qohelet (Sukkot), and Esther (Purim).[8] The Baraita (i.e., a tanaitic tradition that is excluded from the Mishnah but preserved in the Talmudim) in the Babylonian Talmud, *Baba Batra* 14b, locates Esther before the late historical books, Ezra, Nehemiah, and Chronicles, although according to the traditional chronology, these books discuss earlier periods in Israelite history, and should come before it.[9] Most of the oldest codices and the printed editions of the Hebrew Bible follow this tradition, and in many cases the book of Esther appears even before the book of Daniel.[10]

III   Esther through the Generations

The story of Esther was translated into Greek, probably at the last quarter of the second century or the first quarter of the first century BCE, and six additions of a legendary character were attached to it.[11] Certainly,

---

E. Tov (eds.), *Mitte der Schrift? Ein jüdisch-christliches Gespräch: Texte des Berner Symposions vom 6.-12- Januar 1985* (Judaica et Christiana 11; Bern: Peter Lang, 1987), pp. 45–79 esp. 79; Beckwith, *The Old Testament Canon*, p. 323; Ego, *Esther*, p. 76. On this whole issue, see also T. J. Stone, *The Compositional History of the Megilloth: Canon, Contoured Intertextuality and Meaning in the Writings* (Forschungen zum Alten Testament 2/59; Tübingen: Mohr Siebeck, 2013), esp. 140–181.

[8] Machzor Vitry (eleventh century CE; northern France) is first mentioned as a practice to this day: to read the five scrolls in the synagogue at regular times according to an annual reading cycle that begins in the month of Nisan.

[9] Indeed, in the Christian Bible Esther is located *after* Ezra, Nehemiah, and Chronicles; see Chapter 10, §III. For the comparison of the codices, see Paton, *A Critical and Exegetical Commentary on the Book of Esther*, pp. 1–3.

[10] Regardless of whether Esther appears before or after Daniel, these books are related by several similar thematical lines: Both tell stories about Jews who lived in exile, were appointed for top positions in the courts of foreign kings, were under danger of death (and in the case of Esther all the Jews with her), but saved by extraordinary miracles – implicitly (Daniel and his friends) or explicitly (Esther and all the Jews). Fuerst claims that in some manuscripts of the Hebrew Bible, Esther occurs immediately after the Torah; see Fuerst, *The Books of Ruth, Esther, Ecclesiastes, the Song of Songs, Lamentations*, p. 32. However, he did not base this saying on any source, and I could not find any manuscript to support it.

[11] On the two versions of Greek translation of Esther – B-Text and A-Text – including the six additions, as well as on the date of the B-Text, see Chapter 2, §IV, 1–2.

these testify to the popularity of and engagement with the book in the late Second Temple period, in the Land of Israel, where the translation took place (as the colophon at the end of the translation testifies), and the will to spread out the story and the feast of Purim as much as possible among the Hellenistic Jewish communities. Moreover, in his *Jewish Antiquities*, published in 93–94 CE in Rome (*Jewish Antiquities* 20.267), Josephus Flavius devoted an extensive section to recounting Esther's narrative (*Jewish Antiquities* 11.184–296).[12]

In contrast to the absence of the book of Esther among the Dead Sea Scrolls, a great number of fragments of it have been found in the Cairo Genizah, more than any other biblical composition aside from the Torah. This is incontrovertible evidence of the broad liturgical and educational usage of the book in the old Ben-Ezra Synagogue (built in 882 CE) of Fostat-Cairo's Jewish community.[13]

Furthermore, as the following examples indubitably reflect, Jews paid great attention to Esther and adored it in all generations. Thus, some Sages, such as Shemuel of Nehardea (ca. 165–254), expressed the view that "Esther was composed under the inspiration of the holy spirit" (Babylonian Talmud, *Megillah* 7a).[14] Otherwise, how did the author know what Haman thought in his heart (Esth 6:6, "Now Haman thought in his heart, To whom would the king delight to do honor more than to myself?").[15] Other Rabbis even affirmed that "this scroll was given [literally: stated] to Moses at Sinai," and they bridged the hundreds of years that separate the age of Moses from that of Esther by saying, "There are no considerations of early or later in the Torah" (Jerusalem Talmud, *Megillah* 1.5 [7a]). Seemingly, these Rabbis wished to enhance the holiness of the book, which lacks any explicit references to God's name or religious customs and institutions, and to strength its place in the canon and community. The affirmation that this scroll was given to Moses at Sinai also implies that the hatred of Jews and their astonishing survival were already announced to

---

[12] See Marcus, *Josephus with an English Translation*, vol. 6, pp. 403–456; and the discussion by D. Luria, *Josephus on the Book of Esther: The Sources, Intentions and Virtues* (Tel Aviv: Resling, 2015; Hebrew).

[13] See S. C. Reif, *A Jewish Archive from Old Cairo: The History of Cambridge University's Genizah Collection* (Richmond: Curzon Press, 2000), pp. 190, 225; idem (ed.), *The Cambridge Genizah Collections: Their Contents and Significances* (Cambridge University Library Genizah Series 1; Cambridge: Cambridge University Press, 2002), pp. 24, 34, 155, who notes several letters that refer to reading Esther on Purim, including by students.

[14] For the English translation, see M. Simon, *Megillah: Translated into English with Notes, Glossary and Indices* (London: Soncino Press, 1938), pp. 35–36.

[15] Similarly, Rashi comments on Gen 27:41–42 that recounts "Esau *said in his heart*, When the days of mourning for my father are at hand; then will I slay my brother Jacob. And these words of Esau her elder son were told to Rebecca ...," that Rebecca knew these words of Esau by the Holy Spirit.

Moses at the very starting point of Israelite/Jewish nationhood as soon as the covenant between God and Israel had been established. The Galilean Amora, Rabbi Simeon ben Lakish (nickname: Resh-Lakish; ca. 200–275 CE) considered the holiness of Esther to be at the same level as the holiness of the Torah, that is, greater than the books of the Prophets and any other book in the Writings, including Psalms. He maintained that, in time to come, all the books of the Bible would be annulled except the Five Books of Moses and the book of Esther (Jerusalem Talmud, *Megillah* 1.5 [7b]). This meant that, even in the Messianic era, hatred of Jews and the miraculous existence of the Jewish people would be remembered!

In medieval times, several commentaries were dedicated to the book of Esther, such as the Arabic commentary of Rab Saadia Gaon (Rasag; 882–942) *Ketab Alainas* (i.e., *The Book of Society*) of which only some fragments survived. A comprehensive and complete commentary to the book of Esther has survived by the prominent Karaite commentator, Jephet ben/ ibn Ali Halevi (Basra [Iraq] and Jerusalem, active ca. 960–1005).[16] Well-known commentaries on Esther were also composed in northern France, such as those of Rabbi Shlomo Yitzchaki (acronym: Rashi; 1040–1105), his grandson, Rabbi Samuel ben Meir (acronym: Rashbam; 1080–1160), and Rabbi Joseph Kara (ca. 1065–1135).[17] It is especially worthwhile to mention the two commentaries of Rabbi Abraham ibn Ezra (acronym: Raaba; 1089–1164):[18] the first one in Rome, 1140–1142 (published within *Mikraot Gedolot*); and the second one in Ryan (Lombardi, North France), ca. 1156 1157;[19] the commentary of Rabbi Levi ben Gershom (acronym: Ralbag; 1288–1344) from Provence, southern France; and Yalkut Shimoni on Esther – an eclectic selected anthology of midrashim on the book (13 century, probably ca. 1235).[20] Though the famous Rabbi Moshe ben Maimon (Maimonides; 1135–1204) reaffirmed the statement of Resh-Lakish concerning the everlasting existence of the Megillah,[21] it is

---

[16] On Saadia Gaon and Jephet ben Ali Halevi and their literary and exegetical activities, see Kalimi, *The Retelling of Chronicles in Jewish Tradition and Literature*, pp. 191–197, with references to earlier secondary literature; idem, *Fighting over the Bible*, pp. 7–8, 103, 114–116, 231–238. Ben Ali's commentary on Esther has recently been published by M. G. Wechsler, *The Arabic Translation and Commentary of Yefet ben 'Eli the Karaite on the Book of Esther* (Leiden: Brill, 2008).

[17] See J. Kara, *Oṣar Tob: Commentary on the Book of Esther* (published by E. Hübsch, A. Jellinek and A. Berliner; 1878).

[18] On ibn Ezra, see Kalimi, *Fighting over the Bible*, pp. 238–249.

[19] See Mishaly and Zipor, *Abraham Ibn Ezra's Two Commentaries on Megilat Esther*, pp. 9, 15–17. On ibn Ezra's commentaries on Esther, see also M. Gómez Aranda, *Dos Comentarios de Abraham ibn Ezra al Libro de Ester: Edición Crítica, Traducción y Estudio Itroductorio* (Madrid: Instituto de Filologia, 2007).

[20] See D. Börner-Klein, *Jalkut Schimoni zu Esther* (Berlin: De Gruyter, 2019).

[21] See Maimonides, *Mishneh-Torah*, Hilchot Megillah, chapter 2 halachah 18.

uncertain, however, that he also composed a commentary on the book, as is claimed by Joel J. Rivlin.[22]

In later generations the book of Esther was by no means neglected. Verses from it (such as Esth 4:11; 5:13; 6:14) were cited by Jewish Sages in medieval Jewish-Christian disputations.[23] Many commentaries from different point of view have been written on the book. Examples include the commentary on Esther by Rabbi Eleazar of Worms (ca. 1160–ca. 1230), who integrate the rabbinic teachings on the Megillah into the biblical text itself.[24] There is an anonymous commentary on the book of Esther, the earliest copy of which is from the mid-fourteenth century (Paris, National Library, Ms. Hebr. 249), that has been recently published by Aharon Mondschein.[25] Although the identification of the author of the commentary still is unknown, Mondschein claims, however, that there are several indications which point out that it was composed in Provence.[26] Usually, the commentator prefers the *peshat* (the simple, plain, literal meaning) approach over the midrashic one.

There is also the important commentary of Rabbi Abraham Saba (1440–1508).[27] In the opening words to his commentary, Saba compares the day that Megillat Esther was composed, no less than to the day that the Israelite received the Torah on Mount Sinai (Exodus 19–20 // Deuteronomy 5). He stresses that in the latter case they were forced to accept the Torah, while in the time of Esther and Mordecai they willingly accepted the yoke of the Almighty and obliged themselves to keep his Torah.[28] In another place Saba states that "there are profound matters in this Megillah about the hint of our redemption when our Messiah will come" (והנה זאת המגילה ... יש בה ענינים עמוקים על רמז גאולתינו לכשיבא משיחנו).[29]

The kabbalist and commentator, Rabbi Shlomo haLevi Alkabetz (Safed, ca. 1500–1576) wrote a colossal commentary on Esther, namely *Menot*

---

[22] See J. J. Revlin, *The Commentary on the Book of Esther by Maimonides* (Jerusalem: Krynfiss Press, 1950; Hebrew). Revlin also claimed that the commentary was originally written in Arabic, and printed for the first time in Livorno by Antonio Santini, 1759.

[23] See H. Maccoby, *Judaism on Trial: Jewish-Christian Disputations in the Middle Age* (Rutherford, NJ: Fairleigh Dickinson University Press / London: Associated University Press, 1982), pp. 122, 141, 179.

[24] See in detail Ch. S. Koenigsberg, "Accounting for Tradition: Calculations in the Commentary of R. Eleazar of Worms to Esther," *Megadim – Journal of Biblical Studies* 60 (2021), pp. 41–54.

[25] A. Mondschein, *An Anonymous [Provencal] Commentary on the Book of Esther: An Annotated Critical Edition with an Introduction* (Givat Washington (Israel): Academic College Givat Washington, 2019; Hebrew).

[26] See Mondschein, *An Anonymous [Provencal] Commentary on the Book of Esther*, p. 7.

[27] See Abraham Saba, *Ketav Yad Eshkol Hakofer on Megillat Esther* (Drahobyrz: Zupnik, 1903; Hebrew). On Abraham Saba and his exegetical work, see Chapter 9, §I, 5.

[28] See Saba, *Ketav Yad Eshkol Hakofer on Megillat Esther*, pp. 3–12 esp. 3, 12.

[29] Saba, *Ketav Yad Eshkol Hakofer on Megillat Esther*, p. 46.

Halevi.[30] He integrates in his commentary many midrashic sources, while considering them as if they are an integral part of the original story. He struggles also with some Sages' weird homiletic interpretations.[31]

Rabbi Eliyahu of Vilna (the Vilna Gaon, 1720–1797) composed three commentaries on three aspects of Esther: the *peshat*, *remez* (an allusion, a hint at the deeper meaning) and *sod* (a "secret" mystical meaning) of the text.[32] The Vilna Gaon stresses that the miracle related in the book of Esther (Purim) is ranked much higher than that of Hanukkah, though the latter was a very great wonder.[33] It is noteworthy that the very same opinion was already stated by Rabbi Judah Loew ben Bezalel (the Prague Maharal, 1520[?]–1609)[34] in his introduction to *Or Hadash*, dedicated to Megillat Esther.[35] Moreover, the first commentary of Rabbi Meir Libush ben Yechiel Michal (acronym: Malbim; 1809–1879) was on the book of Esther (ca. 1845). Several modern studies and commentaries have been composed on the book by Jewish scholars in Diaspora as well as in the State of Israel, which are scattered throughout this monograph.

IV   The Story of Esther and the Talmudic Rabbis

Due to the importance of the classical rabbinic literature in the formation of the Megillah and Purim, and enormous influence of them on generations of Jews and Jewish spiritual leaders, I would like to expand a bit more on the story of Esther and the talmudic Rabbis.[36] In fact, since they included the book of Esther in the Hebrew canon (ca. 90 CE), the Rabbis made countless efforts to enhance its position among the biblical books

---

[30] The commentary was completed in 1529 and was published (with much additional material that he added into it) for the first time in Venice 1585; see C. Y. Friedman (ed.), *Menot Halevi* (Brooklyn, NY, 1996).

[31] See Walfish "Kosher Adultery?" pp. 316–322. Walfish discusses the strange Midrash on Esth 2:20 which states that Esther had marital relations with Mordecai as well as with Ahasuerus, and shows how Alkabetz struggled with this issue.

[32] See Eliyahu of Vilna, *Megillat Esther* (2nd ed.; Jerusalem: Yeshivat Tiferrat haTalmud, 1991; Hebrew).

[33] See the Vilna Gaon's commentary (*Peshat*) on Esther 1:2 (ibid., pp. 16–18); and his commentary on Babylonian Talmud, *Chullin* 139b.

[34] On the birth date of Maharal, see B. L. Sherwin, *Mystical Theology and Social Dissent: The Life and Works of Judah Loew of Prague* (London: Associated University Presses, 1982; reprinted: Oxford: The Littman Library of Jewish Civilization, 2006), pp. 187–189.

[35] For the paragraph from *Or Hadash*, see A. Karib (ed.), *Selected Writings of Rabbi Judah Loew ben Bezalel* (Jerusalem: Mossad Harav Kook, 1960), vol. 1, pp. 186–191, esp. 189–190 (Hebrew).

[36] Usually, it is difficult to interpret this literature diachronically, since dating many of the texts, as well as the statements credited to particular Rabbis or groups within them, is uncertain. Therefore, I treat this material as a conglomerate without trying to lay out chronological development of the statements and texts within it.

(see above), as well as to adapt it to their own theological worldview and halachic system, and interpret it according to their unique methods.

Various rabbinic writings, both halachic (that is, regarding Jewish religious law) as well as midrashic-aggadic (that is, homiletic and non-legalistic exegetical texts), tanaitic, amoraitic and others later on, in Hebrew and in Aramaic, have been written on the Megillah. In the Mishnah, the Jerusalem Talmud, and the Babylonian Talmud, a special tractate was dedicated to the Megillat Esther and the holiday of Purim that is based on it – *Masechet Megillah*.[37] This tiny book is also not lacking from the Tosefta (that is, the supplement to the Mishnah).

The book of Esther also gained two major Aramaic translations – Targum Rishon, which is mostly a verbatim translation of the Hebrew text with just some midrashic expansions; and Targum Sheni, which is largely midrashic expansions of the text.[38] Presumably these Targums were edited sometime between the sixth and eighth centuries, though they include earlier materials as well. Both Targums have intensive theological tendencies. Thus, like the Greek translations, they also insert God's name and religious elements at several opportunities.[39] There is also the Aramaic translation of Esther, the so-called *Biblia Regia* ("Royal Bible") or Antwerp Polyglot (1569–1572), which eliminates the midrashic elements of the Targums.

The book was also the subject of special homiletical collections. There are about ten such Midrashim on Esther – an additional fact that demonstrates the popularity of the Megillah amongst the Jews. The largest Midrash is *Esther Rabbah* or simply Midrash *Esther*.[40] Some later Midrashim include Midrash *Aba Gurion* (ca. tenth century); Midrash

[37] On classical rabbinic treatment of Esther, see E. Segal, *The Babylonian Esther Midrash: A Critical Commentary* (3 vols.; Atlanta, GA: Scholars Press, 2020). Online resource: https://doi .org/10.26300/10pf-cs60 (Brown University Library). This work consists of a translation and critical commentary on part of the Babylonian Talmud, Tractate *Megillah*.

[38] For a critical edition of the Targum, see Grossfeld, *The Targum Sheni to the Book of Esther*; for a complete English translation of Targum Sheni, see idem, *The Two Targums of Esther*; For a German translation, see B. Ego, *Targum Scheni zu Ester: Übersetzung, Kommentar und theologische Deutung* (Texte und Studien zum Antiken Judentum 54; Tübingen: J. C. B. Mohr [P. Siebeck], 1996). It is a separate question in its own right how much overlap there is between the midrashic expansions and the expansions found in the Greek versions of Esther. M. Zipor, "When Midrash Met Septuagint: The Case of Esther 2,7," *ZAW* 118 (2006), pp. 82–92, discusses one small parallel, but it would be valuable to research if there are any others and why those particularly. For some broad comparisons between the Greek Additions and the Targum Sheni, see also Ego, *Esther*, pp. 78–84.

[39] Examples of these features are noted in several places throughout this volume. See especially Chapter 4, §III; on Targum Sheni see also Chapter 9, §I, 3.

[40] The first part of *Esther Rabbah* is on the first two chapters of the Megillah and comprise six from the ten sections of it. It has early material from the second and third centuries; see J. Tabory, "Esther Rabbah (EstR), Esther Midrashim," *Encyclopedia of the Bible and Its Reception* (Berlin: Walter de Gruyter, 2014), vol. 8, pp. 6–9 esp. 7.

Leqach-Tov on *Esther* (eleventh century);[41] Midrash *Aggadat Esther*, Midrash *Panim Acherot* (Versions A and B). Some midrashim on Esther appear also in midrashic collections such as *Priqe deRabbi Eliezer* and Midrash *Tehillim Shocher-Tov* 22.[42] Certain parts of these sources are parallel or overlap each other with a number of variations.[43] Some examples follow for the treatments of various themes and texts from Esther in the conglomerate corpus of rabbinic literature.

1   Fill in Gaps and Intertextual Allusions

As usual in the rabbinic exegesis, they commonly fill in the gaps in the biblical story of Esther as well. For instance, in the case of Mordecai's discovery of the conspiracy of Bigthan and Teresh, they ask how he learned of it (Babylonian Talmud, *Megillah* 13b, 15b; Targum Rishon to Esth 2:21–23).[44] More than once they took the biblical text far beyond its simple meaning. For example, Esth 8:16, "The Jews had light and gladness and joy and honor," is explained as if it refers to the Torah, phylacteries (*tefilin*), and so on: "Rab Judah said: 'Light' means the Torah ... 'Gladness' means a feast day ... 'Joy' means circumcision ... 'Honor' means the phylacteries ..." (Babylonian Talmud, *Megillah* 16b).

The Rabbis interpreted various biblical verses from outside the book of Esther as if they refer to Mordecai or Haman. They examined the text within its broad biblical contexts and emphasized intertextual allusions. For example:

> "For to the man that is good in his sight he gives wisdom, and knowledge and joy" [Qoh 2:26] – this, he said, is the righteous Mordecai. "But to the sinner he gives the task, to gather and to heap up" [Qoh 2:26] – this is Haman. That he may leave it to him, that is good in the sight of God [Qoh 2:26] – this refers to Mordecai and Esther, as it is written, "and Esther set Mordecai over the house of Haman" [Esth 8:2].
>
> Rabbah bar Ofran introduced his discourse on this section with the following text: "And I will set my throne in Elam and will destroy from there

---

[41] This Midrash was composed by the talmudist and poet Tobiah ben Eliezer.
[42] On these Midrashim, see also M. B. Lerner, "The Works of Aggadic Midrash and the Esther Midrashim," in S. Safrai, Z. Safrai, J. Schwartz, and P. J. Tomson (eds.), *The Literature of the Sages* (Assen: Royal Van Gorcum / Minneapolis: Fortress Press, 2006), part 2, pp. 176–229 esp. 177–193. For further discussion on Esther in different Midrashim and in Josippon (early tenth century), see Cordoni, "Zur mittelalterlichen biblischen Heldin Ester," pp. 42–44.
[43] On some parallel rabbinic texts on Esther, see D. Börner-Klein, *Eine babylonische Auslegung der Ester-Geschichte: Der Midrasch in Megilla 10b–17a* (Judentum und Umwelt 30; Frankfurt am Main: Peter Lang, 1990).
[44] See in detail, Chapter 5, §II, 10.

king and princes" [Jer 49:38]: "King" indicates Vashti, and 'princes' indicates Haman and his ten sons.

Rab Dimi bar Isaac introduced his discourse on this section with the following text: "For we are bondmen; yet God has not forsaken us in our bondage, but has extended mercy to us in the sight of the kings of Persia" [Ezra 9:9]. When was this? In the time of Haman.

Rabbi Hanina bar Papa introduced his discourse on this section with the following text: "You have caused men to ride over our heads, we went through fire and through water" [Ps 66:12]: "through fire" in the days of the wicked Nebuchadnezzar, and "through water" in the days of Pharaoh. "But you brought us out into abundance," – in the days of Haman. (Babylonian Talmud, *Megillah* 10b-11a; and there many more examples).[45]

Thus, according to the Rabbis, at least some events in the book of Esther have been prophesized already a long time before they occurred, by various Israelite Sages, poets, and prophets.[46]

2 Anachronism

Some Rabbis imagined Queen Esther as a righteous Jewish woman of their own talmudic era. They were convinced that Esther and her maidens kept kashrut: "Rab said ... he gave her Jewish food to eat .... Rabbi Yochanan said that he gave her seeds ..." (Babylonian Talmud, *Megillah* 13a). The verse "For Esther did the commandment of Mordecai" (Esth 2:20) was expounded by Rabbi Jeremiah: "[This means] that she used to show the blood of her impurity to the Sages" (Babylonian Talmud, *Megillah* 13b).

Likewise, Mordecai is described as a talmudic Rabbi, who sat in front of other Rabbis and taught them halachot regarding offerings in the Temple: "Then Haman took the apparel and the horse. He went and found [Mordecai with] the Rabbis sitting before him while he showed them the rules of the 'handful' [i.e., a meal-offering that used to be offered as a handful of fine flour; Lev 2:2]" (Babylonian Talmud, *Megillah* 16a). Thus, they present Mordecai anachronistically as if he was one of them in the period of the Mishnah and Talmud. Moreover, even Haman knew to cite a verse from the Jewish Scriptures (ibid.).[47] Esther is described as

---

[45] The English translation adapted from the Soncino Talmud.

[46] In fact, this kind of rabbinic interpretation is not fundamentally different to Christian claims that the Old Testament prophesied about Jesus. After all, many (if not all) of the authors of the material in the New Testament were Jews, who were immersed with Jewish education and interpretive methods.

[47] For additional discussion of some of these rabbinic interpretations, and others, cf. Koller, *Esther in Ancient Jewish Thought*, pp. 170–225.

one who kept the commandment to remove the leavened bread before the Passover holiday (*Qohelet Rabbah* 8:9; see below, §V, 1).

3   Divine Interference

As mentioned already, God's name and religious issues are absent in the Esther story. Talmudic Rabbis attempt to show that still God was there and acted behind the curtains. Thus, Rabbi Eleazar expounded the verse: "And Esther said, 'An adversary and an enemy, even this wicked Haman'" (Esth 7:6), saying: "This informs us that she was pointing to Ahasuerus [that is, Ahasuerus himself is 'an adversary and an enemy'], and an angel came and pushed her hand so as to point to Haman."

Furthermore, the Rabbis affirmed: "For he [i.e., Ahasuerus] went and found ministering angels in the form of men who were uprooting trees from the garden. He said to them, 'What are you doing?' They replied: 'Haman has ordered us.' He came into the house, and there 'Haman was falling' [נפל] upon the couch.' 'Falling'? It should say. 'had fallen'? Rabbi Eleazar said: This informs us that an angel came and made him fall on it. Ahasuerus then exclaimed: 'wow! Trouble inside, trouble outside!'" (Babylonian Talmud, *Megillah* 16a, see also additional example, ibid., 16b).[48]

4   Theodicy

A   The Traumatic Experience of the Jews

The Rabbis attempted to justify why the Jews of that generation should pass such a traumatic experience of near annihilation, and why there was a "hidden face" of God, that is not openly the presence or appearance of him to redeem his people. They claimed that it happened because "Israel indulged, not busying themselves with the Torah, [therefore] the enemy [an euphemism] of the Holy One, blessed be He, became poor" (Babylonian Talmud, *Megillah* 11a). Others explained this as being "because they enjoyed from the feast of that wicked one" or "because they bowed down to the image" (Babylonian Talmud, *Megillah* 12a):

שאלו תלמידיו את רבי שמעון בן יוחאי: מפני מה נתחייבו שונאיהן של ישראל שבאותו הדור
כליה? אמר להם: אמרו אתם - אמרו לו: מפני שנהנו מסעודתו של אותו רשע. - אם כן שבשושן
יהרגו, שבכל העולם כולו אל יהרגו - אמרו לו: אמור אתה - אמר להם: מפני שהשתחוו לצלם.
- אמרו לו: וכי משוא פנים יש בדבר? - אמר להם: הם לא עשו אלא לפנים - אף הקדוש ברוך
הוא לא עשה עמהן אלא לפנים.

---

[48] See also §4, B, "The Case of Vashti."

Rabbi Simon ben Yohai was asked by his disciples: Why were the enemies of Israel [a euphemism for "Israel"] in that generation deserving of extermination? He said to them: Do you answer. They said: Because they participated at the feast of that wicked one [= Ahasuerus]. [He said to them]: If so, those in Susa should have been killed [because only they have been invited and took part in the feast], not those in other parts of the world? They then said, Give your answer. He said to them: It was because they bowed down to the image. They said to him: Did God then show them favoritism [by delivering them]? He replied: They only pretended to worship, and He also only pretended to exterminate them ....

In other words, the traumatic experience of Jews was a punishment for eating non-kosher food at the banquet(s) of King Ahasuerus, or for bowing down to the image (of Haman?),[49] or for not studying Torah.[50]

B   *The Case of Vashti*

In Chapter 2 we discussed the removal of Vashti from her position as queen of Persia despite her noble decision not to appear in front of the king's drunk officials.[51] The Rabbis justified the refusal of Vashti, saying that she has been asked to appear naked, only *with her crown on her head*, in front of the drunk king and officials: להביא את ושתי המלכה לפני המלך בכתר – "Rabbi Abba said: מלכות להראות העמים והשרים את יפיה כי טובת מראה היא That she should appear with nothing on her but the crown, that is, naked" (אמר ר' אבא שלא יהיה עליה כלום אלא הכתר וערומה); *Esther Rabbah* 3:13; Midrash *Abba Gurion* 1). Despite this, they could neither understand nor accept her rebellious behavior against her husband and king. Thus, they searched for some reason to explain her refusal, while attributing it to divine interference. They expounded the case by some legendary and imaginative expositions, while inserting into the story supernatural elements that are completely absent from the biblical story: They explain the refusal of Vashti to appear in front of the king and his high officials: "Why then would she not come? Rabbi Jose ben Haninah said: This teaches that leprosy broke out on her. In a Baraita it was taught that Gabriel came and

---

[49] Differently in Midrash *Leqach Tov* on Esther, in the opening section: על שהשתחוו ישראל לצלם שהקים נבוכדנצר בבקעת דורא, שגלוי וידוע היה לפני כבודו שהם לא עשו אלא לפנים, לפיכך הפחידם השם על ידי המן לפנים, וחזר ונפרע ממנו, והחזיר את עצתו [נוסח אחר: עמו] למוטב. ("Because they bowed down to the figure that Nebuchadnezzar erected at the Valley of Dura [Babylon; Dan 3:1]. It was disclosed and known to his honor that Israel just pretended [but did not really mean to bow down], so he just frightened them by Haman, but he returned to punish Haman, [and thus] he changed his plan [another version: his people] [from bad] to good").

[50] These explanations continued to be maintained also by the medieval Jewish commentators. See, for instance, Saba, *Ketav Yad Eshkol Hakofer on Megillat Esther*, p. 28.

[51] See in detail, Chapter 2, §V, 1.

fixed a tail on her" (פרחה בה צרעת ... בא גבריאל ועשה לה זנב; Babylonian Talmud, *Megillah* 12b; cf. Midrash *Leqach Tov* on Esth 1:12).

The Rabbis also could not tolerate this unjust situation and attempted to balance Vashti's deeds and her punishment. Thus, they sought a way to find a divine justification (theodicy) for this imbalance retribution, saying that God acted measure for measure (cf. Babylonian Talmud, *Megillah* 12b). Accordingly, they looked for some inappropriate behavior that she could be guilty of, which would justify her severe punishment. They expound that she was punished on the seventh day (Esth 1:10), because she used to strip daughters of Israel naked and make them work on the Sabbath: "For a person receives measure for measure. This teaches that the wicked Vashti used to take the daughters of Israel and strip them naked and make them work on the Sabbath ... As she did, so it was decreed concerning her" (Babylonian Talmud, *Megillah* 12b: במדה שהיתה. מלמד שהיתה מודד בה מודדין לו. ושתי הרשעה מביאה בנות ישראל ומפשיטן ערומות ועושה בהן מלאכה בשבת ... כשם שעשתה - כך נגזר עליה).[52] Consequently, they named her "the wicked Vashti" (Babylonian Talmud, *Megillah* 10b). In other words, God punished Vashti exactly in accordance with her accumulated conduct. Nonetheless, this attempt of the Rabbis should be considered no more than a theodicy that justifies God of creation and history, who controls the world and judges the people in exact justice.

Other Rabbis related Vashti's destiny on her as if "Babylonian origin": "Why did this happen to her? Because she would not allow Ahasuerus to give permission to rebuild the Temple, saying to him, 'What my ancestors destroyed you want to rebuild?'" (ולמה עלתה לה כך? לפי שלא היתה מנחת לאחשורוש ליתן רשות לבנות בית המקדש, ואומרת לו מה שהחריבו אבותי אתה מבקש לבנות; *Esther Rabbah* 1 to Esth 2:1). However, these Rabbis are not aware that when Ahasuerus/Xerxes I succeeded to the royal throne of Persia in 486 BCE, the Temple in Jerusalem, which erected in ca. 515 BCE, already existed about thirty years.

V   Esther and Mordecai

Special attention has been given to the central Jewish characters of the Megillah – Esther and Mordecai – in the classical rabbinic literature. The talmudic and midrashic Sages not only avoid criticizing them, but rather praised their personalities and actions on behalf of the Jews. They attribute to them anachronistically some of their own religious manners and

---

[52] See also Targum Rishon to Esther on 1:11.

norms. Thus, they "updated" their portraits and presented them as role models for generations to come.

1 Esther

The Rabbis praised the special beauty of Queen Esther and regarded her as one of the four most beautiful women in the world: Sarah, Rahab, Abigail, and Esther (Babylonian Talmud, *Megillah* 15a). She was called "the virtuous Esther" (אסתר הצדקת) and counted among the seven prophetesses of Israel: Sarah, Miriam, Deborah, Hannah, Abigail, Huldah, and Esther (Babylonian Talmud, *Megillah* 10b, see also 13a, 14a). Accordingly, Esth 5:1: "And it was the third day, and Esther clothed herself in royalty," was expounded by Rabbi Elazar in the name of Rabbi Hanina: "This teaches that Esther was clothed in the divine spirit" (אמר רבי אלעזר אמר רבי חנינא: מלמד שלבשתה רוח הקדש; Babylonian Talmud, *Megillah* 15a).[53] In Midrash Psalms *Shocher-Tov* 22:1, 3 Esther is compared to "the deer of the dawn" (אילת השחר – זו אסתר[54]), and to "the light of Israel" (Isa 10:17; אור ישראל – זו אסתר שהאירה את ישראל כאור שחר).[55] They glorified her faithfulness to Jews and the Jewish cultural life, her righteousness and modesty (Babylonian Talmud, *Megillah* 10b; 13b). Thus, she is described as one who was careful even about the minor commandments that the Sages had fixed, for example: "'Who keeps the commandment shall know no evil thing' [Qoh 8:5a] – this alludes to Esther who was occupied with the commandment to remove the leavened bread (שומר מצוה לא ידע דבר רע – זו אסתר שהיתה עסוקה במצות ביעור חמץ; *Qohelet Rabbah* 8:9).

The Rabbis did not rebuke Esther for her decree to fast on Passover, nor for intermarriage with a non-Jewish man, King Ahasuerus.[56] Most likely because she acted so in an emergency situation in order to save the Jews, and saving life is more important and even cancels all the commandments of the Torah;[57] and because in fact she was taken to the palace by the king's decree (Esth 2:8). Consequently, they attempted also to find some excuses for her behavior as well.

---

[53] This expounding is based also on the rabbinic exegetical rule named *gezeirah shava*, which draws meaning through the analogy of similar words or phrases that appears in two different texts. Here, the word לב"ש appears in Esth 5:1 and in 1 Chr 12:18 (ET, 12:19) regarding to Amasai, who closed with a divine spirit [ורוח לבשה את עמשי], so also happened to Esther who "clothed [ותלבש] herself in royalty."

[54] Cf. also Rashi's commentary on Ps 22:1-7.

[55] See Buber, *Midrash Tehillim*, pp. 180–181; Braude, *The Midrash on Psalms*, vol. 1, pp. 297, 298–299.

[56] See in detail, Chapter 7, §III and §V.

[57] See 1 Macc 2:31–41; 2 Macc 6:11; Mishnah *Shabbath* 18:3; *Yoma* 8:6; and see the discussion by Kalimi, *The Retelling of Chronicles in Jewish Tradition and Literature*, p. 61.

In the Babylonian Talmud, *Megillah* 13a, Rabbi Meir read the biblical word לבת ("as a daughter") in Esth 2:7 as לבית ("to house"), which in rabbinic literature was seen as an equivalent to "wife."[58] But how could Esther be the wife of Mordecai and at the same time also of Ahasuerus? The struggle with this question probably brought them to state weird assertions, such as that "Esther was merely natural soil" (אסתר קרקע עולם היתה), that is, she did not collaborate nor enjoy sexual activity with the king, but she was just the inactive object of Ahasuerus' embraces (Babylonian Talmud, *Sanhedrin* 74b; *Megillah* 15a). Others denied altogether that Esther ever lay with Ahasuerus, saying that God sent to Ahasuerus a female spirit in her image that replaced her.[59] This issue bothered some Rabbis also in later generations, and they attempt to struggle with this difficult issue.[60]

In order to strengthen the position of the Megillah in the canon, Babylonian Talmud, *Chullin* 139b finds allusions for the names Haman, Esther, and Mordecai already in the Torah:

המן מן התורה מנין? - (בראשית ג,יא) "המן העץ."
אסתר מן התורה מנין? - (דברים לא,יח) "ואנכי הסתר אסתיר."
מרדכי מן התורה מנין? - דכתיב (שמות ל,כג) "מר דרור" ומתרגמינן: מירא דכיא.

Where is Haman indicated in the Torah? In the verse: "Is it [*hamin*] from the tree" [Gen 3:11].
"Where is *Esther* indicated in the Torah? – [In the verse,] "and I will surely hide [אסתיר, *asthir*] my face" [Deut 31:18].
Where is Mordecai indicated in the Torah? – In the verse: "Flowing myrrh" [Exod 30:23], which the Targum [Onkelos] renders as *mira dakia*.[61]

This expounding is based on (a) the similarities of words in spelling and in sounds (wordplay): אַסְתִּיר – אֶסְתֵּר, הָמָן – הֲמִן; (b) associatively relating of העץ (= the tree) in Gen 3:11 with העץ (= gallows) in Esth 7:9; (c) using the Aramaic translation of the idiom מר דרור in Exod 30:23 by Onkelos: מִירָא דכיא, which

[58] Interestingly, the Septuagint translates here: ἐπαίδευσεν αὐτὴν ἑαυτῷ εἰς γυναῖκα, that is, "he raised her as his *wife*." On this issue, see in detail the discussion by M. A. Zipor, *Tradition and Transmission: Studies in Ancient Biblical Translation and Interpretation* (Tel Aviv: Hakibbutz Hameuchad, 2001), pp. 211–223 (Hebrew).
[59] See *Zohar*, vol. 3 (*Raa'ya Mehaimana*), 275b: ואי תימרון שום ביש עלה דאסתאבת באחשורוש וכתה לאתלבשא בה רוחא דקדשא הדא הוא דכתיב (אסתר ה) "ותלבש אסתר מלכות" הא אמר קב"ה (ישעיה מב) "אני יי הוא שמי וכבודי לאחר לא אתן ותהלתי לפסילים". ורוחא דקדשא שכינתא חות דאיהי שם דאתלבשת באסתר.
[60] See B. D. Walfish "Kosher Adultery? The Mordecai-Esther-Ahasuerus Triangle in Midrash and Exegesis," *Prooftexts* 22 (2002), pp. 305–333.
[61] Regarding the name of Mordecai, cf. Babylonian Talmud, *Megillah* 10b: אתה קח לך בשמים ראש מר דרור ומתרגמינן: מר דכי ("myrrh, that we translate [in Aramaic], mare deki").

contains the letters of the name מרדכי and sounds like it. In the case of the name "Esther," also the context of the text in Deuteronomy that speaks about the difficulties that will befall the Israelites, helps to relate it with Esther, which talks about the awful situation of the Jews at that time. There are two Aramaic poems from the fourth to the seventh centuries attributed to Queen Esther, who prayed them just before her uninvited appearance before the king (Esth 5:1).[62]

2 Mordecai

The Rabbis in the Babylonian Talmud, *Megillah* 16b, identified Mordecai with the one who holds the same name in the lists of Ezra 2:2 // Neh 7:7, who emigrated from Babylonia to Judea in the time of Cyrus the Great. Since Mordecai lived several generations later, in the time of Xerxes I, obviously it is incorrect. They praised Mordecai no less than Esther, and called him as well "the virtuous Mordecai" (מרדכי הצדיק; Babylonian Talmud, *Megillah* 10b), and stated: "Mordecai in his generation was equal to Moses in his ... Just as Moses stood in the breach ... so did Mordecai, as it is written, 'Seeking the good of his people and speaking peace to all his seed' (Esth 10:3). Moses taught Torah to the Israelites ... so also did Mordecai ..." (*Esther Rabbah* 6:2). Thus, Mordecai is compared to Moses – the core founder and the greatest legislator of the Israelite people, and the savior of them from the Egyptian oppression. Moreover, some Rabbis say that Mordecai was equal to Abraham – the core forefather of the nation – in his generation: "Just as our father Abraham allowed himself to be cast into a fiery furnace and converted his fellowmen and made them acknowledge the greatness of the Holy One, blessed be He ... so in the days of Mordecai men acknowledged the greatness of the Holy One, blessed be He, as it says [Esth 8:17]: 'and many of the people of the land became Jews', and he proclaimed the unity of God's name and sanctified it" (*Esther Rabbah* 6:4).[63] It seems that one cannot receive a greater honor and cultural stature than the one gained by Mordecai.

---

[62] See J. Yahalom and M. Sokoloff, *Jewish Palestinian Aramaic Poetry from Late Antiquity* (Jerusalem: Israel Academy of Sciences and Humanities. Section of Humanities, 1999; Hebrew), pp. 174–180 (poems 27 and 28).

[63] For the English translation, compare M. Simon, *Midrash Rabbah Esther* (3rd ed.; London: Soncino, 1983), pp. 73–74. The notion that Abraham was thrown into a fiery furnace is found already in Pseudo-Philo, *Biblical Antiquities* 6:16–18; cf. also *Genesis Rabbah* 38:13.

VI   Purim and the Remembrance of Amalek

The Rabbis considered Haman the Agagite as an Amalekite descendant. According to the Torah, Amalek memory must be abolished forever (Deut 25:17–19 cf. Exod 17:8–16). Therefore, they made a rule that all the Jewish communities must read annually Exod 17:8–16, the story of the clash between Israel and Amalek at Refidim, as the Torah reading for Purim, and on Sabbath preceding Purim – *Shabbath Zachor* ("Sabbath of remembrance") – the Torah reading from Deut 25:17–19 (Babylonian Talmud, *Megillah* 18a). Furthermore, the *haftarah* reading at that Sabbath is from 1 Sam 15:2–34, which recounts Saul's war with Agag, the king of the Amalekite. The Rabbis connected all these biblical texts with Purim, first and foremost because they share the struggle with Amalek, Agag king of Amalek, and Haman the Agagite. Moreover, they associatively related these texts also due to the appearance of the verbal root זכר ("remember") in all of them: זכרון (Exod 17:14), זכור (Deut 25:17), נזכרים (Esth 9:28).[64] Though in 1 Sam 15:2 the author uses the parallel word פקדתי, he relates his story directly with the one in Exod 17:8–16, saying: פקדתי את אשר עשה עמלק לישראל אשר שם לו בדרך בעלתו ממצרים ("I remember that which Amalek did to Israel, how he laid wait for him in the way, when he came up from Egypt").

VII   Haman, Agag, and Amalek

At this point it is worthwhile discussing the symbolic figures of Haman, Agag, and Amalek in the Esther story as well as in Jewish thought in general. According to Esth 3:8–11, the one who spoke malicious words about the Jews and their religious laws and customs, and initiated the genocide of all the Jews of the empire, was not Ahasuerus, but rather his vizier Haman the Agagite. The term Agagite is an ethnonym, although there is no certainty about the nation labeled by such a name. The narrator associates Mordecai with King Saul (Esth 2:5; cf. 1 Sam 9:1), by relating him to Kish, one of the forefathers of Saul; similarly, Haman the Agagite may be associated with Agag king of Amalek,[65] Saul's enemy, who is mentioned in 1 Sam 15:8, 32–33.[66] Presumably, the narrator viewed Haman

---

[64] See the discussion in the Babylonian Talmud, *Megillah* 18a-b.

[65] Also, it is possible that "Agag" was used as a title of the Amalekite's kings, like "Pharaoh" for the Egyptian kings.

[66] Already Josephus Flavius considered Haman to be of "Amalekite descent" (*Jewish Antiquities* 11.209; Marcus, *Josephus with an English Translation*, vol. 6, p. 415). The talmudic Rabbis drew a genealogical line between Haman and Agag, see Babylonian Talmud, *Megillah* 13a: "that David did not kill Shimei from whom was descended Mordecai who provoked Haman … that Saul did not slay Agag

as a descendant of Agag of the Amalekites, who were considered an old
and eternal enemy of Israel (Exod 17:8–16 esp. 14–16; Deut 25:17–19).[67]
It seems that the narrator of Esther story considers the struggle between
Mordecai and Haman as a struggle between Israel/Saul and Amalek/Agag,
between "good" and "evil," "light" and "darkness." After all, Haman was
an Agagite; and Agag was the king of the Amalekites according to 1 Samuel
15. Furthermore, Haman is used as a symbolic figure of evil in Jewish literature and thought,[68] while Amalek is used as a symbol of evil tribe/
people/nation. Both were – and are – considered bitter enemies of Jews,
not only in the times of Moses, Saul, David, Mordecai and Esther and
the Jews of the Persian Empire, but since forever. The Esther story tells
that when Haman the Agagite attempted to violate the Persian principle
of political tolerance toward others, he was dramatically and completely
foiled by the clever and immediate actions of the empire's queen, Esther,
and the official Mordechai.

VIII   Reading of the Megillah

The Purim festival, which is instituted in the book of Esther, was well
known in the early Maccabean period: 2 Maccabees (ca. 143–140 BCE)
informs that the "Day of Nicanor" (the 13th of Adar) is "the day before
the Day of Mordecai" (2 Macc 15:36).[69] According to the Baraita in the
Babylonian Talmud, *Megillah* 3a, the festival of Purim was recognized by
the Temple authorities. The fact that the *Hallel* (Psalms 113–118) is not read
at Purim might be because it was not considered to be of the same stature of holiness as the feasts commanded in the Torah: Passover, Shavuot
(Weeks/Pentecost), and Sukkot (Booths/Tabernacles).[70]

---

from whom was descended Haman who oppressed Israel"; *Midrash Esther Rabbah*, Petichta [=
Introduction], 7: had Saul not saved Amalekites, there would have been no Haman (והעם שאול ויחמול
שנאמר המן זה זה ואיה בצדיקים ולצנינים בעיניכם לשכים קשים דברים לכם עושה שהוא מיניה קיימא צמחא והא אגג על
ולאבד להרוג להשמיד). This claim simply ignores the statement that "Samuel hacked Agag to pieces
before the Lord" (1 Sam 15:33). See also Targum Sheni to Esther 4:13 (Grossfeld, *The Two Targums
of Esther*, pp. 155–156). For the deliberate relationship between the Esther story and the story of Saul
and the Amalekites in 1 Samuel 15, that is, Saul and Mordecai (who were both descendants of Kish
from the tribe of Benjamin), and Haman the Agagite and Agag, king of the Amalekites, see W.
McKane, "A Note on Esther IX and I Samuel XV," *JTS* 12 (1961), pp. 260–261; Bickerman, *Four
Strange Books of the Bible*, pp. 196–197; Magonet, "The Liberal and the Lady," p. 169.

[67] Note that Agag is also mentioned in Balaam's prophecy, in Num 24:7.
[68] See in detail, Chapter 9.
[69] See Chapter 2, §II.
[70] Contra L. Finkelstein, *The Pharisees* (Philadelphia: Jewish Publication Society of America, 1938),
p. 679. Compare Beckwith, *The Old Testament Canon*, p. 295.

Megillat Esther has also a central place in the Purim liturgy: "It is a person's duty to recite the Megillah at night and to repeat it the next day" (Babylonian Talmud, *Megillah* 4a: חייב אדם לקרות את המגילה בלילה ולשנותה ביום). In other words, the Megillah must be read twice: once at the evening service of Purim, and once again in the following day, at the morning service. Everyone must recite the Megillah:

כהנים בעבודתן, ולוים בדוכנן, וישראל במעמדן - כולן מבטלין עבודתן ובאין לשמוע מקרא מגילה. מכאן סמכו של בית רבי שמבטלין תלמוד תורה ובאין לשמוע מקרא מגילה ...

The Priests at their [Temple] service, the Levites on their platform [on which they stood to sing the daily psalm], the lay Israelites [who were appointed to be present at the offering of the daily sacrifices] at their station, all cease from their service in order to hear the reading of the Megillah. (Babylonian Talmud, *Megillah* 3a; cf. Tosefta, *Megillah* 2:7)

Furthermore, some Rabbis gave priority for reading of the Megillah over any service in the Temple and even study of the Torah – one of the highest principles of Judaism: "Rabbah said: There is no question in my mind that, as between [the Temple] service and the reading of the Megillah, the reading of the Megillah takes priority … between the study of the Torah and the reading of the Megillah, the reading of the Megillah takes priority" אמר רבא: פשיטא לי: עבודה ומקרא מגילה - מקרא מגילה עדיף ...., תלמוד תורה ומקרא) מגילה - מקרא מגילה עדיף; Babylonian Talmud, *Megillah* 3b). Though women are free from many commandments, they "also must recite the Megillah, since they also] profited by the miracle" נשים חייבות במקרא מגילה, שאף הן היו) באותו הנס; Babylonian Talmud, *Megillah* 4a).

The Purim feast is celebrated as memorizing of and thanking for the redemption of the Jewish people from complete annihilation. It is not a celebration of death and revenge. The Jews make these days "the days of feasting and joy, and of sending portions one to another, and gifts to the poor," as ordered in Esth 9:22. As the death decree of Haman was most extreme and conclusive, and the redemption was extraordinary, and because all these run in the Megillah around banquets and drinking, the Rabbis stressed also the unusual amount of drinking in the Purim feast: "A man must drink on Purim until he does not recognize between 'curse is Haman' and 'blessed is Mordecai'" (Babylonian Talmud, *Megillah* 7b).

The practice of wearing costume on Purim is known in the Ashkenazic Jewish communities only since the medieval times. Apparently, it originated among the Italian Jews, particularly in Venice, at the end of the fifteenth century, and was probably copied from the Christian carnivals.

IX The Story of Esther in Jewish Thought

What accounts for the great popularity and highly valued position of the book of Esther among the Jews? Was its appeal only due to its dramatic story, lively descriptions, sharp irony, clear and beautiful style, or its noble characters, such as Esther and Mordecai (aspects that are shared with several other biblical compositions),[71] or is there some additional explanation for this? Indeed, one can interpret the words of Resh-Lakish and Maimonides, which stress the eternal presence of the book of Esther, against the background of Esth 9:27–28:

קימו וקבל היהודים עליהם ועל זרעם ועל כל הנלוים עליהם ולא יעבור להיות עשים את שני
הימים האלה ככתבם וכזמנם בכל שנה ושנה. והימים האלה נזכרים ונעשים בכל דור ודור
משפחה ומשפחה מדינה ומדינה ועיר ועיר וימי הפורים האלה לא יעברו מתוך היהודים וזכרם
לא יסוף מזרעם.

> The Jews ordained, and took upon them, and upon their descendants, and upon all who joined themselves to them, so that it should not fail, that they would keep these two days according to their writing, and according to their appointed time every year. And these days [should be] remembered and practiced in all generations and families and provinces and cities, and these days of Purim shall not fail from among the Jews, nor the memorial of them perish from their descendants.

However, something far beyond a legalistic or halachic expounding of Scripture has made the book of Esther so close to the heart of the Jewish people and so popular and central among them.

The book has an important and unique message for the Jewish people at all times and all places, a message that places it in a central position of Jewish culture, theology, and self-definition. The book of Esther is probably one of the last links in the long chain of biblical texts alluding to the Israelite/Jewish fear of annihilation. In earlier crises, God acted directly on behalf of Israel. Now, the book of Esther recounts that even in those times when the direct interference of God is unseen, God will still support his people and redeem them. This means that God will save Israel/Jews at any time and place, directly and indirectly, not just by unusual miracles, but also by acting "behind the curtain," where the specific details of his acts are invisible. To cite Mordecai: "relief and deliverance will arise for the Jews from another quarter" (Esth 4:14). In other words, in the book of Esther God does not appear openly, but he is still there behind the events, and acts on behalf of the Jews, to redeem them from

---

[71] See Chapters 2 and 3.

annihilation. The book's author preferred to state this notion by avoiding mention of God's name and any religious law or custom. He stressed the apparent absence of God also by frequently mentioning the king and his name, alongside other figures, and many banquets. This highlights the lack of religious features from the book. Esther's message is intended for Jews in general, and for those in the Diaspora in particular, namely, that God is devoted to Israel. Every generation has its "Haman," but God is constantly there to keep his promise and help his people, directly or indirectly, while acting silently "behind the curtain."[72] The author trusts that God's covenant with Israel is everlasting (Deut 7:9). He holds true to the prophetic promises, such as expressed in Isa 54:9–10 and Isa 66:22. Because the existence of the Jewish people is everlasting, he trusts, the execution of the Jews in any form and at any time and place is intolerable to God. He is confident that "Israel *is* holy to the Lord, and all who devour him shall offend (Jer 2:3). This fundamental theme emerging from Esther is similar to the message that is stated later by the Rabbis in the Haggadah of Passover.[73]

Indeed, in the Babylonian Talmud, *Megillah* 11a, Rabbi Yochanan expresses a similar notion to that of Esther, that is, God is loyal to the covenant with Israel and redeems them: זכר חסדו ואמונתו לבית ישראל ראו" כל אפסי ארץ את ישועת אלהינו" (תהלים צח, ג) – אימתי 'ראו כל אפסי ארץ את ישועת אלהינו'? - בימי מרדכי ואסתר, "'He had remembered his *covenant and his faithfulness to the House of Israel*, all the ends of the earth have seen *the salvation of our Lord* [Ps 98:3].' When 'did all the ends of the earth see the salvation of our Lord'? In the days of Mordecai and Esther" (since letters were sent to all provinces of the Persian Empire). The word חסדו, which is usually translated "goodness/kindness/love/mercy," means in this context "his covenant," as in Isa 55:3b, where חסד is parallel to ברית: ואכרתה לכם ברית עולם / חסדי דוד הנאמנים :ברית ("and I will make an everlasting *covenant* with you / even the sure *loving* promises of David"; see also Gen 24:27; 2 Chr 6:42).

In fact, this is the idea also behind the many new "Purims" (that were at times accompanied also by new "*Megillot*"), which numerous Jewish communities celebrated in the Diaspora. As in the story of Esther, their salvation from the hands of various new "Hamans" happened in such unknown and unbelievable ways, that is, miraculously but without obvious and observable miracles.[74]

---

[72] See in detail, Chapter 4.
[73] On this issue, see the details in Chapter 4, §IV (at the end).
[74] See the discussion and examples in Chapter 9.

X   The Esther Story in Art, Play, Music, and Film

Scenes from the book of Esther are recurring subjects in Jewish poetry, art, liturgy, and folk music.[75] This topic is big, and here I would like to list just some bold examples. The earliest surviving pictures of scenes from the book of Esther are those two that have been painted as early as the mid-third century in the synagogue of Dura-Europos (northeast Syria). One shows Haman leading Mordecai through the roads of Shushan (Figure 7), while people greet him. The other displays Esther, Ahasuerus, and Mordecai receiving a report of the numbers killed in Shushan (Figure 8). These scenes are placed immediately at the left side of the Torah Shrine (the niche), in the center of the western wall of the synagogue. The west wall of the synagogue is the direction toward Jerusalem. Here also is located the niche, and toward this wall faced all the prayers in synagogues. Thus, the placing of the scenes on the west wall shows the importance of the theme of Esther and Purim for the local Jewish community of Dura-Europos.[76]

A close look at the latter scene (Figure 8) shows that the throne of King Ahasuerus[77] is presented similarly to that of King Solomon:[78] The same figures of animals are painted on the sides of the steps of both thrones. In fact, the frescoes reflect midrashic sources that affirm that the throne of Ahasuerus was the same as that of Solomon. So, for example, in Targum Sheni to Esth 1:2, על כרסיה יקר מלכותיה – ... הוא כורסייה לאו דידיה ולא דאבהתי אלא כרסיה דמלכא שלמה ("'sat upon his throne' – ... this throne was neither his nor his father's but King Solomon's").[79] Midrash *Esther Rabbah* 1:12, "He [that is, Ahasuerus] thereupon made himself a throne of his own like it [i.e., like that of Solomon]." Midrash *Leqach Tov* on Esth 1:2 (eleventh century) states differently: מלמד שביקש לישב על כסא שלמה המלך ולא היה יכול ("He wished to sit on the throne of King Solomon, but he could not"); similarly in Midrash *Aba Gurion*, parasha 1, pp. 2–8. The clothing of Ahasuerus resembles late Parthian or Palymerian cloth, and Mordecai is dressed like a Parthian gentleman,[80] – a fact that reflects the admiration of the community for him.

---

[75] See, for instance, A. W. Binder, "Purim in Music," in Ph. Goodman (ed.), *The Purim Anthology* (Philadelphia: The Jewish Publication Society of America, 1952), pp. 209–221.

[76] Cf. C. H. Kraeling, *The Synagogue: The Excavations at Dura-Europos – Final Report* (New Haven, CT: Yale University Press, 1956), p. 151; B. Narkiss, "The Story of Megillath Esther in the Synagogue of Dura Europos," in I. S. Recanati (ed.), *Thoughts, Arts, and Construction* (Jerusalem: Israel's Ministry of Education, 2008), pp. 51–69 (Hebrew).

[77] See Kraeling, *The Synagogue*, plates LXIV, and the discussion on pp. 151–164.

[78] See Kraeling, *The Synagogue*, plate XXVII, and the discussion on pp. 88–93.

[79] See Grossfeld, *The Targum Sheni to the Book of Esther*, pp. 26–30 esp. 26.

[80] See the discussion by Stiehl, "Das Buch Esther," p. 4; Altheim and Stiehl, *Die aramäische Sprache unter den Achaimeniden*, pp. 195–197; D. Levit-Tawil, "The Enthroned King Ahasuerus at Dura in Light of the Iconography of Kingship in Iran," *BASOR* 250 (1983), pp. 57–58.

Figure 7   A fresco from the Dura-Europos Synagogue, west wall panel 15 (left detail):
Haman leads Mordechai through the roads of Shushan; the National Museum
of Damascus.

In medieval and modern times, manuscripts of the Megillah are beauti-
fully decorated with artistic paintings describing images and scenes of it,
depicted in the panels at the top and the bottom of the scroll. There are
numerous examples for this fact from all over Jewish Diaspora. The illustrations in Figures 9 and 10 are examples from Italy and India.

Rabbi Yehudah Halevi (1086–1142) composed a lengthy and beautiful
ballad on the book of Esther (מי כמוכך, "Who is like You"), which became a
part of the Sabbath's liturgy prior to Purim in the Sephardic synagogues.[81]
Many Ashkenazic Jewish communities in Europe composed and performed
a Yiddish play based on the Esther story – "Purim-play" (*Purim-spiel*). The
earliest *Purim-spiel* is known from Venice, 1555.[82] Also, many popular songs

[81] See I. Zemorah (ed.), *Complete Poems of Rabbi Jehudah Halevi* (Tel Aviv: Machbarot Lesifrot &
Mesada 1955), pp. 176–180 (Hebrew).
[82] See Ch. Shmeruk, *Yiddish Biblical Plays 1697–1750, Edited from Manuscripts and Printed Versions*
(Jerusalem: The Israel Academy of Sciences and Humanities, 1979; Hebrew); idem, "Purim-Spiel,"
Encyclopedia Judaica (2nd ed.; Jerusalem: Keter, 2007), vol. 16, pp. 742–746 = (Jerusalem: Keter,
1972), vol. 13, pp. 1396–1404; J. Bamberger, "Le-Haman: Ein Frankfurter Purim-Spiel: Edition,

Figure 8   A fresco from Dura-Europos Synagogue: west wall panel 15 (right detail): Esther, Ahasuerus, and Mordechai receive a report of the numbers killed in Shushan; the National Museum of Damascus.[83]

and melodies were composed on Purim and its story. In fact, continued interest in the theme of Esther is still expressed artistically to the present day.[84] Interestingly, the most modern Esther movies have been made by Christian production companies, and present Esther positively as a heroine

Kommentar und Analyse (Vorstellung eines Forschungsprojektes)," *Jiddistik Mitteilungen: Jidistik in Deutschsprachigen Ländern* 40 (2008), pp. 7–12; E. Horowitz, "Esther: Purimspiels," *Encyclopedia of the Bible and Its Reception* (Berlin: Walter de Gruyter, 2014), vol. 8, p. 28; A. Lehnardt (ed.), *Das verbotene Purim-Spiel: Le-Haman aus Frankfurt am Main* (Wiesbaden: Harrassowitz, 2021).

[83] For both frescoes, see Kraeling, *The Synagogue,* plates LXIV and LXV.

[84] For Esther's story in poetry, art, music, songs, etc., see for example, Ph. Goodman, *The Purim Anthology* (Philadelphia: The Jewish Publication Society of America, 1960).

Figure 9　Illustrated Megillat Esther, Ferrara (Italy), 1616, the National Library of Israel, Jerusalem

Figure 10   An illustrated Esther scroll from India, nineteenth century.

of the faith, in distinction to the tradition espoused by Martin Luther and his followers.[85] Thus, for example, an American-Italian religious film, *Esther and the King*, produced and directed by Raoul Walsh (1960). To mention just one more, *The Book of Esther*, an American biblical-drama film, which is directed by David A. R. White (2013). However, in contrast to this positive evaluation in modern Christian films, the Austrian-British-Dutch-Israeli Hebrew-language movie *Esther* (directed by Amos Gitai, 1986) follows in the footsteps of the critique of Esther and the book of Esther that is characteristic of several Christian and a few Reform Jewish interpretations. No wonder that some reviewers of the film were very negative. For instance, Daniel Warth stated that the film "is an artistic pretension which remains nothing but an aesthetical drill with unsophisticated political declarations [regarding the Arab-Israeli conflict]."[86]

To sum up, it appears, therefore, that alongside the Torah and Psalms, the book of Esther – the "Torah of Purim" (or "Letter of Purim," as it is named in the colophon to B-Text/Septuagint, following Esth 9:29)[87] – is one of the most popular biblical compositions among the Jews, nearly at the level of *micro Biblia* (a "miniature Bible"). That is to say, out of all the books included in the Hebrew Bible as a whole, the popularity of the book of Esther among the Jews was and is surpassed only by that of the Torah and Psalms.

Furthermore, the central place of Esther in Judaism emerges especially when one compares it with a similar kind of story about another heroine – Judith – and the book named after her, which is completely ignored in Josephus' writings as well as in the entirety of the rabbinic literature. This is the fact even though many aspects of Jewish religion are mentioned in the book of Judith (the name of God, prayers, Judith's righteousness, and so on),[88] that are completely lacking in the Hebrew version of the book of Esther.[89]

XI   Some Other Jewish Voices

As we will see in the next part of this volume, Christians have often not been sympathetic to the book of Esther and the feast of Purim that is based on it, and usually harshly criticized both.[90] Yet certain Jewish scholars have

---

[85] See Chapters 11 and 12.
[86] D. Warth, "תרגיל אסתטי," *Ha'ir – Tel Aviv-Yafo* (July 9, 1986, in Hebrew): www.cinema.co.il
[87] See Chapter 2, §IV, 2.
[88] See, for example, Judith 5:17–18; 8:4–6; 8:8, 11–27; 10:5; 12:1–5, 19, 7–8; ch. 16 (religious aspects of Judith, such as her prayers and righteousness). The verse numbering in nearly all of these passages differ in the Vulgate and/or the German compared to the Greek and English.
[89] On this issue, see also Chapter 4, §III.
[90] See the detailed discussion in Chapters 11 and 12.

also joined their campaign against the book and the feast, while adopting the Christian anti-Esther approach in accordance with Martin Luther's spirit – though without expressing explicitly or even without being aware of this.[91] It started in Germany, where Jews wished to obtain civil rights and integrate into the Christian society. Thus, the ideologist of the Reform movement, Abraham Geiger (1810–1874) asserted that the book of Esther is "lacking in taste and morality" (*geschmack-und gesinnungslos*).[92] This negative view of Geiger toward Esther is developed – probably indirectly – by three Reform Jewish scholars, in different times and places, as well as in different historical settings. However, generally speaking they were not influenced by the Reform movement as a whole, and there was – and is – even a positive approach toward Esther and Purim among some liberal rabbis.

1 Claude G. Montefiore

At the end of the nineteenth century, the founder of Anglo-Liberal Judaism and the leader of the Anti-Zionist League of British Jews, Claude G. Montefiore (1858–1938), dismissed the entire book of Esther. In his popular book, *The Bible for Home Reading*,[93] Montefiore challenges the "moral and religious worth of the book,"[94] while setting forth an assumption that "the slain apparently included both women and children. There is no fighting, but just as there was to have been a massacre of unresisting Jews, so now there is a massacre of unresisting Gentiles."[95] However, this is based on an inaccurate reading of Esth 8:11, which assumes that "destroy, kill and annihilate" refers to the children and women of the Jew's attackers, whereas it is probably intended to refer to the attackers, from whom the Jews seek to *protect* their women and children.[96] Moreover, Montefiore ignored that "all the rulers of the provinces … helped the Jews" (Esth 9:3a), just after they took their destiny into their own hands to protect themselves: "the Jews gathered themselves together in their cities throughout all the provinces of the king Ahasuerus, to lay hands *on such* as *sought their harm*" (Esth 9:2a). Esther 9:2, 5–16 describes only a defensive action. The rulers did not resist the self-defense of the Jews and even supported

---

[91] See in detail, Chapters 11 and 12.
[92] See L. Geiger (ed.), *Abraham Geiger's Nachgelassene Schriften* (Berlin: Gerschel, 1875–1878), vol. 5, p. 170; the German translation follows Horowitz, *Reckless Rites*, p. 34.
[93] C. G. Montefiore, *The Bible for Home Reading* (London: Macmillan, 1896).
[94] Montefiore, *The Bible for Home Reading*, vol. 2, p. 386.
[95] Montefiore, *The Bible for Home Reading*, vol. 2, p. 403.
[96] For a detailed discussion on this verse, see Chapter 12, §III, 2, with additional references.

them (Esth 9:3b). In any case, there is no explicit evidence that Jews killed any women or children. Montefiore, who studied Christianity and was overly sympathetic to Jesus, and rigorously promoted Jewish–Christian dialogue, was seemingly deeply influenced by the Christian anti-Esther tendency.[97] His assertion that "if the Bible had not included the Book of Esther, it would have gained rather than lost in religious value and moral worth,"[98] brings to mind the famous assertion of Luther, which is cited by his follower Christian theologians.[99]

2   Samuel Sandmel

Some decades later, the book of Esther was challenged once again, this time by an American Reform Rabbi and scholar, Samuel Sandmel (1911–1979). Sandmel taught Hebrew Bible and Hellenistic literature at the Hebrew Union College in Cincinnati, and was deeply involved with Jewish–Christian dialogue, usually adopting an apologetical approach. His view toward Esther was in fact also in accordance with Luther's line, that is, the book has a "vengeful spirit." Like Luther, he declared: "I should not be grieved if the book of Esther were somehow dropped out of Scripture."[100] Elsewhere Sandmel states: "Esther is by religious standards not a noble book. But perhaps it is a knowledgeable book."[101]

3   Schalom Ben-Chorin

In 1937–1939 four writings are published on the book of Esther and the feast of Purim. Three of them were in German: One positive by a Swiss reform pastor, one – the most noxious ever – by an influential Nazi-German journalist, and another negative one by a German Jew, while the fourth one was published in Hebrew, in Poland.

Schalom Ben-Chorin (1913–1999; until 1931: Fritz Rosenthal), was born and grew up in an assimilated family in Munich. Because of the ruthless anti-Jewish oppression of the Nazi regime in Germany, including a personal abuse, in 1935 Schalom emigrated to Jerusalem. In contrast to

---

[97] On this issue see in detail Chapter 11, §II, and Chapter 12.
[98] Montefiore, *The Bible for Home Reading*, vol. 2, p. 405.
[99] For further discussion of Montefiore and his approach to Esther and Purim, see Magonet, "The Liberal and the Lady," pp. 167–176; Horowitz, *Reckless Rites*, pp. 23–45, 251–258, 276–277.
[100] Sandmel, *The Enjoyment of Scripture*, pp. 35, 44; cf. idem, *The Hebrew Scriptures: An Introduction*, p. 497: "the story contains incidents of bloodthirsty revenge." For more details on Luther and the book of Esther, see Chapter 11.
[101] Sandmel, *The Hebrew Scriptures: An Introduction*, p. 504.

the anti-Zionist Claude G. Montefiore in Great Britain and many other reform Jews in European countries and in America, Ben-Chorin was an active Zionist. In Jerusalem he served as a journalist for some German newspapers, and gradually became a thinker of Reform Judaism, while attempting to mediate between Judaism and Christianity.

In 1938 – most likely when he was already a Reform Jew – the 25-year-old Ben-Chorin published an article where he follows (most likely without being aware) Luther's spirit regarding Esther, proposing "to erase the Purim festival from the Jewish calendar and exclude the book of Esther from the canon of the Holy Scriptures. Both, the festival and the book, are unworthy of a people that is willing to bring about its national and moral regeneration under immense sacrifice .... The book of Esther irritates me. It is not inspired by the spirit of holiness, rather it is the Song of Songs for opportunism."[102]

Interestingly, in 1937 Israel Epstein published in Warsaw his *Two Fest Days: I. 11th Adar – The Symbol of Renewed Judaism, II. Purim – The Symbol of Exile Judaism*, where he wanted to abolish Purim, seeing it as a diaspora festival.[103] Was the young Zionist Ben-Chorin aware of Epstein's material and influenced by it? Nonetheless, some months after the publication of Ben-Chorin's article, the Nazi propaganda newspaper, *Der Stürmer*, published in March 1939 the poisonous article by its founder and chief-editor, Julius Streicher of Nuremberg, against the book of Esther, the feast of Purim, and the Jews.[104] Is Ben-Chorin's article somehow related to the one by Streicher, that is, did the latter draw new impulse from the former, or it is just coincidence? It is hard to say. However, Streicher – who was influenced by Luther, as he admitted later on, in the Nuremberg Process of the Nazi war criminals in 1945–1946 – did not need anyone to inflame his sharp Nazi antisemitism. In any case, *certainly it was not* the intention of the great humanist and peace pursuer, Schalom Ben-Chorin, who loved his people and his culture, and he himself was a victim of the German Nazis.

Strikingly, in total contrast to the negative articles by Epstein, Ben-Chorin, and Streicher about Esther and Purim, stands the positive booklet

---

[102] Ben-Chorin, *Kritik des Estherbuches: Eine theologische Streitschrift*, p. 5: "Ich schlage vor, das Purim-Fest vom jüdischen Kalender abzusetzen und das Buch Esther aus dem Kanon der Heiligen Schriften auszuschließen. Fest und Buch sind eines Volkes unwürdig, das gewillt ist, seine nationale und sittliche Regeneration unter ungeheuren Opfern herbeizuführen .... Das Buch Esther ist mir zum Ärgernis geworden. Es ist nicht diktiert vom Geiste der Heiligkeit, sondern es ist das Hohelied der Opportunität."

[103] See I. Epstein (ed.), *Two Fest Days: I. 11th Adar – The Symbol of Renewed Judaism, II. Purim – The Symbol of Exile Judaism* (Warsaw: Betar, 1937), pp. 29–31. Epstein reorganized the biblical text of Esther and on p. 31 he presents a series of questions and notes (Hebrew).

[104] On this article in *Der Stürmer*, see the detailed discussion in Chapter 9, §III, 1.

on Esther published in 1937, in Munich (!), by the Swiss Reform pastor, Wilhelm E. Vischer. In 1933, the latter was forced to give up his academic position in Bethel (Bielefeld) and was expelled from Germany, for resisting the Nazis' abusive approach toward the Jews.[105]

4   Jonathan D. Magonet

The British Reform rabbi and a biblical scholar, Jonathan D. Magonet (born August 2, 1942), is the Vice-President of the World Union for Progressive Judaism. For many years he was the Principal of the Liberal Jewish seminary Leo Baeck College in London and served on the rabbinic staff at West London Synagogue. Magonet evaluated Megillat Esther and the feast of Purim positively. He sharply rejected the negative approach of Claude G. Montefiore and suggested a stimulating reading of the book of Esther.[106] Magonet concludes his essay as follows: "If we are content to treat the Megillah as a funny book to be read once a year, then perhaps we are entitled to dismiss it. But if we are to treat it with the seriousness, imagination, and care with which every book of the Bible should be approached, then it has much to teach, and more important, many profound and far-reaching questions to ask of us."[107]

5   Overall Assessment

It seems that Montefiore, Sandmel, and Ben-Chorin cannot be indicative of the Reform movement both in their time and today. Like every other denomination of Jewish society, the Reform Jewish congregations all over the world never stopped reading the Megillah and celebrating Purim. These sporadic anti-Esther voices were, in fact, marginal even in the Reform movement. Simply put, these scholars failed to read Esther within its genre and contexts, and thus they missed the essence of the book. They misinterpreted Scriptures such as Esth 8:11. Probably, their eagerness to integrate/assimilate with the larger Christian society or at least to become similar to it, caused them to overlook the anti-Jewish lines of the Christian scholars regarding the book of Esther.[108] Thus they began to argue like them, while overlooking or ignoring the broad Christian

---

[105] See Chapter 13, §I.
[106] See Magonet, "The Liberal and the Lady," pp. 167–176.
[107] Magonet, "The Liberal and the Lady," p. 176.
[108] See Chapters 10, 11, and 12.

anti-Jewish theological context. Moreover, for these "progressive" Jews an elimination of a biblical book from among the Jewish biblical canon and condemning the ancient Jewish feast of Purim, was as easy as leaving out many precious pieces of liturgy from the Jewish daily and holidays prayer books (*Siddurim* and *Machzorim*).

Nonetheless, the Rabbi of a Reform congregation in Berlin, Joachim Prinz, stated that after 1933, "people came by the thousands to the synagogue to listen to the story of Haman and Esther," which "became the story of our own lives." Prinz ends: "No one, however sensitive, minded and objected to the passages of revenge, which in the climate of peace and equality seem to have no place in Jewish life."[109] Though there are no "passages of revenge" in Esther but rather self-defense, the general intention of this Reform Rabbi under the Nazi regime is clear. If Montefiore, Sandmel, Epstein, and Ben-Chorin were in a different place at a different time, perhaps they would think differently about the Megillah and the feast, as did Joachim Prinz. Moreover, some liberal rabbis, such as Jonathan Magonet of London, rejected the negative approach toward the book of Esther, and suggested a stimulating and positive reading of it.

XII Conclusion

Like some other books, this one also was named after its core heroine, Esther, who was ready to sacrifice her life to save her people from annihilation. Second Maccabees (143 BCE), and later on Josephus, call the day of the celebration that commemorates the Jews' redemption not "Purim," but "the Day of Mordecai."

The absence of Esther and Mordecai in the Wisdom of Ben Sira possibly indicates that the book was not yet recognized as Scripture by the early second century BCE (at least by some Sages in the Land of Israel), or, alternatively, since Ben Sira does not mention *all* past Jewish figures, perhaps these were not considered as important. But Purim was well known by the early Maccabean period (2 Macc 15:36), and the Baraita in the Babylonian Talmud, *Megillah* 3a makes clear that the festival of Purim was recognized by the Temple authorities.

Esther's story was translated into Greek (the B-Text/Septuagint was translated at the last quarter of the second century or the first quarter of the first century BCE),[110] and six "Additions" were attached to it. Also,

---

[109] For the full citation of Rabbi J. Prinz, see Chapter 9, §III, 3, and the bibliographical references therein.
[110] See, in detail, Chapter 2, §IV, 2.

Josephus devoted an extensive section to recounting Esther's story, and most likely the book was included in his biblical "canon." The existence of the mishnahic tractate *Megillah* leaves no doubt that the book was authoritative by its time. Various rabbinic writings flourished around the book. In the Mishnah, the Jerusalem Talmud, and the Babylonian Talmud, a special tractate was dedicated to it, and its place is not lacking from the Tosefta. Esther was subject of special homiletical collections, such as: Midrash *Esther Rabbah*; Midrash *Aba Gurion;* Midrash *Leqach-Tov on Esther; Aggadat Esther;* Midrash *Panim Acherot* (Version A and B), and two major Targums. The book also has a respectful place in the Purim liturgy. The talmudic Rabbis made enormous effort to adapt it to their own halachic system, midrashic methods of interpretation, and theological worldview. They attempt to elevate the book and its major Jewish characters, rather than rebuke them.

In the medieval period, other kinds of commentaries were dedicated to the Megillah, in various languages, by Rabbanite as well as Karaite scholars. Verses from the book were also cited by Jewish Sages in medieval Jewish–Christian disputations. In fact, the book of Esther was never neglected.

Jo Carruthers describes Esther as "this strange and difficult book."[III] That may be true of the Christian reception of the book, as we will see in later chapters, but it does not reflect the status of the book within Judaism. Throughout the generations, Esther has not been seen as strange by the Jews, but rather it has been adored by them almost everywhere and has received immense attention. It has spawned a large number of all kinds of commentaries, essays, poetry, paintings, music, plays, comedy shows, and other works of art in all times. Alongside the Pentateuch and Psalms, it has been one of the most popular biblical compositions among the Jews, even though God's name and many aspects of Jewish religion are not mentioned in the Hebrew version of it. The great popularity and highly valued position of the Megillah among the Jews is not just due to its being a literary masterpiece, but also – and perhaps particularly – because of its important and specific religious and theological message for the Jewish people, that is: even in those times when the direct interference of God is unseen, God will still support his people and redeem Israel/Jews, and will save them at any time and place, directly or indirectly, either by unusual miracles, or by acting behind the events to redeem them from annihilation. Simply put, most Jews have seen Esther as a preeminent illustration

---

[III] Carruthers, *Esther through the Centuries*, p. 7.

of God's faithfulness to the prophetic promises, such as in Isa 54:9–10; 66:22; Jer 2:3. All these made the Megillat Esther very popular among the Jewish people and close to their heart.

Some liberal Jewish scholars have campaigned against the book of Esther and the feast of Purim, while in fact adopting the Christian anti-Esther approach. However, their voices were and are marginal and their position was not accepted even by the vast majority of Reform Jews.

CHAPTER 9

Identification of Jew-Haters with Haman
New "Hamans," "Purims," and "Megillot"

The defeat of Haman and his followers in the Persian period, which is described in the book of Esther, neither demolished Judeophobia nor ended the Jewish Diaspora. Through most of their subsequent history, the Jews were considered rootless people, who belong to any place or none, because they had been expelled from their homeland, Eretz-Israel (the Land of Israel), which was devastated, neglected, and occupied by strangers. Their attempts to maintain their own unique religion, literature, cultural heritage, and languages wherever they were among the foreign nations, repeatedly evoked xenophobia, Judeophobia, and misanthropy.[1] Almost in every generation, at least some parts of the Jewish Diaspora have experienced oppression and aggression. To paraphrase Qohelet 1:4, a generation goes, and a generation comes, but Jew-haters, antisemites and oppressors persist, either in the old familiar forms or under new covers. In response to their long and bitter exile, the Jews have often reapplied biblical stories of oppression and rescue to their own times. They have identified various later oppressors with biblical Haman, who became as a symbolic figure of evil in Jewish thought, and have accordingly established their own new "Purim" feasts, complete with new "Megillot" that recount their own experiences.

The story of the wicked Haman was frequently used to describe later oppressors of the Jews as "new Haman(s)." The following sections present this phenomenon in two areas: (§I) within creative exposition of the book of Esther, and (§II) within "new Purim" feasts and new concrete "Megillot," created after the downfall of the "new Haman(s)."[2] A third

---

[1] There are, of course, some additional specific reasons in various historical, theological, and economic contexts that caused the hostility against Jews, but this is not the appropriate place to go into detail.

[2] Similarly, various biblical and rabbinic sources, as well as some medieval and modern Jewish literature, refer to "Egypt" metaphorically as the "House of Bondage" (בית עבדים), and use this name to describe oppressors' lands, while "Pharaoh" was used to describe oppressors themselves. The metaphor בית עבדים appears in several places in the Hebrew Bible (Exod 13:3, 14; 20:2; Deut 5:6; 6:12; 8:14;

section then considers one particular case in more detail: The German Nazis were much concerned with the story of Esther, its characters and the feast of Purim, and alluded to them more than once to justify their actions against the Jews. Meanwhile, the link between the events of the Shoah and the story of Esther was also emphasized among the Jews during and after World War II (§III). Following the Conclusion (§IV), the chapter ends with an appendix that discusses Esther's presumed theological message *versus* the historical reality of Jewish history, which reflects further on the theme: theology, history, and us – a post-Shoah reading of the book of Esther (§V).

I Creative Expounding of the Book of Esther

The examples listed below are from various Jewish and non-Jewish translators and commentators of the book of Esther, as well as from some theologians, scholars, and politicians, across many centuries and various places. As a whole, they demonstrate the enduring, widespread reflection of the book within Western societies.

1   The Greek Esther: Haman as a Macedonian

As already discussed, the Greek translations of Esther include several substantial Additions, when compared to the Hebrew.³ One of these Greek Additions (E 10–14 in the B-Text) presents Haman, called "the Agagite" (האגגי) in the Hebrew version of the Megillah, as Haman "the *Macedonian*." Also in Esth 9:24, the translator of the LXX writes Μακεδών ("Macedonian")

Josh 24:17; Jer 34:13; sometimes in place of the name מצרים "Egypt," Deut 7:8; 13:6 [ET, 13:5]; Judg 6:8). Moreover, there are several Egyptian documents that talk about imposing hard work on Asian people (e.g., in agriculture, mines, and public works). For instance, documents from the time of Ramses II (1304–1237 BCE) attest to the building of his capital Per-Ramses ("the House of Ramses") by foreign forced labor. See B. Mazar, "The Exodus and the Conquest," in idem (ed.), *The World History of the Jewish People – First Series: Ancient Times*, Volume III: *Judges* (New Brunswick, NJ: Rutgers University Press, 1971), pp. 69–93 esp. 71; E. Feucht, "Kinder Fremder Völker in Ägypten," *SAK* 17 (1990), pp. 177–204; A. Loprieno, "Slaves," in S. Donadoni (ed.), *The Egyptians* (Chicago: University of Chicago Press, 1997), pp. 185–219 esp. 204–205; E. Bresciani, "Foreigners," in Donadoni (ed.), *The Egyptians*, pp. 221–253 esp. 235; and the references to the sources therein. In modern times, for instance, the *Allgemeine Zeitung des Judentums* described czarist Russia as "a land of hatred and iniquity, the great nineteenth-century Jewish 'House of Bondage,'" because Jews living there were limited within a particular region, and suffered from poverty, hopelessness, and government-inspired antisemitic discriminations and pogroms. See A. Elon, *The Pity of It All: A History of Jews in Germany, 1743–1933* (New York: Metropolitan Books, 2002), pp. 250–251, the quotation as such appears on p. 251.

³ See Chapter 2, §IV.

for the Hebrew האגגי.[4] That is, while the Hebrew version identifies Haman as the descendant of the Jews' bitter enemy, the Amalekites (in Jewish thought Amalek became a symbol of evil people/nation), this Greek version identifies him as a descendant of the Persians' bitter enemy, the Macedonians. According to these alterations, Haman was not only the enemy of Jews, but of the Persians as well. Although the Persian king appointed Haman as a vizier of his Empire, the Greek Addition E, verses 12–14, claims that Haman wished to "transfer the power of the Persians to the Macedonians."[5] Similarly, though Haman is not himself identified as a Macedonian in the A-Text (instead, he is called "a Bougean"; 8:25 = E 10), there also it is affirmed that he intended to betray Persia to the Macedonians (8:26 = E 14). Possibly these additions and emendations have been written in the Maccabean/Hasmonaean period, when the Jews struggled with the Seleucid Empire, an offshoot of the Greek (i.e., Macedonian) Empire of Alexander, which conquered Persia.[6]

2   Josephus' Rephrasing of Haman's Charges

Interestingly, in the first century CE, the Jewish historian, Josephus Flavius, found it necessary to rephrase Haman's accusations as recorded in Esth 3:8 according to such charges against the Jews that were known among several Greco-Roman scholars.[7] In *Jewish Antiquities* 11.212 he rephrases and expounds the charges of Haman in terms familiar from these Hellenistic anti-Jewish authors:

> He [i.e., Haman] went to the king and brought a charge, saying that there was a certain *wicked* nation scattered throughout the habitable land ruled by him, which was *unfriendly and unsocial* [ἀσύμφυλος "incompatible, unsuitable"].[8] They do not have the same religion, nor do they practice the same laws as other people, "but both by its customs and in practices it is the enemy of your people and of all people [ἄπαντες ἄνθρωποι]."[9] (italics added to emphasize the additions of Josephus)

---

[4] Nonetheless, in Esth 3:1 the LXX and Lucian write Γωγαῖος/Βουγαῖος. Esther 9:24 is not included in the A-Text.

[5] See Chapter 10, §I.

[6] Cf. Hengel, *The "Hellenization" of Judaea in the First Century after Christ*, pp. 24–25. Jonathan Thambyrajah suggests that the identification of Haman as Macedonian can best be explained as originating in the Greek Vorlage to the Vetus Latina; see J. Thambyrajah, "A Macedonian in the Persian Court: Addition E of Esther and the Vetus Latina," *VT* 71 (2021), pp. 743–750.

[7] See Chapter 6.

[8] H. G. Liddell and R. Scott, *A Greek-English Lexicon* (9th ed.; revised by H. S. Jones and R. McKenzie; Oxford: Clarendon, 1940), p. 265.

[9] For English translation, compare Marcus, *Josephus with an English Translation*, vol. 6, p. 417 (Greek on p. 416); cf. L. H. Feldman, *"Remember Amalek!" Vengeance, Zealotry, and Group*

3   Targum Sheni to Esther

Targum Sheni to Esther was composed in the Land of Israel. The date of the composition of the Targum is strongly disputed among scholars, ranging from the fourth to the eleventh century CE.[10] Nonetheless, while there are many Greek words and Roman names in this Targum as well as signs of Christian ideas and anti-Christian disputes, it lacks any traces of Islamic or anti-Islamic notions. Thus, it is reasonable to assume that this Targum was composed by the early seventh century, before the rise of Islam.

Targum Sheni ascribes a long speech to Haman, including a detailed expansion of his charges in Esth 3:8, which draws together numerous slanders that resemble those of other anti-Jewish authors.[11] This includes the charge that the Jews maintain unique religious laws different from those of all other peoples, such as refusing to intermarry, practicing circumcision, and – according to the accusation – engaging in unfair business practices.[12] According to this speech, in order to support his false accusations, Haman repeatedly claims that the Jews refuse to uphold the "*work of* the king" (עיבידתיה דמלכא; for the Hebrew text: דתי המלך, "*the laws* of the king"), that they curse the king in their synagogues and at their festivals, and wish him and his governors death.[13] Haman summarizes in this way the liturgies and religious rituals of Passover, the Feast of Weeks, Rosh Hashanah, the Day of Atonement, and the Feast of Tabernacle, while repeating the accusation that the Jews curse the king, call him foolish, and wish him harm (ומטיין למבעי רחמין קדם הא דימות מלכא ויתבר שלטנה).[14] He retells the story of David killing two thirds of the Moabite captives (2 Sam 8:2) as an account of what the Jews wish to do to other peoples:[15]

> We do not marry their daughters, and they do not marry ours. Is any of them taken for the service of the king, he passes the day in idleness, with all kinds of excuses, such as to-day is the Sabbath, to-day is Passover .... The day on which we want to buy something from them they call an unlawful day, and they close the market for us. In the first hour of the day they say,

---

Destruction in the Bible according to Philo, Pseudo-Philo, and Josephus (Cincinnati: Hebrew Union College, 2004), p. 58.

[10] For surveys of different opinions on the date of Targum Sheni, see Grossfeld, *The Two Targums of Esther*, pp. 19–21; Ego, *Targum Scheni zu Ester*, pp. 21–25.

[11] See Grossfeld, *The Targum Sheni to the Book of Esther*, pp. 46–48; Ego, *Targum Scheni zu Ester*, pp. 240–242, and the earlier bibliography there.

[12] Grossfeld, *The Targum Sheni to the Book of Esther*, p. 48.

[13] Grossfeld, *The Targum Sheni to the Book of Esther*, pp. 46, 47, 48.

[14] See Grossfeld, *The Targum Sheni to the Book of Esther*, p. 46. For similar accusations, see also Chapter 6.

[15] For the complete Aramaic text, see Grossfeld, *The Targum Sheni to the Book of Esther*, pp. 46–48.

"We must read the Shema" [Deut 6:4–9]; in the second hour they say, "We must pray"; in the third, "We must eat"; in the fourth they say, "We must thank the God of heaven for having given us bread and water." In the fifth they go out for a walk. In the sixth they come back. In the seventh they go to meet their wives, who say to them, "Here is some soup to refresh you after the heavy toil which the tyrannical king put on you." One day in the week they keep as a day of rest, in which they go to their synagogues, read in their books, interpret their prophets, curse our king, imprecate our rulers ....

Their unclean wives go after seven days ... and defile the water. On the eighth day they circumcise their sons, without any pity upon them, in order, as they say, thereby to differ from other nations .... In the month of Nisan they keep a feast, lasting eight days ... and they call this day Passover, and go to their synagogues, read in their books, interpret their prophets, curse our king, imprecate the governors, and say, "Like the leaven is removed from that which is unleavened, so may the kingdom of the tyrant be removed from among us, and so may we be delivered from this foolish king." In the month of Sivan they keep a feast of two days, in which they go into their synagogues, read the Shema, pray, read their law, interpret their prophets, curse the king, imprecate the governors .... A certain time they call new year, viz. the first of Tishri, in which they go to their synagogues, read their books, interpret their prophets, curse the king, imprecate the governors ... and they say, "On this day [tenth of Tishri] are our sins atoned, yea, our sins are collected and added to the sins of our enemies." They go to their synagogues, read their books, interpret their prophets, curse the king, imprecate the governors, and say, "May this foolish kingdom be blotted out from the world"; and they pray and supplicate that the king may die, that his government may be destroyed ....

When their kingdom was yet standing, there arose a king among them whose name was David, who harboured thought of evil against us, and wished to kill us and to exterminate us from the world. Two parts of us he killed and rooted out, and one part he left. Yet of those he left, he made servants .... [They] say: "We are the children of renowned fathers, and we have never subjected ourselves nor bowed to kings, neither have we obeyed governors." They send letters to every place, asking for prayers to God that the king may die, and that our rule may be destroyed .... [I]n fact, there is not a more poor and faulty people in the world than they are .... Everything they sell, they sell at an overcharged price, and everything they buy, they do not pay its value; they do not observe the laws and ordinances of the king, and the king has no advantage in tolerating them or in allowing them to exist.[16]

Most likely, the Targumist attempts to explain what Haman meant by his saying "they [i.e., the Jews] do not keep the king's laws," and why he

---

[16] For the Aramaic version, see Grossfeld, *The Targum Sheni to the Book of Esther*, pp. 46–48. The English translation is according to Grossfeld, *The Two Targums of Esther*, pp. 309–314.

claimed that "it is not for the king's profit to tolerate them" (ואת דתי המלך
אינם עשים ולמלך אין שוה להניחם; Esth 3:8c), and which arguments he used to
convince the king to accept his genocide plan. According to the Targumist,
Haman stressed the idleness and laziness of the Jews and their zealous devotion to their many religious rituals, holidays, prayers, and scriptural studies,
which consume an enormous waste of time. Thus, he argued that the Jews
are really useless for any king's service, and not even fit for everyday economic activities and trade, where they cheat and steal. In addition, they also
curse the king and wish all the very worst upon him and his servants.
Finally, the Jews are also dangerous to the very existence of the Empire: If
they only could, they would act as David did with the Moabites!

Thus, the Targumist depicts Haman as a representative of the entire
pagan and Christian world that often hates and persecutes Jews. He shows
that the triumph over Haman was a prototype of the Jews' victory over
other bitter enemies. Note that this example, like Josephus' retelling noted
above, does not explicitly link Haman to later oppressors. Instead, the passage is written *as though* Haman had really said it in his own time, without
explicit reference to any later events. It adapts the content of his speech to
reflect widespread accusations leveled against the Jews in later times.

Beate Ego highlights parallels between Haman's charges in Targum Sheni
and pagan and Christian critiques of the refusal to intermarry, the practice
of circumcision, and the motif of cursing the king.[17] Thus, the Roman
historian Tacitus leveled several similar accusations against the Jews. He
stated: "the earliest lesson they [i.e., the Jews] receive is to despise the
gods, to disown their country" (*Histories* 5.1–13 esp. 5.5).[18] Likewise, various Christian writers accused the Jews of cursing Christians in their synagogues, such as Justin Martyr, who charged them with "cursing in your
synagogues those that believe on Christ. For you have not the power to lay
hands upon us, on account of those who now have the mastery, but as often
as you could, you did so" (*Dialogue with Trypho*, 16; cf. 47).[19] Moreover,
Haman's argument in the Targum – that by keeping the Sabbath every
seventh day, as well as by holding their various holidays, the Jews show
their idleness – is also paralleled by anti-Jewish authors from antiquity. For
instance, in *The City of God* 6.11, Augustine of Hippo summarizes a lost

---

[17] See Ego, *Targum Scheni zu Ester*, pp. 244, 246, 247–248.
[18] Cf. Moore, *Tacitus in Five Volumes*, vol. 3, p. 183 (Greek on p. 182); see Ego, *Targum Scheni zu Ester*,
  p. 247, note 463, with additional examples and bibliography. See also Chapter 6, §VII.
[19] A. Roberts and J. Donaldson (eds.), *The Apostolic Fathers, Justin Martyr, Irenaeus* (Ante-Nicene
  Fathers 1; Edinburgh: T. & T. Clark, 1885; reprinted: Peabody, MA: Hendrickson, 1995), p. 202;
  see Ego, *Targum Scheni zu Ester*, p. 247, note 463, with additional examples and bibliography.

work by Seneca (4 BCE–65 CE), who "found fault with the sacred things of the Jews, and especially the Sabbaths, affirming that they act uselessly in keeping those seventh days, whereby they lose through idleness about the seventh part of their life."[20] Though Haman's accusations in Targum Sheni do not precisely match these or other known parallels, they reflect slanders that were widely repeated in later periods.

In addition, there are several interesting similarities between what the author of Targum Sheni ascribes to Haman and the later accusations by Martin Luther in his antisemitic writings, which are discussed in Chapter 11, and often repeated by other antisemites. In other words, those slanders and accusations against the Jews have a long continuity through many centuries in different periods and places, and within various cultural, religious, and political settings.

4   Midrash Esther Rabbah

Midrash Esther Rabbah 7:4 on Esth 3:1 makes analogy between the punishment of Ahasuerus' two servants, Haman and the contemporary enemy of Israel, probably a Christian:

כך מי שהראנו במפלתן של בגתן ותרש תצליבתן, הוא יראה לנו במפלתו של המן, ומי שפרע
מן הראשונים הוא יפרע לנו מן האחרונים. מה כתיב למעלה מן העניין "ויתלו שניהם על עץ,"
אף סופו של אותו האיש ליצלב.

Thus, also shall he who allowed us to see the fall, the crucifixion of the king's two servants, Bigthan and Teresh [Esth 2:21–23], allow us to see Haman's fall. He who revenged us upon the former, will revenge us on the latter also. And what is written "and they both hanged on gallows," also the end of this man will be crucifixion.

No wonder, that the Christian censors in the last quarter of the sixteenth century, the archbishop of Milan, Carlo (Charles) Borromeo (1538–1584), deleted this passage.[21]

5   Saba's Commentary on Esther in Setting of Expulsions

In 1492, King Ferdinand II of Aragon and Queen Isabella I of Castile, forced the Jews of Spain either to convert to Christianity or to move out of

---

[20] Augustine, City of God 6.11; P. Schaff (ed.), St. Augustin's City of God and Christian Doctrine (Nicene and Post-Nicene Fathers 1/2; Edinburgh: T. & T. Clark, 1886; reprinted: Peabody, MA: Hendrickson, 1995), p. 120; cf. Ego, Targum Scheni zu Ester, p. 245, note 454.

[21] See W. Popper, The Censorship of Hebrew Books (New York: Ktav, 1969), p. 85.

their kingdom. Half a decade later, in 1497, the old Jewish communities of Portugal as well as the ones newly established by the exiled Spanish Jews, were also forced to baptize, or leave.

Rabbi Abraham Saba (1440–1508) was one of those Jews who was expelled from Spain, and five years later also from Portugal.[22] Some of Saba's close family – including his wife and two sons – were among those who were forced to convert, while Saba himself, together with some other Jews, refused to accept Christianity, and was jailed for six months in Lisbon. When he was released, he was forced to leave the country, and found himself in Fez, Morocco, where he passed away about a decade later, after suffering a serious illness.[23]

These personal and national traumatic experiences found their expression in Saba's exegetical writings. In his commentary on Megillat Esther, *Eshkol Hakofer*, he cites the verse: "the king's command and his decree were heard, and when many girls were gathered together in Shushan the capital, to the custody of Hegai, that Esther was brought also to the king's palace" (Esth 2:8), and raises a series of questions regarding the behavior of Mordecai – all in light of his own and other Jews' tragic experiences in Portugal of 1497:

מרדכי צדיק וחסיד שמסר עצמו למיתה לבלתי השתחוות להמן ושם כל ישראל בסכנה, ואיך
עתה כששמע כרוז המלך שכל מי שיש לו בת או אחות שיביאה אל המלך להיותם נבעלת
לערל עובד עבודה זרה? למה לא שם עצמו בסכנה להוליכה אל ארץ גיזרה לבוא במערות
צורים או בנקיקי הסלעים עד יעבור זעם, או להוליכה למלכות אחרת, ואם אי-אפשר לעשות
לא זה ולא זה, הנה ראינו בעינינו במלכות פורטגאל בזמן הגירוש שלקחו הבנים והבנות באונס
להעבירם על דת ולהמירם, שהיו חונקים עצמם ושוחטים עצמם ונשותיהם, ובפרט בראשונה
שהגזירה לא פשטה אלא בבנים ובנות, היו לוקחים הבנים והבנות ומשליכים אותם בבורות
להמיתם בחייהם או לחנקם ולשוחטם, ולא שיראו אותם עובדים עבודה זרה. ולמה לא עשה
מרדכי אחד מאלו הדברים שעשו קטני ישראל בפורטגאל? וראוי היה למרדכי ליהרג על דבר
כזה ולא שיראה בעיניו לאסתר ביד גוי עובד עבודה זרה, ולמה המתין עד שלקחוה
בידים?....[24]

Mordecai was righteous and pious, who gave himself up to die, when he did not bow down to Haman and put all of Israel in danger, so how now when he heard the king's proclamation that anyone who has a daughter or a sister should bring her to the king, to be the sexual object of an

---

22 On the expulsion, see for example, Ch. Beinart, *The Expulsion of the Jews from Spain* (translated from Hebrew by J. M. Green; Oxford: The Littman Library of Jewish Civilization, 2002).

23 See Saba, *Ketav Yad Eshkol Hakofer on Megillat Esther*, p. 22. On Abraham Saba, see A. Gross, "R. Abraham Saba 'the Exilant of two Exiles'," in M. Beniyahu (ed.), *The Memorial Volume of Rab Yitzchak Nissim* (Jerusalem: Yad Harav Nissim, 1985), pp. 205–224 (Hebrew); idem, *Iberian Jewry from Twilight to Dawn: The World of Abraham Saba* (Leiden: Brill, 1995), pp. 18–24; Beinart, *The Expulsion of the Jews from Spain*, pp. 272, 274.

24 See Saba, *Ketav Yad Eshkol Hakofer on Megillat Esther*, pp. 39–40.

un-circumcised idolater?[25] Why did he not put himself in danger to lead her to the wilderness to hide in caves or in holes of rocks until the storm passes, or to lead her to another kingdom, and if he could do neither, *we saw with our own eyes in the kingdom of Portugal during the expulsion, that [when] they took the boys and girls and forced them to change religion and convert, that they used to choke themselves and slaughter themselves and their wives, and especially the first time that the decree did not spread except in boys and girls, they would take the sons and daughters and throw them in pits to kill them or choke them and slay them.* Why did Mordecai not do one of these things that the Israelites did in Portugal? Mordecai deserved to be killed for such a thing, and not see with his eyes Esther in the hands of a non-Jew who is an idolater, and why did he wait until they took her away in their hands ....?

Saba explains that Mordecai could not act in any of these ways because it all happened very suddenly:

כל האומר מרדכי ואסתר חטאו אלא אלא טועה, כי יש לך לדעת שלא היה להם שום פנאי
לעשות שום דבר לפי שפתע פתאום נלקחה אסתר ....[26]

Anyone who says Mordecai and Esther transgressed is mistaken, because you have to know that they had no time to do anything, since Esther was taken very suddenly ....

Thus, Saba questions the actions of the biblical character Mordecai in light of the historical experiences of the Jews in Portugal in 1497. Abraham Gross correctly noted that here Saba attempts to justify not only Mordecai, but also himself for allowing his two sons to be forcibly baptized to Christianity.[27]

Similarly, Saba links Haman and his evil plan to annihilate the Jews of the Persian Empire with the expulsion, forced conversions, humiliations and death suffered by the Jews of the Iberian Peninsula. Thus, for example, Saba questions Haman's postponing of his edict to annihilate the Jews a year later. He replies that Haman wished that during those twelve months Jews would be robbed and killed by their neighbors, and the pressure

---

[25] From a different perspective, similar questions are raised independently by the Irish clergyman, Alexander Carson in the nineteenth century, who also denies that trying circumstances justify violation of the Law. He concludes that Mordecai and Esther "were guilty in this affair. But this unaccountable ignorance of their duty prepared them to execute the part that God had allotted them in this wonderful display of his providence." See, A. Carson, *History of Providence as Manifested in Scripture* (4th ed.; New York: E. H. Fletcher, 1854), p. 26, cf. pp. 25–26, and see Chapter 13, §I, for more about Carson's reading of Esther.

[26] Saba, *Ketav Yad Eshkol Hakofer on Megillat Esther*, pp. 40–41.

[27] A. Gross, "The Reflection of Spain and Portugal Expulsions in a Commentary on Megillath Esther," *Proceedings of the Ninth World Congress of Jewish Studies* (Jerusalem: World Union of Jewish Studies, 1986), Division B, vol. 1, pp. 153–158 esp. 157 (Hebrew).

would cause them to abandon their religion in favor of another one, as the
Christians did to the Jews in Spain and Portugal:

וגם היתה כוונתו [של המן] להבהלם ולפחדים זמן רב חייהם תלויים מנגד כדי שמצד הפחד
והדאגה ימירו דתם רבים מישראל להנצל מהמיתה כי ירחמו על נשיהם חרעם ... ואין ראיה
יותר ברורה מהניסיון שראינו בעינינו שעושים האדומים לישראל כל מיני סיבות להבהילם
ולהומם, בענין שירחמו על בניהם וימירו דתם, וזאת היתה כוונת המן.[28]

And the intention [of Haman] was to terrify and frighten them for a long
time while their lives hang on, so that the fear and worry causes many
of the Israelites to change their religion in order to be saved from death,
because they are merciful to their wives and their children …. And there is
no clearer evidence than the experience we saw with our own eyes, that the
Edomites [= Christians] caused to Israel all sorts of reasons to frighten and
overwhelm them, in order that they fought for their sons and changed their
religion, and that was the intention of Haman.

Interestingly, the time from the edict to expel the Jews of Portugal to its
execution, was *eleven months*, very similar to that of Haman – *twelve
months* (Esth 3:12–13).[29] Moreover, the edict regarding the expulsion of the
Jews from Spain was announced in Adar – the month that Esther's story
took place. Though it is uncertain whether Saba composed his commentary
on the book of Esther *because* of his own and his people's bitter experiences,[30]
it is clear that he drew an analogy between the two. Saba's experiences in
the late fifteenth–early sixteenth centuries are anachronistically related to
the interpretation of the biblical text of Esther, as if "the act of the ancestors
was a sign for the sons" (מעשה אבות סימן לבנים). The commentator compares
the present situation of the Jewish people with the one in the past, and
raises difficult theological questions, which left his mind uneasy. Though
according to the Esther Story there was salvation for the Jews, and Haman
and many enemies of the Jews were killed, such salvation did not take
place in the Iberian Peninsula of Saba's time: The Jews were not rescued
and their enemies continued their life, while Jews suffered, were killed or
became baptized. Despite all of this, Saba himself kept his ancestral belief
and trust in God.

---

[28] Saba, *Ketav Yad Eshkol Hakofer on Megillat Esther*, p. 68; cf. Gross, "The Reflection of Spain and
Portugal Expulsions in a Commentary on Megillath Esther," p. 156.

[29] Cf. Gross, "The Reflection of Spain and Portugal Expulsions in a Commentary on Megillath
Esther," p. 156. The time between the edict and expulsion in Spain was three months. See also
Chapter 9, §I, no. 5.

[30] Saba composed, among others, commentaries on the Torah, Five Megillot, and Tractate Abot, already
in Portugal. Because the penalty for keeping Jewish religious books was death, he hid them, and later
was unable to get them back. Accordingly, he recomposed the commentary on Esther (as well as on
Ruth and Abot) in Fez; see his introduction in *Ketav Yad Eshkol Hakofer on Megillat Esther*, p. 22.

6   Christians as Edom and Haman

Above we cited the Spanish-Jewish commentator Abraham Saba saying: "that the Edomites [= Christians] caused to Israel all sorts of reasons to frighten and overwhelm them, in order that they fought for their sons and changed their religion, and that was the intention of Haman." Calling the Christians "Edomites" and considering their evil acts as that of Haman, was not unusual and it was known even to some Christians. Thus, in his *Von den Juden und ihren Lügen* Martin Luther refers to the Jews' complaint that Christians treat them like Haman: "First they complain to God about us, that we hold them prisoner in misery, and fiercely plead that God would save his holy people and beloved children from our violence and imprisonment, call us Edom and Haman, whereby they want God to hurt us very much."[31] While all examples discussed before and after this one are Jewish applications of Esther to their present oppressors, this is a Christian testimony (and accusation) expressed by Luther, which recounts how the Jews consider the Christians' treatment of them – like Haman.

Moreover, to vent their frustration from Christian persecutions, oppressions and hatred, some Jews occasionally compared their religious and non-religious opponents with Haman on the gallows or on a cross, including Jesus and various contemporary Christian leaders. This issue is discussed already by some scholars, and there is no need to repeat their arguments.[32] Just to illustrate the issue, perhaps it is worthwhile adding here a quotation from *History of the Jews* by Philip Henry Gosse (1810–1888): "The smart of personal insult would add pungency to the indignities with which the infuriated and intoxicated Jews would avenge the old and the new quarrel, venting their important malice at once upon Haman and Christ, upon the Amalekites and the Nazarenes; and blasphemies would be uttered, which might make the ears of those who heard tingle" (p. 228).[33] Elliott Horowitz, who cites this quotation, adds that in contemporary times "the concept of Amalek has been amplified to include not only 'Nazarenes' but also Ishmaelites and even some Israelites."[34]

Nevertheless, here I would like to stress particularly regarding Jesus (Hebrew: Joshua): Although he was a Jewish Sage who rebuked his own

---

[31] See WA vol. 53 p. 519. For the original German version, see Chapter 11, §VII, note 120. For additional postbiblical identifications of "Haman" and "Amalek" to various oppressors and adversaries of the Jews, see Horowitz, *Reckless Rites*, pp. 81–106 and 107–146 respectively.

[32] See T. C. G. Thornton, "Crucifixion of Haman and Scandal of the Cross," *JTS* 37 (1986), pp. 419–426; and recently Horowitz, *Reckless Rites*, pp. 16–18, and the additional bibliographical references therein.

[33] See Horowitz, *Reckless Rites*, pp. 17–18 esp. 18.

[34] Horowitz, *Reckless Rites*, p. 18.

people – the Jewish people – most likely because he cared and loved them and wished to bring them to what he considered as a right and good way, he was never an enemy of his people. However, throughout history many Christians discriminated and persecuted Jesus' people while ignoring these facts and abusing the name of Jesus! Yet the comparison of Jesus to Haman by some ignorant and irresponsible Jews is disgraceful. As a fellow Jew, he should not be condemned for the awful attitude of the Church and some thoughtless Christians who abused his name.[35]

7 Leopold Zunz and the German Kaiser Friedrich Wilhelm IV

In 1848, revolutionary movements sprung up all over Europe (the "Spring of Nations"), challenging royal power and demanding civil liberty. In Germany, many Jews joined and sometimes led these movements, which briefly offered the hope of finally attaining equal rights to their Christian counterparts. Among those leaders was Leopold Zunz (1794–1886), who took part in the revolution in Berlin, manned the barricade, and publicly called for the storming of the royal arsenal to arm the people. On March 5, 1848, he wrote a letter in which he states, "The bloody Day of Judgment is at hand for the oppressors of so many nations ... for the day of the Lord draws nigh. Perhaps by Purim, Amalek will be beaten."[36] Similarly, in a letter on March 17, 1848, two days before Purim, Zunz alluded to some recent anti-Jewish riots, then affirmed that "The storming mobs against the Jews in individual areas will pass by without a trace, and the freedom will remain. With these thoughts I celebrate tomorrow the remembrance of Amalek, and the day after tomorrow, Haman."[37] In this way, Zunz appears to equate tyranny with Amalek, and Kaiser Friedrich Wilhelm IV with Haman, who must soon be overcome. Unfortunately, reality proved otherwise, as the revolution was quickly smashed. The next day, on the eve

[35] To follow this line of thought, and without drawing a line between the classical prophets and Jesus, those Jews should compare also many classical prophets – such as Isaiah, Jeremiah, Ezekiel, Amos, and so on – to Haman, just because they sharply rebuked Israel and attempted to improve their moral, social, and religious behavior!

[36] "Also day Weltgericht nahet blutig für die Unterdrücker so vieler Völker ... für der Tag des Herrn nahet. Vielleicht daß künftigigen Purim Amalek schon niedergestreckt ist, Amen"; N. N. Glatzer, "Leopold Zunz and the Revolution of 1848: With the Publication of Four Letters by Zunz," *Leo Baeck Institute Yearbook* 5 (1960), pp. 122–139 esp. 129, 130; translation from Elon, *The Pity of It All*, p. 163, cf. pp. 149–183.

[37] "Die Pöbelstürme gegen Juden in einzelnen Gegenden werden spurlos wie anderer Unfug vorübergehen und die Freiheit wird bleiben. Mit diesem Gedanken feiere ich morgen das Andenken an Amalek und übermorgen das an Haman"; Glatzer, "Leopold Zunz and the Revolution of 1848," p. 132.

of Purim, a battle broke out between protestors in Berlin and the Prussian army, leaving some 230 dead, including 21 Jews, and the barricade was dismantled.[38] Though the protests did force the king to establish a new All-German Assembly in May 1848, it was short-lived, and its gains modest; the monarchy was not overthrown, and the Jews themselves came to be widely blamed for the unrest.[39]

II   Forming New "Purims" and "Megillot"

When a Jewish community was saved, one way or another, from persecution and pogrom, they celebrated it, often with reminiscences of the biblical story of Esther and the festival of Purim. Thus, the evil thoughts or plans were named "Haman's thought" (מחשבת המן).[40] Occasionally, a special scroll was composed to memorialize the event, while imitating the language, style, and literary metaphors of the biblical Scroll of Esther. They described the evil deeds of the "new Haman," and the miraculous salvation of the Jews from his hands, and celebrated the date as a "New Purim," or "Second Purim" (פורים שני) or "Small Purim" (פורים קטן), a parallel feast to the traditional "First Purim," by reading the scroll narrating the rescue and holding a Purim-meal. A special joy and meaning was attached to the feast day when it occurred in the month of Adar on the Hebrew calendar.

Over the centuries, many local Purims sprung up in various places across Europe, around the Mediterranean and elsewhere, though not all of them continued to be maintained long term. Yom-Tov Lewinsky listed about 90 feasts of such Second Purims all over the Jewish world.[41] However, Elliot Horowitz argues that Lewinsky, followed by the *Encyclopedia Judaica* and others, uncritically accepts a number of local Purims for which there is no solid evidence that they were ever actually celebrated, based purely on literary allusions to Purim in medieval literature.[42] The following discusses some well-known examples of such Purims from the Jewish Diaspora, over the centuries. Some of them include legendary elements. However, mostly they are historical or at least reminiscent of a historical core.

---

[38] Elon, *The Pity of It All*, p. 164.
[39] Cf. Elon, *The Pity of It All*, pp. 160–161, 171–183.
[40] See, for example, the Chabad Chasidic discussion of Y. Yitzchak, *Sacred Letters* (אגרות-קדש; New York: KHT, 1985), vol. 12, pp. 131–134 esp. 131, 133 (Yiddish).
[41] See Y.-T. Lewinsky, *The Book of Holidays* (Tel Aviv: Dvir & The Oneg Shabbat Society [Ohel Shem], 1955), vol. 6, pp. 297–321. For an earlier list, see Epstein, *Two Fest Days*, pp. 31–33; see also Shmeruk, "Purim-Spiel," *Encyclopedia Judaica*, vol. 16, pp. 742–744.
[42] Horowitz, *Reckless Rites*, pp. 293–315.

1   Purim Shmuel haNagid

Shmuel haNagid (lit. *Samuel the Prince*; also known as Samuel ibn Nagrela; ca. 993–1056), was an influential Hebrew poet, scholar, statesman, and vizier to King Badis of Granada, in Islamic Spain. Ibn Abbas, vizier to the king of Almeria, became jealous of him, and could not stand that a Jew had become such a powerful person in Iberia. Therefore, he wrote an accusation against Shmuel haNagid and all the Jews supporting him to King Badis. When the latter refused to listen to him and dismiss Shmuel haNagid from his high position, ibn Abbas attacked Granada, but was defeated and executed. Shmuel haNagid composed a song commemorating that event, where he compares the defeat of ibn Abbas with that of biblical Haman, links the redemption of the Jews in Granada with that of the Jews in Shushan, and celebrates the date of the defeat, on the 1st of month Elul, 1039, as a "Second Purim."[43]

The poem, *Eloha 'oz* also alludes to the battle fought on behalf of King Badis, on the 1st of Elul, 1038, to defeat king "Zuhair," the "Slavic" ruler of Almeria and his vizier ibn Abbas. In the poem, Zuhair is repeatedly referred to as "Agag," and his forces are described as "Amalek, Edom, and the sons of Keturah." Their defeat is, therefore, described as ensuring that "Amalek's memory had vanished from Spain," and the poem concludes as follows (lines 145–149):

וּפוּר מִשְׁנֶה עֲשׂוּ לָאֵל אֲשֶׁר קָם / וְסָעֵף בַּעֲמָלֵק צִיץ וּפֶארָה,
וְהַשְׁמִיעוּ בְּאַפְרִיקִי וְצוֹעַן / וְהוֹדִיעוּ בְּנֵי בֵית הַבְּחִירָה,
וְהַגִּידוּ לְזִקְנֵי פּוּם בְּדִיתָא / וְלִישִׁישֵׁי בְּנֵי בֵי רַב בְּסוּרָא,
וְקִרְאוּ אֶת שְׁמָהּ אָחוֹת לְמִקְרֵה / אֲחַשְׁוֵרוֹשׁ וְאֶסְתֵּר הַגְּבִירָה,
וְכִתְבוּהָ בְּסִפְרֵיכֶם, לְמַעַן / תְּהִי לָעַד וּמִדּוֹר דּוֹר זְכוּרָה![44]

A second Purim celebrate in honor of God / who has arisen and slain the mighty of Amalek;
announce it in Africa and Egypt / and tell it to the House of Sons of the Chosen;
and say it to the elders of Pumbedita / and to the old disciples of Rab in Sura;

[43] Cf. Lewinsky, *The Book of Holidays*, p. 305. On Shmuel haNagid, see H. H. Ben-Sasson, *History of the Jewish People*, Volume 2: *Middle Ages* (Tel Aviv: Dvir, 1969), pp. 76–79 (Hebrew); idem, "The Middle Ages," in idem (ed.), *A History of the Jewish People* (translated by G. Weidenfeld; Cambridge, MA: Harvard University Press, 1976), pp. 454–457; Y. Baer, *A History of the Jews in Christian Spain* (translated from Hebrew by L. Schoffman; Philadelphia: Jewish Publication Society, 1971), vol. 1, pp. 32–34; Y. David, "Shmuel haNagid," *Encyclopedia Hebraica* (Jerusalem: Encyclopedia Publishing Company, 1981), vol. 32, pp. 45–47 (Hebrew).
[44] See D. S. Sassoon, *Diwan of Shemuel Hannaghid: Published for the First Time in Its Entirety according to a Unique Manuscript (MS. Sassoon 589) with an Introduction and Index of Poems* (London: Oxford University Press, 1934), pp. 7–11 (Hebrew).

and make it a sister to the festival of / Ahasuerus and Queen Esther;
and write it in your books, so that it shall be / remembered forever.

This is indeed an excellent example of later Jews describing their contemporary adversaries as "Haman" and "Amalekites," and describing their triumph as a "Second Purim," in parallel to that of Esther and Mordecai. However, the idea that Shmuel haNagid founded a "Second Purim" in Granada was claimed for the first time by Haim [Jefin] Schirmann in 1936, and appears to be based solely on Shmuel haNagid's poem. There is no evidence that such a "Second Purim" was ever actually celebrated in Granada, at least not on any ongoing basis. There is no historical record of such an annual festival, at that time nor at any later point in Granada's history, nor is there any other evidence of such a practice so early (200 years earlier than the supposed next earliest "Second Purim," Purim Narbonne; on which see below). Instead, Horowitz claims that this poetic call for a "Second Purim" should be seen as a metaphor, not the actual founding of a new festival.[45] He compares this to another poem of Shmuel haNagid, which describes the defeat of another personal enemy, ibn Abu Musa, and states:

שָׁתוֹק וּכְתוֹב לְךָ טוּרִים / לְזִכָּרוֹן בְּסִפְרֶכָה,
וְתִקְרָאֵם, קְרִיאָתְךָ / בְּיוֹם שַׁבַּת בְּדָתֶכָה,
וְיִהְיוּ עַל לְבָבֶךָ / וְהוֹדַעְתָּם לְבָנֶיכָה.[46]

Now be quiet and write down these verses in your book!
And read them as your reading on Sabbath
They should be in your heart and tell them to your children.   (lines 54–56)

Horowitz states that, just as it would be absurd to think that Shmuel haNagid intended to actually replace or supplement the weekly Torah reading with his own poem, there is no reason to believe that his comparison of the defeat of ibn 'Abbas to a "Second Purim" should be taken literally, and there is no evidence that it ever *was* taken literally (until 900 years later by Schirmann). However, the poem says: read it as your reading on Sabbath (like one might read anything else) – a day that Jews are not working and have plenty of time to dedicate to intellectual activities. It does not say – as Horowitz misinterprets – that it should be read *instead* of the weekly Torah portion on the Sabbath! In any case, what we definitely have here is the earliest surviving reference to a Second Purim, and an explicit comparison of contemporary figures in the eleventh century with Haman, Agag,

---

[45] Horowitz, *Reckless Rites*, pp. 303–305.
[46] The Poem is titled: *Lecha osher*; see Sassoon, *Diwan of Shemuel Hannaghid*, pp. 26–27 esp. 27.

and Amalek. However, it is uncertain whether this came to be celebrated as an annual holiday of "Second Purim."

2 Purim Narbonne

On or before the 20th of Adar, 4596 (= 1236 CE), a Jew from northern France struck a Christian fisherman in Narbonne (Provence, southeastern France), who later died. According to the only surviving Jewish account of the incident, the injury itself was not fatal, but the fisherman's Christian doctor deliberately killed him (which seems doubtful, but who can say).[47] This individual death led the people of Narbonne to storm the entire Jewish neighborhood of the city, plunder their possessions, and threaten to annihilate them altogether. However, Don Aymeric, the governor of Narbonne, arrived with his troops and prevented the fulfillment of that desire. Moreover, he even ordered the stolen property to be returned to their rightful owners. Here is the full text of the only contemporaneous Jewish account of the event and its consequences:

שבח ותהלה לאל נורא הגדול אשר אין חקר לגדלותיו, הגבור אשר אין תכל ל[גבורותיו], הנורא
מצד מעשיו ונפלאותיו הפלא לנו פלאי עליל[ותיו] יום עשרים לחדש שנת תתקצ'ו
וארבעת אלפי[ם] קמו עלינו כל עם העיר הזאת מנרבונה להשמי[דנו] [על]ו ובאו בביתינו
ובחדרי משכבנו ולא השליטם אלהינו לפ[גוע ב]אחד מבני עמנו גם לא לעכב בידם אחד מכלי
חמדתנו כי כאשר יגשו אל שערי הבתים ושברום הכם השם בסנורים וה[יו] בבהלה עצומה
בסבת אדננו השלטון דון איימריק אשר יחי[ה] לעולם אשר עלה אחרייהם פתאם עם שוטריו
ויעציו להפר מחשבותם הרעה אשר חשבו עלינו גם כל גדולי העיר היו על[ים] [ל]עזרנו ולבטל
עאת הקמים עלינו ובביתי עלו תחלה ושברו הדלתים וספר פירוש התורה עם ספרים אחרים בזו
להם והכל [ה]שיב המחזיר אבדה לבעלים לידי. יתברך שמו ויתעלה זכרו עדי עד ולנצח נצחים
והוא אשר הראנו את כל. אל זכנו לבא אריאל חברים עם כל ישראל אמן. זה הנם היה בסבת
[יהודי] צרפתי שהכה שקץ אחד דייג על דאשו בכלי עץ ועשה [ח]בורה ושמו אותו ביד רופא גוי
ואותו רופא הרגו בעצת דייג שהיה שונא ישראל ושמו פָוְזלִינָא. ויקבצו אליו אנשים [רקים] ועשו
מה שכתוב למעלה. למען יהיה זה לזכרון בכל [העיר] ולא יעברו ימי הפורים האלה ככתבם
וכזמנם [בכל] שנה אמן אמן.
אני הכותב מאיר בר יצחק ז"ל.[48]

---

[47] As Horowitz notes (*Reckless Rites*, pp. 293–301), the summary of this incident by David Kaufman, who first suggested that this was an early "Second Purim," adds numerous details that the primary sources say nothing about (such as that the blow resulted from a dispute about business dealings). The only contemporaneous accounts of the incident are a brief note by Meir bar Isaac reproduced below, and a slightly later Christian account that accuses the Jews of ritual murder. Neither mentions any dispute about business dealings. Note also that the date of the 20th of Adar is when the riot occurred, not necessarily when the attack took place.

[48] Bodleian MS Hebrew F. 48, Fol. 63., reproduced in A. Neubauer (ed.), *Mediaeval Jewish Chronicles and Chronological Notes* (2 vols.; Oxford: Clarendon, 1887–1895), vol. 2, p. 251 (Hebrew).

Nina Caputo translates the text as follows:

> Praise and bless the Lord, so awesome that there is no measure for the greatness of his might [paraphrase of Deut 10:17], that there was Hero of who there is no limit to His heroic acts which amazed us on the twentieth day of Adar of the year 4996 [= 1236 CE] when all the people of this city Narbonne rose to destroy us; they rose and came into our homes and into our bedrooms, yet our Lord did not empower them to touch even one son of our nation, neither did they take in their hands even one Torah scroll because as they arrived at the gates of our houses and broke them down God struck them with [temporary] blindness (Gen 19:11). And a great panic spread amongst them as our lord, the Viscount Don Aymaric, may he live forever, suddenly rose against them with his guards and ministers to purge from their minds the evil which they enacted against us; and all of the notable men of the city rose to our aid and to cancel the orders of our attackers. At my house they began breaking down the doors and a book of biblical commentary and some other books were taken, but Don Aymaric returned everything that was lost into the hands of its rightful owner. May his name be blessed and his memory be exalted for eternity and for ever more for it is he who showed us everything. May our righteousness bring to Ariel [Jerusalem] those friends of the people of Israel, Amen.
>
> And this was the miracle that occurred when a French Jew struck an unclean [*sheqetz*, i.e., Christian] fisherman on the head with a wooden instrument and inflicted on him a wound which put him in the hands of a Christian (goy) doctor. The same doctor conspired with another fisherman who was a hater of Israel to kill him [the injured man]. His [the agitator's] name was Paulivina, and he gathered around him a crowd of people who did what is described above; thus this will be kept as a reminder for all that these days of Purim will not come to pass but according to their writing and at their appointed time every year (Esth 9:27), Amen Amen.
>
> I am the scribe Meir bar Isaac, may his memory be blessed.[49]

Some scholars are of the opinion that the Jewish leaders of Narbonne interpreted this salvation as a "Second Purim," and celebrated Adar 21st as a feast day likened to the "First Purim" of Esther and Mordecai.[50] Nevertheless, as Horowitz shows, there is no freliable historical evidence that the Jewish community established a Second Purim on 21st Adar or any other day. That the Jews were rescued from a riot shortly after Purim is clear from Ben Meir's account, but his exhortation that the incident be remembered "in these days of Purim" does not prove that a second Purim

[49] N. Caputo, "Regional History, Jewish Memory: The Purim of Narbonne," *Jewish History* 22 (2008), pp. 97–114 esp. 97–98.

[50] Cf. Lewinsky, *The Book of Holidays*, p. 318; Caputo, "Regional History, Jewish Memory: The Purim of Narbonne," pp. 97–114, with additional bibliography.

was established by anyone.[51] In any case, there is no good reason to doubt the essence of the story as a whole and the rescue of the Jews, given its report by an eyewitness.

3 Purim Castile

In 1339, González Martinez was identified with "the wicked Haman," because he pushed the king of the Christian Kingdom of Castile (Spanish: Castilla) to impose harsh sanctions against the Jews. He accused the Jewish tax collectors of robbing the Spanish nation. The king captured the Jewish tax collectors and tortured them to death. Later, Martinez suggested seizing the possessions of all the Jews in order to finance the war against the Muslims, and expelling them from the entire kingdom. However, "the Queen Esther" – the Christian lover of the king – convinced the king that "the wicked Haman" was undermining him, and that the confiscation of Jewish assets and their expulsion certainly would distress the kingdom. Thus the king arrested Martinez and sentenced him to death.

Solomon ibn Verga describes the incident in his book *Shebet Yehudah* (*The Tribe of Judah*), in the "Tenth Persecution" (השמד העשירי), while intensively echoing the style of the biblical book of Esther. Often, he names Martinez as "the enemy of the Jews" (צורר היהודים), similar to the biblical Haman (Esth 8:1; 9:24).[52] According to Lewinsky, the Jews announced that day as "Second Purim," and celebrated yearly a feast day for all Castilean Jews. They composed "Castile Megillah," which recounted the story of the event and read it publicly on the same day every year.[53]

4 Purim Saragossa

According to "Megillat Saragossa," the Jewish community of Saragossa (Aragon, Spain), was under great danger in 1420, but was miraculously saved: The Jews of the city were commanded to attend a public reception honoring the king with all their Torah scrolls. However, the Rabbis of the community decided that it would be better to remove the scrolls from their cases, because the king would not notice the difference. A converted

---

[51] Cf. Horowitz, *Reckless Rites*, p. 294.

[52] See S. ibn Verga, *The Tribe of Judah* (edited and introduced by Y. Baer; Jerusalem: Bialik Institute, 1947), pp. 52–55, 170–175 (Hebrew). For a detailed account of this incident, and a brief discussion of its association with Esther (though without reference to a Second Purim), see Baer, *The History of the Jews in Christian Spain*, vol. 1, pp. 354–360.

[53] Lewinsky, *The Book of Holidays*, p. 315.

Jew named Marcos informed the authorities of the Rabbis' plan, saying that the Jews do not respect the king, and therefore they are not bringing the real Torah scrolls. The king was furious, and ordered the Jews to open the cases. A fear fell upon the Jews, because the punishment for disobeying the king was very severe, but they had no choice but to open the cases. Behold! They were astonished to find that all of the cases contained the holy scrolls. What they could not have known was that on the previous night, the custodian of the synagogue had a dream in which the prophet Elijah appeared to him and ordered him to replace the scrolls in their cases, and he acted accordingly. Thus, the king admitted that the Jews were blameless, and he ordered Marcos to be killed for his false accusation. The Rabbis established a "Second Purim" and composed the "Megillat Saragossa" to be read and celebrated on the 17th and 18th of Shevat, which is kept in many communities until this day. The Megillah ends with the words: "Damned Marcos, and blessed Ephraim the custodian, damned all the wicked and blessed all Israel ...."[54]

The legendary elements of this account are obvious. Moreover, Horowitz notes that the earliest evidence we have for Megillat Saragossa is from the eighteenth century, and the entire account is thoroughly stylized, so that no direct connection to any historical king can be determined. Some copies give a date of 1380, others of 1420.[55]

5 Megillat Mizrayim

Although "Megillat Mizrayim" (the "Egyptian Scroll") is not explicitly related with the book of Esther or Purim, its name and its story awake a connotation of the latter. It was discovered in the Cairo Genizah of the Ben-Ezra Synagogue which was brought to Cambridge, UK in 1898 by Solomon Schechter. This exists in a number of copies, and has five or six leaves, but is not complete. The Megillah was written in 1012 CE, in Hebrew, probably by Shmuel haShlishi ben Hoshana, and tells in a poetic narrative the story of the community (including himself): "A public disturbance at a Jewish funeral procession provoked violence, mass arrests followed, and a Fusṭāṭ judge sentenced 23 members of the Jewish community to death. As was their right under Islamic law the leaders of the Jewish community appealed directly to the Caliph al-Ḥākim bi-Amr Allāh

---

54 Cf. Lewinsky, *The Book of Holidays*, p. 314; Ch. Beinart, "Saragossa," *Encyclopedia Judaica* (2nd ed.; Jerusalem: Keter, 2007), vol. 18, pp. 41–45 esp. 44.
55 See Horowitz, *Reckless Rites*, pp. 279–286.

in Cairo. He declared that the Muslim witnesses had lied and released the condemned Jews."[56] The story was recited annually in the synagogue to celebrate the occasion:

> ... in the land of Egypt ... In the thirteenth year of his [al-Ḥākim's] reign he guided all of the kingdom with magnanimity and good judgement. He did not need a vizier, nor a counsellor. A number of conspirators conspired against him and a number of adversaries rose up against him, and God cast them down beneath the soles of his feet, because he loved righteousness and hated wickedness. He appointed judges in the land and ordered them to give fair judgements and dispense lawful verdicts. He banished men of violence and turned away the wicked. He abhorred those of perverse ways or shameful deeds. He loved prudent men, the establishing of justice and the right path. Now, on the third day of the month of Ševaṭ in the year four thousand seven hundred and seventy of the Creation of the World ... They trod them down and beat them in the streets. The people were terrified and fled for their lives. Some of them ran away; some of them hid. Some of them offered bribes of money; some of them stripped off their clothes. Some of them were thrown into wells; some of them had their hands chained; and some their legs fettered. From among the people they picked out twenty-three men, and they took them away to prison, [putting them] in two cells. In a space the size of a manger, they remained overnight, hungry as well as thirsty. And they took a few of their clothes in payment for their rations.[57]

6   Purim Mizrayim

Ahmad Pasha of Mizrayim was appointed governor of Egypt by the Turkish Sultan in 1523, but shortly after rebelled against him and declared himself the Sultan of Egypt. In order to pay for his rebellion, this "new Haman" terrorized the Jews and Christians with his decrees and demands of taxes and gifts. According to the earliest Jewish account, written by Elijah Capsali shortly after the events themselves (in his book *Ḥasdei haShem*; completed in ca. 1524), Ahmad Pasha attempted unsuccessfully to extort a huge amount of

---

[56] Fragments 3–4 and fragment 2; for images, transcription and translation of the manuscript T-S 8K10, which is one of the earliest and best-preserved copies, see https://cudl.lib.cam.ac.uk/view/MS-TS-00008-K-00010/1

[57] See Fragments 3–4 and fragment 2. Another copy of the Egyptian Scroll is here: https://cudl.lib .cam.ac.uk/view/MS-TS-00008-J-00034-00003/1. The first person to publish the text was the early twentieth-century historian of the Genizah, Jacob Mann. Yosef Yahalom included an edited version of the Egyptian Scroll in his work on Samuel's poetry: http://cul.worldcat.org/oclc/891808730?referer=brief_results (העשירית במאה בירושלים ההנהגה מראשי :השלישי שמואל רבי יוצרות). For a complete bibliography for the manuscript T-S 8K10, see: https://cudl.lib.cam.ac.uk/bibliographies/genizah/search?query=MS-TS-00008-K-00010&queryType=CLASSMARKID.

money from the local Jewish leader, Abraham Castro, and caused additional hardships and persecutions, turning the usual festivities of Purim to mourning.[58] A slightly later account, written by Joseph ibn Verga in 1553, who claimed to be merely summarizing the fuller account in an already-existing Megillah, states that Ahmad Pasha demanded that the Jews bring him two hundred pieces of silver by the 24th of Adar, or be executed. They were only able to collect a small portion of the required sum, but on the appointed day when they arrived at the palace to give the payment, they were told that Ahmad Pasha had been attacked in his bath and fled. Three days later he was caught and killed by soldiers loyal to the Turkish Sultan, on the 27th of Adar, 1524.[59] Though Capsali does not mention it, already by ibn Verga's time, that day was being celebrated as "Purim Mizrayim" (or "Purim Cairo"), on which they would read the "Megillat Purim Mizrayim" (מגילת פורים מצרים) to commemorate the day of the salvation of the Jews of Cairo. This continued to be celebrated for many generations, eventually becoming a two-day festival from the 27th to the 28th of Adar.[60]

This is one of the earliest local Purims for which we not only have outside attestation for some of the events described in the Megillah (including from Ottoman sources), but also independent evidence of the festival's celebration over many centuries, including the account by ibn Verga from 1553, just 30 years later. References to the annual celebration of the festival also appear in sources from the seventeenth century and later, and it continued into at least the early twentieth century.[61]

7   "Second Purims" in Other Mediterranean Lands

Incidentally, the same Elijah Capsali who described the events in Cairo in 1524 later became the head of the synagogue of Candia, on the Island of Crete, where yet another similar incident occurred in 1538, when the Christian residents of the city responded to a rumor that the Jews were secretly conspiring with the Turks, and stormed the Jewish quarter. Capsali appealed to the island's governor, who intervened to prevent bloodshed on the 18th of Tammuz. Three years later, in 1541, Capsali called for a new

---

[58] Cf. Horowitz, Reckless Rites, pp. 286–287, with bibliography.
[59] This version appears in an appendix to Joseph ibn Verga's father's book Shevat Yehudah, first published in 1553, which claims to be summarizing a fuller account in a Megillah; cf. Horowitz, Reckless Rites, p. 288.
[60] See A. Ben Yoseph (ed.), Megillath Purim of Egypt ([no publisher information], 1997; Hebrew). See particularly on pp. 33–35 where verses from the book of Esther are rewritten. See also A. Ashtor, "Egypt," Encyclopaedia Hebraica (Jerusalem and Tel Aviv: Encyclopaedia Publishing Company, 1972), vol. 24, pp. 237–242 esp. 240 (Hebrew); Horowitz, Reckless Rites, pp. 286–289.
[61] Cf. Horowitz, Reckless Rites, pp. 288–289.

"day of feasting and merrymaking" on the 18th of Tammuz, a practice that appears to have continued until the twentieth century, though Capsali himself did not refer to it as a "Second Purim."[62]

Additional local Purims also appear about the same time elsewhere around the Mediterranean, including the "Purim Edom" (in Arabic, Purim al-Nasara) in Algiers, celebrating the failure of the Spanish King Charles V's attempt to seize the city in 1541, and the Purim Morocco, established under similar circumstances in 1578 (Purim Sebastiano or Purim Cristianos).[63]

8 Purim Frankfurt or the Vintz-Purim

In 1612–1616, the German antisemite Vinzenz Fettmilch[64] led an uprising of the guilds in Frankfurt am Main. On August 22, 1614 he led a crowd that stormed the Jewish neighborhood (i.e., the *Judengasse*, lit. "the Jewish Lane"; see below fig. 11), plundered the property of the 1380 Jews who lived there, while devastating their synagogues and cemetery. According to the text that appears under the engraving by Georg Keller, "1380 persons old and young were counted at the exit of the gate" of the city of Frankfurt, and herded onto ships on the river Main, and expelled.

Later, when the expelled Jews were allowed to return to Frankfurt, one of the members of the Jewish community, Elhanan bar Abraham (Helen), who was an eyewitness of the events, composed *Megilo Efu* (מגילת עפה – היא מגילת עיר פראנקפורט המעטירה), where he tells the story of the persecution, and names the wicked Fettmilch the new Haman.[65] From then on, the date of the return was celebrated annually as the *Vintz-Purim*,[66] for over 200 years, with a merry march of the Purim Qaddish, to commemorate the return.

Christopher R. Friedrichs mentions allusions to Esther in the early Jewish accounts of the incident, and cites a Jewish poem from the period, the "Das Vintz-Haß Lied" (i.e., "Vintz Hatred Poem") recited during the Vintz-Purim, in which Fettmilch would describe himself as "your Haman in these times."[67]

[62] On these events, see Horowitz, *Reckless Rites*, pp. 290–293, with bibliography.

[63] See Horowitz, *Reckless Rites*, pp. 305–306.

[64] The various spellings of "Vintz," "Vinz" or "Vins" all refer to the first name of Fettmilch Vincenz.

[65] See A. Rosenlicht (ed.), *Megilo Efu* (מגילת עפה – היא מגילת עיר פראנקפורט המעטירה; Krakau: A. Rosenlicht, 1880); R. Ulmer, *Turmoil, Trauma and Triumph: The Fettmilch Uprising in Frankfurt am Main (1612–1616) According to Megillas Vintz* (Judentum und Umwelt 72; Bern: Peter Lang, 2001). Ulmer provides a critical edition of the Hebrew and Yiddish text of *Megillas Vintz*, translated into German and English, and accompanied with introduction and bibliography.

[66] S. A. Baron, *A Social and Religious History of the Jews* (2nd ed.; New York: Columbia University Press / Philadelphia: The Jewish Publication Society of America, 1969), vol. 14, pp. 196–197.

[67] C. R. Friedrichs, "Politics or Pogrom? The Fettmilch Uprising in German and Jewish History," *Central European History* 19 (1986), pp. 186–228 esp. 198–199.

Figure 11   Matthäus Merian, Riot in the *Judengasse*, Frankfurt am Main (August 22, 1614), engraving, ca. 1642.

9   *Megillat ha'Atzmaut*

In a radio broadcast on the fifth anniversary of Jewish State independence in 1953, the Israeli Minister of Education, Ben-Zion Dinur, suggested that the 1948 Declaration of Independence (*Megillat ha'Atzmaut*) should be celebrated with candles, flowers, wine and a festive meal, reminiscent of Purim and Megillat Esther.[68] Presumably, it was just a coincidence that they used a term reminiscent of *Megillat* Esther to name their Declaration of Independence, *Megillat ha'Atzmaut*.

10   *Haman, Amalek, Purim, and the Muslim/Arab–Israeli Conflict*

After an attack on the Muslim community in Hebron, on Purim 1994, by Dr. Baruch Goldstein, at least one Rabbi called for a new Purim.[69] Also, a declaration on November 12, 2004 by the group *Pikuach Nefesh*, a group of approximately 200 Rabbis, proclaimed that the death of Yassar Arafat "should be a day of rejoicing," because he was "the Amalek and the Hitler of our generation."[70]

Moreover, the president of the Islamic Republic of Iran from August 3, 2005 to August 3, 2013, Mahmoud Ahmadinejad, who repeatedly called for the complete annihilation of the State of Israel (or, in his words, the "Zionist regime"). He constantly, declared that Israel should be "wiped off the map."[71] Consequently, the Jews all over the world compared and identified Ahmadinejad with the well-known biblical Jew-hater Haman and with that of the modern time, Adolf Hitler.

Turkey Islamist president, Recep Tayyip Erdoğan, asserted numerous antisemitic statements against Israel, its people, army, government, and leaders. His fabricated claims are described as clearly Haman-like. The Israeli newspaper, *The Jerusalem Post*, suggested awarding him with the "Amalek award" for his most outrageous and poisonous antisemitism.[72]

III   The Esther Story, Purim, and the Nazi Germans

Among the many instances of oppression and deliverance through Jewish history, however, one in particular – the Shoah/Holocaust – stands out as

---

[68] Cf. Horowitz, *Reckless Rites*, p. 313, with bibliography.

[69] Horowitz, *Reckless Rites*, p. 315, with bibliography.

[70] Cf. Horowitz, *Reckless Rites*, p. 3, citing the daily Hebrew newspaper *Haaretz*, from November 12, 2004.

[71] See, for example, the article of H. Cooper and D. E. Sanger, in *The New York Times* from June 4, 2006; *The New York Times*, retrieved May 12, 2010; as well as in an address to the United Nations General Assembly on September 23, 2008, and many other occasions.

[72] See the article of S. Weiss in *The Jerusalem Post*, March 25, 2019.

a uniquely significant parallel to Esther. This is not only because it came the closest to fulfilling Haman's genocidal plans, but also because the Jews as well as their persecutors – the German Nazis – appealed to Esther and Purim to explain some situations. On the one hand, the Nazis themselves showed considerable interest in Esther's story, characters, and the feast of Purim. On the other hand, associations between the events of the Holocaust and the story of Esther and between Haman and Hitler were commonly invoked among Jews during and after the Second World War.

1   "The Murder Feast"

Julius Streicher (1885–1946), the founder and chief editor of *Der Stürmer – Deutsches Wochenblatt zum Kampfe um die Wahrheit*, published in March 1939 an essay that calls the Jewish Festival of Purim "The Murder Feast" (*Das Mordfest*).[73] Streicher justified Haman's decree to exterminate the Jews of the Persian Empire, claiming: "At that time the Jews were settled all over Persia, and requisitioned to themselves all trade and commerce. They lived as an alien race, exploiters and destroyers of the culture according to their own special laws."[74] The Jews were saved, continues Streicher, due to a "prostitute" (*Dirne*) called Esther, who made the king crazy, and the latter finally cancelled Haman's decree. The Jews performed a huge massacre of their opponents and became the lords of the land. On Purim, says Streicher, "the Jews celebrate with this festival a mass-murder of 76,000 Persians. And they celebrate with all the hate, with all the vindictiveness and with all the bloodlust that still animates them today."[75] Streicher then quotes a letter from an anonymous German in Tel Aviv, who claims to have witnessed in 1934 a "Purim carnival" in which an effigy of Haman was made to look like Hitler, and carried by a crowd dressed in brown, like the members of the pro-Nazi "Sturmabteilung" (SA), paramilitary supporters of the National Socialist party: "There they then celebrate their Purim-carnival. Already since the Middle Ages it is customary that in connection with the processions, a puppet of Haman is hanged or burned. Such also

---

[73] Julius Streicher, "Das Mordfest," *Der Stürmer: Deutsches Wochenblatt zum Kampfe um die Wahrheit* 17 no. 13 (March 1939), pp. 1–2, available online, Internet Archive: https://archive.org/stream/DerStuermer-DasJahr1939/1939#page/n13/mode/2up

[74] "In dieser Zeit saßen die Juden schon im ganzen Perserland und hatten Handel und Wandel an sich gerissen. Sie lebten als fremdrassige Ausbeuter und Kulturzerstörer nach ihren eigenen Gesetzen"; Streicher, "Das Mordfest," p. 1.

[75] Streicher, "Das Mordfest," p. 2: "Sie feiern mit diesem Fest einen Massenmord, begangen an 76,000 Persern. Und sie feiern es mit all dem Haß, mit all der Rachsucht und mit all der Mordgier, die sie heute noch ebenso beseelen."

occurred in the year 1934 in Tel Aviv. In the procession a whole group of brown-clothed figures marched (who should be our SA men), and then a Haman-puppet was burned, who bore the unmistakable features of our leader [*Führer*, that is, Adolf Hitler]."[76]

Moreover, Streicher adds, "when they mention 'Haman' in the synagogues they think of 'Hitler.'"[77] Streicher claims that the secret Torah of the Jews orders them to slaughter non-Jews on Purim, claiming that in the Talmud, *Megillah* 6b, it is stated that "Two Rabbis, Rabbah and Zera, held a Purim-festival meal together. Because at the Purim festival one should slaughter a non-Jew as replacement for Haman, so Rabbah stood up and slaughtered Zera. He was so drunk, that he could no longer distinguish Jew and non-Jew."[78] This is, in fact, a misquotation or rough paraphrase of a text in the Babylonian Talmud, *Megillah* 7b, which states that:

> Rabbah said: It is the duty of a man to mellow himself [with wine] on Purim until he cannot tell the difference between "cursed be Haman" and "blessed be Mordecai." Rabbah and Rabbi Zera joined together in a Purim feast. They became mellow, and Rabbah arose and cut Rabbi Zera's throat. On the next day he prayed on his behalf and revived him. Next year he said, will your honor come, and we will have the Purim feast together. He replied: A miracle does not take place on every occasion.[79]

The actual text of the Talmud says nothing about any custom of slaughtering a non-Jew on Purim, nor claims that this was the reason Rabbah killed Zera; it only states that they were so drunk that Rabbah unintentionally killed Zera, then miraculously brought him back to life.

In order to show that this obviously legendary account reflects actual practice, however, Streicher then appeals to the infamous story of the murder of Father Thomas of Damascus and his servant in 1840, which

---

[76] "Dort feiern sie dann ihren Purim-Karneval. Schon seit dem Mittelalter ist es üblich, daß man in Verbindung mit den Maskenzügen eine Hamanpuppe aufhängte oder verbrannte. So geschah es auch im Jahre 1934 in Tel Aviv. Im Maskenzug zog eine ganze Reihe braun angezogene Gestalten (es sollten unsere SA-Männer sein) und dann wurde eine Hamanpuppe verbrannt, die unverkennbar die Züge unseres Führers trug." (Streicher, "Das Mordfest," p. 2). Interestingly, Isaac Bashevis Singer describes the atmosphere among the Jews in Warsaw on the eve of the Second World War, where one of his characters calls "the murderers" (= Nazis) "the Hamans, whose end will be bad and bitter, like others before them"; see I. Bashevis Singer, *Shosha* (Tel Aviv: Am Oved, 1978), p. 169 (Hebrew).

[77] Streicher, "Das Mordfest," p. 2.

[78] Cited by Streicher, "Das Mordfest," p. 2, "Zwei Rabbiner, Rabba und Zera, hieltern zusammen das Purimfestmahl ab. Da man am Purimfeste einen Nichtjuden als Ersatz für Haman schlachten soll, so stand Rabba auf und schlachtete Zera. Er war so betrunken, daß er Juden und Nichtjuden nicht mehr unterscheiden konnte."

[79] Translation from I. Epstein, *The Babylonian Talmud: Seder Mo'ed* (London: Soncino, 1938), vol. 4, p. 38.

Streicher claims was performed by the Jews as a ritual slaughter in order to use his blood for cultic rituals. Streicher refers here to the blood-libel of Damascus, where thirteen Jews were imprisoned and tortured due to false accusation of murdering a Christian monk, Father Thomas, for Passover ritual purposes. He ignores the historical fact that an international committee discussed the Damascus blood-libel in Alexandria (August 4–28, 1840) and secured the release and recognition of innocence for the nine prisoners who had survived the tortures. The committee also issued an edict intended to stop the spread of blood-libel accusations in the Turkish Othman Empire. Streicher's repetition of the libel is therefore undeniably a piece of toxic Nazi propaganda in support of a modern Haman, Hitler and his National Socialist party, seeking the "final solution" of the Jews wherever they existed.

The Nazi Streicher did not invent the labeling of Jews as bloodthirsty murderers, nor was he the first to connect this to the Esther story. As will be seen in Chapter 11, already Martin Luther used this kind of expression.[80] Moreover, as detailed in Chapter 12, these kinds of accusations have been made by many Christian scholars, particularly Germans, for a long time before, and occasionally even after, the Shoah. Streicher merely used them to support Nazi antisemitism, as if to say that these "facts" are known already since the Persian period.

On a day following *Pogromnacht/Kristallnacht* (November 10, 1938), Streicher concluded that like "the Jew slaughtered 75,000 Persians" in one night, the same destiny would have befallen the German people had the Jews succeeded in inflaming a war against Germans; the "Jews would have established a new Purim festival in Germany."[81]

2   *"A Second Triumphant Purim"*

In a speech marking the eleventh anniversary of the Third Reich, delivered January 30, 1944, Adolf Hitler predicted that, if the Nazis should be defeated, the Jews would celebrate it as "a second triumphant Purim," implicitly identifying himself with Haman.[82]

Horowitz states that the Nazis "seem to have taken a perverse pleasure in suffusing Jewish holidays with suffering and slaughter." He notes that, among other cases, on Purim 1942, ten Jews were hanged in Zduńska

[80] See, for example, WA, vol. 53, p. 433 lines 15–21; and Chapter 11, §VII esp. note 98.
[81] See R. L. Bytwerk, *Landmark Speeches of National Socialism* (College Station, TX: A&M University Press, 2008), p. 91.
[82] See Horowitz, *Reckless Rites*, p. 91, with bibliography.

Wola (Poland) to "avenge" the hanging of ten sons of Haman.[83] In a similar occasion on Purim 1943, the Nazis in Piotrokow informed the Jews living in the ghetto that there was to be an exchange of Jews for Germans living in the colony of Sarona (near Tel Aviv), and that they needed ten volunteers with university degrees who were willing to emigrate to Palestine, for the exchange. The volunteers, however, were taken to a nearby cemetery to be shot, seemingly in a deliberate inversion of the execution of the ten sons of Haman. That the number ten was deliberate is evident from that fact that only eight volunteers were found, so the Nazi's also executed the cemetery watchman and his wife, to fill out the number.[84]

3   "We Read Haman the People Heard Hitler"

Before, during and after the war, many Jews identified Hitler and the Nazis as the modern (spiritual) descendants of Haman and Amalek, who must be defeated. For example, Joachim Prinz, Rabbi of a Reform congregation in Berlin, stated that after 1933, "people came by the thousands to the synagogue to listen to the story of Haman and Esther," which "became the story of our own lives." He continued:

> It was quite clear that Haman meant Hitler ... When Haman's plot was announced, it bore a strange resemblance to Hitler's plot to wipe out the Jewish people. Many came to ask me if Hitler had ever read the story of Haman. It was so identical with his own designs for the Jewish people. Then the turning point came. Haman was demasked and exposed to disgrace and death .... Every time we read *Haman* the people heard *Hitler*, and the noise was deafening .... Outside in the streets and in the homes, one could not talk against Hitler, but here in the synagogue there was no limit to our rejection. No one, however sensitive, minded and objected to the passages of revenge, which in the climate of peace and equality seem to have no place in Jewish life.[85]

Similarly, in 1941 the Chief Rabbi in Great Britain, Joseph Hertz, gave a sermon that denounced "Amalek's latest spiritual descendant" and argued that the war against him must not merely be left to God, but be "carried

[83] See A. A. Cohen and P. R. Mendes-Flohr (eds.), *20th Century Jewish Religious Thought: Original Essays on Critical Concepts, Movements, and Beliefs* (Philadelphia: Jewish Publication Society of America, 2009), p. 948.

[84] Horowitz, *Reckless Rites*, p. 91, following M. Gilbert, *The Holocaust: A History of the Jews of Europe during the Second World War* (New York: H. Holt, 1986), pp. 552–553, with discussion of additional examples.

[85] J. Prinz, "A Rabbi under the Hitler Regime," in H. A. Strauss and K. R. Grossmann (eds.), *Gegenwart im Rückblick: Festgabe für die Jüdische Gemeinde zu Berlin 25 Jahre nach dem Neubeginn* (Heidelberg: L. Stiehm, 1970), pp. 231–238 esp. 235–236. Prinz notes that similar links were also perceived with Passover and (especially) Hanukkah (ibid., pp. 234–236).

out by ... men and nations filled with an endless loathing of Amalek and all his works and ways."[86]

4 *"Purim Hitler" of Casablanca and Other Holocaust Survivors*

It is not surprising that when the Nazis were defeated, some celebrated this as a new act of divine rescue from Amalek and Haman. For instance, the Jewish community of Casablanca in Morocco was saved from the hands of Nazis by American forces on the second day of Kislev, 5703 (November 11, 1942). To memorialize the event, a special *Megillat Hitler* was composed for public reading, to celebrate this day that the Jews were saved from the hands of "the new Haman," a day that "was turned from sorrow to joy, they should make it a day of feasting and joy, and of sending portions one to another, and gifts to the poor" (cf. Esth 9:22). It concludes: "Damned Hitler, damned Mussolini, cursed Himmler, cursed Goering, damned Goebbels, damned Hess ...."[87]

Many Jews did celebrate the end of the war as a new Purim, and not just in Casablanca. Horowitz remarks that in the Displaced Persons camp in Landsberg (Bavaria), where survivors were gathered immediately after the war, they celebrated a week-long Purim festival in March of 1946, in which they burned a copy of *Mein Kampf* and carried effigies of Hitler. One of the participants later wrote that "It was [a day] of such elation, I have never seen anything like it .... Hitler and Haman now had their due."[88]

IV Conclusion

This chapter discusses identification of Jew-haters with biblical Haman during the history of the Jewish people since the time of Esther. It provides many examples from different times and places for the creative expounding of the story and figures of Esther, as well as the feast of Purim. It also details many cases where new "Hamans" were identified, and their downfall celebrated with new (or Second) "Purims" and new "Megillot." Among these, it especially emphasizes the connections between the Esther story and the Shoah, drawn both by the Nazis themselves and the Jews during and after the Second World War.

---

[86] Quotations from Horowitz, *Reckless Rites*, p. 143.

[87] The citation is from the last chapter of *Megillat Hitler* according to P. Chasin; see Lewinsky, *The Book of Holidays*, p. 309.

[88] Horowitz, *Reckless Rites*, p. 92, quoting T. Blum-Dobkin, "The Landsberg Carnival: Purim in a Displaced Persons Center," in *Purim: The Face and the Mask, Essays and Catalogue of an Exhibition at the Yeshiva University Museum, February–June 1979* (New York: Yeshiva University Museum, 1979), pp. 53–57 esp. 55, 57.

Several rabbinic sources stress the notion that "every generation and [i.e., has] its expounders, every generation and its administrators, every generation and its leaders, every generation and its prophets, every generation and its heroes, every generation and its crimes" (דור דור ופרנסיו, דור דור ודורשיו, דור דור ודורשיו, דור דור ופשעיו, דור דור וגבוריו, דור דור ונביאיו, דור דור ומנהיגיו).[89] To paraphrase this notion: every generation has its "Haman(s)," every generation has its "Esther(s) and Mordecai(s)," and every generation has its "Purim" and "Megillat Purim."

Generation after generation, Jews all over the Diaspora as well as in the Land of Israel identified their own contemporary persecutors and enemies with the biblical Haman and Amalek. They celebrated the day of deliverance as a feast day named "Second Purim," while sending gifts to each other and supporting the poor people, composing the stories of their own "Hamans" and the great miracles of their time, as "new Megillot," and reading them in their synagogues.

However, the Jews as a people – though not always as individuals – have somehow repeatedly been saved from the total annihilation that their enemies prepared for them. They have continued to solidly trust that the God of Israel eternally keeps his covenant with his chosen people, and that he will save them in some way. Generally speaking, the Jews believe that the words in Ps 37:12–15 remain valid forever, as concretely illustrated in the book of Esther: "The wicked plots against the righteous, and gnashes at him with his teeth. The Lord laughs at him; for he sees that his day is coming. The wicked have drawn out the sword, and have bent their bow, to bring down the poor and needy, and to slay those who are of upright ways. Their sword shall enter into their own heart, and their bows shall be broken" (זמם רשע לצדיק וחרק עליו שניו. אדני ישחק-לו כי-ראה כי-יבא יומו. חרב פתחו רשעים ודרכו קשתם להפיל עני ואביון לטבוח ישרי-דרך. חרבם תבוא בלבם וקשתותם תשברנה).

V Appendix: Esther's Theological Message *versus* Historical Reality

As the examples discussed in this chapter demonstrate, more than once Jewish communities have indeed been saved from destruction and annihilation almost miraculously. However, this was not always the case.

---

[89] *Abot deRabbi Nathan*, Version A, ch. 31 (in the name of Rabbi Joshua ben Korchah, fourth generation of the Tannaites). For different versions of the saying, cf. the Babylonian Talmud, *Abodah Zarah* 5a (in the name of Rabbi Simeon Resh-Lakish); *Leviticus Rabbah* ch. 26 (in the name of Rabbi Joshua of Sachnien, fourth generation of the Amorites in the Land of Israel); and *Seder Olam Rabbah*, end of ch. 30 (anonymous).

On other occasions, the deliverance did not come at all or was delayed and came only after many lives had already been destroyed. Across history, Jews have faced repeated pogrom and slaughter, often without rescue, especially – but by no means exclusively – in the Shoah, when more than six million Jews were murdered by the Nazis and their collaborators. Hitler may have fallen, but not before he succeeded in carrying out Haman's plans – and worse – across much of Europe. Consequently, the question arises: Is the claim that God always protects his people from destruction credible,[90] given the numerous times that the Jewish community *has* faced persecution and destruction? In what follows, I will briefly review the presumed theological concept of Esther against the background of Jewish historical reality and present a few examples from the last millennium in which deliverance did *not* occur (no. 1), then concisely review several post-Shoah readings of Esther among contemporary Jews (no. 2).

1   The Historical Reality

Tragically, "relief and deliverance" does not *usually* characterize the Jews' bitter and long exile, despite the prediction by the author of the book of Esther.[91] To quote Rabbi Zera's expression, "a miracle does not take place on every occasion" (Babylonian Talmud, *Megillah* 7b). Sometimes divine salvation happened, as in those cases discussed above, but other times not at all, for example:

In 1096 CE, the Crusaders slaughtered thousands of the Rhineland's Jews and demolished their flourishing institutions and communities, particularly in Mainz, Worms, and Speyer. The motto was: "Cross or Death!" Thousands of Jews were slaughtered, and no divine redemption was seen on the horizon.

Circa 400 years later, a shocking event took place on another side of Europe: the expulsions of the Jews from Spain (1492) and Portugal (1497). All attempts at diplomacy did not make up for the cruel acts of the "Hamans." Then, not only God did not redeem his people, but it seemed as if he even joined the Jews enemies. To cite Isaac Abarbanel: "I saw God face to face fighting with his people, his portion of inheritance" (ראיתי אלהים פנים אל פנים נלחם בעמו חבל נחלתו).[92]

---

[90] See, in detail, Chapter 4. Interestingly, the literary manifestation of this theological feature – including paraphrasing of Esth 3:13 – is used in the modern story "The Act of Rabbi Gadiel the Infant," by the Israeli writer, S. J. Agnon (*Elu veElu* [Complete Writings of Samuel Joseph Agnon 2; Jerusalem: Schocken Publishing House, 1978], pp. 416–420 [Hebrew]).

[91] For some exceptions to this rule, see above, §II.

[92] See in detail, Kalimi, *Fighting over the Bible*, pp. 259–260.

The massacre of the Jews during the Bohdan Khmelnytsky Uprising in Polish-Lithuanian Commonwealth (1648–1649) and the following waves of horrible pogroms and massacres all throughout the Jewish communities that continued until 1657, caused about 100,000 Jews to be slaughtered and 744 Jewish communities to be destroyed.

Furthermore, there was horrific devastation of the Iranian Jewish communities, for example, in Tabriz (at the end of the eighteenth century), as well as forced conversions to Islam in Mashhad (1839) and horrible pogroms in Barporosh (= Babol, Iran, 1865),[93] and massacres in Damascus (1840), and Kishinev (1903, 1905).

During the Second World War (1939–1945), all the worst fears of the Jews became realities in the ghastly *Shoah* (Holocaust). Once again, "relief and deliverance" did not come for the European Jews from any quarter, and Esther's theological view did not turn into reality. Though, despite that, many Jews did celebrate the end of the war as a new Purim,[94] still one-third of the Jewish people had been annihilated in the most horrible machinery genocide in human history! It looks as if God's presence was completely removed: he simply was not there – neither by direct revealing nor by hidden action!

2 *Theology, History, and Us: A Post-Shoah Reading of Esther*

At the time of the expulsion of the Jews from Spain and Portugal, the contemporary Jewish exegete, Abraham Saba, was aware of the paradoxical contradiction between Esther and the historical reality of his time. In his commentary on the book of Esther, he laments that during those evictions, it was not the case that "many of the people of the land became Jews" (Esth 8:17), but rather that thousands of Jews were forced to be baptized, to become Christians. For the others, there was no "joy and gladness, a feast and a good day" as in Esther (8:17), but there was humiliating expulsion or death.

Yet, in our time the question that arises is, are we, the post-Shoah readers of the book of Esther, still supportive of Esther's theological message?

---

[93] Because the fate of the Iranian Jewry is relatively unknown, note the following studies: A. Netzer, "The Fate of the Jewish Community of Tabriz," in M. Sharon (ed.), *Studies in Islamic History and Civilization in Honour of Professor David Ayalon* (Jerusalem: Brill, 1986), pp. 411–419; idem, "Persecution of Iranian Jewry in the 17th Century," *Pe'amim* 6 (1980), pp. 32–56 (Hebrew); idem, "The History of the Forced Converts of Mashhad according to Ya'kov Dilmaniyan," *Pe'amim* 42 (1990), pp. 127–156 (Hebrew); idem, "The Jews in the Southern Coast of Caspian Sea, 1. Jews in Mazandaran until the End of the 19th Century," in A. Haim (ed.), *Society and Community: Proceedings of the Second International Congress for Research of the Sephardi and Oriental Jewish Heritage 1984* (Jerusalem: Mesgav Yerushalayim, 1991), pp. 85–98 (Hebrew).

[94] See above, §III, 3.

Or, in the words of Exod 17:7, "is the Lord among us, or not?"[95] Of course, each of us is entitled to answer such a question from her or his own religious viewpoint and understanding. Nevertheless, there are three main approaches amongst the contemporary Jews toward this issue. The following offers a brief engagement with them:

One approach is characterized as theodicy, that is, justification of God and all his actions throughout history. To cite Ps 145:17 "The Lord is righteous in all his ways, and gracious in all his works" (צדיק יהוה בכל דרכיו וחסיד בכל מעשיו); or in rabbinic dictum: "Whatever the All-Merciful does is for good" (כל דעביד רחמנא לטב עביד)![96] From this perspective, the Shoah happened for the Jews who did not keep the covenant with God, and it is as described already in Deuteronomy 28 (see also 29:13–14).

Others hold the opinion that the Shoah was a test/trial (ניסיון) by God, of the Jews as a collective, just as he tested individuals such as Abraham and Job (Gen 22:1–19; Job 1). Therefore, we should continue to keep the Torah and the commandments even better than before, improving our treatment of each other, and so on. This approach leads, in fact, to self-reproach and religious fundamentalism. The Chasidic Chabad movement explains the tragedy of the Shoah as "the agonizes of Messiah" (חבלי משיח), that is, tortures prior coming of Messiah who will redeem Israel.

Another approach is of the opinion that the absence of God in the Shoah shows that there is no God whatsoever! To cite an Aramaic-rabbinic dictum, "[there is] neither justice nor judge" (לית דין ולית דיין),[97] that is, the world is run in an anarchic and nihilistic way, there is no God who makes order and justice.[98] If God exists, then how could it be that the Shoah took place? If he chose Israel and loves the Jewish people, then why did he create the Crusaders, Khmelnitzky, Hitler, and many others to slaughter them? This approach leads, therefore, to atheism or total secularism and the abandonment of the entire Jewish religious heritage, including its all-essential values, which developed during thousands of years shedding blood, sweat, and tears.

The most common approach takes the "middle road," that is, despite all the horrible historical experiences of the Jews, it is affirmed that the central theological message of Esther remains valid. The Shoah should be considered as stated in Ps 34:20 (ET 34:19): "Many are the afflictions of the righteous, but the Lord rescues them from all" (רבות רעות צדיק, ומכלם

---

[95] Cf. Deut 31:17b: "So that they will say on that day, are not these evils come upon us, because our God is not among us?"

[96] Babylonian Talmud, *Berachot* 60b; and in 60b–61a, it is stated also in Hebrew: כל מה שעשה הקב"ה הכל לטובה.

[97] For this dictum, see *Genesis Rabbah* 26:6; Targum Pseudo-Jonathan (/ Yerushalmi) on Gen 4:7.

[98] For description of such heretical thoughts, see for instance, I. Bashevis Singer, *The Penitent* (Tel Aviv: Sifriat Poalim, 1986), pp. 91–92 (Hebrew).

יציל‍נו יהוה).[99] In fact, after everything and despite all, "the Jewish People are alive!" (עם ישראל חי!). According to this view, God basically kept the promise that is stated in Lev 26:44–45, "And yet for all that, when they are in the land of their enemies, I will not cast them away, nor will I loathe them, to destroy them entirely, and to break my covenant with them; for I am the Lord their God. But I will for their sakes remember the covenant of their ancestors, whom I brought forth out of the land of Egypt in the sight of the nations, that I might be their God; I am the Lord." We are entitled to ask difficult questions but still to continue to hold to our religious belief; to cite Jer 12:1, "O Lord, you are just, but I will dispute with you!" Why? How could you let this happen?

Nevertheless, the Shoah was, first and foremost the failure of human being, particularly of the Western Christian culture, which committed the terrible crime despite the clear-cut divine commandments such as "You shall not kill" (Exod 20:13 // Deut 5:17; cf. Gen 9:5–6), "you shall love your fellow/neighbor as yourself" (Lev 19:18), and "if a stranger sojourns with you in your land, you shall not wrong him, but the stranger who dwells with you shall be to you as one born among you, and you shall love him as yourself" (Lev 19:33–34).

In any case, after the genocide of the European and a portion of the North African Jews, the Jewish community must read the Hebrew Bible in general, and the book of Esther in particular, differently. This reading should not stoop to either fundamentalist theodicy or fall into depression and denial of God, uprooting him from among us. It should be read critically but also with responsibility for current and coming generations; with belief but still with an open mind, and create renewed hopes for the benefit of all.[100]

---

[99] The first part of this verse is cited already in 4 Macc 18:15 (the first half of the first century CE), regarding the story of the martyrdom of the mother and her seven sons.

[100] On this issue, see in general also E. Fackenheim, *The Jewish Bible after the Holocaust: A Rereading* (Bloomington, IN: Indiana University Press, 1990) – in which Haman is likened to Hitler; T. Linafelt (ed.), *Strange Fire: Reading the Bible after the Holocaust* (The Biblical Seminar 71; Sheffield: Sheffield Academic Press, 2000) – this book that discusses different issues and biblical books is relevant in general, but does not discuss Esther; Sweeney, *Reading the Hebrew Bible after the Shoah*. The latter dedicates three and half pages to discuss the book of Esther (pp. 219–222), though in fact most of it is a summary of the biblical story (including some imprecise assertions, such as: "the slaughter of some seventy-five thousand *members of Haman's family*," ibid., p. 219, italics mine) and brief reception history of the book in Judaism and Christianity, while saying too little on post-Shoah reading of Esther in one tiny paragraph (middle of p. 220 that repeats at the end of p. 222). His conclusion regarding the purpose of the composition of Esther is quite inaccurate and stands in opposition to the one that is developed in Chapter 4 of this volume.

It is worthy to note that some Christian scholars – Catholic as well as Protestant – also became aware that after the Shoah it is necessary to read the Bible differently, for example, Friedrich-Wilhelm Marquardt, Franz Mußner, and Erich Zenger; see in detail I. Kalimi, "Religionsgeschichte Israels oder Theologie des Alten Testaments? Das Jüdische Interesse an der Biblischen Theologie," *JBTh* 10 (1995; 2nd ed.: 2001), pp. 45–68 esp. 54; idem, *Early Jewish Exegesis and Theological Controversy*, p. 117.

PART III

Divine or Demon?
Esther among the Christians

CHAPTER 10

Esther in the Christian Canon, Interpretation, Tradition, and Culture

I The Christian "Book of Esther" *versus* the Jewish "Megillat Esther"

Through generations, Jews and Christians have both considered all chapters of the book of Esther as one unit – *Megillat Esther* or the book of Esther – without questioning its literary unity or textual development, as scholars do since the advent of modern critical biblical scholarship. Still, Esther has been preserved in quite different versions among Jews and Christians. While the Jews read the short Hebrew version of the book (the Masoretic Text), it was the longer version of the Septuagint (B-Text) that was primarily used by the Roman Catholic and Eastern Orthodox Christians.[1] Accordingly, whereas the Jews and most Protestants have read the shorter (and probably older) Hebrew version of Esther, Catholic and Orthodox Christians have read the longer (and probably later) version, which includes the six major additions and many minor variations in comparison to the Hebrew text/MT. In other words, there are enormous differences between the Esther story that is read by Jews and the one that has been read by most Christians. Thus, for example, according to the MT version of Esther, Haman asked to destroy all the Jews because Mordecai did not bow down to him (Esth 3:5–6). However, although the refusal of Mordecai to bow appears also in the Greek B-Text, its Addition A – the prologue (before MT Esth 1:1) – claims that the main reason for Haman was because Mordecai brought Bigthan and Teresh to their death by uncovering their conspiracy against the king: "But Haman ... sought to do harm to Mordecai and his people because of the two eunuchs of the king." This is one of many differences in how particular characters are portrayed in the Greek B-Text compared to the Hebrew.

---

[1] As already mentioned above, four medieval manuscripts preserve a shorter Greek version known as the Alpha-Text (A-Text, or the Lucianic [= L] Text). For a detailed discussion of both Greek versions, see Chapter 2, §IV.

Furthermore, while the MT version of Esther lacks any references to God, and Mordecai's actions remain without explicit religious justification, in the Greek, Mordecai is attributed a prophetic dream (like those of Joseph and Daniel) which affirms that the people of Israel will cry out to God and he will redeem them (Addition F, verses 6–9). In Addition C, both Esther and Mordecai pray to God for deliverance. The book concludes with Mordecai's interpretation of his dream, stating that "From God these things have come," and "my nation, this is Israel, who cried out to God and were saved. The Lord has saved his people, and the Lord has rescued us from all these evils, and God has done signs and great wonders that have not happened among the nations" (Addition F, 1, 6).[2] According to Addition C verses 5–7, Mordecai explains that he did not bow down to Haman, "it was not in insolence nor pride nor for any love of glory that I did this, namely, to refuse to do obeisance to this prideful Haman ... But I did this so that I might not set human glory above divine glory, and I will not do obeisance to anyone but you, my Lord." In Addition D, verses 12–21, Esther prays to God and mourns the situation, puts on mourning clothes, and instead of cosmetics, she puts dirt and dung on her head, and leaves her hair unkempt. The same addition states that Esther did not eat from the king's food nor drink his (non-kosher) wine, and that she hated to sleep with the king. Thus, while no form of God's name nor any religious custom and institution are mentioned in the Hebrew version, all these appear in the Greek (and Latin) versions.[3]

The Greek versions also include more positive references to the king, who is identified as Artaxerxes (Ἀρταξέρξης) in the Septuagint, but "Assueros" (Ἀσσυήρος) in the Alpha-Text.[4] For example, they include a second reference to Mordecai discovering the plot against the king, which says that he *did* receive "gifts" for this service (Addition A, verse 16), implicitly denying the negative portrayal of the king as forgetful in the Hebrew version. In Addition B, verse 2, the king even says that, despite having conquered the whole world, he has no presumption of authority, and seeks to rule with moderation and with kindness. In Addition D, the king is described as full of "glory" and "gentleness" (verse 8), and Esther praises him as "wonderful" and "full of graciousness" (verse 14). In Addition B, verse 3, even Haman is represented as one who is "conspicuous among us for his

---

[2] English translation of the Additions here is according to Jobes, "Esther," in Pietersma and Wright (eds.), *A New English Translation of the Septuagint*, pp. 426–440.
[3] For a list of some additional minor – but very important – differences between the Hebrew and the Greek versions, see Chapter 4, §III.
[4] Cf. Hanhart, *Esther*, p. 131.

balanced judgment," a matter that does not appear in the Hebrew version, though in Addition E he is harshly condemned as "being unable to restrain his arrogance, he made it his business to deprive us of our rule and our breath and by the crafty deceit of ruses asked to destroy Mardochaios [i.e., Mordecai], our savior and constant benefactor, and Esther, the innocent companion of our kingdom, together with their whole nation. For when by these methods he had caught us undefended he thought that he would transfer the power of the Persians to the Macedonians" (Addition E, verses 12–14), that is, he betrayed not only the Jews, but the Persians as well.[5] It goes on to conclude that he "has been crucified at the gates of Susa with his whole household, since the God who prevails over all things has recompensed him quickly with the deserved judgment" (Addition E, verse 18).

All in all, the Greek versions present a totally different impression of the story: They begin and end with prophetic dreams of Mordecai, and even the king and Haman are portrayed more positively, while Esther and Mordecai take the time to mourn and pray, and Mordecai gives a religious reason for his refusal to bow down to Haman. Above all, the name of God and his direct involvement are explicit and clear, and the Jewish characters behave according to expected religious norms.[6] Thus, Jews and most Christians each read a very different version of Esther story.

II   Anti-Jewish Trends in Esther's Greek Translations

There was a long hesitation among Christians whether or not to include the book of Esther in the canon, and even far later, some Christian religious leaders (such as Martin Luther) expressed strong animosity toward the book, complaining especially of its "Jewish" character.[7] But the earliest signs of anti-Judaic expansions could be seen already within the Greek translations of Esther and in one of the Additions to the book. For Christians, who read the Greek/Latin version of Esther, their view of Jews was probably influenced from these texts:

(a) In both the Septuagint (B-Text) and the Alpha-Text (A-Text) of Esther, there is an addition (in comparison with the Hebrew version) after verse 3:13 ("Addition B"), which supplies the text of Haman's edict. The

---

[5] Regarding the presentation of Haman as one who betrayed the Persians to Macedonians, see also Chapter 9, §I, 1.

[6] Note the many similarities between some of the Additions in the Greek versions of Esther and the attempts to fill in gaps in the story in the talmudic and midrashic literature; see Chapter 8, §IV, particularly no. 3.

[7] See below, Chapters 11 and 12.

B-Text includes a claim regarding the Jews that: "this nation stands constantly all alone in opposition to all humanity, perversely following an estranging manner of life due to their laws and since it is ill-disposed to our interests, doing the worst harm and in order that our kingdom may not attain stability." In the A-Text, the addition reads, in part: "the nation stands all alone in its way of life which is contrary to every one of humanity on account of an estranging way of life due to their laws and since it is ill-disposed to our commands, it perpetually does the worst harm, in order that we may never be established in the sole-rule directed by us."[8]

These additions in the Greek texts were probably inserted by a Jewish Hellenized translator, who put these accusations in the king's first letter (i.e., in fact, Haman's letter that has been sent to all the people of the empire) in order to exaggerate Haman's accusations even more than that stated in the original Hebrew text, showing how great a Jew-hater he was.[9] Alternatively, did such descriptions of the Jews reflect the anti-Jewish atmosphere in contemporary Alexandria of the later scribes who copied Esther and inserted into it these texts? Or perhaps of a late Christian glossator who revised the text in such a way to present the Jews in a gloomy light? It seems that for the time being these questions should be left open.

(b) According to the Hebrew version of Esth 9:13, Queen Esther requested that the king of Persia allow the Jews of Shushan/Susa "to do according to the edict for today." It means to let Jews of Shushan protect themselves from their enemies in the city, and to hang Haman's sons, in order to frighten others.[10]

In the Alpha-Text this request is stylized as a much more aggressive request, which depicts Esther negatively: "to kill and to plunder whomever they might desire" (A-Text 9:46). In other words, to kill and plunder not only those who frightened the Jews, but anyone, anywhere in the Persian Empire, that they might desire! Note, according to the MT parallel text, Esther does not ask the king to permit the Jews to plunder their enemies, and later the author stresses: "but on the plunder they did not lay their hand" (ובבזה לא שלחו את ידם; Esth 9:15)! In contrast, according to the Alpha-Text, Esther asked the king to allow the Jews also to plunder whomever they wish. Apparently, such sharp "anti-Jewish" words were inserted by a later glossator (perhaps Christian) who revised the text. Regardless, this

---

[8] Both translations from Jobes, "Esther," in *NETS*, p. 430.

[9] Note, Targum Rishon to Esth 3:8–10 exaggerates Haman's accusations more, and Targum Sheni does it even more so by attributing a very long anti-Jewish speech to him.

[10] See the detailed discussion on this verse in Chapter 12, §III, 3.

suggests that at least some of the readers of Esther would think that the killing at the end of the book was not purely defensive but rather for purposes of plundering.[11]

III Authority, Place, and Names of Esther in the Christian Canon

Within mainstream Judaism, Megillat Esther has almost universally enjoyed enormous attention.[12] Though some early Rabbis hesitated whether or not this book should be included in the Hebrew Bible,[13] after its canonization there were almost no further disputes about this issue until the modern period, when a few "liberal" Jews spoke out against it.[14] By contrast, among Christians there was a long dispute about the authority of the book of Esther and its inclusion in the canon. This dispute continued for several hundred years, in fact at least to some extent until today.[15]

Already in the early stages of Christianity in the second century, there were some Christians who argued against the inclusion of the entire Old Testament into the Christian canon of Scriptures. Thus, for instance, Marcion of Sinope (Asia Minor, ca. 85–160 CE), eliminated the whole Old Testament from his collection of Scriptures (together with some parts of the New Testament). According to Marcion, "the Old Testament God cannot be the Father of Jesus. The Old Testament speaks of a creator whose foremost quality is 'righteousness,' 'an eye for an eye' ... his Son ... taught people to overcome the law of righteousness with love and refuted the law of retaliation."[16] In fact, Christians remain divided over

---

[11] For discussion of various perspectives on the end of the book of Esther among Christians, see Chapters 11 and 12.

[12] For more detail, see Chapters 8 and 9.

[13] See further Chapter 8, §II.

[14] See Chapter 8, §XI.

[15] Thus, for instance, in 1950, the American Biblicist, Bernhard W. Anderson notes that many still question the inclusion of Esther in the Christian canon. He summarizes the arguments against it: "the book of Esther seems strangely out of place in the Christian Bible ... most offensive ... is the discordant note which the book strikes in the ears of those accustomed to hearing the Christian gospel"; see Anderson, "The Place of the Book of Esther in the Christian Bible," p. 32. Anderson also denies that Esther and Mordecai should be seen as "models of character, integrity, and piety" (ibid., p. 42). However, his final position is that the book of Esther should *not* be excluded from the Christian canon, but instead has important lessons to teach the Church, including regarding the unique election of Israel.

[16] On this issue as well as on Marcion's biography and writing, see in detail Kalimi, *The Retelling of Chronicles in Jewish Tradition and Literature*, pp. 56–57; idem, *Fighting over the Bible*, pp. 47–48. The citation is according to H. Räisänen, "Marcion and the Origins of Christian Anti-Judaism," *Temenos* 33 (1997), 121–135 esp. 122.

the precise position, meaning, and purpose of the Old Testament within their religion and theology, as well as over its proper relation to the New Testament.[17] Yet, the dispute among Christians about the book of Esther and what many of them call the "vengeance" character of the book, was and still is much sharper and bitter than on the Old Testament in general, as we will see in this part of the volume, particularly in Chapters 11 and 12.

In some early Christian canonical lists, Esther was not mentioned at all.[18] For example, in 170 CE the book was excluded from the list of canonical Scriptures prepared by Bishop Melito of Sardis in Asia Minor (died ca. 180; Eusebius, *Ecclesiastical History* 4:26). Athanasius of Alexandria (295–373) also excluded Esther from his list of canonical books (along with books such as Wisdom of Solomon, Ben Sira, Judith, and Tobit, which are accepted in the majority of pre-Reformation Christian Bibles). He allows that the latter may be used (and cites from them himself elsewhere), in contrast to other "apocryphal writings," which are "an invention of heretics" and have no place in the Church, because they only "lead astray the simple" (Athanasius, *Festal Letter* 39).[19] Esther is excluded also from the canon list of Gregory of Nazianzus (ca. 329–390) archbishop of Constantinople, and from that of Theodore the Interpreter, bishop of Mopsuestia (ca. 350–428). On the other hand, Origen's (185–254) canon list (as preserved by Eusebius, *Ecclesiastical History* 6:25,1–2) is explicitly attributed to "the Hebrews," and affirms that it consists of 22 books, indicating that he is reliant on a similar Jewish tradition in Josephus, and he counts Esther last, then adds Maccabees "in addition to these."[20] Generally speaking, in the East the book of Esther was excluded from the canon, while in the West it was regularly included,[21] but even in the latter it has often been disputed and regularly neglected.

---

[17] See, Kalimi, *Fighting over the Bible*, pp. 20–21, and the bibliography on p. 20 note 8.

[18] See A. Jepsen, "Zur Kanongeschichte des Altes Testaments," *ZAW* 71 (1959), pp. 114–136.

[19] Cf. Anderson, "The Place of the Book of Esther in the Christian Bible," 33; M. Breneman, *Ezra, Nehemiah, Esther* (The New American Commentary 10; Nashville: Bradman & Holman, 1993), pp. 293–294. For Athanasius' 39th Festal Letter, see P. Schaff and H. Wace (eds.), *Athanasius: Select Works and Letters* (Nicene and Post-Nicene Fathers 2/4; Edinburgh: T. & T. Clark, 1891; reprinted: Peabody, MA: Hendrickson, 1995), pp. 551–552 esp. 552.

[20] See P. Schaff and H. Wace (eds.), *Eusebius: Church History, Life of Constantine the Great, and Oration in Praise of Constantine* (Nicene and Post-Nicene Father 2/1; Christian Publishing Company, 1890; reprinted: Peabody, MA: Hendrickson, 1995), p. 272. Origen's canon list is discussed by Brandt (*Endgestalten des Canons*, pp. 73–78), with a comparison to that of Melito of Sardis. About Josephus' "canon" list, see Chapter 8, §II.

[21] Moore, *Esther*, p. xxv; Ego, *Esther*, p. 77.

Basically the Christian canon shares the literary classifications of the Septuagint and places the book of Esther among the historical books. However, since all the copies of the LXX we have (that are long enough to indicate the order of books) come from Christian hands, it is uncertain whether the Septuagint order as we know it is itself a result of Christian arrangement, rather than vice versa. Either way, this arrangement follows a chronological order, so that Esther appears *after* the late historical books of Chronicles, Ezra, and Nehemiah.

In many codices of the Septuagint the book is named: "the Letter of Purim," following the words in Esth 9:26: "Therefore they called these days *Purim* after the name of *Pur.* Therefore, for all the words of this *letter* ...." Sometime afterward, the book was named after its heroine, Esther, as in the Hebrew canon, and this was also adopted in the Vulgate and all later Christian Bibles.

IV Esther in Christian Interpretation, Tradition, and Culture

1 Quotation and Interpretation of Esther

Esther is never directly cited in the most important Scripture of Christianity – the New Testament. Perhaps, Esth 5:3 (//5:6//7:2//9:12, מה לך אסתר המלכה ומה בקשתך עד חצי המלכות וינתן לך) is alluded to in Mark 6:22–23 (that in Hebrew translation: "בַּקְשִׁי מִמֶּנִּי מַה שֶׁתִּרְצִי וְאֶתֵּן לָךְ." הוּא גַּם נִשְׁבַּע לָהּ: "מַה שֶׁתְּבַקְשִׁי מִמֶּנִּי אֶתֵּן לָךְ עַד חֲצִי הַמַּלְכוּת").[22] Indeed, beside Esther there are other Tanakh books that have never explicitly been cited in the New Testament, but rather are alluded to (according to the Nestle–Aland definition of "allusions"): Ruth – five allusions, Song of Songs – two allusions (4:15 in John 7:38; 5:2; Revelation 3:20), Lamentations – seven allusions, and Obadiah – one allusion (Revelation 11:15). Moreover, Five Megillot that take so important a place in Jewish liturgy, are not explicitly referred to in the New Testament. Still, one cannot ignore this fact in overall evaluation of the Christian attitude toward the book of Esther. Is this due to what was believed about its "secular" or "carnivalistic" narrative of Esther; or because of what it does not have, God's name or any religious features? Nevertheless, one should keep in mind that most Catholics and Greek Orthodox knew the book in its Greek or Latin versions, which do contain God's name and religious customs.

---

[22] I refer to the Greek New Testament edited by Nestle–Aland, who gave an appendix with "Loci Citati vel Allegati."

Generally, the book of Esther was either unnoticed or very rarely mentioned by the Church Fathers. Some Church Fathers, such as Jerome, had interpreted themes in Esther allegorically, probably to enhance its status in the Christian canon and endorse their theological views. Usually they regarded Mordecai as Jesus, Esther as the Virgin Mary, or *Ecclesia* (the Church, that is, Christianity), and Vashti as *Synagoga* (the Synagogue, which is Judaism). They interpreted the gallows built by Haman as foretelling the cross of Jesus.[23] Nonetheless, there was no Christian commentary on the book until the one written by Rabanus Maurus Magnentius (ca. 780–856, also known as Hrabanus, or – in inverse of the first two letters – Rhabanus) in the first half of the ninth century.

2   Rabanus Maurus' Commentary

Rabanus Maurus was a Frankish Benedictine theologian who became archbishop of Mainz. Among his many writings, he also composed commentaries on the books of the Old as well as the New Testaments. In 836 he published a short *Exposition on the Book of Esther* (*Expositio in Librum Esther*),[24] where he developed in detail the allegorical method regarding Esther. Thus, in the foreword to his commentary, he writes:

> The book of Esther ... contains truths of Christ and of the Church in the form of mysteries in a manifold way – as Esther herself, in a figure of the Church, frees the people from danger; and after Haman – whose name is interpreted as wickedness – has been killed, she assigns future generations a part in the feast and the festival day.[25]

Thus, Rabanus Maurus also considered the main act of Esther to be an allegory: She killed the representative of "wickedness" and freed the Jews – so also the Church kills evil/sin and frees humanity.

Similarly, Rabanus interprets the glory, power, and extreme wealth of King Ahasuerus, as described in Esth 1:4, 6–8, as follows:

---

[23] Cf. Fuerst, *The Books of Ruth, Esther, Ecclesiastes, the Song of Songs, Lamentations*, pp. 32, 38.

[24] The commentary is translated from Latin into English by Peter Wyetzner, "Commentary of Rabanus Marus on the Book of Esther," *Jerusalem Letters* (December 2015), http://jerusalemletters .com/is-ahashverosh-jesus/

[25] "Liber Esther ... multipliciter Christi et Ecclesie sacramenta in mysterio continet: quia ipsa Esther in Ecclesiae typo populum de periculo liberat, et interfecto Aman, qui interpretatur iniquitas, partem convivii et diem celebrem mittit in posteros." See R. Maurus, "Expositio in librum Esther," in J. P. Migne (ed.), *Patrologiae Latinae* (Paris: Garnier, 1852), vol. 109, pp. 635–670 esp. 635. The translation is from Wyetzner, "Commentary of Rabanus Marus on the Book of Esther," p. 1.

This preparation of the most opulent feast, although it may seem to represent the historical splendor of riches and the luxury of pleasures of a mighty king, should nevertheless symbolize the magnitude of spiritual riches and the excellence of the wealth of life through the very sanctified mystery of our most powerful king, namely the Lord Christ, which he has generously distributed according to the dispensation to each of his faithful ones.[26]

Rabanus continues, with a further identification of Esther with the Church: "For this king of great wealth, who was implored by the entreaties of his most faithful wife to do away with the imminent destruction of the Jews which wicked men were plotting, prefigures no one else than our Redeemer who is showered every day by the prayers of the Holy Church who is his dearest wife [i.e., Esther], and frees his chosen ones from the hands of their enemies, and subjects their adversaries to the deserved punishment. And that Esther prefigures the Church, no one can doubt; nor may she herself in any way be said to be the bride of anyone but Christ."[27]

Like Jerome, Rabanus also interpreted the election of Esther as queen to correspond to the election of the Gentiles (!) as the chosen people instead of Jews. However, he embraced Esther also as a prototype of the Virgin, Mary. He identifies Esther as *Ecclesia* and Vashti as *Synagoga*. He interprets the refusal of Queen Vashti (Esth 1:10–12, 15) as a symbol of the rebellious and stubborn *Synagoga*, while the obedience of Esther is seen as a symbol of the faithful Church, *Ecclesia*.[28]

---

[26] "Haec praeparatio opulentissimi convivii, licet historialiter divitiarum pompam et deliciarum luxus regis potentis demonstrare videatur, tamen sacratiore mysterio potentissimi regis nostri, videlicet Domini Christi, divitiarum spiritualium magnitudinem ac vitalium opum excellentiam, quas ille secundum modum dispensationis suae unicuique fidelium suorum largiter distribuit, significat"; see Migne, *Patrologiae Latinae*, vol. 109, p. 637.

[27] "Nec enim alicui rex ille ditissimus, qui uxoris suæ fidelissimæ precibus exoratus, Judæorum, quem iniqui meditabantur, imminentem removit interitum, quam Redemptori nostro per figuram aptatur, qui quotidie sanctae Ecclesiæ, quæ sponsa ipsius est dilectissima, orationibus interpellatus, liberat electos suos de hostium manibus, atque inimicos eorum dignæ subjicit vindictæ. Quod autem Esther typum Ecclesiæ teneat, nulli dubium est; nec ipsa alicujus sponsa quam Christi ullo modo dicenda est"; Migne, *Patrologiae Latinae*, vol. 109, p. 637. The translation is adopted with some changes from Wyetzner, "Commentary of Rabanus Marus on the Book of Esther," p. 3.

[28] See M.-L. Thérel, "L'origine du thème de la 'synagogue répudiée," *Scriptorium – International Review of Manuscript Studies* 25 (1971), pp. 285–290 esp. 288–289, with references to the original documents and further secondary literature. E. Ann Matter notes that in the surviving manuscripts, the *Glossa ordinaria* of Esther are primarily drawn from Rabanus Maurus' exposition, and that "Glossed books of Tobit, Esther, Judith and Ruth are often found copied together in one codex, making up what seems to be a collection of favorite Bible stories"; E. A. Matter, "The Church Fathers and the *Glossa Ordinaria*," in I. D. Backus (ed.), *The Reception of the Church Fathers in the West*, Volume 1: *From the Carolingians to the Maurists* (Leiden: Brill, 1997), vol. 1, pp. 83–111 esp. 90.

This interpretation of the election of Esther, the Jewish girl, as representative of the gentiles – the Church/Christianity – and the rejection of Vashti, the gentile woman, as representative of the Synagogue/Jews, is similar to and on the same line as the Paulinian theology. Paul's Epistle to the Galatians makes the equally astonishing identification of the Jews (who do not accept Jesus) with Ishmael, the son of the slave and rejected woman of Abraham, Hagar, and believers in Jesus (Jewish and gentile) with Isaac, the son of the free woman, Sarah, and the chosen one who will bear the covenant with God and continue his father's lineage and heritage:

> Abraham had two sons, one by a slave woman and the other by a free woman. One, the child of the slave, was born according to the flesh; the other, the child of the free woman, was born through the promise.[29] Now this is an allegory: these women are two covenants. One woman, in fact, is Hagar, from Mount Sinai, bearing children for slavery. Now Hagar is Mount Sinai in Arabia and corresponds to the present Jerusalem, for she is in slavery with her children. But the other woman corresponds to the Jerusalem above; she is free, and she is our mother …. Now you, my friends, are children of the promise, like Isaac. But just as at that time the child who was born according to the flesh persecuted the child who was born according to the Spirit, so it is now also. But what does the scripture say? "Drive out the slave and her child; for the child of the slave will not share the inheritance with the child of the free woman" [cf. Gen 21:10, 12: "for in Isaac shall your seed be called"]. So then, friends, we are children, not of the slave but of the free woman. (Gal 4:21–31)

A similar line of thought also guides Paul's Epistle to Romans 9:7–13, where Jacob is identified with Christians and Esau with Jews, while citing Gen 25:23, "the elder [i.e., Esau] shall serve the younger [i.e., Jacob]," as well as prophet Malachi who declares: "Was not Esau Jacob's brother? says the Lord; yet *I loved Jacob*, and *I hated Esau*, and laid waste his mountains and gave his heritage to the jackals of the wilderness" (Mal 1:2–3).

This concept of *Synagoga* and *Ecclesia* found expression later also in medieval art. Here, *Synagoga* is described as the rejected and humbled queen, without crown, with a broken scepter in hand and covered eyes, so she cannot see the "right path." She stands beside *Ecclesia* who is presented as the chosen and gloriously enthroned queen with an unbroken scepter in hand and uncovered eyes, (see below fig. 12). Most likely, the biblical Leah, unbeloved

---

[29] See S. K. Williams, "*Promise* in the Galatians: A Reading of Paul's Reading of Scripture," *JBL* 107 (1988), pp. 709–720.

woman who had "weak eyes" (Gen 29:17a), is interpreted allegorically as the covered eyes queen (*Synagoga*), but Rachel, who was "beautiful" (יפת תואר ויפת מראה, 29:17b) and the beloved woman of Jacob (Gen 29:18a), was interpreted as a symbol of the uncovered eyes queen (*Ecclesia*), who reads the Scriptures and interprets it appropriately according to the methods and principles of the Church. These artistic expressions in the form of sculpted portal figures decorate the fronts of numerous medieval European cathedrals (particularly in cities with Jewish populations), such as Paris (Notre Dame), Strasbourg, Freiburg im Breisgau, Erfurt, Bamberg, Mainz, Trier, and the cathedrals of Lincoln, Rochester, and Winchester in the British Isles, among many others.[30]

Nevertheless, this method of allegory came to dominate Christian biblical interpretation. Rabanus interprets Esther allegorically as he does with other biblical texts. Also, he follows the well-known Christian theological line that maintains whatever is "good" or "nice" in the Scriptures to symbolize Christians and Christianity. Thus, Isaac, Jacob, Racheal, and Esther are identified with Christians and Christianity. But all the "bad" or "low" things or rejected personalities and all the prophetic condemnations apply to the heretical Jews.[31] Accordingly, Ishmael, Esau, Leah, and Vashti are identified with Jews and Judaism. Rabanus Maurus, therefore, follows the well-established "rejection" and "replacement" of Christian theology that is rooted already in the New Testament, and led to the disastrous relationship between Christians and Jews, while the latter paid the horrible cost of the hatred.

The allegorical interpretation of some events in Esther theoretically could be explained on the grounds that it was used to justify the presence of such a "secular" book in the Christian canon, just as the allegorical interpretations of the Song of Songs by Christians (and Jews) did.[32] But the truth is that the book of Esther in many Christian canons did not need to be allegorized for this reason, because numerous Christians read Esther in its Greek and Latin forms, which are by no means "secular." Accordingly, it seems that the allegorical interpretation of Esther is just a part of the Christian interpretation of the entire "Old Testament." In fact, Rabanus Maurus, for instance, also expounded acts of Saul, David, Jechoniah, and Cyrus allegorically, and claimed: "They [= the church fathers] reported

---

[30] See the discussion and the many illustrations by N. Rowe, *The Jew, the Cathedral, and the Medieval City: Synagoga and Ecclesia in the Thirteenth Century* (Cambridge: Cambridge University Press, 2011).

[31] On this issue see also Chapter 11, §VI, nos. 1–2.

[32] On this issue, see Chapter 1, §II.

Figure 12   *Ecclesia* (left) and *Synagoga* (right) at the cathedral of Strasbourg, France.

that the words and actions of Pharaoh or Nebuchadnezzar should be understood as prefiguration concerning the enemies of the Church."[33]

3 Martin Luther's Translation and Negation of the Book

In the first quarter of the sixteenth century, Martin Luther (1483–1546), translated the book of Esther into German within the context of his complete translation of the Old Testament.[34] Although Luther refers to the book and its core Jewish figures in his writings, he did not dedicate any special study or commentary to it, as he did not write any commentaries on the late biblical books, Ezra, Nehemiah, and Chronicles. Moreover, despite his sharp criticism of *the book of Esther*, Luther did not dare to exclude the book from his translated German Bible. He preferred to include in the Christian Old Testament canon only those works included in the Hebrew Bible, instead of the fuller collection found in most Latin manuscripts. Since *both* included Esther, his personal doubts about the book were irrelevant to the question of its canonicity, which he does not challenge, even if he might have liked to do so. In contrast, Luther praised the *figures* of Mordecai and particularly Esther, as a prototype of Jesus, as ones who risked themselves in order to save their people. He considered them as a model for Christian believers (see Chapter 11, §I). Nonetheless, his destructive statements against *the book* of Esther had enormous influence on generations of Christian theologians, exegetes, writers, and thinkers, until today, particularly among Protestants.[35] By doing so, Luther just added to the bewilderment regarding Esther that already existed among the Christians, and thereafter the criticisms of the book and harsh assertions against the Jews became regular and frequent.[36]

4 Esther in Christian Liturgy, Theology, Art, and Music

Usually, the validity of the book of Esther in the Christian canon is much disputed and questioned.[37] The book plays nearly no role in Christian liturgy and is little touched or discussed among Christians before Luther. It had almost

---

[33] "Qui dicta vel acta Pharaonis sive Nabuchodonosor typice super hostibus Ecclesiae intelligenda tradiderunt"; Migne, *Patrologiae Latinae*, vol. 109, p. 638.
[34] See Chapter 11 for more details.
[35] See particularly Chapters 11 and 12.
[36] See Chapters 11 and 12.
[37] Gerleman (*Esther*, p. 40), concludes: "The inclusion of the book of Esther in the Christian Bible has been considered at all times as questionable and offensive ..."; see Chapter 12, §I.

no influence on ancient, medieval, or modern Christian theology (or theologies). The common approach was and still implies that Esther has nothing or too little to contribute to Christian religion and culture. This attitude toward the book of Esther is summarized by Frederic W. Bush as follows: "It is an unfortunate fact that in the Christian world at large the book of Esther has not found acceptance. It is indeed an *opus non gratum*, an unacceptable work. True, when the church took over the Bible of the Jews as part of its canon, it did not embrace the book of Esther. But for the most part it has been a cold embrace indeed."[38] One cannot but endorse this regrettable conclusion.[39]

Indeed, the book has been scarcely mentioned in comprehensive Christian volumes on the Old Testament theology, and in fact lies at the margin of Christian theology since forever.[40] It was and continues to be problematic for many Christians, treated as a book without any theological merit and authority. Thus, for instance, Curt Kuhl concludes: "Because of its purely secular nature, the book of Esther was long controversial ... It is the testimony of a narrow-minded and fanatical nationalism. We understand that Luther inwardly rejected this scripture with its 'pagan malady' and was so hostile to it that he would have liked nothing better than if it did not exist. To the Christian Esther has nothing to say religiously."[41]

Still, there are a large number of Christian art works from the late Middle Ages and early modern times. To mention some, for example: The artistic work such as Michelangelo's (1475–1564) "Esther, Ahasuerus and the crucifixion of Haman" in the Sistine Chapel. Also note the works by Filippino Lippi, Theodore Chasserieu, Rembrandt, and Konrad Witz.[42]

---

[38] Bush, "The Book of Esther: *Opus non gratum* in the Christian Canon," p. 39; see also Bush, *Ruth, Esther*, pp. 275–277.

[39] In the summary of his article, Bush ("The Book of Esther: *Opus non gratum*," p. 39) stresses that "Martin Luther expressed contempt for Esther, claiming that it is spoiled by too much 'pagan impropriety.'" For whatever reason, Bush avoids citing (what he does later in this discussion) also the first and no less important part of Luther's claim: "for they [i.e., Esther and 2 Maccabees] show too much Jewishness (or, judaize too greatly)." On Luther's attitude toward Esther and 2 Maccabees, see the detailed discussion in Chapter 11.

[40] A brief look at the following works, for example, makes this point clear: G. von Rad, *Old Testament Theology* (2 vols.; The Old Testament Library; Louisville: Westminster John Knox, 2001); H. D. Preuss, *Old Testament Theology* (2 vols.; translated by D. M. G. Stalker; The Old Testament Library; Louisville: Westminster John Knox, 1996); W. Brueggemann, *Theology of the Old Testament: Testimony, Dispute, Advocacy* (Minneapolis: Fortress Press, 2000); R. W. L. Moberly, *Old Testament Theology: Reading the Hebrew Bible as Christian Scripture* (Grand Rapids, MI: Baker Academic, 2013).

[41] C. Kuhl, *Die Entstehung des Alten Testaments* (Munich: Lehnen Verlag, 1953), pp. 291–294 esp. 294. For the original German citation, as well as a detail discussion of Kuhl's approach, see Chapter 11, §I.

[42] See Z. Gitay, "Esther and the Queen's Throne," in A. Brenner (ed.), *Feminist Companion to Esther, Judith and Susanna* (Sheffield: Sheffield Academic Press, 1995), pp. 136–148.

In music it is worth mentioning especially Georg Friedrich Händel's Oratorio "Esther" (1718, revised 1732). The book is present also in literature and film.[43]

In the last decades, however, a bit more attention has been paid to this book by a handful of Christian theologians, such as Brevard S. Childs in America and Erich Zenger in Germany. As we will see in Chapter 13, they – and some others before them – firmly stood up against the negative trend and attempted to show what Christianity can and must learn from the book of Esther.[44] Interestingly, "in recent novels, sermons, and Bible-study guides, evangelicals and mainline Protestants alike find inspiration in the biblical tale."[45]

V   Conclusion

In line with the Septuagint, the Christian tradition places Esther within the collection of the biblical historical books, after Chronicles, Ezra, and Nehemiah. In contrast to the Jews who read the shorter, Hebrew version of Esther, most Christians (particularly the Roman Catholic and Orthodox Churches) read the longer, Greek version of the book, which differs in many variants from the Hebrew one. Thus, it contains six major "Additions," and in several places it refers to God and various religious themes, such as prayer, divine dreams, kosher food, and drink. The controversy over the issue whether to include or exclude the book of Esther in the Christian canon continued over numerous generations. Nonetheless, even after the decision was made to accept the book of Esther in the canon, some Christian theologians and writers doubted its religious value – even the Greek version of it – and continued to express antagonism toward the book, while others simply neglected it altogether.

In fact, Esther is never referred to in the New Testament, and it is hardly cited by the Church Fathers. It has almost no place in Christian liturgy. As usual, the Church interpreted the book of Esther allegorically,

---

43 On Esther in the Christian literature, visual arts, music, and film, see the appropriate items that were composed by A. Swindell, O. Z. Soltes, J. Carruthers, H. Leneman, and R. Burnette-Bletsch, "Esther," *Encyclopedia of the Bible and Its Reception* (Berlin: Walter de Gruyter, 2014), vol. 8, pp. 39–54.

44 See Childs, *Introduction to the Old Testament as Scripture*, pp. 606–607; E. Zenger, "Esther," in E. Zenger u. a. (ed.), *Einleitung in das Alte Testament* (8th ed. edited by C. Frevel; Stuttgart: W. Kohlhammer, 2012), pp. 376–386 esp. 386. For detailed citations from these and other scholars, see Chapter 13, §§I–II.

45 See R. Phillips, "Christians Have Fallen in Love with Queen Esther, Purim's Jewish Heroine," *Tablet Magazine* (March 12, 2014): www.tabletmag.com/sections/belief/articles/christians-love-queen-esther

as it did with the other books of the Old Testament. The first Christian commentary on the book was written by Rabanus Maurus in 836. He interpreted the book allegorically, while presenting Esther as *Ecclesia* and Vashti as *Synagoga*. Other Christian theologians referred only occasionally to some parts of Esther and figuratively expounded them. Luther translated the book in German, but his sharp criticism of it had an enormous effect on generations of scholars and theologians, particularly Protestants. Esther has had almost no impact on Christian theology and religion, and has made only a small impression on art and music.

CHAPTER II

Esther, the Jews, and Martin Luther

I The Place of Luther's Approach in Christian Reception

The purpose of this chapter is to trace, analyze, and evaluate the attitudes of the Protestant reformer Martin Luther (1483–1546), over the course of his career, toward the biblical figures of Esther and Mordecai, and toward the book of Esther as a whole. Since it can be argued that modern critical study of the Hebrew Bible/Old Testament has its roots within the German Protestant tradition, and because of the broad and decisive influence of Luther's approach to Esther on subsequent Christian reception of the book over generations of Christian – particularly Protestant – biblical scholars, it is necessary to warrant detailed examination and comprehend the complex origins of his interpretive approach within his career, writings, and theology.

Luther's statements concerning Esther are inconsistent. On the one hand, he refers positively to the characters of Esther and Mordecai, mostly early in his career. Later, these positive references become more seldom, limited only to two late references to Queen Esther herself as "(most) pious." On the other hand, Luther makes several sharply negative statements that criticize the book of Esther as a whole and its Jewish character, particularly in the later stage of his career. This chapter argues that the change in Luther's position took place on two overlapping levels:

1. Luther's positive attitude toward the book's Jewish characters – Queen Esther and Mordecai – and his negative attitude toward the book itself, stem from his selective Christian theological usage of the Old Testament heritage.
2. Luther's changed attitude toward the book of Esther reflects his changed attitude toward the Jews in general. Thus, the discussion of Queen Esther and the book named after her is contextualized within an analysis of Luther's religious-historical approach to the Jewish people and Judaism.

These two overlapping levels will be shown through an examination of Luther's letters, "Table-Talks" (*Tischreden*, that is, some informal comments on a variety of topics in discussion around the table), theological writings, and exegetical treatises, as well as his Bible translations and certain compositions regarding Jews. Though Martin Luther never wrote a commentary or a specific study on the book of Esther, he refers to the book and its major Jewish figures in all genres of his writings: exegetical, theological, pastoral, and polemical, as well as in his sermons and letters.[1] These references are found throughout almost his entire career as a Protestant reformer, and occasionally even before.

II   Luther and the Figures of Esther and Mordecai: Positive Characterizations

In the early stage of his career as a reformer and even a bit before, Luther demonstrates a respectful attitude toward Esther and Mordecai as persons.[2] Thus, in 1515–1516, in one of his lectures on the Epistle to the Romans (*Römerbrief*), he discusses the "shame" (*Schande*), which "Jesus gladly took upon himself for us." In this context, Luther refers to additional ancient Israelite figures who acted similarly and risked themselves on behalf of their people and religion, such as Daniel and his friends, Hananiah, Mishael, and Azariah, as well as Esther and Mordecai.[3] In addition, in a letter of December 18, 1519 to his friend, the influential humanist Georg Spalatin,[4] Luther compares Spalatin to Esther in the great "difficulty and danger" he takes on to serve in the Court.[5] Similarly, in 1523, in a sermon on Luke

---

[1] Cf. H. Bardtke, *Luther und das Buch Esther* (Tübingen: J. C. B. Mohr [P. Siebeck], 1964), p. 50.

[2] It is hard to say definitively which version of the book of Esther Luther had in mind when he refers to it and its figures: the larger LXX version that includes six additions, which Christians adopted (also via the Latin translation of Jerome, the Vulgate) and Luther would have grown up with, or the shorter MT version that he later translated into German. Nonetheless, some of Luther's descriptions of Esther, particularly regarding her piety, her jewelry and her humility, seem to indicate knowledge of Additions D and E in the LXX, which emphasize different qualities for the figure of Queen Esther than the Hebrew version does.

[3] See M. Luther, *Vorlesung über den Römerbrief 1515/1516*, in H. H. Borchert and G. Merz (eds.), *Ausgewählte Werke: Ergänzungsreihe* (3rd ed.; Munich: Chr. Kaiser Verlag, 1965), vol. 2, p. 453; Latin original: M. Luther, *Werke: Kritische Gesam(m)tausgabe* (121 vols.; Weimar: Hermann Böhlaus, 1883–2009), vol. 56, p. 516 lines 11–12 (all references to this series below are abbreviated WA): "Igitur sic Deus dedit populo Israel Danielem et sotios eius in captiuitate Babylonis, Sic Hester et Mardocheum in Perside coram Assuero."

[4] Spalatin was the secretary and personal chaplain to Friedrich III der Weise, Elector of Saxony. On this figure, see I. Höss, *Georg Spalatin – 1484–1545: Ein Leben in der Zeit des Humanismus und der Reformation* (Weimar: Hermann Böhlaus Nachfolger, 1956).

[5] WA *Briefwechsel*, vol. 1, pp. 594–595 esp. 595: "Hoc est: in Aulam, sicut hester, vocatus es, ubi populis servias (ubi potes), qui ex hac Aula reguntur. hoc ut est omnium difficillimum & periculosissimum, ita non dubites esse summum & primum" ("It is [so]: you are called in the court, like Esther, when you serve the people (when you can), who rule in the court. And this is the most difficult and dangerous of all, so no doubt the highest and first"; cf. Bardtke, *Luther und das Buch Esther*, p. 64.

16, Luther names Esther as "the beloved daughter of God" (*Gottes liebe Tochter*), because she did not care about her own life but rather about the lives of her people.[6] Thus at that time Luther was sympathetic toward the biblical characters, who risked themselves for the salvation of the Jewish people in the Persian Empire, and he considered that salvation to be the fulfillment of God's will, by the hand of Queen Esther and Mordecai.

In the same year, 1523, Luther published his work *That Jesus Christ Was Born a Jew* (*Dass Jesus Christus ein geborener Jude sei*), where he presents a positive attitude toward the Jews, and strongly condemns their mistreatment by the Church. In that context, he refers positively to Mordecai among other Jewish biblical leaders, stating that, unlike Jesus, "neither Joseph in Egypt, nor Daniel in Babylon, nor Mordecai in Persia became king [over foreigners] although they were certainly great people in the government."[7]

As common among Christian theologians, Luther reads Esther within the context of the complete Christian Bible, and discusses the figures from the New Testament together with those from the Old Testament.[8] The main goal of Luther's comparison in all these sources is clear: He uses the Old Testament figures in order to highlight the New Testament's central hero – Jesus – in contrast to the positions of Joseph, Daniel, and Mordecai. Though the latter may have held important positions in foreign courts, Christ was far beyond them: The Gentiles have accepted Jesus as a king to rule over them, while Joseph, Daniel, and Mordecai were not accepted by the Gentiles as kings. Luther also tried to show that Esther's bravery in placing her own life in danger to save her people should be a model for the Christian community. Thus, because the book of Esther was already part of the Christian Bible, Luther occasionally uses its figures as he uses those from Genesis, Daniel, and other Old Testament books, when it serves his purposes.

There are also a couple of positive references to Queen Esther in Luther's later writings. So, in a sermon that he delivered sometime between 1537 and 1540, on Jesus' saying that it is harder for a rich man to enter the Kingdom of Heaven than for a camel to go through the eye of a needle (Matt 19:16–24), Luther notes the example of "pious Esther" (*frommen Hester*) who

---

[6] In medieval German, Luther's expression is: "wardt [= war] sy [= sie] dannocht [= dennoch] Got [= Gott] ein[e] liebe Tochter darumb [= darum]"; see WA, vol. 12, p. 593 lines 1–5. All quotations from Luther below will preserve his original spelling and grammar, while adding modern equivalents in brackets where necessary.

[7] WA, vol. 11, p. 331 lines 5–10: "Denn ob Joseph ynn [= in] Egypten [= Ägypten] wol [= wohl] eyn [= ein] gros [= großer] man [=Mann] war, dennoch war er nicht herr [= Herr] noch konig [= König] .... Item [= ebenfalls] so ist auch zu Babylonien noch ynn [= in] Persen land [= Persien] widder [= weder] Daniel noch Mardocheus [= Mordechai] konig [= König] gewessen [= gewesen], ob sie wol [= wohl] grosse [= große] leutt [= Leute] ym [= im] regiment waren."

[8] On this issue see also below, §V.

wore jewelry to approach the king, but was humble inside.[9] Similarly, in September 1542, in his letter to Nikolaus von Amsdorf, Luther describes Esther as a "most pious queen" (*piissima regina*), and presents her, together with Jesus, in such a way that they offer models to encourage Nikolaus.[10]

III Luther and the Book of Esther: Negative Characterizations

In 1522, Martin Luther published his translation of the New Testament into German. The translation of the so-called "Historical Books" of the Old Testament, including the book of Esther (in the order as they appear in the Septuagint and Vulgate), was sent to print in January 1524, and in 1534 the complete Christian *Biblia* was available in German.[11] In contrast to his

---

[9] WA, vol. 47, p. 362 lines 2–4: "Also gehets [= gehet] mit der frommen Hester [= Ester], die soll auch unnd [= und] mus [= muss] ohne ihren Dank zum Konig [= König] ihn [= in] ihrem Geschmuck [=Schmuck] gefuret [= geführt] werden, den sie ihn [= in] ihrem Kemmerlein [= Kämmerlein] ni[c]ht ahn hatte [= anhatte], unnd [= und] war ihr Hertz [= Herz] ihndes [= indes] vol[l] Heulens unnd [= und] weinens." See also Bardtke, *Luther und das Buch Esther*, p. 67.

[10] See WA, *Briefwechsel*, vol. 10, no. 3787, p. 139 lines 7–12, "Et Deus nouit cor tuum abhorrentissimum a tali pompa et splendore. Sed memento piissimae reginae Esther, quae inuita gestabat coronam Regni Persarum, vocans eam ostentum et pollutum pannum, Sed propter Regem et Regnum ferebat. Et Christus pompam in die Palmarum non postulabat, Sed ferebat, ipse interim pauper et assiduo mortificatus et crucifixus." (= "God knows your heart is most afraid of such pomp and splendor. But remember the very pious Queen Esther, who reluctantly carried the crown of the Persian kingdom, which she called her 'vain and soiled rag,' but because of king and kingdom she endured. And Christ did not demand a parade on Palm Sunday, but in the meantime he himself endured as a poor person while he was continually mortified and crucified.")

[11] This important project of Luther had an enormous impact not only on biblical and theological studies, but also on German language and literature. As already stated by Johann Gottfried von Herder (1744–1803): "He [= Luther] is the one who awoke the German language, a sleeping giant, and let it loose; he is the one who spilled the scholastic marketplace of words, like those change tables: he raised a whole nation to thinking and feeling through his reformation" ("Er ist, der die deutsche Sprache, einen schlafenden Riesen, aufgewecket, und losgebunden; er ist, der die schlastische Wortkrämerei, wie jene Wechselertische, verschüttet: er hat durch seine Reformation eine ganze Nation zum Denken und Gefühl erhoben"); see J. G. von Herder, *Über die neuere Deutsche Literatur. Fragmente, als Beilagen zu den Briefen, die neueste Litteratur betreffend* (Riga, 1767), vol. 3, p. 23. Similarly, Heinrich Heine (1797–1856) said: "Martin Luther ... created the word for us, the language in which this new literature could speak ... the beautiful literature begins with Luther ... Anyone who wants to discuss modern German literature has to begin with Luther ...." ("Martin Luther ... er uns auch das Wort schuf, die Sprache, worin diese neue Literatur sich aussprechen konnte ... diese Literatur eröffnet, daß diese, und ganz eigentlich die schöne Literatur, mit Luther beginnt ... Wer über die neuere deutsche Literatur reden will, muß daher mit Luther beginnen ..."); see H. Heine, "Zur Geschichte der Religion und Philosophie in Deutschland," in *Revue des deux Mondes* (Hamburg, December 1834), pp. 81–82. Nonetheless, Luther was not the first to translate the Bible into German, nor did he complete the task alone; see S. Michel, "'Luthers Sanhedrin': Helfer und Mitarbeiter an der Lutherbibel," in M. Käßmann and M. Rösel (eds.), *Die Bibel Martin Luther: Ein Buch und seine Geschichte* (Leipzig: Deutsche Bibel Gesellschaft and Evangelische Verlagsanstalt, 2017), pp. 117–135; see also E. Cameron, "The Luther Bible," in E. Cameron (ed.), *The New Cambridge History of the Bible: Volume 3 – From 1450–1750* (Cambridge: Cambridge University Press, 2016), pp. 217–238; K.-H. Göttert, *Luthers Bibel: Geschichte einer feindlichen Übernahme* (Fischer Wissenschaft: Frankfurt am Main: S. Fischer, 2017).

translations of some other biblical books, such as Jeremiah, where occasionally he inserts anti-Jewish notions into his translations,[12] Luther's translation of the book of Esther usually follows the Masoretic Text, without theological bias or anti-Jewish insertions. As we saw above, occasionally he uses the book in his talks and sermons, though he never wrote a commentary or an essay on it. Nevertheless, Luther was uncomfortable with the book as a whole.

At some point during his career as a reformer,[13] Luther began to express more and more hostility toward the book of Esther, and harshly criticized its very existence. In fact, *all* of his negative portrayals relate to the *book* as a whole (about which he never says anything positive), while all of his positive descriptions relate to *figures* within the book, namely Esther and Mordecai (about whom he never says anything negative). Therefore, while there is certainly a shift toward the negative in Luther's references to the book of Esther, this does not necessarily reflect a change in attitude so much as a change in which aspects he emphasizes, since the positive and negative assessments essentially relate to differing aspects. Whether Luther ever liked the book of Esther as a whole (he never says he liked it), he certainly became increasingly hostile toward it as time went on. Indeed, Luther also had doubts about a few books of the New Testament, such as the Pauline authorship of Hebrews and the theological value of James, Jude, and Revelation.[14] However, he criticized no other books as severely as he did the books of Esther and 2 Maccabees.

---

[12] For example, Jeremiah 5 speaks about the sins of *Jerusalem*; Luther gives the chapter the title "the sinful *nation* cannot be forgiven anymore" ("Dem sündigen *Volk* kann nicht mehr vergeben werden"). Jeremiah 6 speaks about the people from the north that come to attack Jerusalem, but Luther summarizes it as "the well-deserved judgment" ("Das wohlverdiente Gericht"); before Jer 8:4–7 he wrote: "Against the blinded *nation* and their seducers" ("Gegen das verblendete *Volk* und seine Verführer"); Jer 9:24–25 talks about God's punishment that will be visited upon uncircumcised people, but Luther wrote before these verses: "*Israel*, an uncircumcised *nation*" ("*Israel*, ein unbeschnittenes *Volk*"). Chapter titles were added to the Luther Bible between 1531 and 1545, and they were known to Luther and accepted by him; see S. Michel, "Die Revision der Lutherbibel zwischen 1531 und 1545," in M. Lange and M. Rösel (eds.), *"Was Dolmetschen für Kunst und Arbeit sei": Die Lutherbibel und andere deutsche Bibelübersetzungen* (Leipzig: Deutsche Bibel Gesellschaft and Evangelische Verlagsanstalt, 2017), pp. 83–106. A different example: Jer 2:3 declares: קדש ישראל ליהוה ראשית תבואתה כל אכליו יאשמו ("Israel *is* holy to the Lord, the first fruits of his harvest"), Luther translates here: "Because Israel *was* holy to the Lord, the first fruit of his harvest" ("Da *war* Israel dem HERRN heilig, die Erstlingsfrucht seiner Ernte"); see Chapter 4, §IV, note 57.
[13] Regarding when this shift occurred, see below §IV.
[14] "Luther wrote no commentary on James but exercised considerable influence over subsequent scholarly interpretation. In the preface to his 1522 German Bible, he dismissed the latter as an 'epistle of straw' compared to the writings that 'show thee Christ.' Luther would therefore not include James among the 'chief books' of the canon, although he admired 'the otherwise many fine sayings in it'"; see L. T. Johnson, "James, Letter of," in J. H. Hayes (ed.), *Dictionary of Biblical Interpretation* (Nashville: Abingdon Press, 1999), vol. 1, pp. 560–561 esp. 561. Moreover, "Luther placed the books of Hebrews, James, Jude, and Revelation at the end of the NT and did not assign them consecutive numbers as he had the other twenty-three books he considered to be 'the true and certain and

As early as the fall of 1525, in his booklet *On the Bondage of the Will* (*De servo arbitrio*), Luther responds to Erasmus of Rotterdam's criticisms of the Old Testament,[15] by pointing out that while the book of Esther is part of the Christian canon, in his personal opinion it is the least deserving of all those included in it.[16] At the time, Luther did not offer any reason for this conclusion, but eight years later, in 1533, he does give a reason in one of his *Tischreden*, where he states:

> I am so hostile to this book [i.e., 2 Maccabees] and Esther, that I wish they did not exist at all, for they show too much Jewishness and contain a lot of pagan impropriety.[17]

Here Luther does not specify what exactly the "too much Jewishness" in the books of Esther and 2 Maccabees is, nor where in these books there is "a lot of pagan impropriety." Nonetheless, Luther binds these two together, and on the same occasion he stresses that the book of Esther has a favorite place among the Jews, who prefer it over the prophetic books

---

chief books of the NT'"; see J. Neyrey, "Jude, Letter of," in J. H. Hayes (ed.), *Dictionary of Biblical Interpretation* (Nashville: Abingdon Press, 1999), vol. 1, pp. 636–637 esp. 636; C. M. Jacobs and E. T. Bachmann (trans.), "Prefaces to the New Testament," in E. T. Bachmann (ed.), *Luther's Works*, Volume 35: *Word and Sacrament I* (Philadelphia: Muhlenberg, 1960), pp. 355–412 esp. 394. Regarding Jude, Luther wrote: "No one can deny that it is an extract or copy of St. Peter's second epistle, so very like it are all the words. He also speaks of the apostles like a disciple who comes long after them and cites sayings and incidents that are found nowhere else in the Scriptures. This moved the ancient fathers to exclude this epistle from the main body of the Scriptures .... Therefore, although I value this book, it is an epistle that need not be counted among the chief books which are supposed to lay the foundations of faith" (Bachmann, *Luther's Works*, vol. 35, pp. 397–398).

15   On *De servo arbitrio*, see recently H. Hoping, "Freiheit und Sünde: Zur Bedeutung von Martin Luthers '*De servo arbitrio*' für die theologische Anthropologie," in C. Danz and J.-H. Tück (eds.), *Martin Luther im Widerstreit der Konfessionen: Historische und theologische Perspektiven* (Freiburg im Breisgau: Herder, 2017), pp. 227–244. On Erasmus of Rotterdam (ca. 1466–1536) and his attitude toward Jews and the Old Testament, see I. Kalimi, "The Position of Martin Luther towards Jews and Judaism: Historical, Social, and Theological Venues," *JR* 103 (2023), §IV, 6, 2.

16   See WA, vol. 18, pp. 551–787 esp. 666 lines 19–24: "Ne cum iactura temporis me involvo disputationi de receptis libris in Canone Ebraeorum, quem tu non nihil mordes ac rides, dum proverbia Salomonis et Canticum (ut scommate ambiguo vocas) amatorium comparas cum libris duobus Esre, Iudith, historiae Susannae et Draconis, Esther, quamvis hunc habeant in Canone, dignior omnibus, me iudice, qui extra Canonem haberetur." ("that I may not lose my time by involving myself in a dispute about the books received into the Hebrew canon: which you ridicule and revile not a little; comparing the Proverbs of Solomon and the Love-song [as you by an ambiguous sort of jeer entitle it] with the two books of Esdras, Judith, the history of Susannah and of the Dragon, and Esther. This last, however, they have received into their canon; although, in my judgment, deserving, more than all the rest, to be excluded"; translation from M. Luther, *On the Bondage of the Will; to the Venerable Mister Erasmus of Rotterdam*, 1525 [translated by E. T. Vaughan; London: Hamilton, Paternoster-Row and Combe, 1823], p. 140).

17   "Ich bin dem Buch [= 2. Makkabäer] und Esther so feind, dass ich wollte, sie wären gar nicht vorhanden; denn sie judenzen zu sehr, und haben viel heidnische Unart"; WA, *Tischreden*, vol. 1, p. 208 lines 30–31.

such as Isaiah and Daniel.[18] Luther does not clarify why Esther has such a great reputation among the Jews; however, he defines this situation as "horrible."[19] In his anti-Jewish manifesto, *On the Jews and Their Lies* (*Von den Juden und ihren Lügen* [Wittenberg, 1543]), Luther explicitly links his hostility to the book of Esther with his anti-Jewish sentiments: "Oh, how much they love the book of Esther which so well fits with their bloodthirsty, vengeful, murderous lust and hope."[20]

IV An Understanding of Luther's Conflicting Attitudes toward Esther

Hans Bardtke (1906–1975) is of the opinion that Luther's positive remarks regarding Esther outweigh his negative ones, and that the latter addressed the ethnic character of the book.[21] However, Bardtke's claim is imprecise. He does not distinguish between Luther's attitude toward the figures – Esther and Mordecai – and the book itself. Therefore, he overlooks the fact that the positive remarks of Luther relate only to the figures, while his negative ones relate to the entire book and to the Jewish people, as will be shown below (in §VI, nos. 2–3). Bardtke also does not explain the basic conflict in Luther's approach toward Esther, which does not appear throughout *Luther's entire life*, as he claims,[22] but mainly at *different stages* of his career as a Protestant reformer: While in the first half of his career Luther speaks positively of *Queen Esther* (and sometimes Mordecai), these positive statements become less frequent in the second half of his career. At the same time, Luther's critical references to the book become more common. Up to and including 1523, Luther refers to Queen Esther and Mordecai positively several times,

---

[18] Had Luther been informed by contemporary rabbis about the everlasting existence of the book of Esther even in messianic times, as stated by Resh-Lakish (Jerusalem Talmud, *Megillah* 1.5 [7b]) and later on by Rabbi Moses ben Maimon (Maimonides, 1138–1204; *Mishneh Torah*, Hilkhot Megillah, chapter 2 halakhah 18; see Chapter 8, §III)?

[19] "Die Jüden [= Juden] halten vom Buch Esther mehr, denn von irgend einem [= irgendeinem] Propheten; den Propheten Daniel und Jesaiam [= Jesaja] verachten sie gar .... Schrecklich ists [= ist es], daß sie, die Jüden, dieser zweyer [= beiden] heiligen Propheten herrlichste Weissagung verachten, da doch der eine Christum [= Christus] aufs Allerreichlichst und Reinest lehret und prediget, der andere aber die Monarchien und Kaiserthum [= Kaisertum], sammt [= samt] dem Reich Christi, aufs Allergewisseste abmalt und beschreibt." (WA *Tischreden*, vol. 1, p. 208 lines 32–36; cf. also the parallel in WA *Tischreden*, vol. 3, p. 302, no. 3391a).

[20] WA, vol. 53, p. 433 lines 17–19; for the full citation of the paragraph and the reference to Luther's writing, see below, §VII.

[21] "Gegenüber den Zitaten, die eine positive Bewertung des Buches Esther enthalten, treten die Bemerkungen einer negativen Bewertung stark zurück" (Bardtke, *Luther und das Buch Esther*, p. 50). He goes on: "Dadurch wird deutlich werden, dass die abwertenden Bemerkungen Luthers den ethnischen Bezug des Buches Esther meinen" (ibid., p. 53).

[22] See Bardtke, *Luther und das Buch Esther*, p. 86.

but after this he does so only twice, once sometime between 1537–1540 and once again in 1542.[23] By contrast, though, in 1525 Luther shows a restrained attitude toward the *book of Esther*, it is first in 1533 and 1543 (together with 2 Maccabees in the first case) that he sharply criticizes the book, both of which serve as a critique of the Jewish people. Thus, while most of his positive references appear by 1523, and are restricted to the persons of Esther and Mordecai, all three of Luther's negative evaluations of the book come after this, in 1525, 1533, and 1543, where they reflect an increasingly hostile attitude toward the book and the Jews. This shift parallels the change in Luther's relationship with the Jews overall, as we will see below (§VI, nos. 2–3).

In addition, Bardtke's conclusion leaves unexplained why Luther could be so critical toward the very existence of the biblical book and desire to erase it and 2 Maccabees entirely, and in the same breath also admire its major Jewish figures. In other words, how could he wish to throw away the stories about the Jews' salvation that these books recount, while still admiring Mordecai and particularly Esther, who contributed so much to the salvation of the Jewish people? If there is no book, there are also no figures from the book! Furthermore, if there is no story about the salvation of the Jews, one cannot praise the people who risked their lives for that salvation.

Also, why did Luther find it necessary to condemn what Bardtke refers to as "the ethnic character of the book"?[24] What specifically is the "too much Jewishness" and "a lot of pagan impropriety" that Luther attributes to the books of Esther and Maccabees? It seems that Luther's contradictory views toward the person of Esther and the book named after her should be examined on two overlapping levels: First, Luther's attitude toward Esther against the background of his approach to the Old Testament in general (§V); and second, against the historical background of his temporary "changing" approach to Jews (§VI).

V   Luther's Attitude toward Esther against the Background of His Approach to the Old Testament

In the second century, Marcion of Sinope (north Asia Minor; 85–160) famously refused to accept the Old Testament as Christian Scripture. Echoes of such an approach can still be heard also in Luther's time: "There are some [people] who have little regard for the Old Testament; they think of it as a book that was given to the Jewish people only and is now out of

---

[23]   See in detail, above, §II.
[24]   Bardtke, *Luther und das Buch Esther*, p. 50.

date, containing only stories of the past. They think they have enough in the New Testament and assert that only a spiritual sense is to be sought in the Old Testament."²⁵ Though Luther considers the Old Testament to be God's word, he thinks as well that it has been given to the Jewish people, and its laws are not valid anymore, except for some natural laws such as in the Ten Commandments (the Decalogue).²⁶ Thus, he states: "The Old Testament, promised under Moses, was fulfilled under Joshua .... The promises of Moses, therefore, do not last longer than the statutes and judgments serve. For this reason, the Old Testament finally had to become obsolete and had to be put aside; it had to serve as a prefiguration of that New and eternal Testament, which began before the ages and will endure beyond the ages. The Old Testament, however, began in time and after a time came to an end."²⁷ Luther challenges here the "Old Testament" in the sense of "Old Covenant" and the ongoing relevance of the Law, but not in the sense of "the Hebrew Bible." He uses the terms Old and New Testament, to refer sometimes to the collections of books, and other times to the covenants described in them,²⁸ as is the case in this citation.

---

²⁵ See WA *Deutsche Bibel*, vol. 8, p. 11 lines 1–5, "DAs [= Das] Alte Testament halten etliche geringe, Als das dem Jüdischen volck alleine gegeben, und nu[n] fort aus sey [= sei], und nur von vergangenen Geschichten schreibe, Meinen, sie haben g[e]nug am newen [= Neuen] Testament, und geben fur [= für] eitel geistliche[n] sinn im alten Testament zu suchen"; for the English translation, see H. Bornkamm, *Luther and the Old Testament* (translated from the original German [Tübingen: P. Siebeck, 1948] by E. W. and R. C. Gritsch; edited by V. I. Gruhn; 2nd ed.; Mifflintown, PA: Sigler Press, 1997), p. 90.

²⁶ See WA, vol. 18, p. 76 lines 1–8; p. 81 lines 4–17; vol. 24, p. 12 lines 3–9. In his *Von den Juden und ihren Lügen*, WA, vol. 53, p. 478 lines 27–36, Luther describes the Jewish understanding of the Old Testament as follows: "Shame on you here, shame on you there, and wherever you are, you damned Jews, that you dare to pull these serious, glorious, comforting words of God so disgracefully on your mortal, decayed, stinginess .... You are not worthy to see the Bible from outside, not to mention that you should read inside of it. You should only read the 'Bible' that is written under the tail of a sow, and swallow and drink the letters that fall out of it. That would be a 'Bible' for such prophets who so piggishly rummage and boarishly tear the words of the divine majesty, which should be heard with all honor, trembling and joy." ("Pfu euch [= Schande über euch] hie, pfu euch dort, und wo jr [= ihr] seid, jr verdampten Jüden, das jr diese ernste, herrliche, tröstliche wort Gottes so schendlich auff ewern [= euern] sterblichen, madichten [= der Verwesung verfallenen] Geitzwanst zi[e]hen thüret [= zu z. waget] .... Seid jr doch nicht werd [= wert], das[s] jr die Biblia von aussen sollet ansehen, [ge] schweige, das[s] jr drinnen lesen sollet. Jr sol[l]tet allein die Biblia lesen, die der Saw [= Sau] unter dem Schwantz stehet, und die buchstaben, so da selbs[t] heraus fallen, fressen und sauffen, das were [=wäre] eine Bibel fur solche Propheten, die der Göttlichen Maiestet wort, so man mit allen ehren, zittern und freuden hören so[l]lt, so sewisch zu wü[h]len und so schweinisch zu reissen.").

²⁷ WA, vol. 14, p. 602 line 37, p. 608 lines 33–36: "Vetus testamentum sub Mose promissum, sub Iosue impletum est .... Ideo Mose latius non promittit, quam donec servant statute et iura. Quae causa fuit, ut ipsum antiquari tandem et aboleri opertuerit et figuram gerere novi et aeterni illius testamenti, quod ante saecula incepit et post saecula duravit. Illud autem in tempore coepit et post tempus aliquod deficit." For the English translation of the paragraph, see Bornkamm, *Luther and the Old Testament*, p. 81. See also WA, vol. 12, p. 275 lines 5–15 (ET, Bornkamm, ibid., p. 84).

²⁸ As Bornkamm correctly notes: "for Luther 'Old Testament' and 'New Testament' were not just the names of two books," but could also serve as synonyms for "law" and "gospel," which are in both parts of the Christian canon. See Bornkamm, *Luther and the Old Testament*, p. 81.

Nonetheless, Luther still considered the Old Testament as a whole to be part and parcel of the Christian Bible, and translated it from Hebrew into German (completed in 1534). He served as *lector in biblia* in the University of Wittenberg, where he concentrated mostly on the Old Testament.[29] To cite Bornkamm, "He occupied himself with the Old Testament far more than with the New Testament,"[30] as shown by the abundant citations from and discussions of the Old Testament scattered throughout Luther's works, and by his several specific works on the Old Testament books, such as his commentaries on Genesis and Psalms.[31]

Like many Christian theologians before and after him, Luther also believed that Christians must read the Old Testament in light of the New Testament. He considered the Old Testament to be full of hints of the promised messianic coming of Jesus.[32] In this, he embraced the Old Testament and rejected Jewish interpretations of it. He insisted on interpreting Scripture alone from itself and in its own right (*sola scriptura*, or, in fact, *prima scriptura*), and limited the allegorical approach only to Christ in the Old Testament.[33] He even considered the "New" Testament to be older than the "Old" Testament, since it was "promised from the beginning of the world, yes, 'before the times of the world' as St. Paul says

---

[29] The term *biblia* was understood more broadly than just "the Bible," and included also church tradition and doctrine; see A. Beutel, "Theologie als Schriftauslegung," in idem (ed.), *Lutherhandbuch* (2nd ed.; Universität-Taschenbücher 3416; Tübingen: Mohr Siebeck, 2010), pp. 444–449 esp. 444; cf. also R. Schwarz, *Luther* (4th ed.; Universität-Taschenbücher; Göttingen: Vandenhoeck & Ruprecht, 2014), p. 38.

[30] See Bornkamm, *Luther and the Old Testament*, p. vii.

[31] Interestingly, several books and articles about Luther's views of the Old Testament were published between 1932 and 1942; see Bornkamm, *Luther and the Old Testament*, pp. vii–ix, notes 1–4, 6. Some scholars attempt to explain how the prominent German theologian – Luther – occupied himself so much with the Jewish Scriptures. Thus, for instance, Johannes Hempel (1891–1964), who was a member of Nationalsozialistische Deutsche Arbeiterpartei (= National Socialist German Workers [or Labour] Party; abbreviated NSDAP), Schutzstaffel (= SS) and other Nazi organizations (see www.catalogus-professorum-halensis.de/hempeljohannes.html [February 23, 2018]), published a pamphlet on *Luther und das Alte Testament* (Bremen: Hauschild, 1935); see also J. Hempel, "Luther und das Alte Testament," *Die Christus bekennende Reichskirche* 4 (1935), pp. 1–16. On Johannes Hempel, see F. W. Bautz, "Hempel, Johannes," *Biographisch-Bibliographisches Kirchenlexikon* (Bautz: Hamm, 1990), vol. 2, pp. 711–712; C. Weber, *Altes Testament und völkische Frage: Der biblische Volksbegriff in der alttestamentlichen Wissenschaft der nationalsozialistischen Zeit, dargestellt am Beispiel von Johannes Hempel* (Forschungen zum Alten Testament 38; Tübingen: Mohr Siebeck, 2010).

[32] See, for example, Beutel, "Theologie als Schriftauslegung," pp. 444–449; R. Schwarz, *Martin Luther: Lehrer der christlichen Religion* (Tübingen: Mohr Siebeck, 2015), 45–73; cf. also S. Raeder, *Grammatica Theologica: Studien zu Luthers Operationes in Psalmos* (Beiträge zur historischen Theologie 51; Tübingen: J. C. B. Mohr [P. Siebeck], 1977), esp. pp. 51–59.

[33] See particularly in his *Lectures on Genesis*; WA, vol. 42, especially pp. 173–174, 367–377. For detailed discussions of this issue, see Bornkamm, *Luther and the Old Testament*, pp. 87–101; A. Beutel, "Wort Gottes," in idem (ed.), *Lutherhandbuch*, pp. 362–371 esp. 367–369; Schwarz, *Martin Luther: Lehrer der christlichen Religion*, pp. 27–44.

to Titus [1:2]."[34] In another place, Luther states that both law and gospel are found in the Old as well as the New Testaments: "There is no book in the Bible that does not contain both. God has placed them side by side in every way – law and promise …. But because there is a heap of [fulfilled] promises in the New Testament and a heap of commandments in the Old, we call one the gospel book and the other the law book."[35]

Nevertheless, Luther had an inconsistent approach to Esther: On the one hand, he wished that the book of Esther (and 2 Maccabees) was never included in the canon.[36] On the other hand, his positive view of Queen Esther and Mordecai fits with his portrayals of other Old Testament heroes, who could be praised as models for Christians. Like many others, Luther considered Christians to be the "True Israel" (*Verus Israel*)/"Israel in Spirit" (in contrast to "Heretical/Talmudic Jews"), and the continuation of "Biblical Israel."[37] Thus, for instance, in both editions of his introduction to the book of Ezekiel (*Luthers neue Vorrede auf den Propheten Hesekiel*; 1541 and 1545), Luther asserts: "[T]he Jews claim for themselves the name 'Israel' and praise themselves as being Israel alone while we are Gentiles. This is true according to the first part [of "the prophecy"][38] and the Old Covenant of Moses, which was fulfilled a long time ago. But according to the other part, the New Covenant, they are no longer 'Israel,' because everything shall be new, and "Israel" had to become new, too.

---

34 See WA, vol. 14, p. 602 lines 34–36, "Testamentum novum est vetustissimum ab initio mundi promissum, imo ante tempora saecularia, ut Paulus ad Titum loquitur, sed tantum sub Christo impletum"; the English translation is from Bornkamm, *Luther and the Old Testament*, p. 81.

35 See WA, vol. 10 (part I, 2), p. 159 lines 7–8, 17–19, "Es ist keyn [= kein] buch ynn [= in] der Biblien [= Bibel], darynnen [= darin] sie nicht beyderley [= beiderlei] sind, gott hatt [= hat] sie alwege [= immer] beyeynander [= beieinander] gesetzt, beyde [= beide], gesetz und tzusagung [= Zusagung]. Denn er le[h]ret durchs gesetz, was tzu [= zu] thun [= tun] ist, und durch die tzusagung [= Zusagung], wo manß [= man es] ne[h]men soll …. Weyl [= weil] aber ym [= im] newen [= neuen] testament die tzusagung [= Zusagung] mit hauffen [= häufig] stehen, und ym allten [= alten] die gesetz[e] mit hauffen [= häufig], nennet man eynß [= eins] Euangelion [= Evangelium], das ander[e] gesetzbuch." (English translation: Bornkamm, *Luther and the Old Testament*, p. 83). See also the similar sentiment in his *Introduction to the Old Testament*, WA *Deutsche Bibel*, vol. 8, p. 12 lines 13–22 (1523 edition), and p. 13 lines 13–22 (1545 edition); cited and discussed by Schwarz, *Martin Luther: Lehrer der christlichen Religion*, p. 56.

36 In contrast, Luther admired the book of Psalms. In his "Zweite Vorrede auf den Psalter" (1528), he calls it: *eine kleine Biblia* ("a little Bible"). He goes on to clarify: "wer die ganze Biblia nicht lesen könnte, hätte hierin doch fast die ganze Summa [*sic*.], verfasst in ein[em] klein[en] Büchlein" ("whoever cannot read the entire Bible, has here almost the entire Summa [i.e., the whole Scripture], composed in a small booklet").

37 See Kalimi, *Early Jewish Exegesis and Theological Controversy*, p. 146 note 36.

38 In this context "the first part" does not refer to the first part of the Christian canon, but instead to the first part of "the prophecy" that Israel will return to its land and be granted a New Covenant. "The first part" refers to the return to the land after the Exile, which Luther says "was fulfilled a long time ago" under Cyrus, king of Persia, and was (according to Luther) followed by the granting of the promised New Covenant, which the Jews rejected.

And only those who embrace the New Covenant (which is established and begun in Jerusalem), are the 'True Israel.'"[39]

This is an all-too-typical traditional Christian supersessionist approach, claiming the biblical promises regarding Israel mostly for the Church, while applying all the prophetical condemnations of Israel to the Jews.[40] For this reason, one cannot simply count up whether Luther says more positive or more negative things about Esther (the person or the book). Instead, while Luther could praise Esther and Mordecai as *people* (or, if you wish, as literary characters),[41] he considered the *book* of Esther as a whole too Jewish and too popular among the Jews to be valuable for Christians. In particular, he used the violence described in the last part of the book as a platform for his anti-Jewish assertions (see below, §VII).

As with everything else in the Old Testament, Luther holds an ambivalent attitude toward Esther, attempting to claim for the Church all that he likes, while attributing to the Jews all that he dislikes. Accordingly, Esther, the humble queen who approaches the Persian king at risk of her own life, is pious and praiseworthy, and can be used as a model of noble and courageous behavior for all Christians. But Esther, the book, which ends with the victory of the Jews over their bitter enemies, and the celebration of their salvation at the festival of Purim (which is based on this book), would have been better never to have been written at all.[42] For Luther, these two views are apparently not seen as contradictory; he expresses both of them at various points in his life without ever reflecting on the tension between them. In short, he thinks he can keep Esther the pious queen, while rejecting Esther the faithful Jewess and the entire book named after her, forgetting that they are one and the same Esther, and that without the book there are no characters(s) from it.

---

[39] "DAS [= dass] die Juden nu[n] so fest stehen auff [= auf] dem namen Israel, und rhümen [= rühmen], wie sie allein Israel, wir aber Heiden sind, Das ist wa[h]r, nach dem ersten stück und nach dem alten bund Mose, der nu[n] lengest [= längst] erfüllet ist. Aber nach dem andern stück, und newen [= neuen] Bund, sind sie nicht mehr Israel, Denn es sol[l] alles New [= neu] sein, und Israel hat müssen auch new [= neu] werden. Und sind allein die der rechte Israel, die den newen [= neuen] Bund (zu Jerusalem gestifftet [= gestiftet] und angefangen) angenommen haben"; WA *Deutsche Bibel*, vol. II.1, p. 401; cf. the earlier parallel text on p. 400; for a different English translation, see C. M. Jacobs (trans.), "Prefaces to the Old Testament," in Bachmann (ed.), *Luther's Works*, vol. 35, pp. 233–333 esp. 287–288.

[40] See L. Diestel, *Geschichte des Alten Testaments in der christlichen Kirche* (Jena: Mauke, 1869), p. 42; Bornkamm, *Luther and the Old Testament*, p. 4; Kalimi, "The Task of Hebrew Bible/Old Testament Theology," pp. 150–151.

[41] As he considers positively Daniel, Hananiah, Mishael, and Azariah; see above, §II.

[42] For the same reason, Luther rejects 2 Maccabees, which describes the Jews' victories over their enemies, and the celebration of the salvation of the Jews at the festival of Hanukkah.

Figure 13   Lucas Cranach the Elder, A Portrait of Martin Luther, probably 1532, Germany.

VI   Luther's Attitude toward Esther against the Background of His Approaches to Judaism and Jews

The general contrast between Luther's views of the person of Esther and the book in which she appears is roughly parallel to Luther's changing attitudes toward the Jews during his career as a reformer. Above we saw that one can trace a shift over the course of Luther's career, from an early period when he rarely says anything negative about the book while often praising its heroes, to a later period when he hardly praises its heroes and harshly criticizes the book. As already mentioned, in 1525 Luther wrote to Erasmus that he personally would prefer that the book of Esther had been excluded from the canon. This was around the same time, in early 1526, when Luther described the Jews themselves as standing beside Satan (see below). Thus, the shift in Luther's attitude regarding Esther in these years seems to correspond to a larger change in his approach toward Jews more generally, as he explicitly connects the two in his *Von den Juden und ihren Lügen*.[43] But prior to discussing this issue, it is worth clarifying Luther's attitude toward Judaism and Jews.

1   Luther and Judaism

Luther's antipathy to Judaism, as a religion and cultural heritage, is much more *outspoken* in the late period than in the early. However, it does not seem to be the case that his basic theological beliefs concerning Judaism ever changed. In fact, he never appreciated Judaism for its own sake, and sought only to convince the Jews to reject it in favor of Christianity.[44] As Thomas Kaufmann puts it: "A normative, post-biblical Jewish tradition is for him [i.e., Luther] just as illegitimate as the [Roman Catholic] Church tradition. In contrast to [Johannes] Reuchlin, he attributed no significance to the post-biblical Jewish literature; in his image of Judaism it played exclusively a negative role. 'Luther's Jews' should concern themselves only with the Old Testament."[45] Further, as early as 1515–1516, Luther's writings describes the Jews as "Godless," and he claims that "their Talmud [is] full of lies and inversions, even perversions of the Scripture."[46] Also, as seen in his later book, *Von den Juden und ihren Lügen* (1543; see below, no. 3), for Luther, the terms "Judaism" and "lies" are deeply connected and they are one unit, standing in contrast to "Christianity" and "truth." Since he considered postbiblical Jewish literature (particularly the rabbinic

---

[43] See in detail, below, §VII.

[44] Heiko A. Oberman emphasizes that Luther's view of the Jews themselves was "constant and indissoluble"; only his "tactical Jewish politics" changed with the circumstances ("Luthers 'Judenschau' [ist] über die Jahre hinweg konstant und unauflösbar mit seiner Geschichtsschau verschlungen. Geändert haben sich hingegen die taktische Judenpolitik"; H. A. Oberman, "Die Juden in Luthers Sicht," in H. Kremers *et al.* [ed.], *Die Juden und Martin Luther – Martin Luther und die Juden: Geschichte, Wirkungsgeschichte, Herausforderung* [Neukirchen-Vluyn: Neukirchener Verlag, 1985], pp. 136–162 esp. 140).

[45] T. Kaufmann, *Luthers Juden* (2nd ed.; Stuttgart: Reclam, 2015), p. 71: "Eine normative nachbiblische jüdische Tradition galt ihm [= Luther] als ebenso illegitim wie die kirchliche Tradition. Im Unterschied zu Reuchlin erkannte er den nachbiblischen jüdischen Literatur keinerlei Bedeutung zu; in seinem Bild des Judentums spielte sie ausschließlich eine negative Rolle. 'Luthers Juden' sollten sich allein auf das Alte Testament beziehen" (cf. ibid., pp. 66–74).

[46] "Que sunt eorum Thalmudica plena mendaciis et inversionibus, immo perversionibus Scripture"; WA, vol. 3, p. 501 lines 8–9; cf. also E. L. Ehrlich, "Luther und die Juden," in Kremers *et al.* (ed.), *Die Juden und Martin Luther*, pp. 72–88 esp. 73.

writings, that are at the heart of Judaism) to be simply lies and errors, he never made any effort to understand the Jews' own perspectives, self-definition, or theology; his only goal was to convince them to accept his own. Even when he read Jewish books, which he seldom did, Luther had no interest in *understanding* the Jewish concepts of grace and faithfulness, only in condemning their rejection of Jesus. For instance, in one of his *Tischreden*, from April 12, 1539, Luther is said to have read a Hebrew book of prayers and festival liturgies, from which he concluded: "They [= the Jews] understand nothing of God's grace, nor of the righteousness of faith, as God is merciful from pure grace, for Christ's sake, and that faith in Christ is just, pious and blessed; of which they know less than nothing."[47] In other words, because the Jews do not look to Jesus for salvation, they – in Luther's mind – cannot understand anything of God's grace. For all Luther's supposed friendliness toward the Jews (see below, no. 2), there is little evidence that he ever attempted to learn *from* them anything beyond the Hebrew language, which was necessary for his German translation of the Old Testament.

Thus, while Luther greatly desired the conversion of the Jews, and for the time being even loudly condemned all those practices that had previously discouraged Jews from converting, he never accepted the postbiblical Judaism itself as legitimate. He only hoped that the Jews would also recognize the illegitimacy of their postbiblical traditions once they recognized the superiority of Christianity and Christians.

2   Luther's Friendly Approach toward Jews

Regarding the Jews as people, those defined by Christians as "Talmudic" or "Heretical" Jews, Luther was kind and tolerant, for a limited time, in the early stage of his career, but hostile and xenophobic particularly later on.[48] In the second half of the tens and through most of the twenties of the sixteenth century, Luther's approach was friendly toward the Jews, while

---

[47] "Sie [= die Juden] verstehen nichts von Gottes Gnade, noch von der Gerechtigkeit des Glaubens, wie Gott barmherzig sey [= sei] aus lauter Gnad[e], um Christus [= Christi] willen, und daß der Glaub[e] an Christum gerecht, fromm und selig mache; davon wissen sie weniger, denn nichts"; WA *Tischreden*, vol. 4, p. 343 lines 27–30; see also Ehrlich, "Luther und die Juden," p. 82.

[48] On the relationship between Luther and the Jews, in addition to those studies noted below, see also R. Lewin, *Luthers Stellung zu den Juden: Ein Beitrag zur Geschichte der Juden in Deutschland während des Reformationszeitalters* (Neue Studien zur Geschichte der Theologie und der Kirche 10; Berlin: Trowitzsch, 1911); Kremers *et al.* (eds.), *Die Juden und Martin Luther*; P. von der Osten-Sacken, *Martin Luther und die Juden* (Stuttgart: Kohlhammer, 2002); E. W. Gritsch, *Martin Luther's Antisemitism: Against His Better Judgement* (Grand Rapids, MI: Eerdmans, 2012); Kalimi, "The Position of Martin Luther towards Jews and Judaism" with further references.

hoping that in this way he would attract at least some of them to convert to the newly reformed Church. This approach is evident from what Luther stated in his "positive" writings, and from what he did not state in his "negative" ones.

On the one hand, in his *Great Confession* (*Bekenntnis,* 1528), Luther did not mention the Jews among the antichrist heretics such as the Tatars, Persians, Turks (Luther's way of referring to "Muslims"), and the Pope.[49] Elsewhere, Luther mentions the Pope and Mohammed as the major enemies of Christianity, while excluding the Jews and Jewish religious leader(s).[50]

On the other hand, in his work *That Jesus Christ Was Born a Jew* (*Dass Jesus Christus ein geborener Jude sei,* 1523), Luther attempts to show that Jesus and Jews are actually from the same root: "I will therefore show, by means of the Bible, the causes which convince me to believe that Christ was born a Jew, from a virgin." "Perhaps," continues Luther, "I will attract some of the Jews to the Christian faith ...."[51] In the same work, Luther also describes the current treatment of Jews by Christians as intolerable:

> The way our fools, the Papists, bishops, sophists, and monks, the big ass-heads, have before now dealt with the Jews, a good Christian might actually have become a Jew. If I had been a Jew and had seen such mugs and block-heads rule and teach the Christian faith, I should rather have turned into a pig than become a Christian. They treat the Jews as if they were dogs[52] and not human beings ....[53]

---

[49] See WA, vol. 26, pp. 499–509 esp. 506–507. On the Turks in Luther's writings, see J. Ehmann, *Luther und die Türken* (Studienreihe Luther 15; Bielefeld: Luther-Verlag, 2017); K.-J. Kuschel, "Martin Luther, die Türken und der Islam: Ein schwieriges Erbe als Auftrag für Heute," in Danz and Tück (eds.), *Martin Luther im Widerstreit der Konfessionen,* pp. 443–468.

[50] Cf. J. Wallmann, "Luther on Jews and Islam," in B. Uffenheimer and H. Graf Reventlow (eds.), *Creative Biblical Exegesis* (Journal for the Study of the Old Testament Supplement Series 59; Sheffield: Sheffield Academic Press, 1988), pp. 149–160 esp. 157–158.

[51] The book, *Dass Jesus Christus ein geborener Jude sei,* is published in WA, vol. 11, pp. 314–336; see esp. p. 314 lines 25–28: "Darum will ich aus der schrifft ertzelen [= erzählen], die ursach[e]n, die mich bewegen, dass Christus eyn [= ein] Jude sey [= sei] von eyner [= einer] jungfrawen [= Jungfrau] geporn [= geboren], ob ich vi[e]lleicht auch der Juden ettliche [= etliche] mocht [= möchte] zum Christen glauben [= christlichen Glauben] reizen."

[52] The simile also appears several times in Luther's writings; see below, §VI, 3. In ca. 1535, John Calvin also referred to Jews as "impure dogs"; see Kalimi, "The Position of Martin Luther towards Jews and Judaism," §IV, 6, 4.

[53] See WA, vol. 11, p. 314 lines 28–30, and p. 315 lines 1–3: "Denn unsere narren die Papste [= Päpste], Bischoff [= Bischöfe], Sophisten und Munche [= Mönche], die groben Esels köpffe [= Eselsköpfe] haben bis her [= bisher] also mit den Juden gefahren [= verfahren], das, wer ein gutter [= guter] Christ were [= wäre] gewetzen [= gewesen], hette [= hätte] wol [= wohl] mocht [= möchten] ein Jude werden. Und wenn ich ein Jude gewesen were und hette solche tolpell [= Tölpel] und knebel gesehen den Christen glauben [= christlichen Glauben], regi[e]r[e]n und lehren, so were ich ehe[r] eine saw [= Sau] [ge]worden denn ein Christen. Denn sie haben mit den Juden gehandelt als weren es hunde und nicht menschen ...."

Thus, the Protestant reformer proposes modifying the merciless Christian behavior toward the Jews. He was opposed to the persecution of Jews and insisted on dealing with them humanely, in order to attract them to Christianity: "I hope that if the Jews are treated kindly and are clearly instructed through the Bible, many of them will become real Christians and come back to the ancestral faith of the prophets and patriarchs."[54] In other words, Luther hopes that the Jews will abandon Judaism (that is, the rabbinic interpretation of "the ancestral faith of the prophets and patriarchs"), and return to the norms of the original "Biblical Israel," of which Christianity is considered the continuation, in contrast to those of the "Talmudic Jews," who (according to such Christians) distanced themselves from it.[55] Therefore, Luther suggests:

> I would advise and beg everyone to deal kindly with the Jews and to instruct them in the Scriptures. In such cases we could expect them to come over to us. If, however, we use brute force and slander them, saying that they need the blood of Christians to get rid of the stench, and treat them like dogs, what good can we expect from them? Finally, how can we expect them to improve if we forbid them to work among us and have social intercourse with us and so force them into interest [from money lending]? If we wish to make them better, we must deal with them not according to the law of the Pope, but according to the law of Christian charity. We must receive them kindly and allow them to compete with us in earning a living, so that they may have a good reason to be with us, and among us, and have an opportunity to witness Christian life and doctrine. Then if some remain stubborn, what of it? Not every one of us is a good Christian.[56]

[54] See WA, vol. 11, p. 315 lines 14–16: "Ich hoff[e], wenn man mit den Juden freundlich handelt und aus der heyligen [= Heiligen] Schrift sie säuberlich unterweytzet [= unterweise], es sollten ihr viel rechte Christen werden, und widder [= wieder] zu yhrer [= ihrer] Väter, der Propheten und Patriarchen Glauben tretten [= treten] ...." Compare also the account of the conversion of a Jew named "Bernhard" (birth name: Jakob Gipher) who was added to an early Latin translation of *Dass Jesus Christus ein geborener Jude sei*, and was intended to encourage other Jews to follow his lead; see Kaufmann, *Luthers Juden*, pp. 63–64, 67.

[55] On this point, see also Kaufmann, *Luthers Juden*, pp. 66–74.

[56] See WA, vol. 11, pp. 307–336 esp. 336 lines 22–34: "Darumb [= Darum] were [= wäre] meyn [= meine] bitt [= Bitte] und rad [= Rat], das[s] man seuberlich [= säuberlich] mit yhn [= ihnen; d.h., Juden] umbgieng [= umginge] und aus der schrifft [= Schrift] sie unterrichtet, so mochten [= möchten] yhr [= von ihnen] ettliche herbey [= hebei] ko[m]men. Aber nu[n] wyr [= wir] sie nur mit gewalt treyben [= treiben] und gehen mit lugen [= Lügen] teydingen [= verleumden] umb [= um], geben yhn [= ihnen] schuld, sie mussen [= müssen] Christen blutt [= christliches Blut] haben, das sie nicht stincken, [= stinken] und weys [= wissen] nicht wes [= was] des narren wercks [= Werkes] mehr ist, das man sie gleich fur hunde hellt [= hält], Was sollten wyr [= wir] guttis [= Gutes] an yhn [= ihnen] schaffen? Item [= Ebenfalls] das[s] man yhn [= ihnen] verbeutt [= verbietet], untter [sic] uns tzu [= zu] erbeytten [= arbeiten], hantieren und andere menschliche gemeynschaft [= Gemeinschaft] tzu [= zu] haben, damit man sie tzu [= zu] wuchern treybt [= treibt], wie sollt[en] sie das bessern? Will man yhn [= ihnen] helffen [= helfen], so mus[s] man

Similarly, Luther writes in his commentary on Psalm 14:

> Please let me know who would adopt our religion, even if he be a most
> humble and patient person, when he sees how cruelly, hatefully, and in
> a cattle-like, rather than Christian-like, fashion they are treated by us? ...
> Most Passion preachers [during the Easter Week] do nothing else but enor-
> mously exaggerate the Jews' misdeeds against Christ and thus embitter the
> hearts of the faithful against them.[57]

Therefore, Luther asks his followers not only to dismiss all the ridiculous false accusations, bias, and negative attitudes to Jews, but also to
replace them with favorable and positive ones. In these ways Luther
wished to fulfill the old and long-awaited dream of the Church,
namely to convert the people of Jesus – the Jews – to the religion of
Jesus – Christianity.

Luther's project to convert the Jews was, first and foremost, a part of
his Christian mission to spread its religious principles and theological concepts (including the belief that salvation is offered only through Jesus).[58]
Seemingly, Luther was convinced that after his reformation of the corrupted papacy and Church, the Jews eventually would convert and accept
the "right," and "spotless" reformed Christianity. Now, he believed, there
was no longer any obstacle for the Jews finally to convert, and to come
back to the original biblical, ancestral, and prophetic values (as interpreted
by the protestant Christians).

It is worthy to stress that Luther's goal was not just a utopian dream of
the new Christian reformer, but was probably based on some historical
reality: "Jewish apostasy was a serious and not uncommon phenomenon in
late fifteenth- and sixteenth-century Germany, and affected a wide range

---

nicht des Bapsts [= Papstes], sonder[n] Christlicher liebe gesetz [= Liebesgesetz] an yhn [= ihnen]
uben [= üben] und sie freuntlich [= freundlich] annehmen, mit lassen [= erlauben] werben und
erbeytten [= arbeiten], da mit [= damit] sie ursach [= Ursache] und raum [= Raum] gewynnen
[=gewinnen], bey [= bei] und umb [= um] uns tzu [= zu] seyn [= sein], unser Christlich[e] lere [=
Lehre] und leben [= Leben] tzu [= zu] horen [= hören] und sehen. Ob ettliche [= etliche] hallstar-
rig [= halsstarrig/stur] sind, was li[e]gt d[a]ran? sind wyr [= wir] doch auch nicht alle gutte [=
gute] Christen."

57   "Quis rogo ad nostram religionem transeat, vel benignissimae patientissimae mentis, qui tam atroc-
iter et hostiliter et non modo non christianiter, sed plusquam feraliter sese a nobis videat tractari? ...
Nec aliud etiam agunt passionis dominicae declamatores plurimi, quam ut Iudaeorum in Christum
ferociam aggravent et in eos exasperent fidelium corda." See WA, vol. 5, p. 429, lines 7–9.12–14.
See also S. W. Baron, A Social and Religious History of the Jews (2nd ed.; New York: Columbia
University Press/Philadelphia: The Jewish Publication Society of America, 1969), vol. 13, p. 217
(Baron mistakenly refers to Psalm 22, following the mistake of Heinrich Graetz).

58   On Luther's desire to convert the Jews, as well as his skepticism about insincere conversion, and
his denial of the legitimacy of Judaism as an acceptable alternative to Christianity, see Kaufmann,
Luthers Juden, pp. 63–86.

of Jews, even if the most notorious cases seem to have come from a particular group of Jews."⁵⁹

This was, among others, the socio-religious historical background of
Luther's positive attitude toward the Jews in general, and probably also
toward their beloved biblical figures – Esther and Mordecai – in particular.
But this was only a temporary change. Even in his *That Jesus Christ Was
Born a Jew*, Luther concluded that this positive approach to Jews should
only be followed "until I see what I have accomplished."⁶⁰ That is, it was
for Luther a temporary measure aimed at the conversion of Jews as people,
not a fundamental change in attitude toward Judaism.⁶¹

The new approach of Luther gained positive reactions from some Jews and
various Jewish scholars.⁶² Indeed, despite its missionary goal, this attitude of
Luther could have been a dramatic historical turning point in Christian–
Jewish relations, with tremendous and lasting consequences for both sides.
Nevertheless, we should not overstate Luther's time limited tolerance.

3   Luther's Hostile Approach toward Jews

When Luther admitted that although the Jews appreciated his kind words
that improved the general attitude toward the Jews,⁶³ most would not leave
Judaism, even after his reform of the Church, then his friendly attitude
toward them was overturned, and a hostile one – even worse than that of
the Catholic Church – replaced it. The longer he lived and the less likely
the mass conversion of the Jews appeared, the more harshly Luther voiced
poisoned assertions against them and their culture and religion, emphasizing the wrath of God against unrepentant, heretical Jews.

---

⁵⁹ See D. P. Bell, *Sacred Communities: Jewish and Christian Identities in Fifteenth-Century Germany*
(Studies in Central European Histories; Leiden and Boston: Brill, 2001), p. 215, and there, on pp.
213–223, examples of some Jews who converted. For Luther's motivations to convert the Jews, see
Kalimi, "The Position of Martin Luther towards Jews and Judaism" §II.

⁶⁰ WA, vol. 11, p. 336 line 35 ("Hie[r] will ichs di[ese]s mall [= Mal] lassen bleyben [= bleiben], bis
ich sehe, was ich gewirckt [= bewirkt] habe"); cf. WA *Briefwechsel*, vol. 8, pp. 89–91 esp. 89–90
lines 2–13, which is cited below, and see also Kaufmann, *Luthers Juden*, p. 74, who emphasizes
that this conclusion should not be ignored: Luther's positive proposals were only ever *meant* to be
temporary.

⁶¹ See in detail, Kalimi, "The Position of Martin Luther towards Jews and Judaism" §§II–III.

⁶² For instance, Rabbi Abraham haLevi; see P. E. Lapide, "'Der Mann, von dem alle sprechen':
Der Junge Luther aus zeitgenössischer Sicht," *Lutherische Monatshefte* 14 (1975), pp. 527–530. See
in detail, H. H. Ben-Sasson, "Jewish-Christian Disputation in the Setting of Humanism and
Reformation in the German Empire," *HTR* 59 (1966), pp. 369–390; and cf. Wallmann, "Luther on
Jews and Islam," pp. 153–154; P. Johnson, *A History of the Jews* (London: Weidenfeld and Nicolson,
1987), p. 241.

⁶³ See H. H. Ben-Sasson, "The Reformation in Contemporary Jewish Eyes," *Proceedings of the Israel
Academy of Science and Humanities*, vol. 4 (1971), pp. 239–326 esp. 266–267.

The earliest sign of this appears already in 1526, when Luther spoke very sharply against the Jews and linked them with Satan.[64] In one of his sermons in 1531, he lists the Jews alongside the Papists and Turks as stereotypical examples of those who reject God's grace and strive to achieve salvation through human effort, all of whom he associates with the devil.[65] In my opinion, Luther's aforementioned harsh remark on the books of Esther and 2 Maccabees in 1533, which according to Luther "show too much Jewishness," are in line with his growing hostility.

Four years later, in his letter of June 11, 1537, to the Advocate of the Jewish Communities in the Holy Roman Empire and Poland, Josel von Rosheim (Alsace),[66] Luther blames the Jews for misusing his good will and his service for them:

> It is true, I would have acted against my gracious Lord on your behalf, both through the word and the letter, as my writings have long served the Jewish people. But since your people abused my service so shamefully and take such things of the Christians of which they dislike, they themselves have taken away all my demands to Prince and Lord.
>
> Because my heart was, and still is, of the opinion that one should treat the Jews in a friendly manner, whether God will one day look to them with grace and bring them to their Messiah, and not of the opinion that they should be strengthened and angered in their error through my favor and support.[67]

---

[64] For example, WA, vol. 19, p. 599 lines 10–11, where he states that "It is not reason nor human blindness, which would be manageable, but as they stand, Satan stands to their right" ("Nicht vernufft [= Vernunft] noch menschliche blindheit, denn die were [= wäre] zu lencken [= lenken]; sondern, wie hie[r] stehet, Satan stehet zu yhrer [= ihrer] rechten"); cf. also pp. 607–608; Kaufmann, *Luthers Juden*, pp. 98–99.

[65] For example, J. G. Walch (ed.), *Dr. Martin Luthers sämtliche Schriften* (2nd ed.; 24 vols.; Saint Louis, MO: Concordia, 1880–1910/reprinted: Gross Oesingen: H. Harms, 1987), vol. 8, pp. 77–88 esp. 79, where he refers to trust in human righteousness as "der Teufel, und eine jüdische Lehre"). The same sermon affirms that "the Pope, Turks, Jews, nasty men and factious spirits do not recognize it [= the word of Christ; i.e. John 7:37]; therefore they will die of this thirst, and they must die inside" ("der Papst, Türke, Juden, gemeine Mann und Rottengeister erkennen ihn [= das Wort Christi] nicht; darum wird sie dieser Durst tödten [= töten], und sie müssen drinnen sterben"; ibid., pp. 79–80).

[66] On Rabbi Josel von Rosheim (or Joseph ben Gershon Loanz, 1476–1554), see S. Stern, *Josel von Rosheim: Befehlshaber der Judenschaft im Heiligen Römischen Reich Deutscher Nation* (Stuttgart: Deutsche Verlags-Anstalt, 1959); V. Galle (ed.), *Josel von Rosheim: Zwischen dem Einzigartigen und Universellen. Ein engagierter Jude im Europa seiner Zeit und im Europa unserer Zeit* (Worms: Worms Verlag, 2013).

[67] "Ich wollt[e] wohl gerne gegen meinen gnädigsten Herrn für Euch handeln, beide mit Worten und Schriften, wie denn auch meine Schrift der ganzen Jüdischheit gar viel gedienet hat; aber dieweil [= da] die Euren solches meines Diensts so schändlich mißbrauchen und solche Ding für nehmen, die uns Christen von ihnen nicht zu leiden sind, haben sie selbst damit mir genommen alle Forderung, die ich sonst hätte bei Fürsten und Herrn können tun. Denn mein Herz ja gewesen ist, und noch, daß man die Jüden sollt freundlich halten, der Meinung, ob sie Gott dermaleins wollt gnädiglich ansehen und zu ihrem Messia bringen, und nicht der Meinung, daß sie sollten durch mein Gunst und Forderung in ihrem Irrtumb gestärkt und ärger werden"; WA *Briefwechsel*, vol. 8, pp. 89–91 esp. 89–90 lines 2–13.

Luther does not detail how the Jews "abused" his service, but at least part of his complaint seems to be tied to his disappointed hope for their conversion. Thus, elsewhere in the letter Luther states that "Because for the sake of the crucified Jew [= Jesus], whom no one should take from me, I would gladly do the best for all of you Jews, excepting that you should use my favor for your stubbornness."[68] As Ernst L. Ehrlich notes, "Luther expresses it openly: Help from him for the Jews is not to be expected if they do not convert,"[69] but instead persist in their "stubbornness" in keeping Judaism. Ehrlich goes on to conclude correctly that Luther's "good will towards the Jews was never unconditional, but rather always had a concrete goal: to lead them to Jesus. The Jews, however, had not only shut out Luther's arguments, but had nothing to say about Jesus except that he 'was a crucified, condemned Jew,' a formulation that Luther uses explicitly in his letter to Josel of Rosheim."[70] The hope to convert the Jews was always Luther's primary purpose in offering to help them, and as soon as it became obvious that their conversion was unlikely, he refused to continue to aid them in their "stubbornness." Accordingly, the following year, in a letter *Wider die Sabbather* (1538), Luther concluded that the Jews' refusal to accept Jesus is their fundamental sin, which explains both the destruction of their Temple and their long exile.[71]

From his side, Josel von Rosheim blamed Luther for the expulsion of the Jews of Saxony in 1536. Indeed, despite Josel's strong petition, Luther not only refused to convince his chief sponsor John Frederick I, the Elector of Saxony, to revoke the expulsion of the miserable homeless Jews, but even pushed for it. Thus, in 1537, animosity between the two leaders – Luther and Josel – was growing. On the one side, Josel participated in 1539 in a religious debate between Jews, Catholics, and Protestants (including John Calvin and Martin Bucer [1491–1551]) in Frankfurt am Main. He singled

---

[68] "Denn ich umb [= um] des gekreuzigten Jüdens [= Judens; i.e., Jesus Christus] willen, den mir niemand nehmen soll, Euch Jüden allen gerne das Beste tun wollte, ausgenommen, daß Ihr meiner Gunst zu Euer Verstockung [ge]brauchen sollt"; WA *Briefwechsel*, vol. 8, pp. 89–91 esp. 91 lines 57–59; see also Ehrlich, "Luther und die Juden," p. 78.

[69] "Luther spricht es unverhohlen aus: Hilfe von ihm für Jüden ist nicht zu erwarten. wenn sie sich nicht bekehren"; Ehrlich, "Luther und die Juden," p. 78.

[70] "Sein Wohlwollen gegenüber den Juden war nie bedingungslos, sondern hatte immer ein konkretes Ziel: sie zu Jesus zu führen. Die Juden jedoch hätten sich nicht nur Luthers Argumenten verschlossen, sondern über Jesus nichts anders zu sagen gehabt, als daß er 'ein gekreuzigter, verdammter Jude sei', eine Formulierung, die Luther ausdrücklich in seinem Brief an Josel von Rosheim verwendet"; Ehrlich, "Luther und die Juden," p. 79. The expression "verdampten gekreuzigten Jüden" appears in WA *Briefwechsel*, vol. 8, p. 90, line 24.

[71] *Wider die Sabbather* appears in WA, vol. 50, pp. 309–337; cf. p. 313. See Ehrlich, "Luther und die Juden," pp. 79–80; Kaufmann, *Luthers Juden*, p. 99.

out the Lutheran party as particularly antagonistic when he wrote in his diary that he had "to stand up before many gentile scholars and prove to them from our Holy Torah [the groundlessness of the anti-Jewish accusations], against the words of Luther, Bucer, and his faction."[72] On the other side, in a letter to his friends, dated December 31, 1539, Luther expresses his frustration and bitterness regarding the Jews:

> I cannot convert the Jews. Our Lord Jesus Christ also did not succeed in doing so; but I can shut their mouths so that there will be nothing for them to do but sprawl down on the floor and stay there unable to move.[73]

Here Luther overlooks the fundamental fact that Jesus himself as well as his early followers belonged to the Jewish people, a fact that he acknowledged in his 1523 treatise, *That Jesus Christ Was Born a Jew*. Moreover, although Jesus attempted to attract as many of his people as possible to his ideas, he never thought in terms of founding a "new religion" or of "converting" the Jews. Furthermore, as we saw above, Luther himself elsewhere emphasizes the essential continuity between the Old and New Testaments, and even claimed that the New Testament is nothing more than the public proclamation of the Gospel already announced in the Old Testament.[74] But he was convinced that the Jews, in rejecting this, had missed the entire point of their own Scriptures.[75] He sought to convince them to see Christ and the Scriptures as Christians do. When he failed to do so, Luther reverted to the traditional Roman Church's aggressive treatment of Jews and severely escalate it.[76] He frequently asserted hatred against Jews and Judaism in his letters, *Tischreden,* biblical interpretations, and in specific anti-Jewish manifestos.[77] Only twenty years after his positive pamphlet, *That Jesus Christ Was Born a Jew*, and just three years prior

---

[72] See Baron, *A Social and Religious History of the Jews*, vol. 13, p. 289.

[73] "Ich kann die Juden nicht bekehren; unser Herr Jesus Christus hat es auch nicht vermocht. Aber ich kann ihnen ihren Schnabel schließen, so daß ihnen nichts anderes übrigbleibt, als auf dem Boden ausgestreckt bleiben zu müssen"; for the quotations, see L. Poliakov, *Geschichte des Antisemitismus* (translated by R. Pfisterer; Worms: Georg Heintz, 1978), vol. 2, p. 125.

[74] Compare WA, vol. 10 [part I, 1], p. 181 lines 15–22.

[75] See the discussion by Bornkamm, *Luther and the Old Testament*, pp. 1–10.

[76] In this context it is worth mentioning the brutal expulsion of all the Jews of England by Edward I in 1290, and of Spain and Portugal by Ferdinand and Isabella, with the support of the Church, in 1492 and 1497.

[77] In addition to the examples discussed above and below, compare, for example, Luther's commentary on Ps 24:3; E. Mülhaupt (ed.), *Martin Luthers Psalmen Auslegung* (Göttingen: Vandenhoeck & Ruprecht, 1959), vol. 1, p. 327. On Luther's *Tischreden*, see R. Buchwald, *Luther im Gespräch. Aufzeichnungen Seiner Freunde und Tischgenossen* (Stuttgart: Alfred Kröner Verlag, 1983), pp. 144, 348–349. For a collection of Luther's statements against the Jews in his Table-Talks, see Walch, *Martin Luthers Sämtliche Schriften*, pp. 1570–1591.

to his death, Luther composed three racist and antisemitic manifestos (all published in Wittenberg, 1543): *Von den Juden und ihren Lügen* (*On the Jews and Their Lies*),[78] *Vom Schem Hamphoras und vom Geschlecht Christi* (*On the Unknowable Name [Schem Hamphoras, the Tetragrammaton] and the Generations of Christ*),[79] and *Von den letzten Worten Davids* (*On the Last Words of David*). These writings of Luther are among the first and the most destructive manifestos of Protestant antisemitism.[80]

In *Vom Schem Hamphoras*, Luther attacks the Jews in several ways. He insults them with malicious stories,[81] and calls them horrible names, such

---

[78] *Von den Juden und ihren Lügen* is republished in WA, vol. 53, pp. 417–552 (with an introduction on pp. 412–416); on this work, see also R. Süss, *Luthers Theologisch Testament: Over de Joden en hun leugens* (Amsterdam: VU University Press, 2006).

[79] For this book, see WA, vol. 53, pp. 579–648. For an English translation, see G. Falk, *The Jew in Christian Theology: Martin Luther's Anti-Jewish Vom Schem Hamphoras, Previously Unpublished in English, and Other Milestones in Church Doctrine Concerning Judaism* (Jefferson, NC: McFarland, 1992).

[80] Some prefer to describe premodern forms of hostility toward Jews, especially when religiously motivated, by the term *anti-Judaism*, as opposed to *antisemitism*, which implies that the hostility is racially motivated. However, "in spite of all the differences there are also shocking continuities or fluid transitions between older and more recent forms of hostility towards Jews" ("trotz aller Differenzen auch schockierende Kontinuitäten bzw. fließende Übergänge zwischen älteren und jüngeren Formen der Judenfeindschaft"); see A. Pangritz, *Theologie und Antisemitismus: Das Beispiel Martin Luthers* (Frankfurt am Main: P. Lang, 2017), pp. 225, 232 esp. 234–235. This means that one should consider a gradual transformation of anti-Jewish concepts and it is not possible to maintain such a strong distinction between *anti-Judaism* and *antisemitism* (which both apply to Luther in any case). Thus, the term "antisemitism" is used here in the sense of "hostility of every kind towards Jews and Judaism" ("Feindschaft aller Art gegen Juden und das Judentum," ibid., p. 242, cf. the extensive discussion of this topic on pp. 225–253). The church historian Thomas Kaufmann refers to the late medieval stereotypes of hostility toward Jews used by Luther as "elements of a *specifically early modern*" or "pre-modern, protoracist anti-Semitism" ("Elemente eines *frühneuzeitspezifischen*" bzw. eines "vormodernen, protorassistischen Antisemitismus"); see T. Kaufmann, *Luthers "Judenschriften": Ein Beitrag zu ihrer historischen Kontextualisierung* (Tübingen: Mohr Siebeck 2011), pp. 131–132; 157; cf. also M. Morgenstern, "Erwägungen zu einem Dokument der Schande," in *Martin Luther und die Kabbala. Vom Schem Hamephorasch und vom Geschlecht Christi* (Berlin: Berlin University Press, 2017), pp. 251–276 esp. 267.

[81] For instance, Luther recounts: "Here at Wittenberg, in our parish church, there is a sow carved into the stone under which lie young pigs and Jews who are sucking; behind the sow stands a rabbi who is lifting up the right leg of the sow, raises the behind of the sow, bows down and looks with great effort into the Talmud under the sow, as if he wanted to read and see something most difficult and exceptional; no doubt they gained their *Shem Hamphoras* from that place" ("Es ist hie[r] zu Wittenberg an unser Pfarrkirchen eine Saw jnn [= in] stein gehawen, da li[e]gen junge Ferckel und Jüden unter, die saugen, Hinder der Saw stehet ein Rabin, der hebt der Saw das rechte bein empor, und mit seiner lincken hand zeucht er den pirtzel uber sich, bückt und kuckt mit grossen vleis der Saw unter dem pirtzel jnn den Thalmud hinein, als wolt er etwas scharffes und sonderlichs lesen und ersehen. Daselbsher haben sie gewislich jr [= ihr] Schem Hamphoras"). For the original German text and an illustration, see WA, vol. 53, pp. 600 lines 26–35; for the English translation, see Falk, *The Jew in Christian Theology*, pp. 182–183. Images of "Jew-Sow" (*Judensau*) were carved on the outside walls of many European cathedrals (or as woodcuts inside of them), such as Brandenburg, Bamberg, Cologne (Köln), Erfurt, Magdeburg, Nuremberg (Nürnberg), Regensburg, Freising, Colmar, Uppsala, and a painting on the old bridge tower of Frankfurt am Main.

as "devils,"[82] "disgusting bugs" and "a pest in the heart of our territories." He states that "to convert the Jews ... is about as possible as converting the Devil .... For a Jew or a Jewish heart is so stock, stone, iron, Devil hard, that it cannot be moved by any means."[83] Here Luther packs the Jews together with devils, Turks and "all the godless who misuse God's name continually and violate the commandment."[84] Again, though the rhetoric is shocking in its harshness, it did not come from nowhere: already by 1526, Luther was willing to say that Satan stood at the right hand of the Jews.[85]

In *Von den Juden und ihren Lügen*, Luther once again demonizes the Jews by describing them as "devils." He accuses them of still considering the messianic prophecies of the Old Testament unfulfilled, failing to recognize the real Messiah, Jesus, and murdering him. However, Luther does not answer the question: why should the Jews consider the messianic prophecies of the Old Testament otherwise? Does mankind really enjoy worldwide peace and prosperity as prophesized for the messianic era (for example, Isa 2:1–5//Mic 4:1–7; Isa 11:1–10)?[86] In addition, Luther overlooks the fact that Jesus was killed by the Roman governor, Pontius Pilate, rather than by the Jews. Most likely, he is influenced by the passion

---

[82] For *Luther, belief* in the *devil (Teufel)* was rational. The roots of this accusation stem from verses such as John 8:31–59, esp. 8:44, "You are from your father the devil ...." On Luther's views of the devil and their cultural background, cf. H. A. Oberman, *Martin Luther: Mensch zwischen Teufel und Gott* (Munich: Deutscher Taschenbuch Verlag, 1986), esp. pp. 11–21, 260–284.

[83] In order to set the citation in its context, I cite it more fully here: "Because, as I stipulated in a pamphlet, it is not my idea to write against the Jews, as if I hoped to convert them; therefore I did not wish to call that pamphlet *Against the Jews*, but instead *On the Jews and Their Lies*, so that we Germans may know from historical evidence what a Jew is so that we can warn our Christians against them as we warn against the Devil himself in order to strengthen and honor our belief; [the intent is] not *to convert the Jews, which is about as possible as converting the Devil ... For a Jew or a Jewish heart is so stock, stone, iron, Devil hard, that it cannot be moved by any means*" ("Denn wie ich jnn [= in] jhenem [=einem] Büchl[e]in bedingt, ist mein[e] meinung nicht, wider die Jüden [= Juden] zu schreiben, als hoffet ich sie zu beke[h]ren, hab[e] darumb [= darum] dasselb[e] buch nicht wollen nennen: Widder [= Wider] die Jüden, Sondern: Von den Jüden und jren [= ihren] lügen, Das[s] wir Deutschen historien weise auch wissen möchten, was ein Jüde sey [= sei], unser[e] Christen fur [= vor] jhnen [= ihnen], als fur [= vor] den Teuffeln [= Teufeln] selbs[t], zu warnen, unser[e]n glauben zu stercken [= stärken] und zu ehren, nicht *die Jüden zu beke[h]ren, Welch[e]s eben so müglich [= möglich] ist, als den Teuffel zu beke[h]ren ... Denn ein Jüde odder [= oder] Jüdisch[es] hertz [= Herz] ist so stock, stein, eisen, Teuffel hart, das[s] mit keiner Weise zu bewegen ist*"); for the German, see WA, vol. 53, p. 579 lines 9–16, 21–22 (italics mine); for another English translation, see Falk, *The Jew in Christian Theology*, pp. 166–167.

[84] "Was helffen [= helfen] sie den Teuffel [= Teufel], Türcken [= Türken], Jüden [= Juden] und alle Gottlosen, so solcher Buchstaben, auch Gottes Namens, ohne [= ohne] unterlas [= Unterlass] misbrauchen [= missbrauchen], wider das ander[e] Gebot?"; WA vol. 53, p. 592 lines 1–3; cf. Falk, *The Jew in Christian Theology*, pp. 175, 233.

[85] See WA, vol. 19, p. 599 lines 10–11.

[86] For further discussion on this issue, see Kalimi, *Fighting over the Bible*, pp. 108–109.

narratives in the Gospels (Mark 14–15; Matthew 26–27; Luke 22–23; John 18–19).[87]

In *Von den letzten Worten Davids* Luther defends a Christological reading of 2 Sam 23:1–7, against Jewish readings of the passage, whom he calls "children of darkness, that is, of the devil," and accuses them of being "despoilers, robbers, and perverters of Holy Scripture":

> [T]hese false and unknown Jews or Israelites, who have wrought no miracle these 1500 years, who have interpreted no writings of the prophets, who have perverted everything, who have done nothing in the open but underhandedly and clandestinely, like children of darkness, that is, of the devil, have practiced nothing but blasphemy, cursing, murder, and lies against the True Jews and Israel, that is, against the apostles and prophets. And they continue this daily and thus prove that they are not Israel or Abraham's seed but venomous and devilish foes of the True Israel and Abraham's children and in addition despoilers, robbers, and perverters of Holy Scripture. Therefore, it behooves us to recover Scripture from them as from public thieves wherever grammar warrants this and harmonizes with the New Testament.[88]

[87] The passion narratives in the Gospels claim that *some* Jewish authorities in Jerusalem pushed in that direction. However, this claim was expressed in a hostile polemical context between the minority group of the early Jewish-Christians and their Jewish opponents, who rejected Jesus as Messiah. Furthermore, on the one hand, the Jewish leaders themselves were forced to maintain the peace, including by disposing of "troublemakers" like Jesus, or they risked that the entire nation would be punished with them by Rome. On the other hand, it was also convenient for the Gospel writers not to blame Rome directly for Jesus' death (and for later Christian interpreters, Rome was Christian), but rather their religious opponents, the Jewish leaders. At any rate, one cannot collectively blame all the Jews of that era, and certainly not all those of the following centuries, for Jesus' death. Moreover, in contrast to Jeremiah, who asked God "do not forgive their iniquity [of those plotting to kill him], do not blot out their sin from your sight" (Jer 18:23), according to Luke 23:34, Jesus himself begged God to forgive those who caused his death, because "they know not what they do." Unfortunately, even this statement is absent – whether deliberately or not – from some early New Testament manuscripts, such as P[75], B and D*; see E. J. Epp, "Early Christian Attitudes toward 'Things Jewish' as Narrated by Textual Variants in Acts: A Case Study of the D-Textual Cluster," in I. Kalimi (ed.), *Bridging between Sister Religions: Studies in Jewish and Christian Scriptures Offered in Honor of Prof. John T. Townsend* (Brill Reference Library of Judaism 51; Leiden and Boston: Brill, 2016), pp. 141–171 esp. 153. Besides, even if they had been guilty, how many millions of innocent Jews should be killed in their stead to clear the balance? For extensive bibliography on anti-Judaism in the New Testament and its interpretation, see for example, I. Kalimi, "History of Israelite Religion or Hebrew Bible/Old Testament Theology? Jewish Interest in Biblical Theology," in *Early Jewish Exegesis and Theological Controversy: Studies in Scriptures in the Shadow of Internal and External Controversies* (Jewish and Christian Heritage 2; Assen: Royal Van Gorcum [now under: Brill, Leiden and Boston], 2002), pp. 107–134 esp. 115–117; J. D. Crossan, *Who Killed Jesus? Exposing the Roots of Anti-Semitism in the Gospel Story of the Death of Jesus* (New York: HarperCollins, 1995), esp. pp. 147–159; A.-J. Levine, *The Misunderstood Jew: The Church and the Scandal of the Jewish Jesus* (New York: HarperCollins, 2006), esp. pp. 87–118.

[88] "[Sollten wir glauben] den falschen unbekandten Jüden oder Israeliten, die diese 1500. jar kein wunder gethan, kein Schrifft der Propheten ausgelegt, alles verkeret und im liecht offentlich nichts gethan, Sondern in jrem winckel meuchlinges wie die Kinder des finsternis, das ist des Teuffels, eitel lestern, fluchen, morden und liegen wider die rechten Jüden und Israel (das ist, wider die

Paradoxically, Luther blames the Jews for robbing the Scriptures, but the latter is the *Jewish* Scriptures, so how can they rob them? It is possible that Luther means that Jews robbed the Scriptures by "misinterpreting" them. Still, it has been Christians like Luther who have taken the Bible over for their own use and often allegorical interpretation of it, while denying the Jews' right to read the Scriptures for themselves.

These anti-Jewish assertions and actions of Luther continued until the very last days of his life. In his final letters to his wife, Katharina von Bora ("die Lutherin," 1499–1552), on February 1 and 7, 1546, Luther blames the Jews for his illness and dizziness, because he had passed by their residential area in a village near Eisleben (today: Lutherstadt Eisleben). Accordingly, he planned to expel all the Jews from that area. In his letter of February 1, he writes:

> I have been weak on my way near Eisleben, which was my fault. But if you [= Katharina] had been here you would have said, it was the Jews or their God's fault.[89] We had to pass through a village near Eisleben, where many Jews live; maybe they blew so harshly towards me. In this hour there are more than fifty Jews living here in the town of Eisleben. And it is true that when I was near the village, such a very cold wind came through the back of my cart on my head under my hat, as if it tried to freeze my brain. This may have helped a bit to make me dizzy ....[90]

Apostel und Propheten) geübet haben, und noch üben teglich, damit sie uber weiset, das sie nicht Israel, noch Abrahams samen, Sondern gifftige, Teufelissche feinde sind, des rechten Israels und Abrahams kinder, dazu der Heiligen schrift diebe, reuber und verkerer. Darum man als von offentlichen dieben wider nehmen sol die Schrift, wo es die Grammatica gerne gibt und sich mit dem Newen Testament reimet"; Martin Luther, *Von den letzten Worten Davids*; WA, vol. 54, pp. 16–100 esp. p. 93, lines 14–24; English translation from M. H. Bertram, "Treatise on the Last Words of David: 2 Samuel 23:1–7," in J. Pelikan and H. C. Oswald (eds.), *Luther's Works* (Saint Louis: Concordia, 1972), p. 344. Mark U. Edwards states that this work of Luther is not really an anti-Jewish treatise per se, but rather a work of exegesis with a few anti-Jewish comments; see M. U. Edwards, Jr., *Luther's Last Battles: Politics and Polemics, 1531–46* (Ithaca and London: Cornell University Press, 1983), p. 134. Nonetheless, Edwards' claim that "the few critical asides in the treatise are aimed at rabbinic exegesis and not at contemporary Jews in general" is inaccurate, in light of Luther's depiction of "false ... Jews or Israelites" as blasphemers, murderers, liars, and robbers, as cited above.

[89] This could imply that Katharina von Bora was even more anti-Jewish than her husband, Martin Luther, or it could simply be that Luther is projecting his own prejudice onto her, which is a common phenomenon.

[90] "Ich bin ia [= ja] schwach gewesen auff [= auf] dem weg hart vor Eisleben, Das war meine schuld. Aber wenn du [= Katharina] werest [= wärest] da gewest [= dagewesen], so hettestu [= hättest du] gesagt, Es were [= wäre] der Juden oder i[h]res Gottes schuld gewest [= gewesen]. Denn wir mus[s]ten durch ein Dorff [= Dorf] hart vor Eisleben, da viel Juden innen wo[h]nen; vielleicht haben sie mich so hart angeblasen. So sind hie[r] in der Sta[d]t Eisleben itzt [= jetzt] diese Stund[e] uber [= über] funffzig [= fünfzig] Juden wohnhaftig [= wohnhaft]. Und wa[h]r ists, do [= da/als] ich bey [= bei] dem Dorff [= Dorf] fuhr, gieng [= ging] mir ein solcher kalter wind hinden [= hinten] zum Wagen ein auff [= auf] meinen Kopff, Durchs Barret, als wol[l]t mirs das Hirn zu eis machen. Solch[e]s mag mir zum Schwindel etwas geholffen [= geholfen] haben"; see WA, *Briefwechsel*, vol. 11, pp. 275–276, Brief Nummer 4195 lines 4–12.

Luther continues and concludes: "When the main issues are resolved, I must start to expel the Jews." He also states how he is going to implement this.[91] How serious Luther considered these issues emerges also from his letter of February 7, 1546, to his wife, where he associates Jews with devils and repeats his plan:

> I think that hell and the whole world must be free of all devils, who could have perhaps all have come here to Eisleben on my account, so bad and harsh are things here. So are there also Jews here, about fifty, in one house, as I wrote to you before.[92]

These letters reveal the courageous reformer and gifted theologian, Luther, as a believer in superstitions. The fifty poor Jews of Eisleben are accused of causing the physical problems of an old man traveling in icy cold winter! So far had Luther's hatred of the Jews come.

Furthermore, Luther gave his very last sermon on February 15, 1546, that is, just two days before his death, on the night of February 17/18. Here he describes Jews as Christians' enemies, accuses them of defaming and mocking the core saints of Christianity, and attributes to Jews a homicidal character: "The Jews are our public enemies. They never stop defaming our Lord Christ, calling the Virgin Mary a whore and Jesus Christ the son of a whore ... If they could, they would gladly kill us all."[93] In this sermon, Luther attempts once again to promote his mission to convert the Jews: "Still we wish to practice Christian love toward them, and ask them to convert, [and] accept the Lord .... When the Jews wish to convert to us and give up their heresy and whatever else they have done to us, we will gladly forgive them, but if not, we will not tolerate nor suffer that they should be in our midst."[94]

---

[91] "Wenn die Heuptsachen [= Hauptsachen] geschlichtet weren [= wären], so mus[s] ich mich dran legen, die Juden zu[ ]vertreiben"; see WA *Briefwechsel*, vol. 11, p. 276 lines 16–17.

[92] "Ich denke, das[s] die Helle [Hölle] und [die] gantze Welt musse [= müsse] itzt [= jetzt] ledig sein von allen teuffeln [= Teufeln], die vi[e]lleicht alle umb [= um] meinen willen hie[r] Zu Eisleben Zu sammen[ge]kom[m]en sind, So fest und hart stehet die Sache. So sind auch hie[r] Jüden [= Juden], bey [= bei] fuffzig [= fünfzig] ynn [= in] einem hause, wie ich dir zuuor [= zuvor] geschrieben"; see WA *Briefwechsel*, vol. 11, pp. 286–287 (Brief Nummer 4201) lines 13–16.

[93] "Sie [= die Juden] sind unsere öffentliche[n] Feinde, hören nicht auff [= auf] unser[e]n HErrn [= Herrn] Christum [= Christus] zu lestern [= lästern], Heissen [= nennen] die Jungfraw [= Jungfrau] Maria eine Hure, Christum [= Christus] ein Hurenkind .... und wenn sie uns kondten [= könnten] alle tödten [= töten], so theten [= täten] sie es gerne"; WA, vol. 51, p. 195 lines 28–32.

[94] WA, vol. 51 p. 195, lines 39–49, p. 196, lines 14–17; "Noch wollen wir die Christliche liebe an i[h]nen uben und vor sie bitten, das sie sich beke[h]ren, den HErrn [sic!] anne[h]men .... Wollen sich die Jüden zu uns beke[h]ren und von i[h]ren lesterung [= Lästerung], und was sie uns sonst gethan [getan] haben, auffhören, so wollen wir es i[h]nen gerne vergeben, Wo aber nicht, so sollen wir sie auch bey [= bei] uns nicht dulden noch leiden." On this sermon and its conclusion, cf. Oberman, "Die Juden in Luthers Sicht," pp. 157–158.

This text shows that despite Luther's knowing that he could not convert the Jews (as seen above), in fact he never gave up on this issue. This confirms again Luther's aggressive stance toward the Jews as a whole and especially toward those who refuse to be converted (that is, toward the vast majority of them).

Regarding Luther's complaint that the Jews defame Christ and the Virgin Mary: Is he alluding here to those talmudic texts, which he might have heard about from Jewish apostates or even from Jews themselves, which call Jesus "ben Stada," "ben Padira," or "ben Pandera" (that is, regarding him as a son of a human being rather than the offspring of the "Holy Spirit")?[95] Or perhaps, Luther refers here to the satiric and vulgar anti-Christian writing, *The Life Story of Jesus* (*Toledot Yeshu*), that attempts to defame Jesus and Mary?

Nonetheless, this very last sermon dovetails with other anti-Jewish assertions of Luther and shows that his anti-Jewishness stems from his (proto-)racist approach,[96] fear and hatred of strangers in German society (xenophobia), as well as from his deep Christian theological worldview.[97]

VII   Luther, the Book of Esther, and the "Ethnic Character" of the Jews

In the following paragraphs, I will attempt to show that the culmination of Luther's hatred that occurred when he came to the conclusion that the Jews would never accept his calls for conversion, developed together with his attitude toward the book of Esther (and 2 Maccabees). Luther was particularly hostile to the texts that narrate the Jews' struggles to defend themselves from their enemies (Esth 9:2–16; 2 Maccabees 8–10). For example, in his *Von den Juden und ihren Lügen* Luther states:

> And all their hearts' uneasy sighing, longing and hoping go in the direction that one day they wish to deal with us Gentiles as they dealt with the Gentiles in the time of Esther in Persia. Oh, how much they love the book of Esther which so well fits with their bloodthirsty, vengeful, murderous lust and hope. There is no nation that is so bloodthirsty and vengeful under the

[95] See Babylonian Talmud, *Sanhedrin* 43a; 67a; 104b; 107b (usually deleted in medieval copies by Christian censors); S. G. Wilson, *Related Strangers: Jews and Christians 70–170 C.E.* (Minneapolis, MN: Fortress Press, 1995), pp. 183–193 ("Jewish Allusions to Jesus and Christians").

[96] See above, note 80.

[97] It is worth noting that since Luther expressed himself so badly against the peasants in 1525, when he was young and healthy, and later on against the Jews, seemingly it has something to do also with his temper and basic character; see below next paragraph.

sun than those who think that they are God's people, that they must slay the pagans and suppress them.[98]

"Therefore," suggests Luther: "Dear Christian, beware of the Jews ... you can admit how the wrath of God has consigned them to the devil, who has robbed them not only of a proper understanding of the Scripture, but also of common human reason, modesty and sense ...." "Accordingly," he advises, "when you see a real Jew, you may, with a good conscience, cross yourself, freely and surely, saying: 'There goes a living devil!'"[99] Furthermore, Luther details seven practical pieces of advice on how one can shut the mouths of Jews, that is, to silence them, including burning to ashes their synagogues and schools, prayer-books and Talmuds, taking possession of their properties, and completely expelling them from the German territories forever.[100]

It is inaccurate to state, as Thomas Kaufmann does, that Luther did not advocate physical elimination of the Jews themselves.[101] Although Luther did not call explicitly for mass murder of the Jews, he calls them "disgusting bugs" and "a pest in the heart of our territories" in his *Vom Schem Hamphoras* (see above, §VI, no. 3). Everybody knows what should be done with bugs and pests: totally exterminate them.[102] Also, in *Von den Juden und ihren Lügen* he calls Jews "miserable people" and "mad dogs" who

[98] "Und alle irs [= ihre] hertzen [= Herzen] engstlich [= ängstlich] seufftzen [= seuftzen] und sehnen und hoffen gehet dahin, das sie [= die Juden] ein mal [= einmal] möchten mit uns Heiden umbgehen [umgehen], wie sie zur Zeit Esther in Persia mit den Heiden umbgiengen [= umgingen]. O, wie lieb haben sie das Buch Esther, das so fein stimmet auff [= auf] ire [= ihre] blutdürstige, rachgyrige [= rachgierige], mörd[er]ische begir [= Begier] und hoffnung [= Hoffnung], Kein blutdürstiger[e]s und rachgyrigers [= rachgierigeres] Volk hat die Sonne je beschienen, als die sich dünken lassen, Sie seien darumb [= darum] Gottes Volk, dass sie sollen und müssen die Heiden morden und würgen"; WA, vol. 53, p. 433 lines 15–21.

[99] "Darumb [= Darum] hüte dich, lieber Christ, fur [= vor] den Jüden [= Juden], die du hieraus si[e]hest, wie sie durch Gottes zorn [Zorn] dem Teufel ubergeben [= übergeben] sind, Der sie nicht allein des rechten verstand[e]s in der Schrifft, sondern auch gemeiner menschlicher vernunfft [=vernunft], scham und sinn, beraubt hat ... Darumb [= Darum], wo du einen rechten Jüden si[e]hest, magst[d]u mit gutem gewissen ein Creuz [= Kreuz] fur [= für] dich schlahen [= schlagen] und frey [= frei] sicher sprechen: Da gehet ein leibhafftiger [= leibhaftiger] Teufel!" WA, vol. 53, p. 479 lines 24–35.

[100] See Luther, *Von den Juden und ihren Lügen*, WA, vol. 53, pp. 523–526, also reaffirmed on pp. 536–539. The eviction of all Jews "in eternal times" ("auf ewige Zeiten") that was documented in the local history of the city, took place before Luther, under Frederick the Wise in 1494. See Ingetraut Ludolphy, *Frederick the Wise: Elector of Saxony 1463–1525* (reprint of the first edition in 1984, Leipzig: Leipziger Universitätsverlag, 2006), pp. 314–315.

[101] "Einer physischen Eliminierung der Judenheit hat Luther das Wort nicht geredet"; see Kaufmann, *Luthers 'Judenschriften*," p. 145.

[102] Interestingly, several centuries later, the German Emperor Wilhelm II, who was immensely influenced by Luther, asserted in 1927: "The press, the Jews and mosquitoes are a plague, which humankind has to rid itself of one way or the other – I believe the best would be gas" ("Die Presse, die Juden und Mücken sind eine Pest, von der sich die Menschheit so oder so befreien muss – I believe the best would be gas" [sic!]); see J. C. G. Röhl, "Der Kaiser und die Juden," *Wilhelm II.: Der Weg in den Abgrund 1900–1941* (Munich: C. H. Beck, 2008), pp. 1291–1297 esp. 1295.

must not be shown mercy, and handle them with all heartlessness, "as Moses did in the wilderness and struck three thousand dead":

> Our rulers, who have Jews under them, I wish and ask that they might exercise a sharp mercy against these miserable people, as said above, [to see] whether [this] might help (as difficult as this is). As the motivated doctors do, when gangrene has gotten into a leg, they proceed without mercy and cut, saw, and burn flesh, veins, bones, and marrow. Thus, also one does here. Burn their synagogues, forbid everything that I have explained above, force them to work, and handle them with all mercilessness, as Moses did in the wilderness and struck three thousand dead so that the whole house would not be spoiled. They truly know not what they do. Like possessed people, they do not want to know, hear, or learn it. Therefore, one cannot practice mercy here, to strengthen them in their character. If this does not help, we must drive them out like mad dogs, so that we do not become participants in their dreadful blasphemy and all vices, earning God's wrath and being damned with them.[103]

Luther justifies treating the Jews mercilessly by appealing to Moses' slaughtering of 3000 Israelites who worshipped the Golden Calf (Exod 32:28). In contrast to his early writings, in which Luther complains that the Roman Church treats the Jews as if they were "dogs," in his later writings he himself calls for them to be treated even worse: "we must drive them out like mad dogs."[104] Elsewhere Luther details what should be done with "mad dogs": In May 1525, when the German peasants rebelled against the princes and demanded some reduction in taxes and housing rent, fishing privileges and the like, Luther stood behind the aggressive princes, and urged them to crush the peasants' rebellion ruthlessly. He compares the peasants to "*a*

---

[103] WA, vol. 53, p. 541 line 25, p. 542 line 2; "UNSern [= Unseren] Ober Herrn, so Jüden [= Juden] unter sich haben, wündsche [= wünsche] ich und bitte, das sie eine scharffe [= scharfe] barmhertzigkeit [= Barmherzigkeit] wol[l]ten gegen diese elende Leute uben [= üben], wie droben gesagt, obs [= ob es] doch etwas (wiewo[h]l es mi[s]slich ist) helffen [= helfen] wol[l]te, Wie die treiven [= getriebenen] Ertzte [= Ärtzte] thun [= tun], wenn das heilige Feivr [= Rotlauf; St. Anthony's Fire] in die bein[e] kom[m]en ist, Fa[h]ren sie mit unbarmhertzigkeit [= Unbarmherzigkeit] und schneiten [= schneiden], segen [= sägen], brennen fleisch [= Fleisch], adern [= Adern], bein [= Beine] und marck [= (Knochen-)Mark] abe [= ab]. Also thu [= tut] man hie[r] auch. Verbrenne i[h]r[e] Synagogen, Verbiete alles, was ich droben erzelet [= erzählt] habe, Zwinge sie zur erbeit [= Arbeit], Und gehe mit i[h]nen umb [= um] nach aller unbarmhertzigkeit [= Unbarmherzigkeit], wie Mose thet [= tat] in der Wüsten und schlug drey tausent [= dreitausend] tod [= tot], das nicht der gantze [= ganze] hauffe [= Haufen] verderben mus[s]te. Sie wissen wa[h]rlich nicht, was sie thun, Wollens dazu, wie die besessen Leute, nicht wissen, hören noch lernen. Darumb [= Darum] kann[n] man hie[r] keine barmhertzigkeit [= Barmherzigkeit] uben [= üben], sie in jrem [= ihrem] wesen zu stercken [= stärken]. Wil[l] das nicht helffen [= helfen], So müssen wir sie, wie die tollen hunde [= Hunde] aus jagen [= wegjagen], damit wir nicht, jrer [= ihrer] greulichen lesterung [= Lästerung] und aller laster teilhafftig [= teilhaftig], mit jnen [= ihnen] Gottes zorn [= Zorn] verdienen und verdampt [= verdammt] werden."

[104] See WA, vol. 53, p. 541 line 35, p. 542 line 1.

mad dog that *must be killed*; if you would not attack and kill the rebel first, he will attack you and the whole country with you" (italics added).[105] Is this not sufficiently clear allusion to physical elimination of the Jews? In this case, the biblicist Luther did not appeal to the prophetic calls for social justice, such as Isa 5:8; 58:6–7; Amos 4:1; and 6:3–6. Instead, he acted as "those who call evil good, and good evil …" (Isa 5:20).

Furthermore, in the same manifesto, *Von den Juden und ihren Lügen*, Luther describes all the Jews as nothing but "thieves and robbers" who should be hanged: "For a usurer is an arch-thief and a robber who should rightly be hanged on the gallows seven times higher than other thieves."[106] At another point, Luther states: "If I had power over the Jews, as our princes and cities have, I would deal severely with their lying mouth." He even proposes cutting off the tongues of rabbis if they fail to prove "their lies are true."[107] Further Luther states in *Von den Juden und ihren Lügen*:

> So, it is also our fault that we have not avenged the great innocent blood that *they* have spilled from our Lord and from Christians for three hundred years after the destruction of Jerusalem, and since then, the blood of children (whose eyes and skin still shine). [It is our fault] that *we do not slay them*, but instead for all their murder, cursing, slander, lies and shame, we leave them confused,

---

[105] See WA, vol. 18, pp. 344–361 esp. 358 lines 10–18, particularly 16–18: "gleich als wenn man eynen [= einen] tollen Hund todschlahen [= totschlagen] mus[s], schlegstu [= schlägst du] [ihn] nicht, so schlegt [= schlägt] er dich und [d]ein ganzt[es] land mit dyr [= dir]." See in detail, Kalimi, "The Position of Martin Luther towards Jews and Judaism" §IV, 3. On the Peasants' War (*Bauernkrieg*), that actually erupted in Thüringen, at 1524, see I. Dingel, *Geschichte der Reformation* (Theologische Bibliothek 5; Göttingen: Vandenhoeck & Ruprecht, 2018), pp. 231–238, and the additional earlier bibliography on p. 231, note 2.

[106] "Auch wenn sie nicht so stock starr blind weren [= wären], Sol[l]t[en] sie jr [= ihr] eigen, auch das gar grobe eusserlich [= äußerliche] leben wo[h]l uberzeugen [= überzeugen], was sie fur [= für] busse [= Buße] thun [= tun]. Denn sie voller zeuberey [= Zauberei], geucherey, mit zeichen, figuren und des namens Tetragrammaton [= Tetragramm] stecken (das ist Abgötterey [= Abgötterei]), vol[l] neides und stoltz[e]s, dazu eitel *Diebe und Reuber*, die teglich [= täglich] nicht einen bissen essen, noch einen faden antragen, den sie uns nicht gestolen und geraubet [= geraubt] haben, durch jren [= ihren] verdampten [= verdammten] wucher, Leben also teglich [= täglich] von eitel Diebstal und Raub mit Weib und Kind, als die Ertzdiebe und Landreuber [= Landräuber], in aller unbusfertigen [= unbußfertiger] sicherheit. *Den ein Wucherer ist ein Ertzdieb und Landreuber [= Landräuber], der billich [billig] am Galgen sieben mal [= siebenmal] höher, denn andere Diebe hangen [= hängen] sol[l]t[e].* Ja fur war [= fürwahr], von solcher schönen busse und verdienst müs[s]te Gott von Hi[m]mel durch seinen heiligen Engel weissagen, und so ein schendlicher [= schändlicher], lesterlicher Lügener [= Lügner] werden, umb [= um] der edlen blut[e]s und beschnitten[er] Heiligen willen, das sich durch Gottes gebot geheiliget [= geheiligt] rhümen [= rühmen], und doch die selbigen alle mit füssen [= Füßen] tretten [=treten], und keins nicht halten"; WA, vol. 53, p. 502 lines 1–14.

[107] "WENN ich macht hette [= hätte] uber [= über] die Jüden [= Juden], wie unser Fürsten und Stedte [= Städte] haben, Wo[l]lt ich diesen ernst mit jrem [= ihrem] lügen maul [= Lügenmaul] spielen …. Darumb [= Darum], wenn ich uber [= über] sie gewalt hette [= hätte], wol[l]t[e] ich jre [=ihre] gelerten und besten versamlen und jnen [= ihnen] aufflegen [= auferlegen], bey [= bei] verlust der zungen hinden [= hinten] zum halse [= Halse] heraus"; WA, vol. 53, p. 539 lines 9–10 and 31–32.

we protect and shield their schools, houses, bodies, and goods. We make them lazy and secure, and help them to feel comforted as they suck out our money and goods, for which they mock us, [and] spy on us [i.e., to the Turks], [to see] whether they can in the end overpower us, and for such a great sin, to slay all of us, take everything good, as they daily ask and hope. (italics mine)[108]

Ironically, Luther laments that the Christians "have not avenged" the Jews and in fact calls for vengeance against them, even while accusing the Jews collectively of being the most "bloodthirsty and vengeful" people among all those on which the sun shines! He explicitly repeats the blood-libel, which falsely accuses Jews of killing Christian children to use their blood to bake unleavened bread (Passover *matzot*).[109] It is puzzling how Luther repeats and spreads this vulgar, antisemitic lie, although as professor of Christian Bible/theology and a Bible translator, he knew that the Torah not only forbids any murder of a human being (e.g., Gen 9:5–6; Exod 20:13//Deut 5:17), but also eating of any blood: "You shall eat no kind of blood ... any person who eats any kind of blood, that person shall be cut off from his people" (Lev 7:26–27).[110] Thus, Luther spreads lies about the Jews, within a book where he blames them for lying, and calls for vengeance against the Jews, while accusing them of vengefulness.

Seemingly, Luther was unable to conceive a pluralistic religious society. As such, he rejects his own earlier policy of tolerance toward the Jews and shows himself even worse than the "Papist" attitudes that he earlier condemned. In fact, no Pope in Christian history ever reached Luther's peak of hostility.[111] Note, Luther not only polemicizes against

---

[108] "So ists [= ist es] auch unser schuld [= Schuld], das[s] wir das grosse unschüldige [= unschuldige] Blut, so sie an unser[e]m Herrn und den Christen bey [= bei] dreyhundert [= dreihundert] ja[h]ren nach zerstörung [der Zerstörung] Jerusalem, und bis daher, an Kindern vergossen (welch[e]s noch aus jren [= ihren] augen und haut scheinet) nicht rechen [= rächen], *sie nicht todschlahen* [=totschlagen], Sondern fur [= für] alle jren [= ihren] mord [= Mord], fluchen, lestern [= lästern], liegen, schenden [= schänden] frey [= frei] bey [= bei] uns sitzen lassen, jre [=ihre] Schule[n], heuser [= Häuser], leib [= Leib] und gut [= Gut/Güter] schützen und schirmen, damit wir sie faul und sicher machen und helffen [= helfen], das[s] sie gestrost [= getrost] unser geld [= Geld] und gut [= Gut/ Güter] uns aussaugen, dazu unser spotten, uns anspeien [= anspucken], ob sie zuletzt kündten [= könnten] unser mechtig [= mächtig] werden, Und fur [= für] solche grosse Sünde uns alle todschlahen [= totschlagen], alles gut ne[h]men, wie sie teglich [= täglich] bitten und hoffen"; WA, vol. 53, p. 522 lines 8–17; Falk, *The Jew in Christian Theology*, pp. 272, 292.

[109] On this issue, see D. O'Brien, *The Pinnacle of Hatred: The Blood Libel and the Jews* (Jerusalem: Magnes Press, 2011); M. Teter, *Blood Libel: On the Trail of an Antisemitic Myth* (Cambridge, MA: Harvard University Press, 2020).

[110] See also Lev 3:17; and Gen 9:4.

[111] On Luther's place in the history of religions as well as in the history of the European religious reformations, see Kalimi, "The Position of Martin Luther towards Jews and Judaism" and the detailed discussion of Luther's contemporary theologians and reformers, such as Erasmus of Rotterdam, Huldrych (Ulrich) Zwingli and John Calvin.

Jews and Jewish religion on theological matters, but also dehumanizes them on the level of their *national character*. In all these cases he is not talking about an individual Jew or a specific group of Jews, but rather about "*the* Jews," "they," "these miserable people," as a collective, and calls them "devils," "thieves and robbers," "mad dogs," *the* most "bloodthirsty and vengeful" nation.

Against this background of Luther's general anti-Jewish position, his hostility toward the book of Esther becomes clear. Luther's claim that "the book of Esther ... so well fits with their [= Jews'] bloodthirsty, vengeful, murderous lust and hope,"[112] is most likely an allusion to the climax of the Esther story, which is described as "a day when the Jews would gain power over their foes. The Jews gathered in their cities throughout all the provinces of King Ahasuerus to lay hands on *those who had sought their ruin* .... The other Jews who were in the king's provinces also gathered to *defend their lives*, and gained relief from their enemies, and killed seventy-five thousands of those who hated them" (Esth 9:1–2, 16).[113] Luther, who greatly wished to convert the Jews, certainly could not tolerate that: "many of the peoples of the land professed to be Jews [מתיהדים],[114] because the fear of the Jews had fallen upon them" (Esth 8:17).

These verses may be part of what Luther calls "too much Jewishness," or what Bardtke (and other followers of Luther, including many theologians and biblical scholars) describes as "the ethnic character of the book of Esther," which is present also in the book of 2 Maccabees.[115] This might imply that Luther not only hated Jewish triumphs, but also denied the fundamental right of Jews to defend their existence from the genocidal plan of Haman and the religious persecutions of Antiochus IV, Epiphanes (175–164 BCE; see below, §VIII). These scholars consider, for example, claims such as that the Jews "gained power *over their foes* ... laid hands on *those who had sought their ruin* ... gathered *to defend their lives*, and gained relief from *their enemies*" to be illegitimate and unacceptable.[116]

---

[112] See WA, vol. 53, p. 433, lines 15–21, and earlier in this section's text as well as note 97.
[113] The LXX (or B-Text) reads here: *"fifteen thousand,"* and in the Greek Alpha Text of Esther the number is: *"seventy thousand and one hundred."* See in detail, Chapter 12, §III, 1.
[114] Interestingly, the Greek version (LXX) writes here: περιετέμνοντο ("were circumcised"), which was considered to be a proper *nota Iudaica*; for details and bibliography, see I. Kalimi, "He Was Born Circumcised," in *Early Jewish Exegesis and Theological Controversy*, pp. 61–76 esp. 72 and note 41.
[115] See in detail, below, §VIII.
[116] See the detailed discussion in Chapter 12.

VIII   Haman, Antiochus Epiphanes, and Martin Luther

Luther targeted the books of Esther and 2 Maccabees from among all the ancient Israelite literary heritage and wished to discard them from the canon.[117] Yet, both Esther and 2 Maccabees describe amazing victories of Jews over those who attempted to eliminate them physically or culturally. According to the Esther story, Haman desired to annihilate all the Jewish people, but he failed due to Esther's and Mordecai's actions. In the case of 2 Maccabees, it was Antiochus IV who sought to assimilate the Jews, by forbidding their ancestral traditions, such as keeping Sabbath and the Jewish feasts, circumcision, and the dietary laws (2 Maccabees 6), which in fact meant undermining their religious-cultural legacy. He also plundered the Temple vessels, slaughtered many Jews and sold many others as slaves (2 Macc 5:11–26), polluted the Temple, and renamed it Jupiter Olympius (2 Maccabees 6–7). He vowed to turn Jerusalem "into a cemetery of Jews" (2 Macc 9:4; a statement made when Antiochus heard of his troops' defeat), but he also failed due to the Maccabean victory over him.[118] Most likely, Luther felt some empathy for Antiochus' plan to Hellenize the Jews, or even for Haman's plan to annihilate them. Luther similarly desired that Judaism and Jewish interpretations and approaches to the Hebrew Bible/Old Testament would disappear, sooner rather than later: Either by assimilating/converting to Christianity, which would imply perishing spiritually, religiously, and culturally, or by being eliminated physically by the process that he suggested in his shocking writings against the Jews, particularly in his manifestoes *Von den Juden und ihren Lügen* and *Vom Schem Hamphoras*.[119] Thus, part of what Luther disliked about both Esther and 2 Maccabees was probably that they both describe successful Jewish efforts to defend themselves and defeat those who would try to assimilate or annihilate them, precisely the path that Luther himself dares to tread in his writings. He simply could not stand the Jewish triumphs over their

---

[117] See WA *Tischreden*, vol. 1, p. 208, lines 30–31.

[118] On this issue, see in detail Kalimi, *How the Mighty Have Fallen*.

[119] Nearly 400 years later, on the anniversary of Luther's birth, precisely this advice was literally and systematically implemented by the German Nazis and their collaborators on the so-called *Reichskristallnacht* (actually, *Reichspogromnacht*), November 9/10, 1938, and in the following years. On the line that leads from Luther's *Von den Juden und ihren Lügen* to Richard Wagner's "Das Judenthum in der Musik" and Adolf Hitler's *Mein Kampf*, see Kalimi, "The Position of Martin Luther towards Jews and Judaism," §VIII. That Luther's anti-Jewish writings played a decisive roll in the Nazi propaganda, and in fact were a model for Hitler's "Final Solution" (*Endlösung*), see also H. Lehmann, "Luther und die Juden: Stolpersteine auf dem Weg zur Fünfhundertjahrfeier der Reformation 2017," in Danz and Tück (eds.), *Martin Luther im Widerstreit der Konfessionen*, pp. 428–442 esp. 428–431, 436–437, 439–440, and the additional bibliography therein.

enemies in the Persian and Hasmonaean periods, and the feasts based on them – Purim and Hanukkah – that the Jews celebrate every year. Moreover, in his sermon of February 15, 1546, Luther calls Jews "our public enemies." Perhaps in view of what the Jews did to their enemies in the past, as recounted in Esther and 2 Maccabees, he states that: "If they [= the Jews] could, they would gladly kill us all" as well. Obviously, Luther did not wish for himself the same final fate of Haman or the other enemies of the Jews, as described in Esther and 2 Maccabees. Admittedly, these are not the only two biblical books that describe great acts of salvation for God's people, but others include Exodus, many stories in the book of Judges, and the rescue of Jerusalem from Sennacherib. Nevertheless, Esther and 2 Maccabees stand out as cases where the threatened destruction was specifically linked to the people's identity as *Jews* (יהודים) while the earlier cases involved "Biblical Israel," from Luther's perspective. In both Esther and 2 Maccabees, it is explicitly stated that the Jews are a people who keep their religious laws, which separate them from all others. In addition, in these books the Jews themselves act to protect their own instead of relying on direct interference by divine powers. Since Luther's antagonism toward the Jews was linked specifically to their refusal to give up their religious laws and traditions, it makes sense that he would especially single out these books for opposition.

In fact, in *Von den Juden und ihren Lügen* Luther refers explicitly to the Jews' complaint that Christians treat them like Haman: "First they complain to God about us, that we hold them prisoner in misery, and fiercely plead that God would save his holy people and beloved children from our violence and imprisonment, *call us Edom and Haman*, whereby they want God to hurt us very much."[120] Luther, of course, does not accept these charges. He goes on to state that he would willingly claim Edom as father, but he says nothing further regarding Haman. Nevertheless, the bitter irony is too great to miss. In his earlier writings, Luther himself had blasted the Church for precisely this kind of treatment of the Jews, and even here in his late writings, he acknowledges the Jews' grievance that Christians have repeated the sins of Haman. Yet none of this stops Luther from urging precisely the same measures against the Jews, just a few pages later in his book.

---

[120] "Erstlich klagen sie fur [= vor] Gott über uns, das[s] wir sie im Elende gefangen halten, Und bitten hefftiglich [= heftig], das[s] Gott wol[l]t[e] sein heiliges Volk und lieben Kinder von unser[er] gewalt [= Gewalt] und gefengnis [= Gefängnis] erlösen, Heissen [= nennen] uns Edom und Haman, damit sie uns fur [= vor] Gott wollen seer [= sehr] wehe gethan [= wehgetan] haben"; *Von den Juden und ihren Lügen*, WA, vol. 53 p. 519.

Therefore, how could Luther accuse the Jews in Esther's and Judah Maccabeus' times, as well as in his own day, as "bloodthirsty," while making statements of his own such as: "It is also our fault that ... we do not slay them [= the Jews]"? Similarly, when he admits that Christian oppression of the Jews was seen by them as a continuation of the persecution of Haman, did he not see the irony in his own calls for further persecution as an implicit wish to deliver the Jews to the same destiny that Haman had sought for them? Yet Luther explicitly condemned Haman on at least two occasions: In a letter on May 2, 1528, he compares Haman's desire to wipe out the Jewish people with Satan's desire to wipe out the Gospel, and in one of his *Tischreden* from 1538 he calls Haman a "blasphemer" or "slanderer" (*Lästerer*).[121] Apparently, Luther did not hold himself to the same standard.

How then can the shift in Luther's attitude toward the Jews generally, and the books of Esther (and 2 Maccabees) particularly, be explained? A variety of factors contributed to Luther's shifting portrayals of Jews over the course of his career, from positive and encouraging, to violent and intolerant. Some have attempted to explain this change as a reflection of the antisemitic aspects of his own culture, or as a poor reaction to trauma, old age, or illness. Even if all of those had an influence on him, they cannot fully explain, much less excuse, his extreme antisemitism. More directly, it reflects Luther's longstanding antipathy toward Judaism itself, combined with the failure of his hopes that the Jews might finally convert to his newly reformed church. That failure convinced him that Jewish stubbornness was too ingrained to be overcome, and he came to see the Jews' continued refusal to convert not only as a nuisance, but as a threat to the Church, as I discuss in detail elsewhere.[122]

IX   Conclusion

Martin Luther refers to the book of Esther and its Jewish figures in all kinds of his writings. Though Luther showed a respectful attitude toward the book's Jewish heroes, especially in the early stage of his career as a reformer, later he severely criticized the very existence of the book and used it to support his antisemitic attacks against the Jews. These contradictory views are examined in this chapter against the background of Luther's

---

[121]   WA *Briefwechsel*, vol. 4, p. 449, line 41; WA *Tischreden*, vol. 4, p. 127, line 37, cf. line 4; see Bardtke, *Luther und das Buch Esther*, pp. 59–62, with additional references.

[122]   On all these issues, see Kalimi, "The Position of Martin Luther towards Jews and Judaism," §II and §V, with detailed engagement with original sources and the earlier literature.

general attitude toward the Old Testament on the one hand, and Jews and Judaism on the other.

Regarding Esther within the Old Testament: Whereas Luther could praise Esther and Mordecai as *people*, much as he commended other Old Testament heroes as models for Christians, he considered the *book* of Esther, as a whole, too Jewish and too popular among the Jews to be valuable for Christians. Thus, his attitudes toward Esther (the book and the person) appear inconsistent, attempting to claim for the Church all that he liked, while attributing to the Jews all that he disliked, but his attitudes also gradually shifted over the course of his life.

Luther never tolerated nor recognized postbiblical Judaism. However, in the last four decades of his life and career, Luther's approach toward the Jews shifted from tolerant and welcoming in the early stage, to xenophobic and antisemitic later on. Similarly, Luther's praise of the Jewish characters in the book of Esther appears most commonly in the early stage of his career, while his harshest statements about the book appear especially in his late writings, where he explicitly uses it to accuse the Jews of being bloodthirsty murderers.

Most likely these two themes run together, side by side, in Luther's life as a reformer: Luther's sympathy especially toward Esther the person (as a model of piety) – particularly in the early stage his career – and his later hostility toward Esther the book (along with 2 Maccabees) are part of and parallel to his early friendly and later anti-Judaic polemics. In other words, Luther's growing hostility to the book of Esther specifically can be seen as a reflection of his growing hostility to those Jews who would not abandon Judaism. Luther seems to assume that the Jewish people, instead of accepting his reformed Christianity and joining him, were still longing for a day when – as in the time of Esther – they would once again be vindicated by God, defeat their enemies (i.e., Christians), practice their "false" religion and "lies" at will, and even cause Gentiles to convert.

Luther's own failure to convert the Jews seems to have deepened his dislike of the Jews' victory over Haman and their triumph over Antiochus IV. Presumably, because of this failure, Luther called for the decline and death of the Jewish people in a manner comparable with Haman's own attempt to annihilate the Jews. Thus, the Jews' success in foiling Haman's plan and demolishing their enemies was repugnant to Luther. His hatred of the feast of Purim, which is based on the book of Esther and celebrates Jewish rescue from annihilation, as well as of the feast of Hanukkah, which is based on 2 Maccabees, and celebrates Jewish religious-cultural and spiritual salvation and triumph over their enemies, is all tied to his broader antagonism toward the continued persistence of the Jewish faith. Like Apion of Alexandria, who blamed the Jews that they hate Greeks (*Against Apion* 2.95; cf. 2.121), Luther blanketly blamed the Jews that they hate Christians.[123]

Let me end this chapter by paraphrasing Josephus Flavius' final words on his contemporary Jew-hater, Apion of Alexandria: "A wise man's duty is to be scrupulously faithful to the religious laws of his religion, and to refrain from abuse of those of others" (*Against Apion* 2.144).[124] Luther was a defaulter of his religion's laws (e.g., love your fellow person; Lev 19:18; Matt 5:43–48; Rom 12:14, 20) and told lies about the religion of others, while talking *On the Jews and Their Lies*, and misinterpreting the book of Esther and using it against the Jews.

---

[123] On Apion of Alexandria, see the discussion in Chapter 6, §V.

[124] English translation follows Thackeray, *Josephus: The Life, Against Apion*, p. 349 (Greek: p. 348).

CHAPTER 12

Christian Anti-Esther and Judeophobic Interpretation

The view of Theodor Mommsen that "The hatred of Jews and Jew-baiting are as old as the Diaspora itself,"[1] is not one that I share. After all, there is no sign of Israelite/Jew hatred *per se* – at least not documented – after the fall of Samaria and exile of the Israelites in 720 BCE by Sargon II, king of Assyria, or after the exile of the Judahites by Sennacherib in 701 BCE, or those of them in 597 and 587/6 BCE by Nebuchadnezzar II, king of Babylon. Nonetheless, the story of Esther, the Egyptian attack on the Jewish mercenary community in Elephantine (410 BCE),[2] the persecutions of the Jews by Antiochus IV (168–165 BCE),[3] and the devastating statements of some Greco-Roman writers, such as the rhetorician Apollonius Molon (the first half of the first century BCE), the Hellenized Egyptian, Apion of Alexandria (30–20 BCE–ca. 45–48 CE), and the Roman historian, Tacitus (ca. 55–117 CE), demonstrate that Judeophobic views and acts existed prior to Christianity (and, of course, Islam).[4] However, Christians in general and Martin Luther in particular not only charged the Jews, *collectively*, as the killers of "God's son," but also demonized them as the enemies of God and mankind, and portrayed them as the most bloodthirsty and vengeful nation on the earth, and thus increased the hostility toward Jews and anti-Judaism to the highest level ever. Moreover, many Christians implemented their hostility toward the Jews and in fact moved to perform pogroms and persecutions over many centuries.

---

[1] "Der Judenhass und die Judenhetzen sind so alt wie die Diaspora selbst"; see T. Mommsen, *Römische Geschichte* (Munich: Deutscher Taschenbuch Verlag, 1976), vol. 7, p. 219 (a reprint of the 5th ed, 1904, vol. 5, p. 519).
[2] See Chapter 5, §II, 11.
[3] See Chapter 11, §§VI–VII.
[4] On these and other writers and relevant citations from their works, see in detail Chapter 6 and the bibliography listed there in note 7.

I   Christian Repudiations of Esther, Jews, and Judaism

In the centuries following Luther's era, his hostile attitudes toward the book of Esther, Jews, and Judaism spread rapidly, and became almost a formative belief among Christian thinkers, theologians, and biblical commentators, particularly German Protestants. Many of them have repeated Luther's criticism of Esther and the Jews, and as if that were not enough, they even added further negative words and anti-Jewish assertions of their own. Indeed, as the Swedish exegete, Gillis Gerleman (1912–1993), concludes: "The inclusion of the book of Esther in the Christian Bible has been considered *at all times as questionable and offensive* …. The critique [of Martin Luther on Esther] has never been silenced" (italics mine).[5] Indeed, after Luther's time, the next period in which anti-Esther sentiment becomes especially prominent was in the modern biblical critical scholarship in the eighteenth–nineteenth and the vast part of the twentieth centuries. It rose for the most part – but not only – in Germany at a time in which political questions were being debated about the Jews' civil rights within Christian society, and viewpoints similar to those of Haman were in fact common, as we will see below in §II. It continued as racism and antisemitism rose immensely, particularly in the "Third Reich," and even after Shoah it did not stop.

To demonstrate this, the following presents a collection of twenty-five commentaries representative of anti-Esther interpreters. These commentaries harshly judge the book from various angles, often based on their Christian theology, in comparison to the New Testament, from political and antisemitic perspectives.

The third section of this chapter provides detailed engagement with these scholars' accusations that Esther is characterized by "hatred," "bloodshed," and "vengeance," to show the extent to which these charges distort aspects of the book of Esther itself. It shows that these and other scholars did not grasp the very central content and the essential message of the book of Esther. They ignored or did not read the biblical text precisely as it is and did not let the book or any other historical data restrain them. Instead, they maintained their own non-scholarly agendas which have often been driven by anti-Judaism or antisemitism, and then read them into the biblical text (eisegesis).

Let us begin with Johannes Brenz (or Brentio/Brentius; 1499–1570) who was a contemporary and early follower of Luther (they met in Heidelberg

---

[5] See Gerleman, *Esther*, p. 40: "Die Zugehörigkeit des Estherbuches zur christlichen Bibel ist zu allen Zeiten als fragwürdig und anstößig betrachtet worden …. Die Kritik ist nicht verstummt."

in 1518). He spent much of his life promoting the Reformation in southern German territories, especially in Heidelberg, Schwäbisch Hall, and Württemberg. In a Latin commentary on Esther, first published in 1543, Brenz simultaneously accused the Jews of longing to take revenge against Christians as their ancestors did in Persia, and identifies them with Haman the Amalekite, while identifying Christians as true Israelites:

> The Jews, who take pride in this name in our time, marvelously please themselves in the reading of this story. And if any pious magistrate treats them rather sharply and drives them out of his borders, they give him the name of Aman, and this only they hope and breathe for that they may be allowed to take revenge on their enemies, that is, on the Christians, among whom they live, as this story bears record that the Jews in Persia took vengeance on their enemies. This is the thankfulness of the wicked Jews, which they return to the Christians for their hospitality – namely, for a maximum benefit they return maximum evil deeds, that is murder and robbery. But they have no reason to take pride in the story of Esther at this time. For this story belongs to the people and Church of God. But the Jews, because they have cast off Christ, the true seed of Abraham, they are no more the people of God nor his Church but they belong to Ismael and Esau who always persecuted the true seed of Abraham. And because they pursue the true Israelites, who are the Christians, with the same hatred with which Aman pursued them in the past, it is clear that they are the cousins and kindred of Aman the Amalekite – a nation which always with extreme hatred breathed for the bitter destruction of the Israelites. As the Jews, who now live, are far from being able to expect their deliverance and the destruction of the Christians from this book so that Aman rather stands out as a clear example that, when they have begun to fall before the Church of Christ, they will never be able to raise themselves again unless they convert to Christ who alone is our only salvation.[6]

---

[6] The original Latin is: "Iudæi, qui nostro tempore hoc nomine gloriantur, mirum in modum sibi placent lectione huius Historiæ. Et si pius quispiam magistratus tractauerit ipsos severiter, ac eijciat eos è finibus suis, tribuunt ei cognomen Aman, & hoc unum sperant ac spirant, ut liceat ipsis vindictam sumere de hostibus suis, hoc est, Christianis, inter quos vitam agunt, quemadmodum haec Historia testatur Iudæos de hostibus in Persia vindctam sumpsisse. Haec est impiorum Iudæorum gratitudo, quam rependunt Christianis pro hospitio, pro maximo scilicet beneficio, maxima malefacta, hoc est, caedem & latrocinia. At non habent, quod hoc tempore de Historia Esther glorientur. Pertinet enim haec Historia ad populum & Ecclesiam Dei. Iudæi autem, quia abiecerunt Christum, verum semen Abrahæ, non sunt amplius populus Dei, nec Ecclesia eius, sed pertinent ad Ismael & Esau, qui semper verum semen Abrahæ persecuti sunt. Et quia ueros Israelitas, qui sunt Christiani, eodem odio prosequuntur, quo quondam Aman eos prosecutus est, manifestum est ipsos esse cognatos & affines Amani Amalechitæ, quæ gens summa semper invidia extremam Israelitarum internecionem spiravit. Quare tantum abest, ut Iudæi, qui nunc sunt, possint sibi aliquam spem liberationis suae & exitij Christianorum ex hoc libello polliceri, ut magis in Amano extet manifeſtum exemplum, quod cùm cœperint cadere ante Ecclesiam Christi, numquam poterunt sese erigere, nisi convertantur ad Christum, qui solus est salus nostra." See Ioanne Brentio [Johannes Brenz], *In Epiſtolam Pauli ad Philemo, nem, et in Historiam Esther, Commentarioli* (Frankfurt am Main: Petri Brubachij, 1570; first published 1543), pp. 275–276.

In this passage, Brenz sounds very similar to Luther, and most likely he was enormously influenced by the latter's assertions and writings against the Jews and against the book of Esther, as cited in the previous chapter. He twists the Jews' symbolic usage of "Esau" as a description of "Christians" who oppress the Jews, and uses it against the Jews themselves, as if they were the ones attempting to persecute "the true seed of Abraham" (i.e., Christians)! Moreover, Brenz's accusation that the Jews "belong to Ismael [that is, Muslims/Turks] … who always persecuted the true seed of Abraham," resembles a similar one of Luther's own assertion that the Jews joined the Turks to spy on Christians, to see "whether they could in the end overpower us."[7] These accusations were asserted against a political background in which the Islamic power of the Turks had been frightening European Christians for centuries.

Also, Brenz repeats well-known Christians dogmas, such as the belief that the Jews could only be saved if they accepted Christianity. Obviously, his characterization of the Jews as a bitter enemy of Christians and the Church, accusing them of "murder and robbery" and evil thoughts against Christians, deepened the animosity of the latter against the former, and contributed to the oppression of the Jewish communities.

Strikingly, Brenz claims that the story of Esther belongs not to the Jews but "to the people and Church of God." This was probably because some Church Fathers interpreted Esther using allegorical methods, as was discussed above in Chapter 10, §IV.

In the dawn of modern Protestant biblical scholarship in the early nineteenth century, Wilhelm Martin Leberecht de Wette (1780–1849), attributed to the book of Esther a "bloodthirsty spirit of revenge and persecution."[8] His contemporary theologians were no less harsh. Thus, in his *Introduction to the Old Testament*, Friedrich Bleek (1793–1859) declares that the book of Esther reflects a "very narrow-minded and Jewish spirit of revenge and persecution," that is "far removed … from the spirit of the Gospel."[9] And the

---

[7] See Chapter 11, §VII.

[8] See de Wette, *Lehrbuch der historisch-kritischen Einleitung*, vol. 1, pp. 273–277 esp. 276 ("der blutdürstige Rache- und Verfolgungsgeist des Buches"); English: idem, *A Critical and Historical Introduction*, vol. 2, pp. 336–349 esp. 346.

[9] Bleek affirms that "in dem Buche ein sehr engherziger Jüdischer Rache und Verfolgungsgeist herrscht und keine andere Schrift des A[ltes] T[estaments] von dem Geiste des Evangeliums so fern ist wie diese"; F. Bleek, *Einleitung in die Heilige Schrift*, Volume 1: *Einleitung in das Alte Testament* (3rd ed; edited by J. Bleek and A. Kamphausen; Berlin: G. Reimer, 1870), p. 407; English: idem, *An Introduction to the Old Testament* (2 vols.; edited by J. Bleek and A. Kamphausen; translated from the 2nd German edition of 1865 by G. H. Venables; London: Bell and Daldy, 1869), vol. 1, p. 450. Horowitz (*Reckless Rites*, p. 15), refers to Heinrich Ewald (1803–1875), who asserted about the book of Esther: "we fall as it were, from heaven to earth."

German historian and orientalist, Alfred von Gutschmid (1835–1887) dismisses Esther as "an extremely stupid and immoral book."[10] Ernst Bertheau (1812–1888) not only fully supports Luther's grave statement concerning Esther, but expands it further in the spirit of Bleek:

> It [that is, the book of Esther] stands further away from the spirit of Old Testament revelation and of the Gospel than any other book of the Old Testament. Esther and Mordecai are full of a vengeful spirit of hostility not against the pagan nature but against pagans [themselves], full of cruelty and of the godless faith in victory over the world through secular power and the use of worldly means, in a spirit that found more and more space in the Jewish people in the last centuries before the birth of Christ.[11]

The Old Testament scholar, Karl Budde (1850–1935) makes a comparison between the books of Jonah and Ruth on the one hand and the book of Esther on the other while criticizing the latter: "There [i.e., in Jonah and Ruth] broadminded tolerance, yes, warm affection for other peoples; here [in Esther] furious hatred against *all non-Jews*, satisfied only by terrible bloodshed" (italics added).[12]

Yet it was not only in the early modern period that such views were expressed. At the very beginning of the twentieth century, D. C. Siegfried opens the new era with the old animosity against the biblical book of Esther. According to Siegfried, "In the book of Esther there is no trace of the religious enthusiasm and hope that was typical for the time after the Exile and led to a new foundation of Judaism. National exclusiveness and fanaticism, hatred against the pagans, amongst whom they live, characterize the book."[13]

---

[10] "Ein äußerst dummes und unmoralisches Buch"; see A. von Gutschmid, "Vorlesungen über Josephos' Bücher gegen Apion," *Kleine Schriften* (edited by F. Rühl; Leipzig: B. G. Teubner, 1893), vol. 4, pp. 336–589 esp. 404.

[11] E. Bertheau, *Esra, Nechemia und Ester* (Kurzgefasstes Exegetisches Handbuch zum Alten Testament 17, Leipzig: Verlag von S. Hirzel, 1862), p. 287: "Es [d.h. das Buch Esther] steht dem Geiste der alttestamentl. Offenbarung und des Evangeliums ferner als irgendein anderes Buch des A[lten] T[estament]s. Ester und Mordochai [*sic.*] sind erfül[l]t von dem Geiste der Rache, der Feindschaft nicht gegen heidnisches Wesen, sondern gegen die Heiden, der Grausamkeit und des gottlosen Vertrauens auf den Sieg über die Welt durch weltliche Macht und Gebrauch weltlicher Mittel, von dem Geiste, der in den letzten Jahrhunderten vor der Geb[urt] Chr[isti] im jüdischen Volke immer weiteren Raum gewann." Bertheau was followed by Carl Friedrich Keil, *Biblischer Commentar über die Nachexilischen Geschichtsbücher: Chronik, Esra, Nehemia und Esther* (Leipzig: Dürffling und Franke, 1870), p. 613.

[12] "Dort [i.e., in Jona und Ruth] weitherzige Duldung, ja warme Zuneigung zu andern Völkern, hier wütender Hass gegen *alle Nichtjuden*, der sich nur in furchtbarem Blutvergießen Genüge tun kann"; Budde, *Geschichte der althebräischen Literatur*, p. 237.

[13] "Im Esterbuche ist keine Spur von der religiösen Erregung und Hoffnung, welche die ersten Zeiten nach dem Exil auszeichnete und zur Neugründung des Judentums führte. Nationale Abgeschlossenheit und nationaler Fanatismus, Hass gegen die Heiden, in deren Mitte man wohnt, charakterisieren es." See D. C. Siegfried, *Esra, Nehemia und Esther* (Handkommentar zum Alten Testament; Göttingen: Vandenhoeck & Ruprecht, 1901), p. 141.

Siegfried does not base his severe critique of the biblical canonical book on explicit textual evidence. Perhaps for him, if Luther spoke likewise, it is already enough!

In the same decade, in the 6th and 7th editions of his influential *Einleitung in die kanonischen Bücher des Alten Testaments* (1908, 1913), Carl Heinrich Cornill (1854–1920), professor of theology at the University of Halle (Saale), states in the spirit of Luther, although without clear reference to him: "It is characteristic of the Judaism of the last pre-Christian era that this questionable book [that is, the book of Esther] became the most popular one [among the Jews], more than Psalms and the Prophets, and even was equal to the Torah."[14] He defines the writing in Esther 9 as "the bloodthirsty revenge against the Gentiles."[15]

Cornill's accusation that the Jews prefer Esther to the Prophets, recalls Luther's own accusation that the Jews prefer Esther over the prophetic books such as Isaiah and Daniel.[16] The term "bloodthirsty revenge" that he uses, appears also in Luther's assertions about Esther. Furthermore, Cornill does not say how he measures that in the pre-Christian period the book of Esther was more popular among the Jews than the book of Psalms. Besides, it is inaccurate to say so, because like the Torah (and some prophetical books), Psalms was already very popular before 70 CE, as reflected in the numerous copies of it – altogether 39 (partly fragmentary) – are found at Qumran and in countless quotations across the full spectrum of Second Temple Judaism. Although Esther enjoyed some popularity among Hellenistic Jews – as attested by the six additions, two translations of it in Greek, and many minor insertions into the book – it was rarely alluded to in other Second Temple period Hebrew sources, and was not preserved among the Dead Sea Scrolls.[17] Later, the book of Esther became

---

[14] "Es charakterisiert das Judentum der letzten vorchristlichen Zeit, wenn gerade dies bedenkliche Buch sich der größten Beliebtheit erfreute, ja über Psalmen und Propheten, und der Thora gleichgestellt wurde." See C. H. Cornill, *Einleitung in die kanonischen Bücher des Alten Testaments* (Grundriss der Theologischen Wissenschaften; 6th ed.; Tübingen: J. C. B. Mohr [P. Siebeck], 1908), pp. 153–156 esp. 155 (= 7th revised ed.; Tübingen: J. C. B. Mohr [P. Siebeck], 1913), vol. 2, pp. 148–151 esp. 150). For an English translation of an earlier version of the book, see idem, *Introduction to the Canonical Books of the Old Testament* (translated by G. Box; New York: Williams and Norgate, 1907), p. 257.

[15] "Die in Kap[ital] 9 sich äußernde blutdürstige Rachgier gegen die Heiden"; Cornill, *Einleitung in die kanonischen Bücher des Alten Testaments*, p. 154 (7th ed.; p. 149). Interestingly, Carl Steuernagel, who served as professor of theology at the same university, and published his *Lehrbuch der Einleitung in das Alte Testament* in 1912, in the same city and by the same publisher (Tübingen: J. C. B. Mohr [P. Siebeck]), did not use such sharp language toward the book of Esther and Jewish people; see Steuernagel, *Lehrbuch der Einleitung in das Alte Testament*, pp. 433–439 esp. 434.

[16] See Chapter 11, §III, esp. note 19.

[17] On attitudes toward Esther at Qumran and in later Jewish literature, see Chapters 7 through 9.

(and still is) very popular among the Jews, but even then by no means more than the Psalms, which after the Torah, is the most popular book in everyday Jewish life and liturgy.[18]

It was not only among German scholars that Esther was critiqued, however. Although the distinguished British scholar, Samuel R. Driver (1846–1914), who was professor of Hebrew and canon of Christ Church at Oxford University, does not express the same level of uncontrolled invective against the book of Esther as some of the above, he is still sharply critical of certain aspects of the book, in line with other Christian scholars:

> Much fault has been found with the temper displayed in the Book of Esther: it is said, for instance, to breathe a spirit of vengeance and hatred, without any redeeming feature; and to be further removed from the spirit of the gospel than any other Book of the O[ld] T[estament]. It is impossible altogether to acquit it of this accusation ... [I]t seems consequently impossible to acquit Mordecai of permitting, and the Jews of engaging in, an *unprovoked* massacre. Nor, as it seems, can the request in 9[13] be excused.[19]

The American scholar Louis B. Paton, published a comprehensive commentary in 1908 on the book of Esther, where he decisively states: "There is not one noble character in this book ... Morally Esther falls far below the general level of the Old Testament, and even of the Apocrypha. *The verdict of Luther is not too severe* ... The book is so conspicuously lacking in religion that it should never have been included in the Canon of the Old Testament, but should have been left with Judith and Tobit among the apocryphal writings" (italics mine).[20]

Two years later, in 1910, the prominent German Protestant biblical scholar, Hermann Gunkel (1862–1932),[21] wrote similarly in an encyclopedia article: "Luther's pure spirit justifiably found it [i.e., the book of Esther] to be too 'Judaizing'."[22] Gunkel details his opinion of Esther in his books:

---

[18] See further, I. Kalimi, "The Centrality and Interpretation of Psalms in Judaism Prior to and during Medieval Times: Approaches, Authorship, Genre and Polemics," *RRJ* 23 (2020), pp. 229–259 esp. 229–233.

[19] See Driver, *An Introduction to the Literature of the Old Testament*, pp. 485–487 esp. 485, 486.

[20] See Paton, *A Critical and Exegetical Commentary on the Book of Esther*, pp. 96–97. He is also of the opinion that Esther should have interceded on behalf of her fallen enemy – Haman (Esth 7:8; ibid., p. 264) – as if the latter did not plan to annihilate the entire Jewish people. Following such an absurd line of ethics, a Holocaust survivor should intercede on behalf of Hitler in April 1945, or on behalf of the Nazi criminals in the Nuremberg process!

[21] On Gunkel, see recently K. Hammann, *Hermann Gunkel: Eine Biographie* (Tübingen: Mohr Siebeck, 2014).

[22] See H. Gunkel, "Estherbuch," *Die Religion in Geschichte und Gegenwart* (Erste Auflage; Tübingen: J. C. B. Mohr [P. Siebeck], 1910), pp. 647–653 esp. 653: "Luthers reiner Geist fand es mit Recht zu sehr 'judenzend'."

Typical for the spirit of this novel [that is, Esther] is the hatred towards the enemies of the Jews, the one-sided prejudice for fellow Jews [that is, their ethnic group] – all light is on the Jew and all shadow on the gentile – and the belief that the Jew certainly will have victory over the gentile/pagans. There is no word about moral or religious principles, but simply the natural egotism of a nation which is determined to succeed even under demeaning conditions and by all possible means.[23]

Gunkel does not read Luther's verdict on the book of Esther with open eyes, as an objective and critical scholar should. Instead, he justifies Luther's word in its entirety: Esther contains too much "Jewishness." In addition, like Luther, Gunkel also reflects this racism in what he calls "the natural egotism of the Jewish nation," as a whole.

No less offensive and disgraceful are the antisemitic words of Max Haller in 1914: "much more common are the bad, even repulsive traits of this *national character*, above all the uncontrolled desire for revenge, which lets their imagination, with true Oriental savagery, *swim and rejoice in the blood* of their foes" (italics mine).[24] Haller ignores that the Jews rejoice in their salvation from national annihilation and not in what he describes as the blood of their foes.

The campaign against the book of Esther, Jews, and Judaism continued also in the thirties and forties of the twentieth century, that is, shortly

---

[23] "Für den Geist dieses Romans [d.h., Esther] ist bezeichnend der Haß gegen die Judenfeinde, die einseitige Parteinahme für die Volksgenossen – auf den Juden liegt alles Licht, auf den Heiden aller Schatten – und die Überzeugung, dass der Jude notwendiger Weise gegen die Heiden den Sieg gewinnt. Von sittlichen oder religiösen Gedanken ist nicht die Rede, sondern einfach von dem natürlichen Egoismus einer Nation, die entschlossen ist, sich auch unter unwürdigen Verhältnissen auf jeden Fall zu behaupten, mit welchen Mitteln es auch sei." See H. Gunkel, *Esther* (Religionsgeschichtliche Volksbücher, 2. Reihe, Heft 19/20, Tübingen: Mohr Siebeck, 1916), p. 76. See also ibid., p. 51: "And equally to be understood is the murderous decree of the state against the enemies of the Jews: pogroms against the Jews were an unfortunate reality at that time; but such a reverse pogrom against all the nations that beset Judaism is nothing but a bloody dream of souls seeking vengeance." ("Und so ist auch der Morderlaß des Staates gegen die Judenfeinde zu erklären: Judenpogrome sind damals eine leidige Wirklichkeit; aber ein solcher umgekehrter Pogrom gegen alle Völker, die das Judentum bedrängen, ist nichts als ein blutiger Traum rachedürstiger Seelen.").

[24] M. Haller, *Das Judentum: Geschichtsschreibung, Prophetie und Gesetzgebung nach dem Exil* (Schriften des Alten Testament 2/3; Göttingen: Vandenhoeck & Ruprecht, 1914), p. 278: "Viel zahlreicher aber sind die schlimmen, ja widerwärtigen Züge dieses Volkscharakters, vor allem die ungebändigte Rachsucht, die ihre Phantasie mit richtiger orientalischer Wildheit im Blute des Gegners schwimmen und schwelgen läßt." Moreover, on p. 279 Haller describes Judaism as follows: "For these Jews, religion means loyalty towards their nationhood (Esth 8:6). The idea of loyalty to God is immersed in the concept of loyalty to the nationhood. God is there for the human being, not the human being for God. Salvation, the very real and worldly image of salvation, is the content of their religion, not the glory of God. The Jew himself has become the real God" ("Religion heißt bei diesen Juden: Treue gegen sein Volkstum [Esth 8,6]. Der Gedanke der Treue gegen Gott ist in diesem andern, konkreteren untergetaucht. Gott ist für die Menschen da, nicht der Mensch für Gott. Das Heil, und zwar ein sehr wirklich und diesseitig gedachtes Heil, ist der Inhalt der Religion, nicht die Ehre Gottes. Der Jude ist sich selber zum Gott geworden").

before, during, and even after the Holocaust, as if nothing had happened meanwhile, as a result of centuries of such insidious antisemitic declarations by theologians and scholars. Thus, in 1919 Johannes Meinhold (1861–1937) classified Esther as a "bloodthirsty story," and asserted: "This book, where the name of God ... is not even mentioned, is a shocking testimony to what state of neglect mind and feeling, to what distortion, the religion of the Jews was driven under Syrian pressure."[25]

Johannes Hempel (1891–1964), did not lag behind, and wrote as follows: "[It] is shown in the hate-filled dream of the book of Esther: the Jewish Queen and the Jewish Prime Minister work together to misuse the royal authority to save the Jews, with the King's seal to give permission for a Jewish pogrom against their 'enemies,' and in this way [their] proselytizing has a powerful boost."[26] Hempel's book was published for the first time in 1938, that is, in the midst of "Third Reich" Germany; then its second revised edition was published twice after the war: about twenty years later, in 1964, and reprinted in 2019! In all editions of the book, Hempel's attitude toward Esther is the same. Hempel was deeply involved with Nazism. He established the Evangelical "German Christians" (*Deutsche Christen*), was a member of the Nazi party (NSDAP = Nationalsozialistische Deutsche Arbeiterpartei, that is, National Socialist German Workers Party), and of "the professors of German colleges and universities profession of loyalty to Adolf Hitler and the National Socialist state,"[27] which was founded in November 1933. As the editor of *Zeitschrift für die alttestamentliche Wissenschaft (ZAW*; 1927–1959), he published an article there, where he presents the "Third Reich" struggling with Judaism: "The more the racial and ethnic awakening prevails and the more vigorously in the political arena the opposition between the Third Reich and

---

[25] See the first edition of Meinhold, *Einführung in das Alte Testament*, p. 306 (in the 3rd ed., 1932, p. 360): "dies Buch, in dem Gott ... überhaupt nicht erwähnt wird, ist ein abschreckendes Zeugnis dafür, bis zu welcher Verwilderung von Geist und Gemüt, bis zu welcher Entstellung die Religion der Juden unter syrischen Druck getrieben ward." See also his assertion cited in Chapter 2, §III, and note 29.

[26] "Wohin die Phantasie der Rachsucht sich dabei verlieren kann, zeigt der haβ druch glühte Wunschtraum des Esterbuches: im Zusammenspiel der jüdischen Königin mit dem jüdischen Ministerpräsidentten wird die königlische Vollmacht, die Juden zu retten, dazu miβbraucht, mit des Königs Siegel die Erlaubnis zu einem Pogrom der Juden an ihren ‚Feinden' zu erteilen und so der Proselyten-macherei einen kräftigen Auftrieb zu haben"; see J. Hempel, *Das Ethos des Alten Testaments* (Beihefte zur Zeitschrift für die alttestamentliche Wissenschaft 67; Berlin: Alfred Töpelmann, 1938; 2nd revised ed. published by Walter de Gruyter, 1964, and reprinted in 2019), p. 30, see also p. 105: "... wie in den blutrünstigen Pogromschilderungen des Esther-Buches" ("... as in the bloodthirsty pogrom portrayals of the book of Esther"); cf. Horowitz, *Reckless Rites*, p. 15.

[27] "Das Bekenntnis der Professoren an den deutschen Universitäten und Hochschulen zu Adolf Hitler und dem nationalsozialistischen Staat."

Judaism as a life and death struggle becomes visible ...."[28] Hempel's position regarding Esther and the Jews therefore is not surprising at all. What is astounding, however, is that despite all his Nazi activities, in 1955 he was appointed an Honorary Professor at the University of Göttingen.[29]

The negation of Esther and the Jews is seen in Nazi Germany, not only in scholarly writings but also in papers for a more general public that spread the anti-Jewish propaganda of the Third Reich. For instance, in March 1939, Julius Streicher, the founder and chief editor of the newspaper *Der Stürmer*, published an anti-Jewish article and dropped poisonous remarks against the book of Esther, the feast of Purim, and the Jews. Although Streicher himself was not a theologian, the hostile atmosphere toward Esther among the German theologians was, most likely, not unfamiliar to him.[30]

During the Second World War, in 1941, Robert H. Pfeiffer of Boston (1892–1958) described the author of Esther as characterized by a "passionate sanguinary patriotism." He continued: "His chauvinistic loyalty to his race, as in the case of some modern Zionists, has no relation to religion. Likewise, his bitter hatred for the heathen, probably unparalleled in ferocity, is dictated by political rather than religious motives ...." "From the moral point of view," Pfeiffer said, "the book has little to commend it to civilized persons enjoying the benefits of peace and freedom, whatever their race ... The book is morally neither better nor worse than the violent 'hymns of hatred' .... Such a secular book hardly deserves a place in the canon of Sacred Scriptures, even when provided with the pious additions

---

[28] "Je stärker das rassische und völkische Erwachen sich durch setzt und je energischer in der politischen Lage der Gegensatz zwischen dem Dritten Reiche und dem Judentum als ein Kampf auf Leben und Tod hervortritt ..."; see J. Hempel, "Chronik," *ZAW* 59 (1942/43), pp. 209–215 esp. 212.

[29] On Hempel, see R. Smend, "Die älteren Herausgeber der *Zeitschrift für die alttestamentliche Wissenschaft*," *ZAW* 100 Suppl. (1988), pp. 1–21 esp.17–20; F. W. Bautz, "Hempel, Johannes," *Biographisch-Bibliographisches Kirchenlexikon* (Hamm, Westf.: Verlag Traugott Bautz, 1990), vol. 2, pp. 711–712; C. T. Begg, "Hempel, Johannes," in J. H. Hayes (ed.), *Dictionary of Biblical Interpretation* (Nashville: Abingdon Press, 1999), vol. 1, p. 493.

[30] See in detail, Chapter 9, §III, 1. In this atmosphere, no wonder that the Berliner Dr. Reinhold Krause could propose in 1933 to abandon the entire Old Testament, "with its tales of cattle merchants and pimps" ("von diesen Viehhändler- und Zuhältergeschichten"); see W. L. Shirer, *The Rise and Fall of the Third Reich: A History of Nazi Germany* (London: Secker and Warburg, 1961), p. 237. This approach is also found in the contemporary, largely Protestant, movement of the so-called "German Christians" (*Deutsche Christen*), of which Krause was a leader (*Obmann*). That movement wanted a de-Judaization of Christianity to fit in with Nazi ideology. In so doing they took up the project, begun already some years before Hitler, of creating a "Germanic Bible" – one that would eliminate the Old Testament and "Jewish" passages of the New Testament and add various selections from German folkloristic literature. See D. L. Bergen, *Twisted Cross: The German Christian Movement in the Third Reich* (Chapel Hill: University of North Carolina Press, 1996); S. Heschel, *The Aryan Jesus: Christian Theologians and the Bible in Nazi Germany* (Princeton: Princeton University Press, 2008).

of the LXX and the Targums ...."[31] Thus Pfeiffer follows Luther's assertion regarding Esther and questions the decision of those who included Esther among Scriptures. He claims that the author of Esther is characterized by a "chauvinistic loyalty to his race," at the time when the Nazi racists were murdering and burning Jews in the gas chambers in Christian Europe. He does not explain why someone who defends his or her people from slaughter should be accused of chauvinism and racism.

In March 1947, Otto Weber (1902–1966) published his "5th fully revised version" of *Bibelkunde des Alten Testaments*, where he concludes his discussion on the book of Esther as follows: "[T]his book stands in a strange way 'on the boundary between true and false beliefs,' and at least *one* line also led from it to those people who prided themselves on their direct descent from Abraham and in that way restricted in an inadmissible way the covenant with God."[32] Obviously, by the "true faith" Weber refers to Christianity, while by the "false belief" to Judaism, which is held by the Jewish people, who consider themselves to be the direct descendants of the biblical Abraham. This is the way a professor of theology at the University of Göttingen, where he served after the war also as the Dean of the Faculty of Theology (1950–1951 and 1957–1958) and as the Rector of the University (1958–1959) expresses himself. Also, from 1963 to 1965, Weber served as the State Synodal (*Landessynodaler*) of the Reformed Protestant Church of North Germany. This fundamental textbook on the Bible was printed at least eight times – four after the Second World War, before the blood of Holocaust victims had dried! No wonder Weber had already joined the Nazi party NSDAP by 1933 and also belonged to the "German Christians," who lined up with the antisemitic and racist principles of Nazism. Apparently, Weber did not really read the book of Esther itself, but rather was mentally and religiously under the influence of the Protestant Church following the *Führerprinzip*.

Nevertheless, Weber was not the only Shoah and post-Shoah scholar who spoke in such a way. Approximately half a decade later, in 1953, Curt Kuhl (1890–1959) ends his chapter on the book of Esther with these words:

> Because of its purely secular character, the book of Esther has long been controversial, until it gradually rose to great popularity. It is the testimony

---

[31] See Pfeiffer, *Introduction to the Old Testament*, pp. 743–744, 747.

[32] Otto Weber, *Bibelkunde des Alten Testaments: Ein Arbeitsbuch* (Tübingen: Furche-Verlag, 1947), p. 250. In the 8th edition of the book (Hamburg: Furche-Verlag, 1959), p. 349, Weber repeats in the same words: "dieses Buch auf eine eigentuemliche Weise ‚auf der Grenze zwischen wahrem und falschem Glauben' stehe und daß von ihm her jedenfalls *eine* Linie auch zu jenen Männern führte, die sich ihrer fleischlichen Abrahamskindschaft rühmten und darin den Bund Gottes unzulässig einengten."

of a narrow-minded and fanatical nationalism. We understand that Luther inertly had to reject this book with its 'pagan improprieties,' and was so hostile to it that he would prefer to wish that it did not exist at all. For Christians the book of Esther has nothing religious to say.[33]

Thus, this biblical scholar, whose National Socialist German Workers Party (NSDAP) had just devastated Europe, caused the Second World War, and annihilated one-third of the Jewish people, defines the book of Esther as "the testimony of a narrow-minded and fanatical nationalism"! As though nothing had changed since the time of Friedrich Bleek, who used the same words! But no surprise, Kuhl was an active Nazi. In 1933, he officially joined the NSDAP. He already was a member of the *Sturmabteilung* (SA) that was the paramilitary fighting organization of that party during the Weimar Republic, and belonged to the "German Christians."[34] Apparently, Kuhl's Nazi background and antisemitic approach influenced his scholarly writings.

There were several other scholars who expressed themselves in a similar way, for example: Although the commentary on Esther in the first edition of *Peake's Commentary on the Bible* (by Archibald Duff in 1920), rejected the common view that Esther is "revengeful" and "irreligious,"[35] *Peake's Commentary* was "completely revised" in 1962, and Duff's entry was replaced with one by L. E. Brown, who harshly condemned the book of Esther. Reversing the positive defense of the book and Judaism by Duff, Brown claimed: "The Book of Esther occupies the same place in sacred scripture as the villainous rogue in a story or play which has been written with a moral purpose. In the whole book there is no mention of God or religion, and no noble character. Even Esther, who in some sense is the heroine of the story in that she risks her life to save the Jews from destruction, is expressly said to have done so only after Mordecai had threatened that she herself would not escape the massacre."[36]

---

[33] Kuhl, *Die Entstehung des Alten Testaments*, pp. 291–294 esp. 294: "Wegen seines rein weltlichen Charakters war das Estherbuch lange umstritten, bis es allmählich zu großer Beliebtheit aufstieg. Es ist das Zeugnis eines engherzigen und fanatischen Nationalismus. Wir verstehen, daß Luther diese Schrift mit ihren 'heidnischen Unarten' innerlich ablehnen mußte und ihr so feindlich gesonnen war, daß er am liebsten gewollt hätte, daß sie gar nicht vorhanden wäre. Dem Christen hat das Buch Esther religiös nichts zu sagen."

[34] Still, after the War, all these did not prevent Evangelical-Theological Faculty of the University of Bonn to grant him an "Honorary Doctor" (1956), and the University of Göttingen hired him to teach. See K. Pegler, "Pfarrer Dr. Lic. Curt Kuhl," *Frohnauer Geschichte*, http://klauspegler.de/texte/blickpunkt-frohnau/pfarrer-dr-lic-curt-kuhl/ (accessed April 18, 2018).

[35] A. Duff, "Esther," in A. S. Peake and A. J. Grieve (eds.), *A Commentary on the Bible* (New York: T. Nelson & Sons, 1920), pp. 336–340 esp. 340. For detailed discussion of Duff's positive assessment of the book, see Chapter 13, §I.

[36] L. E. Brown, "Esther," in A. S. Peake, M. Black, and H. H. Rowley (eds.), *Peake's Commentary on the Bible* (revised edition; London: T. Nelson, 1962), pp. 381–384 esp. 381; cited by Carruthers, *Esther through the Centuries*, p. 10.

The Danish-Lutheran biblical scholar, Aage Bentzen (1894–1953), was professor of theology in the University of Copenhagen. He published his influential *Introduction to the Old Testament* in 1952. Here he follows the judgement of Luther regarding the book of Esther, and adds: "The book is a very unpleasant example of how persecution and suppression have poisoned the soul of a nation, a part at least of the Jewish nation living, and breathing in wishful dreams of a *revanche*" (italics original).[37] Further, Bentzen criticizes Esther's behavior: "Morally unsound is that Esther conceals her nationality and so secures her high position or at least avoids an unpleasant handicap. Her silence in 7,8, when the king misunderstands the position of her enemy, is an act of untruthfulness." However, in the next sentence he attempts, despite all, to find an excuse for her: "But … we cannot overlook the description of the lonely Jewish woman taking a personal risk for her people in a critical situation."[38]

The first edition of Bentzen's book is published in 1948, just three years after the Shoah, while the second edition "with corrections and a supplement" (from which is the above quotation) was published in 1952, only seven years after the annihilation of millions of Jews. Still, astonishingly Bentzen expresses himself as he did. Interestingly, what he would say about his contemporary and current Jews: How much the Shoah "poisoned the soul of [the] nation"? Are the Holocaust survivors also "breathing in wishful dreams of a *revanche*"?

In 1963, Ernst Haenchen (1894–1995) published an article titled "Hamans Galgen und Christi Kreuz," in which he concludes: "Luther was right when he judged the book of Esther in accordance with his *theologia crucis* [i.e., theology of the cross]: it shows too much Jewishness and contains a lot of pagan impropriety. That is not nice, but it is true."[39] Haenchen does not bother to tell his audience why and on which basis he concludes that "it is true." As a New Testament scholar, who in 1939 willingly joined the Nazi Party (NSDAP), perhaps it was self-explanatory.

Another renowned German scholar, Otto Eissfeldt (1887–1973), wrote in 1964:

> A book which was so closely bound up with the national spirit and which indeed the people itself regarded as a source of its power, could not be

---

[37] A. Bentzen, *Introduction to the Old Testament* (2nd ed.; Copenhagen: G. E. C. Gad Publisher, 1952), vol. 2, p. 194.

[38] Bentzen, *Introduction to the Old Testament*, vol. 2, p. 194.

[39] E. Haenchen, "Hamans Galgen und Christi Kreuz," in H. Gerdes (ed.), *Wahrheit und Glaube: Festschrift für Emanuel Hirsch* (Itzehoe: Die Spur, 1963), pp. 113–133 esp. 129: "Nein, Luther hat schon recht gehabt, als er von seiner theologia crucis aus über das Estherbuch urteilte, es juditze zu sehr und habe viel heidnische Unart. Das ist freilich nicht erbaulich. Aber es ist wahr."

excluded by the religion which was bound up with it. This we can understand. But Christianity, extending as it does over all peoples and races, has neither occasion nor justification for holding on to it. For Christianity, Luther's remark should be determinative, a remark made with reference to II Maccabees and Esther in his Table-Talk ....[40]

Also Eissfeldt, who served as a professor of Old Testament studies at Martin Luther University Halle-Wittenberg, was well immersed in Luther's anti-Jewish legacy against the people, religion, and "national spirit" of Israel. Moreover, he took upon himself the authority to speak not only in the name of all Lutherans, but the whole of "Christianity," including Catholic and Orthodox Churches, in all times and places. He ignored, or was unaware, that at least some other Christian theologians suggested positive and even pro-Jewish interpretation of Esther, as we will see in the next chapter.

Georg Fohrer (1915–2002) of Friedrich-Alexander-Universität Erlangen-Nürnberg, was not so far removed from Eissfeldt's critical assertions. In his *Introduction to the Old Testament*, he completely revised Sellin's work; like other Christian theologians, he also doubted the religious and theological value of Esther. Fohrer claimed that the book is "the product of a nationalistic spirit, seeking revenge upon those that persecute the Jews, which has lost all understanding of the demands and obligations of Yahwism, especially in its prophetical form." In the next sentence he expresses a certain understanding: "In this respect, it is an accusation and warning, as it makes the effects of the persecution of Jews clear within Judaism itself."[41]

Interestingly, after his retirement from the University in 1979, Fohrer converted to Judaism and moved to the Jewish Quarter of the Old City in Jerusalem, where he lived until his death in 2002. So, this German theologian ended his life among "the very narrow-minded" Jews, whose ancestors had supposedly "lost all understanding of the demands and obligations of Yahwism." Presumably, in the end Fohrer emended his view of Esther, Jews, and Judaism. However, this is not

---

[40] See O. Eissfeldt, *Einleitung in das Alte Testament* (3rd ed.; Tübingen: J. C. B. Mohr [P. Siebeck], 1964), pp. 692–693 esp. 693: "Ein mit dem Volkstum so innig verwachsenes, ja von ihm als ein Quell seiner Kraft gewertetes Buch ließ sich durch eine an dieses Volkstum gebundene Religion nicht verdrängen. Das ist verständlich. Aber das über den Völkern und Rassen stehende Christentum hat zu gleicher Haltung weder Veranlassung noch Recht. Vielmehr wird ihm Luthers Wort maßgebend bleiben müssen, das er in einer seiner Tischreden über II Makkabeer und Esther gesprochen hat ...." For the English version, see his *The Old Testament: An Introduction*, pp. 511–512.

[41] See E. Sellin and G. Fohrer, *Einleitung in das Alte Testament* (12th ed.; Heidelberg: Quelle & Meyer, 1979), p. 275: "Es ist das Erzeugnis eines antionalen Geistes, der die Rache an den Verfolgern begehrt und darüber das Verständnis für die Forderungen und Aufgaben des Jahweglaubens, insbesondere in seiner prophetischen Ausprägung, verloren hat. Insofern ist es eine Ankage und Mahnung, indem es die Auswirkungen der Judenverfolgung innerhalb des Judentum selbst deutlich macht."

the case with many other biblical scholars and theologians in Germany and elsewhere who have made devastating attacks on the book of Esther and the Jewish people, even in the years after the Holocaust had eliminated over six million Jews and almost wiped them out of the European continent!

A similar spirit is reflected likewise in the fifth "improved version" of Artur Weiser's *Introduction to the Old Testament*, where he repeats the well-known derogatory note of Martin Luther, and adds: "The Book of Esther ... is a monument to the *nationalist spirit of Judaism, which born from Jew-baiting, has lost all connection with the great tasks that the prophets have put before their people* ... It is a testimony to the impartial clarity of Christian judgment if Luther was 'hostile' to this book and was deeply opposed to it as a 'Jewish' book with 'pagan garbage'" (italics mine).[42] But where exactly are the signs of "Judaism" in the book of Esther? Where is the "nationalist spirit of Judaism" mentioned in Esther? Does Esther really represent "*Judaism*" in the sense that Weiser assumes? Is this not an anachronistic imposition onto the book? And what anyway, is the "nationalist spirit of Judaism"? Weiser simply follows the anti-Jewish and anti-Judaism lines of the Protestant reformer, as if nothing had happened since those dark times.

Even in the Bonn of 1995, the Protestant Old Testament theologian Werner H. Schmidt continues in a similar unacceptable approach, and writes:

> To be sure, Mordecai and Esther hold fast to Judaism in an exemplary way, in a dangerous situation, but *does the book not emphasize too much the superiority of Judaism* (6:13)? Why must rescue from extinction escalate to triumph over their enemies? Retribution by your own hand is certainly an understandable wish of the one who is persecuted, but a theologically illegitimate hope. (italics mine)[43]

Schmidt takes this as self-evident and does not explain how the book of Esther actually "emphasizes too much the superiority of Judaism." Again, does Esther really represent "*Judaism*" in the sense that Schmidt assumes? In fact, the term "Judaism" (Judentum) was invented in the

---

[42] See Weiser, *Einleitung in das Alte Testament*, p. 273: "Das Estherbuch ... ist ein Denkmal des nationalistischen Geist des Judentums, der, durch die Judenhetze erzeugt, jegliche Verbindung verloren hat mit den grossen Aufgaben, welche die Propheten ihrem Volk vor Augen gestellt haben ... Es ist ein Zeugnis für unbefangene Klarheit des christlichen Urteil, wenn Luther diesem Buch ‚feind' war und ihm als einem ‚judenzenden' Buch mit ‚heidnischer Unrat' innerlich ablehnend gegenüberstand."

[43] W. H. Schmidt, *Einführung in das Alte Testament* (5th ed.; Berlin: Walter de Gruyter, 1995), p. 323: "Gewiß halten Mordechai und Ester auch gefaerlicher Situation vorbildlich am Judentum fest; *stellt das Buch aber nicht zu sehr die Überlegenheit des Judentums* (6,13) heraus? Warum muß die Rettung vor dem Untergang zum Triumph über die Feinde gesteigert werden? Vergeltung aus eigener Hand ist ein gewiß verständlicher Wunsch der Verfolgten, aber eine theologisch illegitime Hoffnung" (italics added).

nineteenth century as a counterpart to "Christianity" (Christendom; and also Islam). It never existed or was used before. Thus, Schmidt uses the term anachronistically and reads it into the biblical book. He refers in parenthesis to Esth 6:13, where Haman's advisers and wife declare: "If Mordecai, before whom your downfall has begun, is of the Jewish people, you will not prevail against him, but will surely fall before him." But this is no more than a part of Esther's ironic and humoristic style, which is one of the main features of the book: instead of encouraging him, Haman's advisers and wife add to his agony by prophesying a coming disaster. Moreover, "Judaism" (as a religious practice) is precisely what Esther does not emphasize, since there is virtually no mention of religious practice at all in the book. It is not "Judaism" but "the Jewish people" that Esther describes as undefeatable, and that is not at all the same thing as emphasizing the "superiority" of Judaism. Furthermore, the legitimate self-defense that Esther describes cannot be considered as "vengeance" as we will see below in §III.

There are also some other scholars, such as the American historian and biblicist, John Bright (1908–1995), who consider Esther to be a book that "exhibits a most vengeful spirit,"[44] although he states this as a critique of the book rather than of the Jews as a whole. Similarly, the noted Presbyterian biblical scholar, Elizabeth Achtemeier wrote in 1998 that the "slaying of Haman and his ten sons, as well as seventy-five thousand enemies of the Jews – [is] hardly biblically ethical according to most of the Bible's standards of morality."[45] Achtemeier does not question whether the number "seventy-five thousand" is realistic or hyperbolic. Also, she does not refer to the various versions of the number of the dead in the old translations of the Bible (see below). Moreover, although she refers to that number as "enemies of the Jews," she does not ask if the Jews should have simply waited to be slaughtered by "Haman and his ten sons," as well as by their "enemies." Would this be "biblically ethical" enough? Likewise, Achtemeier does not explain what exactly she means by the words "biblically ethical."[46]

---

[44] J. Bright, *The Authority of the Old Testament* (Grand Rapids, MI: Baker Book House, 1977), p. 157.

[45] E. Achtemeier, *Preaching Hard Texts of the Old Testament* (Peabody, MA: Hendrickson, 1998), pp. 86–91 esp. 87.

[46] Is Achtemeier referring to the ethical norm emphasized in the second part of the Christian Bible (though it is certainly already found in the Hebrew Bible, for instance, 2 Chr 28:8–15), such as of Matt 5:38–39, where Jesus exemplifies metaphorically the idea that one should not repay evil with evil: "Do not resist an evildoer. But if anyone strikes you on the right cheek, turn the other also; and if anyone wants to sue you and take your coat, give your cloak as well; and if anyone forces you to go one mile, go also the second mile"? But if this is the biblical ethical ideal that Achtemeier refers to, then the church's own history of violence against its "enemies" (including the Jews) is nothing less than a *rejection* of Jesus' call to "love your enemies and pray for those who persecute you" (Matt 5:44; cf. Luke 6:27–30).

Of course, not every critique of the book of Esther is inherently anti-semitic and it need not be assumed that all the above scholars were themselves antisemitic. Nevertheless, many of these critiques extend beyond the book itself to the Jewish people, equating what these scholars see as "the negative aspects of the book" with "the Jewish character" in general. In such cases, these accusations of Esther and the Jews as "vengeful," "blood-thirsty," or "chauvinistic" do not reflect a normal academic diversity of views, but rather a double standard: one for Jews and another for the rest of the world – particularly Christians. This approach has caused colossal harm to the Jewish people and to their religious, cultural, and literary heritage. Doubtless, the prejudicial hatefulness of so many of these Christian "interpreters" is a manifestation of a broader and deeper mistrust and hate of Judaism and Jews in the history of Christianity.

What is true regarding Luther is true also regarding many of his followers: they do injustice to the book of Esther, to the Jewish people, and to Judaism. They misread the book and judge (or even reject) it because of – what they call – the absence of overt religious matters and because of the violence described in the last part of the book which they define as "vengeance," "national spirit," and "Jewish character." But, in fact, they fail to interpret the book as a whole according to its literary merits and historical contexts. Many of them portray the violence described in the book as characteristic of the entire Jewish people. By doing so they reveal their ignorance of the book and of the Jewish people and their heritage. Their negative words against the Jews reflect, no less, their arrogance – as if they represented the superior religion and have the right to judge and condemn the inferior (in their view!) religion and nation. But there is no religion greater than dignity and righteousness. And even within Christianity, is not such antisemitism itself a violation of the principles emphasized in texts like the Sermon on the Mount (Matthew 5–7)? No one who truly takes Matthew 5–7 seriously could possibly enact a crusade or a pogrom, much less (in quantity) than the Shoah. Even if someone mistakenly assumes that the book of Esther celebrates violence or vengeance, even then, based on ethical, as well as theological norms, this is no justification for using the book to condemn the whole Jewish people.

Furthermore, it is striking that so many German scholars in particular, including Brenz, de Wette, Bertheau, Bleek, Siegfried, Cornill, Gunkel, Kuhl, Haenchen, Eissfeldt and Schmidt, would condemn the "very narrow-minded and Jewish spirit of revenge and persecution," when it was their own "open-minded" people who led humanity (including other European peoples) to its deepest and darkest moral and spiritual level ever. Did the "very narrow-minded" Jews cause the most horrible persecutions and bloodsheds under the sun or was it those who think that they carry out "the spirit of the Gospel" (which was, by the way, written by Jews), when they totally failed to follow it? It is simply tragic and ironic how these scholars, whose nation spilled more innocent blood than any other in human history, blame their victims – the Jewish people – for being "bloodthirsty," although in reality the Jews have repeatedly been the scape-goats and victims of boundless forced-conversions, expulsions, pogroms, and persecutions, up to and including the Holocaust and even in the time beyond it.[47]

Had the pre-Shoah scholars known where their antisemitism would lead, perhaps some of them would have refrained from expressing it. However, none of the Nazi era, Shoah, and post-Shoah scholars could profit from such a doubt. Even in the contemporary world, antisemitism still shows its ugly face under the cover of "scholarly" biblical interpretation.

II   Political Background and Parallels to These Anti-Jewish Accusations

What then can explain the deep animosity toward the Jews and the book of Esther found among these Christian interpreters? As §III below demonstrates, these interpretations cannot be seen as straightforward readings of the book of Esther itself, which they repeatedly distort; but they do not come out of nowhere. Not only do the interpretations discussed above reflect the theological lines favored by the Church and especially by the Protestant reformer Martin Luther and his followers, but at least some of them may also reflect broader political debates occurring – particularly in Germany – in the modern period. Aspects of this political background have already been discussed in this and earlier chapters with regards to the sixteenth century and the Nazi period in the twentieth century,[48] but a number of the above-mentioned scholars did not live in either of those periods, but instead in the eighteenth and nineteenth centuries, during a time in which the status and civil rights (*Bürgerrechte*) of the Jews within Christian society were sharply disputed. It is therefore worth noting that similar ideas about the Jews as antisocial were also circulating during that time, even without

---

[47] See also the catalogue in the booklet by W. Herrmann, *Ester im Streit der Meinungen* (Beiträge zur Erforschung des Alten Testaments und des antiken Judentums 4; Frankfurt am Main: Peter Lang, 1986); Bush, "The Book of Esther," pp. 39–41.
[48] See Chapter 9, §III and ii, §VI.

reference to Esther, but still broadly reminiscent of Haman's accusations in the book. The following examples will illustrate these parallels.

1   Johann Gottlieb Fichte

The German philosopher Johann Gottlieb Fichte (1762–1814) follows Luther's anti-Jewish attitude and expresses strong Judeophobic statements. He says that the Jews weaken German society and therefore they should be isolated and expelled. Fichte's main arguments against the Jews are comparable to those of Haman, although his conclusion is different from that of Haman's radical genocide.

Fichte is of the opinion that because of their unique religious and cultural laws and customs, the Jews should be considered as a state within a state in Germany as well as in other European countries: "Are you not then reminded of the state within the state? Does the understandable thought not occur to you that the Jews, who are without you citizens of a state that is more stable and mightier that all of your, if you grant them citizenship in your states as well, will crush your other citizens completely under foot?"[49] Fichte stresses that "in almost all countries of Europe, a powerful hostile government spreads, which continuously at war with all others, and in some oppresses the citizens mightily; it is Judaism." Therefore, Fichte concludes that giving civil rights to Jews would only be possible if one succeeded "to cut off all their heads in one night, and to set other ones on their shoulders, in which there is not a single Jewish idea." Fichte continues, "In order to protect ourselves from them, I do not see any other option but to conquer their promised Land for them and send them all there."[50]

Other scholars go in a similar direction to Fichte. Thus, Friedrich Rühs believes that by keeping their laws, the Jews "serve two masters" – one

---

[49] "Erinnert ihr euch denn hier nicht des Staats im Staate? Fällt euch denn hier nicht der begreifliche Gedanke ein, daß die Juden, welche ohne euch Bürger eines Staats sind, der fester und gewaltiger ist, als die eurigen alle, wenn ihr ihnen auch noch das Bürgerrecht in euren Staaten gebt, eure übrigen Bürger völlig unter die Füße treten werden." See J. G. Fichte, *Beitrag zur Berichtigung der Urteile des Publikums über die Französische Revolution* (first published 1793), in R. Lauth and H. Jacob (eds.), *J.-G. Fichte-Gesamtausgabe* I/1 (Stuttgart: Friedrich Frommann Verlag, 1964), p. 292.

[50] "Fast durch alle Länder von Europa verbreitet sich ein mächtiger, feindselig gesinnter Staat, der mit allen übrigen im beständigen Kriege steht, und der in manchen fürchterlich schwer auf die Bürger drückt; es ist das Judentum … Aber ihnen Bürgerrechte zu geben, dazu sehe ich wenigstens kein Mittel, als das, in einer Nacht ihnen allen die Köpfe abzuschneiden, und andere aufzusetzen, in denen auch nicht eine jüdische Idee sey, um uns vor ihnen zu schützen, dazu sehe ich wieder kein andre Mittel, als ihnen ihr gelobtes Land zu erobern, und sie alle dahin zu schicken." See Fichte, *Beitrag zur Berichtigung der Urteile des Publikums über die Französische Revolution*, in Lauth and Jacob, *J.-G. Fichte-Gesamtausgabe* I/1, pp. 292, 293.

their religious laws and leaders, and the other the state laws – and demand conversion of the Jews as a primary condition to offer them German citizenship. Let us turn our attention to this issue in a bit more detail.

2   Friedrich Rühs

There is also no direct indication that the German historian Friedrich Rühs (1781–1820) was influenced by Haman's accusations, nevertheless, his line of thinking similarly resembles Haman's plot. Thus, in 1815 he wrote an article "On the Jewish Claims to German Citizenship" ("Über die Ansprüche der Juden auf das deutsche Bürgerrecht"),[51] in which he denies them this right if they do not convert to Christianity. Rühs insisted that the Jews should wear a distinctive sign, as used to be the case during the High Middle Ages. He asserted that because the Jews are scattered among the nations and form a separate state controlled by the Rabbis, they are disqualified from any citizenship, which requires unity of sentiment, language, and faith. Furthermore, he argued: "If they [i.e., the Jews] would like to become citizens of another country *without giving up Judaism, they are delivered into a collision of obligations, which is very problematic, and which in many cases are impossible to reconcile.* Nobody can serve two masters, and it is in fact a strange contradiction that a citizen of the Jewish state or empire at the same time wishes to be a citizen of a Christian country."[52]

Moreover, at least in this case it may be that Haman's accusation became a model for Rühs, with or without his being aware of the text in Esther. Like Haman's claims in Esth 3:8, Rühs stresses the fact that the Jews are dispersed among many nations. They live within their communities, led by their own religious leaders, and prefer to keep their unique laws that often contradict the laws of the state, all of which made them unbearable to people like Rühs, who condemn them as separatists, a nation within a nation, or a state within a state. Unlike Haman, however, Rühs did not wish to annihilate the Jews altogether but just to discriminate against them

---

[51] The article was published, for the first time, in *Zeitschrift für die Neueste Geschichte, die Staaten- und Völkerkunde* (Berlin, February 1815), pp. 129–161; reprinted as a separate booklet – F. Rühs, *Ueber die Ansprüche der Juden an das deutsche Bürgerrecht* (2nd ed.; Berlin: Realschulbuchhandlung, 1816).

[52] Rühs, *Ueber die Ansprüche der Juden auf das deutsche Bürgerrecht*, p. 5, "wenn sie Mitglieder eines andern Staats seyn wollen, ohne dem Judenthume zu entsagen, sie in eine Collision von Pflichten gerathen, die höchst bedenklich ist, und die in vielen Fällen unmöglich ausgeglichen werden können; Niemand kann zweien Herren dienen, und es ist doch in der That ein sonderbarer Widerspruch, daß ein Bürger des jüdischen Staats oder Reichs zugleich Bürger eines christlichen Staats seyn will." Compare also his *Die Rechte des Christentums und des deutschen Volkes: verteidigt gegen die Ansprüche der Juden und ihrer Verfechter* (Berlin: Realschulbuchhandlung, 1816).

and prevent them from holding any citizenship or the rights and privileges that come with it. Furthermore, like Luther who made his friendly attitude to Jews conditional on their acceptance of his reformed Christianity (that is, conversion), Rühs insisted that a condition for Jews to obtain citizenship is "giving up their Judaism," which would have amounted to religious-cultural suicide.

3   Jakob Friedrich Fries

About a year after Rühs' article was published, a student of Fichte, the philosopher Jakob Friedrich Fries (1773–1843), circulated a booklet in 1816, *Polemic on the Danger Posed by the Jews to the Prosperity and Character of the Germans* (*Polemik über die Gefährdung des Wohlstandes und Charakters der Deutschen durch die Juden*). In this booklet Fries described the Jews – as already done by Luther[53] – as a closed and conspiring society within the states where they live. He argued that "the Jewish society includes four very different elements. Namely, the Jews are: 1. a separate nation, 2. a political union, 3. a religious party, 4. a caste of brokers and junk dealers."[54] Thus, Fries identified the Jews as being not only a different *religious* entity living in various Christian countries, as they had been seen until then, but also as a *nation* like many other nations in Europe. Furthermore, Fries believed that the Jewish religion is a sign of separatism, a self-governing state society. "In its form," says Fries, "this society is subject to the strictest aristocratic tyranny of the Rabbis ... this political society spread over the entire world, is a caste of brokers, small shopkeepers and junk dealers. They are a caste of small shopkeepers and junk dealers tightly bound by theocratic despotism, sworn together by their own religion ...."[55] Fries challenges his audience with a rhetorical question: "What can be more corrupting than a society that practices such an innately dangerous trade, what's more tightly sworn together across the entire world by their inherited relationships, by

[53] WA, vol. 53, p. 522 lines 8–17; see Chapter 11, §VII, and note 108.
[54] "Die Gesellschaft der Juden vereinigt in sich vier sehr verschiedene Elemente. Die Juden nämlich sind 1. Eine eigene Nation, 2. Eine politische Verbindung, 3. Eine Religionspartei, 4. Eine Mäkler und Trödlerkaste." J. F. Fries, *Über die Gefährdung des Wohlstandes und Charakters der Deutschen durch die Juden* (Heidelberg: Mohr und Winter, 1816), p. 15.
[55] "Diese Religion ist nun eigentlich nur eine Zugabe zu einer eigenen, sich selbst regierenden Staatsgesellschaft. Der Form nach ist diese Gesellschaft dem strengsten aristokratischen Despotismus der Rabbiner unterworfen ... dass diese politische Gesellschaft eine über die ganze Erde verbreitete Mäkler-, Krämer- und Trödlerkaste ist. Sie sind eine durch theokratischen Despotismus eng verbundene, durch eine eigene Religion zusammen verschworene Krämer und Trödlerkaste." Fries, *Über die Gefährdung des Wohlstandes und Charakters der Deutschen durch die Juden*, p. 18.

a politically aligned constitution, grounded in their own religion, which requires them to hate foreigners and cancels all laws allowing rights and moral treatment for them?"[56] Thus, Fries recommends German leaders to treat the Jews as Pharaoh had done in Egypt. He suggests imposing harsh laws upon Jewish trade, legally nullifying their papers, blocking their civil rights, and expelling them from the country.[57]

Although Fries initially attacked the collective nature of Jewish societies in terms of their religion, from which the individuals should be rescued, he soon blamed them for their financial activities and advocated a distinct sign on their clothing and eventual expulsion from Germany. Here Fries demands less than the biblical Haman but much more than his contemporary Rühs. Thus, the solutions that these scholars suggest for "the Jewish Question" are not the same as those of Haman but run smoothly in a similar direction.

All these are examples of anti-Jewish rhetoric from the eighteenth and nineteenth centuries, the same period during which harsh criticism of Esther also flourished among scholars such as de Wette, Bleek, and Bertheau. As we have already seen in this and previous chapters, neither antisemitism in general, nor anti-Jewish readings of Esther in particular, are limited to those centuries of the modern period; they also continued long after. Is this approach toward the Jews not parallel to or in the same line as that of biblical Haman, who claimed that by keeping their own (religious) laws the Jews are unable to keep the laws of the empire, and therefore they should be annihilated? It is unclear why Jews, who keep their religious laws and rituals, should be outlined in political terms, and embraced in the category of "state within a state." Why should they be expelled from the places they lived for hundreds of years or be annihilated, just for keeping their religious and cultural identity? Are these not instances of Christian Judeophobic and supersessionist attitudes toward Jews and Judaism; examples of the dominant religion wishing to dismiss the different way of life and thinking? Would these scholars consider a group of Catholic Christians, living among Protestant Germans, Dutch, or in any other Protestant – or even Islamic – dominated country in the

---

[56] "Was kann verderblicher sein als eine Gesellschaft, welche ein an sich so gefährliches Gewerbe treibt, nun noch über die ganze Erde eng verschworen durch innere erbliche Verbindung, durch politisch geordnete und auf eigene Religion gegründete Verfassung bei einem durch die Religion vorgeschriebenen Hass gegen die Fremden und Aufhebung aller Gesetze des Rechtes und der Sittlichkeit gegen sie?" Fries, *Über die Gefährdung des Wohlstandes und Charakters der Deutschen durch die Juden*, p. 21.

[57] Fries, *Über die Gefährdung des Wohlstandes und Charakters der Deutschen durch die Juden*, pp. 23, 26–27.

world, as those who "serve two masters" or have "dual loyalty" – one for the Pope in Vatican and the other to the state where they live? After all, the Jews were quite loyal and productive citizens, and did not get involved with any terror, and did not attempt to conquer any land or to impose their religious laws on the countries where they lived (as, for instance, currently some Muslims try to impose their *sharia* laws on the Christian European countries).

III   An "Antisemite Pogrom of the Jews" or Legitimate Self-Defense?

Can one really describe the struggles of the Jews against their pagan persecutors in the book of Esther as "bloody revenge" (*blutige Rache*), as de Wette and many others over the centuries have done?[58] Is this truly a story of an "antisemite pogrom" (*Antisemitenpogrom*) of the Jews against their gentile persecutors in which "not the Jews but their persecutors were killed," as asserted by Jan Assmann?[59] Is there any basis in the book of Esther itself for such harsh accusations? Or, in fact, was the violence depicted at the end of the book a necessary act of legitimate self-defense by the Jews to escape from their sworn bitter enemies?

As Moses Maimonides has stated, "The gates of interpretation are not sealed to us" (ולא שערי הפירוש סתומים בפנינו).[60] Indeed, a careful, open-minded, and unprejudiced reading of the Esther story, in light of biblical, ancient Near Eastern and Mediterranean story-telling practices and their socio-cultural contexts, leaves no space for any of these allegations and the inaccurately and devastating critiques of the book, Jews, and Judaism. In the following paragraphs, I will describe some of the basic context for the large number claimed to have been killed and consider several additional factors that must be considered for any interpretation of the book, in particular Esther chapter 9.

---

[58] See de Wette, *Lehrbuch der historisch-kritischen Einleitung*, vol. 1, p. 273; idem, *A Critical and Historical Introduction*, vol. 2, p. 337. See above, §I, and below, §III, for example, Gunkel, Nöldeke, Cornill.

[59] See J. Assmann *Das kulturelle Gedächtnis* (8th ed.; Munich: C. H. Beck, 2013), p. 83, "Was hier erzählt wird, ist nichts anderes als ein Antisemitenpogrom. Nicht die Juden, sondern ihre Verfolger werden umgebracht." Assmann's words take us back to those of Johannes Hempel on the book of Esther in 1938: "[die] blutrünstigen Pogromschilderungen" ("the bloodthirsty pogrom"); see above, §II, where he quoted saying that the story of Esther is "a Jewish pogrom against their 'enemies'."

[60] M. Maimonides, *The Guide for the Perplexed* 2:25; see J. Ben-Shlomo (ed.), *Moreh Nevuchim* (Jerusalem: Bialik Institute, 1968), p. 126 (Hebrew).

1   How Many Enemies Were Killed?

An ancient written source preserved through a process of scribal transmission does not always present the original work itself but sometimes only a secondary form of it. It could contain words or numbers that do not present in the original text. Hence, any discussion of events described in an ancient written source must open with a textual examination of that source.

Now, the Masoretic Text (MT) of Esth 9:16 affirms that the Jews killed *"seventy-five thousand"* of their enemies. However, in the Greek Alpha Text (or A-Text, sometimes referred to as the Lucianic Text) of Esther the number is: *"seventy thousand and one hundred,"* and the LXX (or B-Text) gives a different number altogether, which is one fifth that of the MT: *"fifteen thousand."* It is difficult to know if in front of us we have an effort by the Greek translators to reduce the number given in their Hebrew *Vorlage* (perhaps because they were worried about the potentially hostile reaction of their gentile readers/neighbors), or whether at least one of these numbers in the Greek texts reflects an older and original Hebrew version. Thus, all in all the number of the enemies that were killed by the Jews is uncertain and it could be much less than that recounted in the MT version of the book, even if one takes the reported figures literally.

Moreover, all the versions of the number of enemies who were killed by the Jews should be considered hyperbolic. They are enormously exaggerated and therefore improbable, like several other exaggerated numbers in the book of Esther. These numbers are part of the book's literary character, rather than a reflection of historical reality.[61] The intention of the author is clear: He wished to say that numerous enemies of the Jews were killed. It is doubtful that he had an exact number of them (who counted them anyway?). He inflates the number of dead enemies in order to highlight the greatness of the divine salvation and triumph of the Jews, as well as the decisive defeat of the enemy. Indeed, the phenomenon of overstated numbers in Esther is not exceptional in the ancient world. There are many biblical, ancient Near Eastern, and Greco-Roman examples of such exaggerations.[62]

Furthermore, it is difficult to imagine that such an uprising in the entire Persian Empire took place in which the Jews killed such a huge number of Gentiles and neither the Persian nor the Greek sources preserve even

---

[61] See Chapter 3, §X.

[62] See, for example, 2 Sam 24:9; 2 Kgs 19:35; 1 Chr 29:7; 2 Chr 13:3, 17; 14:8 and those from other semitic and nonsemitic sources that are listed by Kalimi, "Placing the Chronicler in His Own Historical Context," pp. 181–182.

a hint of it.[63] Thus, these large numbers in the book of Esther should be considered to be purely imaginary creative elements.

Also, it is important to put the number of those killed within the appropriate context: The number refers not to one specific place only, or even to a group of towns and cities, but rather to total casualties in the entire Persian Empire "from India to Ethiopia/Nubia" (Esth 1:1; 8:9). Indeed, the number is still high, but awareness of this point sets the issue in proportion.

Besides, one should be very skeptical regarding the historicity of *the extent* of the descriptions of the violent plans of the Gentiles as well as the reaction of the Jews as recounted in Esther. Simply put, it is unlikely that the king allowed the Jews to wage a civil war within his capital, Shushan (Esth 9:11–15). Thus, Esth 9:16 is one of several fictional elements in the book of Esther (though generally set in a real historical context).[64] Accordingly, one should note with Theodor Nöldeke: "If the decree of extermination of all the Jews in the entire Empire is unimaginable, how can one believe in such nonsense, that the Jews would be allowed to massacre 75,000 subjects of the king? This aspect, which is the point of the whole story, determines sufficiently that it is ahistorical."[65]

Of course, any indiscriminate killing of a group of people is evil at any time and any place, but ancient accounts of this sort must be read first and foremost according to the textual evidence, historical reasonableness and reliability, and the literary and cultural conventions of the society in which they were written. It makes no difference if the number is actually a different number and a much smaller one. After saying all this, I must stress that regardless which number reflects the earliest version of the book, and of whether that number is real or enormously exaggerated, the question to us seems to be ethically: Was this loss of lives – again, in whatever number – the result of justified self-defense, or was it for "bloodthirsty revenge" and

---

[63] Except for the names "Ahasuerus," which is usually identified with the Persian King Xerxes I (485–465 BCE; see above, Chapter 5, §II, 2), and Mordecai (see above, Chapter 5, §II, 4), there is no direct extrabiblical parallel or archaeological find that confirms the existence of any individual or event referred to in the book of Esther.

[64] See Chapter 5, §II.

[65] See Nöldeke, "Esther," p. 84: "Wenn schon der Befehl zur Ausrottung der Juden im ganzen Reich undenkbar ist, wie kann man gar an einen solchen Unsinn glauben, daß es den Juden verstattet wäre, 75,000 Unterthanen des Königs niederzumachen? Dieser Umstand, der doch die Pointe der ganzen Erzählung ist, entscheidet schon hinlänglich für ihre Ungeschichtlichkeit." However, I do not accept Nöldeke's general conclusion that the whole story of Esther is fiction. Similarly, de Wette already defined this number of dead – "75,000" – as "unbelievable" or "incredible" (*unglaublich*); see de Wette, *Lehrbuch der historisch-kritischen Einleitung*, vol. 1, p. 274; idem, *A Critical and Historical Introduction*, vol. 2, p. 339.

for looting purposes? In any case, the distance between this depiction in ancient literary work and accusations and antisemitic characterizations of entire Jewish people is immense.

2 Who Was Killed and Why?

Some scholars, such as Ruth Stiehl, paraphrase the Hebrew text of Esth 8:11 as follows: "It allows the Jews to take revenge on their enemies. Cruelly the Jews carry out what had been granted to them."[66] Similarly, Lewis B. Paton writes, "they [that is, the Jews] fall upon their enemies, slay their wives and children, and plunder their property (8ᴵᴵ 9²⁻¹⁰)."[67] Jon Levenson also concludes that "The substance of the new edict is that the Jews are now permitted to gather in self-defense, to slay the women and children of any that attack them, and to take booty (8:11) … It is probably also colored by old cultic conceptions of combat."[68]

These kinds of paraphrases and expositions are misleading. They are ethically not preferable, and philologically impossible. As already noted above in Chapter 3 (§III), Esth 8:11 is part of a traditional-style repetition of the book: it repeats 3:13. Indeed, Levenson himself is aware of this: "This [i.e., 8:11] closely mirrors the substance of the first edict (3:13). The killing of women and children, offensive to any decent moral sensibility today, is dictated by the symmetry of the two decrees, which in turn heightens the expectations of the day of decision."[69] Moreover, as already noted by several scholars, the phrase "their women and children" in Esth 8:11 refers to *the Jews* who defend themselves against those enemies who strive to annihilate them and their women and children.[70] The correct

---

[66] "[E]s gestattet den Juden, sich an ihren Feinden zu rächen. Grausam vollziehen die Juden, was ihnen zugebilligt"; see Stiehl, "Das Buch Esther," p. 5. She repeats again and again the word "Rache" ("revenge"), that the Jews supposedly took on the Gentiles; see also ibid., pp. 6, 7.

[67] See Paton, *A Critical and Exegetical Commentary on the Book of Esther*, p. 96.

[68] Levenson, *Esther: A Commentary*, pp. 110–111.

[69] Levenson, *Esther: A Commentary*, p. 111.

[70] See, for example, R. Gordis, "Studies in the Esther Narrative," *JBL* 95 (1976), pp. 43–58 esp. 49–53; Magonet, "The Liberal and the Lady," p. 168; R. Kessler, "Die Juden als Kindes- und Frauenmörder? Zu Est 8,11," in E. Blum, Ch. Macholz, and E. W. Stegemann (eds.), *Die hebräische Bibel und ihre zweifache Nachgeschichte: Festschrift für Rolf Rendtorff zum 65. Geburtstag* (Neukirchen-Vluyn: Neukirchener Verlag, 1990), pp. 337–345 esp. 337–339; R. Achenbach, "Vertilgen – Töten – Vernichten (Est 3,13). Die Genozid-Thematik im Estherbuch," *ZABR* 15 (2009), pp. 282–315 esp. 306–309; idem, "'Genocide in the Book of Esther,'" in R. Albertz and J. Wöhrle (eds.), *Between Cooperation and Hostility: Multiple Identities in Ancient Judaism and the Interaction with Foreign Powers* (Journal of Ancient Judaism Supplements 11; Göttingen: Vandenhoeck & Ruprecht, 2013), pp. 89–114, which also sees 8:11 as a statement of the Jews' right to defend themselves. See also the recent discussion by Ego, *Esther*, pp. 349–351.

translation of the verse is, therefore: "to stand for their life, to destroy, to slay, and to annihilate, any armed force of any people or province that might attack them, [their] children and women," rather than: "to stand for their life, to destroy, to slay and to cause to perish, all the power of the people and province that would assault them, both little ones and women" (King James Version); or as Carey A. Moore translates Esth 8:11: "to wipe out, slaughter, and annihilate every armed force of any people or province that was hostile to them, along with their children and women, and to plunder their personal property,"[71] though there is no equivalent for the words "along with their" in the Hebrew text; or as Levenson translates: "to slay the women, and children of any that attack them."[72] Regardless, the book of Esther never states that the Jews *did* kill women or children (Haman's sons are not children) and the biblical narrator explicitly stresses that the Jews "laid no hands on the plunder" (Esth 9:10, 15, 16), although Mordecai's contra-edict explicitly allowed them to do so.

If there is any voice of "Nationalism" or the "national spirit" in the book of Esther it is understandable when one keeps in mind that the Jews as a collective were in danger of annihilation. It presents, as noted by Jan Alberto Soggin, "the frustration of a people constantly under foreign domination, which was often felt to contrast greatly with the mission they felt they had received from God."[73] However, Soggin concludes, "this theme should not be exaggerated."[74]

3   Self-Defense or Revenge?

Martin Luther as well as his old and new followers emphasize the death of pagans/Gentiles at the end of Esther. However, they overlook the central theme of the book – that because of a personal clash that Haman had with

---

[71] Moore, *Esther*, p. 76.

[72] Levenson, *Esther: A Commentary*, p. 100.

[73] J. A. Soggin, *Introduction to the Old Testament: From Its Origins to the Closing of the Alexandrian Canon* (Old Testament Library; 3rd ed.; Louisville, KT: Westminster John Knox, 1989), p. 470. Anderson ("The Place of the Book of Esther in the Christian Bible," p. 35) makes this point clear: "By building a wall around its communal life, and thus sharpening the separateness of the Jew from his neighbors, Judaism excited against itself a suspicion and hatred which have led to Haman-like pogroms on the part of Greeks and Romans, Spanish and Russians, and lately the Nazis of Germany. These persecutions, in turn, have produced a deepening group consciousness on the part of the Jew and therefore a further retreat into the protecting walls of the community .... Quite apart from the problem of the historicity of the Book of Esther or any part of it, the real issue of the book, viz., the tension between Jew and gentile, is clearly 'historical' and is as old as the phenomenon of Judaism itself."

[74] Here one recalls, for example, the exaggeration of Stiehl ("Das Buch Esther," p. 6), who writes: "in fact, the book of Esther is a song of songs of national Judaism" ("Tatsächlich ist das Estherbuch ein Hoheslied nationalen Judentums").

Mordecai, he desired to "destroy all the Jews ... throughout the whole
kingdom of Ahasuerus." The book narrates how at Haman's command
"letters were sent to all the king's provinces, giving orders to destroy, to
kill, and to annihilate all Jews, young and old, women and children, in one
day" (Esth 3:13; cf. 3:6, 8–9; 7:4; 8:5–6; 9:24). This means an immediate
and complete extermination – genocide – of the entire Jewish people
wherever they may be found. Luther and his followers ignore the fact that
the Jews were under great danger of extermination and that they were
seriously threatened and thus they attempted to *protect* themselves. Even if
the account of Haman's decree is historically exaggerated in the book, still
the Jews were entitled to defend themselves against their enemies. Should
they just ignore the threat of their enemies and presume that it is not going
to happen, as many Jews did on other occasions and finally find themselves
dead? In fact, the king could not completely cancel the evil decree that was
sent by Haman to annihilate the Jews, because "for the decrees which are
decreed in the king's name, and sealed with the king's ring, no man can
revoke" (8:8b; cf. Dan 6:16). The narrator clearly emphasizes that the
contra-decree that Mordecai authorized to send in the name of the king,
gave the Jews the permission to assemble and protect themselves from
those who will attack them. The threat was not yet over, and the fighting
of the Jews was an act of legal *self-defense*. King Ahasuerus gave permission:
"to gather themselves together, and *to stand for their life*, to destroy, to kill,
and to annihilate, *any armed force* of any people or province *that might
attack* [or: *oppress*] *them*" (להקהל ולעמוד על נפשם להשמיד ולהרוג ולאבד את כל חיל
עם ומדינה הצרים [/ הצוררים] אתם; Esth 8:11).

Note, the authorization of Mordecai to the Jews: "to destroy, to kill and
to annihilate" (להשמיד ולהרוג ולאבד)), is exactly as it appears in the decree of
Haman in Esth 3:13 (and in the citation of the decree by Esther in 7:4). The
narrator formed the counter-decree of Mordecai according to his literary
motif of "the reversal of fate" (ונהפוך הוא).[75] Nevertheless, this is not a
complete inversion because while Haman's order commands them "to
destroy, to kill, and to annihilate *all Jews, young and old, women and
children*," Mordecai's order applies only to "*any armed force ... that might
attack* [or: *oppress*] *them*, *[their] children and women.*" Thus, the king's edict
that granted the Jews permission to protect themselves was formulated in
contrast to that of Haman, but it was not simply an inverted *implementation*
of Haman's evil decree; instead, it was the necessary act to allow the Jews
to defend themselves and *prevent* its implementation, which would have

---

[75] On this literary feature of the Esther story, see Chapter 3.

resulted in their annihilation. Indeed, as Gerleman points out, the difference between the defensive edict in Esth 8:11 and Haman's extermination decree in Esth 3:13–14, is clear: The second edict gave the *possibility of self-defense* to the Jews, while Haman's decree provided *a command to kill* – everyone in every place.[76]

Moreover, although the king's decree permits the Jews to plunder their enemies' possessions (Esth 8:11b), they did not implement this part of the edict. They were concerned with self-defense and security, not booty. The narrator stresses that the Jews "laid no hands on the plunder" (וּבַבִּזָּה לֹא שָׁלְחוּ אֶת יָדָם; Esth 9:10, 15, 16). But they "gathered to lay hands on those *who had sought their ruin*" (נִקְהֲלוּ הַיְּהוּדִים בְּעָרֵיהֶם...לִשְׁלֹחַ יָד בִּמְבַקְשֵׁי רָעָתָם, Esth 9:2), as permitted by the king (Esth 8:11a). This point is repeated five times in the book, including: Esth 9:1, "the Jews had rule over those *who hated them*"; in verse 9:5; and once again in verse 9:16, which stresses that the Jews "gathered in their cities to *defend their lives*, and gained relief from their *enemies ... those who hated them*" (וּשְׁאָר הַיְּהוּדִים...נִקְהֲלוּ וְעָמֹד עַל נַפְשָׁם וְנוֹחַ מֵאֹיְבֵיהֶם וְהָרוֹג בְּשֹׂנְאֵיהֶם). Now, how can one describe these purely defensive actions of the Jews as "bloody revenge" or as a story of an "antisemite pogrom" of the Jews against their gentile persecutors? The destiny of the Jewish communities, for example, in the Rhineland (Speyer, Worms, and Mainz) during the First Crusade (1096), in Poland-Lithuanian in 1648–1649, in Kishinev (1904–1905), in Germany and Austria of 1938, and in entire Europe in 1939–1945, may perhaps have been different if they had the permission and the possibility of legal self-defense, such as the Jews had in the time of Ahasuerus.

At first glance, Esther's request to let the Jews of Susa "do according to the edict for today" and to hang Haman's sons (Esth 9:13) is troubling. Particularly when one reads this issue in the Greek Alpha-Text (that many Christians read), where the translator stylized it as a very aggressive request that depicts Esther negatively: "to kill and to plunder whomever they might desire" (A-Text 9:46).[77] Nevertheless, Esth 9:12 presents the request not as Esther's own free initiative, but coming as a reply to the king's leading question. It is not necessarily "a wild desire for blood and revenge" (*wilde Blutgier und Rache*), as put, for instance, by Theodor Nöldeke (1836–1930).[78] Presumably, the request was due to the presence of many enemies of the Jews in Susa "who hated them [that is, the Jews]," in order to weaken the power of the enemies, frighten them, and prevent potential danger or

---

[76] Gerleman, *Esther*, p. 129.
[77] On this text, see in detail Chapter 10, §II.
[78] Nöldeke, "Esther," pp. 86–87.

intimidation of the Jews in the present or in the near future. It could be also self-protection from a visible contra-attack of the Jew haters. It is unlikely that the king gave his permission to act in this way without good reason (Esth 9:14; although one must admit that the king does not have good grounds for some of his other decisions reported in the book). The conduct of the Jews in Susa was, therefore, primarily defensive, though it did not exclude offensive acts in the interest of self-protection. Moreover, as is noted earlier in this chapter, there are many exaggerations in the book of Esther, and the number of the dead among the Jews' enemies in Shushan is just another one (note the typological number "three hundred," Esth 9:15).

Esther and Mordecai did not permit, and the Jews did not engage in, any revenge, unprovoked homicide, or plundering of non-Jews. Assertions – such as those of Cornill about "the bloody revenge of the Jews against their foes … the bloodthirsty longing for revenge against the pagans,"[79] and Konrad Hammann's description of the defensive acts of the Jews in the Persian Empire as "the horrible revenge" of Jews on the Gentiles[80] – are not found in any biblical or other text. Where in the book of Esther does the author speak about "vengeance" by the Jews "on their enemies," much less of "revenge against pagans" in general? All that the book claims is that in the face of urgent circumstances, the Jews stood up and protected themselves from their enemies. Were they not entitled to do so? According to the double standards of these scholars (which are unfortunately common in the history of the Jewish people, as well as nowadays), the answer is obvious: The Jews' enemies can persecute them, but they have no right to defend themselves.

4   Killing and Hanging of Haman's Sons

The killing of the ten sons of the archenemy Haman (Esth 9:7–10) was not just because of their father's sins, that is, his anti-Jewish activities. Assertions such as that of Hermann Gunkel, who describes Esther's request as a "thirst for revenge" (*Rachedurst*), and remarks that "to Haman is not yet done enough. His sons shall be defiled even in death and hanged on the gallows,"[81] are misleading. Can anyone guarantee that Haman's sons were innocent? Perhaps

---

[79] Cornill, *Einleitung in die kanonischen Bücher des Alten Testaments*, p. 154: "die ganz profane Geschichte, wie die Adoptivtochter des jüdischen Exulanten Mordechai … den Juden blutige Rache an ihren Gegnern verschafft … Die Kap[ital] 9 sich äußernde blutdürstige Rachgier gegen die Heiden …."

[80] See Hammann, *Hermann Gunkel: Eine Biographie*, pp. 272, 273: "[die] furchtbare Rache."

[81] See Gunkel, *Esther*, p. 44: "auch an Haman ist noch nicht genug geschehen. Seine Söhne sollen noch im Tode geschändet und an den Galgen gehängt werden." See also Kuhl, *Die Entstehung des Alten Testaments*, p. 291: "Haman hat sein Leben verwirkt, und seine Familie wird zur Bestrafung in Esthers Hand gegeben."

they were killed among other enemies of the Jews in Susa because of their own animosity and hatred of the Jews or even because of a potential danger of violence. The biblical author stresses this fact: "the Jews struck all their *enemies* with the stroke of the sword ... and did what they would to *those who hated them*" (Esth 9:5). In all probability, Haman's sons were included in the circle of "his wife Zeresh and all those who loved him," who advised Haman to hang Mordecai on a "gallows fifty-cubits-high" (Esth 5:14).[82] Esther who redeemed her people from annihilation, attempted to ensure their protection, and to put an end to their persecution.

The hanging of Haman's sons' corpses, that Esther requests (Esth 9:13– 14), was done according to a common Persian custom toward betrayers (Esth 2:23) or enemies who were killed in conflicts, as testified by Herodotus in several places (*Historia* 3.16; 3.79; 3.125; 7.238; 9.79).[83] This custom, which was intended to humble and to frighten the enemy, is known also from other biblical texts regarding Egyptians (Gen 40:19); Philistines (1 Sam 31:10//1 Chr 10:10); and Israelites (Deut 21:22–23 – who restrict the custom; Josh 10:26). It is also well documented in Assyrian royal inscriptions and stelae. For example, Sennacherib king of Assyria recounts that in his third campaign to Ḥatti (701 BCE), he "killed the officials and patricians

---

[82] In addition, generally speaking this kind of judgment that Gunkel attributes to Esther was (and is) totally beyond the Israelite/Jewish theological worldview (*Weltanschauung*). The latter stresses – again and again – that one should not "sweep away good and bad together" (Gen 18:23), and "you shall not seek revenge, or cherish anger" (Lev 19:18). Also, the biblical law states clearly: "The fathers shall not be put to death for the children, nor shall the children be put to death for the fathers; every man shall be put to death for his own sin" (Deut 24:16; cf. 2 Kgs 14:6//2 Chr 25:4; Jer 31:28–29; Ezek 18:2, 20). On this point it is noteworthy that the bitter enemy of Israel, the Arameans of the monarchic era, state after their defeat: "And his servants said to him, Behold now, we have heard that the kings of the house of Israel are merciful kings; let us, I beg you, put sackcloth on our loins, and ropes upon our heads, and go out to the king of Israel; perhaps he will save your life" (1 Kgs 20:31). In fact, the king of Israel saved his life! Though this is not an appropriate place to discuss in detail biblical passages such as Deut 7:1–2; 20:16–18; and Joshua 6–7 regarding the *ḥerem* of the seven nations of Canaan, it should be noted that in fact it never occurred, as clearly is reflected in Judg 1:19, 21, 27, 28–35. The purpose of these Deuteronomistic texts was presumably to warn the Israelites that if they will sin as the Canaanites, their destiny in the land will be as that of the Canaanites who inherited the land prior to them! The order in Deut 25:17–19 regarding the Amalekites, who attacked the Israelites in the wilderness, and whose descendants constantly attacked and plundered the Israelite's inhabited land (Exod 17:8–13; Judg 6:1–6, 33; 1 Sam 30:1–2, 13–18), is also an exception to this line of the Israelites' ethics, and actually is also never completely implemented, as is clear even from the story of the war of Saul against the Amalekites in 1 Samuel 15. Despite the allusions to Agag king of Amalek (1 Sam 15:8–9, 20, 32–33) in Esth 3:1; 8:3, it is hard to say whether Haman's sons were considered here to be Amalekite descendants, or whether they were killed for that reason. Certainly, the story of Esther does not call for the implementation of *ḥerem*. Because, if it were indeed so, then one would expect the destruction of the complete family and property of Haman, as the Deuteronomic law and the story in 1 Samuel 15 demand – and not only his sons.

[83] See I. Hofmann und A. Vorbichler, "Herodot und der Schreiber des Esther-Buches," *Zeitschrift für Missionswissenschaft und Religionswissenschaft* 66 (1982), pp. 294–302 esp. 299–300.

[of Ekron] who had committed the crime and hung their bodies on poles surrounding the city."[84] Thus, Esther's request in this regard is not unusual when one evaluates it in the context of ancient Near Eastern and Mediterranean norms rather than modern Western cultural ones. She requested the implementation of a customary measure also regarding the enemies of the Jews, as had been done to other enemies and betrayers. Since there is no available information regarding how long the corpses of Haman's sons stayed on the gallows, it is unknown whether Esther reflects a violation of the biblical law in Deut 21:22–23.

5   Purim Feast: Celebration of Deliverance

The feast of Purim is not "The Murder Feast" (*Das Mordfest*), as the Nazi Julius Streicher presented it.[85] Likewise, in April 2011 the anti-Zionist Reverend Ted Pike (Clackamas, Oregon, USA) wrote on his website: "Every book in the Bible condemns the violent racism of modern Zionism … except one: the book of Esther. The source of the annual feast of Purim, Esther celebrates the Jews' slaughter of more than 75,000 Gentiles (which included women and children) … It celebrates the triumph of Jews who obtain peace not by faith in God, but by slaughter."[86]

However, these are misleading interpretations of the feast. Purim does not celebrate the Jews' killing of Gentiles or elimination of Jews' enemies. It does not permit anyone to be attacked or harmed. It is not a feast of revenge and hatred, but a feast of deliverance from annihilation, liberation from cruel oppression. Purim was not established to remember or celebrate the slaying of the Jews' enemies, but rather to remember the day of grief, curse, and destruction that turned out to be the day of relief from the threat of death (Esth 9:21–22). The feast of Purim is a celebration of divine redemption (or salvation) of the Jewish people from ethnic annihilation – genocide – and therefore also a day of happiness, joy, and restoration (Esth 9:17–18, 22).[87] It celebrates the triumph of light over dark, right over wrong.

---

[84] See *ANET*, p. 288a; for an illustration of this practice used by the Assyrians against a city in Judah, see J. B. Pritchard, *Ancient Near Eastern Pictures Relating to the Old Testament* (Princeton: Princeton University Press, 1954), p. 131, no. 373: at the bottom, on the right side of the picture, three nude bodies from the city of Lachish are impaled on poles.

[85] See Chapter 9, §III, no. 1, and the bibliographical references therein.

[86] See T. Pike, "The Pseudo-Biblical Book of Esther: Mainspring of Zionism," *National Prayer Network* (April 5, 2011), http://truthtellers.org/alerts/PseudoBibicalEsther.html

[87] In this sense Esth 9:17–18, 22 reminds one of the curses of Balaam son of Beor, which God turned to blessings; see Numbers 22–24; Deut 23:5–6 [ET, 23:4–5]; cf. Neh 13:1–2; Mic 6:5.

From this viewpoint, this feast resembles somewhat the feast of Passover, when Jews celebrate the redemption from Egyptian slavery and oppression. Then also many Egyptians died (Exod 12:29; 14:29, 30; 15:1, 4, 9–10). However, that is also not the focus of the Passover festival, but rather the result is – Israel's deliverance. Similarly, in Purim the Jews remember the divine redemption by twice reading the Esther story – the *Megillah* – partying, sharing food with each other, and giving gifts to the poverty-stricken (Esth 9:18–19, 22). As such, it is compatible with other classical biblical festivals (which commemorate historical moments in Israelite history), as well as with the ethical and humanistic values of the Hebrew Bible (for example, Exod 23:11–12; Lev 19:9–10, 18; Deut 14:29; 16:14).

Certainly, there is no room or justification for any violence for its own sake, at any time and in any place, nor for a celebration of the death of a human being. However, in extreme cases, the death of the tyrant is often necessary, otherwise he would remain a potential danger to society, and most likely there would be no complete salvation and peace. To illustrate my point with an example from modern history, I would say that the celebration of the downfall of Hitler and his Third Reich at the end of the Second World War, was a celebration of liberation from the murderous Nazi oppression, rather than of the death of many German Nazis and their collaborators, even though that liberation would not have been possible without the elimination of those evil powers. These issues are linked together: Without the final and complete downfall of the wicked, liberation is utopian and most often impossible. Yet should we eliminate celebration of salvation and liberation, just because they are related to the final fall and death of ruthless tyranny and its followers and supporters? In this category also, leaders like the biblical Haman should be included.[88]

To sum up this crucial point: the Purim festival follows the effort of self-defense and is celebrated not through violence but through generosity – sharing food, gifts to the poor, and showing solidarity and friendship to each other by sending portions of food – days of feasting and joy (לאביונים ומתנות לרעהו איש מנות ומשלוח ושמחה משתה ימי; Esth 9:22). Thus, any other interpretation of the Purim feast is simply false and

---

[88] A similar idea is expounded in the opening section of Midrash *Leqach-Tov* on Esther: בטוב" כתוב צדיקים תעלוץ קריה ובאבוד רשעים רנה" (משלי יא, י), אמר טוביהו ב"ר אלעזר ז"ל פסוק זה מתגלגל והולך משנברא העולם ועד סופו ... למדנו ששקט לרשעים רע להם ורע לעולם ... וכן המן הרשע לא קם לאבד את עם ה', אלא מתוך עושר ... ושלום. והשקט ("It is written: 'When it goes well with the righteous, the city rejoices; and when the wicked perish, there is jubilation' [Prov 11:10] – Rabbi Tobiyahu son of Rabbi Elazar, blessed be his memory, said: This verse has been rolling on since the creation of the world and forever ... peace for the wicked is bad for them and for the world ... similarly Haman the wicked who arose to annihilate God's people just when he was wealthy, and had serenity and peaceful conditions ....").

misleading. Furthermore, Soggin correctly notes that "The very connection between the book and a carnival tends to show the absurd, ridiculous and humorous side of events rather than their cruelty. On the other hand, the history of the people of Israel shows that the distance between tragedy and humor is not great."[89]

In the light of the careful reading of the book of Esther and certainly the cumulative weight of all the points discussed here, interpreters of Esther would be wise to adopt the saying of the Second Temple period sage, Abtalion: "[You] sages, be careful with your words, lest ... the disciples that come after you drink of them and die ..." (אבטליון אמר: חכמים הזהרו בדבריכם שמא ... ישתו התלמידים הבאים אחריכם וימותו; Mishnah, *Abot* 1:11). The irresponsible words of those scholars have unfortunately had dire consequences on later generations of students, scholars, clergy, and laypeople.

IV   Conclusion

Over centuries, a broad range of Christian interpreters have repeatedly questioned the inclusion of Esther in the Christian canon,[90] while anti-Jewish interpretation of the book has been common since at least the medieval period. Martin Luther's hostility toward the book of Esther, the Jews, and Judaism generally[91] has been especially influential and has been followed and paralleled by generations of Christian biblicists, theologians, writers, and laypeople, across territorial, ethnical, and cultural boundaries. Luther's aggressive assertions and accusations and those of influential modern scholars such as de Wette, Cornill, Bleek, Gunkel, Paton, Haller, J. Meinhold, Hempel, Pfeiffer, O. Weber, Kuhl, Eissfeldt, and Weiser, have caused immense harm to the Jewish people and to their cultural legacy. Overlooking the central theme and context of the Esther story and ignoring the great danger that the Jews were in, these and other scholars have illegitimately denied the Jews the right to defend themselves and unjustly condemned the book and the Jews as "bloodthirsty." These harsh condemnations, which over-emphasize the violence of the book's conclusion, have used Esther as a podium for the justification of antisemitism, that had existed in the Christian society anyhow for centuries. In line with the

---

[89] Soggin, *Introduction to the Old Testament*, p. 471.
[90] In addition to the scholars mentioned in this chapter, see also Chapters 10 and 11, and also Haenchen, "Hamans Galgen und Christi Kreuz," p. 125.
[91] See the detailed discussion in Chapter 11.

anti-Jewish political and philosophical[92] rhetoric of some of their contemporaries, these and later modern scholars have interpreted Esther inaccurately, ignored ancient textual witnesses of some verses, and made it a platform to advance their own biased, anti-Jewish agendas.

Indeed, as Luther expressed, "an accurate interpretation is a special gift of God."[93] However, many interpreters – including Luther himself – seem to lack that "special gift" or have lost it, at least when they come to the book of Esther or touch somehow on Jews and Judaism, while they violate elementary religious, ethical and moral principles, and intellectual righteousness. Their assertions and critiques of Esther are *eisegesis* rather than *exegesis* of the biblical text.[94]

None of this should blind us to the fact that a range of scholars, Jewish as well as Christian, have attempted to wrestle with what they define as the "ethical questions" raised by the book. Of course, it is possible to criticize a biblical text or book without necessarily being anti-Jewish, ignorant, or self-serving. The book of Esther is no more immune to critique than any other biblical or nonbiblical text should be, and critique does not prove automatically that the critic is anti-Jewish. Also, not everyone who criticizes nationalism or violence is automatically antisemitic. However, Esther is not a hymn for nationalism or violence, and it is not more ethically problematic than some other biblical writings (such as Deut 7:1–2; 13:18; 20:16–18; Josh 7:24–26; 11:11, 14; 1 Sam 15:1–3), which also depict "enemies" as uniformly wicked and use this as a justification for their mass slaughter. If that were reason enough to exclude Esther from the canon, a lot of other biblical books would have to follow, and that would rob us of works that are in many other ways admirable and valuable.

To cite the tannaitic Sage, Rabbi Yosi ben Dormaskit (that is, from Damascus) to Rabbi Judah, "How long can you distort us in the Scriptures?" (עד מתי אתה מעוית עלינו את הכתובים?).[95] As the third section of this chapter reveals, there is nothing in Esther that justifies antisemitic readings of the

---

[92] Such as that of Johann G. Fichte discussed above, and Georg W. F. Hegel's essay "Der Geist des Christentums und sein Schicksal," where he paints the core of Judaism in the blackest colors and describes the Jews as slaves of the Mosaic Law.

[93] See M. Luther, *Tischrede* of August 9, 1532, WA *Tischreden*, vol. 3, pp. 243–244 no. 3271b, esp. p. 244 lines 9–16.

[94] The one-sided criticism of the biblical script by some scholars is tantamount to the phrase of William Shakespeare (1564–1616): "The devil can cite Scripture for his purpose / An evil soul producing holy witness / Is like a villain with a smiling cheek / A goodly apple rotten at the heart." See W. Shakespeare, *The Merchant of Venice*, Act 1, Scene 3, p. 5. Most likely, *The Merchant of Venice* was written between 1596 and 1598.

[95] See *Sifre Deuteronomy*, piska 1 (L. Finkelstein [ed.], *Sifre on Deuteronomy* [New York: The Jewish Theological Seminary of America, 1969], p. 7; another version: למה אתה מעוית ...); see also Rashi's commentary on Gen 41:43.

book, which paint *all* Jews everywhere as bloodthirsty murderers. The fact that the entire history of the Jewish reception of Esther emphasizes *first and foremost* the deliverance from annihilation (and only the death of enemies enabled it) confirms this.

A close reading of Esther from various perspectives, within its broad biblical and general extrabiblical contexts, as well as within its proximate and comprehensive settings, leaves no room for such harsh criticism, and definitely not for any anti-Judaic, inaccurate, and biased interpretations of the book. This reading shows that the book emphasizes the self-defense and deliverance of the Jews in the face of murderous Jew-haters. The justified self-defense of the Jews in standing firm against the danger and absolute pure evil of annihilation, was most likely necessary and even mandatory. The Jews simply chose life over death or mortal danger.

CHAPTER 13

Christian Pro-Esther Interpretation

Indeed, "No book in the Old Testament has occasioned more antipa-thy for some readers, and more enjoyment for others, than the book of Esther."[1] Thus, though the Christian reception of the book of Esther has been mostly negative, as discussed in the previous chapters, there are also some positive pro-Esther voices. This chapter demonstrates that the latter have been much less prominent than the former, and that even these more appreciative readings of the book are still fundamentally shaped by the interpreters' Christian convictions.

Here it is important to distinguish between those few Christian schol-ars who spoke in favor of Esther and its depiction of the Jews before the Holocaust, and those who spoke out after the Holocaust, though it took some decades for most of them to do so.

I   Before the Holocaust

Among the advocates in Christian society, one who stands out is the English scholar and clergyman, Matthew Henry (1662–1714), who composed an influential commentary that highly praises the book of Esther:

> We find in this Book, that even those Jews which were scattered in the provinces of the heathen, were taken Care of, as well as those who were gathered in the Land of Judea, and were wonderfully preserved, when doomed to Destruction, and appointed as Sheep for the Slaughter .... The narrative [is] of a plot laid against the Jews to cut them all off, and wonderfully disappointed by a Concurrence of Providences .... But though the name of God be not in it; the finger of God is, directing many Minute Events for the bringing about of his people's deliverance. The Particulars are not only surprising and very entertaining, but edifying

[1] Fuerst, *The Books of Ruth, Esther, Ecclesiastes, the Song of Songs, Lamentations*, p. 32.

and very encouraging to the Faith and Hope of God's people, in the most difficult and dangerous Times: We cannot now expect such miracles to be wrought for us, as were for Israel when they were brought out of Egypt, but we may expect that in such ways as God here took to defeat Haman's plot he will still protect his people. ... The whole story confirms the Psalmist's observation (Ps. 37. 12, 13), *The Wicked plotteth against the Just, and gnashes upon him with his teeth. The Lord shall laugh at him; he sees that his Day is coming.*[2]

This positive account of God's rescue of the Jews in the time of Esther does not stand on its own. It serves as an example of how God will continue to protect his people, including the Christians of Henry's own time. Indeed, the purpose of the commentary as a whole is not just to interpret what the Bible says, but to explain "what is this to us?"[3] That is, his purpose is to indicate what the Scriptures mean for his contemporary Christian audience. Thus, he concludes that the feast of Purim serves as a "*Memorial* of the great things God has done for his Church," and refers to "Esther's good Services *to the Church*" (emphasis original). By contrast, he sharply criticizes the way contemporary Jews celebrate the feast through drinking and carnival, as described in "their Talmud," practices which he calls "corrupt and wicked" distortions of what was "at first well intended."[4] Nevertheless, this is not a condemnation of the Jews in general, but merely a legitimate critique of how some have celebrated the salvation of God's people.

This does not mean that Henry has rejected the common Christian view that the Jews, like all peoples, can only be saved by Jesus, and those who reject him are "children of the devil," as Henry states in his interpretation of John 8:47.[5] Nevertheless, he straightforwardly praises the book of Esther and its Jewish characters, and affirms their right "to stand upon their own defense," and that they "relied on the Goodness of their God, [and] the Justice of their Cause," while praising their "kindness" in refusing to take advantage of the second decree by plundering their enemies.[6]

---

[2] M. Henry, *An Exposition of the Old and New Testament: With Practical Remarks and Observations* (6 vols.; London: J. Clark *et al.*, 1721–1725), vol. 2, p. 647. There are many editions of this commentary, each with differing page numbers; the citation comes from Henry's introduction to Esther. On Matthew Henry and his commentary, see A. W. Wainwright, "Henry, Matthew (1662–1714)," in J. H. Hayes (ed.), *Dictionary of Biblical Interpretation* (Nashville: Abingdon, 1999), vol. 1, p. 495, with additional bibliography.
[3] For the quotation, see Wainwright, "Henry, Matthew," p. 495.
[4] Henry, *An Exposition of the Old and New Testaments*, vol. 2, p. 665.
[5] See Henry, *An Exposition of the Old and New Testaments*, vol. 5, pp. 508–510.
[6] See Henry, *An Exposition of the Old and New Testaments*, vol. 2, pp. 661, 662.

Similarly, the Irish scholar Adam Clark (ca. 1762–1832) wrote in his *Commentary on the Bible* (1831):

> Though some Christians have hesitated to receive the book of Esther into the sacred canon, yet it has always been received by the Jews, not only as perfectly authentic, but also as one of the most excellent of their Sacred Books. They call it *Megillah*, the Volume, by way of eminence; and hold it in the highest estimation. That it records the history of a real fact, the observation of the feast of Purim, to the present day, is a sufficient evidence.[7]

Clark's analysis of the actions of the Jews as described in the book of Esther is even-handed, stressing the legality and legitimacy of their response to Haman's decree: "the Jews had as much authority to slay their enemies, as their enemies had to slay them ... whether this was right or wrong, it was the custom of the people, and according to the laws."[8]

Like Henry, Clark criticizes some aspects of the celebration of Purim among contemporary Jews, who pound so hard on the furniture during the reading of the *Megillah* that they "are sure to have considerable labor at the conclusion, to repair the damages done among the seats etc., in the synagogue. It seems, overall, that the feast is by no means a religious one .... Indeed, the Jews, bad as they might have been before the feast of Purim, are much less *children of Abraham* at the conclusion than they were before."[9] He also affirms that "It is only the Gospel which will not admit of coercion for the propagation and establishment of its doctrines ... If the kingdom of Christ were of this *world*, then would his servants *fight*. But it is not from hence."[10] Yet while Clark maintains his Christian dogmas and values, and criticizes some aspects of the customary behavior of some Jews during the Purim feast, he is fundamentally approving of the book of Esther, the right of the Jews to defend themselves, and their salvation within the book.

Another eighteenth- to nineteenth-century scholar, the English Catholic, George Leo Haydock (1774–1849), published an influential commentary with the Douay-Rheims translation of the Vulgate. It also explicitly defends Esther against "the boldness of many Lutherans ... who represent the whole work as a mere fiction. The Jews have a greater respect for it than for any of the prophets; whose works, they say, will perish at the coming of the Messiahs: whereas this will subsist with the books of Moses,

---

[7] A. Clark, *The Holy Bible Containing the Old and New Testaments* (Baltimore: J. J. Harrod, 1834), vol. I, p. 1019.

[8] Clark, *The Holy Bible Containing the Old and New Testaments*, vol. I, p. 1029.

[9] Clark, *The Holy Bible Containing the Old and New Testaments*, vol. I, p. 1031.

[10] Clark, *The Holy Bible Containing the Old and New Testaments*, vol. I, p. 1029.

and the feast of Purim will never be abolished."[11] Like Henry and Clark, however, Haydock's view is not entirely positive, defending the actions of the Jews at the end of the book as justifiable self-defense, yet also sharply criticizing certain aspects of the Jewish celebration of Purim as a gratification of "their vanity and vengeful spirit."[12] In particular, he emphasizes the practice of burning a straw model of Haman on a cross, which he says was banned by the Christian emperors due to the belief that it was a symbolic attack on Christ.[13]

Haydock's contemporary, the Irish Baptist minister, Alexander Carson (1776–1844), described the book of Esther as exceptionally focused on God's providence:

> In it we see the people of God providentially brought to the very brink of ruin, and delivered without a single miracle. The means employed by their enemies to affect their destruction are by Providence employed as the means of their exaltation and glory. The hand of God in his ordinary Providence has linked together a course of events as simple and as natural as the mind can conceive, yet as surprising as the boldest fictions of romance.[14]

Carson even devoted an entire volume to the theme of God's providence in Esther, in which he highly praised the book, and used it as a model for Christians. For example:

> [I]n the book of Esther we are not only to attend to the wonderful interpositions of Providence manifested in the facts of history. From the manner of revelation, in innumerable other instances, we are warranted to consider this history as prophetical and typical. In the deliverance of the Jews on this occasion, we may see God's method of preserving his church in the time of the fourth beast; and the final triumph of the saints of the Most High .... In Haman we see a striking type of the man of sin; he seeks to destroy the whole Israel of God; but his effort will only bring on his own ruin.[15]

Carson does not criticize the book of Esther and argues against those who deny its value and inspiration, strongly affirming both.[16] He does criticize

---

[11] The commentary was first published in 1811; the quotation apparently comes from the 1855 edition: G. L. Haydock, *The Holy Bible, Translated from the Latin Vulgate, with Useful Notes, Critical, Historical, Controversial, and Explanatory* (New York: E. Dunigan, 1855), p. 624. For another positive treatment of the book of Esther, see F. W. Schultz, *Die Bücher, Esra, Nehemia und Esther* (Theologisch-homiletisches Bibelwerk: Des Alten Testaments, Neunter Teil; Bielefeld: Verlag von Belhagen und Klasing, 1876), pp. 218–302 esp. 282, 293, 296.

[12] Haydock, *The Holy Bible*, p. 632.

[13] Haydock, *The Holy Bible*, p. 633.

[14] Carson, *History of Providence*, pp. 176–177.

[15] A. Carson, *Providence Unfolded: Comprising the History of Providence as Unfolded in the Book of Esther* (2nd ed.; New York: E. H. Fletcher, 1852), p. 96.

[16] Carson, *Providence Unfolded*, pp. 99–107.

Esther and Mordecai as individuals, for instance for violating the law against the intermarriage with Gentiles,[17] but not for their actions at the end of the story. He concludes that "While in Mordecai we find something to blame, we may find in him much more to praise."[18]

In 1885, the British philologist and Assyriologist, Archibald Henry Sayce (1845–1933), who taught at the University of Oxford, published *An Introduction to the Books of Ezra, Nehemiah, and Esther.*[19] He declared that the book of Esther "has been made an instrument through which God has revealed His will to us, and prepared the way for the work of Christ."[20]

As briefly noted in the previous chapter, in 1920 the English biblicist, Archibald Duff (1845–1934) published a short commentary on Esther in *Peake's Commentary on the Bible.* Duff denied that Esther is "revengeful" and "irreligious," in part because he thought the Greek version is closer to the original than the Hebrew is: "It is said that Esther is revengeful, and so also were the Jews in those generations. Is this true, or is it a traditional but unfortunate way of uttering ill will against the folk among whom Jesus was killed? It is said, moreover, that the book is irreligious, for it never speaks of God. Is this true?"[21] Though these are presented as questions, the rest of his commentary makes clear that Duff views these accusations as unfair. Thus, he concludes that:

> The story was for the ordinary folk, and is honoured among these for the generous Jewish treatment of poor by rich, and even of enemies by the suffering Israelites. The people abhorred bloodthirst and selfish spoiling of conquered persons. They were deeply religious, attributing all guidance to Yahweh, and they expected to rule the whole world for Him. The common fancy that Esther is a cruel book is entirely mistaken, even when the short Hebrew edition is taken as authoritative."[22]

However, in the second edition of Peake's Commentary (1962), Duff's contribution is replaced by a different one, by L. E. Brown, which is highly negative, as noted in the previous chapter.

It is worthy to mention here also an example of the appreciation of Esther in the nineteenth-century American literature. In her book, *The Book of Esther and the Typology of Female Transfiguration in American*

---

[17] Carson, *Providence Unfolded*, pp. 25–26. On this issue see also Chapter 7, §III and Chapter 8, §III.
[18] Carson, *Providence Unfolded*, p. 98.
[19] A. H. Sayce, *An Introduction to the Books of Ezra, Nehemiah, and Esther* (London: Religious Tract Society, 1885; 4th ed., 1893).
[20] Sayce, *An Introduction to the Books of Ezra, Nehemiah, and Esther*, p. 120.
[21] Duff, "Esther," pp. 336–340 esp. 336.
[22] Duff, "Esther," p. 340.

Literature, Ariel Clark Silver focuses on Esther as a figure of female redemption, particularly in the works of Nathaniel Hawthorne and Henry Adams. She shows how Queen Esther is used as the figure of an ancient woman who functions as a wise female for the salvation of American society and culture.[23]

1   The Case of Wilhelm Eduard Vischer

A unique example appears in the most unexpected period, place, and social climate. In the Munich of 1937, under the Hitler regime and against the background of its brutal anti-Jewish persecution, Wilhelm Eduard Vischer published the text of his inaugural lecture at the University of Basel, on the book of Esther,[24] in which he uses it to challenge the Nazi attitude toward the Jews. Indeed, it is not a coincidence that he published his booklet on Esther first and foremost in Munich, then later in Zurich.

Vischer, who was born in Davos, Switzerland, in 1895 and died in Montpellier, France, in 1988, was a Swiss Reformed pastor and Old Testament scholar.[25] He taught in Bethel (Bielefeld, Germany), until he was stripped of his position and expelled from the country in 1933, for opposing the Nazis and insulting Hitler, including by calling him a "Balkanesen." He returned to and remained in Basel as a pastor and *Privatdozent* until 1947 when he moved to Montpellier and became a professor of the Old Testament.

In contrast to the Nazi's racist handling of "the Jewish question" (*Judenfrage*), Vischer rejects the view that the Jews are unlike all other peoples. He stresses that "the blood and the morals of Jews are not so different from the blood and the morals of the rest of mankind." Therefore, he suggests that only "God the Lord himself ... can give an answer" to this question, and not Hitler with his "Final Solution" (*Endlösung*):

---

[23] See Silver, *The Book of Esther and the Typology of Female Transfiguration in American Literature*. There is much more to do on such subjects, which are projects in their own right, however they are beyond the scope of this volume.

[24] See W. Vischer, *Esther* (Theologische Existenz Heute 48; Munich: Chr. Kaiser Verlag, 1937). It was also published in Zurich the following year (both in German), then in English: "The Book of Esther," *Evangelical Quarterly* 11 (1939), pp. 3–21.

[25] For a summary of Vischer's life and work, see S. Felber, "Vischer, Wilhelm Eduard," in F. W. Bautz and T. Bautz (eds.), *Biographisch-Bibliographisches Kirchenlexicon* (Herzberg: Verlag T. Bautz, 2000), vol. 17, pp. 1493–1504. For more detail, see idem, *Wilhelm Vischer als Ausleger der Heiligen Schrift: Eine Untersuchung zum Christuszeugnis des Alten Testaments* (Forschungen zur systematischen und ökumenischen Theologie 89; Göttingen: Vandenhoeck & Ruprecht, 1999); R. Smend, "Wilhelm Vischer," *Kritiker und Exegeten: Porträttskizzen zu vier Jahrhunderten alttestamentlicher Wissenschaft* (Göttingen: Vandenhoeck & Ruprecht, 2017), pp. 770–793.

The approach to the Jewish question as natural history trivializes it .... For the blood and the morals of Jews are not so different from the blood and the morals of the rest of mankind that therefore the Jews should be perceived as unbearable ... Even with the absolute sovereign power of the Persian king and moreover the whole apparatus of the Persian imperial administration available to him for this purpose, the 'enemy of the Jews' Haman had as little success resolving the Jewish question by the extermination of the Jews, as before him the Pharaoh of Egypt with his brutal methods failed, or as shortly afterwards the Greeks and the Romans and the Spanish and the Russians and the Germans. Why not? Simply because the Jewish question is the question of [the chosen people of biblical] Israel, that is: because it is God the Lord himself created this question, and only he can give an answer.[26]

Arguably, the fact that Vischer compares the "Final Solution" initiated by Hitler to Haman's attempt to exterminate the Jews, may also imply that Hitler's destiny would be like that recounted in Esther regarding Haman. Vischer considers the book of Esther as an integral part of the Christian Bible. His positive approach to it was part of his much broader embrace of the Old Testament as God's Word, and of the Jews/Israel as God's chosen people.[27] In response to the Nazi affirmation that "The Jews are our misfortune" (*Die Juden sind unser Unglück*),[28] Vischer published a memorandum in October 1938, just a month before the *Reichskristallnacht* (November 9–10, 1938), titled "Salvation Comes from the Jews" ("Das Heil kommt von den Juden"), while citing John 4:22. In other works, he emphasized that Jesus was himself a Jew, that the true church is recognized by its inclusion of the Jews, and that hatred

---

[26] "Die naturgeschichtliche Betrachtung der Judenfrage ist eine Verharmlosung .... Denn das Blut und die Moral der Juden sind nicht dermaßen verschieden vom Blut und der Moral der übrigen Menschen, daß deswegen die Juden als unerträglich empfunden werden müßten ... Trotzdem ihm die absolute Herrschergewalt des Perserkönigs und überdies der ganze Apparat der persischen Reichsverwaltung für diesen Zweck zur Verfügung standen, ist es dem 'Judenfeind' Haman ebenso wenig gelungen, die Judenfrage durch die Vertilgung der Juden zu lösen, wie vor ihm dem Pharao von Ägypten mit seinen brutalen Methoden, und ebenso wenig später den Griechen und den Römern und den Spaniern und den Russen und den Deutschen. Warum nicht? Weil eben die Judenfrage die Frage Israels ist, und das heißt: weil Gott der Herr es ist, der diese Frage gestellt hat und der sie allein beantworten kann"; see Vischer, *Esther*, pp. 14–15 see also pp. 23–24: "... der Judenfrage als der Frage, die er [= Gott] mit der Auserwälung Israels gestellt hat und nur er selbst beantworten kann" ("... the Jewish question as the question he [= God] created, when Israel was chosen, and only he can answer it"). For a slightly different English translation, see Vischer, "The Book of Esther," pp. 8–9.

[27] On this issue and Vischer's argues with E. Brunner and W. Zimmerli, see E. Busch, *Unter dem Bogen des einen Bundes: Karl Barth und die Juden 1933–1945* (Neukichen-Vluyen: Neukirchner Verlag, 1996), pp. 359–399; Smend, "Wilhelm Vischer," p. 789.

[28] This expression was coined by the German historian Heinrich von Treitschke; see H. von Treitschke, "Unsere Aussichten," *Preußische Jahrbücher* 44.5 (November 1879), pp. 559–576 esp 575.

of the Jews is a greater attack against humanity than any other kind of hate, due to God's unique election of Israel.[29] This was not merely an academic issue for Vischer, it was also a practical one: he was President of the "Society of the Friends of Israel" (*Verein der Freunde Israels*) in Switzerland, beginning in 1937, and actively worked to receive and support Jewish refugees from Germany.

Thus, Vischer used the interpretation of the biblical book of Esther as a political and ideological challenge to the Nazis and Nazism, with their actively hostile approaches toward the Jewish people. Vischer identified Haman's plan as one of the oldest attempts to implement the "Final Solution," and thereby anticipated the horror of the forthcoming Holocaust.

II After the Holocaust

Despite the Holocaust, it was some time before such alternative readings of Esther became common, but by the 1980s, some Christian scholars categorically rejected the anti-Jewish readings of Esther. For example, the American scholar, Mervin Breneman writes: "Esther says to the Christian that anti-Jewish hostility is intolerable to God."[30] Another eminent American theologian and biblical scholar, Brevard S. Childs (1923–2007), states: "the book of Esther provides the strongest canonical warrant in the whole Old Testament for the religious significance of the Jewish people in an ethnic sense. The inclusion of Esther within the Christian canon serves as a check against all attempts to spiritualize the concept of Israel."[31] Similarly the English biblical scholar David Clines stated: "Esther may perform a valuable critical function for the Christian reader as a test case for whether one truly accepts the Old Testament as a legitimate and necessary part of the Christian Scriptures."[32]

Among German scholars, the Catholic Erich Zenger (1939–2010) made a clear-cut and most courageous assertion. The Christian scholars who negate the book of Esther, says Zenger, "are terrifying judgment of Christianity itself, which often played in history the role of Haman.

---

[29] For details, see Felber, "Vischer, Wilhelm Eduard," pp. 1496–1497. This position directly opposes the mainstream view of the so-called "German Christians," as reviewed in Chapter 12, §I, and note 30.
[30] Breneman, *Ezra, Nehemiah, Esther*, p. 297.
[31] Childs, *Introduction to the Old Testament as Scripture*, pp. 606–607. See also Meinhold, *Das Buch Esther*, pp. 107–108; Rendtorff, *The Old Testament: An Introduction*, p. 270.
[32] Clines, *Ezra, Nehemiah, Esther*, p. 256.

For this dark side of Church history, reading of the book of Esther is a necessary examination of conscience and the call to its reversal." "On the other hand," stresses Zenger, "Christianity can learn from the book of Esther that the God of Israel holds faith to his chosen people also as the hidden God, because he is a God of delivery. Because and if this is true for Israel, it is also true as an oath of loyalty to the Church."[33]

Zenger, who was a child when the Holocaust took place, compares that horrible act of the German Nazis and their other collaborators as playing "the role of Haman," not only in planning, but also in actively executing, the "Final Solution."

III   Conclusion

There were and are also positive – or at least not negative – voices regarding the book of Esther and the Jewish people among some Christian scholars, which should not be overlooked. Among them, a few spoke out prior to the Holocaust (such as Henry, Clark, Carson, and Duff), or very close to it (Vischer), and a few wrote some decades after (such as Breneman, Childs, Clines, and Zenger). Some of them stress that Christianity can and should learn from the book of Esther that God saves Israel and punishes those who attempt to eliminate his people. These scholars are a minority who swim against the stream of general hostility of most theologians and interpreters toward the book of Esther.

Comparing the examples in this chapter with the previous one, a geographic and cultural distinction can be seen: Most of the harshest criticisms of the book of Esther are found among German Protestants since the Reformation. By contrast, many Anglo-Saxon commentators have maintained a much more positive view of both the book itself and its Jewish characters. This is true both of Protestant and Catholic writers since at least the seventeenth century. Though they also sometimes criticize aspects of the book, as well as elements of later Jewish celebrations of Purim, they praise the book's merit and inspiration, and embrace its conclusion as an example of God's deliverance, without condemning the Jews for

---

[33] See Zenger, "Das Buch Esther," p. 388: "Die bis in die Gegenwart von christlichen Exegeten propagierten Auffassungen … sind ein erschreckendes Urteil über das Christentum selbst, das in der Geschichte vielfach die Rolle des Haman gespielt hat. Für diese dunkle Seite der Kirchengeschichte ist die Lektüre des Buches Ester eine notwendige Gewissenserforschung und die Aufforderung zur Umkehr. Andererseits kann das Christentum aus dem Esterbuch lernen, dass der Gott Israels auch als der Verborgene seinem Volk die Treue hält, *weil* er ein Gott der Rettung ist. Weil und wenn dies für Israel gilt, ist diese Treue-Zusage auch für die Kirche wahr."

defending themselves. This further supports the conclusion that Martin Luther's devastating judgment against the book had major consequences in shaping the subsequent critique of Esther, which was much more widespread among Lutheran Christians than among other Christian groups. Certainly, there are exceptions on both sides – positive and negative – but the general tendency is evident.

CHAPTER 14

Synthesis and Conclusion

This volume comprises an introduction, three core parts, and the current chapter that synthesizes and concludes the volume as a whole. Part I focuses on the book of Esther itself and its place in scholarship, while Parts II and III concentrate on the history of interpretation and reception of the book among Jews and Christians through centuries. The examination of the book is based on the Hebrew Bible – the Masoretic Text, which is probably the oldest and the closest one to the original version of the story – though the incompatible Greek and Aramaic versions are discussed on various occasions in the volume. Also, we examined some presumed late additions to the story.

I The Book of Esther

The first part of the volume discusses the date and place of the book's composition, its virtuosity, literary style, features, and methods, its structure, extent and unity, its textual development, as well as its noble characters (Vashti, Esther, and Mordecai). This part also handles the presumed key theological view of the book, as well as its historical setting and the question of its historicity, and sheds new lights on these matters. It argues that the primary story of Esther was written in Susa, sometime during the reign of the historic figure Ahasuerus/Xerxes I, or a generation or two after (ca. 475–425 BCE). Further, it claims that it would be inappropriate to dismiss the entire story of Esther as an ahistorical fantasy, or to accept it completely as a reliable history. Although the book contains several fictional elements, overstatements, exaggerated numbers, humoristic scenes, satires, and the like that cannot be accepted as trustworthy historical information – "history" in the sense of, to cite Leopold von Ranke (1795–1886), "as it actually happened" (*wie es eigentlich gewesen ist*),[1] – still, the core story of the book is genuine.

---

[1] See L. Ranke, *Geschichte der romanischen und germanischen Völker von 1494 bis 1535* (Leipzig and Berlin: G. Reimer, 1824), pp. v–vi (Leopold Ranke became Leopold *von* Ranke when he was knighted in 1865).

That is, despite the general Persian tolerance toward different minorities in the Empire, probably there was some unusual terrifying hostility toward the Jews. The Esther story embodies the first "Final Solution" – the annihilation of the entire Jewish people – which was initiated by a top imperial official, who manipulated the drunken king of Persia. The Jews were rescued somehow, thanks to the decisive and rapid actions of a few of them who held high positions in the royal court – Esther and Mordecai. The long and tragic history of the Jewish people, as well as the several parallels from the ancient world for Haman's false accusations against Jews in the statements of many Jew-haters in different times and places as discussed in Chapter 6, strengthen the argument that the accusations of Haman presented in the book of Esther are not an imaginary tale of the storyteller that could not have happened, as some scholars have asserted. A comparison of the accusations of Haman with those in a wider range of other literature demonstrates that similar charges were often laid against the Jews. Particularly the allegation that by keeping their specific religious laws, rituals, and cultural identity the Jews become separatists who ignored the communal, social, and civil laws. The parallels appear in the biblical book of Daniel, several Greco-Roman sources, as well as some modern anti-Jewish writings. Thus, Haman's accusations are just the earliest form that has reached us. Usually, these kinds of accusations by ancient and modern antisemites did not remain theoretical, abstract illusions. As is stated by Plutarch, "a word is a deed's shadow" (*Moralia* 1:10a): The false accusations have been used frequently to justify discrimination, horrific repression, and violence against Jewish communities.

Furthermore, several significant aspects of the book reflect reliable historical information about the Persian Achaemenid Empire: The name of the king, the size of the empire, its administrative hierarchy, the harem, the rich palace in Susa and the probability that the king spent the spring there; the danger of conspiracy and attempted murder at the royal court; existence and usage of imperial-royal annals, archives, and the postal system. These things are largely in accordance with other biblical, Greek, and Persian written sources, as well as with various archaeological finds.

Even with its secular character on the surface, the story of Esther is not a secular book. The absence of religious institutions, rituals, and the explicit name of God – in any form – from the Hebrew version of the book, does not mean that the author has no interest in theological matters. He encapsulates and addresses the worst fear of the Israelite/Jewish people: the threat of complete annihilation. The story is one of the links in a long chain which presents a fear of annihilation that has accompanied the Israelites/Jews throughout ages, as several biblical sources testify and extrabiblical documents support. Through a highly effective humoristic style and other literary features, the author tells his story, while leading the audience delicately to his fundamental theological concept that God rules all the events behind the curtain and is devoted to saving his people when they are confronted with an ultimate threat. In other words, even when God's actions are unseen, still he keeps his covenant with Israel/Jews and continuously stands on their side and redeems them.

The book of Esther has always sparked sharp controversies in biblically oriented societies. Thus, the second and third parts of the volume focus on the "after life" (*Nachleben*) of the book and its history of interpretation and reception in Jewish and Christian societies, religions, cultures, and thoughts from the earliest times to the contemporary period.

II Esther and the Jews

There are only a few sporadic exceptions of small groups of Jews who have questioned or rejected the book of Esther and the celebration of the redemption that it recounts – Purim – with it, each group with its own logic and set of reasons. Among them is the isolated and marginal Jewish community of Qumran, on the edge of the Judean Dessert, which most likely excluded Esther from among their collection of sacred books. They do not appear to have copied or studied the book and did not celebrate the feast of Purim. Also, in modern times, a few Reform Jewish scholars have joined – though without uttering this explicitly – with many Christians to negate the book of Esther and Purim altogether.

Nevertheless, through the ages, the book of Esther gained overall a great popularity and has long been one of the most beloved biblical books in all Jewish communities, despite its lack of any direct mention of God. It has been considered a highly valued sacred Scripture; along with the Five Books of Moses and the Five Books of David (that is, Psalms), Esther is one of the most esteemed, well-cherished, and admired biblical books among the Jews. Jewish societies have adored and sanctified Megillat Esther and believe that it is an everlasting Scripture. Thus, the Rabbis rank it nearly as highly as the holiest Scripture of Judaism, the Torah, and even before all the prophetic and other hagiographic books – a fact that was harshly condemned by the Protestant reformer, Martin Luther, in the sixteenth century.

Esther has therefore received enormous attention among Jews. They have devoted a significant number of diverse studies, translations, and interpretations to the book. All these have inspired Jewish thoughts, legends and folklore, art (such as painting), music, plays and humoristic theater pieces, as well as prose and poetic literature in many languages in almost all Jewish communities around the globe. The Esther story was translated into Greek, and six "Additions" were attached to it. Further, the first-century Jewish historian, Josephus Flavius, dedicated an extensive section of his work to rewriting the story, and the book was probably included in his "canon" of twenty-two Jewish Scriptures. The existence of the tractate *Megillah* in the Mishnah leaves no doubt that it was accepted as an authoritative text a long time before its inclusion in that codex, surely in the first to second centuries. Many rabbinic compositions flourished around the book of Esther. A special tractate was dedicated to it not only in the Mishnah, but also in the Tosefta, the Jerusalem Talmud, and the Babylonian Talmud. Esther was the subject of several special homiletical collections (such as Midrash Esther Rabbah), and at least two Aramaic translations (Targum Rishon and Targum Sheni). The talmudic Rabbis integrated it into their halachic system, midrashic methodologies of interpretation, and unique theologies. In the Middle Ages, different kinds of commentaries were written on the Megillah, in Hebrew as well as in Arabic, both by the Rabbanite and Karaite exegetes, by Sephardi as well as Ashkenazi scholars. This trend has continued also up to modern times. The book was also used by the Jews in their disputes with Christians.

Through the centuries, Jews have made connection between the story of Esther and their own situation in different foreign lands. They have regularly associated their contemporary enemies with those whose anti-Jewish policies have been overcome within the book, seeing them all as repeated manifestations of the same anti-Jewish oppression shown by "Haman." They have also looked to the book of Esther as a model for understanding their ongoing experiences of exile and have frequently anticipated salvation through the downfall of their opponents, while comparing them to Haman, who is killed along with his sons and many other enemies, as recounted at the end of the book of Esther. Thus, the story of the evil Haman was usually utilized to describe later Jews' oppressors as "new Haman(s)," in almost all Jewish communities, and Jews who have faced their own contemporary oppressors and foes have often looked to Esther for models to describe their own experiences. They have celebrated the day of release and deliverance from the hands of those enemies, and called it a "Second Purim," while sending presents to each other and assisting the poor and weak members of society, writing the stories of their own "Hamans," and the great miracles of their time, as "new Megillot," and reading them publicly. They have continued to trust that the God of Israel will keep his covenant with his people eternally and somehow will save them.

Thus, this centrality of the book within Jewish reception history may be attributed to several factors that have been combined to bring the book of Esther to such high esteem. Here plays, first and foremost, the central theological message of the book that implicitly emphasizes the eternal covenant between Israel and God in any place and time, and under any circumstances. Add to this the relevance of the story for almost every generation and in every place, that illustrates the extraordinary existence of the Jewish people despite all the hostilities, evil plans, and acts of Jew-haters. Indeed, as shown in Chapter 9, the book of Esther has been paradigmatic for Jewish confrontations with threat throughout the ages, including both during and after the Holocaust. The understanding of Esther as a blueprint provides hope to an exiled community living during precarious times that, no matter how bad the situation, there is always hope for redemption and salvation. Hence, it is a deeply theological book despite the apparent absence of the divine from the narrative. To these significant reasons one can add also the great literary and stylistic qualities of the book, which is considered as one of the world's masterpieces, and certainly attracts the audience. Also, Esther and Mordecai – the noble characters who were committed to saving their people while taking high personal risk – used role models of reputable leaders who never forget to whom they belong and always rise up to help their people. Indeed, Esther is viewed as one of the seven prophetesses and Mordecai is compared to the greatest biblical figures and the core father of the nation – Abraham.

The feast of Purim is based on an outcome of the Esther story. It was inaugurated at that time and has since been celebrated every year everywhere by the Jews and has an important role in the feast liturgy. Like the Torah, Megillat Esther is also written on parchment and read publicly twice every year in the synagogue. As the Megillah commands, Jews celebrate the Purim feast by sending food and gifts to each other, especially to poor people, and by eating and drinking, singing, and dancing. Purim is considered a celebration of the redemption of the Jews from annihilation. In any case, it is definitely not a celebration of revenge and murder.

A question in its own right is whether Esther's presumed theological message can be coordinated with the historical reality of Jewish experience, particularly in the Shoah: Do post-Shoah readers of the book of Esther still accept Esther's apparent central theology that God is always loyal to his covenant with Israel? Or, after the horrendous genocide of the Jews in the Second World War, should we read the book of Esther differently?

III   Esther and the Christians

The position of Esther among Christians and in Christianity is completely different from that among the Jews and in Judaism. In contrast to the general enthusiastic embracement of the book of Esther by the Jews, the Christian reception of it, in the past and present, has rarely been positive, and most often was and still is widely negative and neglectful. This part of the volume therefore contrasts the theological and paradigmatic centrality of Esther in Judaism with the book's – at best marginal – place within Christian religion, theology, and culture, which has tended to assess the book quite negatively, particularly since time of Martin Luther. It painstakingly unwraps the neglect of the book through the ages and Luther's influence on the field of biblical studies and on the development of an antisemitic hermeneutics of reading Esther. While there have been some positive Christian evaluations of the book in modern scholarship, the list of those damning the work in antisemitic terms is depressingly long. In this manner, this part of the volume is an indictment of traditional Christian approaches to Esther, which stand in such stark contrast to traditional Jewish ones.

There is a vital distinction to be made between the Christian "Book of Esther" and the Jewish "Megillat Esther": Jews read the short version of Esther, the Hebrew text. In contrast, most Christians (particularly the Roman Catholic and Orthodox Churches) read the long version of the book, Greek or Latin, which contain six major "Additions" and differ in many important variants from the Hebrew one. The Greek version, followed by the Latin, refers also to God and several religious themes, such as prayers, divine dreams, and kosher food and drink, which do not appear in the Hebrew version preserved by the Jews. It is hard to imagine that the name of God was mentioned explicitly in the original Hebrew version and later someone simply deleted it. Though it is most likely that the Greek version(s) were also formerly produced by Jews, but they were only preserved by Christians.

Esther is never referred to in the New Testament and is hardly cited by the Christian Church Fathers. Early Christians hesitated for a long time whether to include the book in their scriptural canons or exclude it altogether. Even when, finally, the book became a part of the Christian biblical canon, the dispute over it still continued for many generations, and some Christian thinkers and writers doubted its religious value and expressed sharp hostility toward it, while others simply ignored or dismissed it altogether. The first Christian commentary on the book was not written until the ninth century, by Rabanus Maurus of Mainz. He presented Queen Esther positively, as a symbol of the Church, in contrast to Vashti, who was removed from her position, and identified with the Synagogue, which was rejected and replaced by the Church. Otherwise, Esther received very little – if any – attention until the Reformation, when it was referred to in the works of Martin Luther and some of his followers.

In the last four decades of his life, Martin Luther's approach toward the Jews as a people shifted, from tolerant and welcoming in the early stages (while hoping in this way to convert them to the reformed Christianity), to sweepingly xenophobic and antisemitic later on. Likewise, his views of Esther also shifted: Luther praises especially *Queen* Esther (but also Mordecai) mostly in the early stage of his career, while his harshest statements about the *book* of Esther appear particularly in his late writings, where he uses the book to accuse the Jews of being cruel murderers and bloodthirsty enemies of the Christians. These two themes run alongside each other in Luther's life as a reformer: His sympathy especially toward Esther the person as a model of piety, and his later hostility toward Esther the book (along with 2 Maccabees) is part of and runs parallel to his early friendly and later anti-Jewish polemics.

Luther claimed that the book of Esther shows "too much Jewishness and contains a lot of pagan impropriety." According to him, the book reflects a vengeful and bloodthirsty spirit. Though Luther translated the book into German in his complete translation of the Christian Bible, he declares that it is too popular among the Jews to be adopted and should not be appreciated by Christians. Luther's failure to convert the Jews seems to have deepened his hatred toward them and their triumphs over Haman and over Antiochus IV. His abhorrence of the Purim feast and its celebration of the Jews' rescue from extermination, is all tied in with broader antipathy toward the continued existence of Jews and Judaism, which he neither tolerated nor recognized as a legitimate religion with its own worth, alongside Christians and Christianity.

Luther's harsh criticism of the book of Esther and his aggressive and destructive assertions concerning the Jews and their faith had an enormous effect on generations of theologians, writers, thinkers, and politicians, particularly in the Protestant Christian world, but not only there. They have led to widespread misinterpretation and misrepresentations of the book – that it celebrates revenge and mass murder, using it to demonize the Jews as the enemies of God and mankind. Esther's ethical and moral norms have been claimed to be far below those of any other biblical books, particularly those of the New Testament's Gospels. It has been considered not to be a religious book, one that is unworthy of Christian study and theology. Many Christian theologians, commentators, and scholars have condemned the book and used it as a platform to express their own bias, Judeophobic or antisemitic agendas, and propagate their prejudice and hatred toward the "People of the Book" – the Jews – and their cultural and religious heritage – Judaism.

Of course, it is not necessarily illegitimate to criticize a biblical text, nor must a critique be anti-Jewish or antisemitic. Esther's story is not protected from critique more than any other biblical or other text should be, and many Jews, Christians, and others have wrestled with the historical, theological, ethical, and other questions raised by the book. But Esther is no more ethically problematical than some other biblical texts/books, and even if it were, that would not justify condemning for that reason the entire Jewish people at all times and in all places along with it. While there is no justification of brutality for its own sake, nor should the death of a human being be celebrated for itself; too many Christian exegetes have overstated the violence in the Esther story and drawn from it and loaded on it antisemitic conclusions. A close analysis of its context and main theme, its textual variants, its genre, and the common ancient literary conventions that stand behind it would exclude such condemnations of the book and the Jews. The Esther story does not celebrate violence; it stresses self-defense and the deliverance of the Jews from freighting annihilation in the face of brutal Jew-haters.

Just a handful of Christian scholars – before, during, and some decades after the Shoah – have called for a positive evaluation of the book of Esther. Some of them even stress that Christians should learn from the book of Esther that God protects Israel and punishes those who try to persecute it.

All in all, this volume presents the book of Esther within its own merit, context, and complexity. It shows its literary features and virtuosity; historical background and the extent of its historical plausibility; and its key theological position, as well as its various difficulties. Further, it discusses the place of the book and its figures in the sister monotheistic religions and cultures of Judaism and Christianity. It demonstrates how and why different Jewish denominations have approached the book and the feast based on it as they did, and how its story and characters have been used throughout the centuries as models for their own reality and destiny (this point is common to Jews and Christians as well). The volume also engages with the place of Esther among Christians and in Christianity; its negligence and the roots of their widespread antagonism toward the book, the usage of it by many Christian theologians, commentators, and politicians as a basis for their own anti-Jewish and antisemitic agenda. The fact that just a handful Christian scholars has treated the book positively speak also for itself.

Thus, both Jews and Christians have regularly used the book of Esther and its characters either to symbolize and glorify their own religion and communities, or to demonize their religious and political opponents. Each have, in their own ways, used the book of Esther as an instrument to attack, condemn, and mock the other.

Bibliography

This bibliography comprises the studies that were used in the monograph. For comprehensive bibliographies on the book of Esther see the lists below, by M. Riegler, as well as E. Lubetski and M. Lubetski.

Achenbach, R. "'Genocide' in the Book of Esther," in R. Albertz and J. Wöhrle (eds.), *Between Cooperation and Hostility: Multiple Identities in Ancient Judaism and the Interaction with Foreign Powers* (Journal of Ancient Judaism Supplements 11; Göttingen: Vandenhoeck & Ruprecht, 2013), pp. 89–114.

Achenbach, R. "Vertilgen – Töten – Vernichten (Est 3,13). Die Genozid-Thematik im Estherbuch," *ZABR* 15 (2009), pp. 282–315.

Achtemeier, E. *Preaching Hard Texts of the Old Testament* (Peabody, MA: Hendrickson Publishers, 1998).

Agnon, S. J. "The Act of Rabbi Gadiel the Infant," *Elo veElo* (Complete Writings of Samuel Joseph Agnon 2; Jerusalem: Schocken Publishing House, 1978), pp. 416–420 (Hebrew).

Aharoni, Y. *Arad Inscriptions* (Jerusalem: Bialik Institute and Israel Exploration Society, 1975; Hebrew).

Albright, W. F. "The Lachish Cosmetics Burner and Esther 2:12," in H. N. Bream, R. D. Heim, and C. A. Moore (eds.), *A Light unto My Path: Old Testament Studies in Honor of Jacob M. Myers* (Philadelphia: Temple University Press, 1974), pp. 25–32.

Albright, W. F. "The Moabite Stone," in Pritchard, *ANET*, pp. 320–321.

Altheim, F. and R. Stiehl, *Die aramäische Sprache unter den Achaimeniden* (Frankfurt am Main: Vittorio Klostermann, 1960).

Anderson, B. W. "The Place of the Book of Esther in the Christian Bible," *JR* 30 (1950), pp. 32–43.

Ashtor, A. "Egypt," *Encyclopedia Hebraica* (Jerusalem and Tel Aviv: Encyclopaedia Publishing Company, 1972), vol. 24, pp. 237–242 (Hebrew).

Assmann, J. *Das kulturelle Gedächtnis* (8th ed.; Munich: C. H. Beck, 2013).

Avnery O. "Gender, Ethnicity, Identity: Duality in the Book of Esther," in P. Machinist, R. A. Harris, J. A. Berman, N. Samet, and N. Ayali-Darshan (eds.), *Ve-'Ed Ya'aleh (Gen 2:6): Essays in Biblical and Ancient Near Eastern Studies Presented to Edward L. Greenstein* (Atlanta: SBL Press, 2021), vol. 2, pp. 1099–1121.

Bachmann, E. T (ed.), *Luther's Works* – Volume 35: *Word and Sacrament I* (Philadelphia: Fortress Press, 1960).

Baer, Y. *A History of the Jews in Christian Spain* (2 vols.; translated from Hebrew by L. Schoffman; Philadelphia: Jewish Publication Society, 1971).

Balcer, J. "The Athenian *episkopos* and the Achaemenid King's Eye," *AJP* 98 (1977), pp. 252–263.

Bamberger, J. "Le-Haman: Ein Frankfurter Purim-Spiel: Edition, Kommentar und Analyse (Vorstellung eines Forschungsprojektes)," *Jiddistik Mitteilungen: Jidistik in Deutschsprachigen Ländern* 40 (2008), pp. 7–12.

Bardtke, H. *Luther und das Buch Esther* (Tübingen: J. C. B. Mohr [P. Siebeck], 1964).

Bar-Ilan, M. *Biblical Numerology* (Reḥovot: Association for Jewish Astrology and Numerology, 2005; Hebrew).

Bar-Kochva, B. "On the Festival of Purim and Some of Succot Practices in the Period of the Second Temple and Afterwards," *Zion* 62 (1997), pp. 387–407 (Hebrew).

Bar-Kochva, B. "The Jewish Ethnographic Excursus by Hecataeus of Abdera," *The Image of the Jews in Greek Literature: The Hellenistic Period* (Hellenistic Culture and Society 51; Berkeley: University of California Press, 2010), pp. 90–135.

Bar-Kochva, B. "The Anti-Jewish Ethnographic Treatise by Apollonius Molon," *The Image of the Jews in Greek Literature: The Hellenistic Period* (Hellenistic Culture and Society 51; Berkeley: University of California Press, 2010), pp. 469–516.

Baron, S. W. *A Social and Religious History of the Jews* (vol. 13; 2nd ed.; New York: Columbia University Press / Philadelphia: The Jewish Publication Society of America, 1969).

Baron, S. A. *A Social and Religious History of the Jews* (vol. 14; 2nd ed.; New York: Columbia University Press / Philadelphia: The Jewish Publication Society of America, 1969).

Bashevis Singer, I. *Shosha* (Tel Aviv: Am Oved, 1978; Hebrew).

Bashevis Singer, I. *The Penitent* (Tel Aviv: Sifriat Poalim, 1986; Hebrew).

Bautz, F. W. "Hempel, Johannes," in F. W. Bautz (ed.), *Biographisch-Bibliographisches Kirchenlexikon* (Hamm: Traugott Bautz, 1990), vol. 1, pp. 711–712.

Beal, T. *The Book of Hiding: Gender, Ethnicity, Annihilation and Esther* (Biblical Limits; London and New York: Routledge, 1997).

Beckerath, J. von, *Chronologie des Pharaonischen Ägypten* (Münchner Ägyptologische Studien 46; Mainz: P. von Zabern, 1997).

Beckwith, R. *The Old Testament Canon of the New Testament Church and Its Background in Early Judaism* (London: SPCK, 1985).

Begg, C. T. "Hempel, Johannes," in J. H. Hayes (ed.), *Dictionary of Biblical Interpretation* (Nashville: Abingdon Press, 1999), vol. 1, p. 493.

Beinart, Ch. "Saragossa," *Encyclopedia Judaica* (2nd ed.; Jerusalem: Keter, 2007), vol. 18, pp. 41–45.

Beinart, Ch. *The Expulsion of the Jews from Spain* (translated from Hebrew by J. M. Green; Oxford / Portland: The Littman Library of Jewish Civilization, 2002).

Bell, D. P. *Sacred Communities: Jewish and Christian Identities in Fifteenth-Century Germany* (Studies in Central European Histories; Leiden and Boston: Brill, 2001).

Ben-Chorin, S. *Kritik des Estherbuches: Eine theologische Streitschrift* (Jerusalem: Salinger, 1938).

Ben-Dov, J. "A Presumed Citation of Esther 3:7 in 4QD^b*," *DSD* 6 (1999), pp. 282–284.

Ben-Sasson, H. H. *History of the Jewish People*, Volume 2: *Middle Ages* (Tel Aviv: Dvir, 1969; Hebrew).

Ben-Sasson, H. H. "Jewish-Christian Disputation in the Setting of Humanism and Reformation in the German Empire," *HTR* 59 (1966), pp. 369–390.

Ben-Sasson, H. H. "The Reformation in Contemporary Jewish Eyes," *Proceedings of the Israel Academy of Science and Humanities* 4 (1971), pp. 239–326.

Ben-Sasson, H. H. "The Middle Ages," in H. H. Ben-Sasson (ed.), *A History of the Jewish People* (translated by G. Weidenfeld; Cambridge, MA: Harvard University Press, 1976).

Ben-Shlomo, J. (ed.), *Moreh Nevuchim* (Jerusalem: Bialik Institute, 1968), p. 126 (Hebrew).

Ben Yoseph, A. (ed.), *Megillath Purim of Egypt* ([no publisher information], 1997; Hebrew).

Bentzen, A. *Introduction to the Old Testament* (2nd ed.; Copenhagen: G. E. C. Gad Publisher, 1952).

Berg, S. B. *The Book of Esther: Motifs, Themes and Structure* (Society of Biblical Literature Dissertation Series 44; Missoula, MN: Scholars Press, 1979).

Bergen, D. L. *Twisted Cross: The German Christian Movement in the Third Reich* (Chapel Hill: University of North Carolina Press, 1996).

Bergey, R. "Late Linguistic Features in Esther," *JQR* 75 (1984), pp. 66–78.

Berlin, A. *Esther: A Commentary* (Mikra Leyisra'el; Jerusalem: Magnes Press / Tel Aviv: Am Oved, 2001; Hebrew).

Berlin, A. "The Book of Esther and Ancient Storytelling," *JBL* 120 (2001), pp. 3–14.

Bertheau, E. *Esra, Nechemia und Ester* (Kurzgefasstes Exegetisches Handbuch zum Alten Testament 17, Leipzig: Verlag von S. Hirzel, 1862).

Bertram, M. H. "Treatise on the Last Words of David: 2 Sam 23:1–7," in J. Pelikan and H. C. Oswald (eds.), *Luther's Works* (Saint Louis: Concordia, 1972), vol. 15, pp. 265–352.

Beutel, A. "Theologie als Schriftauslegung," in A. Beutel (ed.), *Lutherhandbuch* (2nd ed.; Universität-Taschenbücher 3416; Tübingen: Mohr Siebeck, 2010), pp. 444–449.

Beutel, A. "Wort Gottes," in A. Beutel (ed.), *Lutherhandbuch* (2nd ed.; Universität-Taschenbücher 3416; Tübingen: Mohr Siebeck, 2010), pp. 362–371.

Bickerman, E. J. "The Colophon of the Greek Book of Esther," *JBL* 63 (1944), pp. 339–362.

Bickerman, E. J. *Four Strange Books of the Bible* (New York: Schocken, 1967).

Bickerman, E. J. *The Jews in the Greek Age* (Cambridge, MA: Harvard University Press, 1988).

Binder, A. W. "Purim in Music," in Ph. Goodman (ed.), *The Purim Anthology* (Philadelphia: The Jewish Publication Society of America, 1952), pp. 209–221.

Bleek, F. *Einleitung in die Heilige Schrift*, Volume 1: *Einleitung in das Alte Testament* (3rd ed.; edited by J. Bleek and A. Kamphausen; Berlin: G. Reimer, 1870).

Bleek, F. *An Introduction to the Old Testament* (2 vols.; edited by J. Bleek and A. Kamphausen; translated from the 2nd German edition of 1865 by G. H. Venables; London: Bell and Daldy, 1869).

Bloch, R. S. *Antike Vorstellungen vom Judentum: Der Judenexkurs des Tacitus im Rahmen der griechisch-römischen Ethnographie* (Historia: Einyelschriften 160; Stuttgart: Steiner, 2002).

Blum-Dobkin, T. "The Landsberg Carnival: Purim in a Displaced Persons Center," in *Purim: The Face and the Mask, Essays and Catalogue of an Exhibition at the Yeshiva University Museum, February–June 1979* (New York: Yeshiva University Museum, 1979), pp. 53–57.

Boccaccini, G. *Beyond the Essene Hypothesis: The Parting of the Ways between Qumran and Enochic Judaism* (Grand Rapids, MI: W. B. Eerdmans, 1998).

Bolin, T. "The Temple of יהו at Elephantine and Persian Religious Policy," in D. V. Edelman (ed.), *The Triumph of Elohim: From Yahwisms to Judaisms* (Contributions to Biblical Exegesis & Theology 13; Kampen: Kok Pharos, 1995), pp. 127–144.

Börner-Klein, D. *Eine babylonische Auslegung der Ester-Geschichte: Der Midrasch in Megilla 10b-17a* (Judentum und Umwelt 30; Frankfurt am Main: Peter Lang, 1990).

Bornkamm, H. *Luther and the Old Testament* (translated from the original German [Tübingen: P. Siebeck, 1948] by E. W. and R. C. Gritsch; edited by V. I. Gruhn; 2nd ed.; Mifflintown, PA: Sigler Press, 1997).

Borst, J. (ed.), *P. Cornelius Tacitus Historien: Latain-Deutsch* (Zurich and Munich: Artemis Verlag, 1984),

Brandt, P. *Endgestalten des Kanons. Das Arrangement der Schriften Israels in der jüdischen und christlichen Bibel* (Bonner Biblische Beiträge 131; Berlin and Vienna: Philo, 2001).

Braude, W. G. *The Midrash on Psalms* (Yale Judaica Series 13; New Haven, CT: Yale University Press, 1959; 3rd ed., 1976).

Breneman, M. *Ezra, Nehemiah, Esther* (The New American Commentary 10; Nashville: Bradman & Holman, 1993).

Brenner, A. (ed.), *A Feminist Companion to Esther, Judith and Susanna* (Feminist Companion to the Bible; Sheffield: Sheffield Academic Press, 1995).

Brentio, I. [Brenz, J.], *In Epiftolam Pauli ad Philemo, nem, et in Historiam Esther, Commentarioli* (Frankfurt am Main: Petri Brubachij, 1570; first published 1543).

Bresciani, E. "Foreigners," in S. Donadoni (ed.), *The Egyptians* (Chicago and London: University of Chicago Press, 1997), pp. 221–253.

Briant, P. *Darius in the Shadow of Alexander* (translated by J. M. Todd; Cambridge, MA and London: Harvard University Press, 2015).

Briant, P. *From Cyrus to Alexander: A History of the Persian Empire* (Winona Lake, IN: Eisenbrauns, 2002).

Briggs, C. A. and E. G. Briggs, *A Critical and Exegetical Commentary on the Book of Psalms* (International Critical Commentary; Edinburgh: T. & T. Clark, 1907).

Bright, J. *The Authority of the Old Testament* (Grand Rapids, MI: Baker Book House, 1977).

Brown, F., S. R. Driver and C. A. Briggs, *A Hebrew and English Lexicon of the Old Testament* (Oxford: Clarendon Press, 1907).

Brown, L. E. "Esther," in A. S. Peake, M. Black and H. H. Rowley (eds.), *Peake's Commentary on the Bible* (rev. ed.; London and New York: T. Nelson, 1962), pp. 381–384.

Brownback, L. *Esther: The Hidden Hand of God* (Flourish Bible Study; Wheaton, IL: Crossway Books, 2020).

Brueggemann, W. *Theology of the Old Testament: Testimony, Dispute, Advocacy* (Minneapolis, MN: Fortress Press, 2000).

Buber, S. *Midrash Tehillim* (Vilna: Reem, 1891; reprinted, Jerusalem: Ch. Wagschal, 1977; Hebrew).

Buchwald, R. *Luther im Gespräch. Aufzeichnungen Seiner Freunde und Tischgenossen* (Stuttgart: Alfred Kröner Verlag, 1983).

Budde, K. *Geschichte der althebräischen Literatur* (Leipzig: C. F. Amelangs, 1906; 2nd ed. 1909).

Busch, E. *Unter dem Bogen des einen Bundes: Karl Barth und die Juden 1933–1945* (Neukichen-Vluyen: Neukirchner Verlag, 1996).

Bush, F. W. *Ruth, Esther* (Word Biblical Commentary 9; Dallas, TX: Word Books, 1996).

Bush, F. W. "The Book of Esther: *Opus non gratum* in the Christian Canon," *BBR* 8 (1998), pp. 39–54.

Bytwerk, R. L. *Landmark Speeches of National Socialism* (College Station, TX: A&M University Press, 2008).

Cameron, E. "The Luther Bible," in E. Cameron (ed.), *The New Cambridge History of the Bible: Volume 3 – From 1450–1750* (Cambridge: Cambridge University Press, 2016), pp. 217–238.

Cameron, G. G. *The Persepolis Treasury Tablets* (Chicago: University of Chicago Press, 1948).

Cameron, G. G. "The Persian Satrapies and Related Matters," *JNES* 32 (1973), pp. 47–56.

Caputo, N. "Regional History, Jewish Memory: The Purim of Narbonne," *Jewish History* 22 (2008), pp. 97–114.

Carroll, R. P. *Jeremiah: A Commentary* (The Old Testament Library; Philadelphia: Westminster Press, 1986).

Carruthers, J. *Esther through the Centuries* (Blackwell Bible Commentaries; Victoria: Blackwell, 2008).

Carson, A. *History of Providence as Manifested in Scripture* (4th ed.; New York: E. H. Fletcher, 1854).

Carson, A. *Providence Unfolded: Comprising the History of Providence as Unfolded in the Book of Esther* (2nd ed.; New York: E. H. Fletcher, 1852).

Cassel, P. *An Explanatory Commentary on Esther* (Clark's Foreign Theological Library 34; Edinburgh: T. & T. Clark, 1888).

Cazelles, H. "Note sur la composition du rouleau d'Esther," in H. Gross and F. Mussner (eds.), *Lex tua veritas* (Festschrift Hubert Jonker; Trier: Paulinus, 1961), pp. 17–29.

Childs, B. S. *Introduction to the Old Testament as Scripture* (Philadelphia: Fortress Press, 1979).

Clark, A. *The Holy Bible Containing the Old and New Testaments* (Baltimore: J. J. Harrod, 1834).

Clines, D. J. A. *Ezra, Nehemiah, Esther* (New Century Bible Commentary; Grand Rapids, MI: Wm. B. Eerdmans / London: Marshall, Morgan & Scott, 1984).

Clines, D. J. A. *The Esther Scroll: The Story of the Story* (Journal for the Study of the Old Testament Supplement Series 30; Sheffield: JSOT Press, 1984).

Cohen, A. A. and P. R. Mendes-Flohr (eds.), *20th Century Jewish Religious Thought: Original Essays on Critical Concepts, Movements, and Beliefs* (Philadelphia: Jewish Publication Society of America, 2009).

Cohen, A. D. "'Hu Ha-Gural': The Religious Significance of Esther," *Judaism* 23 (1974), pp. 87–129.

Collins, J. J. *A Commentary on the Book of Daniel* (Hermeneia; Minneapolis, MN: Fortress Press, 1993).

Collins, J. J. *Beyond the Qumran Community: The Sectarian Movement of the Dead Sea Scrolls* (Grand Rapids, MI: W. B. Eerdmans, 2010).

Colson, F. H. *Philo in Ten Volumes, with an English Translation* (vol. 9; The Loeb Classical Library; London: W. Heinemann / Cambridge, MA: Harvard University Press, 1967).

Cordoni, C. "'Wenn du in diesen Tagen schweigst' (Est 4,14): Zur mittelalterlichen biblischen Heldin Ester," in C. Bakhos and G. Langer (eds.), *Das jüdische Mittelalter* (Die Bibel und die Frauen 4,2; Stuttgart: W. Kohlhammer, 2020), pp. 37–56.

Cornill, C. H. *Einleitung in die kanonischen Bücher des Alten Testaments* (Grundriss der Theologischen Wissenschaften; 6th ed.; Tübingen: J. C. B. Mohr [P. Siebeck], 1908; 7th rev. ed., 1913).

Cowley, A. *Aramaic Papyri of the Fifth Century b.c.* (Oxford: Clarendon Press, 1923).

Coxon, P. W. "Shadrach," in D. N. Freedman *et al.* (eds.), *The Anchor Bible Dictionary* (New York: Doubleday, 1992), vol. 5, p. 1150.

Craigie, P. C., P. H. Kelley and J. Drinkard, *Jeremiah 1–25 (Word Biblical Commentary 26*; Dallas, TX: Word Books Publisher, 1991).

Crossan, J. D. *Who Killed Jesus? Exposing the Roots of Anti-Semitism in the Gospel Story of the Death of Jesus* (New York: HarperCollins, 1995).

Dalley, S. *Esther's Revenge at Susa: From Sennacherib to Ahasuerus* (Oxford and New York: Oxford University Press, 2007).

Daube, D. *Civil Disobedience in Antiquity* (Edinburgh: Edinburgh University Press, 1972).

David, Y. "Shmuel haNagid," *Encyclopedia Hebraica* (Jerusalem and Tel Aviv: Encyclopedia Publishing Company, 1981), vol. 32, pp. 45–47 (Hebrew).

Day, L. *Three Faces of a Queen* (Journal for the Study of the Old Testament Supplement Series 186; Sheffield: Sheffield Academic Press, 1995).

Demsky, A. *Literacy in Ancient Israel* (Biblical Encyclopedia Library 28; Jerusalem: Bialik Institute, 2012; Hebrew).

Diestel, L. *Geschichte des Alten Testaments in der christlichen Kirche* (Jena: Mauke, 1869).

Dingel, I. *Geschichte der Reformation* (Theologische Bibliothek 5; Göttingen: Vandenhoeck & Ruprecht, 2018).

Dommershausen, W. *Die Estherrolle: Stil und Ziel einer alttestamentlichen Schrift* (Stuttgarter Biblische Monographien; Stuttgart: Verlage Katholisches Bibelwerk, 1968).

Donner, H. and W. Röllig, *Kanaanäische und aramäische Inschriften*, Volume I: *Texte* (3rd ed.; Wiesbaden: Otto Harrassowitz, 1971).

Driver, S. R. *An Introduction to the Literature of the Old Testament* (9th ed.; Edinburgh: T. & T. Clark, 1913).

Duff, A. "Esther," in A. S. Peake and A. J. Grieve (eds.), *A Commentary on the Bible* (New York: T. Nelson & Sons, 1920), pp. 336–340.

Edwards, M. U. Jr., *Luther's Last Battles: Politics and Polemics, 1531–46* (Ithaca and London: Cornell University Press, 1983).

Ego, B. *Esther* (Biblischer Kommentar Altes Testament 21; Göttingen: Vandenhoeck & Ruprecht, 2017).

Ego, B. "The Book of Esther: A Hellenistic Book," *JAJ* 1 (2010), pp. 279–302.

Ego, B. *Targum Scheni zu Ester: Übersetzung, Kommentar und theologische Deutung* (Texte und Studien zum Antiken Judentum 54; Tübingen: J. C. B. Mohr [P. Siebeck], 1996).

Ehmann, J. *Luther und die Türken* (Studienreihe Luther 15; Bielefeld: Luther-Verlag, 2017).

Ehrlich, E. L. "Luther und die Juden," in H. Kremers *et al.* (eds.), *Die Juden und Martin Luther – Martin Luther und die Juden: Geschichte, Wirkungsgeschichte, Herausforderung* (Neukirchen-Vluyn: Neukirchener Verlag, 1985), pp. 72–88.

Eissfeldt, O. *Einleitung in das Alte Testament* (3rd ed.; Tübingen: J. C. B. Mohr [P. Siebeck], 1964).

Eissfeldt, O. *The Old Testament: An Introduction* (New York: Harper and Row, 1965).

Eliyahu of Vilna (Vilna Gaon). *Megillat Esther* (2nd ed.; Jerusalem: Yeshivat Tiferrat haTalmud, 1991; Hebrew).

Ellens, J. H. *Sex in the Bible: A New Consideration* (Westport, CT and London: Praeger, 2006).

Elon, A. *The Pity of It All: A History of Jews in Germany 1743–1933* (New York: Metropolitan Books, 2002).

Emmerson, G. I. "Esther," in R. J. Coggins and J. L. Houlden (eds.), *A Dictionary of Biblical Interpretation* (London: SCM Press, 1990), pp. 204–205.

Epp, E. J. "Early Christian Attitudes toward 'Things Jewish' as Narrated by Textual Variants in Acts: A Case Study of the D-Textual Cluster," in I. Kalimi (ed.), *Bridging between Sister Religions Studies in Jewish and Christian Scriptures Offered in Honor of Prof. John T. Townsend* (Brill Reference Library of Judaism 51; Leiden and Boston: Brill, 2016), pp. 141–171.

Epstein, I. (ed.), *Two Fest Days: I. 11th Adar – The Symbol of Renewed Judaism, II. Purim – The Symbol of Exile Judaism* (Warsaw: Betar, 1937).

Epstein, I. *The Babylonian Talmud: Seder Mo'ed* (London: Soncino, 1938).

Even-Shoshan, A. *A New Concordance of the Bible* (3rd ed.; Jerusalem: Kiryat Sefer, 1988).

Fackenheim, E. *The Jewish Bible after the Holocaust: A Rereading* (Bloomington, IN: Indiana University Press, 1990).

Falk, G. *The Jew in Christian Theology: Martin Luther's Anti-Jewish Vom Schem Hamphoras, Previously Unpublished in English, and Other Milestones in Church Doctrine Concerning Judaism* (Jefferson, NC and London: McFarland, 1992).

Felber, S. *Wilhelm Vischer als Ausleger der Heiligen Schrift: Eine Untersuchung zum Christuszeugnis des Alten Testaments* (Forschungen zur systematischen und ökumenischen Theologie 89; Göttingen: Vandenhoeck & Ruprecht, 1999).

Felber, S. "Vischer, Wilhelm Eduard," in F. W. Bautz and T. Bautz (eds.), *Biographisch-Bibliographisches Kirchenlexicon* (Herzberg: Verlag T. Bautz, 2000), vol. 17, pp. 1493–1504.

Feldman, L. H. *"Remember Amalek!" Vengeance, Zealotry, and Group Destruction in the Bible according to Philo, Pseudo-Philo, and Josephus* (Cincinnati: Hebrew Union College, 2004).

Feucht, E. "Kinder Fremder Völker in Ägypten," *Studien zur altägyptischen Kultur* 17 (1990), pp. 177–204.

Fichte, J. G. *Beitrag zur Berichtigung der Urteile des Publikums über die Französische Revolution* (first published 1793), in R. Lauth and H. Jacob (eds.), *J.-G. Fichte-Gesamtausgabe* I/1 (Stuttgart: Friedrich Frommann Verlag, 1964).

Finkel, J. "The Author of Genesis Apocryphon Knew the Book of Esther," in Y. Yadin and C. Rabin (eds.), *Essays on the Dead Sea Scrolls in Memory of E. L. Sukenik* (Jerusalem: The Shrine of the Book, 1962), pp. 163–182 (Hebrew).

Finkelstein, L. *The Pharisees* (Philadelphia: Jewish Publication Society of America, 1938).

Finkelstein, L. (ed.), *Sifre on Deuteronomy* (New York: The Jewish Theological Seminary of America, 1969).

Fleet, J. "History and Meaning of the Word 'Holocaust': Are We Still Comfortable with This Term?" Huffington Post (March 28, 2012): www.huffingtonpost .com/2012/01/27/the-word-holocaust-history-and-meaning_n_1229043.html

Flint, P. W. "David," in L. H. Schiffman and J. C. VanderKam (eds.), *Encyclopedia of the Dead Sea Scrolls* (Oxford: Oxford University Press, 2000), vol. 1, pp. 178–180.

Flint, P. W. *The Dead Sea Psalms Scrolls and the Book of Psalms* (Studies on the Texts of the Desert of Judah 17; Leiden and Boston: Brill, 1997).

Fowler, H. N. and W. R. M. Lamb, *Plato, Volume VIII: The Statesman, Philebus, Ion* (Loeb Classic Library 164; Cambridge, MA: Harvard University Press, 1925; reprinted 2006).

Fox, M. V. *Character and Ideology in the Book of Esther* (2nd ed.; Grand Rapids, MI: W. B. Eerdmans / Eugene, OR: Wipf & Stock, 2001).

Fox, M. V. *The Redaction of the Books of Esther: On Reading Composite Texts* (Society of Biblical Literature Monograph Series 40; Atlanta: Scholars Press, 1991).

Frahm, E. "Family Matters: Psychohistorical Reflections on Sennacherib and His Times," in I. Kalimi and S. Richardson (eds.), *Sennacherib at the Gates of Jerusalem: Story, History and Historiography* (Culture and History of the Ancient Near East 71; Leiden and Boston: Brill, 2014), pp. 163–222.

Friedlander, G. *Pirke de Rabbi Eliezer* (2nd ed.; New York: Hermon Press, 1965).

Friedman, C. Y. (ed.), *Menot Halevi* (Brooklyn, NY, 1996).

Friedrichs, C. R. "Politics or Pogrom? The Fettmilch Uprising in German and Jewish History," *Central European History* 19 (1986), pp. 186–228.

Fries, J. F. *Über die Gefährdung des Wohlstandes und Charakters der Deutschen durch die Juden* (Heidelberg: Mohr und Winter, 1816).

Fuerst, W. J. *The Books of Ruth, Esther, Ecclesiastes, the Song of Songs, Lamentations: The Five Scrolls* (Cambridge Bible Commentaries on the Old Testament; Cambridge: Cambridge University Press, 1975).

Furley, D. J. "On the Cosmos," in E. S. Forster and D. J. Furley, *Aristotle*, Volume 3: *On Sophisticated Refutations, On Coming-To-Be and Passing-Away, On the Cosmos* (Loeb Classical Library 400; Cambridge, MA: Harvard University Press, 1955; reprinted 2000).

Galle, V. (ed.), *Josel von Rosheim: Zwischen dem Einzigartigen und Universellen. Ein engagierter Jude im Europa seiner Zeit und im Europa unserer Zeit* (Worms: Worms Verlag, 2013).

Gambetti, S. *The Alexandrian Riots of 38 C.E. and the Persecution of the Jews: A Historical Reconstruction* (Supplements to the Journal for the Study of Judaism 135; Leiden and Boston: Brill, 2009).

Gan, M. "The Book of Esther in the Light of the Story of Joseph in Egypt," *Tarbiz* 31 (1961–1962), pp. 144–149 (Hebrew).

García Martínez, F. and J. C. Trebolle Barrera, *The People of the Dead Sea Scrolls: Their Writings, Beliefs and Practices* (translated by W. G. E. Watson; Leiden and Boston: Brill, 1995).

Gaster, T. H. *The Festivals of the Jewish Year* (New York: William Sloane Associate Publishers, 1953), pp. 215–232.

Gehman, H. "Notes on the Persian Words in the Book of Esther," *JBL* 43 (1924), pp. 321–328.

Geiger L. (ed.), *Abraham Geiger's Nachgelassene Schriften* (Berlin: Gerschel, 1875–1878).

Gelb, I. J. *et al.* (eds.), *The Assyrian Dictionary of the Oriental Institute of the University of Chicago* (= *CAD*; 20 vols.; Chicago: The Oriental Institute; Glückstadt: J. and J. Augustin, 1956–2010).

Gerleman, G. *Esther* (Biblischer Kommentar Altes Testament 21; Neukirchen-Vluyn: Neukirchener Verlag, 1973).

Gerleman, G. *Ruth. Das Hohelied* (Biblischer Kommentar Altes Testament 18; Neukirchen-Vluyn: Neukirchner Verlag, 1965).

Gertoux, G. "Dating the Reigns of Xerxes and Artaxerxes," www.academia.edu/2421036/ (accessed February 1, 2016).

Gertoux, G. "The Book of Esther: Is It a Fairy Tale or History?" www.academia.edu/8233800/ (accessed February 1, 2016).

Gesenius, W. *Hebräisches und Aramäisches Handwörterbuch über das Alte Testament* (Berlin and Heidelberg: Springer, 2013).

Gibson, J. C. L. *Textbook of Syrian Semitic Inscriptions*, Volume 1: *Hebrew and Moabite Inscriptions* (Oxford: Clarendon Press, 1973).

Gilbert, M. *The Holocaust: A History of the Jews of Europe during the Second World War* (New York: H. Holt, 1986).

Ginsberg, H. L. "Elephantine Papyri," in Pritchard, *ANET*, p. 492.

Gitay, Z. "Esther and the Queen's Throne," in A. Brenner (ed.), *Feminist Companion to Esther, Judith and Susanna* (Sheffield: Sheffield Academic Press, 1995), pp. 136–148.

Glatzer, N. N. "Leopold Zunz and the Revolution of 1848: With the Publication of Four Letters by Zunz," *Leo Baeck Institute Yearbook* 5 (1960), pp. 122–139.

Godley, A. D. *Herodotus with an English Translation* (4 vols.; Loeb Classical Library; London: William Heinemann / Cambridge, MA: Harvard University Press, 1920–1925).

Goethe, J. W. von, "Paralipomena," in E. Beutler (ed.) *Gedenkausgabe der Werke, Briefe und Gespräche* (Zurich: Artemis Verlag, 1949), vol. 5, pp. 539–619.

Goethe, J. W. von, *Sämtliche Werke nach Epochen seines Schaffens* (Munich: Carl Hanser Verlag, 1987).

Golb, N. *Who Wrote the Dead Sea Scrolls: The Search for the Secret of Qumran* (New York: Simon & Schuster, 1995).

Gómez Aranda, M. *Dos Comentarios de Abraham ibn Ezra al Libro de Ester: Edición Crítica, Traducción y Estudio Itroductorio* (Madrid: Instituto de Filologia, 2007).

Goodman, Ph. *The Purim Anthology* (Philadelphia: The Jewish Publication Society of America, 1960).

Gordis, R. *Megillat Esther: The Masoretic Hebrew Text* (New York: Ktav, 1974).

Gordis, R. "Studies in the Esther Narrative," *JBL* 95 (1976), pp. 43–58.

Göttert, K.-H. *Luthers Bibel: Geschichte einer feindlichen Übernahme* (Fischer Wissenschaft; Frankfurt am Main: S. Fischer, 2017).

Greenfield, J. C. "Aramaic Language in the Persian Period," in H. Tadmor (ed.), *The History of the Jewish People: The Restoration – The Persian Period* (Jerusalem: Am Oved, 1983), pp. 224–228, 310–311 (Hebrew).

Greenstein, E. L. "A Jewish Reading of Esther," in J. Neusner, B. A. Levine, and E. S. Frerichs (eds.), *Judaic Perspectives on Ancient Israel* (Philadelphia: Fortress Press, 1987), pp. 225–243.

Gritsch, E. W. *Martin Luther's Antisemitism: Against His Better Judgement* (Grand Rapids, MI: Eerdmans, 2012).

Gross, A. "R. Abraham Saba 'the Exilant of two Exiles'," in M. Beniyahu (ed.), *The Memorial Volume of Rab Yitzchak Nissim* (Jerusalem: Yad Harav Nissim, 1985), pp. 205–224 (Hebrew).

Gross, A. "The Reflection of Spain and Portugal Expulsions in a Commentary on Megillat Esther," *Proceedings of the Ninth World Congress of Jewish Studies* (Jerusalem: World Union of Jewish Studies, 1986), Division B, vol. 1, pp. 153–158 (Hebrew).

Gross, A. *Iberian Jewry from Twilight to Dawn: The World of Abraham Saba* (Leiden and Boston: Brill, 1995).

Grossfeld, B. *The Targum Sheni to the Book of Esther: A Critical Edition Based on MS. Sassoon 282 with Critical Apparatus* (New York: Sepher-Hermon Press, 1994).

Grossfeld, B. *The Two Targums of Esther: Translated, with Apparatus and Notes* (The Aramaic Bible 18; Collegeville, MN: Liturgical Press, 1991).

Gunkel, H. "Estherbuch," in *Die Religion in Geschichte und Gegenwart* (Erste Auflage; Tübingen: J. C. B. Mohr [P. Siebeck], 1910), pp. 647–653.

Gunkel, H. *Esther* (Religionsgeschichtliche Volksbücher, 2. Reihe, Heft 19/20, Tübingen: Mohr Siebeck, 1916).

Gutschmid, A. von, "Vorlesungen über Josephos' Bücher gegen Apion," in F. Rühl (ed.), *Kleine Schriften* (Leipzig: B. G. Teubner, 1893), pp. 336–589.

Haag, E. H. *Daniel* (Die Neue Echter Bibel; Würzburg: Echter, 1993).

Haenchen, E. "Hamans Galgen und Christi Kreuz," in H. Gerdes (ed.), *Wahrheit und Glaube: Festschrift für Emanuel Hirsch* (Itzehoe: Die Spur, 1963), pp. 113–133.

Haller, M. *Das Judentum: Geschichtsschreibung, Prophetie und Gesetzgebung nach dem Exil* (Schriften des Alten Testament 2/3; Göttingen: Vandenhoeck & Ruprecht, 1914).

Hallo, W. "The First Purim," *BA* 46/1 (1983), pp. 19–29.

Hallock, R. T. *Persepolis Fortification Tablets* (Chicago: University of Chicago Press, 1969).

Hammann, K. *Hermann Gunkel: Eine Biographie* (Tübingen: Mohr Siebeck, 2014).

Hanhart, R. (ed.), *Esther* (Septuaginta: Vetus Testamentum Graecum Auctoritate Academiae Litterarum Gottingensis editum 8,3; Göttingen: Vandenhoeck & Ruprecht, 1966; 2nd ed., 1983).

Hartman, L. F. and A. A. Di Lella, *The Book of Daniel: A New Translation with Notes and Commentary* (Anchor Bible 23; Garden City, NY: Doubleday, 1978).

Harvey, C. D. *Finding Morality in the Diaspora? Moral Ambiguity and Transformed Morality in the Books of Esther* (Beihefte zur Zeitschrift für die alttestamentliche Wissenschaft 328; Berlin: Walter de Gruyter, 2003).

Haydock, G. L. *The Holy Bible*, Translated from the Latin Vulgate, with Useful Notes, Critical, Historical, Controversial, and Explanatory (New York: E. Dunigan, 1855).

Heine, H. "Zur Geschichte der Religion und Philosophie in Deutschland," *Revue des deux Mondes* (December 1834), pp. 81–82.

Hempel, J. *Luther und das Alte Testament* (Bremen: Hauschild, 1935).

Hempel, J. "Luther und das Alte Testament," *Die Christus bekennende Reichskirche* 4 (1935), pp. 1–16.

Hempel, J. *Das Ethos des Alten Testaments* (Beihefte zur Zeitschrift für die alttestamentliche Wissenschaft 67; Berlin: Alfred Töpelmann, 1938; 2nd rev. ed. published by Walter de Gruyter, 1964, and reprinted in 2019).

Hempel, J. "Chronik," *ZAW* 59 (1942/43), pp. 209–215.

Hengel, M. *The "Hellenization" of Judaea in the First Century after Christ* (London: SCM Press / Philadelphia: Trinity Press International, 1989).

Henry, M. *An Exposition of the Old and New Testament: With Practical Remarks and Observations* (6 vols.; London: J. Clark, 1721–1725).

Hentschel, G. *1. Könige* (Echter Bibel 10; Würzburg: Echter Verlag, 1984).

Heschel, S. *The Aryan Jesus: Christian Theologians and the Bible in Nazi Germany* (Princeton: Princeton University Press, 2008).

Herder, J. G. von, *Über die neuere Deutsche Literatur. Fragmente, als Beilagen zu den Briefen, die neueste Litteratur betreffend* (Riga, 1767).

Herrmann, W. *Ester im Streit der Meinungen* (Beiträge zur Erforschung des Alten Testaments und des antiken Judentums 4; Frankfurt am Main: Peter Lang, 1986).

Higger, M. "Pirke Rabbi Eliezer," *Horeb* 10 (1948), p. 243 (Hebrew).

Hoffman, Y. "Holy Is Israel to God," in M. Haran (ed.), *Companion to the Biblical World*, Volume II: *The Book of Jeremiah* (Ramat Gan: Revivim, 1983), p. 29 (Hebrew).

Hofmann, I. and A. Vorbichler, "Herodot und der Schreiber des Esther-Buches," *Zeitschrift für Missionswissenschaft und Religionswissenschaft* 66 (1982), pp. 294–302.

Holm, T. L. "Memories of Sennacherib in Aramaic Tradition," in I. Kalimi and S. Richardson (eds.), *Sennacherib at the Gates of Jerusalem: Story, History and Historiography* (Culture and History of the Ancient Near East 71; Leiden and Boston: Brill, 2014), pp. 295–323.

Hoping, H. "Freiheit und Sünde: Zur Bedeutung von Martin Luthers 'De servo arbitrio' für die theologische Anthropologie," in C. Danz and J.-H. Tück (eds.), *Martin Luther im Widerstreit der Konfessionen: Historische und theologische Perspektiven* (Freiburg im Breisgau, Basel and Vienna: Herder, 2017), pp. 227–244.

Horowitz, E. *Reckless Rites: Purim and the Legacy of Jewish Violence* (Jews, Christians, and Muslims from the Ancient to the Modern World; Princeton and Oxford: Princeton University Press, 2006).

Horowitz, E. "Esther: Purimspiels," *Encyclopedia of the Bible and Its Reception* (Berlin: Walter de Gruyter, 2014), vol. 8, p. 28.

Horst, P. W. van der, *Philo's Flaccus: The First Pogrom* (Philo of Alexandria Commentary Series 2; Leiden and Boston: Brill, 2003).

Horst, P. W. van der, "The Myth of Jewish Cannibalism: A Chapter in the History of Antisemitism," *Israel Academy of Sciences and Humanities Proceedings* (Jerusalem: Israel Academy of Sciences and Humanities, 2008), vol. VIII (no. 3), pp. 43–56.

Hoschander, J. *The Book of Esther in the Light of History* (Ph.D. Dissertation, Dropsie College; Philadelphia, 1923).

Höss, I. *Georg Spalatin – 1484–1545: Ein Leben in der Zeit des Humanismus und der Reformation* (Weimar: Hermann Böhlaus Nachfolger, 1956).

Howard, C. B. R. "When Esther and Jezebel Write: A Feminist Biblical Theology of Authority," in P. K. Tull and J. E. Lapsley (eds.), *After Exegesis: Feminist Biblical Theology: Essays in Honor of Carol A. Newsom* (Waco, TX: Baylor University Press, 2015), pp. 109–122.

Hubbard R. L., "Vashti, Amestris and Esther 1,9," *ZAW* 119 (2007), pp. 259–271.

Humphreys, W. L. "A Life-Style for Diaspora: A Study of the Tales of Esther and Daniel," *JBL* 92 (1973), pp. 211–223.

Hunger, H. (ed.), *Astronomical Diaries and Related Texts from Babylonia: Volume V, Lunar and Planetary Texts* (Vienna: Verlag der Österreichischen Akademie der Wissenschaften, 2001).

Hutter, M. *Iranische Namen in Semitischen Nebenüberlieferungen – Faszikel 2: Iranische Personalnamen in der Hebräische Bibel* (Vienna: Verlag der Österreichischen Akademie der Wissenschaft, 2015).

Ibn Verga, S. *The Tribe of Judah* (edited and introduced by Y. Baer; Jerusalem: Bialik Institute, 1947; Hebrew).

Jacobs, C. M. (trans.), "Prefaces to the Old Testament," in E. T. Bachmann (ed.), *Luther's Works,* Volume 35: *Word and Sacrament I* (Philadelphia: Muhlenberg, 1960), pp. 233–333.

Jacobs, C. M. and E. T. Bachmann (trans.), "Prefaces to the New Testament," in E. T. Bachmann (ed.), *Luther's Works,* Volume 35: *Word and Sacrament I* (Philadelphia: Muhlenberg, 1960), pp. 355–412.

Janzen, J. G. *Studies in the Text of Jeremiah* (Harvard Semitic Monographs 6; Cambridge, MA: Harvard University Press, 1973).

Jensen, P. "Elamitische Eigennamen: Ein Beitrag zur Erklärung der elamitischen Inschriften," *WZKM* 6 (1892), pp. 47–70, 209–226.

Jensen, P. *Moses, Jesus, Paulus: Drei Varianten des babylonisches Gottmenschen Gilgamesh* (2nd ed.; Frankfurt am Main: Neuer Frankfurter Verlag, 1909).

Jepsen, A. "Zur Kanongeschichte des Altes Testaments," *ZAW* 71 (1959), pp. 114–136.

Jobes, K. H. *The Alpha-Text of Esther: Its Character and Relationship to the Masoretic Text* (Society of Biblical Literature Dissertation Series 153; Atlanta: Scholars Press, 1996).

Jobes, K. H. "Esther," in A. Pietersma and B. G. Wright (eds.), *A New English Translation of the Septuagint and the Other Greek Translation Traditionally Included under that Name* (= *NETS*; New York and Oxford: Oxford University Press, 2007), pp. 424–440.

Johnson, L. T. "James, Letter of," in J. H. Hayes (ed.), *Dictionary of Biblical Interpretation* (Nashville: Abingdon Press, 1999), vol. 1, pp. 560–561.

Johnson, P. *A History of the Jews* (London: Weidenfeld and Nicolson, 1987).

Jones, B. W. "Two Misconceptions about the Book of Esther," *CBQ* 39 (1977), pp. 171–181.

Jones, C. P. *Philostratus: The Life of Apollonius of Tyana Books V–VIII* (Loeb Classic Library; Cambridge, MA: Harvard University Press, 2005).

Jones, H. L. *The Geography of Strabo with an English Translation* (vol. 7; Loeb Classical Library; London: Heinemann / Cambridge, MA: Harvard University Press, 1961).

Junker, H. "Konsonantenumstellung als Fehlerquelle und textkritischer Hilfsmittel im massoretischen Text," in P. Volz, F. Stummer and J. Hempel (eds.), *Werden und Wesen des Alten Testaments* (BZAW 66; Berlin: Alfred Töpelmann, 1936), pp. 162–174.

Kahana, H. *Esther: Juxtaposition of the Septuagint Translation with the Hebrew Text* (Contributions to Biblical Exegesis and Theology 40; Leuven and Boston: Peeters, 2005).

Kalimi, I. *An Ancient Israelite Historian: Studies in the Chronicler, His Time, Place, and Writing* (Studia Semitica Neerlandica 46; Assen: Royal Van Gorcum [now under: Brill, Leiden], 2005).

Kalimi, I. "The Centrality and Interpretation of Psalms in Judaism Prior to and during Medieval Times: Approaches, Authorship, Genre and Polemics," *RRJ* 23 (2020), pp. 229–259.

Kalimi, I. *Das Chronikbuch und seine Chronik: Zur Entstehung und Rezeption eines biblischen Buches* (Fuldaer Studien 17; Freiburg im Breisgau, Basel and Vienna: Herder Verlag, 2013).

Kalimi, I. *Early Jewish Exegesis and Theological Controversy: Studies in Scriptures in the Shadow of Internal and External Controversies* (Jewish and Christian Heritage Series 2; Assen: Van Gorcum [now under: Brill, Leiden], 2002).

Kalimi, I. *Fighting over the Bible: Jewish Interpretation and Polemic from Temple to Talmud and Beyond* (The Brill Reference Library of Judaism 54; Leiden and Boston: Brill, 2017).

Kalimi, I. "Go, I Beg You, Take Your Beloved Son and Slay Him!: Binding of Isaac in Rabbinic Literature and Thought," *RRJ* 13 (2010), pp. 1–29.

Kalimi, I. "He Was Born Circumcised," *Early Jewish Exegesis and Theological Controversy: Studies in Scriptures in the Shadow of Internal and External Controversies* (Jewish and Christian Heritage 2; Assen: Royal Van Gorcum [now under: Brill, Leiden and Boston], 2002), pp. 61–76.

Kalimi, I. "History of Israelite Religion or Hebrew Bible/ Old Testament Theology? Jewish Interest in Biblical Theology," *Early Jewish Exegesis and Theological Controversy: Studies in Scriptures in the Shadow of Internal and External Controversies* (Jewish and Christian Heritage 2; Assen: Royal Van Gorcum [now under: Brill, Leiden and Boston], 2002), pp. 107–134.

Kalimi, I. *How the Mighty Have Fallen: The Disastrous Destiny of Arrogant Leaders in Ancient Mediterranean Cultures* (in press).

Kalimi, I. "Jewish Bible Translations," in K. J. Dell (ed.), *The Biblical World* (2nd ed.; London: Routledge, 2021), pp. 889–905.

Kalimi, I. "The Position of Martin Luther towards Jews and Judaism: Historical, Social, and Theological Venues," *JR* 103 (2023).

Kalimi, I. *Metathesis in the Hebrew Bible: Wordplay as a Literary and Exegetical Device* (Peabody, MA: Hendrickson Publishers, 2018).

Kalimi, I. "Persepolis," in K. D. Sakenfeld (ed.), *The New Interpreter's Dictionary of the Bible* (Nashville, TN: Abingdon Press, 2009), vol. 4, pp. 450–451.

Kalimi, I. "Placing the Chronicler in His Own Historical Context: A Closer Examination," *JNES* 68 (2009), pp. 179–192.

Kalimi, I. "Religionsgeschichte Israels oder Theologie des Alten Testaments? Das Jüdische Interesse an der Biblischen Theologie," *JBTh* 10 (1995; 2nd ed. 2001), pp. 45–68.

Kalimi, I. *The Reshaping of Ancient Israelite History in Chronicles* (Winona Lake, IN: Eisenbrauns, 2005; reprinted 2012).

Kalimi, I. *The Retelling of Chronicles in Jewish Tradition and Literature: A Historical Journey* (Winona Lake, IN: Eisenbrauns, 2009).

Kalimi, I. "Salem," in *Das wissenschaftliche Bibellexikon im Internet* (Stuttgart: Deutsche Bibelgesellschaft Stuttgart, 2015): www.bibelwissenschaft.de/stichwort/25882/

Kalimi, I. "'So Let Him Go Up [to Jerusalem]!': A Historical and Theological Observation on Cyrus' Decree in Chronicles," *An Ancient Israelite Historian: Studies in the Chronicler, His Time, Place, and Writing* (Studia Semitica Neerlandica 46; Assen: Van Gorcum [now under Brill, Leiden and Boston] 2005), pp. 143–157.

Kalimi, I. "The Task of Hebrew Bible/ Old Testament Theology: Between Judaism and Christianity," *Early Jewish Exegesis and Theological Controversy: Studies in Scriptures in the Shadow of Internal and External Controversies* (Jewish and Christian Heritage 2; Assen: Royal Van Gorcum [now under: Brill, Leiden and Boston], 2002), pp. 135–158.

Kalimi, I. *Zur Geschichtsschreibung des Chronisten* (Beihefte zur Zeitschrift für die alttestamentliche Wissenschaft 226; Berlin and New York: Walter de Gruyter, 1995).

Kara, J. *Oṣar Tob: Commentary on the Book of Esther* (published by E. Hübsch, A. Jellinek and A. Berliner; 1878).

Karib, A. (ed.), *Selected Writings of Rabbi Judah Loew ben Bezalel* (Jerusalem: Mossad Harav Kook, 1960; Hebrew).

Kaufmann, T. *Luthers Juden* (2nd ed.; Stuttgart: Reclam, 2015).

Kaufmann, T. *Luthers "Judenschriften": Ein Beitrag zu ihrer historischen Kontextualisierung* (Tübingen: Mohr Siebeck 2011).

Kaufmann, Y. *History of the Religion of Israel: From Its Beginnings to the Babylonian Exile* (vol. 8; Jerusalem and Tel Aviv: Bialik Institute and Dvir, 1972; Hebrew).

Keil, C. F. *Biblischer Commentar über die Nachexilischen Geschichtsbücher: Chronik, Esra, Nehemia und Esther* (Leipzig: Dürffling und Franke, 1870).

Keil, C. F. *The Books of Ezra, Nehemiah, and Esther* (Edinburgh: T. & T. Clark, 1873).

Kessler, R. "Die Juden als Kindes- und Frauenmörder? Zu Est 8,11," in E. Blum, Ch. Macholz, and E. W. Stegemann (eds.), *Die hebräische Bibel und ihre zweifache Nachgeschichte: Festschrift für Rolf Rendtorff zum 65. Geburtstag* (Neukirchen–Vluyn: Neukirchener Verlag, 1990), pp. 337–345.

Kissinger, H. *World Order: Reflections on the Character of Nations and the Course of History* (London: Penguin, 2014).

Kittel, R. *Die Psalmen übersetzt und erklärt* (Kommentar zum Alten Testament 13; 6th ed.; Leipzig: A. Deichertsche Verlagsbuchhandlung D. Werner Scholl, 1929).

Koch, H. *Persepolis: Glänzende Hauptstadt des Perserreichs* (Mainz: von Zabern, 2001).

Koch, K. *Daniel* (Biblischer Kommentar Altes Testament 22.1; Neukirchen-Vluyn: Neukirchener Verlag, 1986).

Koenigsberg, Ch. S. "Accounting for Tradition: Calculations in the Commentary of R. Eleazar of Worms to Esther," *Megadim – Journal of Biblical Studies* 60 (2021), pp. 41–54.

Koller, A. *Esther in Ancient Jewish Thought* (Cambridge: Cambridge University Press, 2014).

Kottsieper, I. "Die Religionspolitik der Achämeniden und die Juden von Elephantine," in R. G. Kratz (ed.), *Religion und Religionskontakte in Zeitalter der Achämeniden* (Veröffentlichungen der Wissenschaftlichen Gesellschaft für Theologie 22; Gütersloh: Gütersloher Verlagshaus Gerd Mohn, 2002), pp. 150–178.

Kottsieper, I. *Zusätze zu Ester* (Altes Testament Deutsch Apokryphen 5; Göttingen: Vandenhoeck & Ruprecht, 1998).

Kraeling, C. H. *The Synagogue: The Excavations at Dura-Europos – Final Report* (New Haven, CT: Yale University Press, 1956).

Kraus, H.-J. *Psalms 60–150: A Continental Commentary* (translated by H. C. Oswald; Minneapolis: Augsburg Fortress, 1989).

Kremers, H., L. Siegele-Wenschkewitz, and B. Klappert (eds.), *Die Juden und Martin Luther – Martin Luther und die Juden: Geschichte, Wirkungsgeschichte, Herausforderung* (Neukirchen-Vluyn: Neukirchener Verlag, 1985).

Kuhl, C. *Die Entstehung des Alten Testaments* (Munich: Lehnen Verlag, 1953).

Kuhrt, A. *The Persian Empire: A Corpus of Sources from the Achaemenid Period* (London and New York: Routledge, 2007).

Kuschel, K.-J. "Martin Luther, die Türken und der Islam: Ein schwieriges Erbe als Auftrag für Heute," in C. Danz and J.-H. Tück (eds.), *Martin Luther im Widerstreit der Konfessionen: Historische und theologische Perspektiven* (Freiburg im Breisgau, Basel and Vienna: Herder, 2017), pp. 443–468.

LaCocque, A. "The Different Versions of Esther," *BibInt* 7 (1999), pp. 301–322.

LaCocque, A. "Haman in the Book of Esther," *HAR* 11 (1987), pp. 207–222.

Lapide, P. E. "'Der Mann, von dem alle sprechen': Der Junge Luther aus zeitgenössischer Sicht," *Lutherische Monatshefte* 14 (1975), pp. 527–530.

Lehmann, H. "Luther und die Juden: Stolpersteine auf dem Weg zur Fünfhundertjahrfeier der Reformation 2017," in C. Danz and J.-H. Tück (eds.), *Martin Luther im Widerstreit der Konfessionen: Historische und theologische Perspektiven* (Freiburg im Breisgau, Basel and Vienna: Herder, 2017), pp. 428–442

Lehnardt, A. (ed.), *Das verbotene Purim-Spiel: Le-Haman aus Frankfurt am Main* (Wiesbaden: Harrassowitz, 2021).

Lerner, M. B. "The Works of Aggadic Midrash and the Esther Midrashim," in S. Safrai, Z. Safrai, J. Schwartz, and P. J. Tomson (eds.), *The Literature of the Sages* (Assen: Royal Van Gorcum / Minneapolis, MN: Fortress Press, 2006), part 2, pp. 133–230

Levenson, J. D. *Esther: A Commentary* (The Old Testament Library; Louisville, KT: Westminster John Knox Press, 1997).

Levit-Tawil, D. "The Enthroned King Ahasuerus at Dura in Light of the Iconography of Kingship in Iran," *BASOR* 250 (1983), pp. 57–58.

Levine, A.-J. *The Misunderstood Jew: The Church and the Scandal of the Jewish Jesus* (New York: HarperCollins, 2006)

Levy, J. H. *Studies in Jewish Hellenism* (Jerusalem: Bialik Institute, 1960; Hebrew).

Lewin, R. *Luthers Stellung zu den Juden: Ein Beitrag zur Geschichte der Juden in Deutschland während des Reformationszeitalters* (Breslau, 1911; reprinted: Aalen, 1973).

Lewinsky, Y.-T. *The Book of Holidays* (Tel Aviv: Dvir & The Oneg Shabbat Society [Ohel Shem], 1955).

Lewy, J. "Nāḫ et Rušpān," *Mélanges syriens offerts à monsieur René Dussaud* (Paris: Geuthner, 1939), vol. 1, pp. 273–275.

Liddell, H. G. and R. Scott, *A Greek-English Lexicon* (9th ed.; revised by H. S. Jones and R. McKenzie; Oxford: Clarendon Press, 1940).

Linafelt, T. *Ruth* (Brit Olam; Collegeville, MN: Liturgical Press, 1999).

Linafelt, T. (ed.), *Strange Fire: Reading the Bible after the Holocaust* (The Biblical Seminar 71; Sheffield: Sheffield Academic Press, 2000).

Lindenberger, J. M. "What Ever Happened to Vidranga? A Jewish Liturgy of Cursing from Elephantine," in P. M. Michèle Daviau (ed.), *The World of the Aramaeans III: Studies in Language and Literature in Honour of Paul-Eugène Dion* (Journal for the Study of the Old Testament Supplement Series 326; Sheffield: Sheffield Academic, 2001), pp. 134–157.

Liver, J. "Cyrus," *Encyclopedia Biblica* (Jerusalem: Bialik Institute, 1962), vol. 4, pp. 55–64 (Hebrew).

Llewellyn-Jones, L. and J. Robson, *Ctesias' History of Persia: Tales of the Orient* (Routledge Classical Translations; London and New York: Routledge, 2010).

Loewenstamm, S. E. "Esther 9:29—32: The Genesis of a Late Addition," *HUCA* 42 (1971), pp. 117–124.

Loprieno, A. "Slaves," in S. Donadoni (ed.), *The Egyptians* (Chicago and London: University of Chicago Press, 1997), pp. 185–219.

Lubetski E. and M. Lubetski, *The Book of Esther: A Classified Bibliography* (Sheffield: Phoenix Press, 2008).

Ludolphy, I. *Frederick the Wise: Elector of Saxony 1463–1525* (reprint of the first edition in 1984, Leipzig: Leipziger Universitätsverlag, 2006).

Luria, D. *Josephus on the Book of Esther: The Sources, Intentions and Virtues* (Tel Aviv: Resling, 2015; Hebrew).

Luther, M. *On the Bondage of the Will; to the Venerable Mister Erasmus of Rotterdam, 1525* (translated by E. T. Vaughan; London: Hamilton, Paternoster-Row and Combe, 1823).

Luther, M. "Vorlesung über den Römerbrief 1515/1516," in H. H. Borchert and G. Merz (eds.), *Ausgewählte Werke: Ergänzungsreihe* (vol. 2; 3rd ed.; Munich: Chr. Kaiser Verlag, 1957).

Luther, M. *Werke: Kritische Gesam(m)tausgabe* (= WA; 121 volumes; Weimar: Hermann Böhlaus Nachfolger, 1883–2009).

Luzatto, S. D. *Erläutungen über einen Theil der Propheten und Hagiographen* (Lemberg: Verlag A. Isaak Menkes, 1876; Hebrew).

Maccoby H. *Judaism on Trial: Jewish-Christian Disputations in the Middle Age* (Rutherford, NJ: Fairleigh Dickinson University Press / London and Toronto: Associated University Press, 1982).

Machinist, P. "Achaemenid Persia as Spectacle, Reactions from Two Peripherical Voices: Aeschylus, *The Persians* and the Book of Esther," *Eretz-Israel* 33 (L. E. Stager Volume; Jerusalem: Israel Exploration Society, 2018), pp. 109*–123*.

Magness, J. *The Archaeology of Qumran and the Dead Sea Scrolls* (Grand Rapids, MI and Cambridge: W. B. Eerdmans, 2002).

Magonet, J. "The Liberal and the Lady: Esther Revisited," *Judaism* 29 (1980), pp. 167–176.

Marcus, R. *Josephus with an English Translation* (vol. 6; Loeb Classical Library; London: William Heinemann / Cambridge, MA: Harvard University Press, 1958).

Marcus, R. *Josephus with an English Translation* (vol. 9; Loeb Classical Library; London: William Heinemann / Cambridge, MA: Harvard University Press, 1943; reprinted 2006).

Matter, E. A. "The Church Fathers and the *Glossa Ordinaria*," in I. D. Backus (ed.), *The Reception of the Church Fathers in the West*, Volume 1: *From the Carolingians to the Maurists* (Leiden and Boston: Brill, 1997), pp. 83–111.

Maurus, R. "Expositio in librum Esther," in J. P. Migne (ed.), *Patrologiae Latinae* volume 109 (Paris: Garnier, 1852), pp. 635–670.

Mazar, B. "The Exodus and the Conquest," in B. Mazar (ed.), *The World History of the Jewish People – First Series: Ancient Times*, Volume III: *Judges* (New Brunswick, NJ: Rutgers University Press, 1971), pp. 69–93.

McClain-Walters, M. *The Esther Anointing: Becoming a Woman of Prayer, Courage, and Influence* (Lake Mary, FL: Charisma House, 2014).

McKane, W. *A Critical and Exegetical Commentary on Jeremiah* (2 vols.; International Critical Commentary; Edinburgh: T. & T. Clark, 1986).

McKane, W. "A Note on Esther IX and I Samuel XV," *JTS* 12 (1961), pp. 260–261.

Meek, T. J. "Review of *the Book of Esther in the Light of History* by J. Hoschander," *The American Historical Review* 29 (1924), pp. 744–745.

Meinhold, A. *Das Buch Esther* (Zürcher Bibelkommentare; Zurich: Theologischer Verlag, 1983).

Meinhold, A. "Die Gattung der Josephsgeschichte und des Estherbuches: Diasporanovelle," *ZAW* 87 (1975), pp. 306–324; 88 (1976), pp. 72–93.

Meinhold, A. "Esther/ Estherbuch," in H. D. Betz *et al.* (ed.), *Religion in Geschichte und Gegenwart* (4th ed.; Tübingen: Mohr Siebeck, 1999), vol. 2, pp. 1594–1597.

Meinhold, J. *Einführung in das Alte Testament: Geschichte, Literatur und Religion Israels* (3rd ed.; Die Theologie im Abriß 1; Gießen: Alfred Töpelmann, 1932).

Melton, B. N. *Where Is God in the Megilloth? A Dialogue on the Ambiguity of Divine Presence and Absence* (Oudtestamentische Studiën 73; Leiden and Boston: Brill, 2018).

Michel, S. "Die Revision der Lutherbibel zwischen 1531 und 1545," in M. Lange and M. Rösel (eds.), *"Was Dolmetschen für Kunst und Arbeit sei": Die Lutherbibel und andere deutsche Bibelübersetzungen* (Leipzig: Deutsche Bibel Gesellschaft and Evangelische Verlagsanstalt, 2017), pp. 83–106.

Michel, S. "'Luthers Sanhedrin': Helfer und Mitarbeiter an der Lutherbibel," in M. Käßmann and M. Rösel (eds.), *Die Bibel Martin Luther: Ein Buch und seine Geschichte* (Leipzig: Deutsche Bibel Gesellschaft and Evangelische Verlagsanstalt, 2017), pp. 117–135.

Millard, A. R. "The Persian Names in Esther and the Reliability of the Hebrew Text," *JBL* 96 (1977), pp. 481–488.

Miller, W. *Xenophon Cyropaedia with an English Translation* (Loeb Classical Library; London: Heinemann / Cambridge, MA: Harvard University Press, 1961).

Mishaly, A. and M. A. Zipor, *Abraham Ibn Ezra's Two Commentaries on Megilat Esther: An Annotated Critical Edition* (Ramat Gan: Bar-Ilan University Press, 2019; Hebrew).

Moberly, R. W. L. *Old Testament Theology: Reading the Hebrew Bible as Christian Scripture* (Grand Rapids, MI: Baker Academic, 2013).

Mommsen, T. *Römische Geschichte* (Munich: Deutscher Taschenbuch Verlag, 1976, vol. 7; a reprint of the 5th ed., 1904, vol. 5).

Mondschein, A. *An Anonymous [Provencal] Commentary on the Book of Esther: An Annotated Critical Edition with an Introduction* (Givat Washington (Israel): Academic College Givat Washington, 2019; Hebrew).

Montefiore, C. G. *The Bible for Home Reading* (London: Macmillan, 1899).

Montgomery, J. A. *The Book of Daniel* (International Critical Commentary; Edinburgh: T. & T. Clark, 1927).

Moore, C. A. Daniel, *Esther and Jeremiah: The Additions: A New Translation with Introduction and Commentary* (Anchor Bible 44; Garden City, NY: Doubleday, 1977).

Moore, C. A. *Esther: Translated with an Introduction and Notes* (Anchor Bible 7b; Garden City, NY: Doubleday, 1971).

Moore, C. H. *Tacitus in Five Volumes*, volume 3: *The Histories, Books IV–V* (Loeb Classical Library; London: William Heinemann / Cambridge, MA: Harvard University Press, 1969).

Morgenstern, M. "Erwägungen zu einem Dokument der Schande," in *Martin Luther und die Kabbala. Vom Schem Hamephorasch und vom Geschlecht Christi. Neu bearb. u. komm. v. M. Morgenstern* (Berlin: Berlin University Press, 2017), pp. 251–276.

Mülhaupt, E. (ed.), *Martin Luthers Psalmen Auslegung* (Göttingen: Vandenhoeck & Ruprecht, 1959).

Murray, J. A. H. *The Oxford English Dictionary* (Oxford: Clarendon Press, 1933).

Narkiss, B. "The Story of Megillath Esther in the Synagogue of Dura Europos," in I. S. Recanati (ed.), *Thoughts, Arts, and Construction* (Jerusalem: Israel's Ministry of Education, 2008), pp. 51–69 (Hebrew).

Netzer, A. "The Fate of the Jewish Community of Tabriz," in M. Sharon (ed.), *Studies in Islamic History and Civilization in Honour of Professor David Ayalon* (Jerusalem and Leiden: Brill, 1986), pp. 411–419.

Netzer, A. "The History of the Forced Converts of Mashhad according to Ya'kov Dilmaniyan," *Pe'amim* 42 (1990), pp. 127–156 (Hebrew).

Netzer, A. "The Jews in the Southern Coast of Caspian Sea, I. Jews in Mazandaran until the End of the 19th Century," in A. Haim (ed.), *Society and Community: Proceedings of the Second International Congress for Research of the Sephardi and Oriental Jewish Heritage 1984* (Jerusalem: Mesgav Yerushalayim, 1991), pp. 85–98 (Hebrew).

Netzer, A. "Persecution of Iranian Jewry in the 17th Century," *Pe'amim* 6 (1980), pp. 32–56 (Hebrew).

Neubauer, A. (ed.), *Mediaeval Jewish Chronicles and Chronological Notes* (2 vols.; Oxford: Clarendon Press, 1887–1895; Hebrew).

Neyrey, J. "Jude, Letter of," in J. H. Hayes (ed.), *Dictionary of Biblical Interpretation* (Nashville: Abingdon Press, 1999), vol. 1, pp. 636–637.

Niditch, S. "Esther: Folklore, Wisdom, Feminism and Authority," in A. Brenner (ed.), *Feminist Companion to Esther, Judith and Susanna* (Sheffield: Sheffield Academic Press, 1995), pp. 26–46.

Noth, M. *Könige* (Biblischer Kommentar Altes Testament 9,1; Neukirchen-Vluyn: Neukirchner Verlag, 1968).

Nöldeke, Th. "Esther," *Die Alttestamentliche Literatur in einer Reihe von Aufsätzen dargestellt* (Leipzig: Verlag von Quant & Händel, 1868), pp. 81–91.

Nötscher, F. *Die Psalmen, Die Heilige Schrift in deutscher Übersetzung* (Echter-Bibel; Würzburg: Echter Verlag, 1947).

Oberman, H. A. "Die Juden in Luthers Sicht," in H. Kremers *et al.* (ed.), *Die Juden und Martin Luther – Martin Luther und die Juden: Geschichte, Wirkungsgeschichte, Herausforderung* (Neukirchen-Vluyn: Neukirchener Verlag, 1985), pp. 136–162.

Oberman, H. A. *Martin Luther: Mensch zwischen Teufel und Gott* (Munich: Deutscher Taschenbuch Verlag, 1986).

O'Brien, D. *The Pinnacle of Hatred: The Blood Libel and the Jews* (Jerusalem: Magnes Press, 2011).

Oldfather, C. H. *Diodorus of Sicily with an English Translation* (vol. 1; Loeb Classical Library; London: William Heinemann / Cambridge, MA: Harvard University Press, 1960).

Oldfather, C. H. *Diodorus of Sicily with an English Translation* (vol. 4; Loeb Classical Library; London: William Heinemann / Cambridge, MA: Harvard University Press, 1961).

Oppenheim, A. L. "Babylonian and Assyrian Historical Texts," in Pritchard, *ANET*, pp. 265–317.

Oppenheimer, A. "The Historical Approach: A Clarification," *Zion* 61 (1996), pp. 225–230 (Hebrew).

Oppenheimer, A. "Love of Mordechai or Hatred of Haman? – Purim in the Days of the Second Temple and Afterwards," *Zion* 62 (1997), pp. 408–418 (Hebrew).

Osten-Sacken, P. von der, *Martin Luther und die Juden* (Stuttgart: Kohlhammer, 2002).

Panaino, A., R. Abdollahy and D. Balland, "Calendars," *Encyclopaedia Iranica* (New York: Bibliotheca Persica Press, 1990) vol. 4, pp. 658–677; online: www.iranicaonline.org/articles/calendars.

Pangritz, A. *Theologie und Antisemitismus: Das Beispiel Martin Luthers* (Frankfurt am Main: Peter Lang, 2017).

Pardes, I. *The Song of Songs: A Biography* (Princeton, NJ: Princeton University Press, 2019).

Paton, L. B. *A Critical and Exegetical Commentary on the Book of Esther* (International Critical Commentary; Edinburgh: T. & T. Clark, 1908).

Pegler, K. "Pfarrer Dr. Lic. Curt Kuhl," *Frohnauer Geschichte*; online: http://klauspegler.de/texte/blickpunkt-frohnau/pfarrer-dr-lic-curt-kuhl/ (accessed April 18, 2018).

Pelletier, A. *In Flaccum* (Les Oeuvres de Philon d'Alexandrie 31; Paris: Cerf, 1967).

Perrin, B. *Plutarch's Lives with an English Translation* (11 vols.; Loeb Classical Library; London: William Heinemann / Cambridge, MA: Harvard University Press, 1950–1968).

Pfeiffer, R. H. *Introduction to the Old Testament* (New York: Harper & Brothers, 1941).

Phillips, R. "Christians Have Fallen in Love with Queen Esther, Purim's Jewish Heroine," *Tablet Magazine* (March 12, 2014): www.tabletmag.com/sections/belief/articles/christians-love-queen-esther

Pike, T. "The Pseudo-Biblical Book of Esther: Mainspring of Zionism," *National Prayer Network*, April 5, 2011, http://truthtellers.org/alerts/PseudoBibicalEsther.html

Poliakov, L. *Geschichte des Antisemitismus* (translated by R. Pfisterer; Worms: Georg Heintz, 1978).

Popper, W. *The Censorship of Hebrew Books* (New York: Ktav, 1969).

Porten, B. *The Elephantine Papyri in English: Three Millennia of Cross-Cultural Continuity and Change* (2nd ed.; Studies in Near Eastern Archaeology and Civilization; Atlanta: Society of Biblical Literature, 2011).

Posner, E. *Archives in the Ancient World* (Cambridge, MA: Harvard University Press, 1972).

Preuss, H. D. *Old Testament Theology* (2 vols.; translated by D. M. G. Stalker; The Old Testament Library; Louisville: Westminster John Knox, 1996).

Prinz, J. "A Rabbi under the Hitler Regime," in H. A. Strauss and K. R. Grossmann (eds.), *Gegenwart im Rückblick: Festgabe für die Jüdische Gemeinde zu Berlin 25 Jahre nach dem Neubeginn* (Heidelberg: L. Stiehm, 1970), pp. 231–238.

Pritchard J. B. (ed.), *Ancient Near Eastern Pictures Relating to the Old Testament* (Princeton: Princeton University Press, 1954).

Pritchard, J. B. (ed.) *Ancient Near Eastern Texts Related to the Old Testament* (= ANET; 3rd ed. with Supplement; Princeton, NJ: Princeton University Press, 1969).

Rad, G. von, *Old Testament Theology* (2 vols.; translated by D. M. G. Stalker; The Old Testament Library; Louisville: Westminster John Knox, 2001).

Radday, Y. T. "Chiasm in Joshua, Judges and Others," *LB* 3 (1973), pp. 6–13.

Radday, Y. T. "Esther with Humour," in A. Brener and Y. T. Radday (eds.), *On Humour and the Comic in the Hebrew Bible* (Journal for the Study of the Old Testament Supplement Series 92; Sheffield: Almond Press, 1990), pp. 295–313.

Raeder, S. *Grammatica Theologica: Studien zu Luthers Operationes in Psalmos* (Beiträge zur historischen Theologie 51; Tübingen: J. C. B. Mohr [P. Siebeck], 1977).

Rainey, A. F. "Israel in Merneptah's Inscription and Reliefs," *IEJ* 51 (2001), pp. 57–75.

Rainey, A. F. "Satrapy of 'Eber-Hanahar'," in H. Tadmor (ed.), *The History of the Jewish People: The Restoration – The Persian Period* (Jerusalem: Am Ovid, 1983), pp. 105–116, 277–280 (Hebrew).

Räisänen, H. "Marcion and the Origins of Christian Anti-Judaism," *Temenos* 33 (1997), 121–135.

Ranke, L. *Geschichte der romanischen und germanischen Völker von 1494 bis 1535* (Leipzig and Berlin: G. Reimer, 1824).

Reif, S. C. (ed.), *The Cambridge Genizah Collections: Their Contents and Significances* (Cambridge University Library Genizah Series 1; Cambridge: Cambridge University Press, 2002).

Reif, S. C. *A Jewish Archive from Old Cairo: The History of Cambridge University's Genizah Collection* (Richmond: Curzon Press, 2000).

Rendtorff, R. *The Old Testament: An Introduction* (Philadelphia: Fortress Press, 1991).

Revlin, J. J. *The Commentary on the Book of Esther by Maimonides* (Jerusalem: Krynfiss Press, 1950; Hebrew).

Reynolds, G. S. *The Qur'ān and the Bible: Text and Commentary* (New Haven, CT: Yale University Press, 2018).

Riegler, M. *Bibliography on the Five Scrolls* (Jerusalem: The Israeli Center for Libraries, 2006), pp. 56–71 (Hebrew).

Roberts, A. and J. Donaldson (eds.), *The Apostolic Fathers, Justin Martyr, Irenaeus* (Ante-Nicene Fathers 1; Edinburgh: T. & T. Clark, 1885; reprinted: Peabody, MA: Hendrickson, 1995).

Rofé, A. *Introduction to the Literature of the Hebrew Bible* (translated by H. N. Bock and J. H. Seeligmann; Jerusalem Biblical Studies 9; Jerusalem: Simor, 2009).

Rofé, A. "Isaiah 59:19: Read: 'A messenger (ציר) will come as light' – The Vision of Redemption by Trito-Isaiah," in Y. Segev (ed.), *The Religion of Israel and the Text of the Hebrew Bible* (Jerusalem: Carmel, 2018), pp. 382–389 (Hebrew).

Röhl, C. G. "Der Kaiser und die Juden," *Wilhelm II.: Der Weg in den Abgrund 1900–1941* (Munich: C. H. Beck, 2008), pp. 1291–1297.

Rosenberg, A. J. *Book of Jeremiah: A New English Translation* (Judaica Books of the Prophets; New York: Judaica Press, 1985).

Rosenlicht, A. (ed.), *Megilo Efu* (פראנקפורט עיר המעטירה – היא מגילת עפה מגילת עפה; Krakau: A. Rosenlicht, 1880).

Rosenthal, L. A. "Die Josephsgeschichte mit den Büchern Ester und Daniel vergleichen," *ZAW* 15 (1895), pp. 278–284.

Rowe, N. *The Jew, the Cathedral, and the Medieval City: Synagoga and Ecclesia in the Thirteenth Century* (Cambridge: Cambridge University Press, 2011).

Rudolph, W. *Das Buch Ruth. Das Hohe Lied. Die Klagelieder* (Kommentar zum Alten Testament 17,1–3; Gütersloh: Gütersloher Verlaghshaus Gerd Mohn, 1962).

Rudolph, W. *Jeremia* (Handbuch zum Alten Testament 12; Tübingen: J. C. B. Mohr [P. Siebeck], 1947).

Rühs, F. *Die Rechte des Christentums und des deutschen Volkes: verteidigt gegen die Ansprüche der Juden und ihrer Verfechter* (Berlin: Realschulbuchhandlung, 1816).

Rühs, F. *Ueber die Ansprüche der Juden an das deutschen Bürgerrecht* (2nd ed.; Berlin: Realschulbuchhandlung, 1816).

Rühs, F. "Über die Ansprüche der Juden auf das deutsche Bürgerrecht," *Zeitschrift für die Neueste Geschichte, die Staaten- und Völkerkunde* (Februar 1815), pp. 129–161.

Saba, A. *Ketav Yad Eshkol Hakofer on Megillat Esther* (Drahobyrz: Zupnik, 1903; Hebrew).

Sandmel, S. *The Enjoyment of Scripture: The Law, the Prophets, and the Writings* (New York: Oxford University Press, 1972).

Sandmel, S. *The Hebrew Scriptures: An Introduction to Their Literature and Religious Ideas* (New York: Oxford University Press, 1978).

Sassoon, D. S. *Diwan of Shemuel Hannaghid: Published for the First Time in Its Entirety according to a Unique Manuscript (MS. Sassoon 589) with an Introduction and Index of Poems* (London: Oxford University Press, 1934; Hebrew).

Sayce, A. H. *An Introduction to the Books of Ezra, Nehemiah, and Esther* (London: Religious Tract Society, 1885; 4th ed., 1893).

Schäfer, P. *Judeophobia: Attitudes towards the Jews in the Ancient World* (Cambridge, MA: Harvard University Press, 1997).

Schaff, P. (ed.), *St. Augustin's City of God and Christian Doctrine* (Nicene and Post-Nicene Fathers 1/2; Edinburgh: T. & T. Clark, 1886; reprinted: Peabody, MA: Hendrickson, 1995).

Schaff, P. and H. Wace (eds.), *Athanasius: Select Works and Letters* (Nicene and Post-Nicene Fathers 2/4; Edinburgh: T. & T. Clark, 1891; reprinted: Peabody, MA: Hendrickson, 1995).

Schaff, P. and H. Wace (eds.), *Eusebius: Church History, Life of Constantine the Great, and Oration in Praise of Constantine* (Nicene and Post-Nicene Father 2/1; Christian Publishing Company, 1890; reprinted: Peabody, MA: Hendrickson, 1995).

Schaudig, H. *Die Inschriften Nabonids von Babylon und Kyros' des Großen samt den in ihrem Umfeld entstandenen Tendenzschriften: Textausgabe und Grammatik* (Alter Orient und Altes Testament 256; Münster: Ugarit-Verlag, 2001).

Schep, L. J., R. J. Slaughter, J. A. Vale, and P. Wheatley, "Was the Death of Alexander the Great Due to Poisoning? Was it *Veratrum album?*" *Clinical Toxicology* 52 (2014), pp. 72–77.

Scheper, G. L. *The Spiritual Marriage: The Exegetic History and Literary Impact of the Song of Songs in the Middle Ages* (Ph.D. dissertation; Princeton University, 1971).

Schmid, K. *Theologie des Alten Testaments* (Tübingen: Mohr Siebeck, 2019).

Schmidt, W. H. *Einführung in das Alte Testament* (5th ed.; Berlin and New York: Walter de Gruyter, 1995).

Schmitt, R. "Amestris," *Encyclopaedia Iranica* (New York: Bibliotheca Persica Press, 1973), vol. 1, pp. 936–937; online: www.iranicaonline.org/articles/amestris-gr

Schmitt, R. *Die altpersischen Inschriften der Achaimeniden* (Wiesbaden: Reichert Verlag, 2009).

Schmitt, R. "Otanes" *Encyclopaedia Iranica*: www.iranicaonline.org/articles/otanes

Schreiner, J. *Jeremia 1–25,14* (Die Neue Echter Bibel; Würzburg: Echter Verlag, 1981).
Schultz, F. W. *Die Bücher, Esra, Nehemia und Esther* (Theologisch-homiletisches Bibelwerk: Des Alten Testaments, Neunter Teil; Bielefeld und Leipzig: Verlag von Belhagen und Klasing, 1876).
Schürer, E. *The History of the Jewish People in the Age of Jesus Christ (175 B.C.–A.D. 135)*. A new English version revised and edited by G. Vermès, F. Millar, and M. Goodman (Edinburgh: T. & T. Clark, 1986), vol. 3,1, pp. 598–600.
Schwarz, R. *Luther* (4th ed.; Universität-Taschenbücher; Göttingen: Vandenhoeck & Ruprecht, 2014).
Schwarz, R. *Martin Luther: Lehrer der christlichen Religion* (Tübingen: Mohr Siebeck, 2015).
Segal, E. *The Babylonian Esther Midrash: A Critical Commentary* (3 vols.; Atlanta, GA: Scholars Press, 2020).
Segal, M. Z. *An Introduction to the Hebrew Bible* (vol. 3; Jerusalem: Kiryat Sepher, 1967; Hebrew).
Sellin, E. and G. Fohrer, *Einleitung in das Alte Testament* (12th ed.; Heidelberg: Quelle & Meyer, 1979).
Semler, J. S. *Abhandlung von freier Untersuchung des Canon* (Halle: Hemmerde, 1772).
Shapur Shahbazi, A. "Harem: i. In Ancient Iran," *Encyclopaedia Iranica* (New York: Bibliotheca Persica Press, 2003), vol. 11, pp. 671–672 and vol 12, pp. 1–3; online: www.iranicaonline.org/articles/harem-i
Shapur Shahbazi, A. *Persepolis: Die altpersiche Residenzstadt* (Darmstadt and Mainz: Wissenschaftliches Buchgesellschaft, 2013).
Shea, W. H. "Esther and History," *Concordia Journal* 13 (1987), pp. 234–248.
Sherwin, B. L. *Mystical Theology and Social Dissent: The Life and Works of Judah Loew of Prague* (London: Associated University Presses, 1982; reprinted: Oxford and Portland, OR: The Littman Library of Jewish Civilization, 2006).
Shirer, W. L. *The Rise and Fall of the Third Reich: A History of Nazi Germany* (London: Secker and Warburg, 1961).
Shmeruk, Ch. "Purim-Spiel," *Encyclopedia Judaica* (2nd ed.; Jerusalem: Keter, 2007), vol. 16, pp. 742–746 = (Jerusalem: Keter, 1972), vol. 13, pp. 1396–1404.
Shmeruk, Ch. *Yiddish Biblical Plays 1697–1750, Edited from Manuscripts and Printed Versions* (Jerusalem: The Israel Academy of Sciences and Humanities, 1979; Hebrew).
Siegfried, D. C. *Esra, Nehemia und Esther* (Handkommentar zum Alten Testament; Göttingen: Vandenhoeck & Ruprecht, 1901).
Silver, A. C. *The Book of Esther and the Typology of Female Transfiguration in American Literature* (Lanham, MD: Lexington Books, 2018).
Silverstein, A. "The Book of Esther and the *Enūma Elish*," *BSOAS* 69 (2006), pp. 209–223.
Silverstein, A. *Veiling Esther, Unveiling Her Story: The Reception of a Biblical Book in Islamic Lands* (Oxford Studies in the Abrahamic Religions; Oxford: Oxford University Press, 2018).
Simon, M. *Megillah: Translated into English with Notes, Glossary and Indices* (London: Soncino Press, 1938).
Simon, M. *Midrash Rabbah Esther* (3rd ed.; London: Soncino Press, 1983).

Smelik, K. A. D. "Nehemiah as a 'Court Jew,'" in I. Kalimi (ed.), *New Perspectives on Ezra-Nehemiah: History and Historiography, Text and Literature* (Winona Lake, IN: Eisenbrauns, 2012), pp. 61–72.

Smend, R. "Die älteren Herausgeber der *Zeitschrift für die alttestamentliche Wissenschaft*," *ZAW* 100 Suppl. (1988), pp. 1–21.

Smend, R. "Wilhelm Vischer," *Kritiker und Exegeten: Porträttskizzen zu vier Jahrhunderten alttestamentlicher Wissenschaft* (Göttingen: Vandenhoeck & Ruprecht, 2017), pp. 770–793.

Soggin, J. A. *Introduction to the Old Testament: From Its Origins to the Closing of the Alexandrian Canon* (Old Testament Library; 3rd ed.; Louisville, KT: Westminster John Knox, 1989).

Stern, M. *Greek and Latin Authors on Jews and Judaism* (Jerusalem: Israel Academy of Sciences and Humanities, 1974–1984), vols. 1–3.

Stern, S. *Josel von Rosheim: Befehlshaber der Judenschaft im Heiligen Römischen Reich Deutscher Nation* (Stuttgart: Deutsche Verlags-Anstalt, 1959).

Steuernagel, C. *Lehrbuch der Einleitung in das Alte Testament* (Sammlung Theologischer Lehrbücher; Tübingen: J. C. B. Mohr [P. Siebeck], 1912).

Stiehl, R. "Das Buch Esther," *WZKM* 53 (1957), pp. 4–22.

Stone, T. J. *The Compositional History of the Megilloth: Canon, Contoured Intertextuality and Meaning in the Writings* (Forschungen zum Alten Testament 2/59; Tübingen: Mohr Siebeck, 2013).

Streicher, J. "Das Mordfest," *Der Stürmer – Deutsches Wochenblatt zum Kampfe um die Wahrheit* 17.13 (March 1939), pp. 1–2, available online, Internet Archive: https://archive.org/stream/DerStuermer-DasJahr1939/1939#page/n13/mode/2up

Striedl, H. "Untersuchung zur Syntax und Stilistik des hebräischen Buches Esther," *ZAW* 55 (1937), pp. 73–108.

Süss, R. *Luthers Theologisch Testament: Over de Joden en hun leugens* (Amsterdam: VU University Press, 2006).

Sweeney, M. A. *Reading the Hebrew Bible after the Shoah* (Minneapolis, MN: Fortress Press, 2008).

Swindell A., O. Z. Soltes, J. Carruthers, H. Leneman, and R. Burnette-Bletsch, "Esther," *Encyclopedia of the Bible and Its Reception* (Berlin: Walter de Gruyter, 2014), vol. 8, pp. 39–54.

Tabory, J. "Esther Rabbah (EstR), Esther Midrashim," *Encyclopedia of the Bible and Its Reception* (Berlin: Walter de Gruyter, 2014), vol. 8, pp. 6–9.

Tadmor, H. "Rabshakeh," *Encyclopedia Biblica* (Jerusalem: Bialik Institute, 1976), vol. 7, pp. 323–325.

Tadmor, H. "Was the Biblical sārîs a Eunuch?" in Z. Zevit, S. Gitin and M. Sokoloff (eds.), *Solving Riddles and Untying Knots: Biblical, Epigraphic, and Semitic Studies in Honor of Jonas C. Greenfield* (Winona Lake, IN: Eisenbrauns, 1995), pp. 317–325.

Talmon, S. "Heiliges Schrifttum und kanonische Bücher aus jüdischer Sicht: Überlegungen zur Ausbildung der Grösse 'Die Schrift' im Judentum," in M. Klopfenstein, U. Luz, S. Talmon and E. Tov (eds.), *Mitte der Schrift? Ein jüdisch-christliches Gespräch: Texte des Berner Symposions vom 6.-12- Januar 1985* (Judaica et Christiana 11; Bern: Peter Lang, 1987), pp. 45–79.

Talmon, S. "Was the Book of Esther Known at Qumran?" *Eretz-Israel* 25 (Joseph Aviram Volume; 1996), pp. 377–382 (Hebrew).

Talmon, S. "'Wisdom' in the Book of Esther," *VT* 13 (1963), pp. 419–455.

Tanner, J. P. "The History of Interpretation of the Song of Songs," *BibSac* 154 (1997), pp. 23–46.

Teter, M. *Blood Libel: On the Trail of an Antisemitic Myth* (Cambridge, MA: Harvard University Press, 2020).

Thackeray, H. St. J. *Josephus with an English Translation*, volume 1: *The Life, Against Apion* (Loeb Classical library; London: W. Heinemann and New York: G. P. Putnam's Sons, 1926).

Thambyrajah, J. "A Macedonian in the Persian Court: Addition E of Esther and the Vetus Latina," *VT* 71 (2021), pp. 743–750.

Thérel, M. -L. "L'origine du theme de la 'synagogue répudiée," *Scriptorium – International Review of Manuscript Studies* 25 (1971), pp. 285–290.

Thompson, J. A. *The Book of Jeremiah* (New International Commentary on the Old Testament; Grand Rapids, MI: W. B. Eerdmans, 1980).

Thornton, T. C. G. "Crucifixion of Haman and Scandal of the Cross," *JTS* 37 (1986), pp. 419–426.

Torrey, C. C. "The Older Book of Esther," *HTR* 37 (1944), pp. 1–40.

Tov, E. (with collaboration of S. J. Pfann), *The Dead Sea Scrolls on Microfiche, Companion Volume: A Comprehensive Facsimile Edition of the Texts from the Judean Desert* (Leiden and Boston: Brill, 1993).

Tov, E. "The 'Lucianic' Text of the Canonical and Apocryphal Sections of Esther: A Rewritten Biblical Book," *Textus* 10 (1982), pp. 1–25.

Trebolle Barrera, J. *The Jewish Bible and the Christian Bible* (Leiden and Boston: Brill / Grand Rapids, MI: Eerdmans, 1998).

Treitschke, H. von, "Unsere Aussichten," *Preußische Jahrbücher* 44, 5 (November 1879), pp. 559–576.

Ulmer, R. Turmoil, *Trauma and Triumph: The Fettmilch Uprising in Frankfurt am Main (1612–1616) According to Megillas Vintz* (Judentum und Umwelt 72; Bern and Frankfurt am Main: Peter Lang, 2001).

Ulrich, E. [C.] (ed.), *The Biblical Qumran Scrolls: Transcriptions and Textual Variants* (Supplements to Vetus Testamentum 134; Leiden and Boston: Brill, 2010).

Ulrich, E. C. "An Index of the Passages in the Biblical Manuscripts from the Judean Desert (Part 2: Isaiah-Chronicles)," *DSD* 2 (1995), pp. 86–107.

Ungnad, A. "Keilinschriftliche Beiträge zum Buch Esra und Esther," *ZAW* 58 (1940–41), pp. 240–244.

VanderKam, J. C. "Authoritative Literature in the Dead Sea Scrolls," *DSD* 5 (1998), pp. 400–402.

VanderKam, J. C. *The Dead Sea Scrolls Today* (Grand Rapids, MI: W. B. Eerdmans, 1994).

VanderKam, J. C. "Jubilees, Book of," in D. N. Freedman *et al.* (eds.), *The Anchor Bible Dictionary* (New York: Doubleday, 1992), vol. 3, pp. 1030–1032.

VanderKam, J. C. "Jubilees, Book of," *Encyclopedia of the Dead Sea Scrolls* (Oxford: Oxford University Press, 2000), vol. 1, p. 435.

VanderKam, J. C. "The Jubilees Fragments from Qumran Cave 4," in J. Trebolle Barrera and L. Vegas Montaner (eds.), *The Madrid Qumran Congress: Proceedings of the International Congress on the Dead Sea Scrolls, Madrid 18–21 March, 1991* (Leiden and Boston: Brill, 1992), vol. 2, pp. 635–648.

Vischer, W. E. "The Book of Esther," *Evangelical Quarterly* 11 (1939), pp. 3–21.

Vischer, W. E. *Esther* (Theologische Existenz heute 48; Munich: Chr. Kaiser Verlag, 1937).

Wahl, H. M. *Das Buch Esther: Übersetzung und Kommentar* (Berlin and New York: Walter de Gruyter, 2009).

Wainwright, A. W. "Henry, Matthew (1662–1714)," in J. H. Hayes (ed.), *Dictionary of Biblical Interpretation* (Nashville: Abingdon, 1999), vol. 1, p. 495.

Walch, J. G. (ed.), *Martin Luthers Sämtliche Schriften* (2nd ed.; Saint Louis, MO: Concordia, 1880–1910 / reprinted: Gross Oesingen: H. Harms, 1987).

Walfish, B. D. *Esther in Medieval Garb: Jewish Interpretation of the Book of Esther in the Middle Ages* (Albany, NY: SUNY Press, 1993).

Walfish, B. D. "Kosher Adultery? The Mordecai-Esther-Ahasuerus Triangle in Midrash and Exegesis," *Prooftexts* 22 (2002), pp. 305–333.

Wallmann, J. "Luther on Jews and Islam," in B. Uffenheimer and H. Graf Reventlow (eds.), *Creative Biblical Exegesis* (Journal for the Study of the Old Testament Supplement Series 59; Sheffield: Sheffield Academic Press, 1988), pp. 149–160.

Walton, F. R. *Diodorus of Sicily: The Library of History* (Loeb Classical Library; Cambridge, MA: Harvard University Press, 2001).

Wassén, C. "The Importance of Marriage in the Construction of a Sectarian Identity in the Dead Sea Scrolls," in S. Byrskog, R. Hakola and J. Jokiranta (eds.), *Social Memory and Social Identity in the Study of Early Judaism and Early Christianity* (Novum Testamentum et Orbis Antiquus / Studien zur Umwelt des Neuen Testaments 116; Göttingen: Vandenhoeck & Ruprecht, 2016), pp. 127–150.

Watzinger, C. *Tell el-Mutesellim* (Leipzig: J. C. Hinrichs'sche Buchhandlung, 1929), vol. 2.

Weber, C. *Altes Testament und völkische Frage: Der biblische Volksbegriff in der alttestamentlichen Wissenschaft der nationalsozialistischen Zeit, dargestellt am Beispiel von Johannes Hempel* (Forschungen zum Alten Testament 38; Tübingen: Mohr Siebeck, 2010).

Weber, O. *Bibelkunde des Alten Testaments: Ein Arbeitsbuch* (5th ed., Tübingen: Furche-Verlag, 1947; 8th ed., Hamburg: Furche-Verlag, 1959).

Wechsler, M. G. *The Arabic Translation and Commentary of Yefet ben 'Eli the Karaite on the Book of Esther* (Leiden and Boston: Brill, 2008).

Weill, M.-D. "Le livre d'Esther et la face cachée de Dieu, *Hester Panim*. Une lumière sur la Shoah," *NRTh* 138 (2016), pp. 367–384.

Weiser, A. *Einleitung in das Alte Testament* (5th ed.; Göttingen: Vandenhoeck & Ruprecht, 1963).

Weiser, A. *The Psalms: A Commentary* (translated by H. Hartwell; The Old Testament Library; Philadelphia: Westminster, 1962).

Weiss, R. "The Language and Style of Megillath Esther," *Mashot beMikra* (Jerusalem: Reuben Mass, [1976]; Hebrew).

Welles, C. B. *Diodorus of Sicily with an English Translation* (vol. 8; Loeb Classical Library; London: William Heinemann / Cambridge, MA: Harvard University Press, 1963).

Wette, W. M. L. de, *A Critical and Historical Introduction to the Canonical Scriptures of the Old Testament* (translated by T. Parker; Boston: H. B. Fuller, 1850).

Wette, W. M. L. de, *Lehrbuch der historisch-kritischen Einleitung in die Bible, Alten und Neuen Testamentes* (5th ed.; Berlin: G. Reimer, 1840).

Whedbee, J. W. *The Bible and the Comic Vision* (Cambridge: Cambridge University Press, 1998).

White Crawford, S. A. *The Additions to Esther: Introduction, Commentary and Reflections* (The New Interpreter's Bible 3; Nashville, TN: Abingdon Press, 1999).

White Crawford, S. A. "Esther: A Feminine Model for Jewish Diaspora," in P. L. Day (ed.), *Gender and Difference* (Minneapolis: Fortress Press, 1989), pp. 161–177.

White Crawford, S. A. "Esther, Book of," in L. H. Schiffman and J. C. VanderKam (eds.), *Encyclopedia of the Dead Sea Scrolls* (Oxford: Oxford University Press, 2000), vol. 1, pp. 269–270.

White Crawford, S. A. "Esther," in C. A. Newsom, S. H. Ringe, and J. E. Lapsley (eds.), *Woman's Bible Commentary* (3rd ed.; Louisville, KY.: Westminster John Knox, 2012), pp. 201–207.

White Crawford, S. A. "Has *Esther* Been Found at Qumran? *4Qproto-Esther* and the *Esther* Corpus," *RevQ* 17 (1996), pp. 307–325.

Wiebe, J. M. "Haman," in D. N. Freedman *et al.* (eds.), *The Anchor Bible Dictionary* (New York: Doubleday, 1992), vol. 3, p. 33.

Williams, S. K. "*Promise* in the Galatians: A Reading of Paul's Reading of Scripture," *JBL* 107 (1988), pp. 709–720.

Wills, L. M. *The Jew in the Court of the Foreign King: Ancient Jewish Court Legends* (Harvard Dissertations in Religion 26; Minneapolis, MN: Fortress Press, 1990).

Wilson, J. A. "Hymn of Victory of Mer-ne-Ptah (The 'Israel Stela')," in Pritchard, *ANET*, pp. 376–378.

Wilson, S. G. *Related Strangers: Jews and Christians 70–170 C. E.* (Minneapolis, MN: Fortress Press, 1995).

Wintermute, O. S. "Jubilees: A New Translation and Introduction," in J. H. Charlesworth (ed.), *The Old Testament Pseudepigrapha* (The Anchor Bible Reference Library; New York: Doubleday, 1985), vol. 2, pp. 35–142.

Winton Thomas, D. "A Consideration of Some Unusual Ways of Expressing the Superlative in Hebrew," *VT* 3 (1953), pp. 209–224.

Wyetzner, P. "Commentary of Rabanus Marus on the Book of Esther," *Jerusalem Letters* (December 2015), online: http://jerusalemletters.com/is-ahashverosh-jesus/

Yahalom, J. and M. Sokoloff, *Jewish Palestinian Aramaic Poetry from Late Antiquity* (Jerusalem: Israel Academy of Sciences and Humanities. Section of Humanities, 1999; Hebrew).

Yamauchi, E. M. *Persia and the Bible* (Grand Rapids, MI: Baker Book House, 1990).

Yardeni, A. and B. Porten, *Textbook of Aramaic Documents from Ancient Egypt,* Volume 2: *Contracts* (Jerusalem: Academon, 1989).

Yavetz, Z. *Judenfeindschaft in der Antike* (Munich: Verlag C. H. Beck, 1997).

Yitzchak, Y. *Sacred Letters* (אגרות-קודש; vol. 12; New York: KHT, 1985; Yiddish).

Younger, K. L. Jr. *Ancient Conquest Accounts: A Study in Ancient Near Eastern and Biblical History Writing* (Journal for the Study of the Old Testament Supplement Series 98; Sheffield: JSOT Press, 1990).

Zadok, R. "Notes on Esther," *ZAW* 98 (1986), pp. 105–110.

Zadok, R. "The Historical Background of Megillat Esther," *Beit Mikra* 30 (no. 100; 1985), pp. 186–189 (Hebrew).

Zemorah, I. (ed.), *Complete Poems of Rabbi Jehudah Halevi* (Tel Aviv: Machbarot Lesifrot & Mesada 1955; Hebrew).

Zenger, E. "Esther," in E. Zenger u.a. (ed.), *Einleitung in das Alte Testament* (8th ed.; edited by C. Frevel; Stuttgart: W. Kohlhammer, 2012), pp. 376–386.

Zimmern, H. "Zur Frage nach dem Ursprunge des Purimfestes," *ZAW* 11 (1891), pp. 157–169.

Zipor, M. A. *Tradition and Transmission: Studies in Ancient Biblical Translation and Interpretation* (Tel Aviv: Hakibbutz Hameuchad, 2001; Hebrew).

Zipor, M. A. "When Midrash Met Septuagint: The Case of Esther 2,7," *ZAW* 118 (2006), pp. 82–92.

Zunz, L. *Die vier und zwanzig Bücher der heiligen Schrift* (Berlin: Verlag von Beit, 1838).

Authors Index

378 *Authors Index*

Names and Subjects Index

Sources Index

1. Hebrew Bible/ Old Testament

NB: Except where otherwise specified, all the biblical references refer to the Masoretic Text, according to the numbering in *BHS*.

396

Terms and Expressions Index

CPSIA information can be obtained
at www.ICGtesting.com
Printed in the USA
LVHW040924190723
752503LV00042B/146